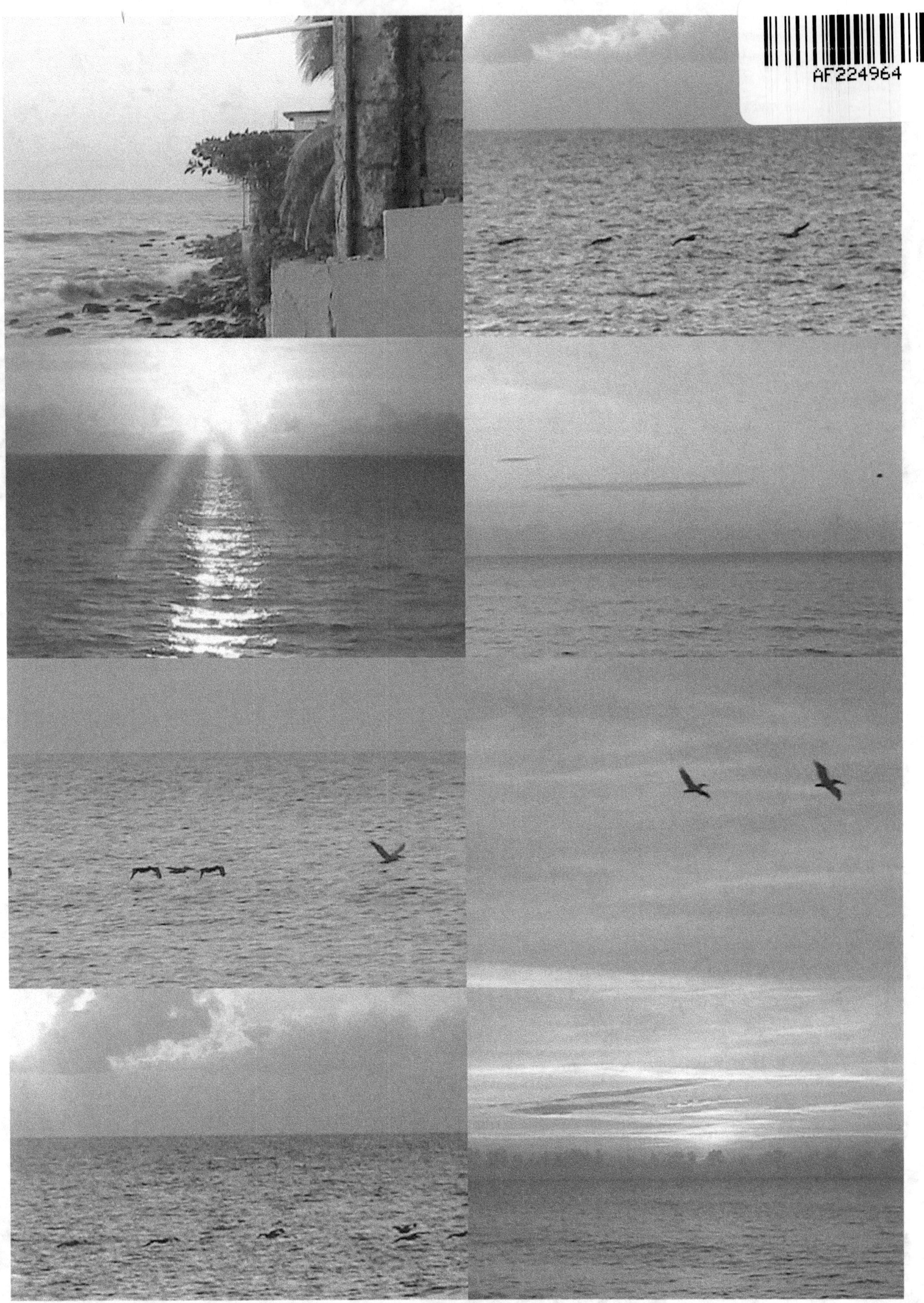

Sunset Views from Gouyave

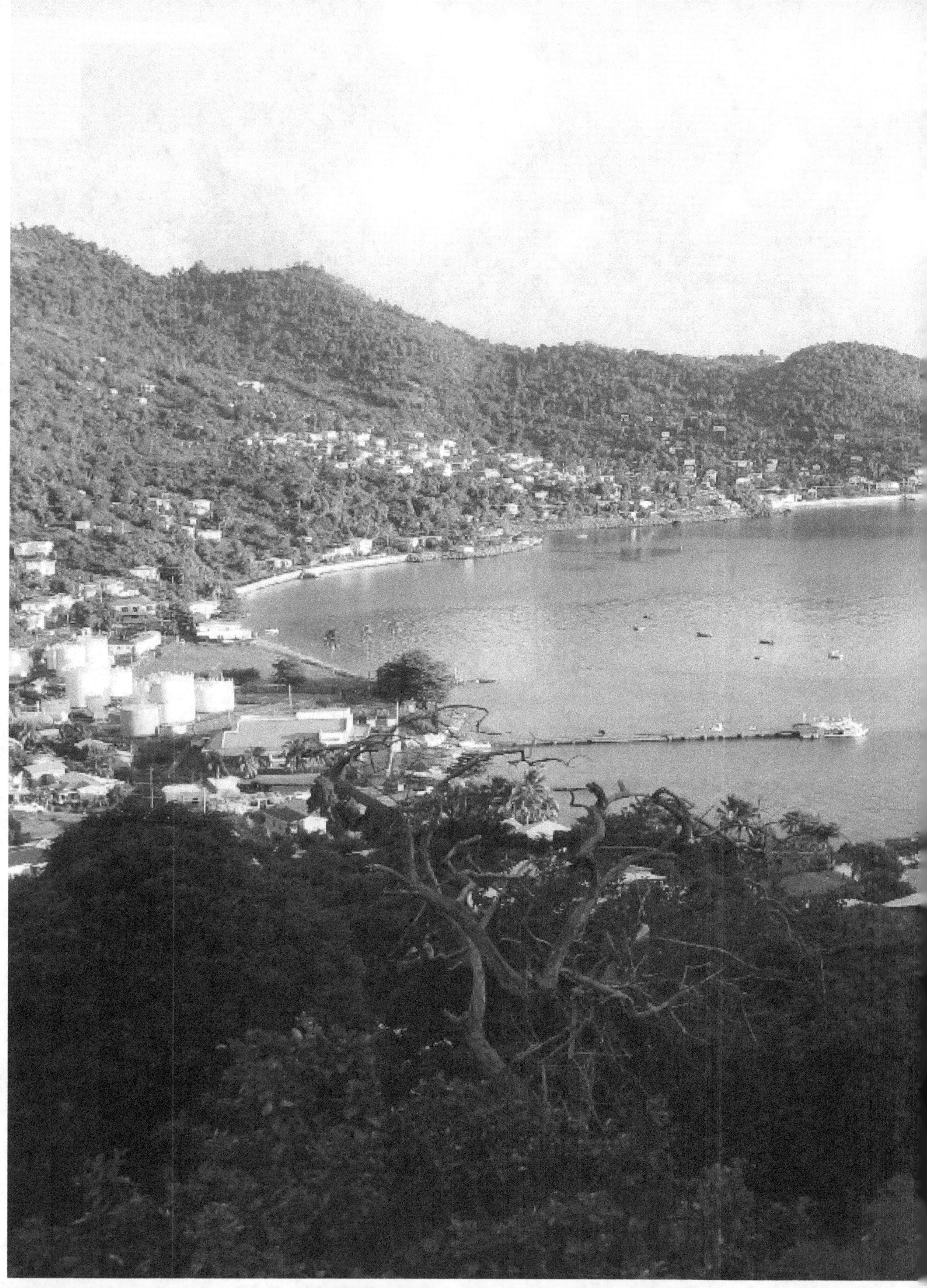

Grenada Uncovered

An uncommon view of the island's geocultural beauty

BLACK AND WHITE EDITION

RAYMOND D. VIECHWEG

Ordering Information:

For orders and inquiries, please contact:
1-888-404-1388
www.goldtouchpress.com
book.orders@goldtouchpress.com

Printed in the United States of America

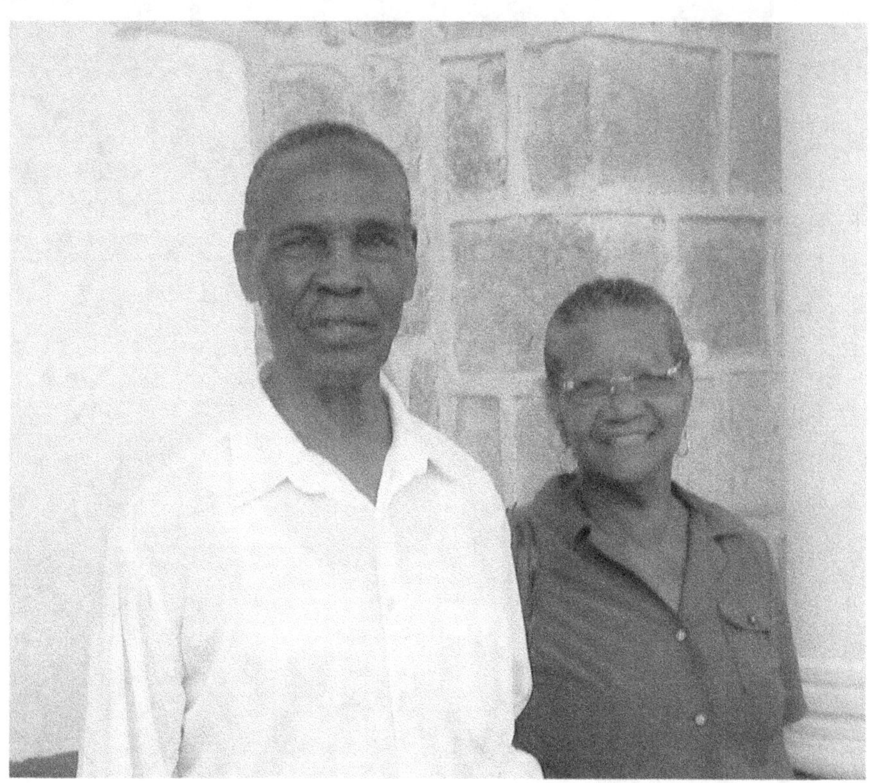

To my parents, Valentine and Erma Viechweg

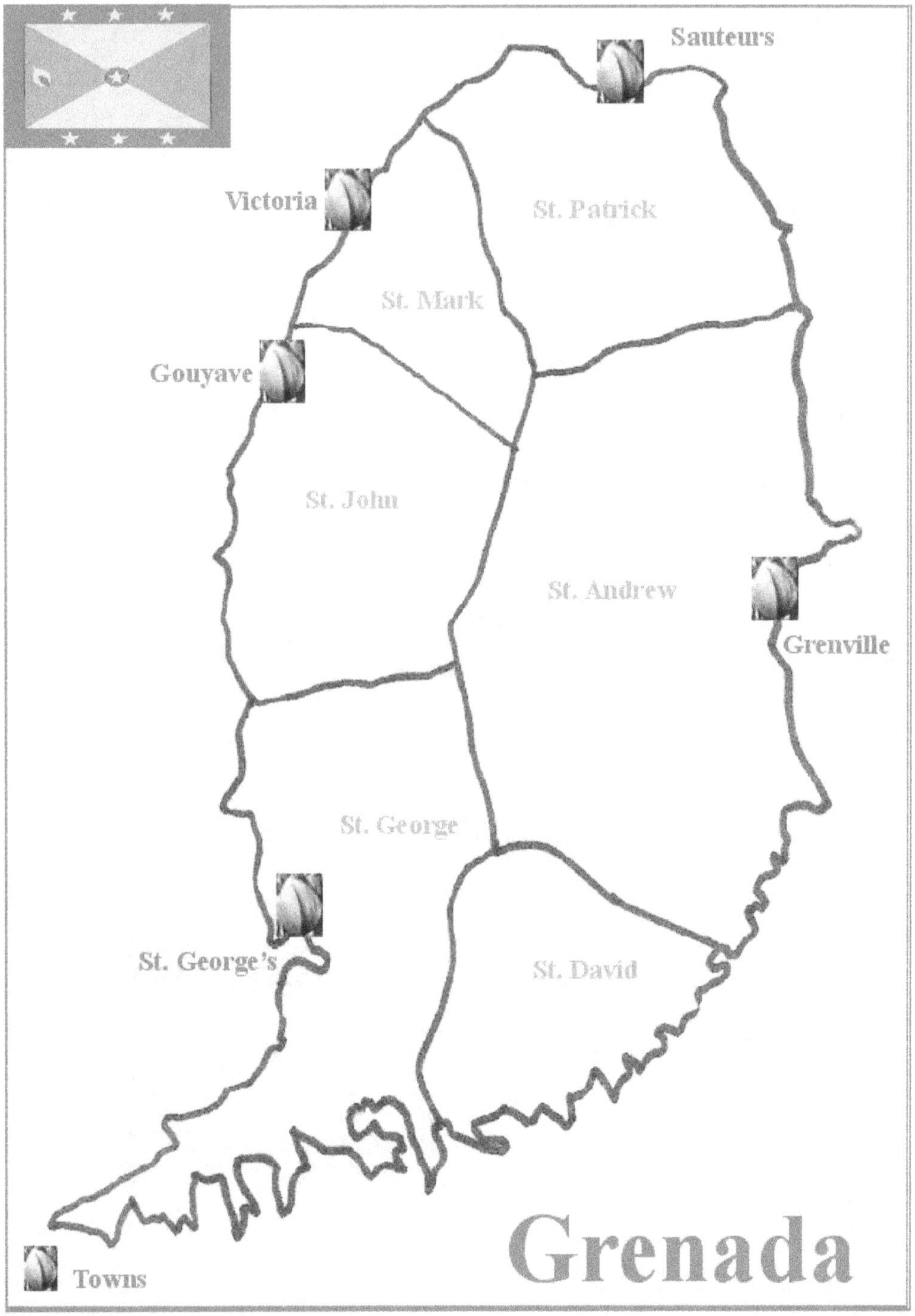

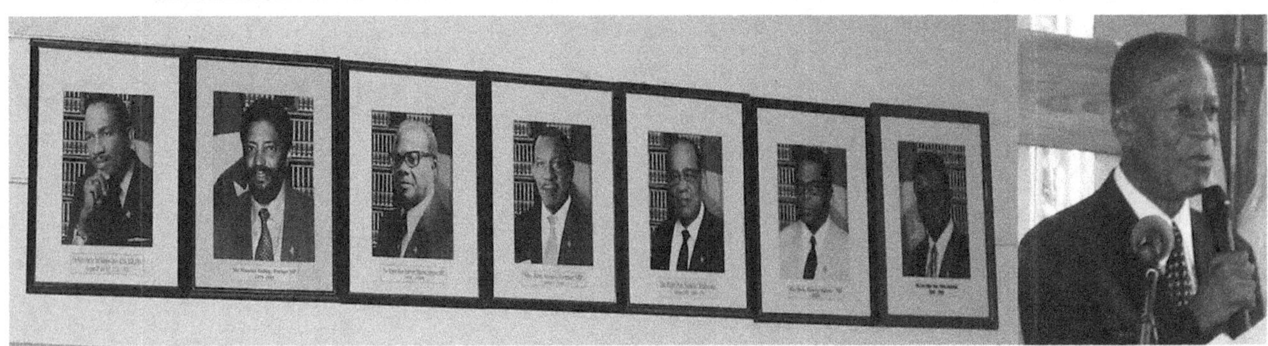

Grenadian heads of state since 1954

About Grenada

Grenada is a tropical Caribbean island of 120 square miles, located at 12.03 degrees North and 61.45 degrees West. St. George, with a beautiful, almost land-locked harbor, is the capital. The population of Grenada is approximately 105,000. The Grenadian economy is supported mainly by agriculture, tourism, and light industries. Its modern international airport at Point Salines facilitates transportation to and from Grenada. Its flourishing visitor and trading seaports at St. George, likewise, are busy points of contact with the rest of the world.

Grenada's recorded history begins in 1498 when Christopher Columbus, on his third voyage, encountered Grenada and named it Conception Island. The Spaniards also named it Granada. Grenada's indigenous inhabitants were an Amerindian people called Caribs, from whom the Caribbean derives its name. The Carib name for Grenada was Camerhogne. The French called the island L' Isle de la Grenade, but today it is known as Grenada, the Isle of Spice. A wide assortment of spice plants, including cinnamon, cloves, and nutmegs, abound on Grenada's rich soils. After many years of reliance on the export of cocoa and bananas, the island has begun to diversify its economic focus to include agro-industries and geo-tourism.

Grenada is today an independent island, with a democratic political system based on the Westminster parliamentary model. Grenada is the largest of a tri-island nation. The other two islands are Carriacou (13 sq. miles) and Petite Martinique (586 acres), both islands of the Grenadines, a geographical unit of smaller islands between Grenada and St. Vincent.

On the opposite page is an arrangement of Grenadian heads of state since 1954, from Lt. to Rt.: Sir Eric M. Gairy of the Grenada United Labour Party (GULP) led Grenada to Independence in 1974, was Chief Minister in 1954, 1958, and 1961. Gairy was Prime Minister from 1967-1979; Maurice R. Bishop of the New Jewel Movement (NJM) was Grenada's only socialist head of state (1979-1983); Herbert A. Blaize of the Grenada National Party (GNP) was Chief Minister from 1962-1967, and Prime Minister from 1984-1989; Ben J. Jones of the New National Party (NNP) was Prime Minister from 1989-1990; Nicholas A. Brathwaite of the National Democratic Congress (NDC) was Prime Minister from 1983-1984 and 1990-1995, George I. Brizan (NDC) was Prime Minister in 1995; Dr. Keith C. Mitchell (NNP) was Prime minister from 1995-2008 and 2013 -); Tillman J. Thomas (NDC) was Prime Minister from 2008 to 2013.

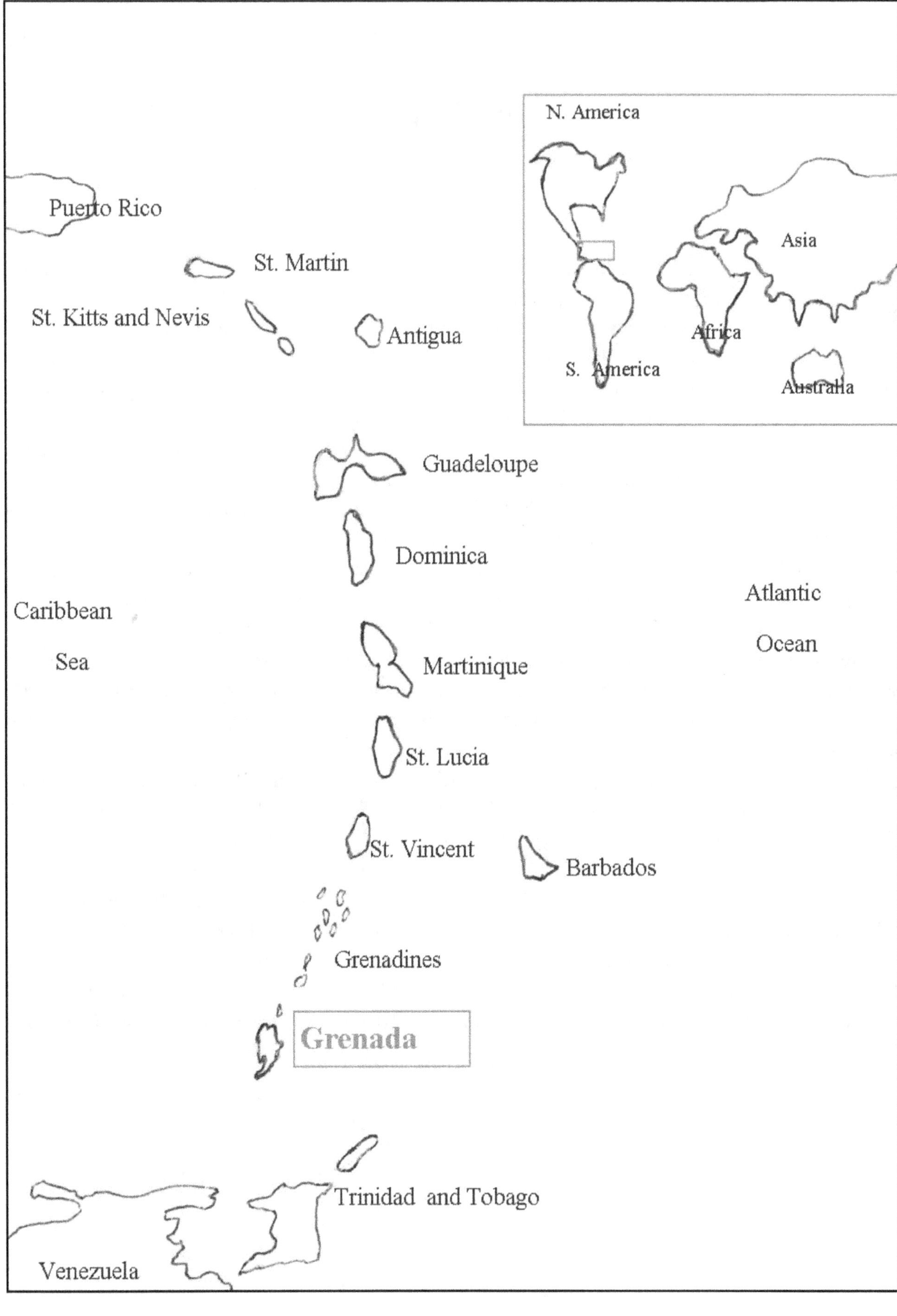

Puerto Rico
St. Martin
St. Kitts and Nevis
Antigua
N. America
Asia
Africa
S. America
Australia
Guadeloupe
Dominica
Caribbean
Sea
Atlantic
Ocean
Martinique
St. Lucia
St. Vincent
Barbados
Grenadines
Grenada
Trinidad and Tobago
Venezuela

CONTENTS

Preface

Grenada Uncovered assembles an assortment of views that I hope will help uncover Grenada's distinctiveness, history, and people. Readers will see pictures of Grenada, some taken recently, and some from further back. Hurricanes Ivan and Emily devastated Grenada in 2004 and 2005. Despite some evidence of the damage, it is the continued recovery that characterizes the scenes. The recovery of Grenada speaks volumes about the island and its people.

I do not focus on hotel complexes and structures that are sometimes mistakenly equated with success and progress. I instead caution against the wholesale compromise of Grenada's uniqueness and natural habitat. Developers must be mindful of Grenada's fragile oceanic existence, where volcanic explosions have produced a tranquil landscape and fertile soils.

In Grenada, tourism accounts for about half of the GDP; it is inevitable and even necessary that this sector continues its development. Yet, there must be a careful negotiation of the delicate balance among economic advancement, historic preservation, culture, and ecological protection. This book's pictorial choices reflect this negotiation, where the spotlight is on the undamaged environment bequeathed to us by our ancestors. Not only is it a sign of sound national character, but I believe Grenadians honor their ancestors when they work to preserve the evidence of their noble existence.

Grenada Uncovered is relatively scant in its portrayal of Grenadian faces, opting to represent Grenadian character mainly through its landscape. Grenada realizes that preserving all life forms must be central to its politics, industry, and entertainment; it can no longer take the land and its generosity for granted. Ultimately, being good custodians of the earth will make people better neighbors to each other. In crafting a new attitude towards its geographical resources, a holistic form of tourism must evolve to incorporate ordinary Grenadians' cultural input. National Geographic's Geo-tourism, which integrates culture with other sustainable forms of tourism, including eco-tourism, describes this new attitude reasonably well.

The presented landscape is one that mirrors the great potential of Grenadians. If the landscape adequately represents its people, Grenada Uncovered says to the world that Grenadians are a beautiful people, ready to accelerate in their roles as custodians, leaders, and benefactors of earth's resources. So that Grenada achieves a broader self-definition, the Grenadian Diaspora will also have to embrace Grenada's cause as enthusiastic stakeholders. For its part, the Government must studiously craft roles for its expatriates' participation and contribution. Grenada Uncovered has focused on the Grenadian landscape to engender a spirit of appreciation for what nature has given and on appealing to Grenadian planners to chart developmental courses and alliances that ultimately protect the land.

Acknowledgments

These are some of the many people I must thank for their assistance: Miss Lorna of Plains for letting me photograph her pomegranate trees; The Sauteurs Museum guide for allowing me to photograph the Carib artifacts; Carol-Anne for the suggestions and technical assistance she provided on the overall project; Raphael and Regis for helping me cut a path to the Carib Stone; Steve, for accompanying me to La Sagesse; My family members, including my wife Judy and sister Denise who encouraged me; Nick, who helped me identify some Carriacou locations; Emmanuel for finding some of the medicinal bushes.

Raymond D. Viechweg

Grenada *means* Pomegranate

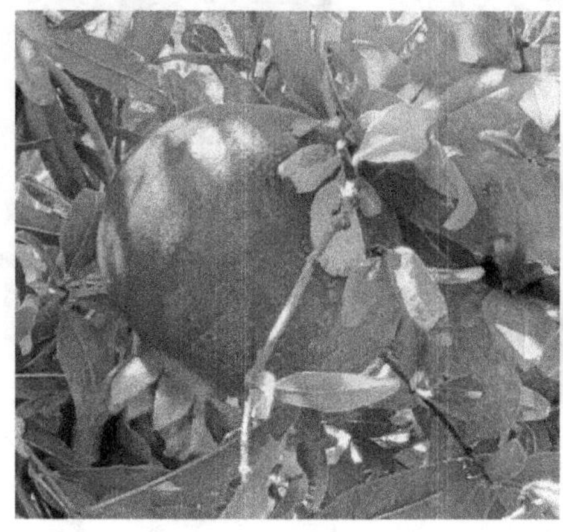

A Pomegranate

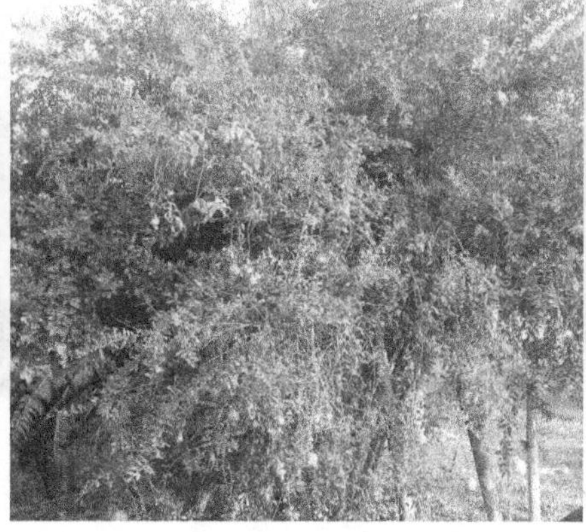

Pomegranate trees in Plains,
St. Patrick

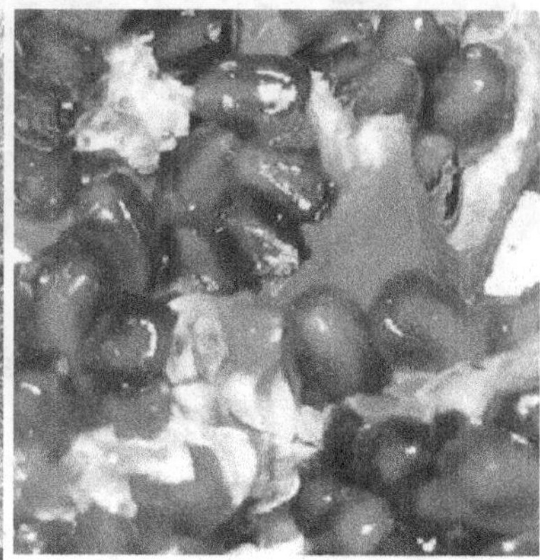

The juicy seeds inside

Grenada derives its name from the pomegranate. The Latin name for pomegranate is pomum granatum, meaning seeded or grained apple. In Spanish, pomegranate is granada, and in French, it is grenade. Colonial Britain seems to have synthesized the French grenade and Spanish granada into Grenada. All three words, coming successively from the Spanish, French, and English claimants to the island, are linked to the pomegranate fruit, precisely its seed (granatum).

The first European explorers of Grenada were the Spanish. They came under Italian Christopher Columbus on his third voyage in 1498. Spanish sailors found Grenada's hills reminiscent of their homeland in Granada, Spain, and named the island Granada. Later came the French to colonize the island, and they translated the name to La Grenade, keeping with the pomegranate meaning. Then came the English, and they synthesized the Spanish (Granada) and French (Grenade) into Grenada, keeping within the pomegranate meaning. The words granada, grenade, and grenada all mean pomegranate, so dubbing the pomegranate the grenada is quite understandable. I am proceeding to use grenada, lower case g, in place of pomegranate. Through the island of Grenada's linkage to the pomegranate, we begin to uncover Grenada's resonances in world religions, history, and mythology. In this discussion, I will substitute grenada, spelled with the lower case "g," for pomegranate.

The grenada has a thick, often red rind that encloses sweet, mildly acidic packets of juicy pulp around its many seeds. The seeds are internally chambered, like how pellets are chambered in a hand grenade, explaining how the hand grenade derived its French name. The ancient world used grenadas as medicine and as food. Grenadine syrup, widely used in drinks, is among the by-products of the grenada. With its high antioxidant content, we use grenadas mostly for food and as medicine.

There are other parts of the world called Grenada or Granada, but Moorish and Spanish conquerors

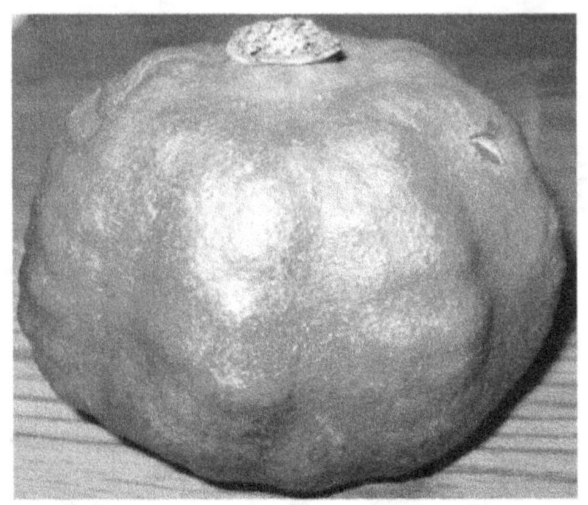

The grenade-like segments of the dried grenada

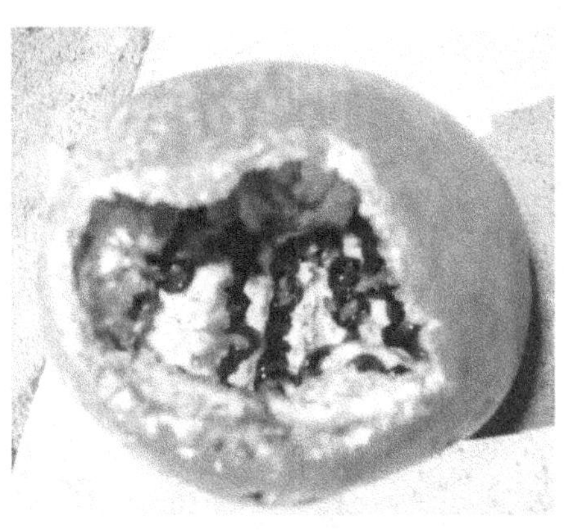

The grenade-like internal chambers of the grenada

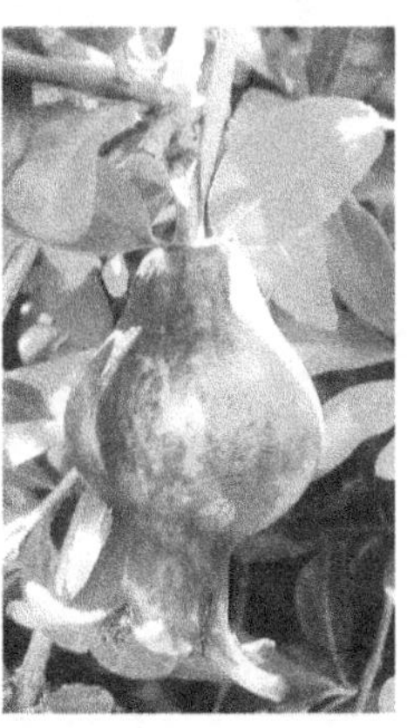

A young grenada showing its distinctive crown

respectively named Granada, Spain and Grenada, West Indies. Conquerors named both places. The Moors were impressed by the abundance of grenadas in the region before founding Spanish Granada. Likewise, the hills of Grenada reminded the Spaniards of their home, and they named it Granada.

Today ironically, grenadas are not common in Grenada. They are unacceptably scarce on this island that so clearly bears their name. Yet, in Grenada's earlier history, during slavery, there seemed to have been grenadas growing abundantly on the island. Henry Nelson Coleridge, nephew, and editor to the great English writer and poet, Samuel Taylor Coleridge, observed on his 1825 trip to Grenada:

"they [Grenadians] give turtle, porter, and champagne in abundance and perfection, they lend horses, and send pines and pomegranates on board your ship, in short they are right pleasant Christians."

The Spaniards were known to have spread grenada plants throughout the New World territories they encountered in the 15th century. It appears that Coleridge saw grenadas in Grenada when he visited in 1825.

Even centuries before the Spanish explored the Caribbean; there were an old-world history and mythology associated with the grenada. The grenada's history preceded its Moorish introduction to Spain; it is a history that echoes in the traditions of the great religions. In Judaism, the grenada is considered a symbol of righteousness. Many believe the grenada has 613 seeds corresponding to the Torah's 613 commandments (Mitzvot). In some artistic depictions, Jesus' mother Mary has a grenada in her hand. The Quran describes grenada as one of God's select fruit and fruit from the Garden of Paradise. Reportedly Prophet Muhammed said that whoever eats a grenada, Allah will light his heart forty nights. The grenada is one of the three blessed fruits of Buddhism. The grenada also has a rich history in Rome, China, Persia, Egypt, and Greece. One of the oldest medical texts known, the Ebers Papyrus (circa 100 BC) from Egypt, discussed the grenada's medicinal properties.

According to ancient Greek culture, the grenada is at the center of a spectacular myth concerning the seasons' origin. The ancient Greek myth of the grenada, the Persephone myth, links Grenada to world mythology.

In the Persephone myth, the myth of the Underworld's dark goddess, grenada is central. While playing, Persephone was abducted by Hades, the god of the Underworld, and brought there as his wife. Persephone's mother, Demeter, goddess of the Harvest, went into mourning for her abducted daughter and stopped all plants from growing. Zeus, the highest authority among the Greek gods, could not allow crops to die eternally, so he commanded Hades to return Persephone to her mother. By the time Hades returned Persephone to Demeter, it was too late to stop Earth's seasonal divides.

During Persephone's time, Ancient Greeks believed that fate would doom her to eternity if she ate food in the Underworld. Since Persephone refused to eat or drink during her abduction in the Underworld, Hades tricked her into eating six seeds from a grenada, and therefore, fate condemned her to spend six months in the Underworld every year. It was during these six months of Persephone's condemnation to the Underworld, while her mother Demeter mourned for her, that Earth's fertilization ceased. The unfertilized six-month period of Persephone's captivity corresponds to the six months of Fall and Winter. The fertilized six-month period of her release back to her mother corresponds to the six months of Spring and Summer. Thus, the myth of Persephone, featuring the grenada, became central to ancient Greek accounting for the origin of seasons.

Grenada stands to benefit immensely from the cultivation of grenadas. From a marketing standpoint, every by-product of the grenada can conceivably enjoy a fast-track marketing advantage: The natural name of the fruit (pomegranate) corresponds directly with the island's name (Grenada). Should Grenada eventually seize the opportunity to use the grenada commercially, it may signal the island nation's readiness to highlight its uniqueness as the only country bearing the pomegranate's name.

Raymond D. Viechweg

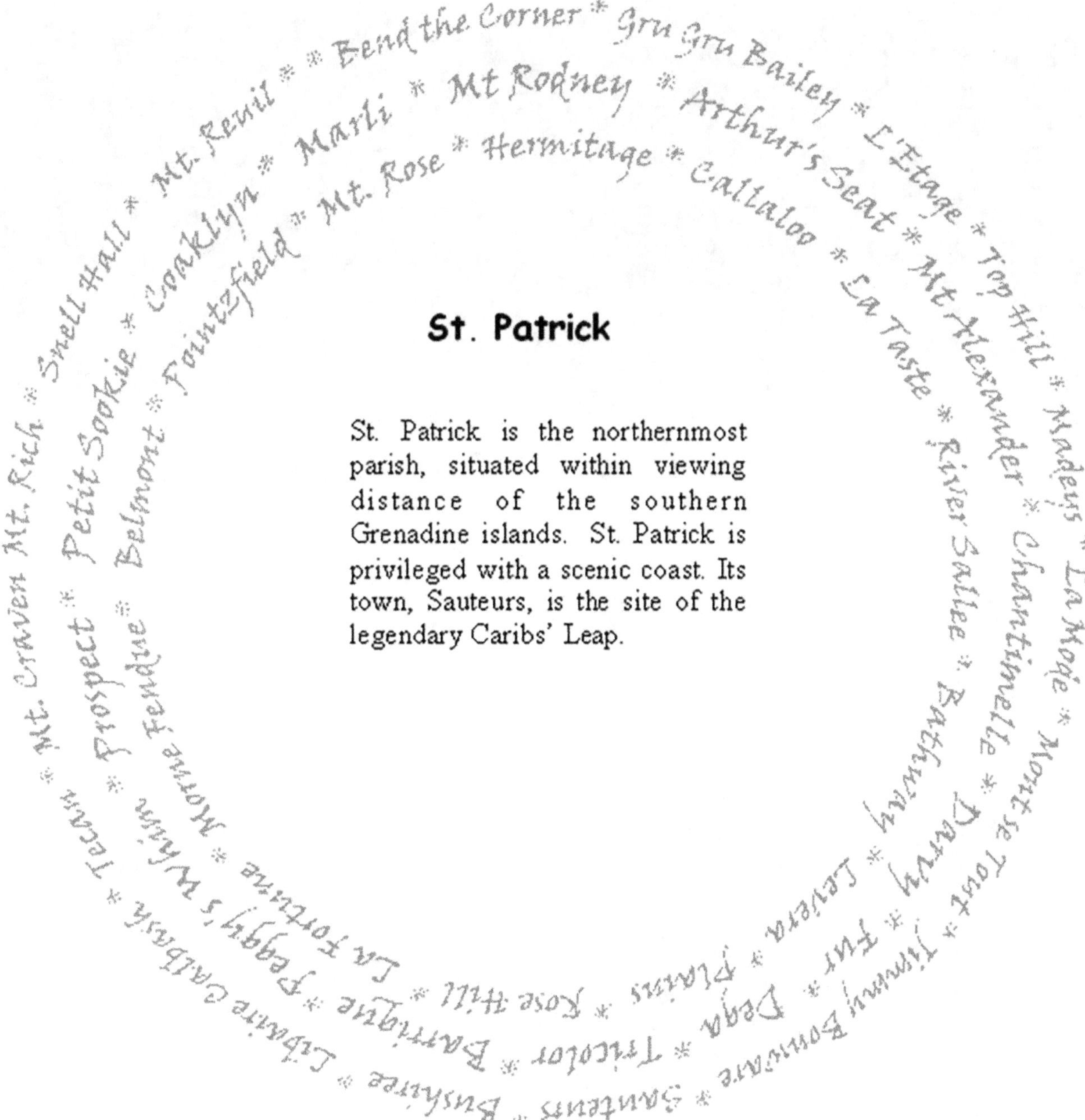

St. Patrick

St. Patrick is the northernmost parish, situated within viewing distance of the southern Grenadine islands. St. Patrick is privileged with a scenic coast. Its town, Sauteurs, is the site of the legendary Caribs' Leap.

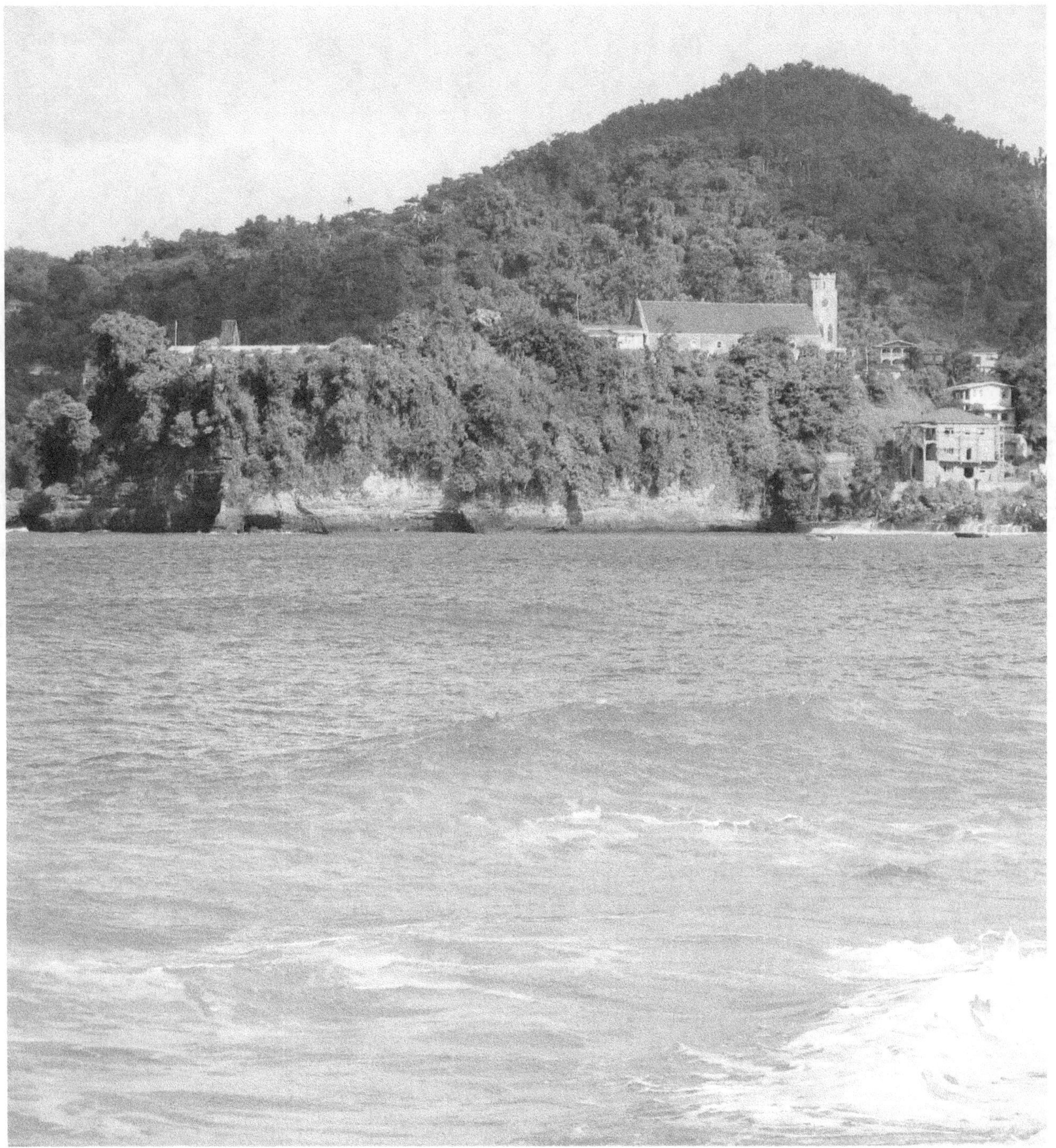

Leapers' Hill is a prominent part of Sauteurs.

The rock from which the last indigenous inhabitants of Grenada, the Amerindian Caribs, reportedly leaped to their deaths rather than submit to French colonizers in 1651. As a result, the rock above was named Le Morne des Sauteurs, which means Hill of the Leapers. The local town is named Sauteurs after the historic site.

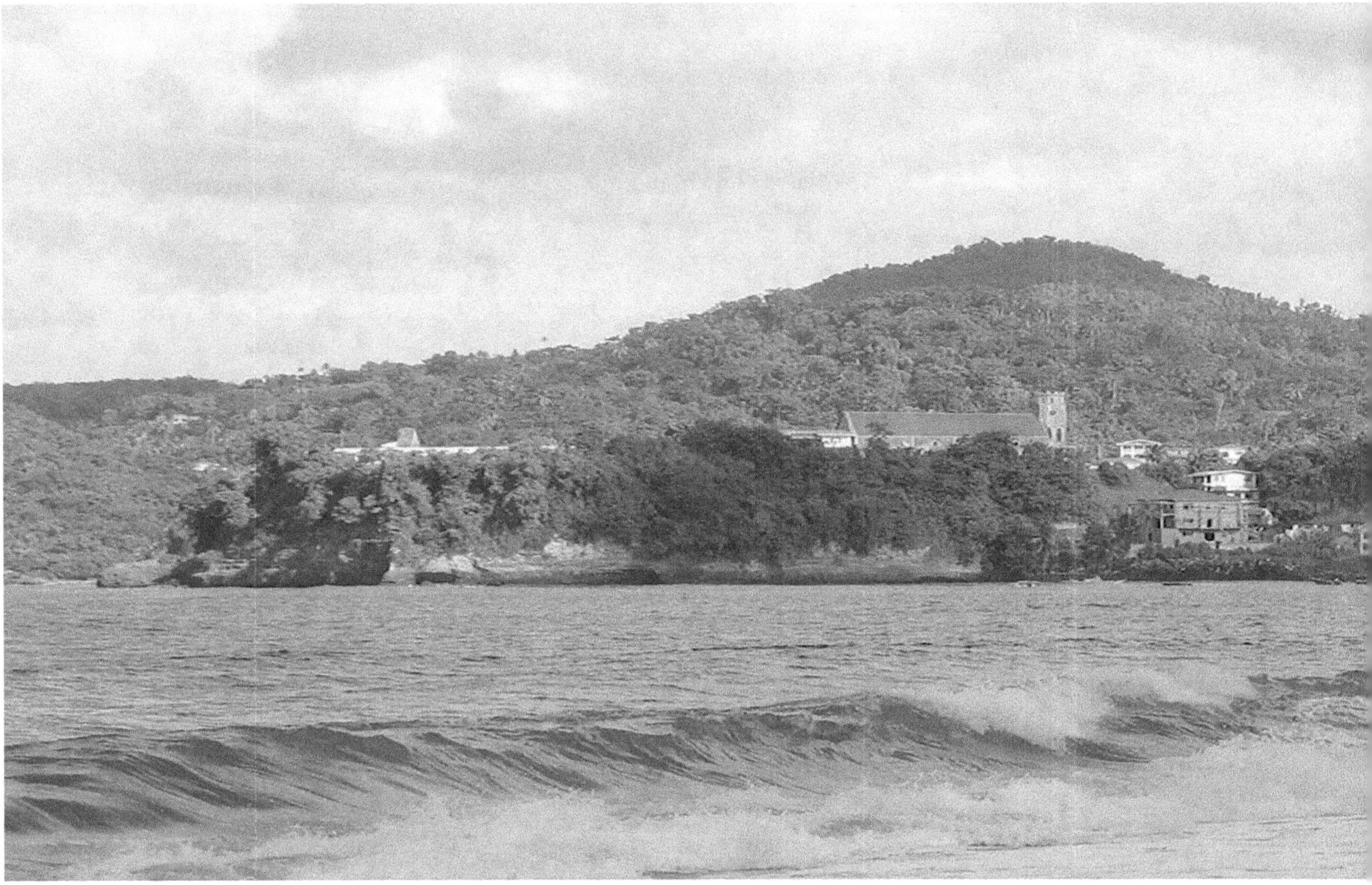

Mc Donald College campus overlooking Sauteurs. It is one of the
secondary schools that serve the parish of St. Patrick.

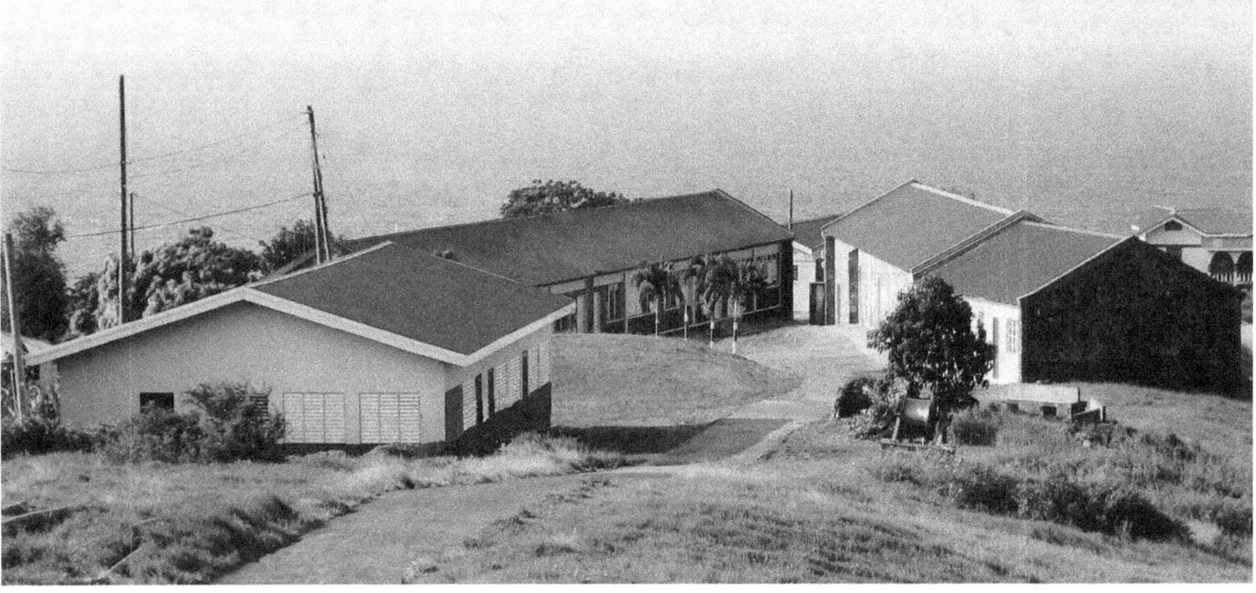

Sauteurs is a historic town situated at the center of Grenada's northern coast.

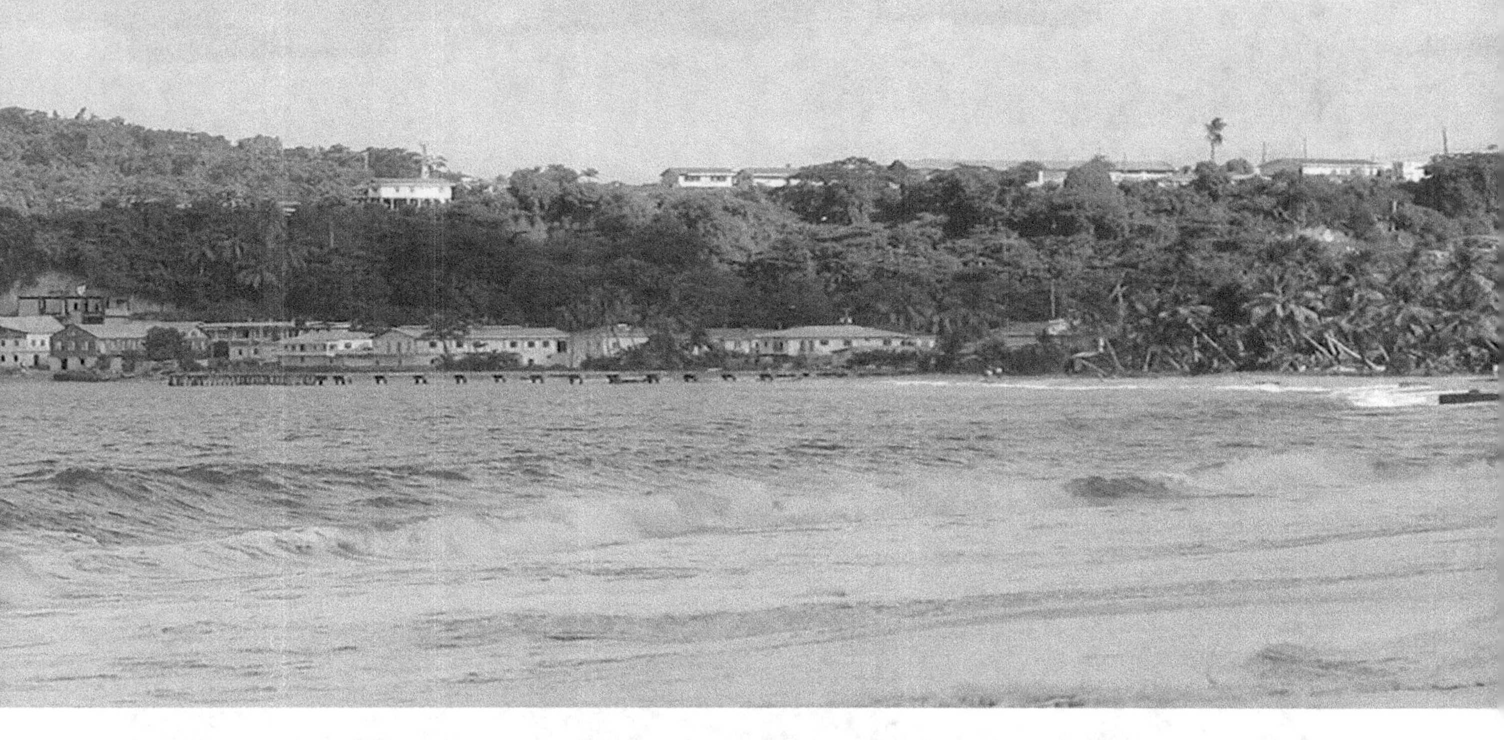

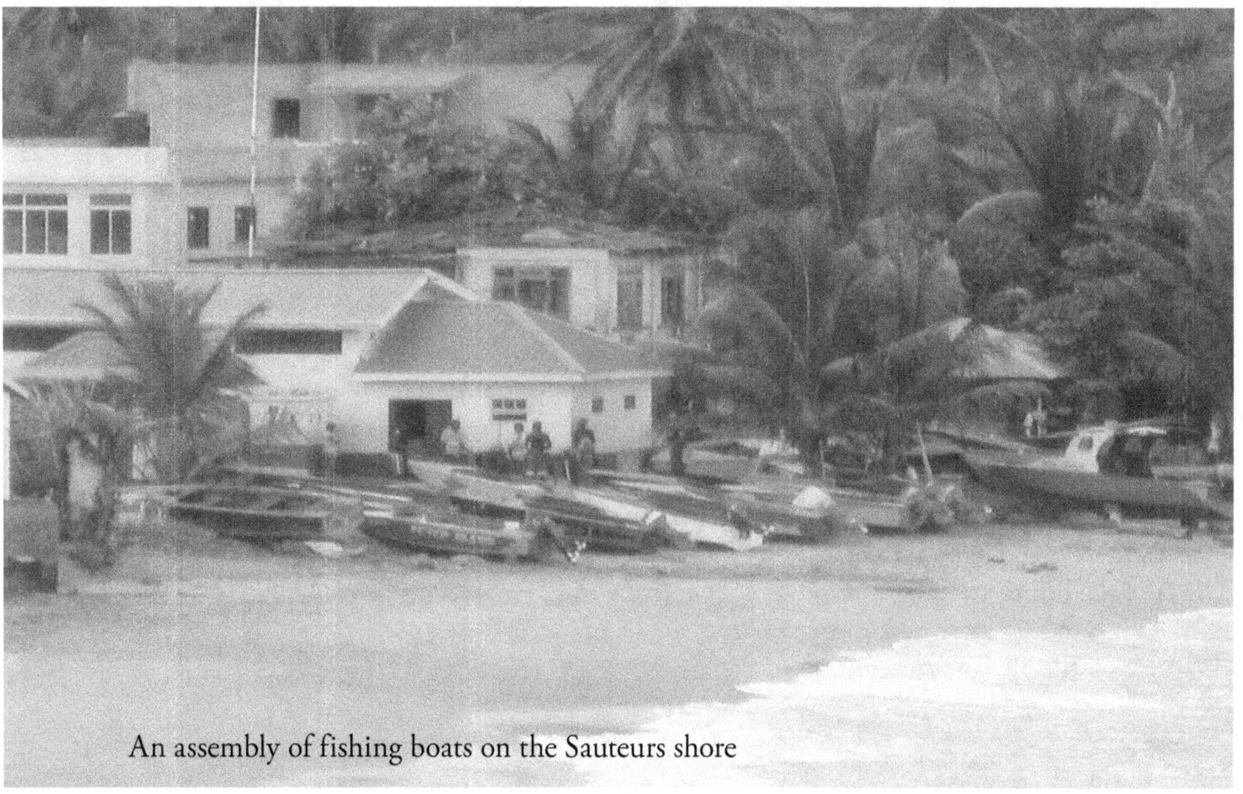

An assembly of fishing boats on the Sauteurs shore

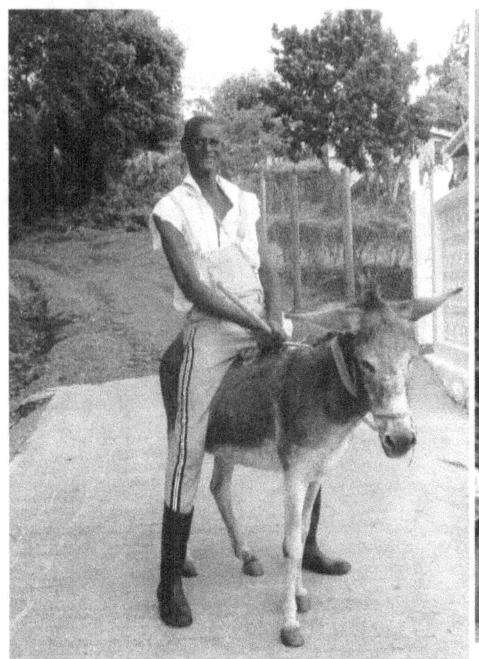

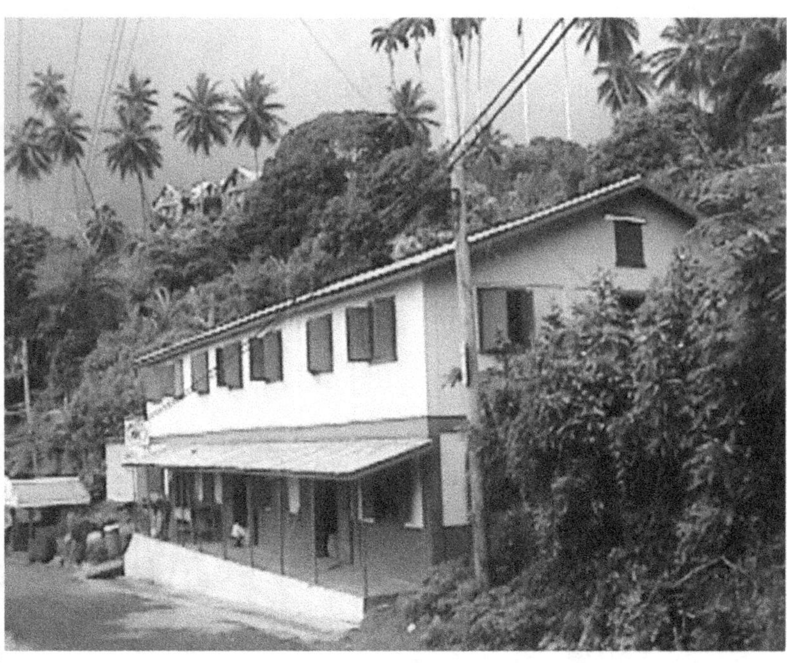

This farmer occasionally uses his donkey to carry his nutmeg harvest to the processing station (pool).

A nutmeg pool. Nutmeg is Grenada's most valuable cash crop. The nutmeg is featured on Grenada's national flag.

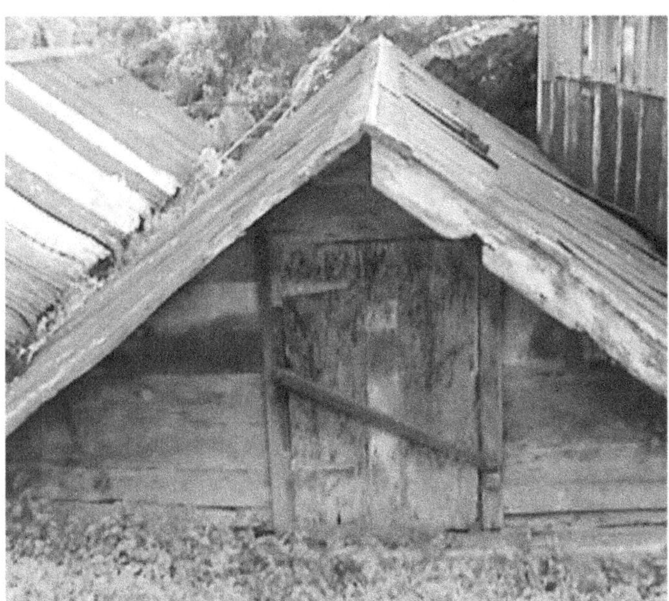

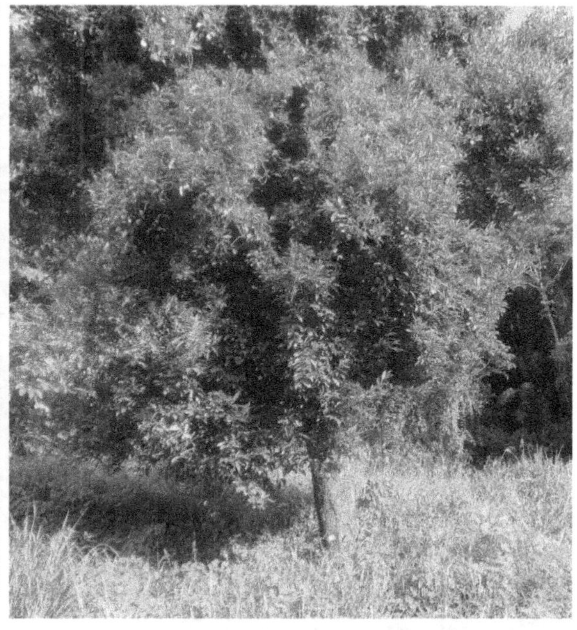

An old slide drawer in Hermitage once used to dry cocoa beans in the sun is mounted on rails. The visible housing once slid back and forth along the rails to expose the beans to sunlight or protect them from rain. As it is locally known, this cocoa slide is a relic of the village's agricultural past.

A nutmeg pool. Nutmeg is Grenada's most valuable cash crop. The nutmeg is featured on Grenada's national flag.

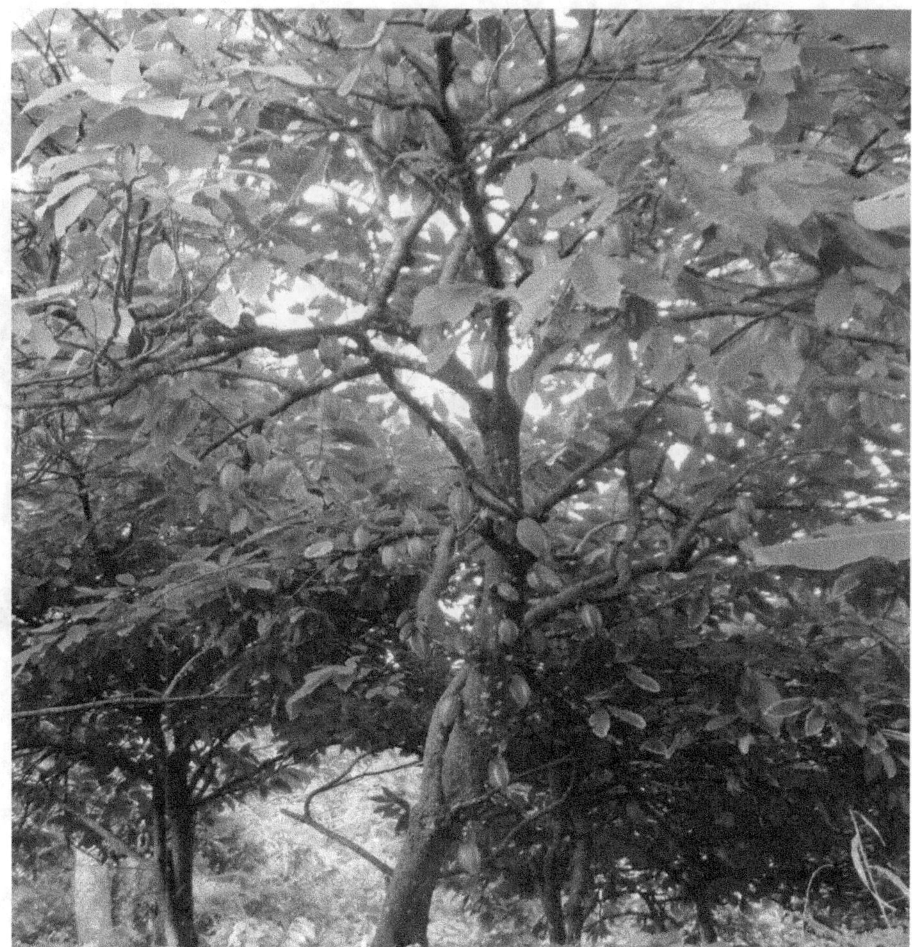

Cocoa Trees

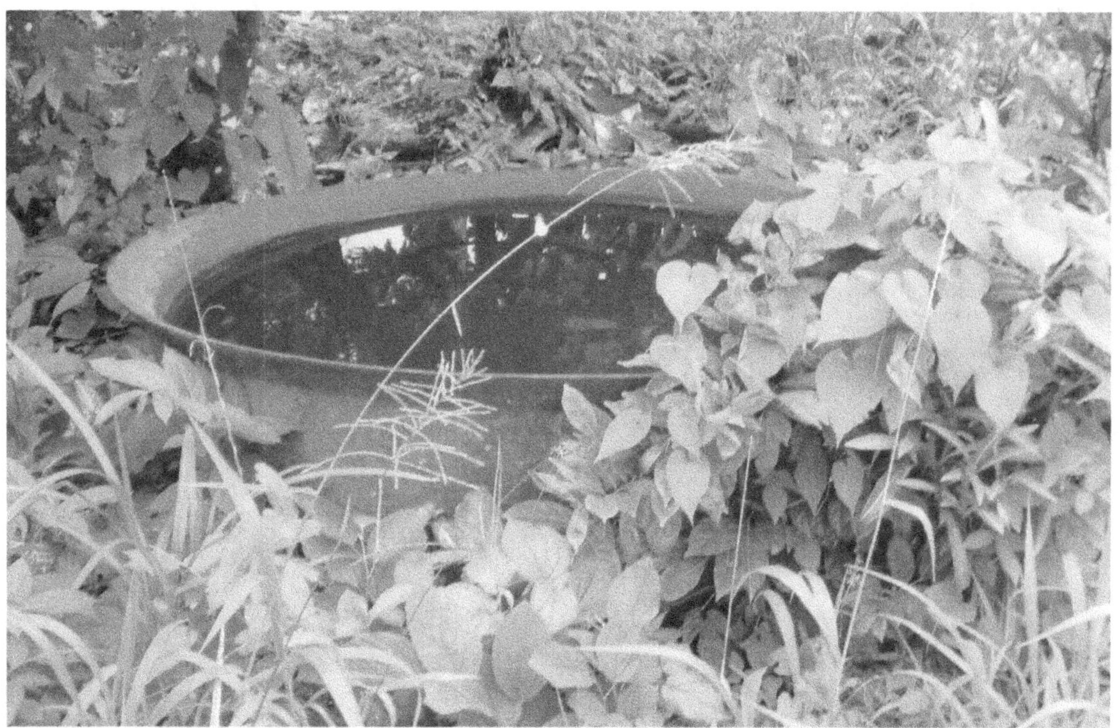

Copper pots once used on Grenada's sugar plantations

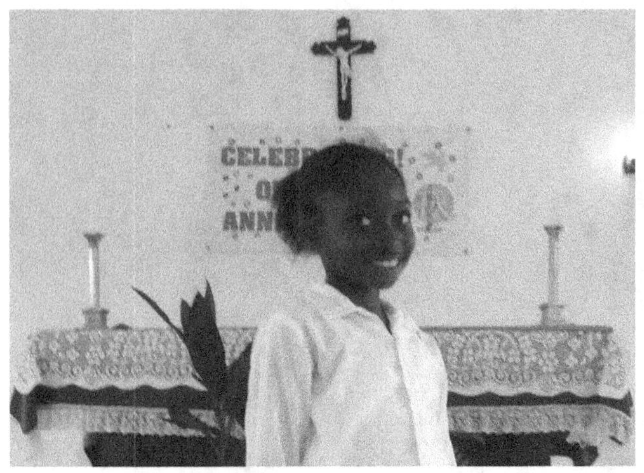

A young parishioner at Hermitage R.C. Church

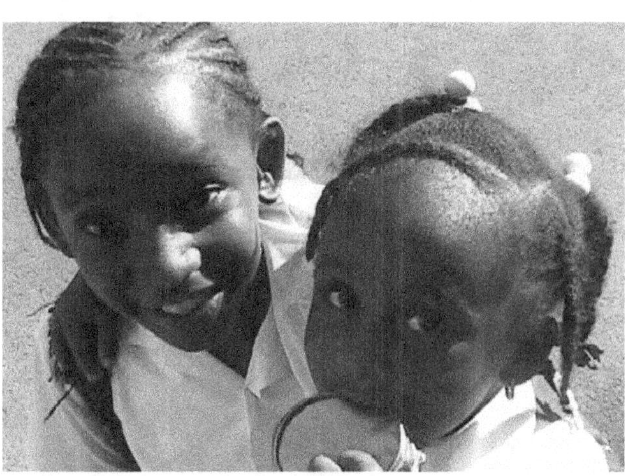

The joy of sisterhood

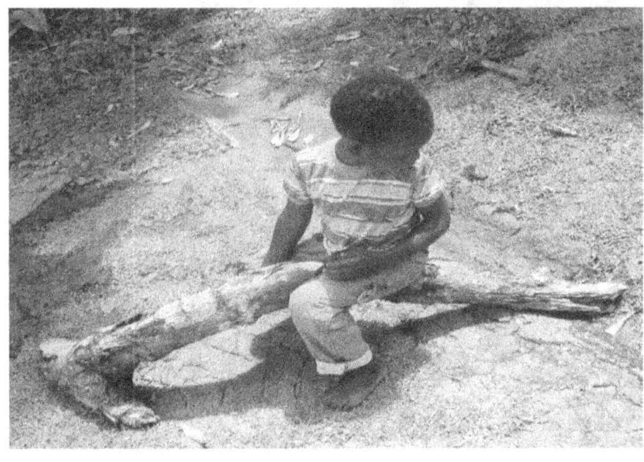

Kid playing Horsy. The hind leg is stuck.

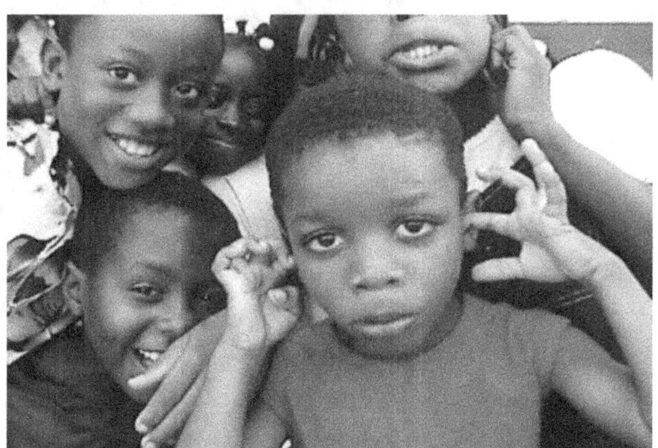

Making faces

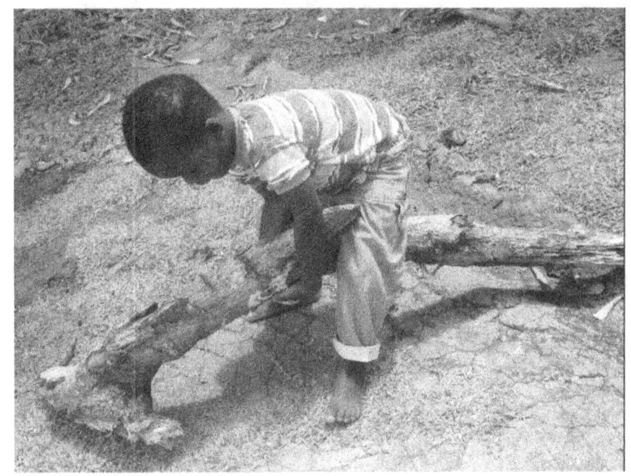

Horsy is helped out of the rut.

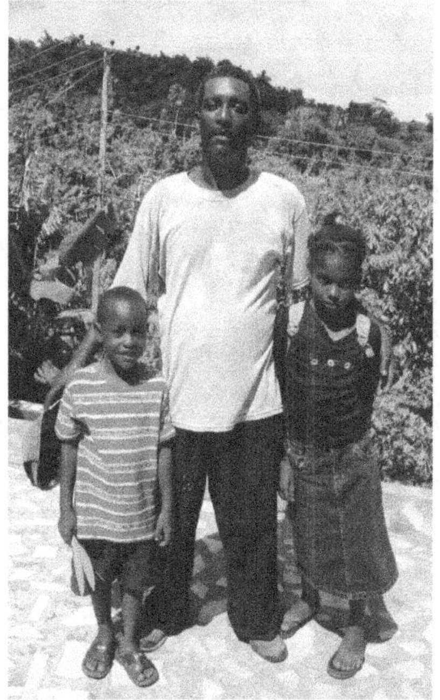

A day with dad

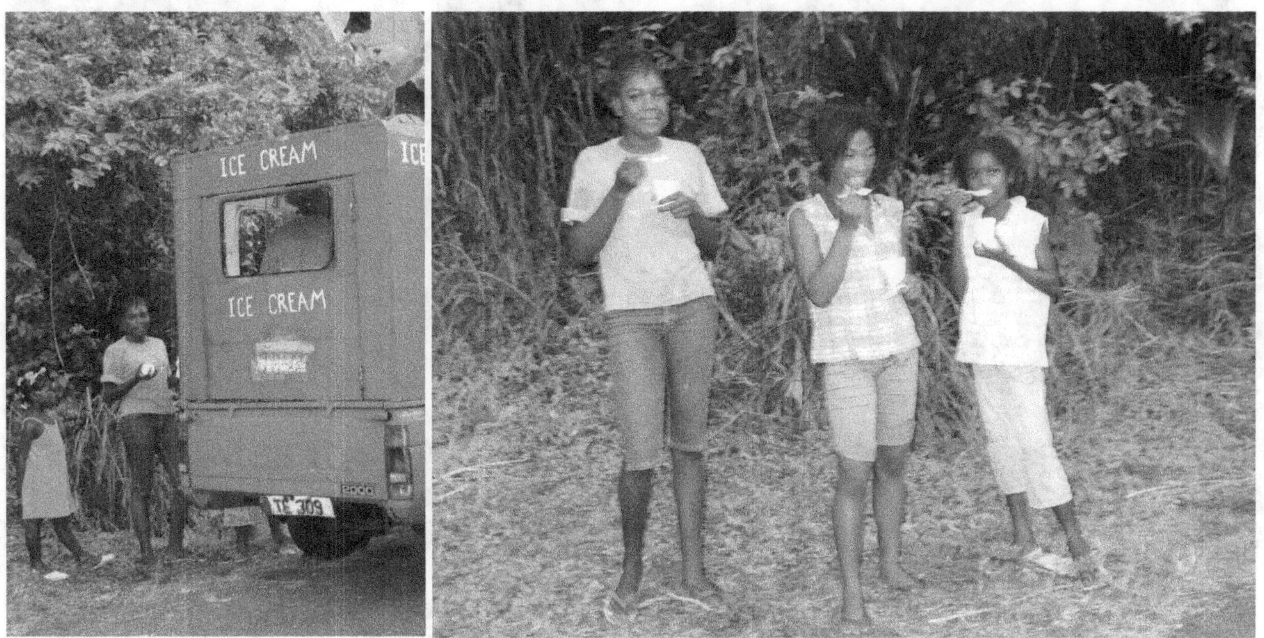

An ice cream van makes a village stop at Gru-gru Bailey hilltop and brings smiles to these young faces.

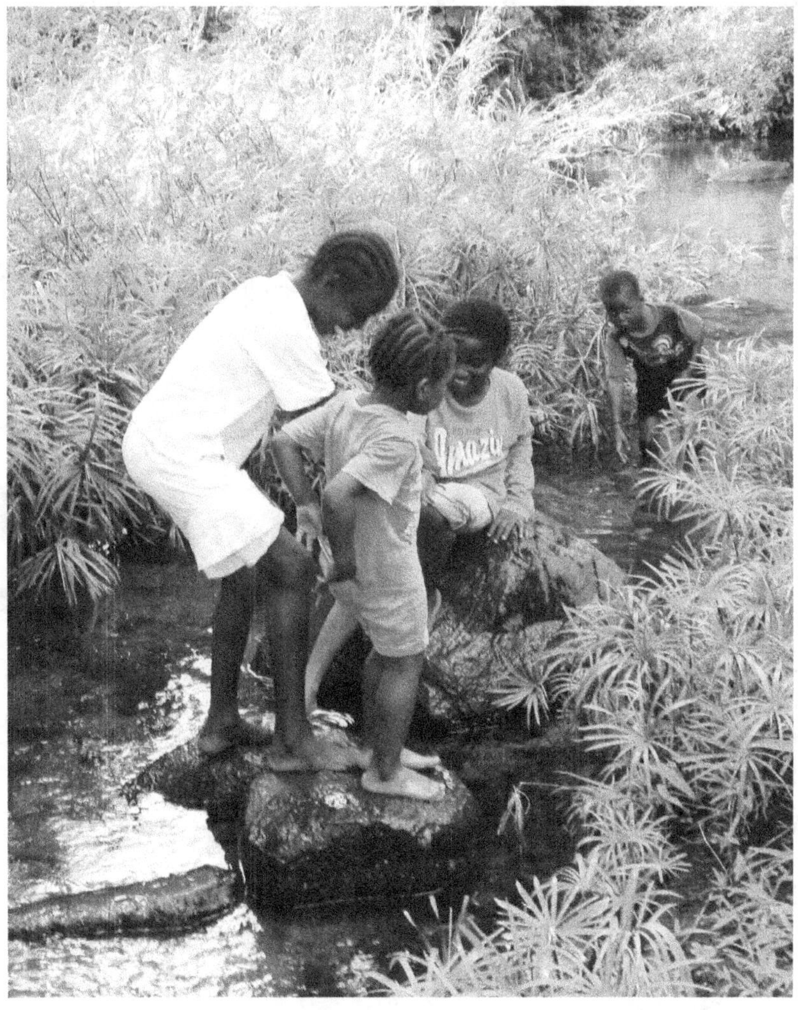

Kids playing in the stream

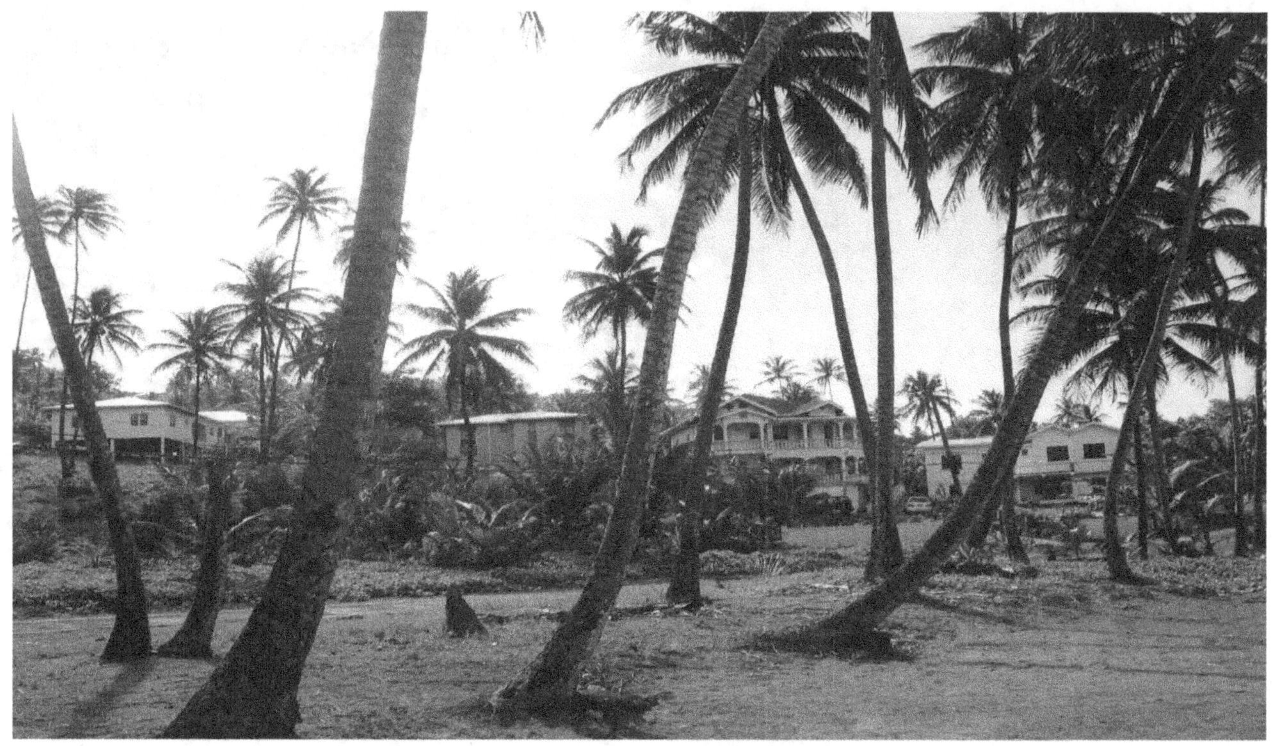

Homes among the palms near Mt. Rodney Beach

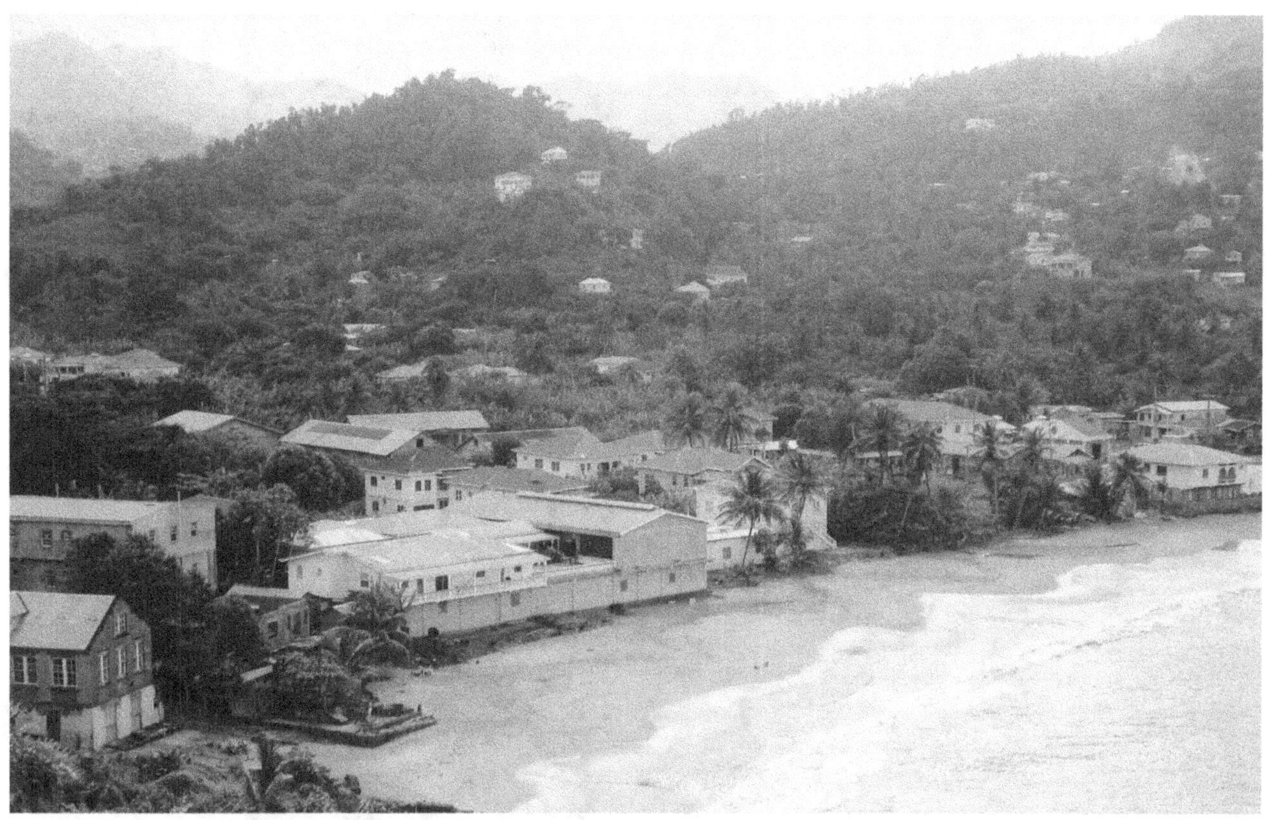

The lower end of Sauteurs, near the pier and fish market, has become an important interconnection point for transportation along Grenada's east and west coasts.

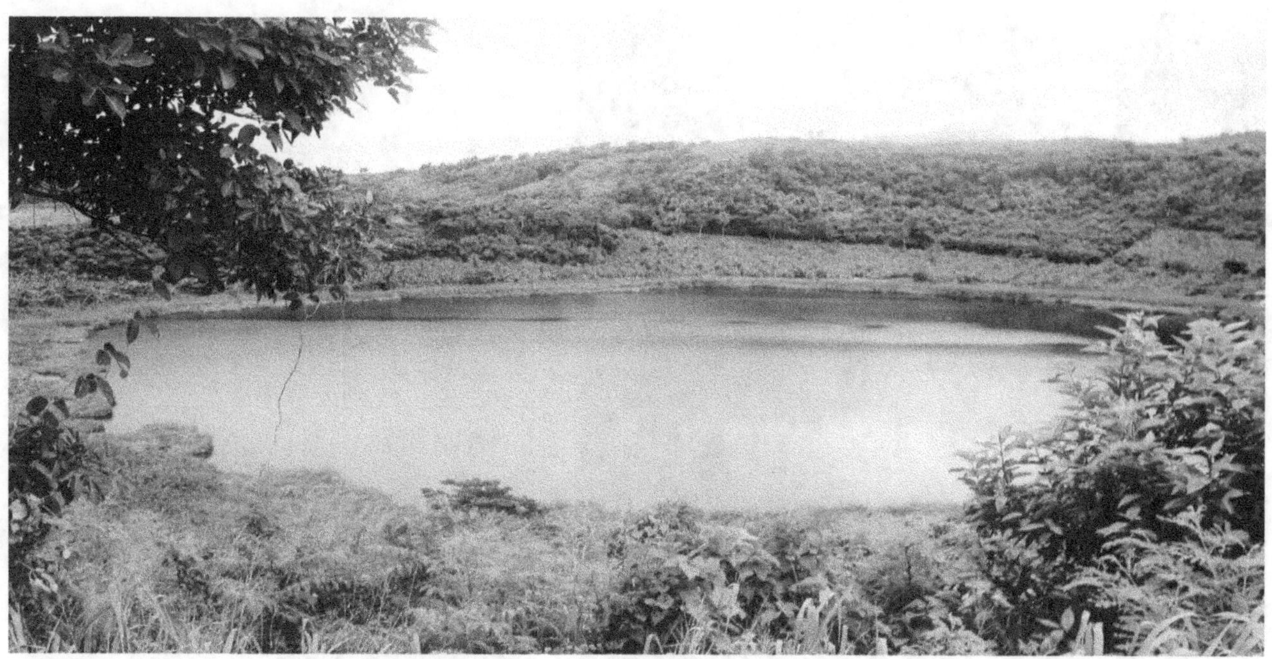

Lake Antoine is one of two volcanic lakes in the parish of St. Patrick.
Sugarcane thrives in the rich soils around.

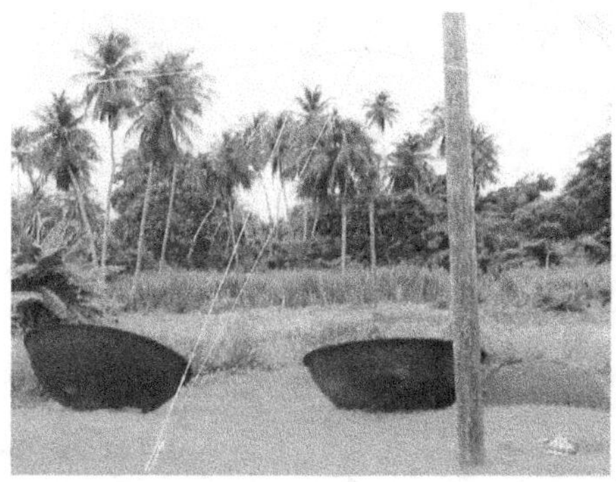

Copper pots in the factory yard

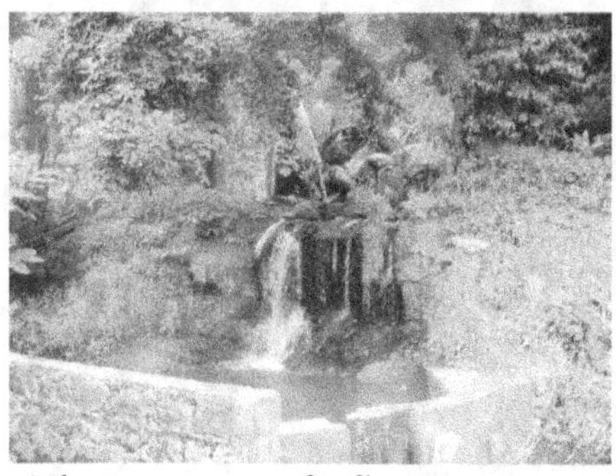

The proximity of a flowing stream
was necessary for turning the water
wheel during manufacturing.

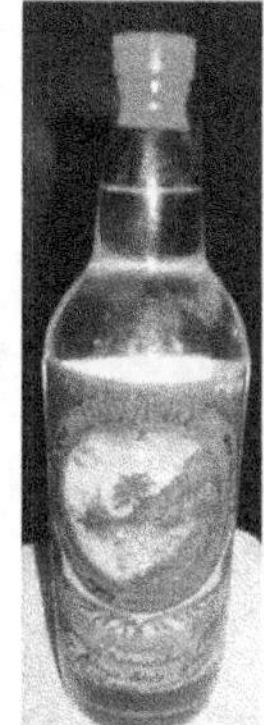

Rivers, named after its
River Antoine location,
is the brand of white
rum produced.

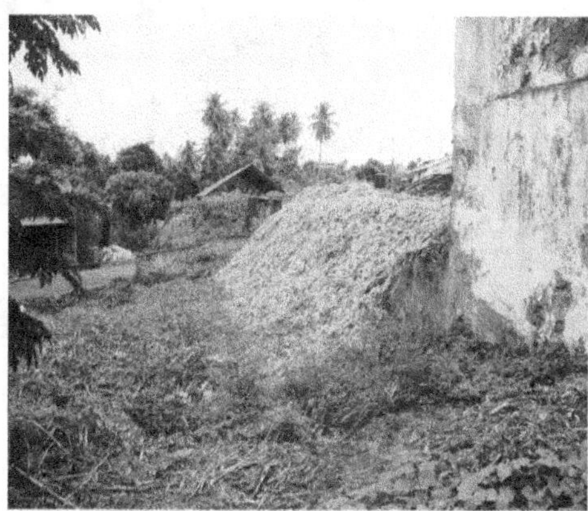

Bagasse is the dried sugar cane stalks after
they extract the juice. They use the bagasse
as fuel for the boiler.

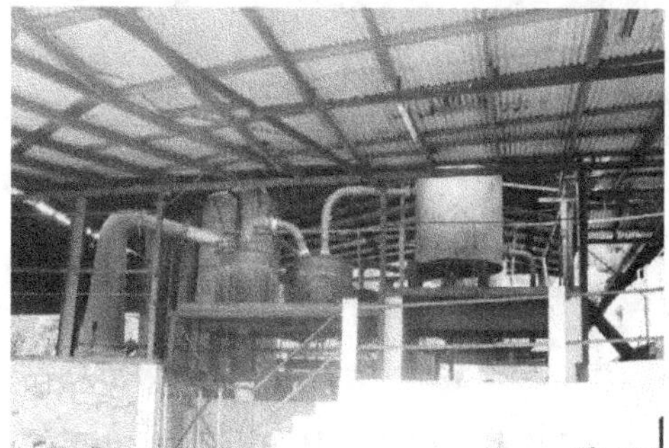

Rum manufacturing at River Antoine
factory. The factory was opened in 1785 and
has produced sugar during slavery and rum
subsequently. The manufacturing procedure
has remained the same throughout the years.

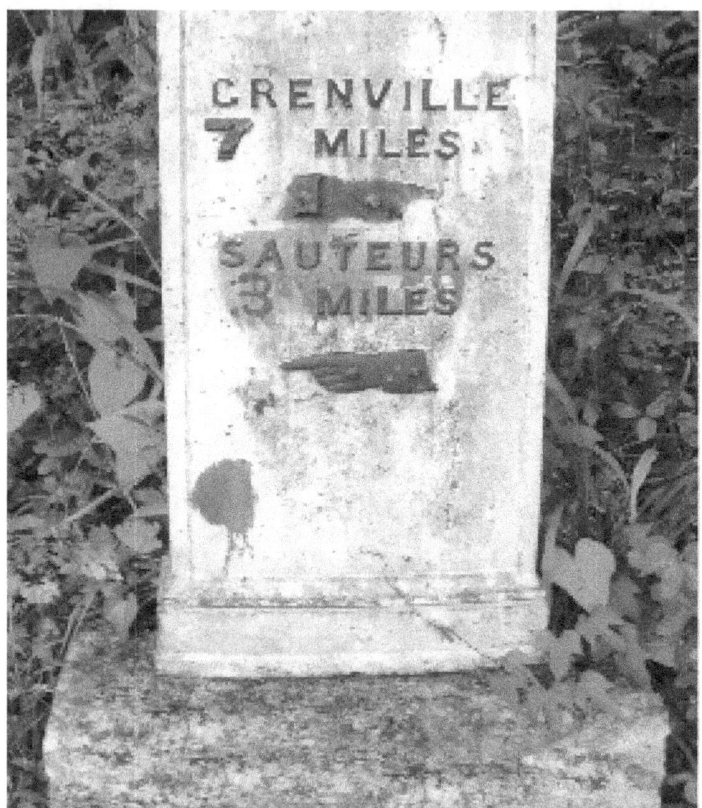

A colonial-era milestone at Gru-Gru Bailey hilltop. This is an item worthy of preservation.

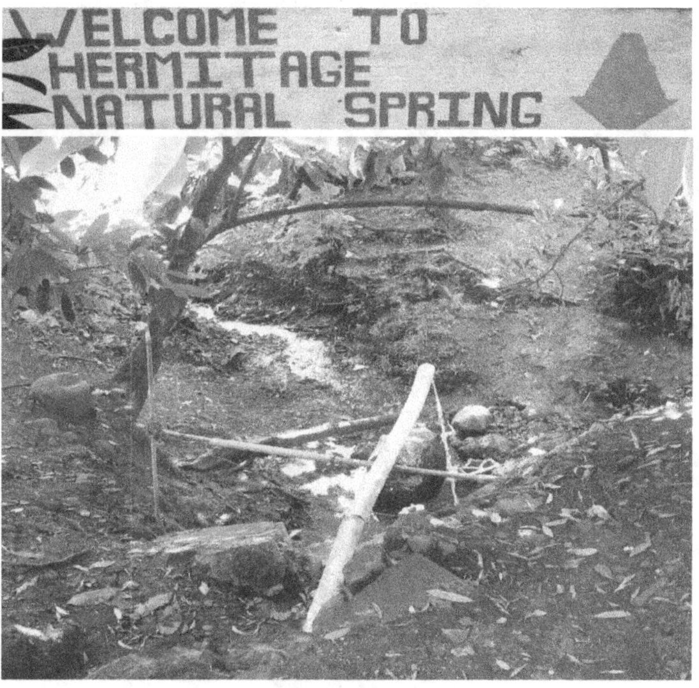

At this nearby location in Hermitage, water issues from an underground spring. This spring has met the emergency needs of the village for over a century. The area is called La Source because of its water source.

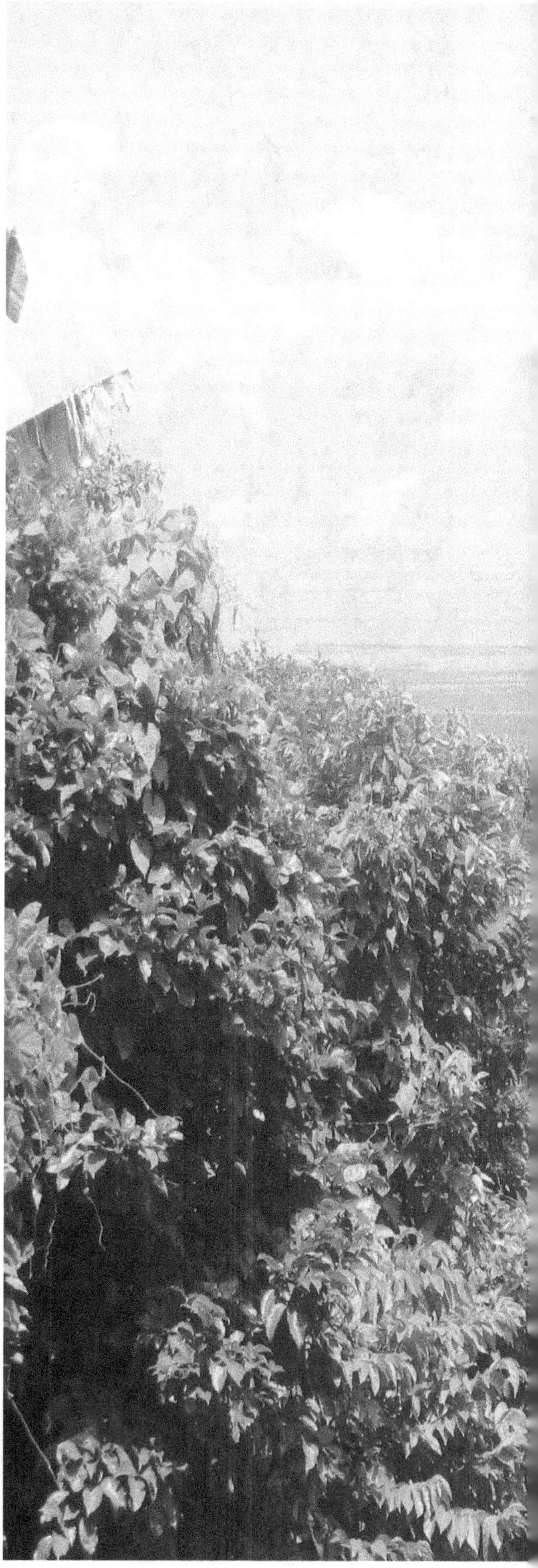

Tivoli and Conference Bay, viewed from Patterson Hill in Hermitage

Grenada has chosen to celebrate its carnival in August, a departure from the pre-Lenten dates on which other countries celebrate the festival. Here, we have presented a glimpse of carnival celebration from the countryside. Grenadian culture is enhanced by the village traditions that attract masqueraders such as 'wild' Amerindians, singing cowboys, historians, Jab Jabs, Maypole dancers, clowns, and others. Those who cannot join the crowds in the towns can enjoy the carnival entertainment that the masqueraders provide from village to village.

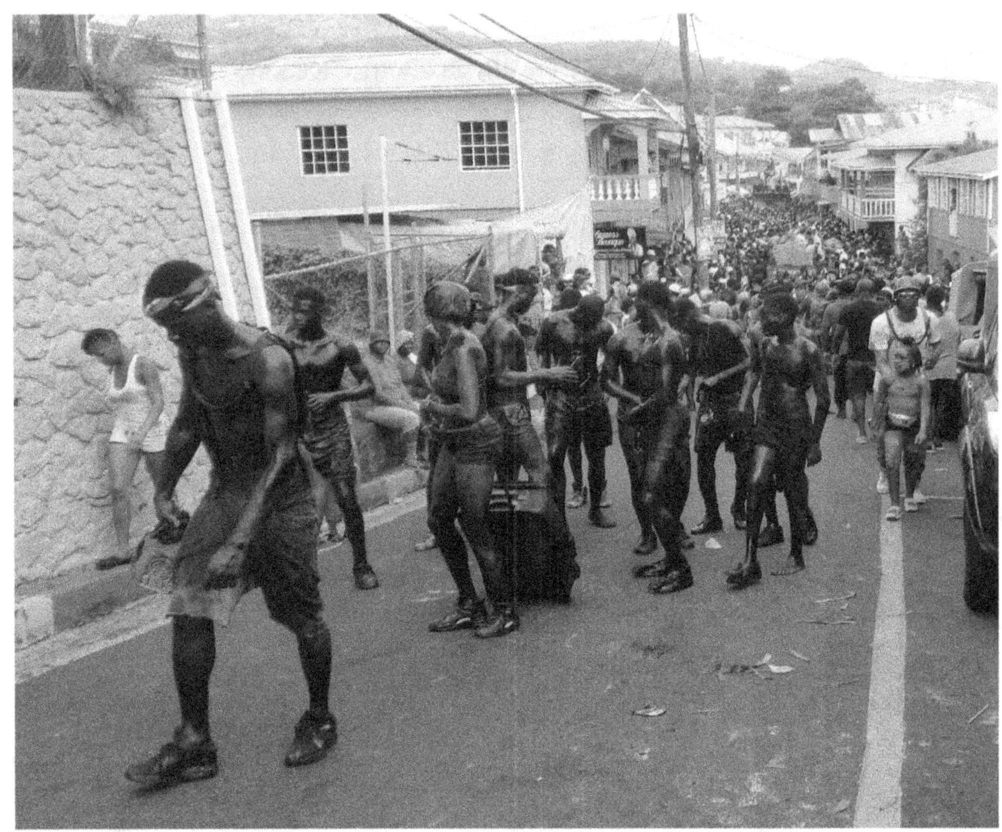

Black-painted jab jab masqueraders drum and chant through the streets of Sauteurs.
Jab-jab is a colloquial expression that is likely of the French, *diable* (devil).

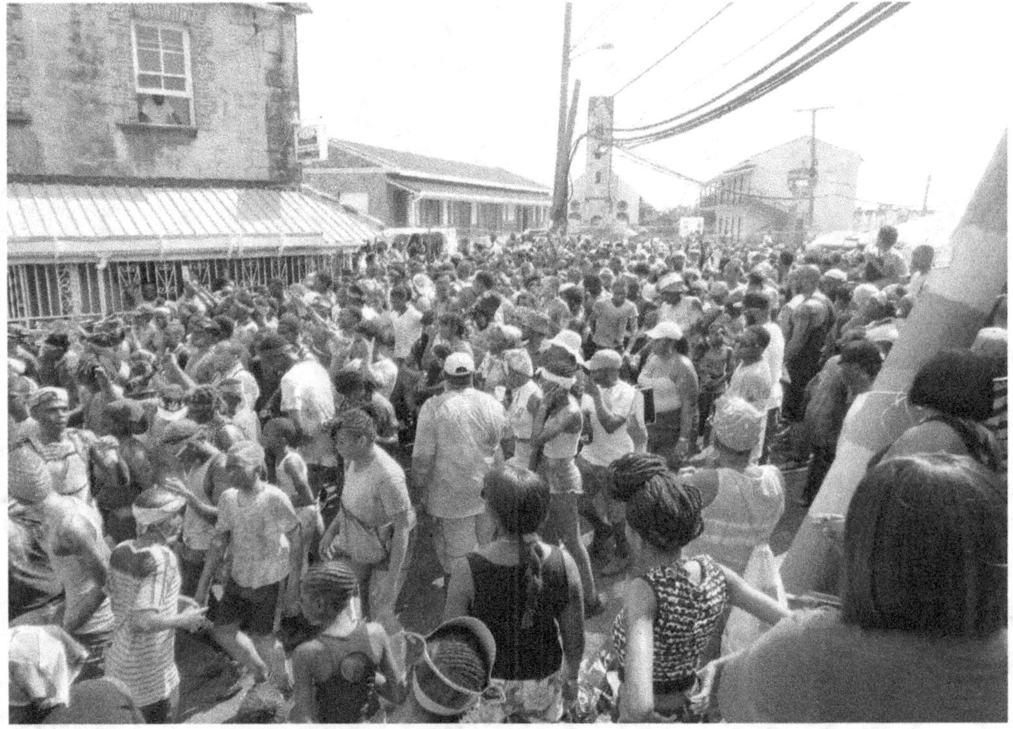

Crowds of onlookers mingle with the masqueraders.

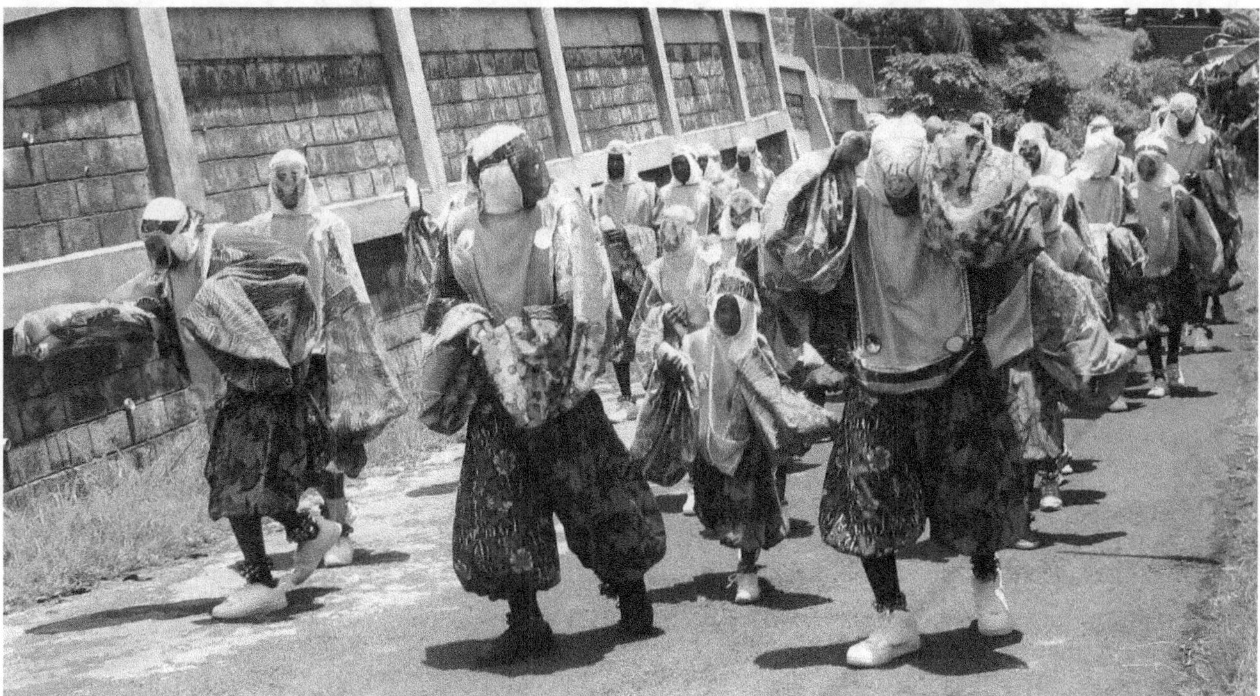

Short-knees: A short-knee band dances and sings its lyrical compositions in the streets of Hermitage. Short knees quite likely originated in the masquerade tradition of the speech-making Pierrot Grenade. The short-knee also has a practice rooted in the bravery of men who once defended their villages from outsiders.

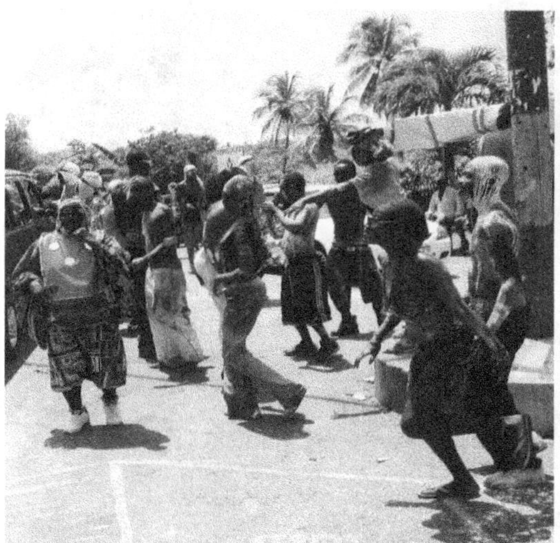

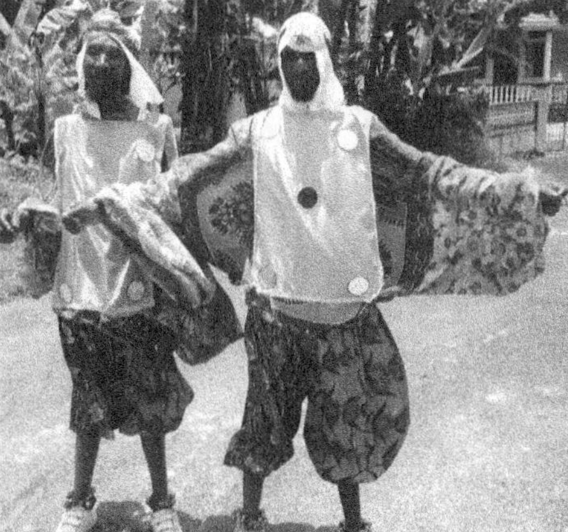

Two short-knee masqueraders, colorfully dressed in puffed attire, stockings, mirrors, bells around their ankles (called willows), and masks temporarily raised above their heads, take some time away from the band to approach the camera.

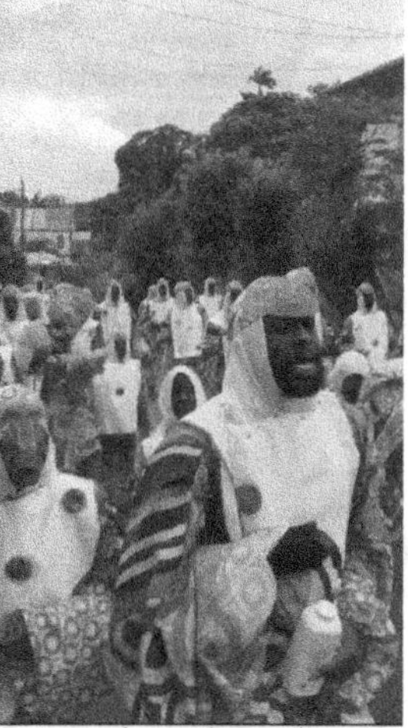

Another short-knee band

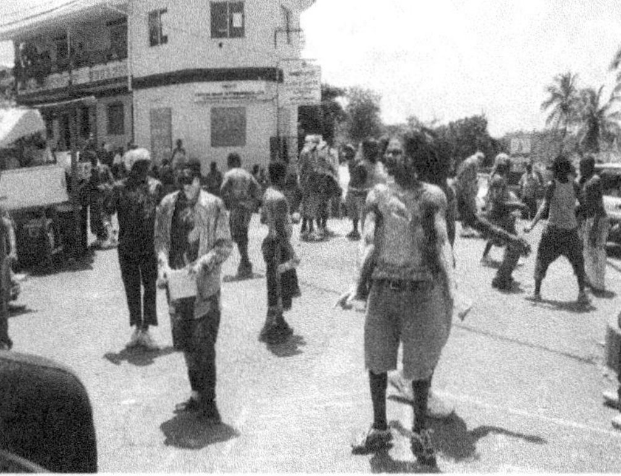

River Sallee villagers celebrate carnival.

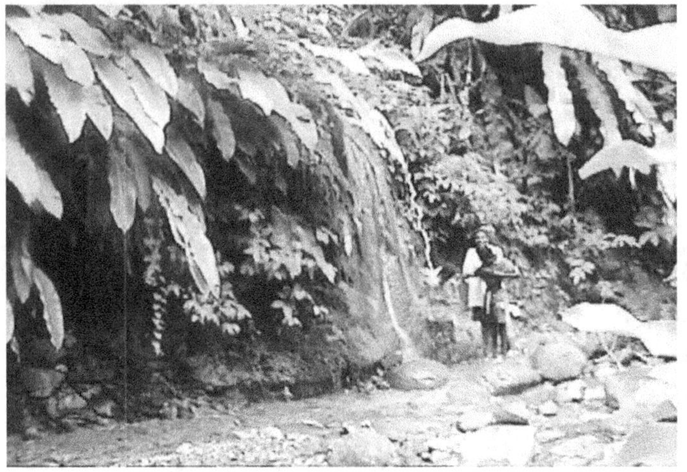

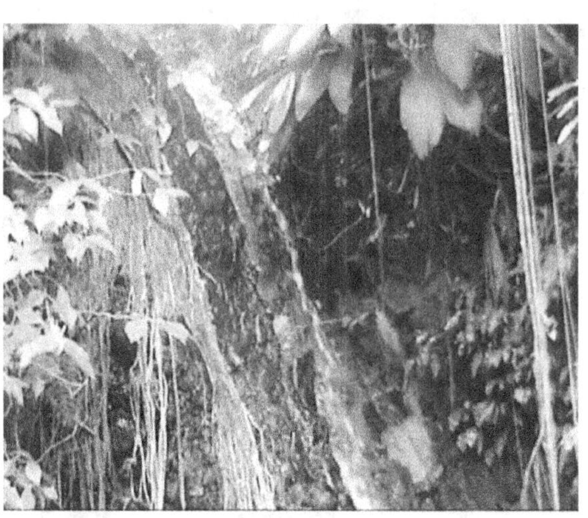

Sulphur deposits give the warm water a copper tone, providing evidence of the island's volcanic past.

Cascading warm water from Cha Cha's boiling spring

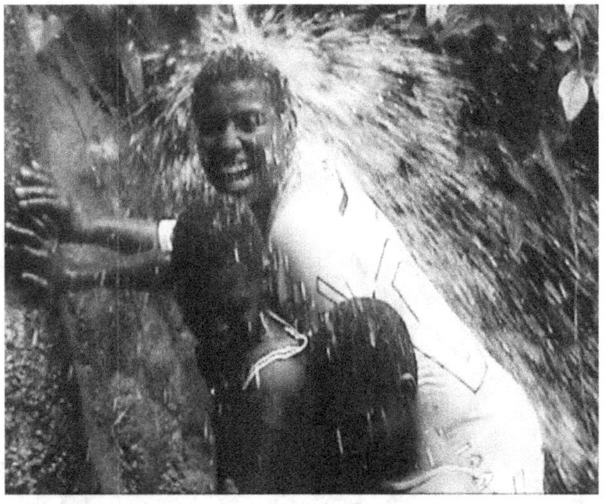

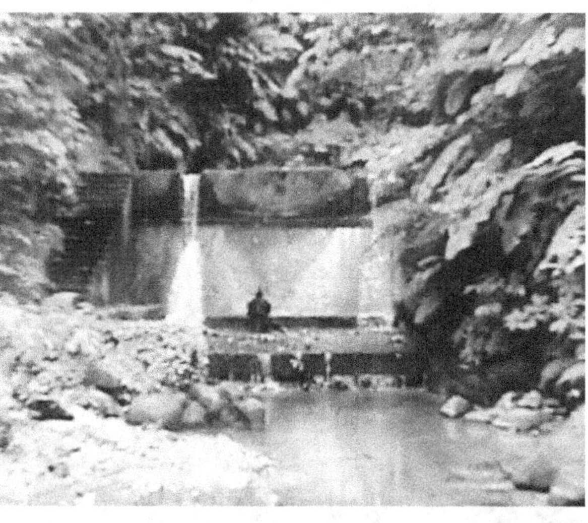

Boys having fun in the warm waterfall

A dam located upstream from the boiling spring

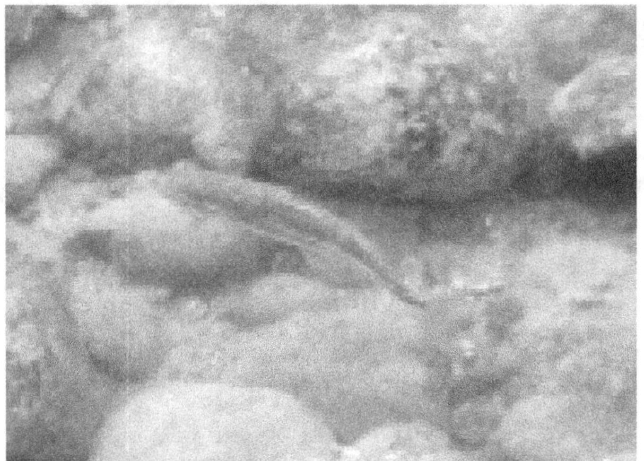

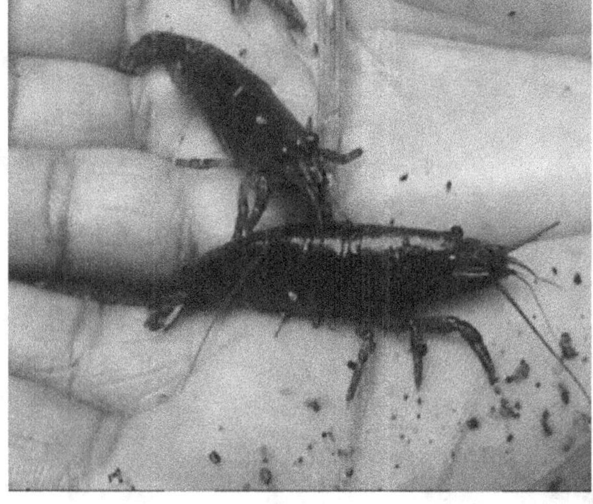

A mullet swims downstream in the River. It is another variety of Grenada's freshwater fish.

The boys in the picture to the left have caught these crayfish, locally called books, in a nearby stream.

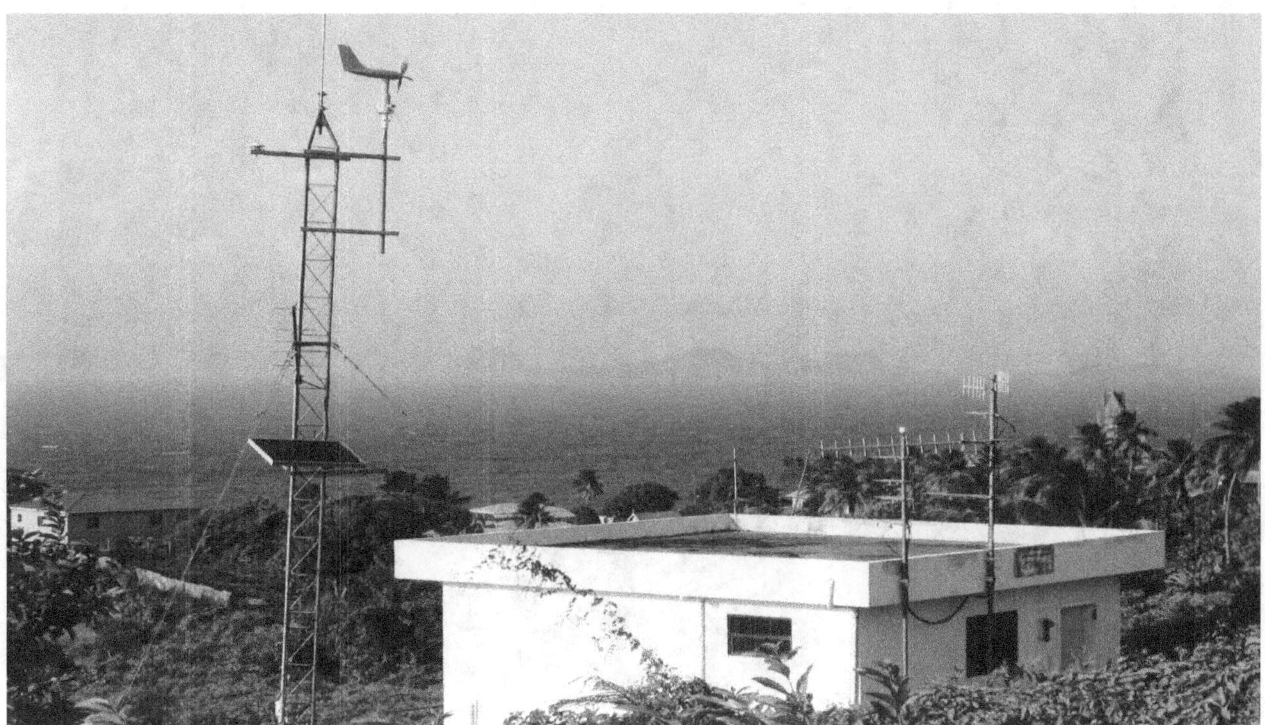

This volcano monitoring station is at Marli. Seismologists located the station at an elevated point some seven miles offshore from Kick 'em Jenny, an underwater volcano that erupts on rare occasions. In addition to its facilitation of research, the monitoring station is part of a mechanism that may provide early warning if needed.

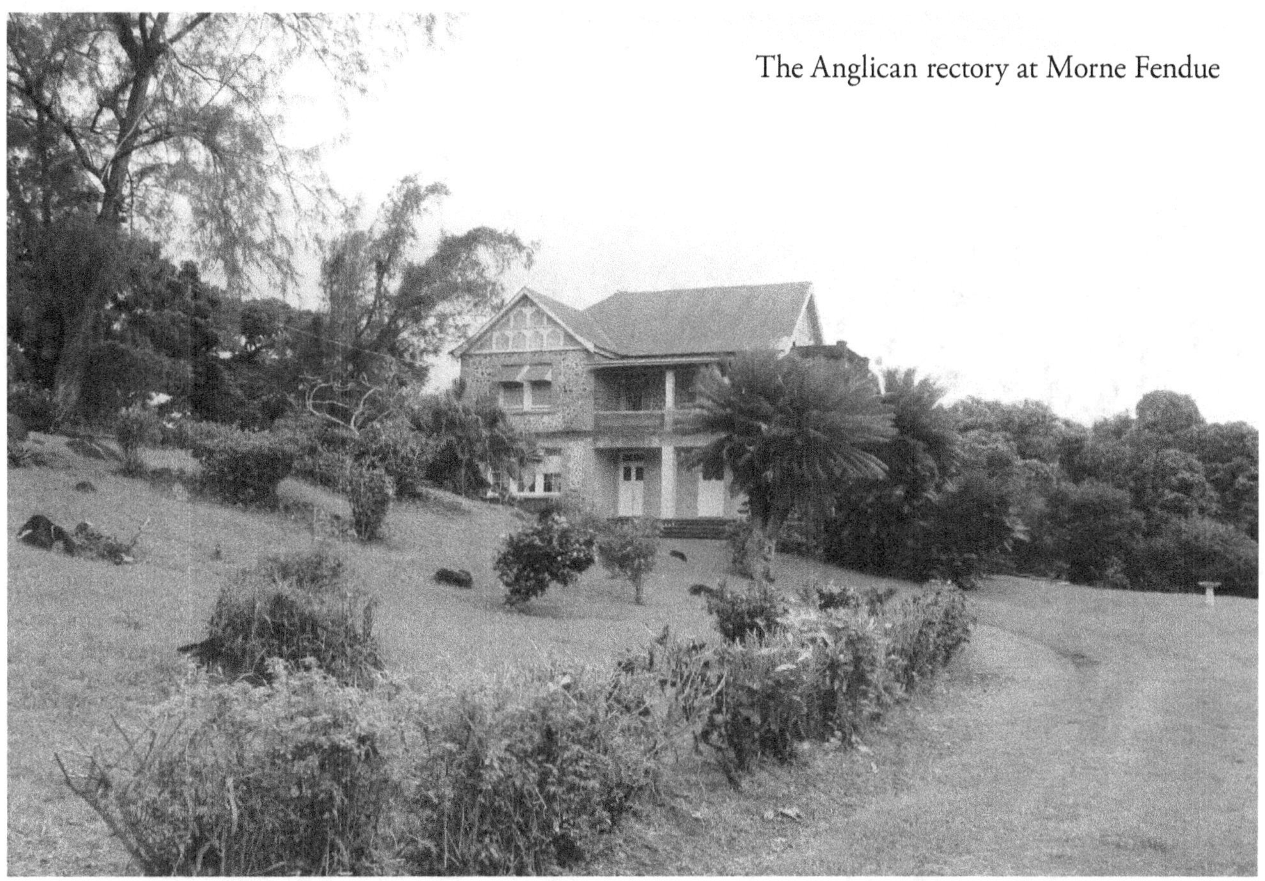

The Anglican rectory at Morne Fendue

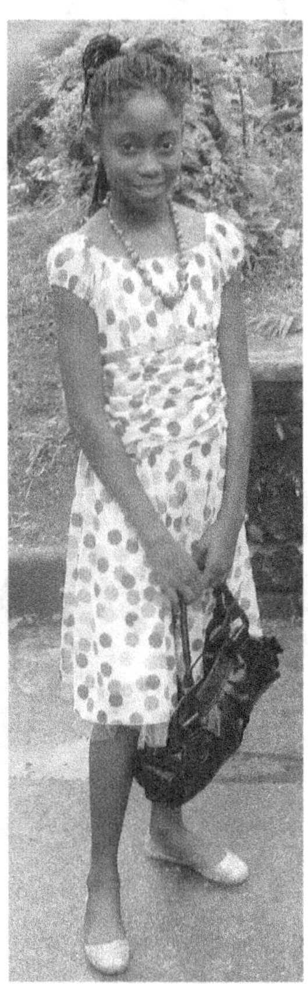

A young parishioner

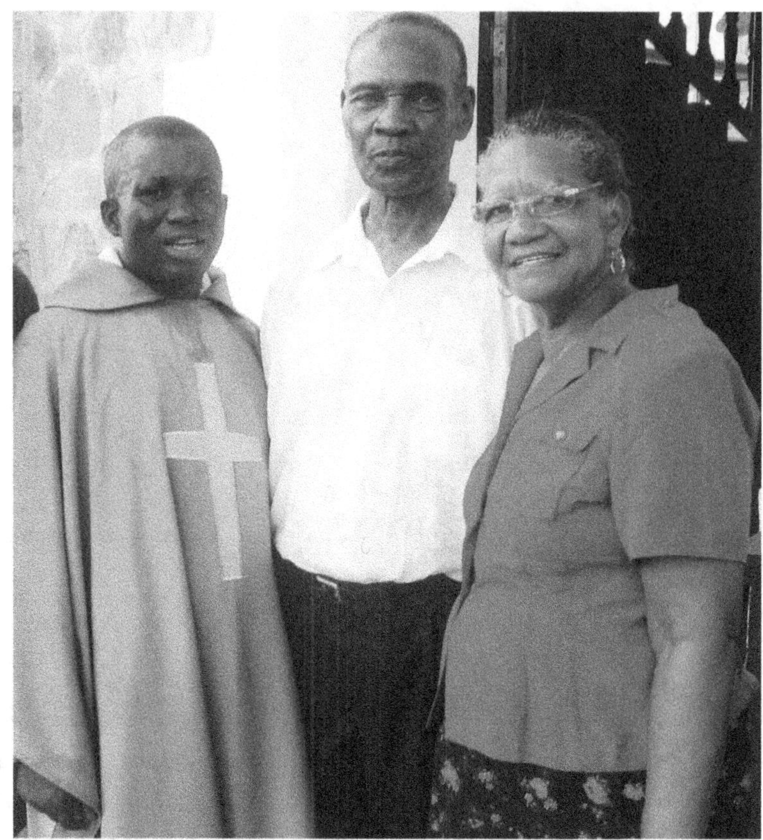

Here is an after-church celebration of kinship between a Roman Catholic priest from Nigeria and his Afro-Grenadian parishioners from Hermitage, a celebration once prohibited by the foreboding Atlantic Ocean and five hundred years of separation.

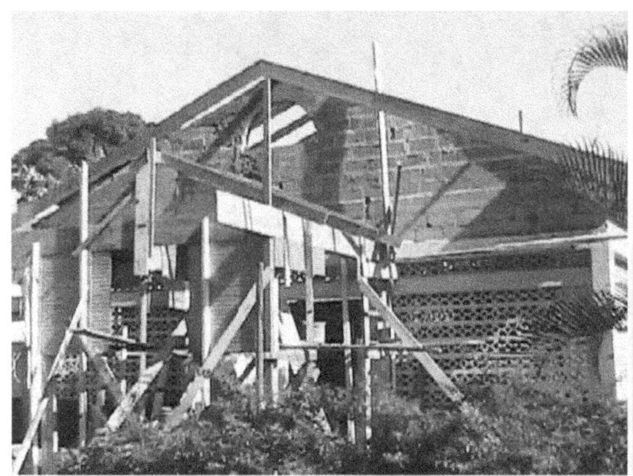

Rebuilding Hermitage R.C. Church after Hurricane Ivan in 2004. Wind and water damaged the roof and interior.

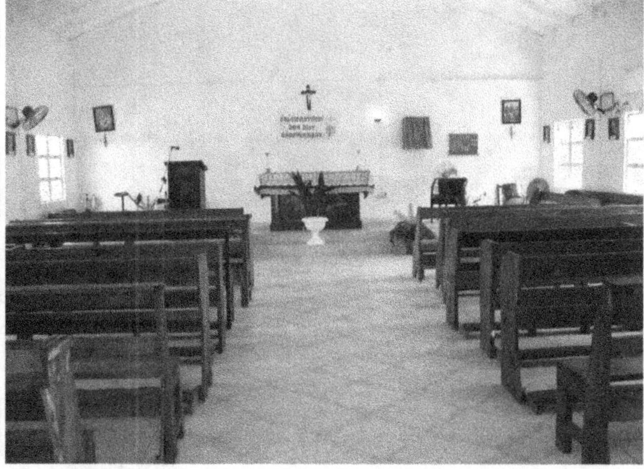

Hermitage R.C. Church after repairs from Hurricane Ivan's damage. Like many other damaged structures in Grenada, this roof is rebuilt better and stronger.

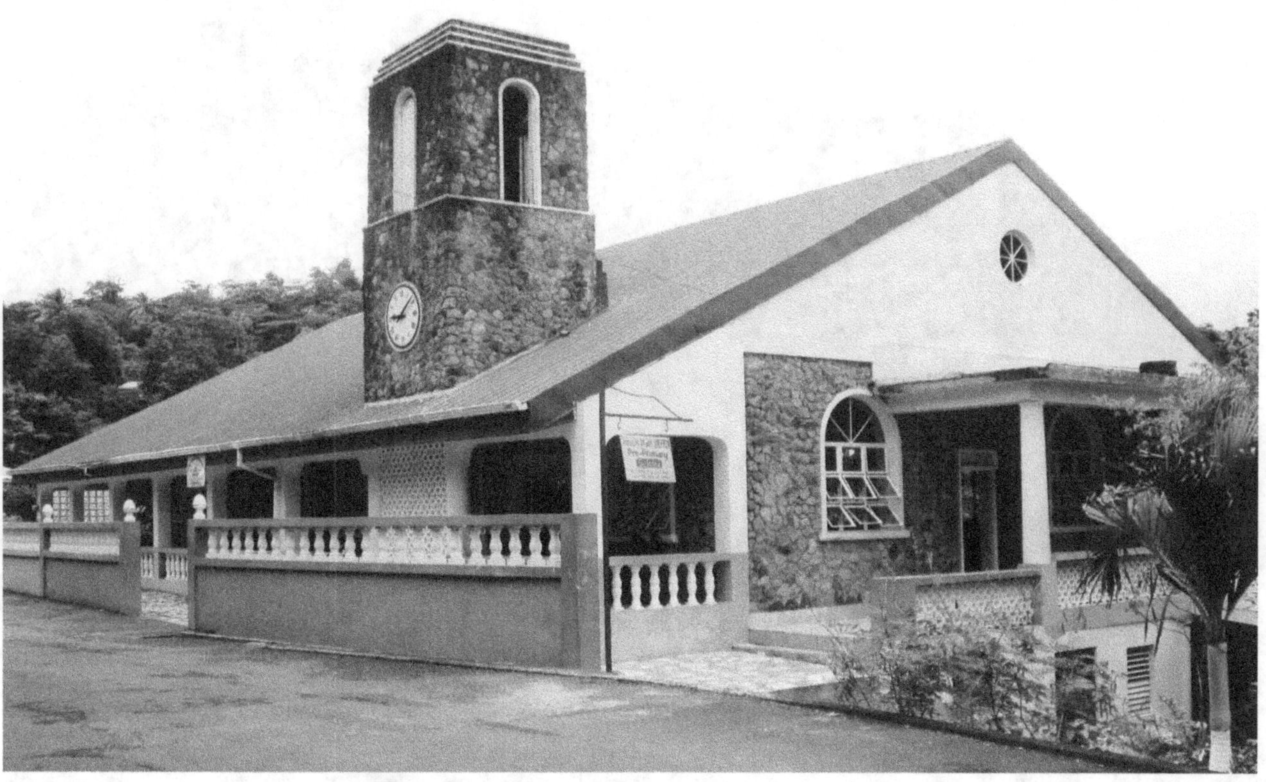

Snell Hall Seventh Day Adventist (SDA) Church

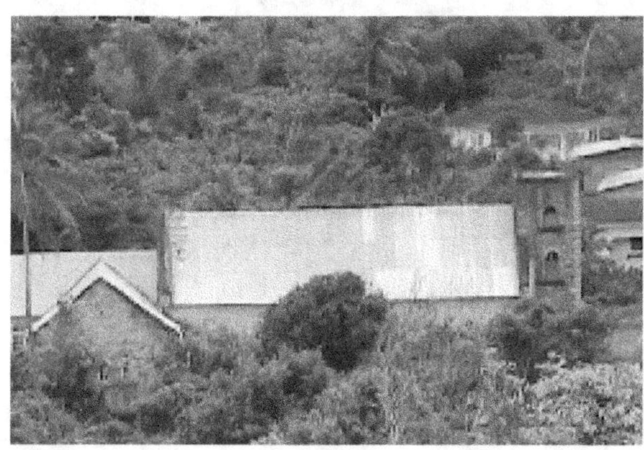

Hermitage Anglican church

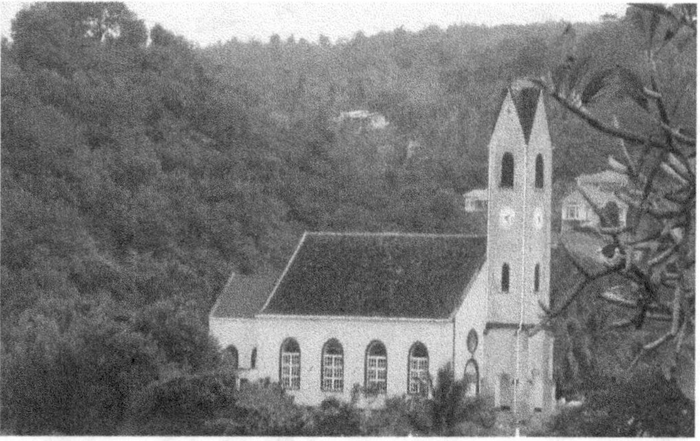

St. Patrick's Anglican Church, post - Hurricane Ivan

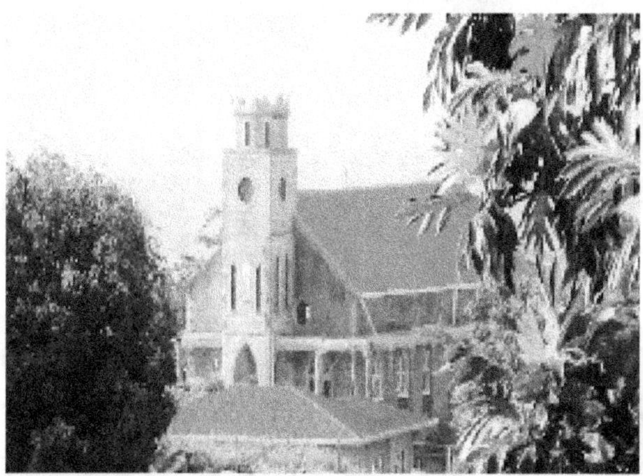

Sauteurs R.C. Church

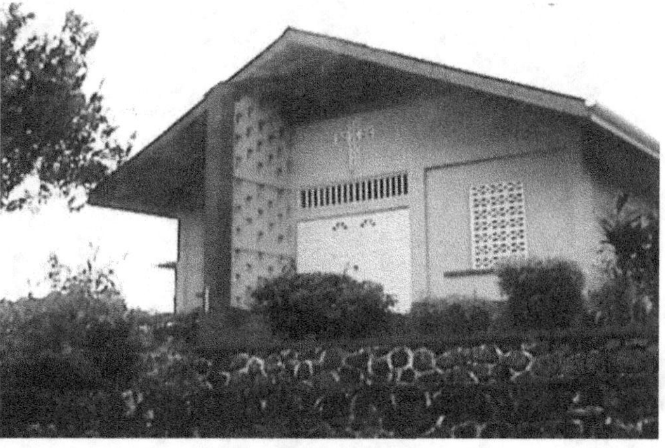

Hermitage Evangelical Church

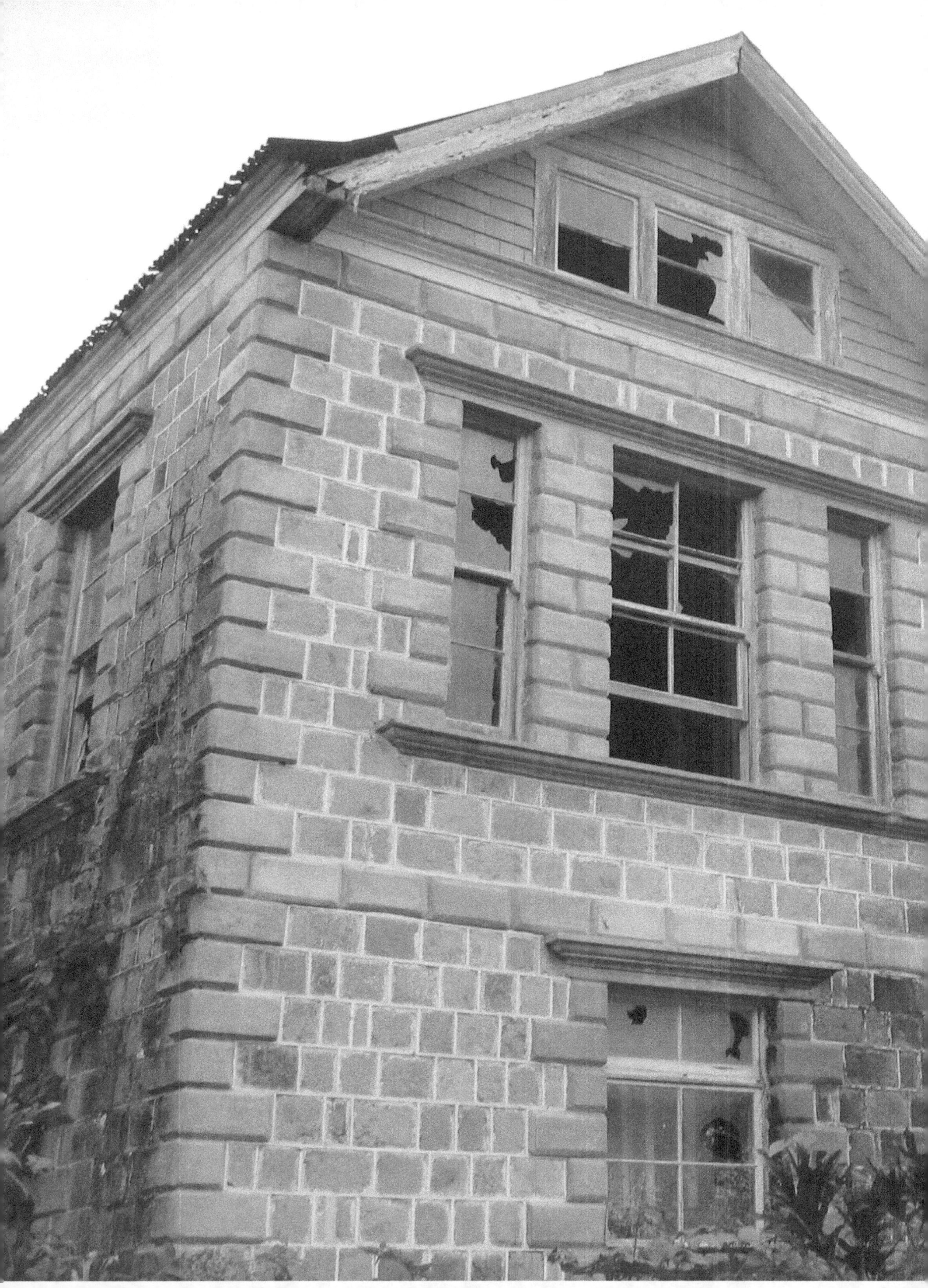

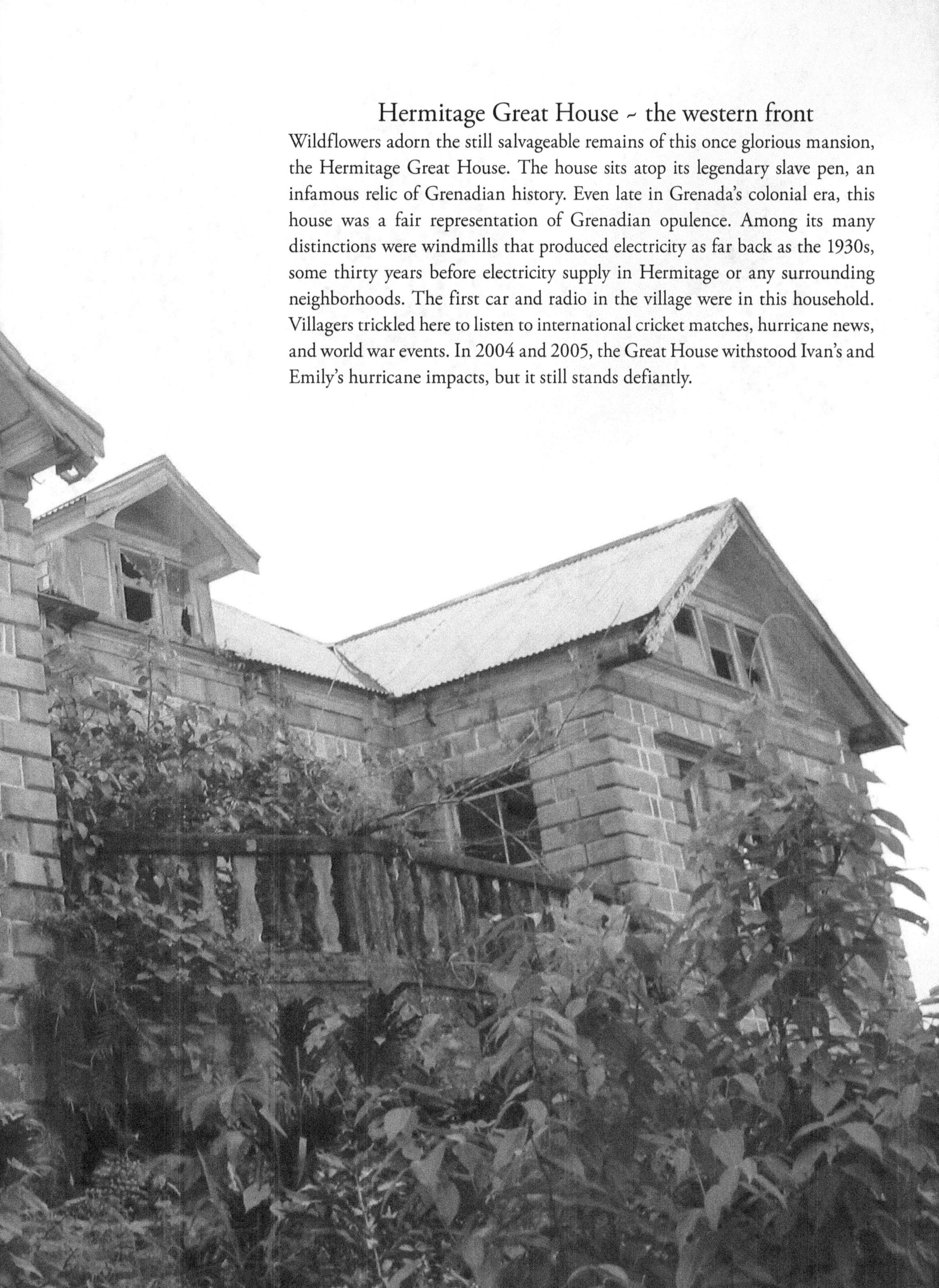

Hermitage Great House ~ the western front

Wildflowers adorn the still salvageable remains of this once glorious mansion, the Hermitage Great House. The house sits atop its legendary slave pen, an infamous relic of Grenadian history. Even late in Grenada's colonial era, this house was a fair representation of Grenadian opulence. Among its many distinctions were windmills that produced electricity as far back as the 1930s, some thirty years before electricity supply in Hermitage or any surrounding neighborhoods. The first car and radio in the village were in this household. Villagers trickled here to listen to international cricket matches, hurricane news, and world war events. In 2004 and 2005, the Great House withstood Ivan's and Emily's hurricane impacts, but it still stands defiantly.

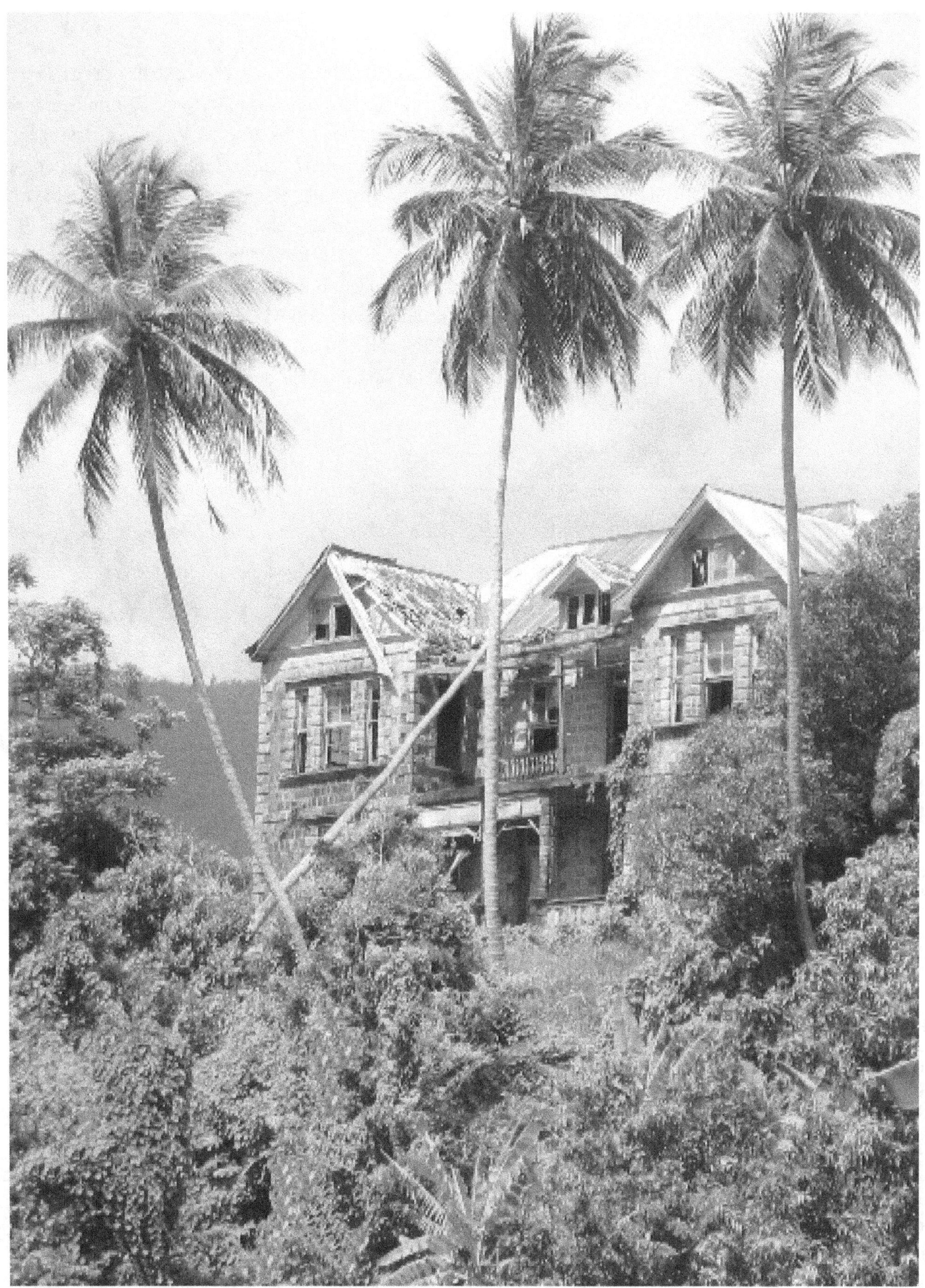

Hermitage Great House — the eastern front

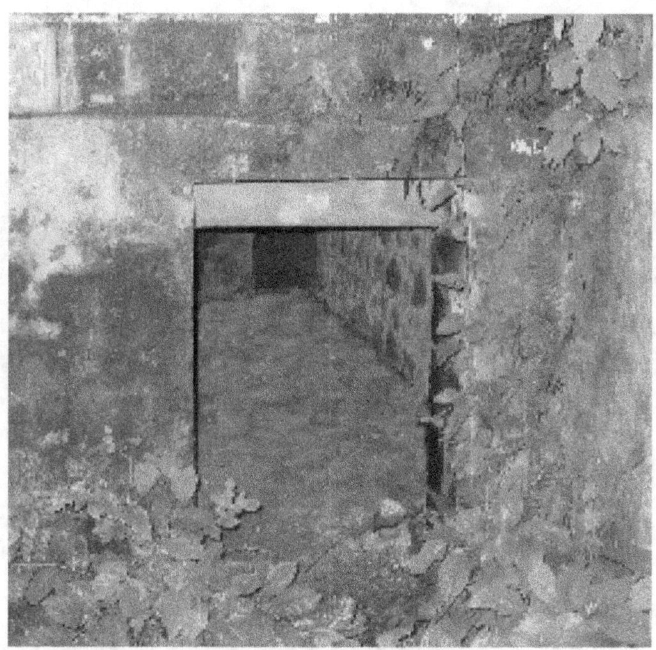

The Hermitage Slave Pen

This pen sits at the bottom of the Hermitage Great House; it would have been a dreaded entrance to the slaves they brought in for punishment. Hopefully, there are plans to refurbish or restore much of this historical site.

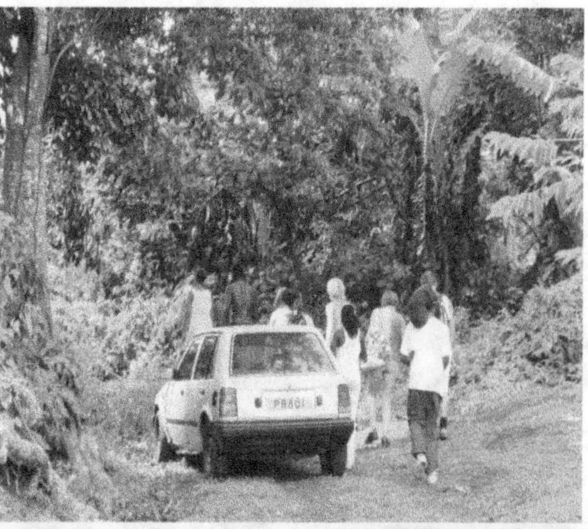

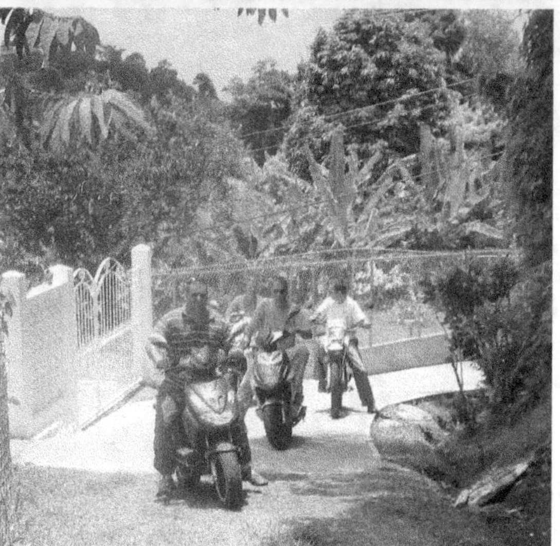

Above, visitors walk and ride towards the Hermitage slave pen.

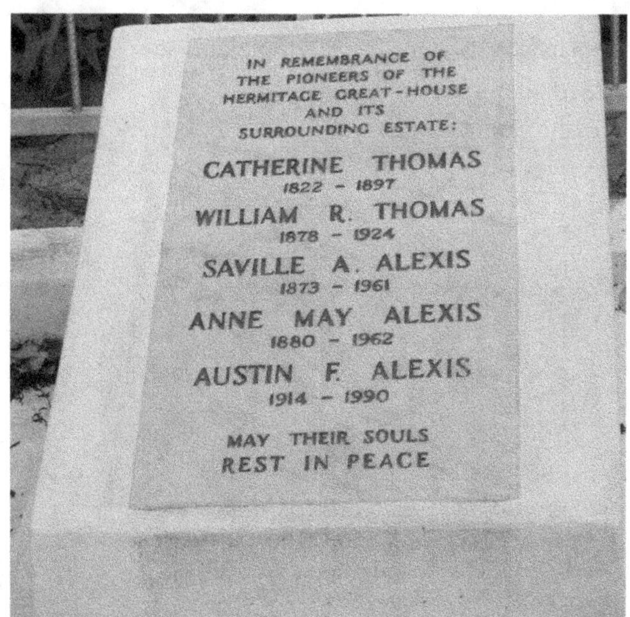

According to information on the family tombstone above, Catherine Thomas (1822-1897) would have been alive before Britain abolished slavery in 1834. Catherine's parents were slave owners at the Hermitage Great House.

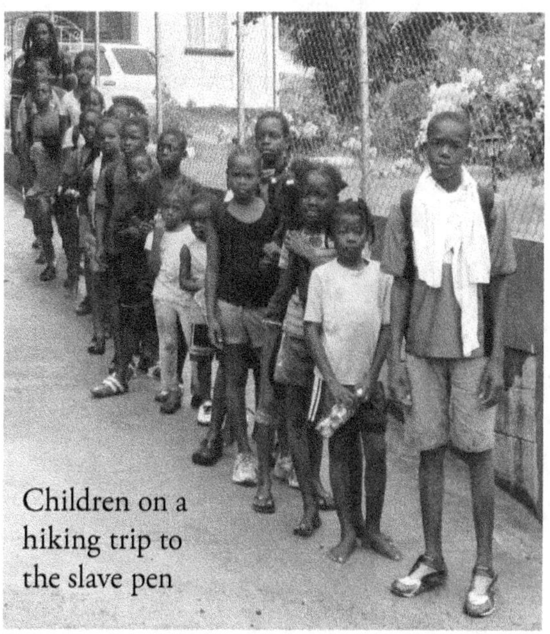

Children on a hiking trip to the slave pen

CALLALOO VILLAGE

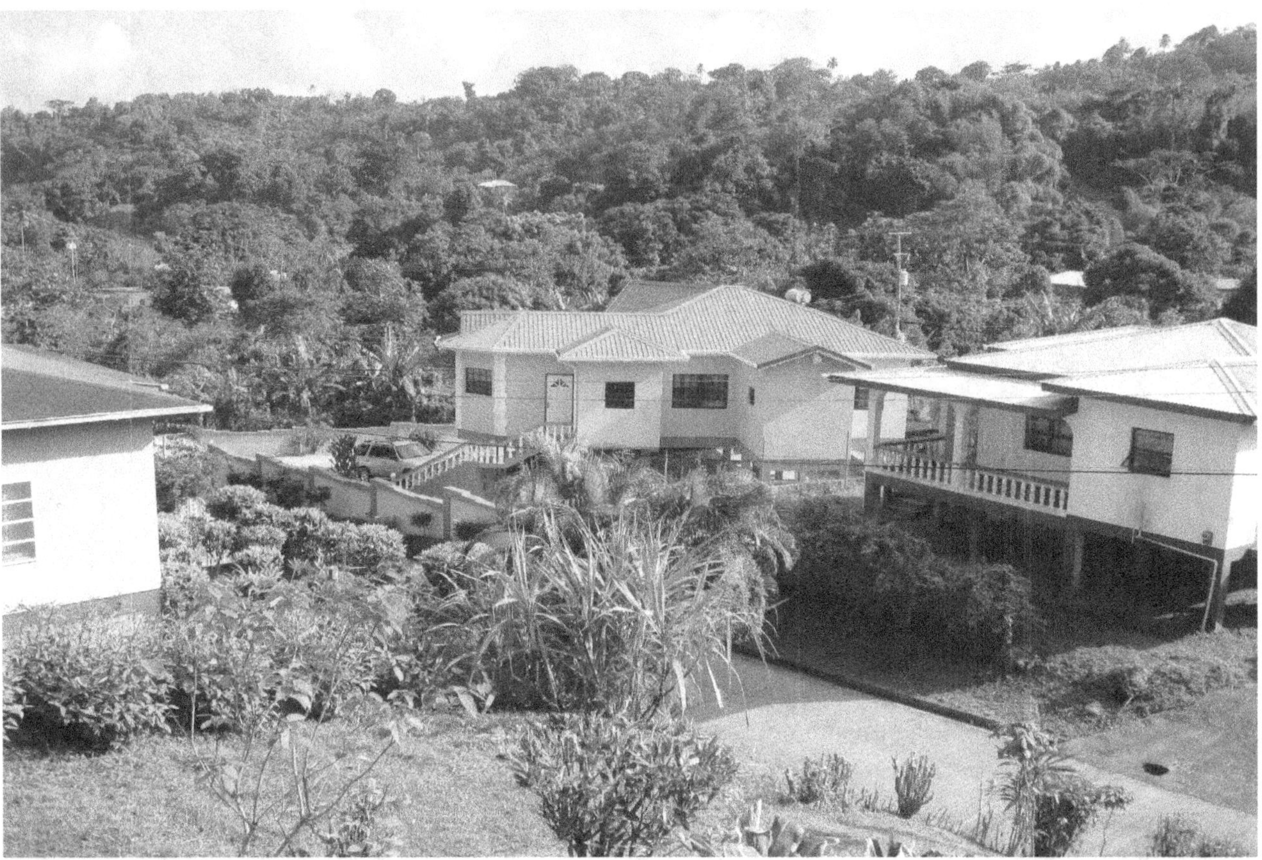

Here are homes in the village of Callaloo. The village gets its name from the callaloo plant (see facing page), which once occupied a large section along the nearby roadsides.

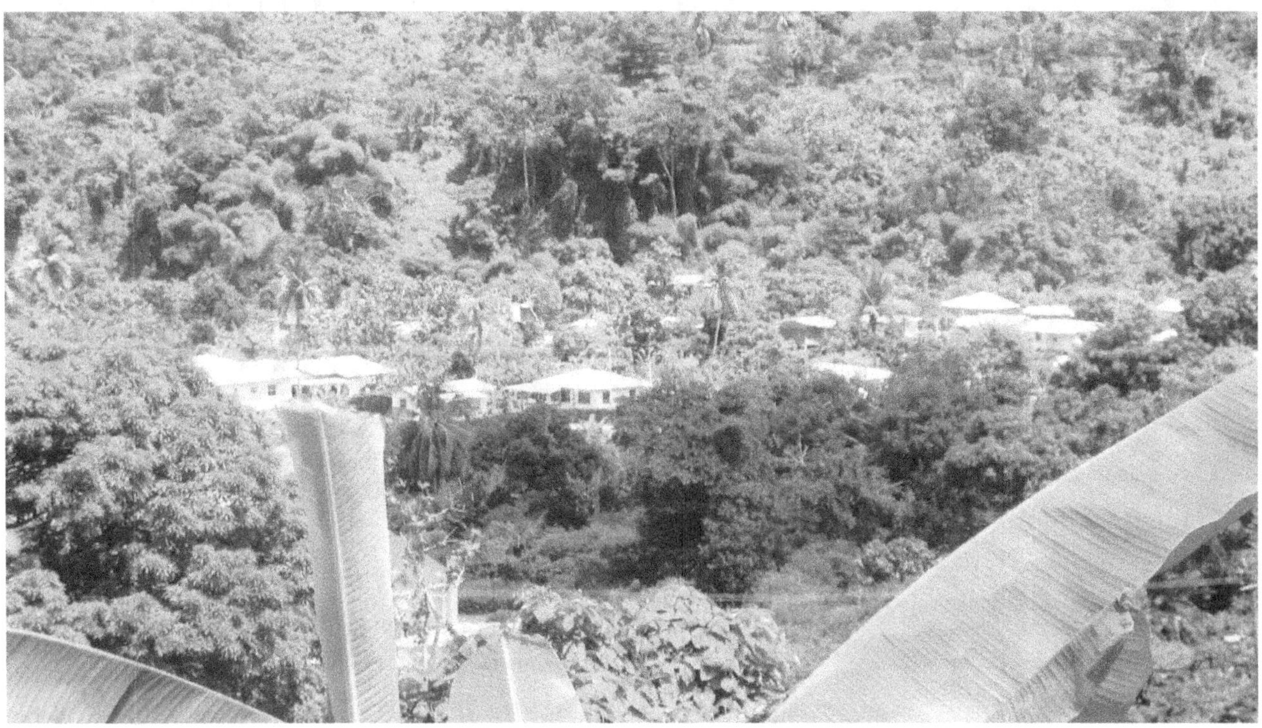

CALLALOO PLANT

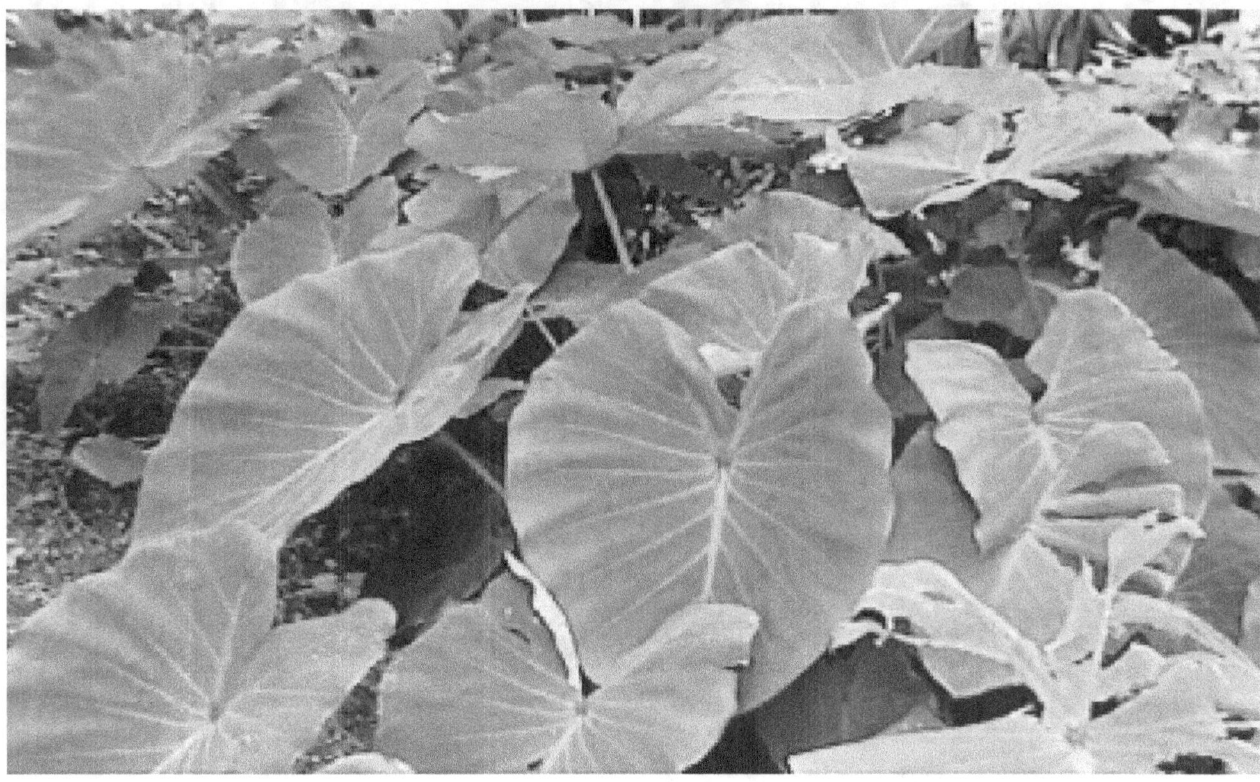

Callaloo plants

In Grenada, callaloo is a large-leaf vegetable that grows best in, or near, running water. The leaf forms the above-ground extension of the edible taro root. Taro is locally known as dasheen. The name, callaloo, may have been derived from the Spanish term calulu, which described a dasheen variant called tannia.

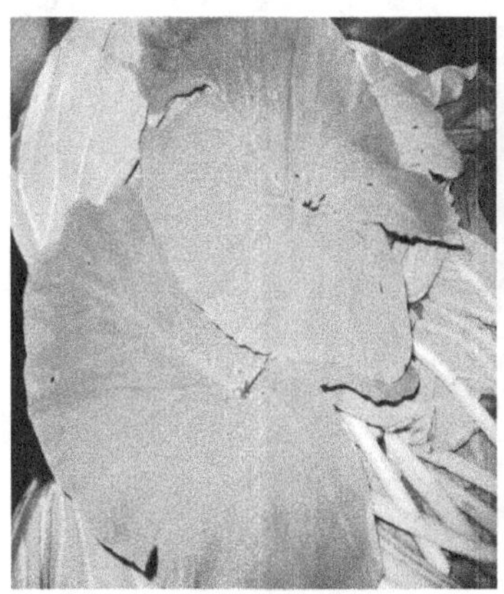

Callaloo leaves, ready to be cleaned for cooking

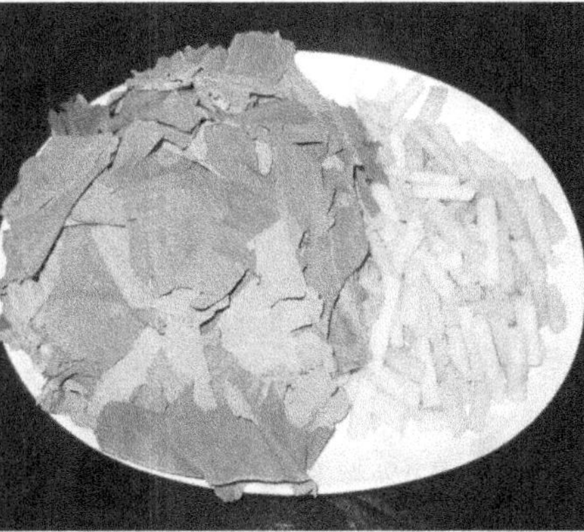

Leaves and stem, cleaned and chopped, ready for cooking

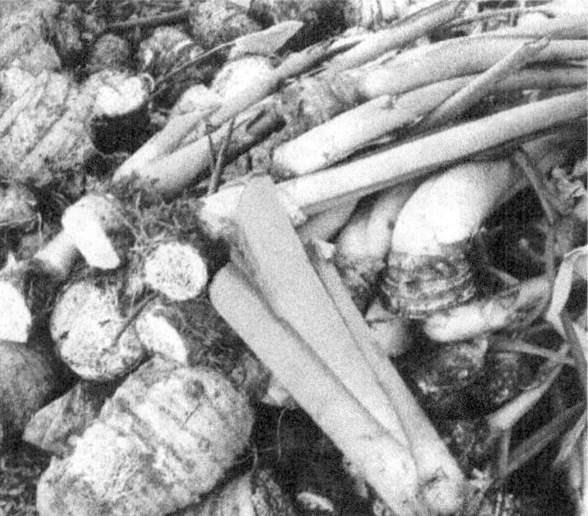

Dasheen, the root of the callaloo, is a widely used vegetable in Grenada.

Popular callaloo dishes are callaloo soup, stewed callaloo, crab and callaloo, coo-coo and callaloo, and callaloo as an indispensable oil-down ingredient in Grenada's national dish.

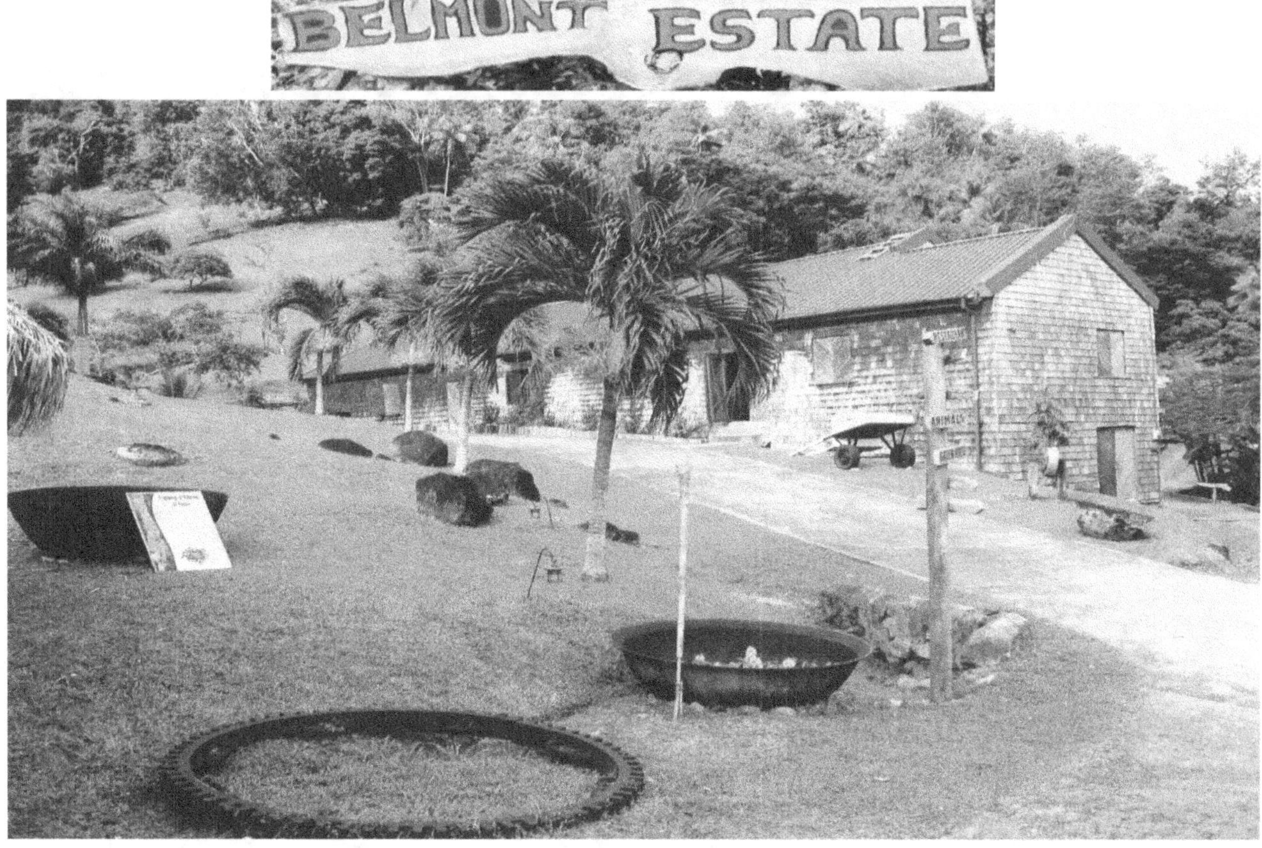

Belmont Estate management has restored the boucan above, and it functions as the estate museum. Among the estate's attractions are a restaurant featuring local dishes, cultural performances, a local thrift store, and cocoa processing demonstrations.

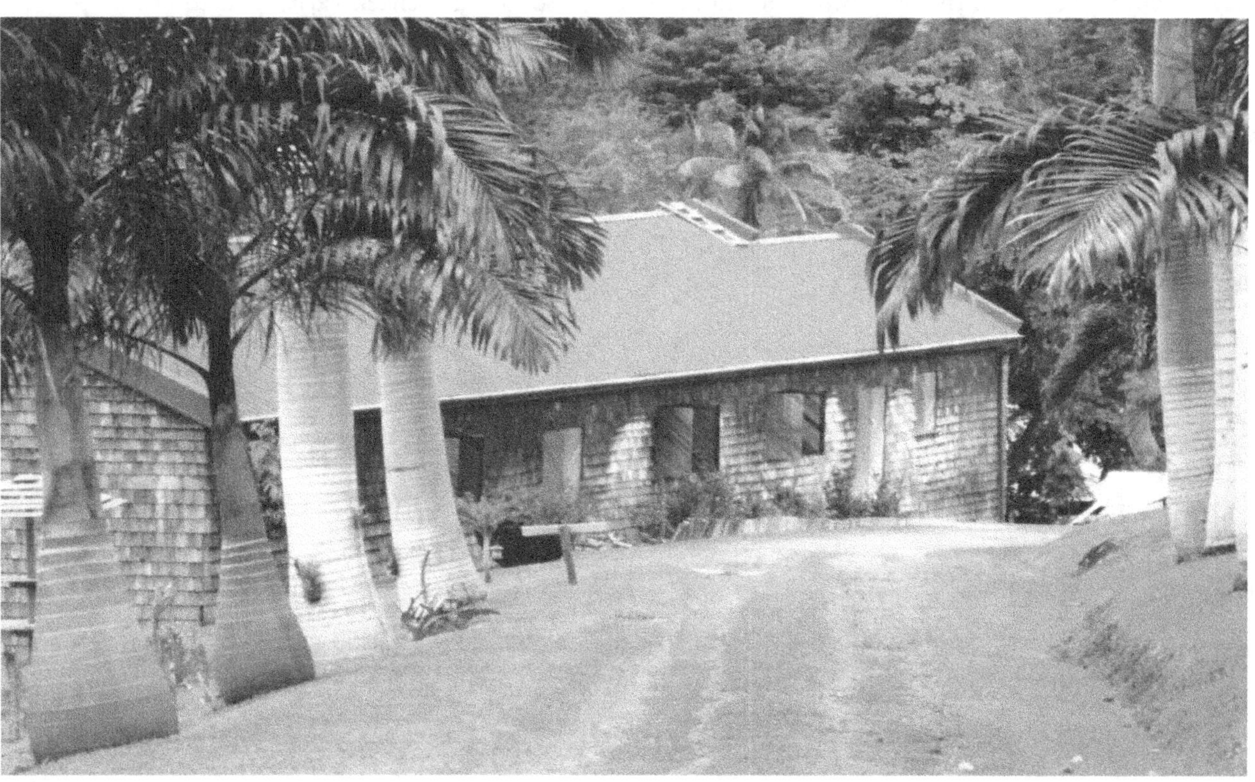

The estate uses the main building for processing cocoa beans. This facility provides an exhibition of artifacts that highlight essential aspects of Grenada's cocoa processing history.

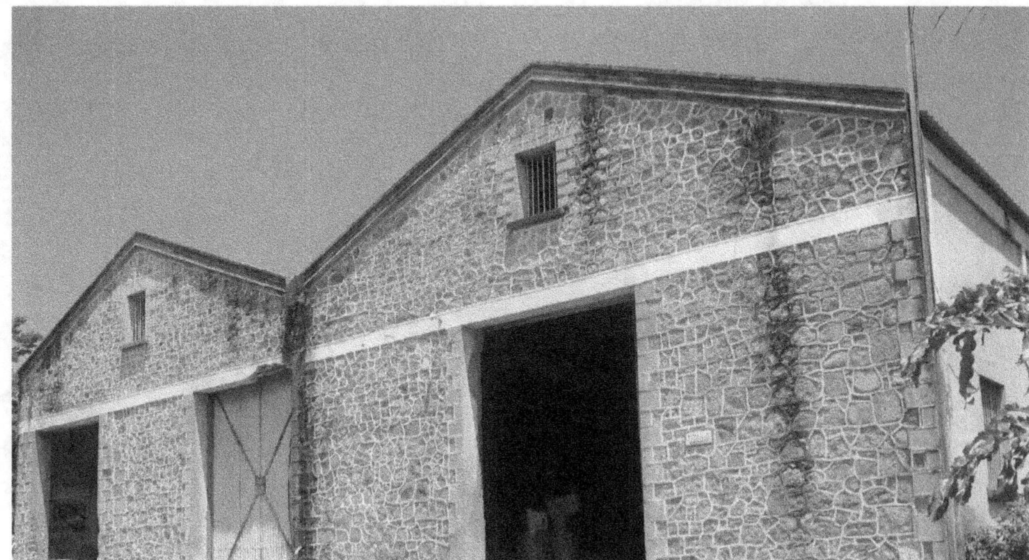

Belmont Estate

A horse takes a stroll on the estate grounds. While horses are rare in Grenada today, they were a more familiar sight when horse racing was an active sport in the 1950s and 1960s.

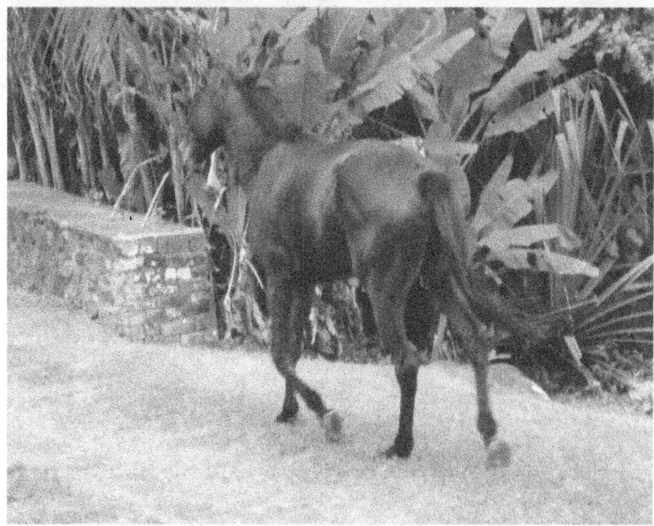

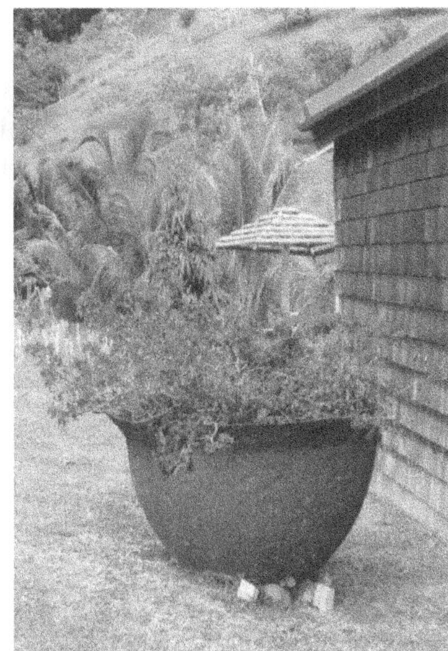

Copper pot with flowers

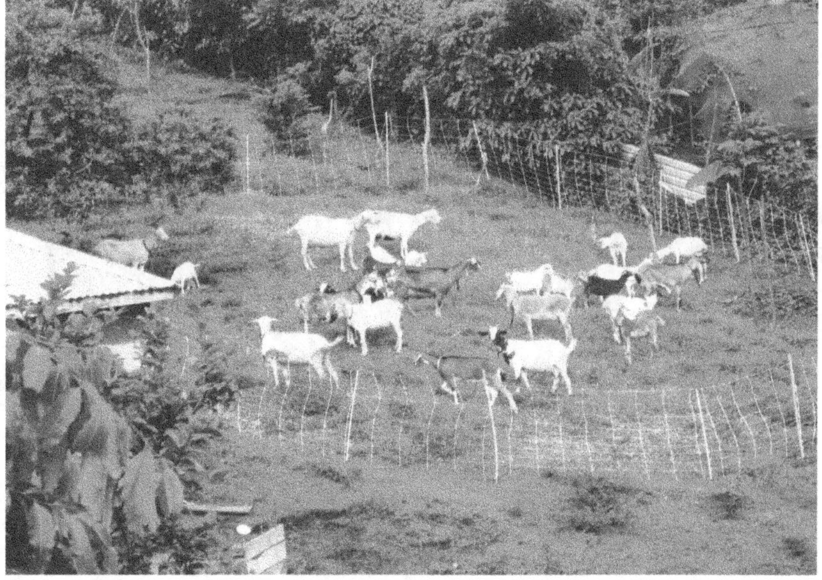

Goats are among the various animals reared on the estate.

The Beautiful floral sights of Belmont help decorate its history-bearing location. Belmont Estate is now an attractive place for visiting, weddings, parties, and other functions.

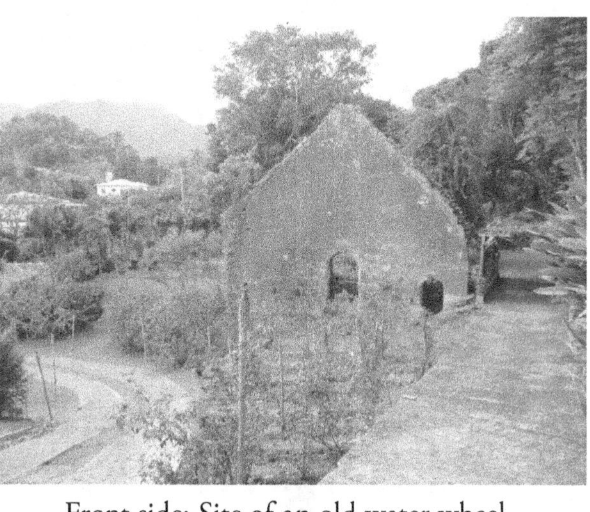

Front side: Site of an old water wheel

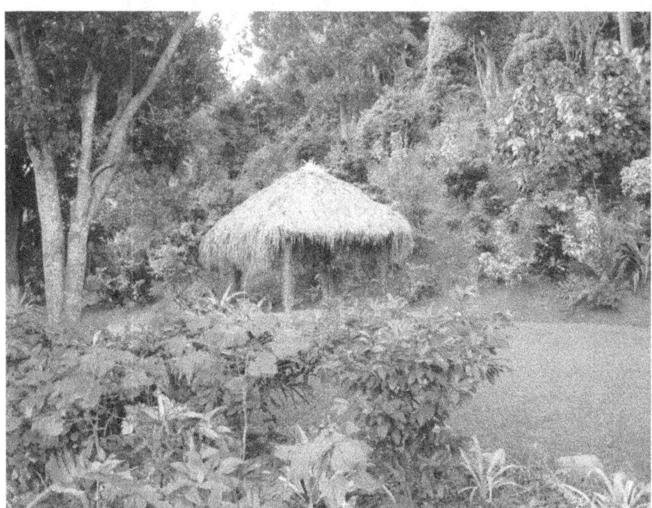

Thatched cabana, reminiscent of a native Amerindian ajoupa

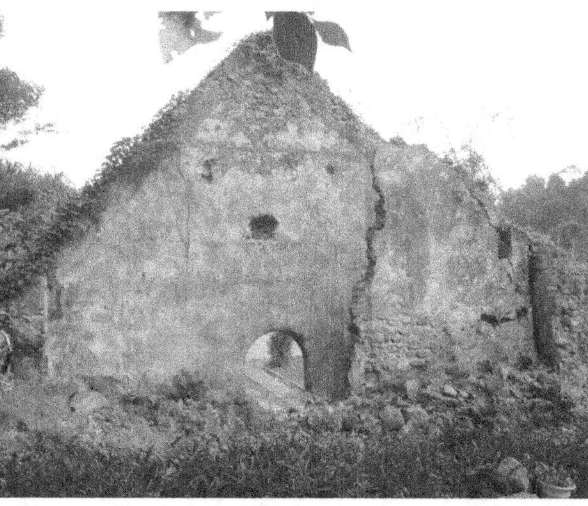

Back side: The reinsertion of a wheel will be an interesting endeavor.

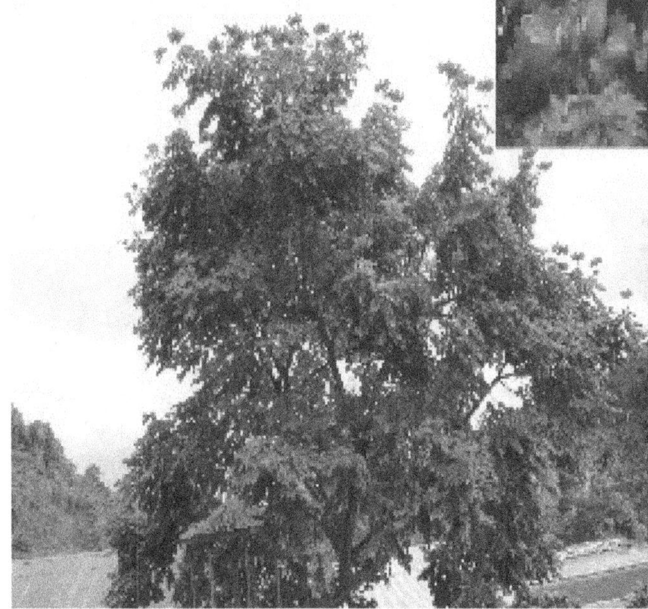

African Tulip

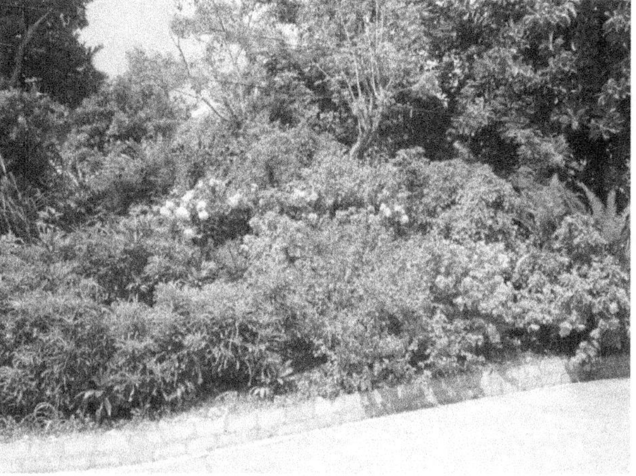

Curbside flowers

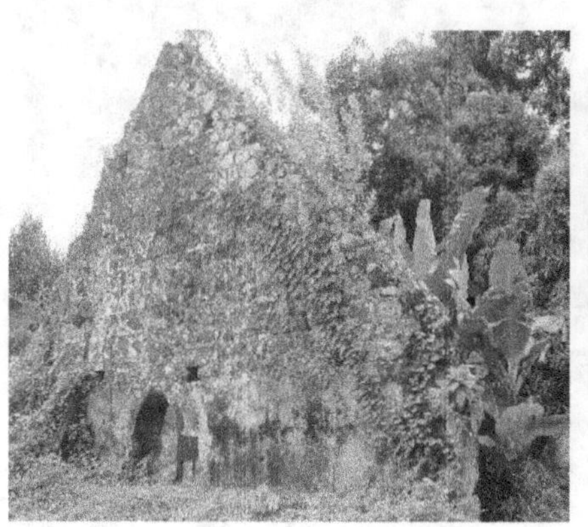
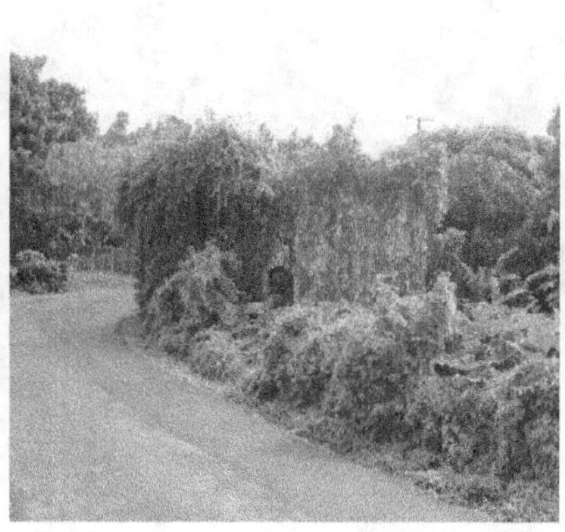
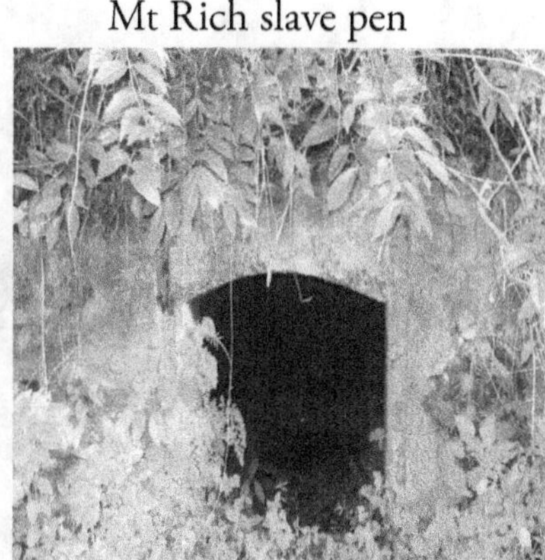

Mt Rich slave pen

Plantation ruins of St. Patrick (above)

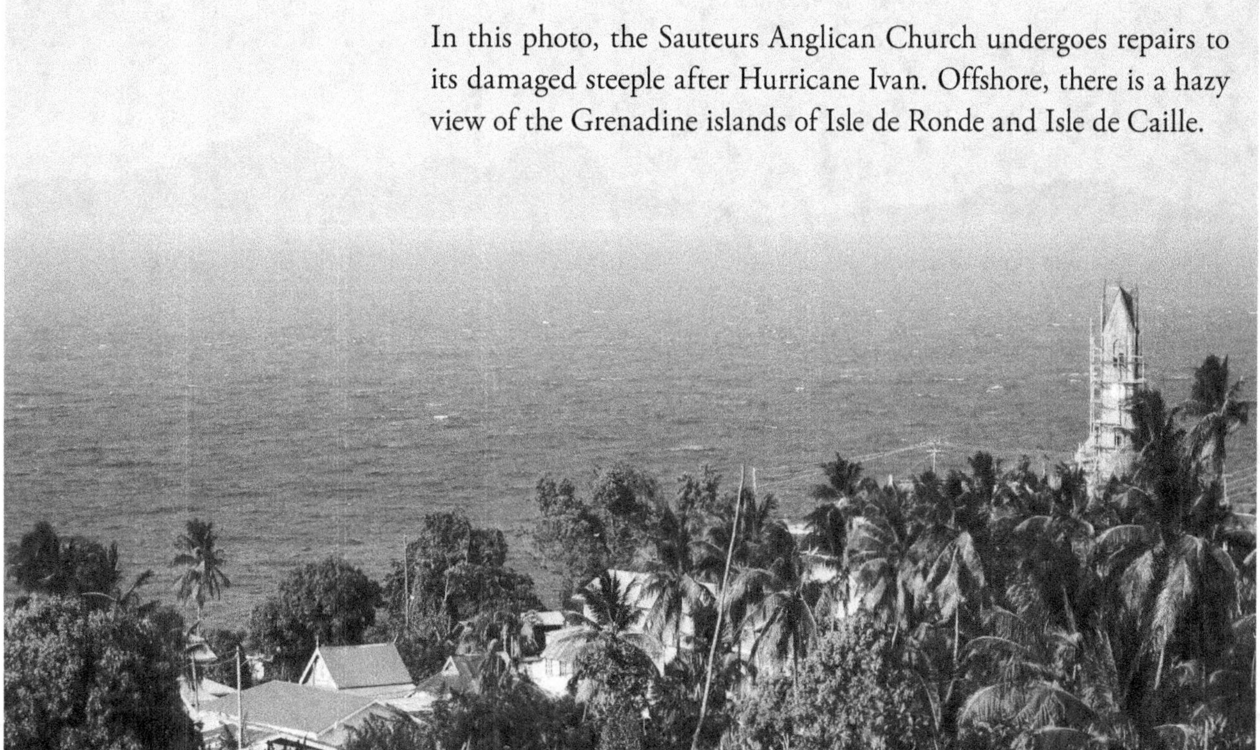

In this photo, the Sauteurs Anglican Church undergoes repairs to its damaged steeple after Hurricane Ivan. Offshore, there is a hazy view of the Grenadine islands of Isle de Ronde and Isle de Caille.

Views of Piton

From River Sallee

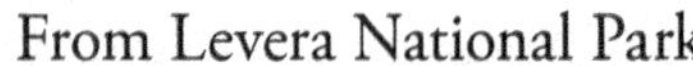

From Levera National Park

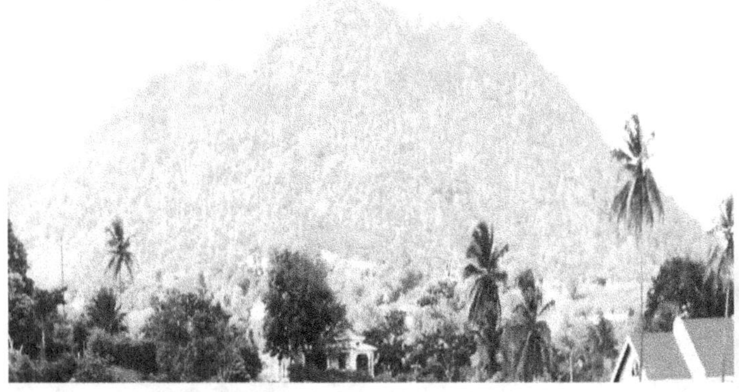

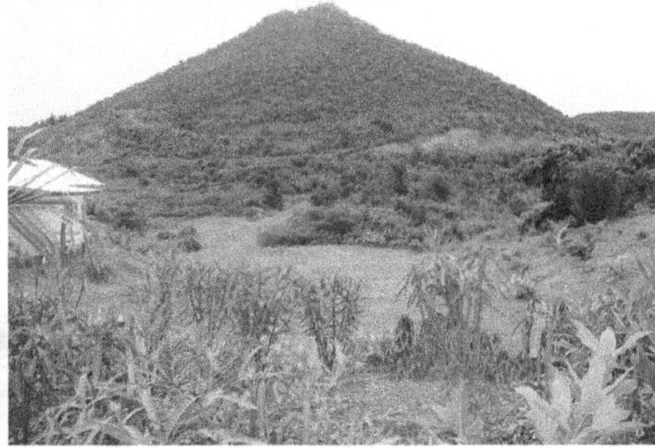

From Bathway

From Levera Beach

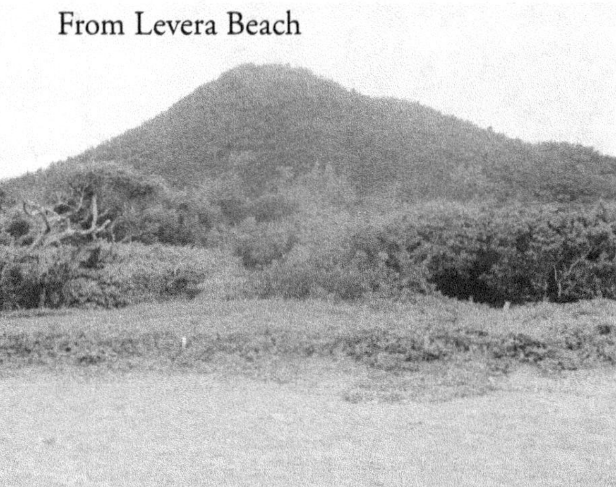

Above: Four different views of the 848 ft. high Levera Hill, locally known as Piton

Levera Island, a remnant of past volcanic activity, rises abruptly just yards off Levera Beach. Levera Island is sometimes called Sugarloaf Island.

Views from Piton's hilltop

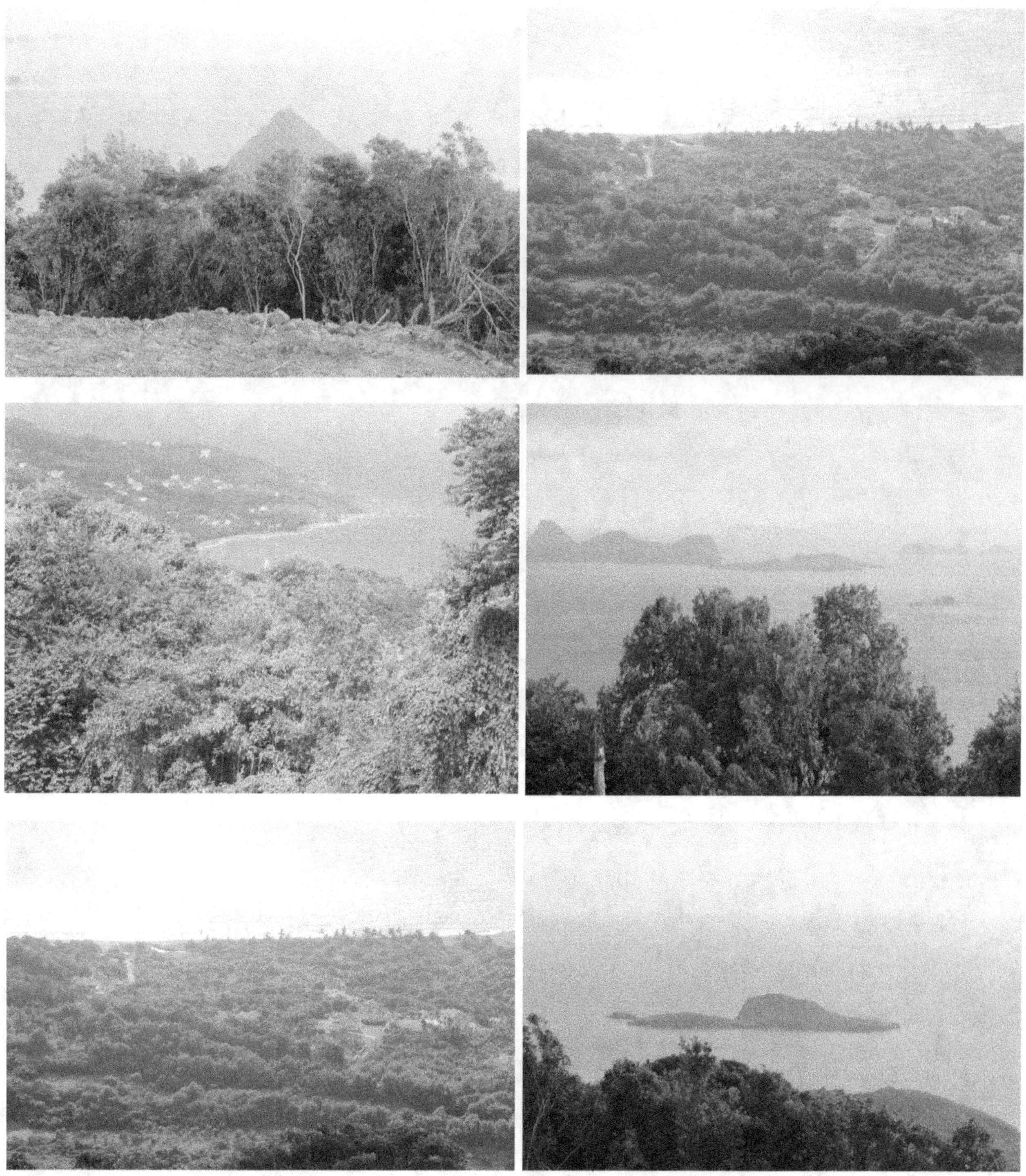

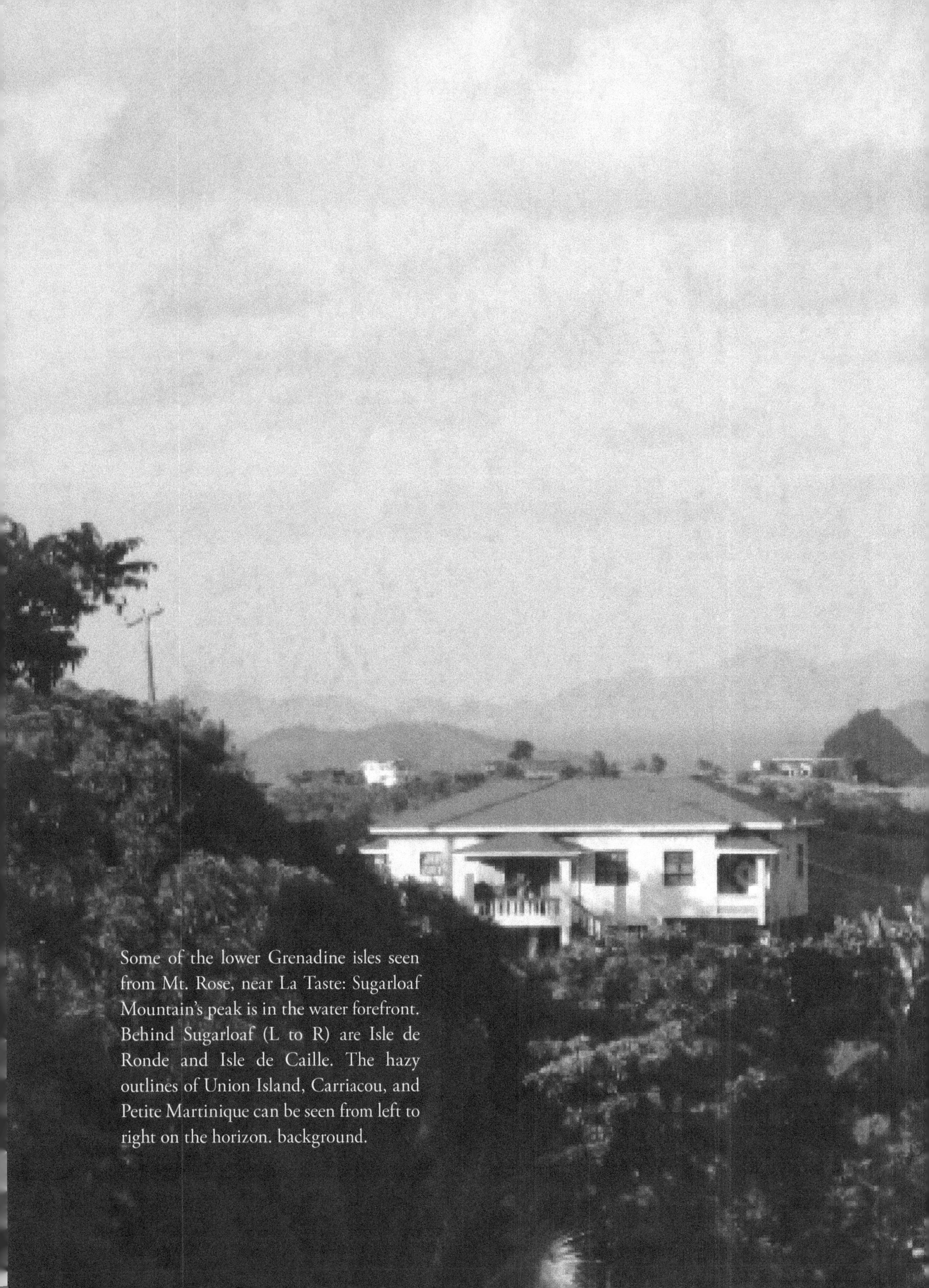

Some of the lower Grenadine isles seen from Mt. Rose, near La Taste: Sugarloaf Mountain's peak is in the water forefront. Behind Sugarloaf (L to R) are Isle de Ronde and Isle de Caille. The hazy outlines of Union Island, Carriacou, and Petite Martinique can be seen from left to right on the horizon. background.

St. Mark's

St. Mark's is the smallest parish in Grenada. A quaint Victoria, also known as the Sunset City, is the parish's town. St. Mark's boasts a lovely coast, overhung by magnificent rocks. From several locations in St. Mark's, one gets a privileged view of Mt. St. Catherine, Grenada's highest mountain.

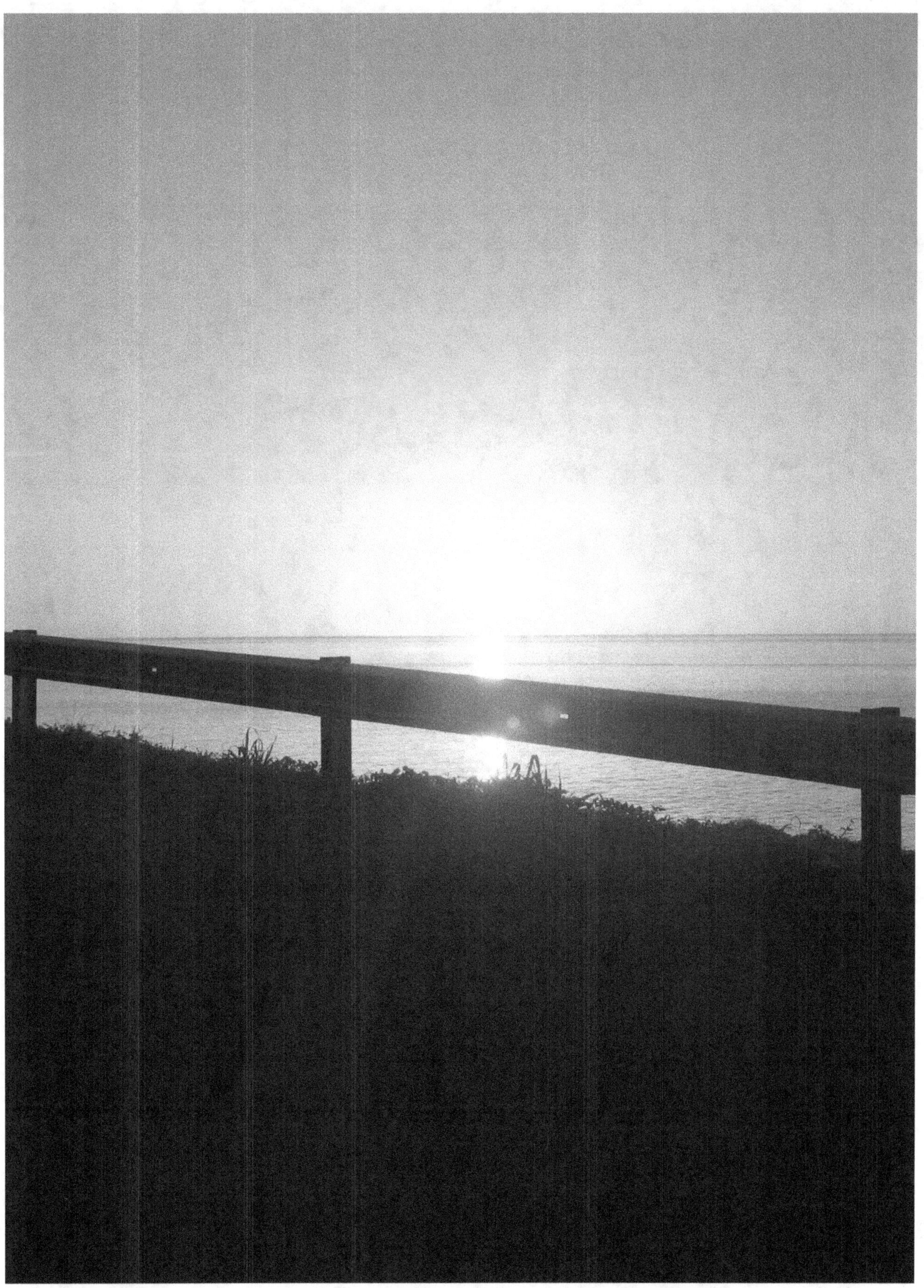

Along the roadside near Victoria, Grenada's Sunset City

The hills over Victoria command a magnificent view of Grenada's mountainous spine. Mt. St. Catherine, Grenada's highest peak, projects from that spine.

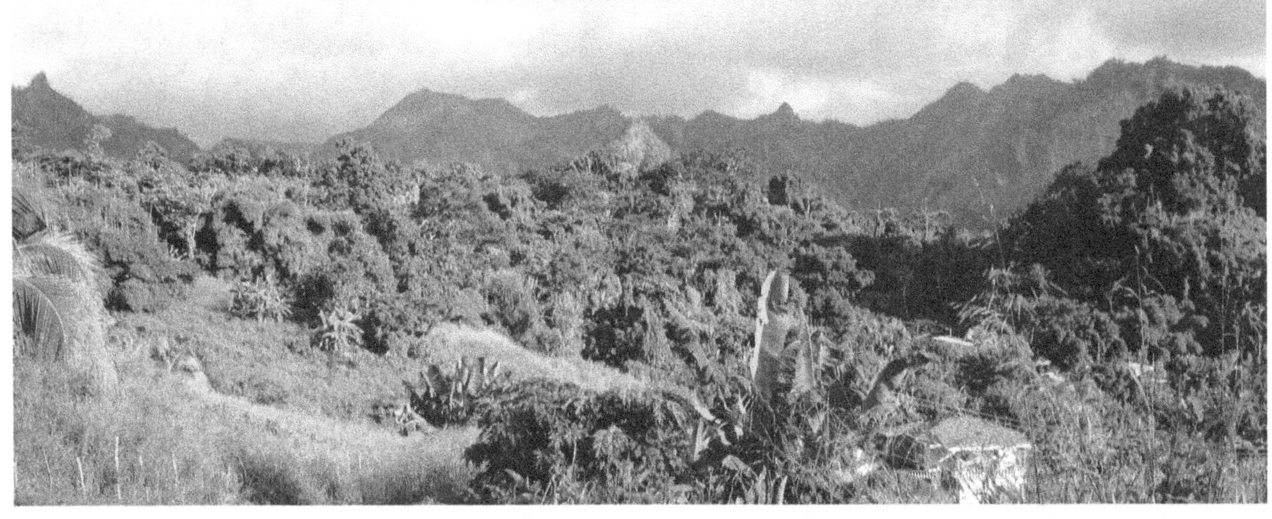

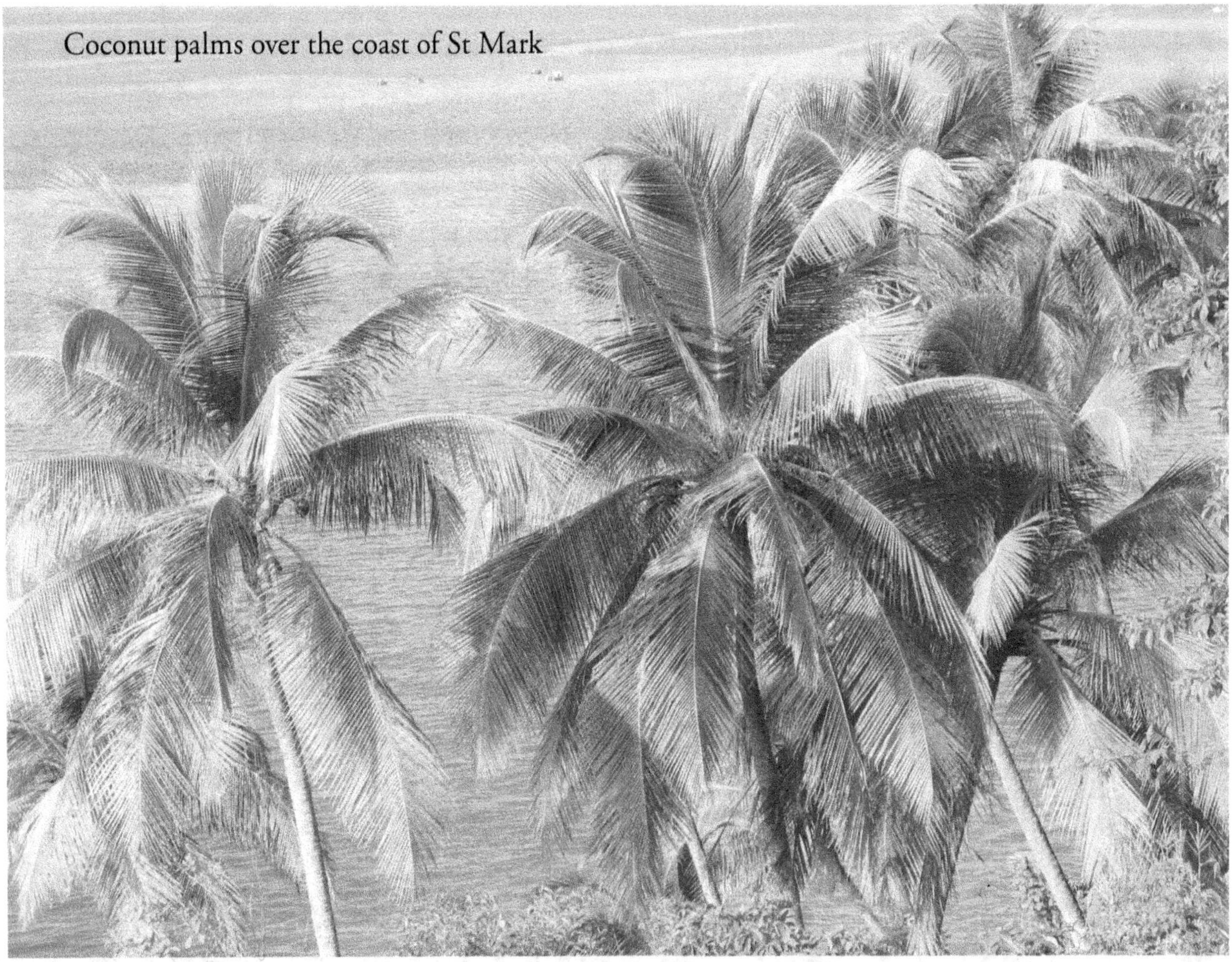

Coconut palms over the coast of St Mark

Diamond Estate Boucan

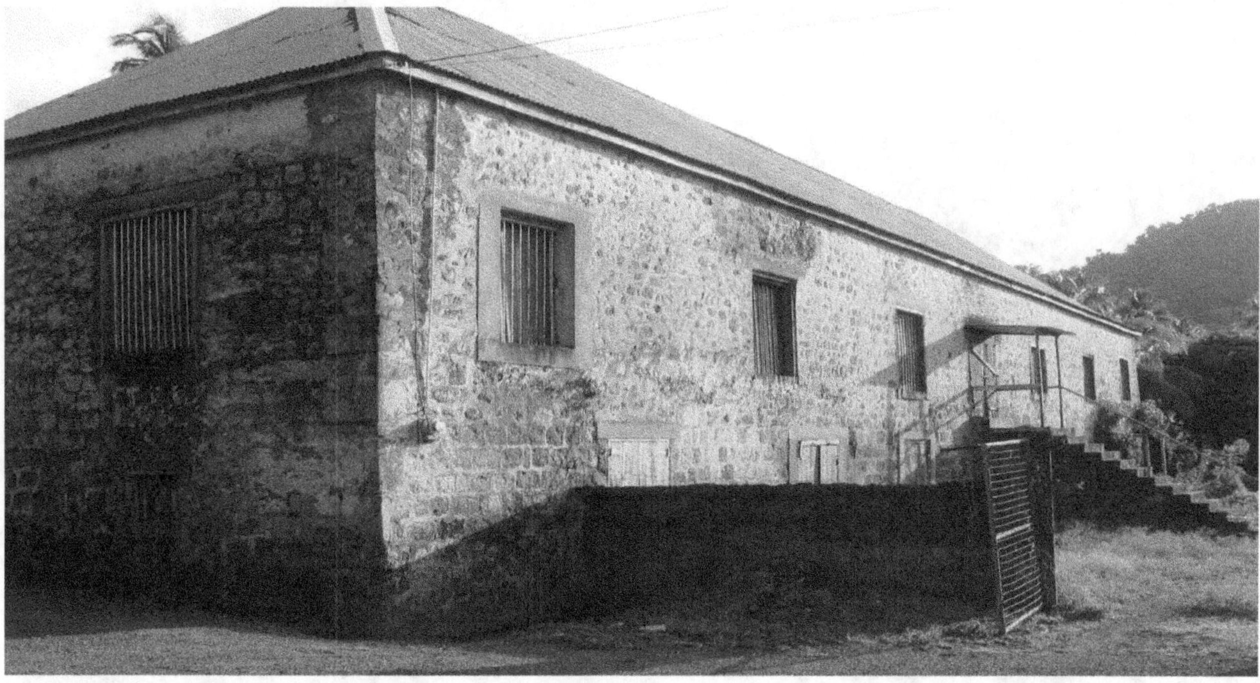

Slave planters built Diamond Estate boucan (1774) before the American Independence (1776) and before the French Revolution (1789). It existed before the Grenadian slave rebellion led by Julien Fedon of Belvidere.

They built Diamond Estate boucan before Henri Christophe, a Grenadian slave who served at sea under a French slave owner, became King of Haiti (1811). In some accounts, Christophe briefly returned home to Grenada from the American War of Independence, where he allegedly served and was wounded.

Diamond Estate Boucan preexisted Fort Frederick (1787) in St. George's and came only 123 years after the French extermination of Grenada's aboriginal Caribs. They have used the boucan as a receiving station, emergency shelter, and chocolate factory over the years.

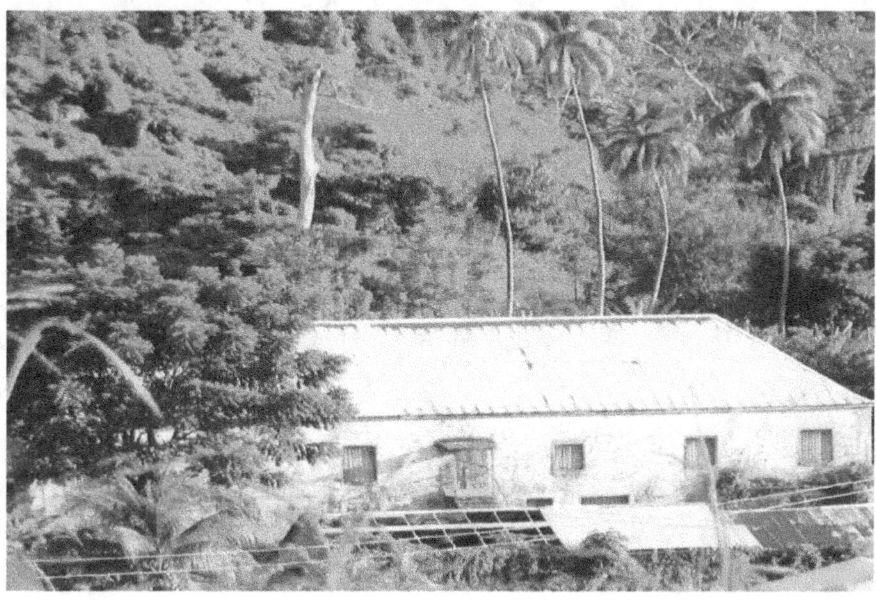

Nonpareil coast looking north

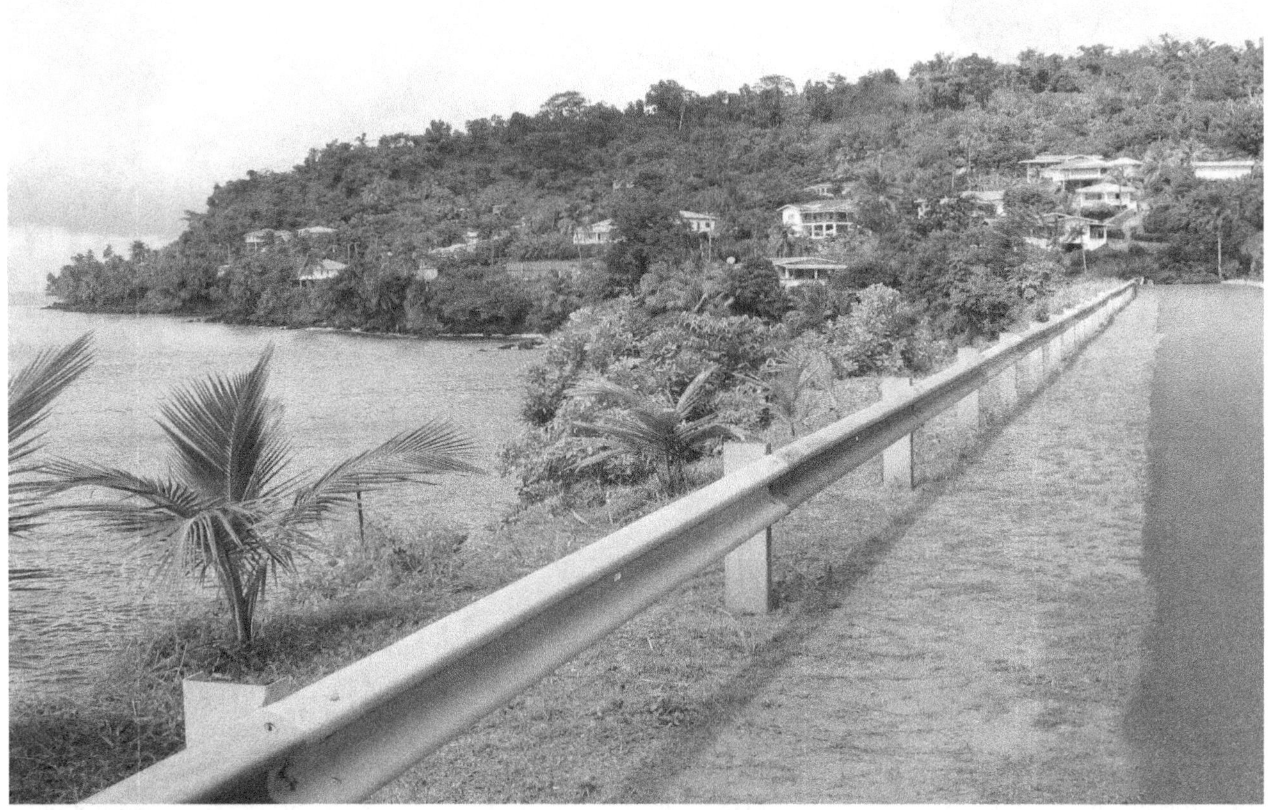

Dwelling on the water's edge

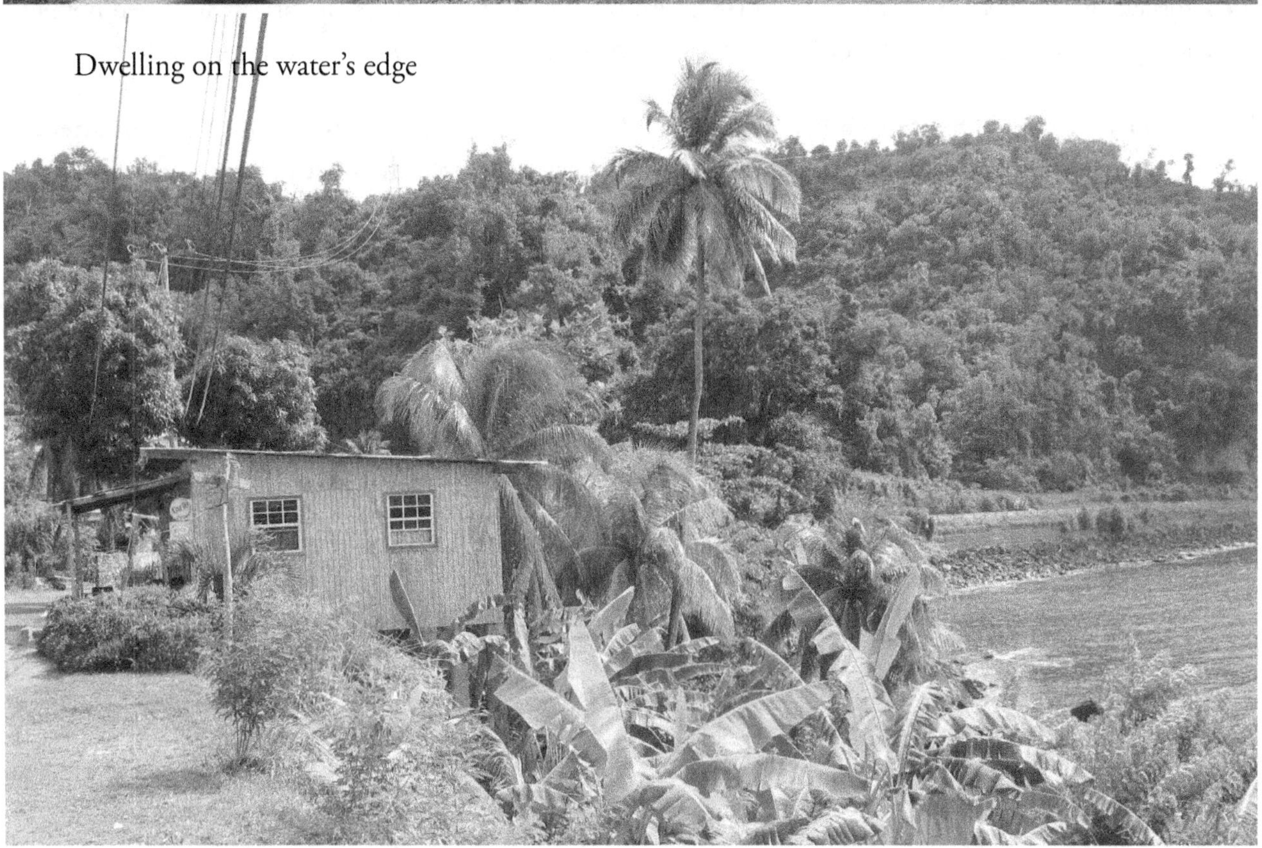

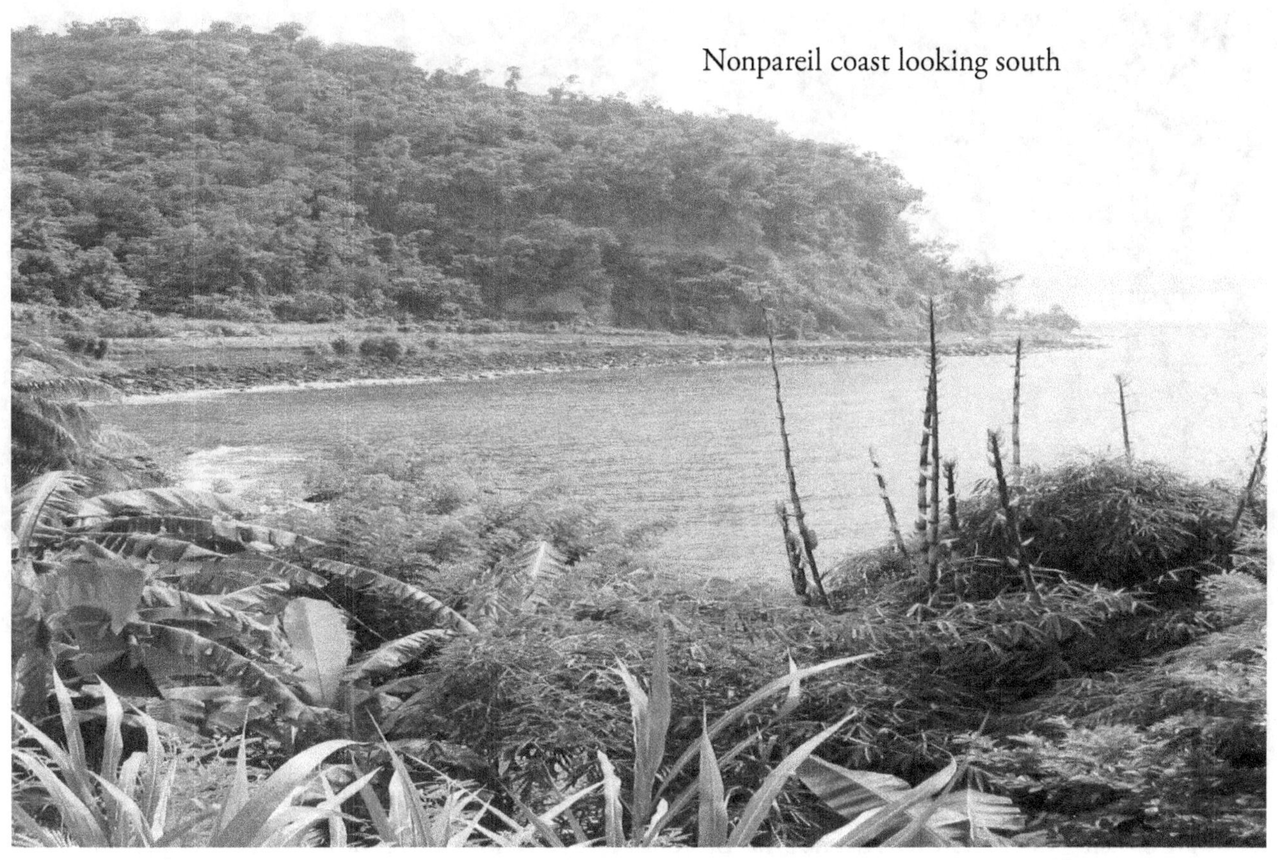

Nonpareil coast looking south

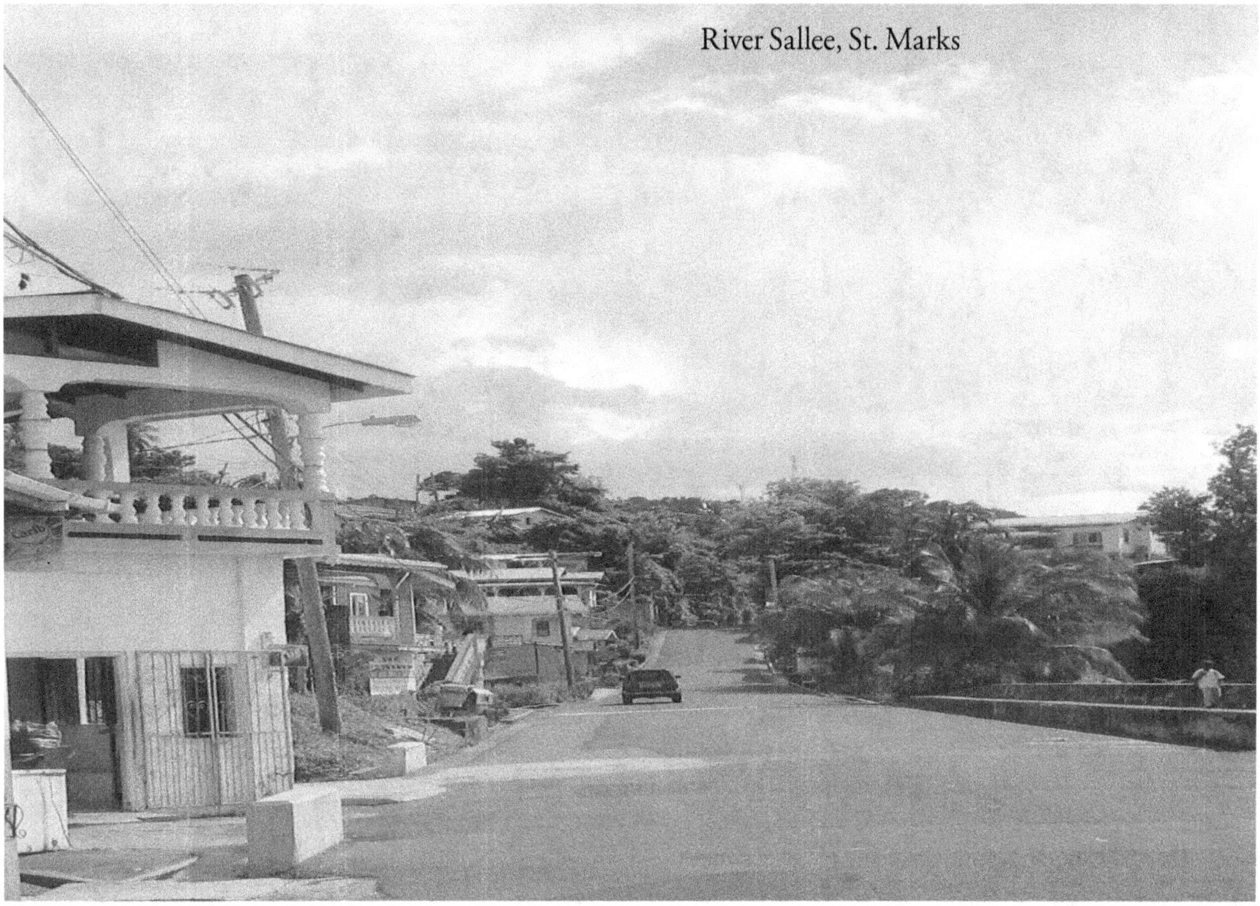

River Sallee, St. Marks

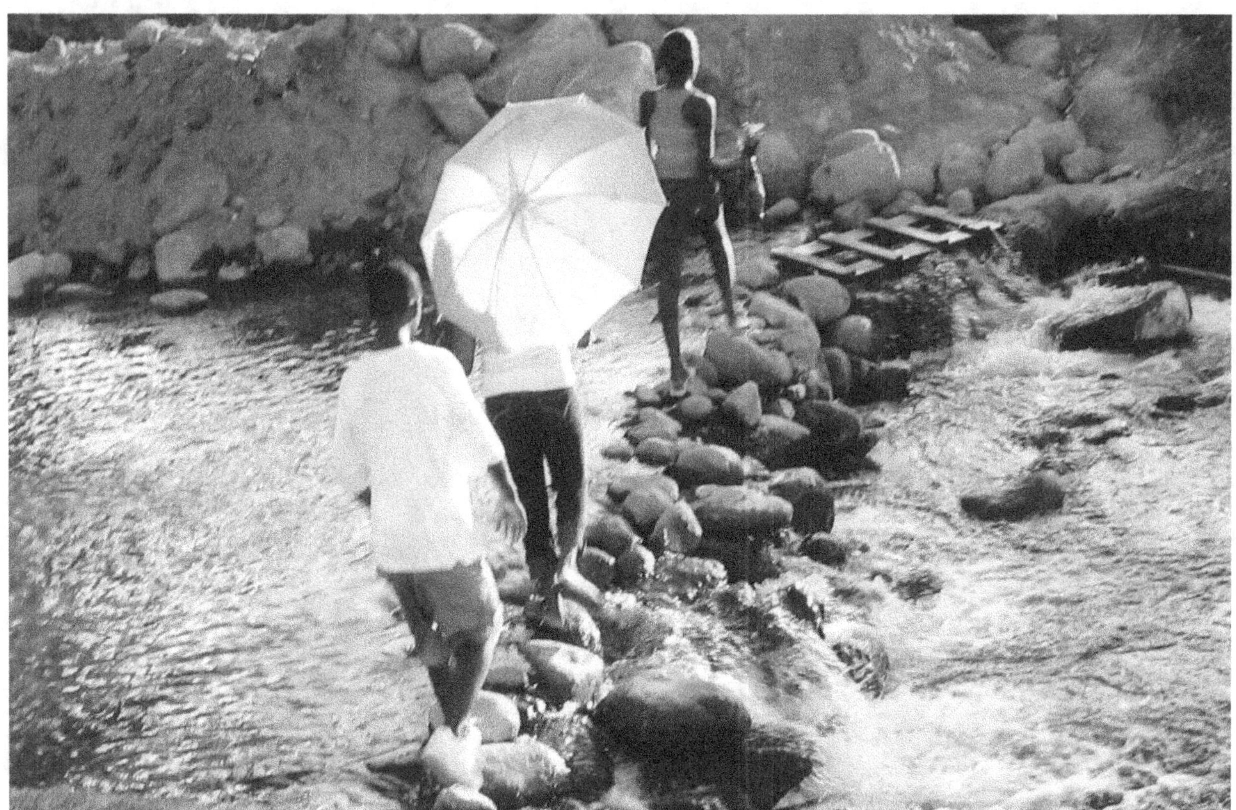

They are crossing the Bonair River. The array of stones across the local River provides a convenient shortcut for these Victorian youngsters.

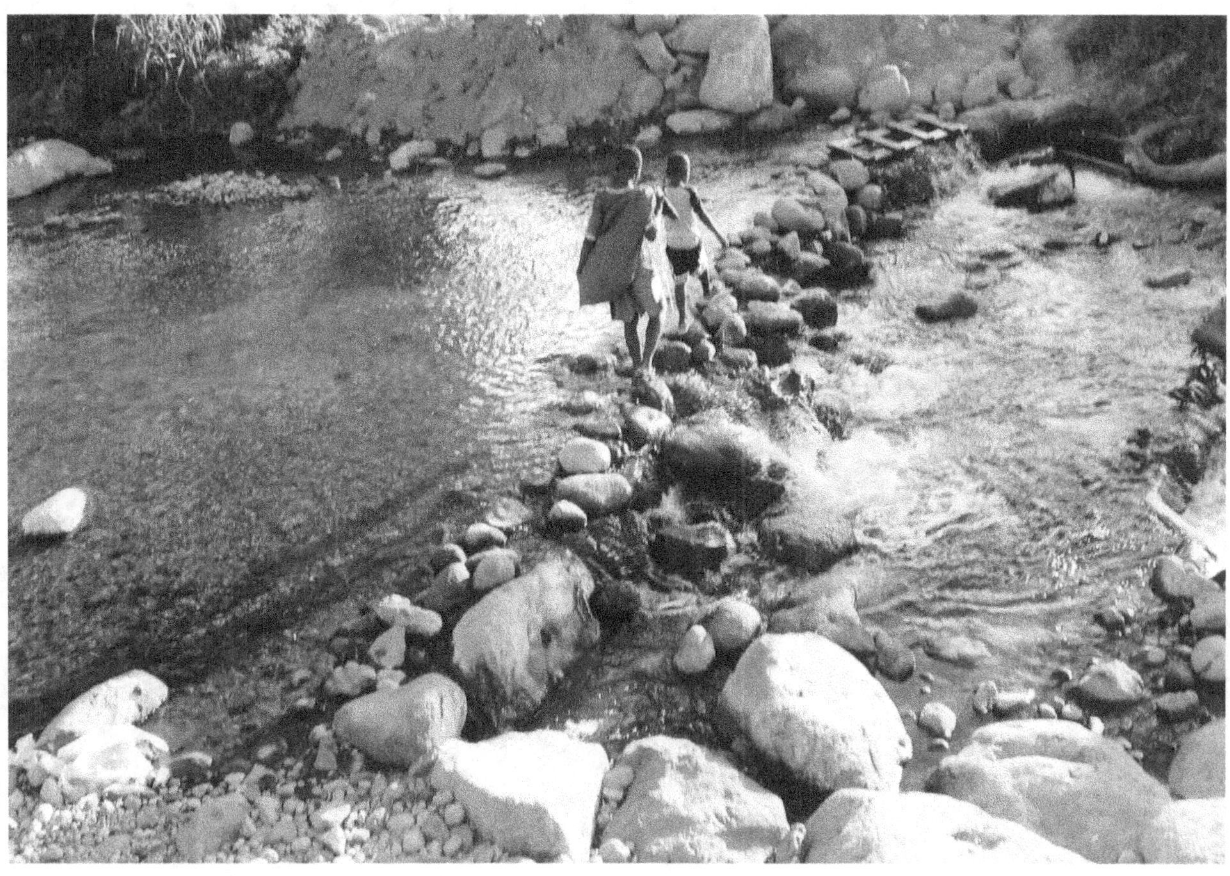

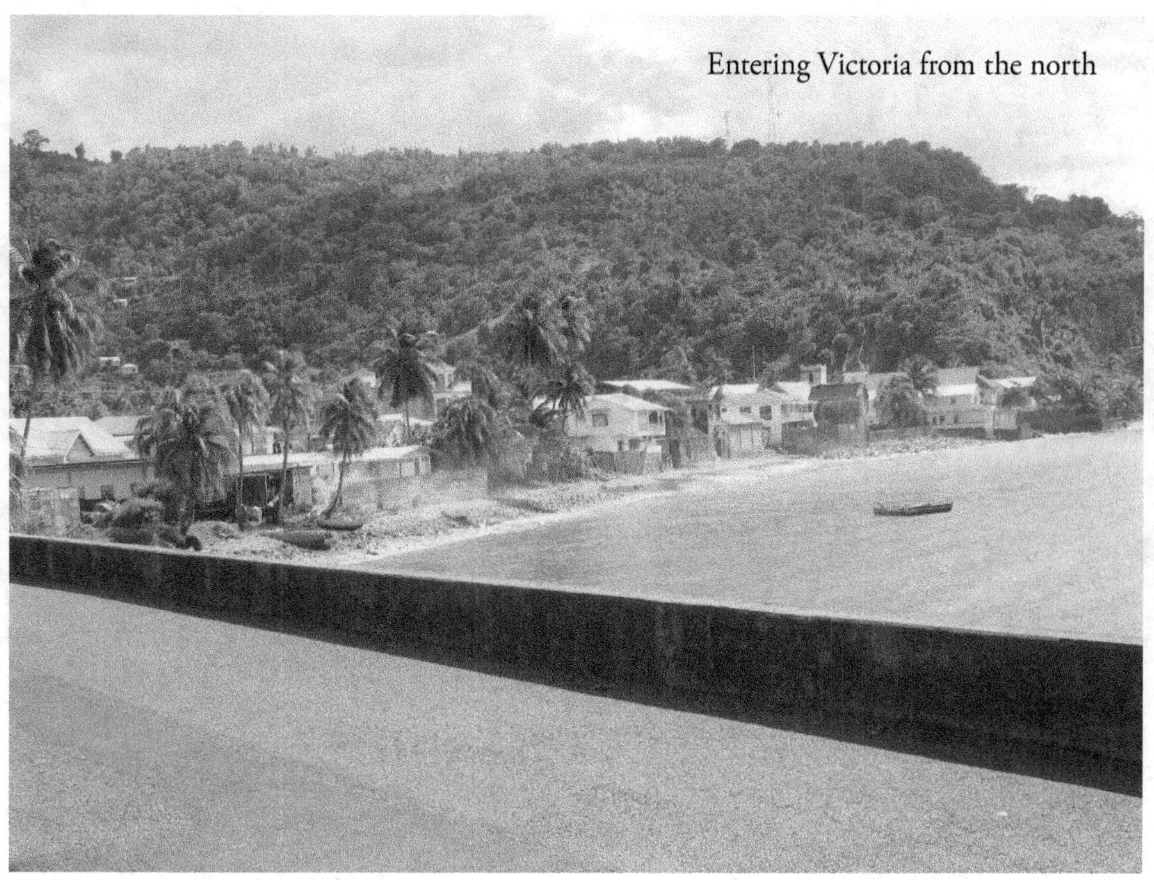

Entering Victoria from the north

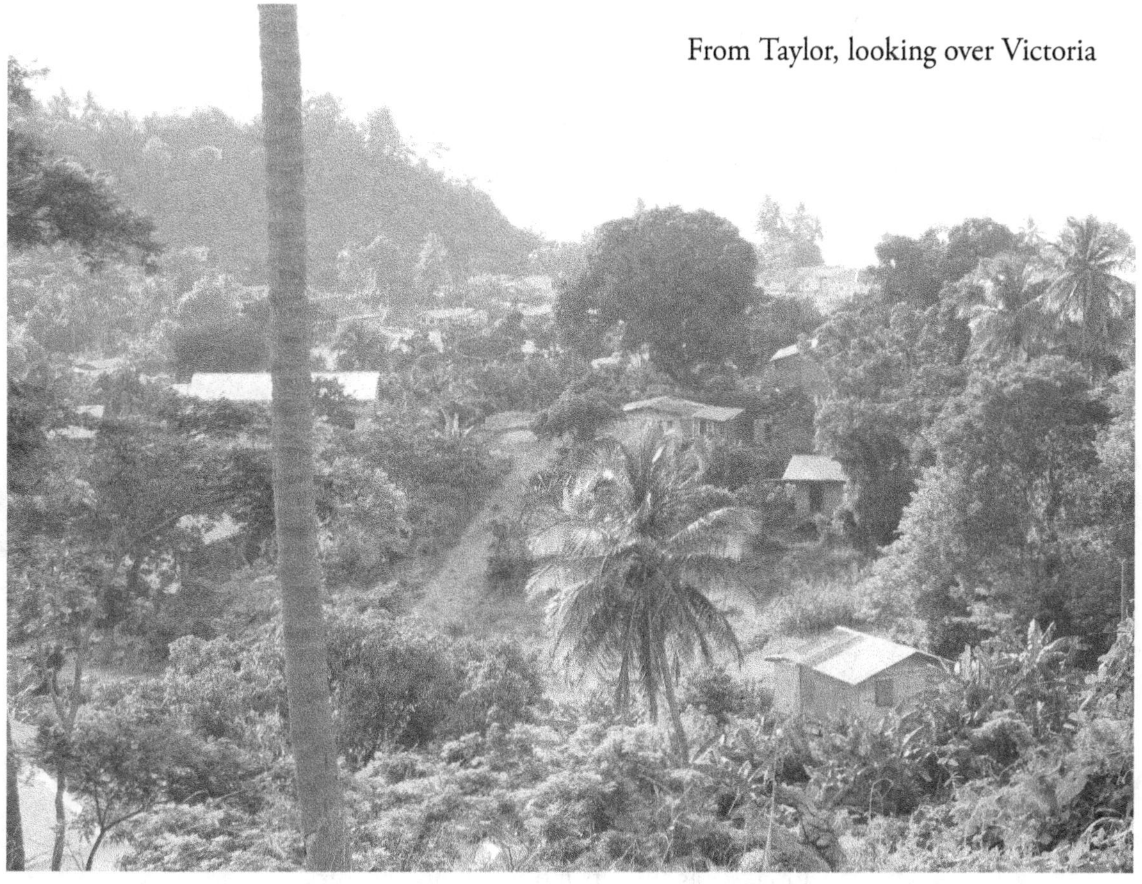

From Taylor, looking over Victoria

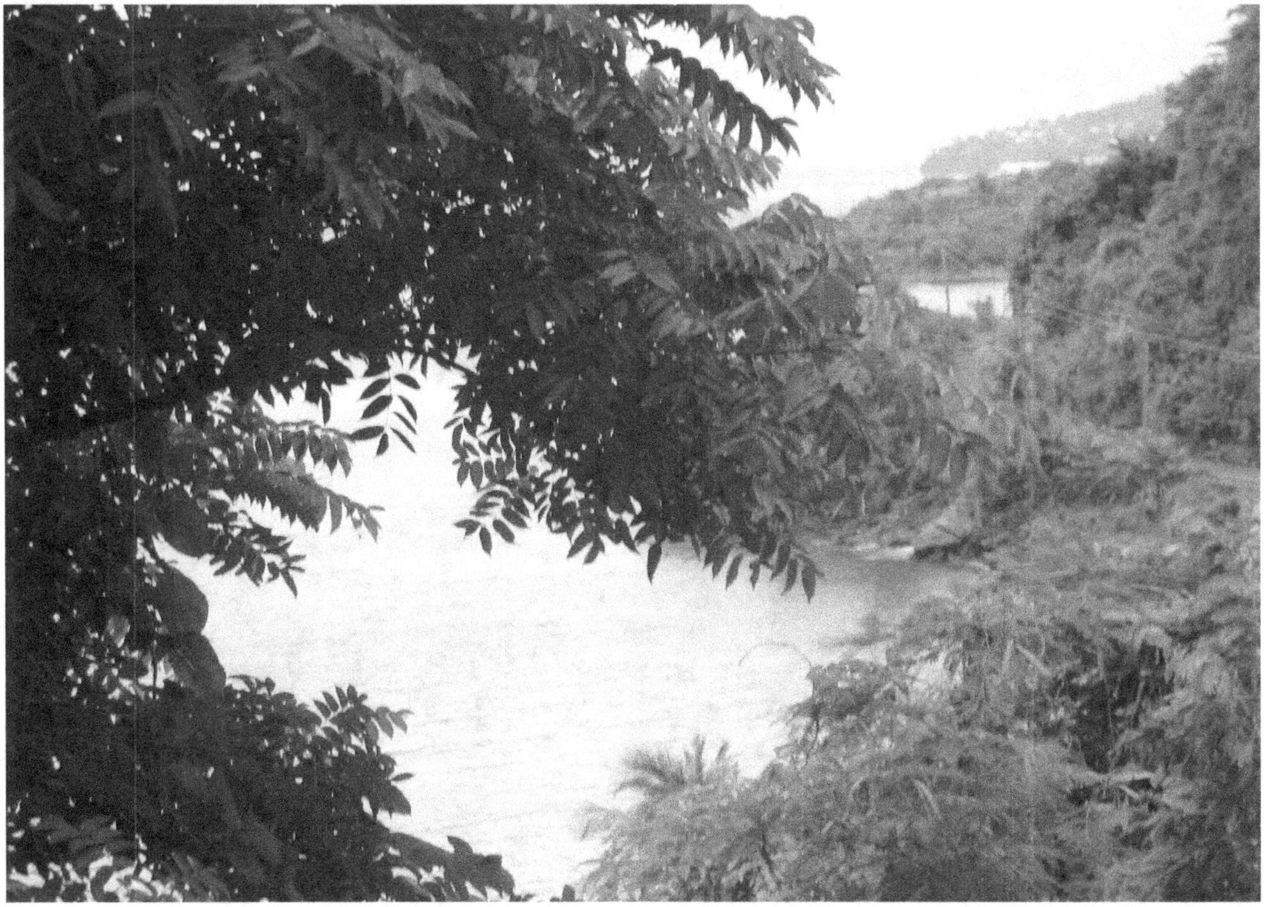

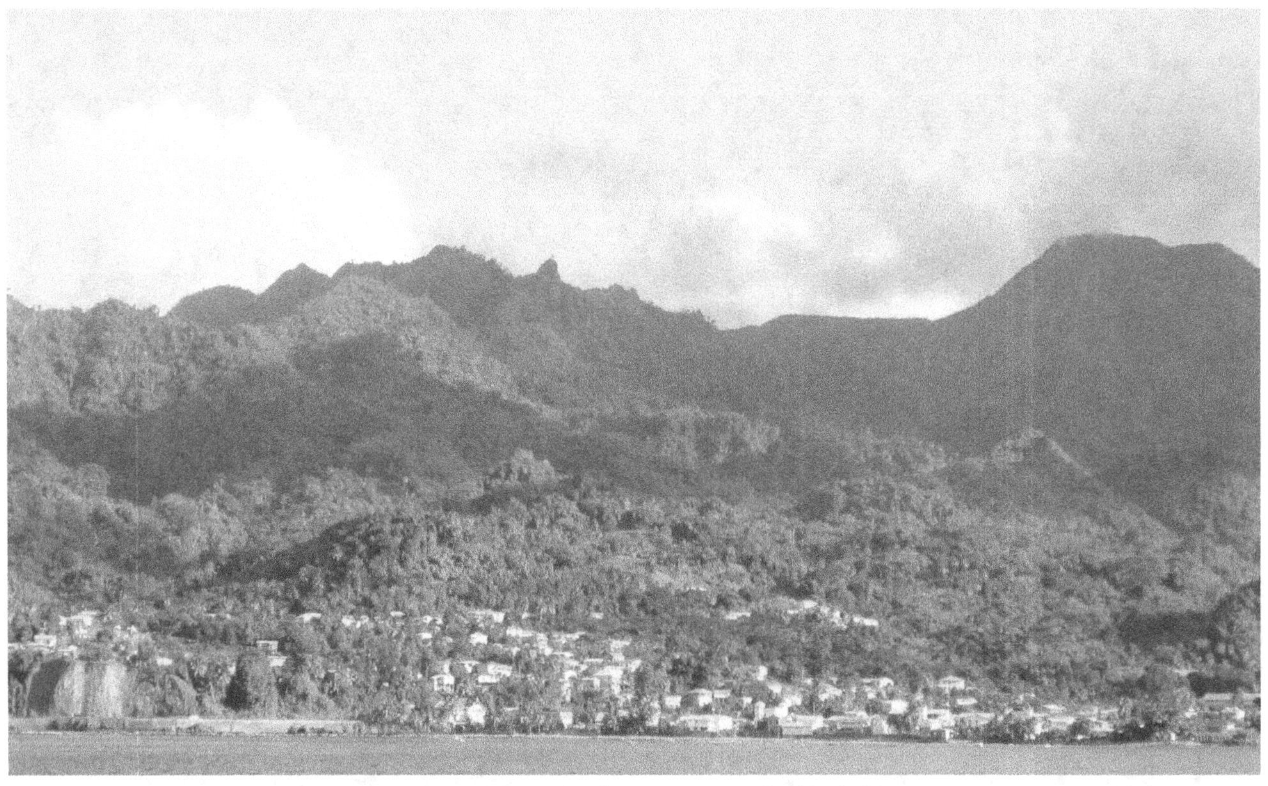

Peeping into the Caribbean Sea coast of St. Mark

Victoria, set against its mountainous backdrop

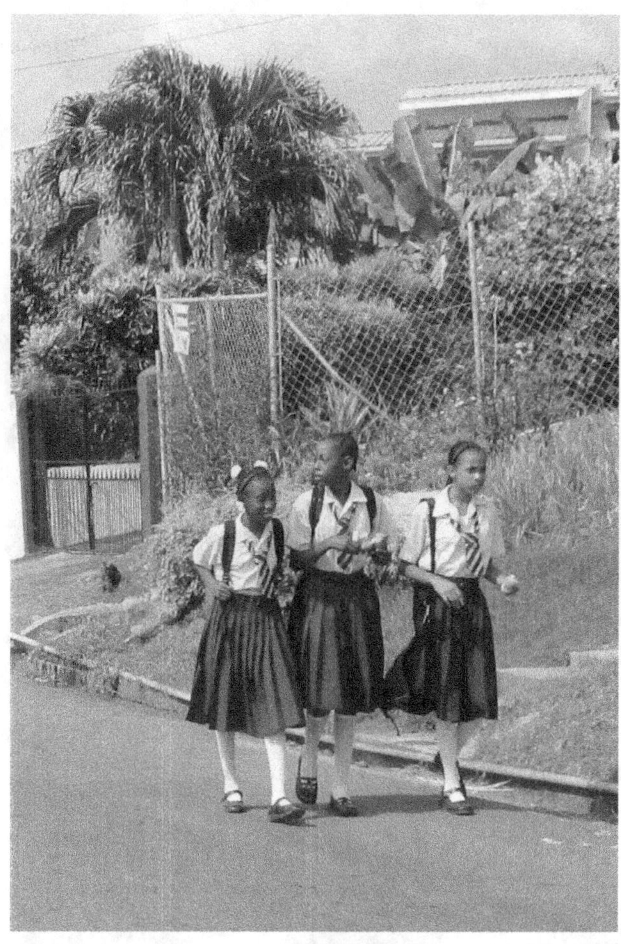

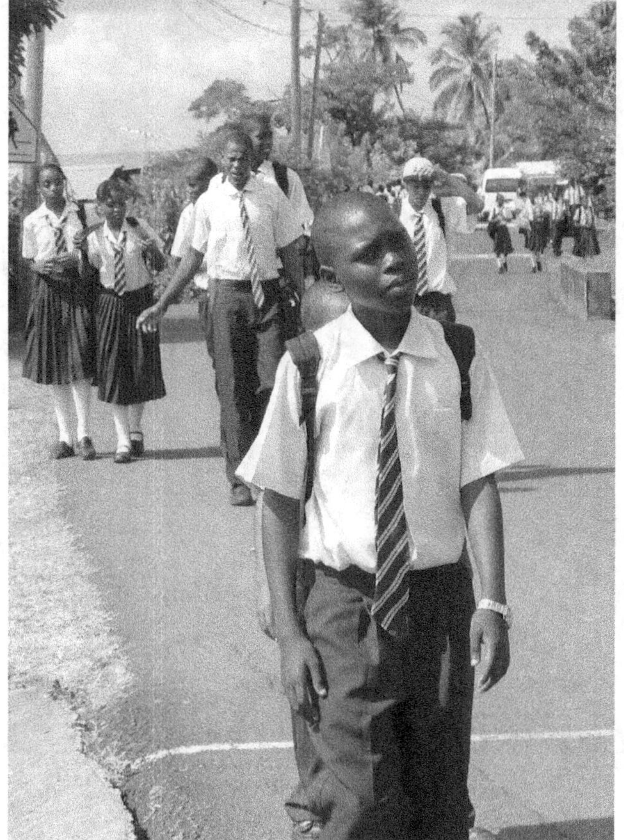

Waltham
Secondary School
students at the end
of a school day

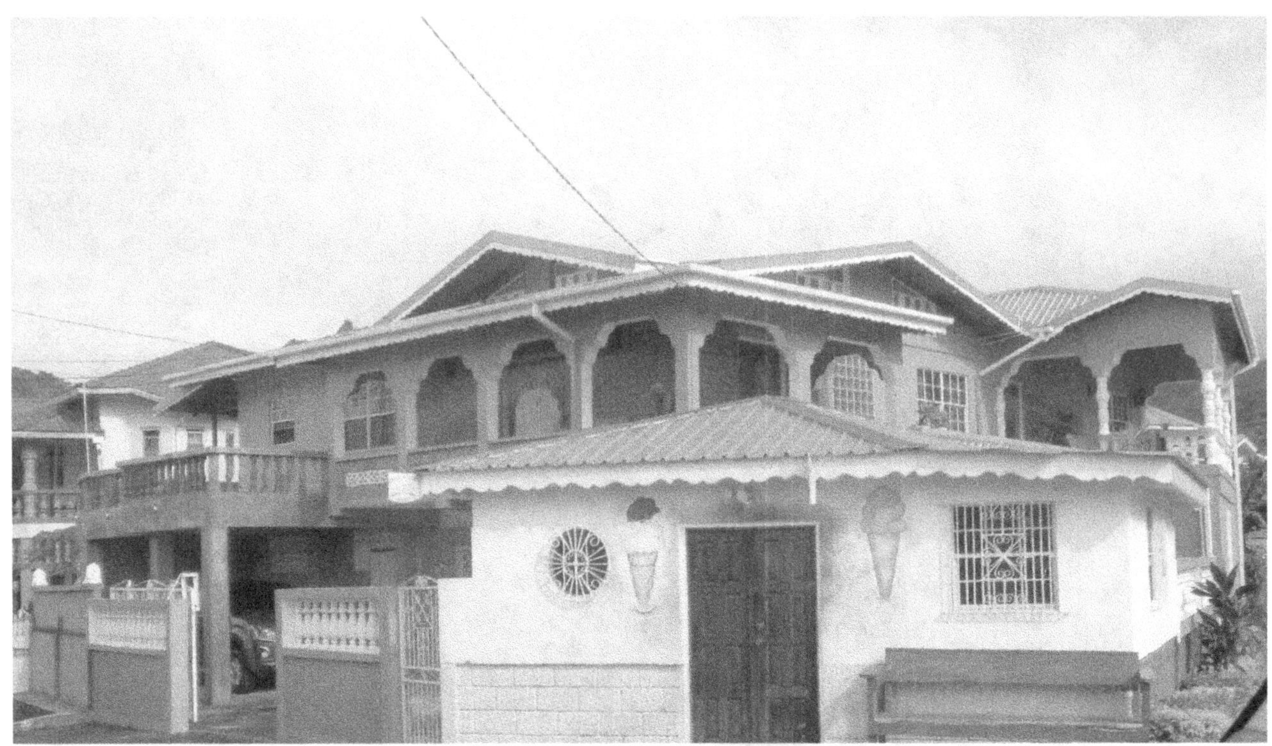

Dwelling and shop in Victoria

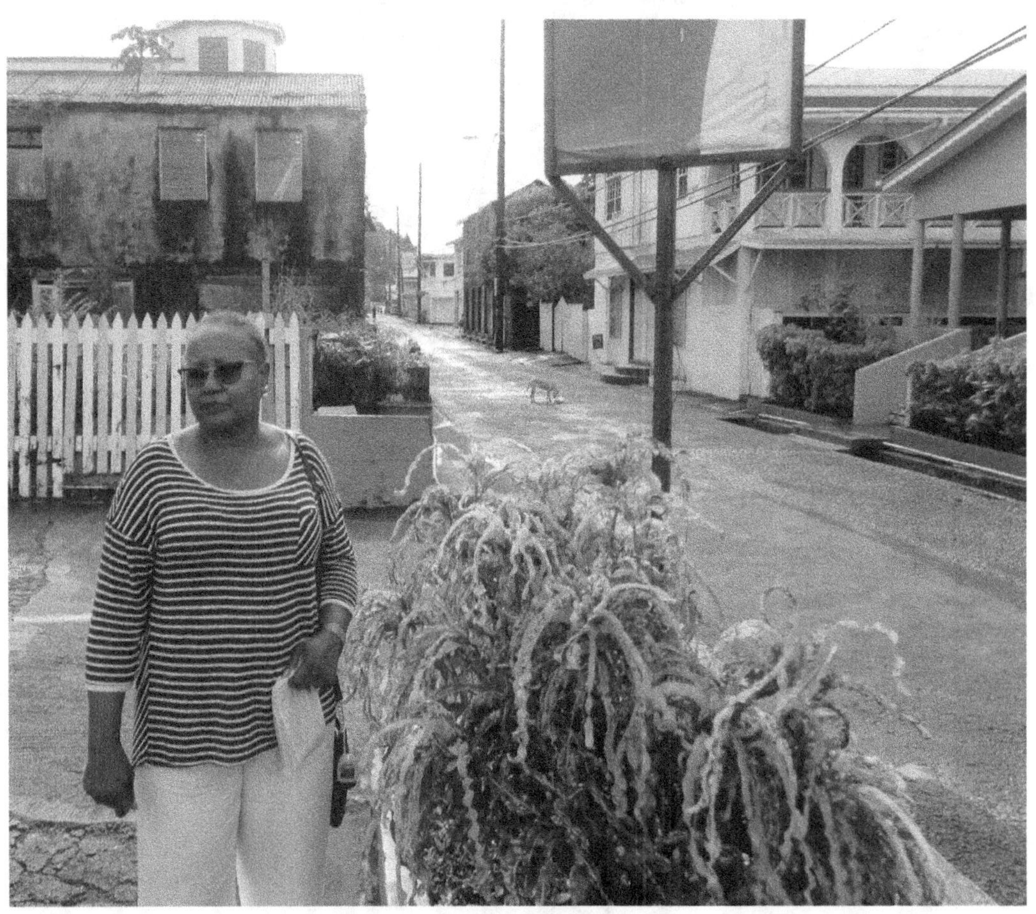

A lone shopper after a little rain in Victoria

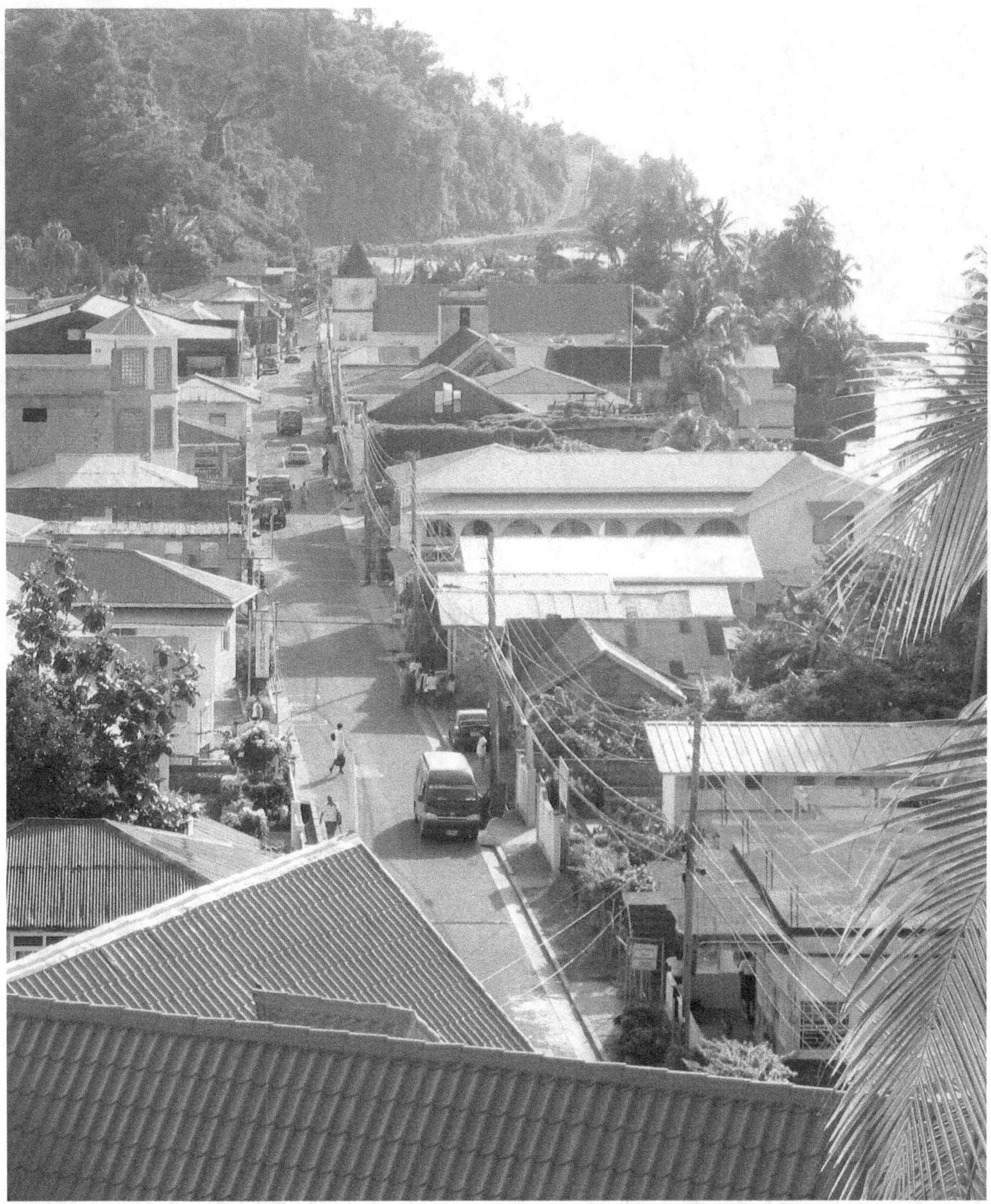

Morning activities begin on Queen Street, Victoria. From the top of the picture, La Source Hill descends into Queen Street.

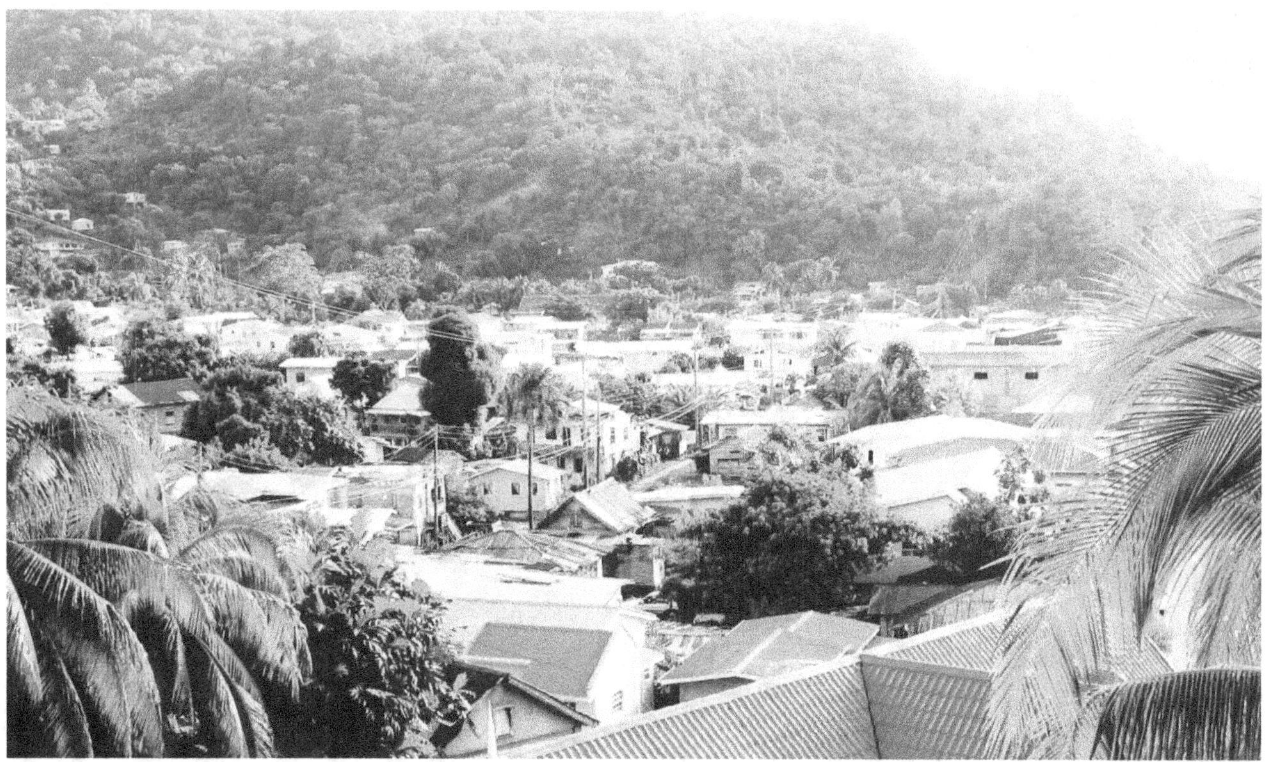

Victoria town as seen from Coast Guard

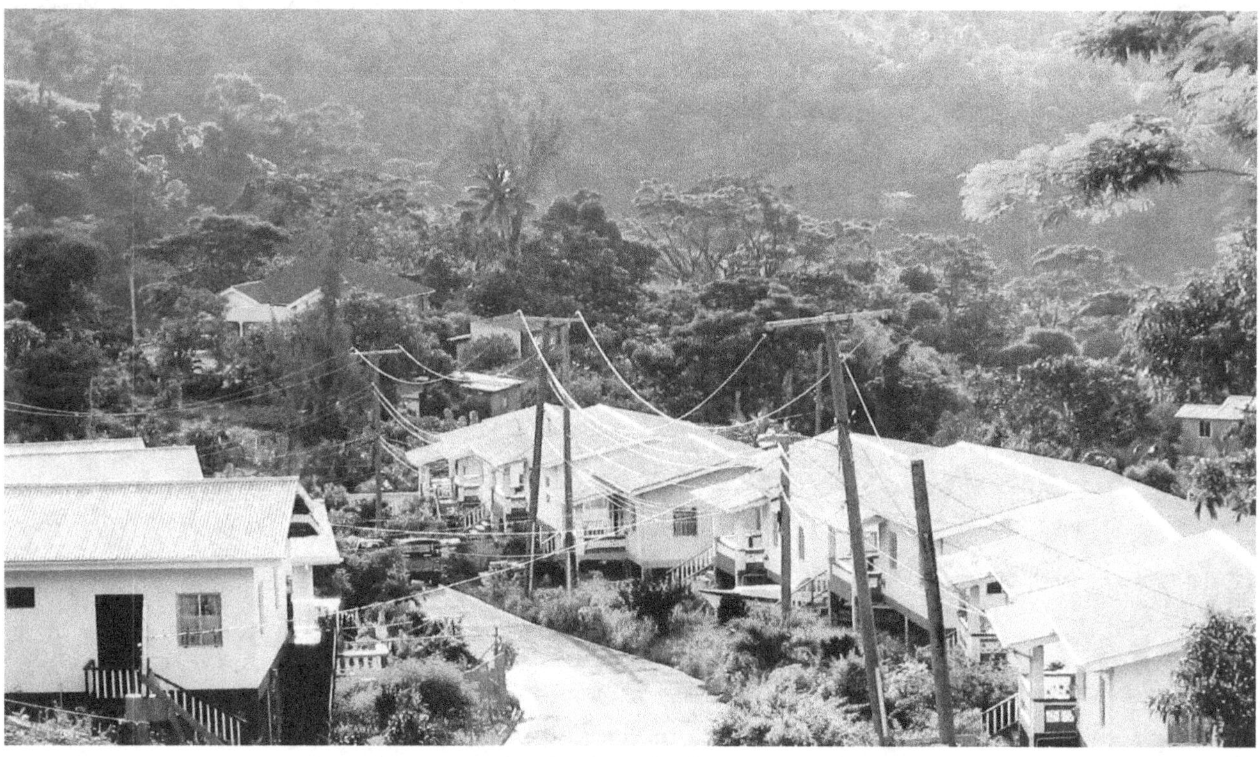

Homes at Taylor, high in the hills above Victoria

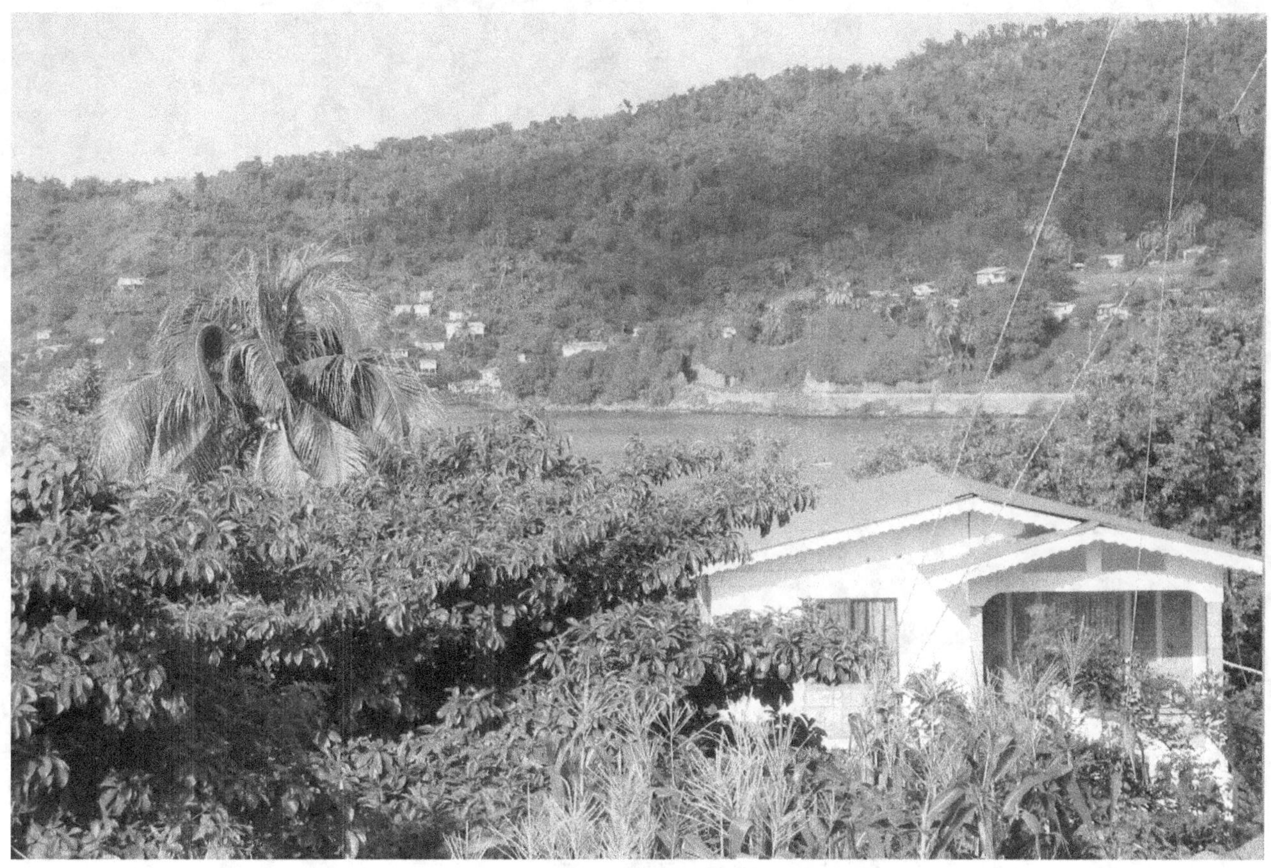

On the outskirts of Victoria

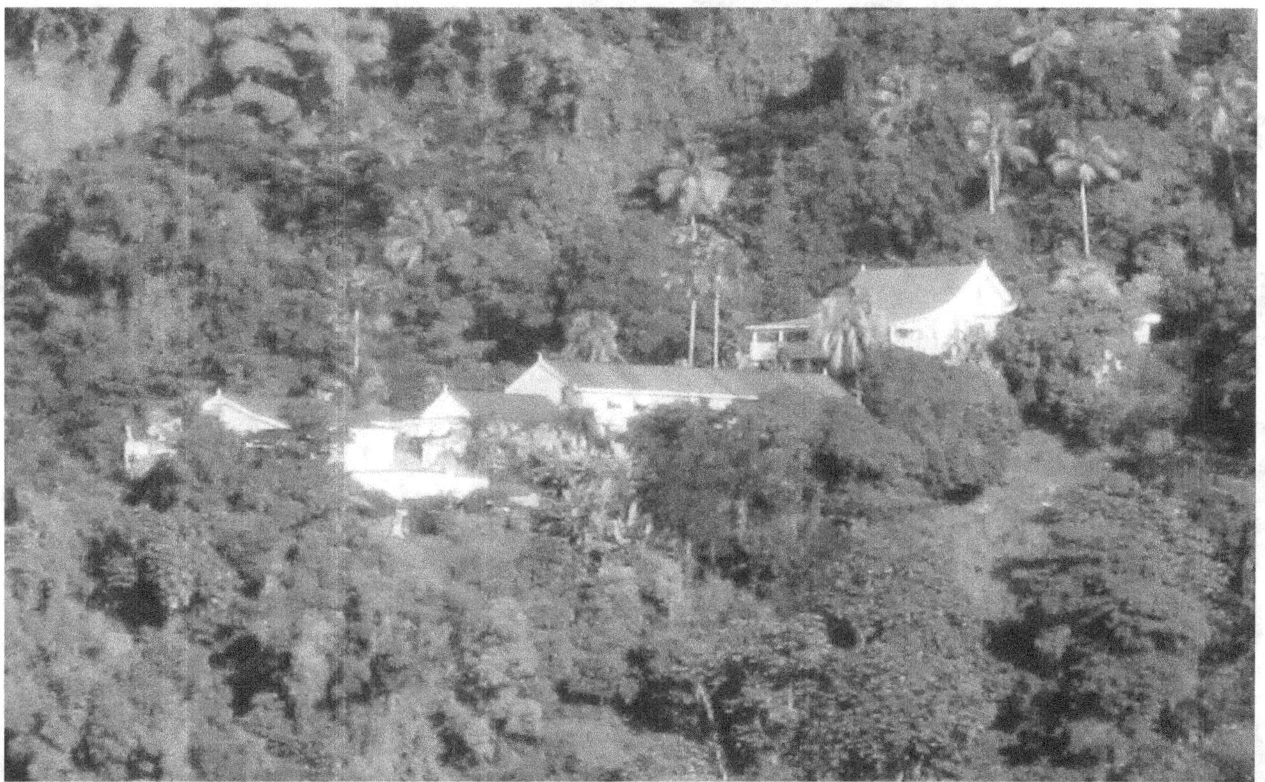

Mt. Edgecombe plantation house is a restored property that now provides accommodation for those who want to relax in the quiet of Grenada's lush, eco-forested interior.

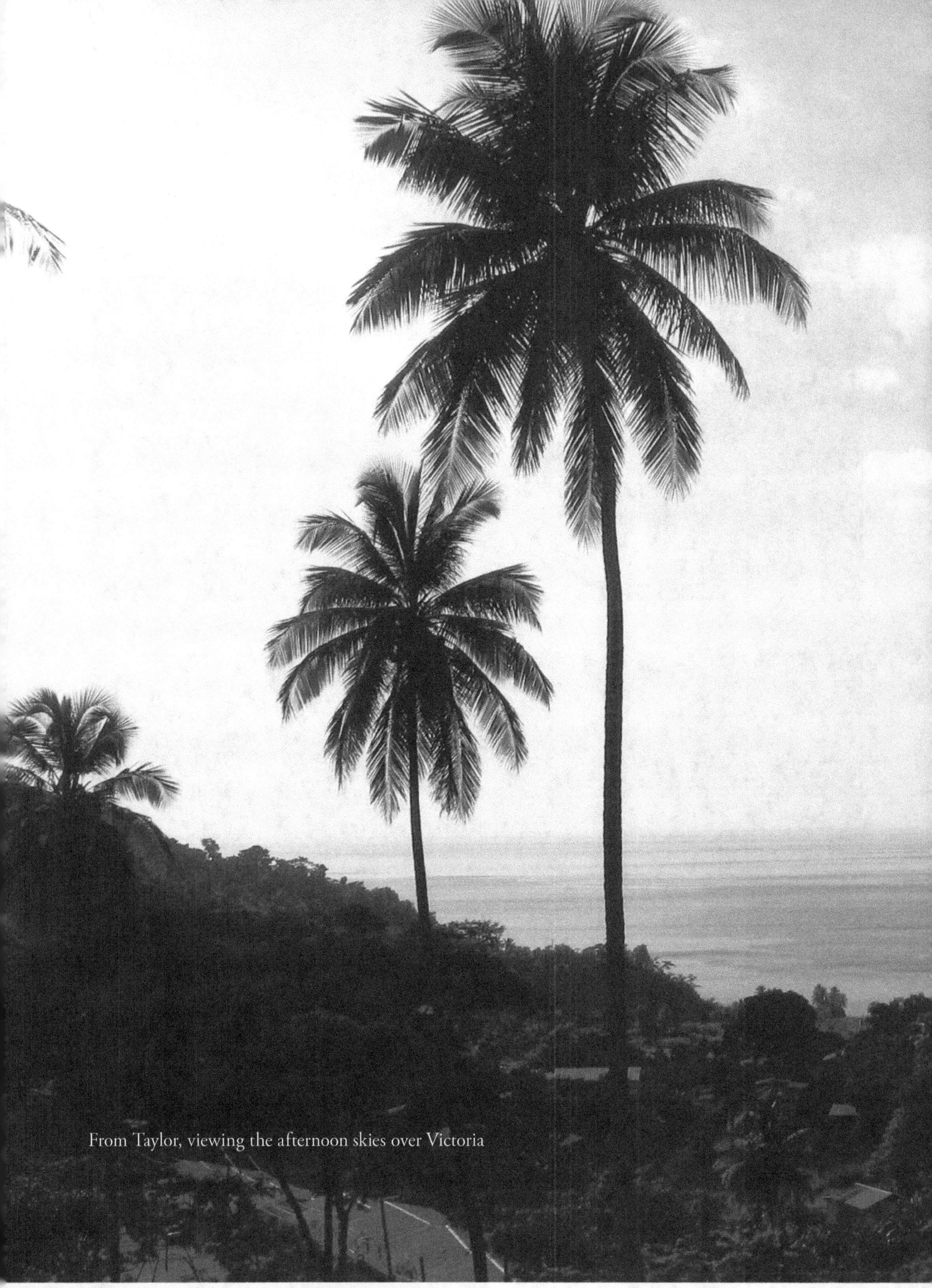

From Taylor, viewing the afternoon skies over Victoria

Mabouya * Mt. Granby * Mt. Nesbit * Maran * Brothers * Woodford * St. Mary * Mt. Plasir * Mt. D'or * Morne Jaloux * Palmiste * Dougaldston * Woodford * Waterloo * Donaldston * Dothan * Marigot * Belle Gou * Loretto * Gross Point * Paradise * Brooklyn * Florida * Clozier * Gouyave * Concord * Black Bay * Rosemont * Clozier

ST. JOHN

St. John's parish, particularly the town of Gouyave, is well known for its fishing. St. John reports a greater fish catch than many of the other parishes. Fishing has influenced local culture where, today, *Fish Friday* has become a weekly festivity that attracts many people to the local food, art and culture of St. John.

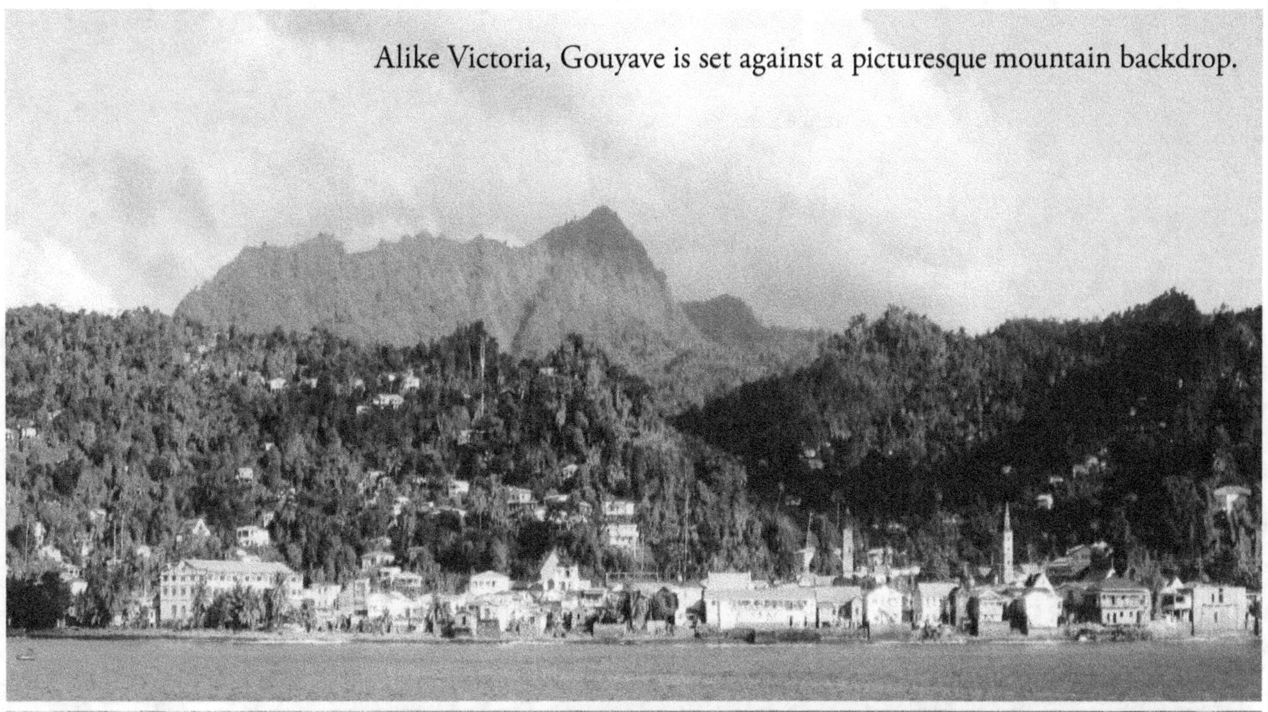

Alike Victoria, Gouyave is set against a picturesque mountain backdrop.

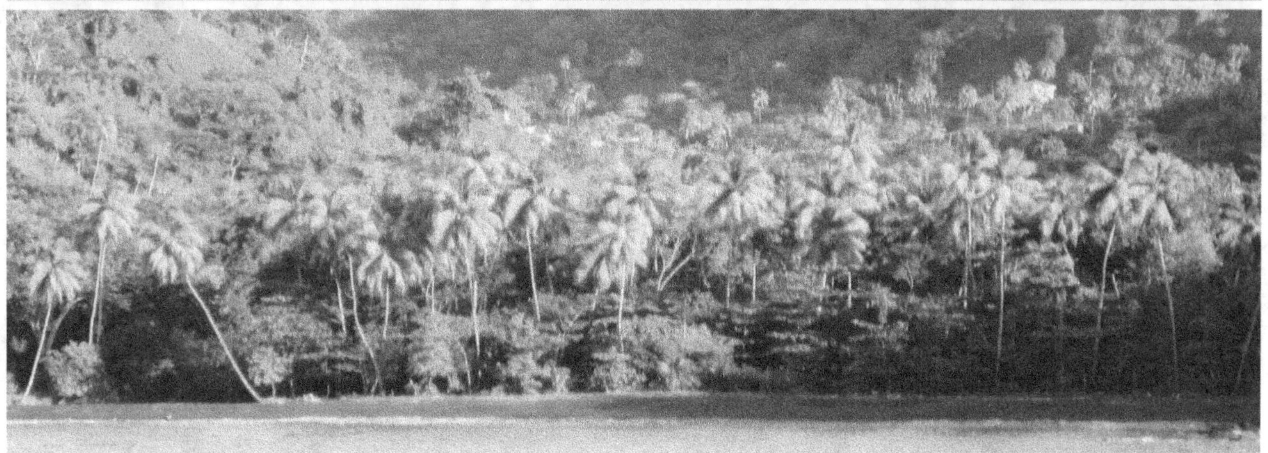

Beautiful Black Bay Beach is composed of dark volcanic sands.

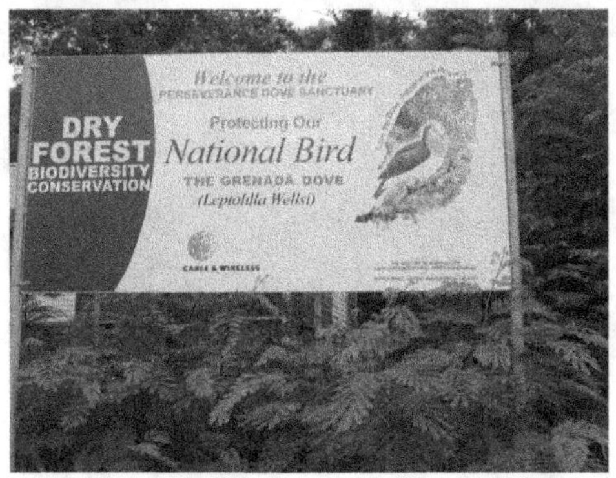

Here at Perseverance is an example of Grenada's declared commitment to the preservation of its national bird, the Grenada Dove (leptolilla Wellsi)

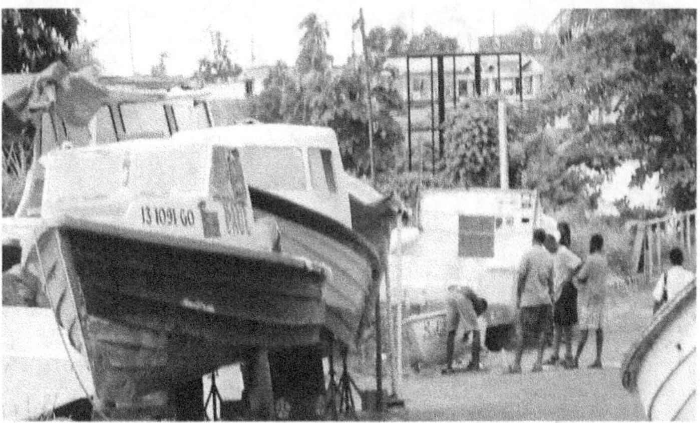

Boat painting at Gouyave

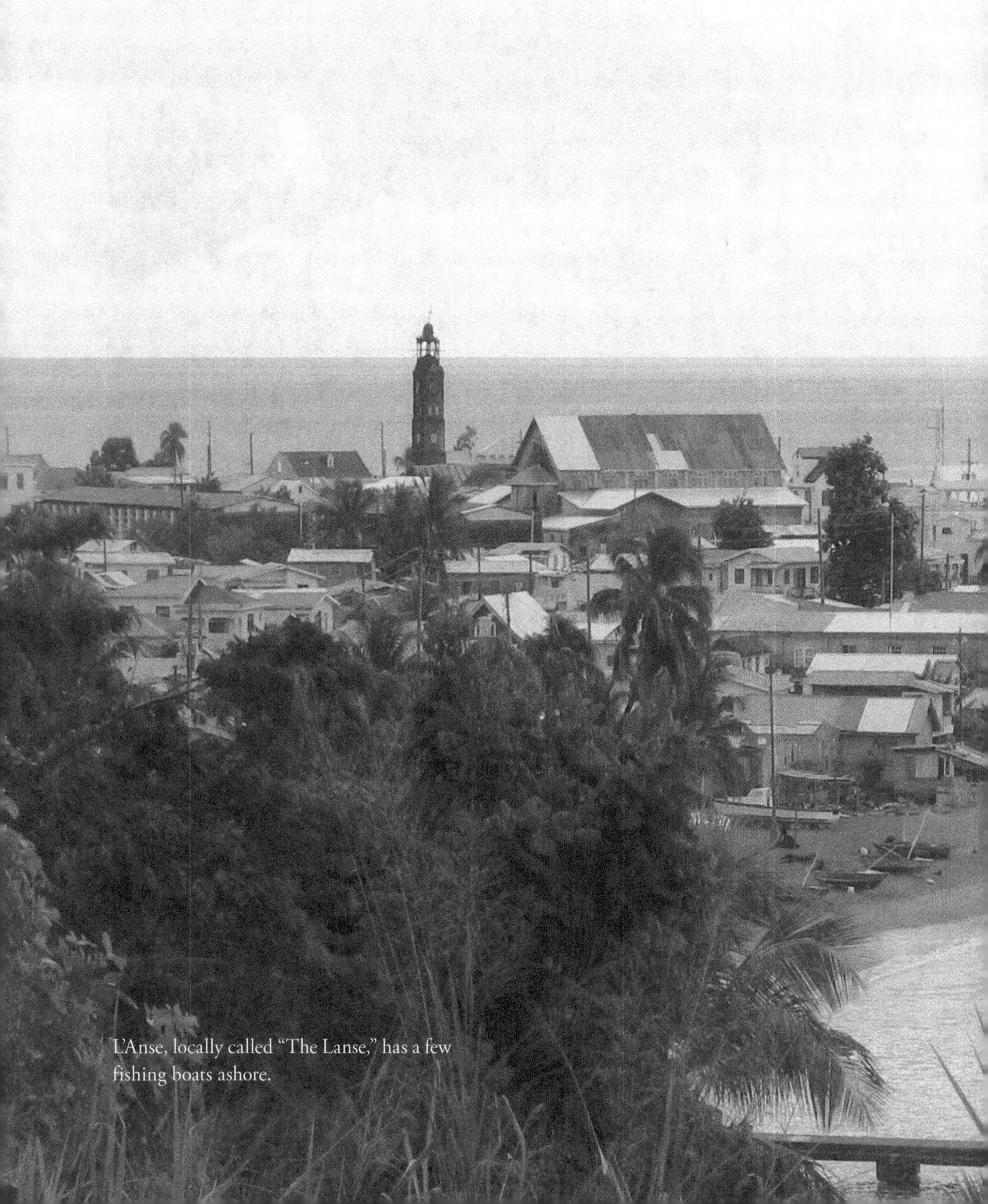

L'Anse, locally called "The Lanse," has a few
fishing boats ashore.

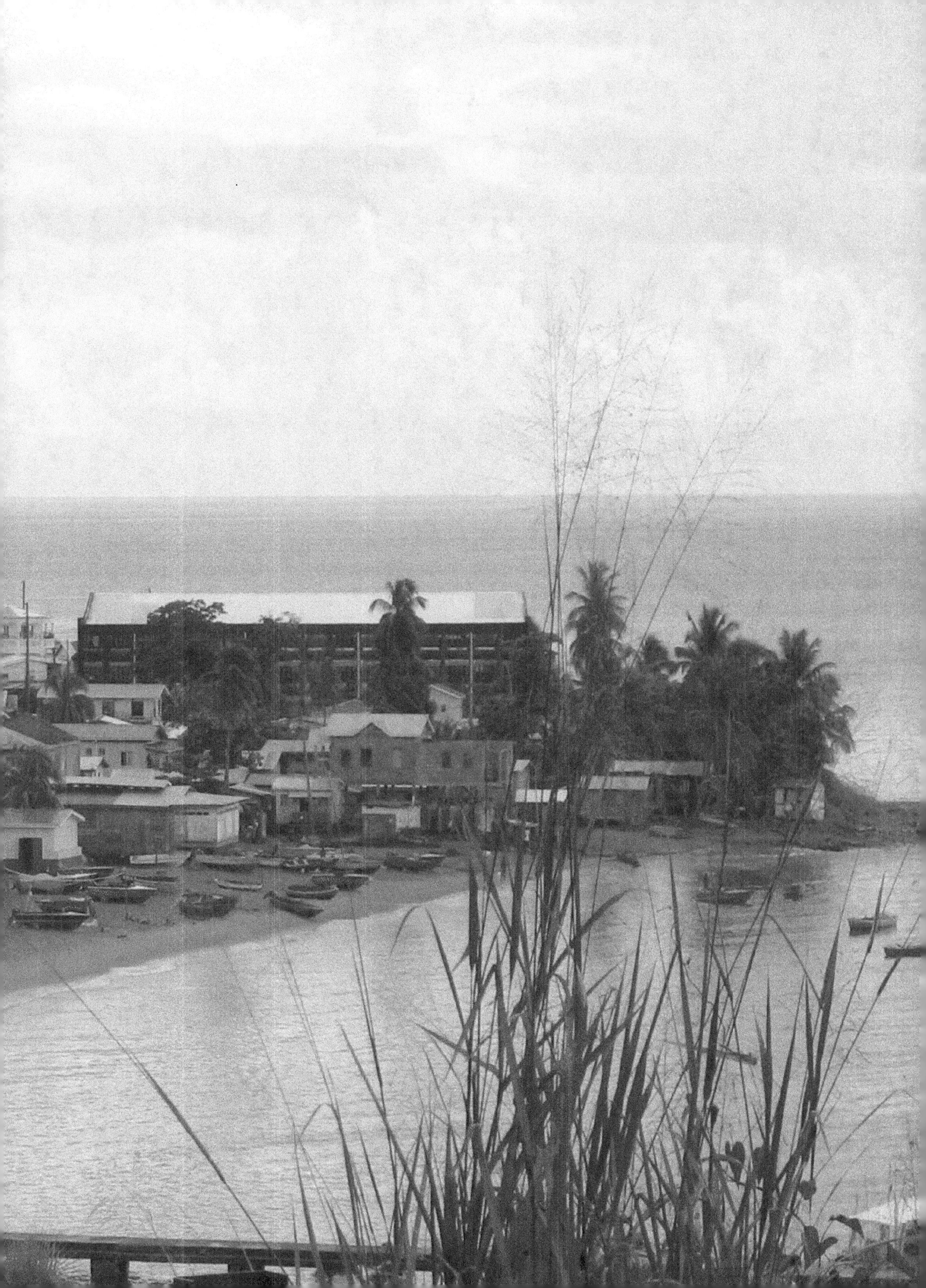

CLOZIER

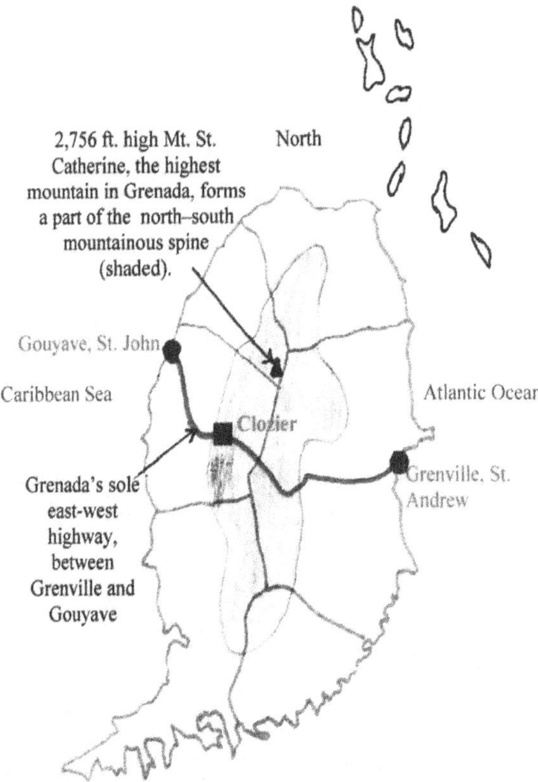

Clozier is a village located on Grenada's only east-west roadway, running between Grenville on St. Andrew's Atlantic coast and Gouyave on St. John's Caribbean coast. Eighteenth-century Grenadian slave rebels traveled through the east-west corridor, including Clozier, as they maneuvered between the seacoasts. Before the automobile, many farmers from Gouyave and Grenville would travel some ten miles by foot over the mountainous east-west access to sell their produce on each other's coasts. Clozier today is one of the villages with a small concentration of Indo-Grenadians.

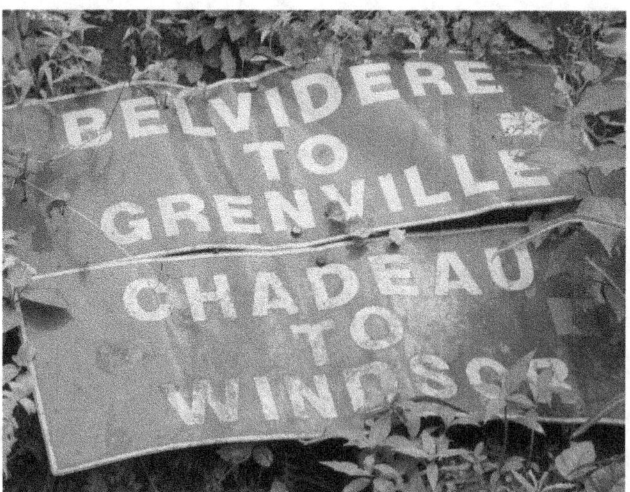

The fallen road sign indicates directions to Grenville town and the nearby villages of Chadeau, Windsor, and historic Belividere, the home of Grenada's anti-slavery rebel, Julien Fedon.

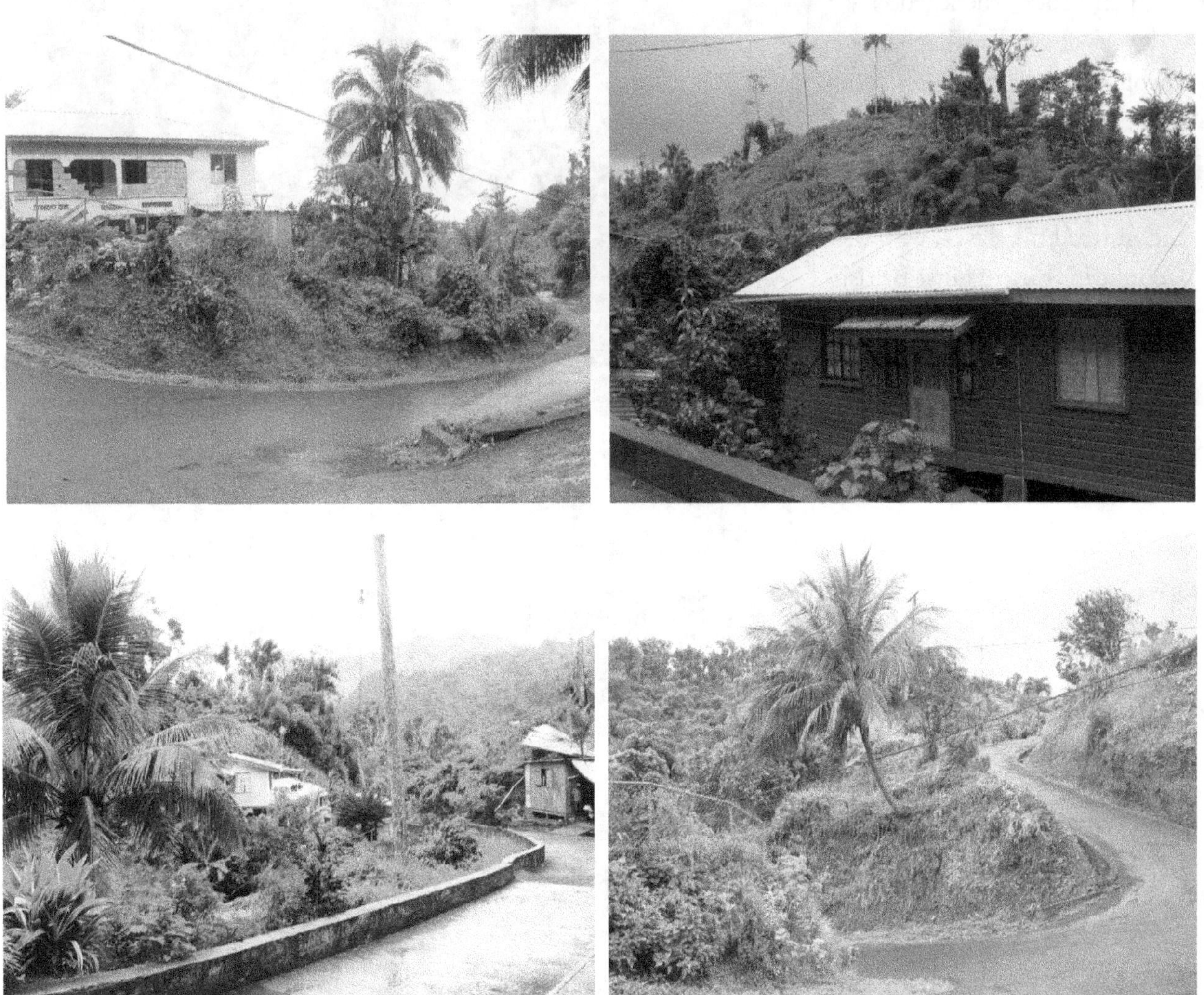

Clozier village (above pictures) is in Grenada's mountainous interior.

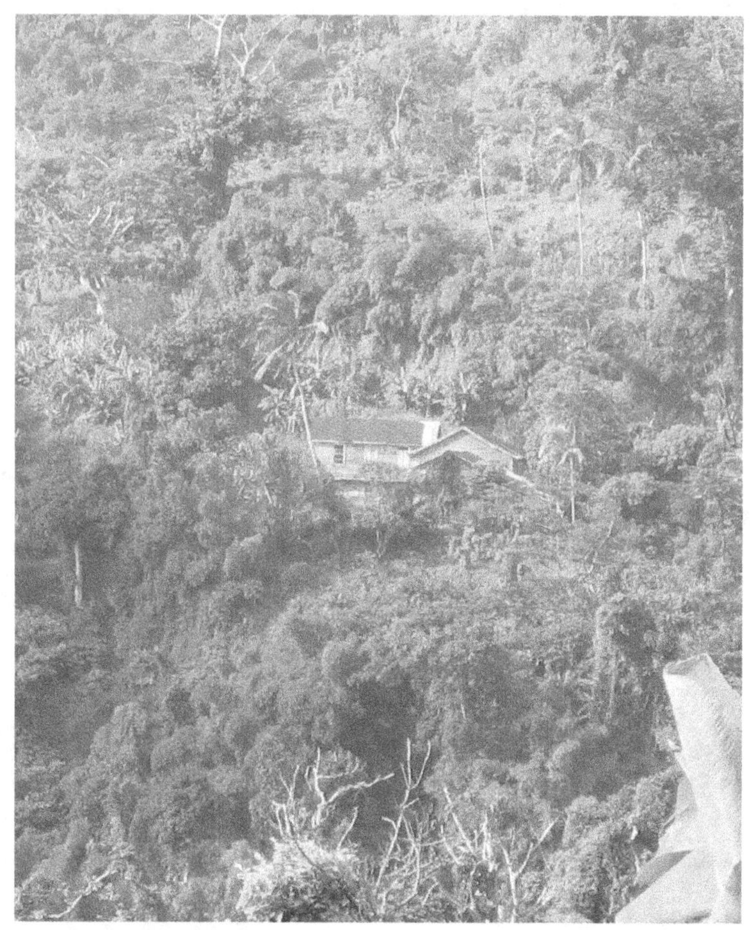

This picture is a section of Belvidere Estate, located near the St. John and St. Andrew border.

Julien Fedon, the legendary leader of a Grenadian slave revolt, was a French Grenadian colored (petit blanc) who owned Belvidere Estate.

Fedon freed his slaves, who then fought for him against British slavery in Grenada. At one point, Fedon had conquered most of Grenada except St. George's.

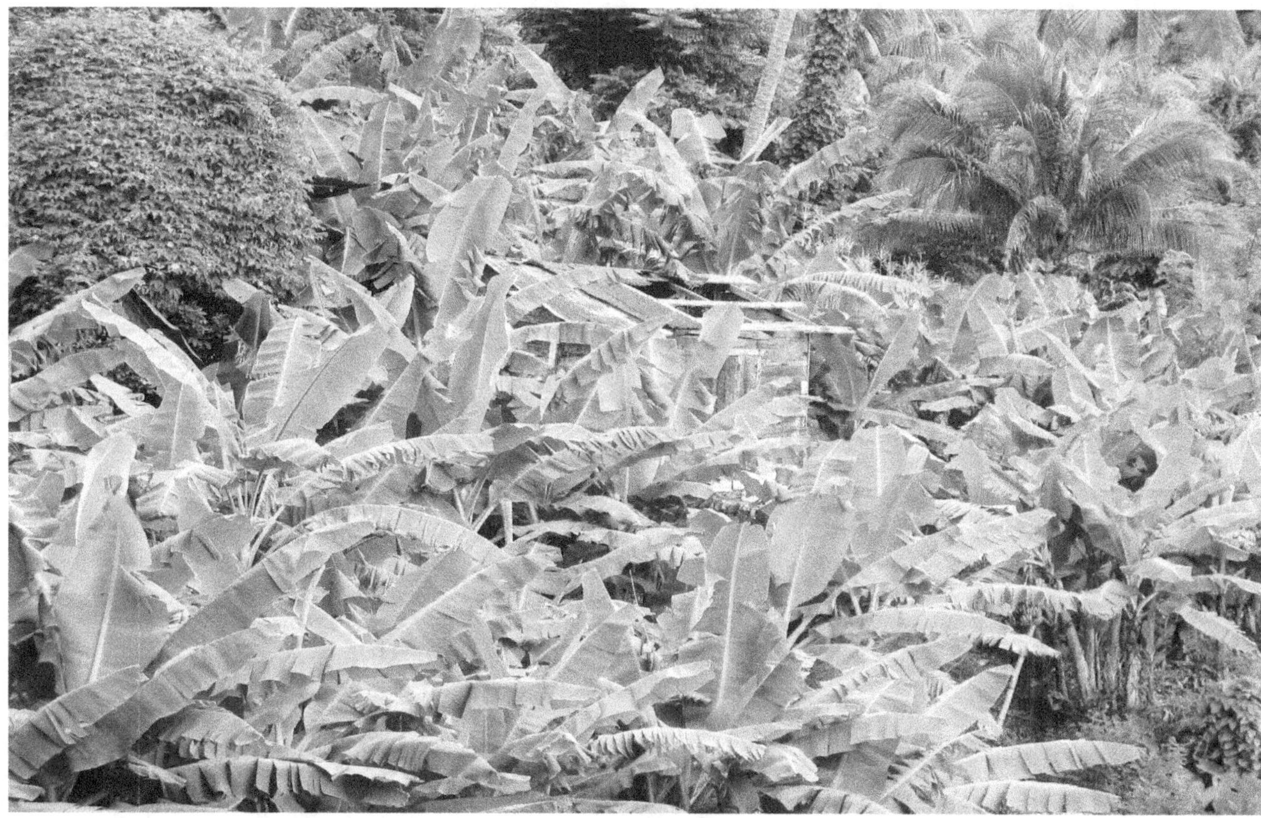

Banana trees in the Black Bay area surround an abandoned house.

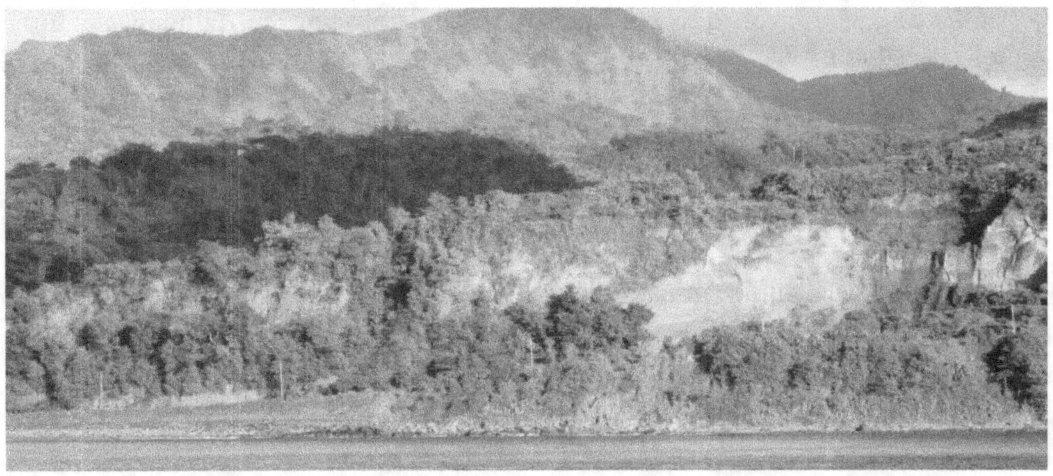

Mabouyah Rock drops steeply towards the Western Main Road.

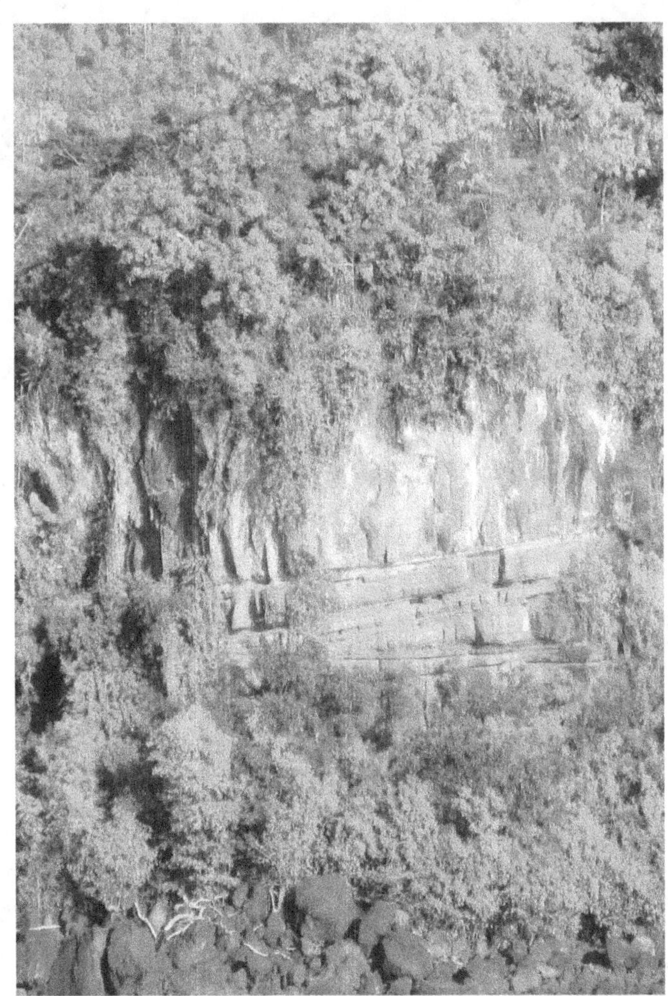

Color diversity in the rock layers along the western coast

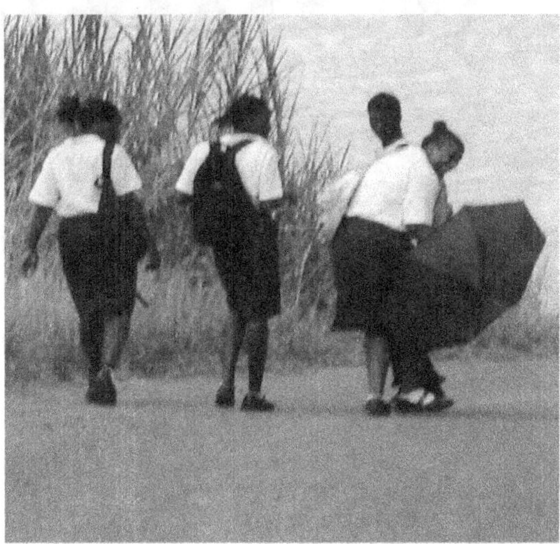

School children near Mabouyah Rock get ready to share an umbrella as a drizzle begins.

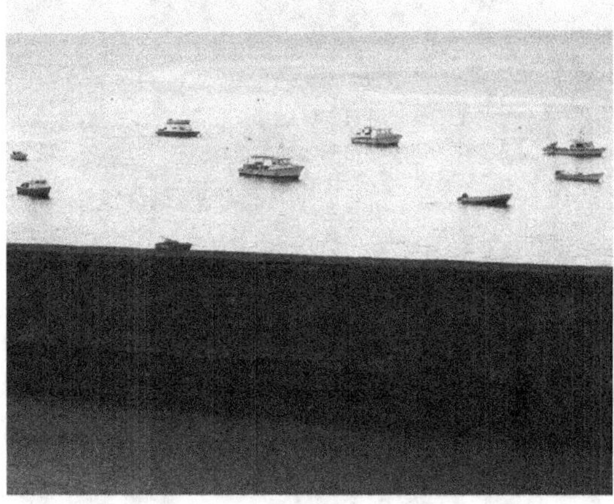

Fishing boats at Maran

Gouyave derives its name from the French *goyave* (guava), because of the abundance of guavas found in the area. French colonizers first called the location Charlotte Town, in honor of the French Queen, Charlotte.

Gouyave, as seen from the south

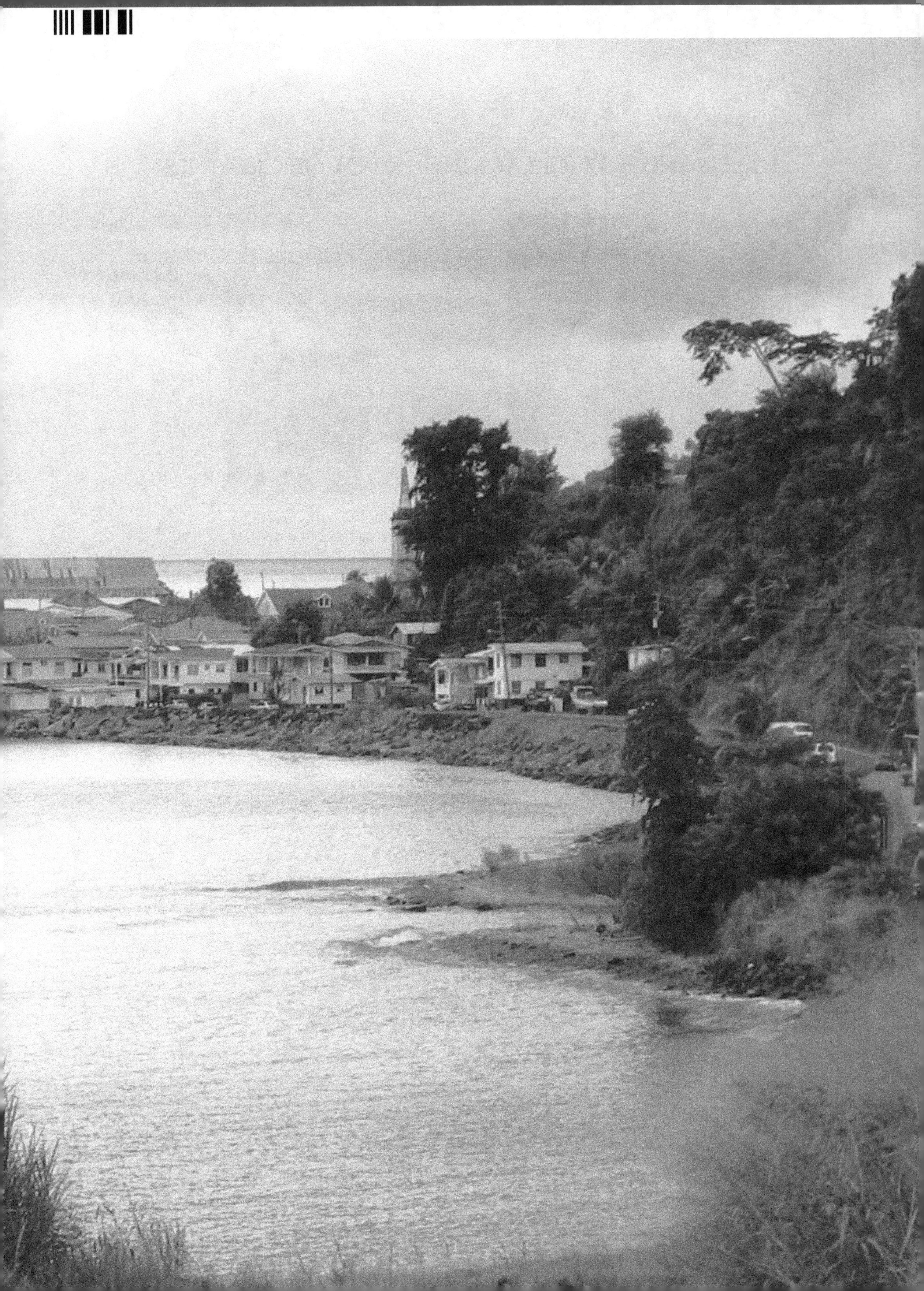

GRAND ROY (GREAT KING), ROOT OF GREATNESS

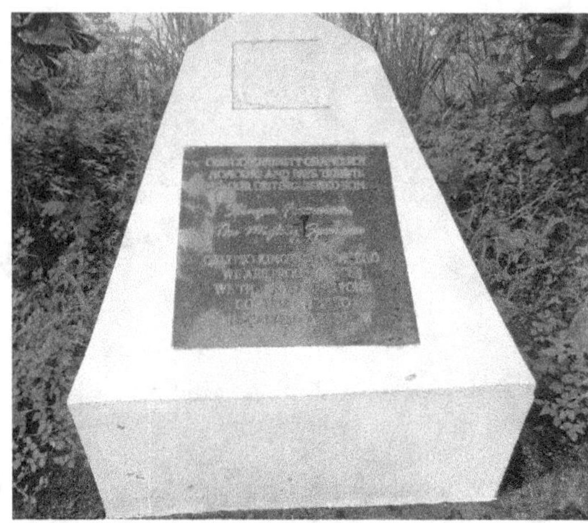

This monument reads, "Our Community Grand Roy honours and pays tribute to our distinguished son Slinger Francisco The Mighty Sparrow Calypso King of the world. We are proud of you; we thank you for your contribution to the Calypso art form.

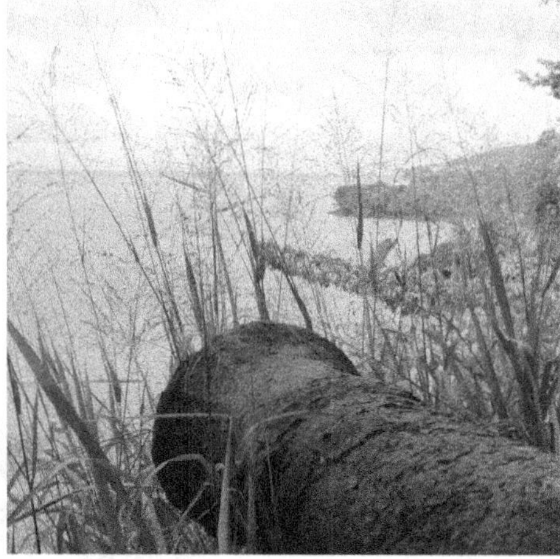

Remains of a centuries-old colonial cannon mounted next to The Mighty Sparrow's monument

Lewis Hamilton, with 92 Grand Prix victories as of October 2020, is the world record holder in Formula 1 race car driving. His paternal grandparents are from Grand Roy. Regarding Grenada's independence, he once posted:

"Happy Independence Day, Grenada. My heritage and a big part of who I am today. #LOVE #Greneda #SpiceIsland."

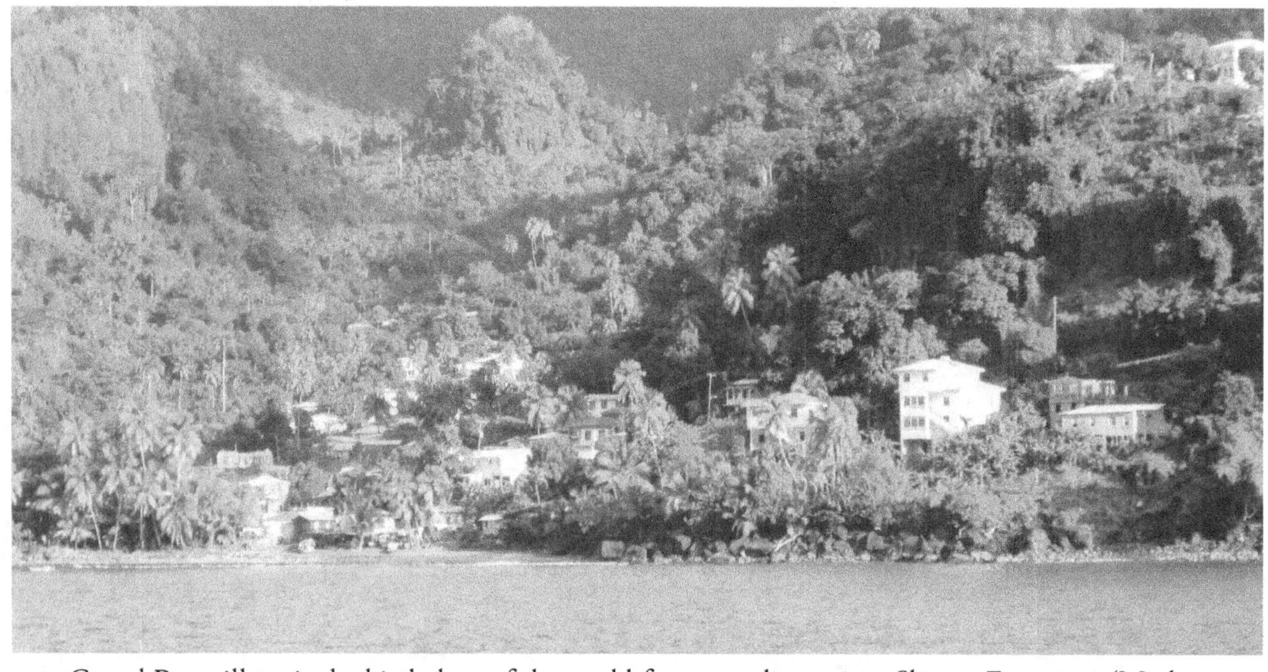

Grand Roy village is the birthplace of the world-famous calypsonian, Slinger Francisco (Mighty Sparrow). It is also the birthplace of Lewis Hamilton's paternal grandparents.

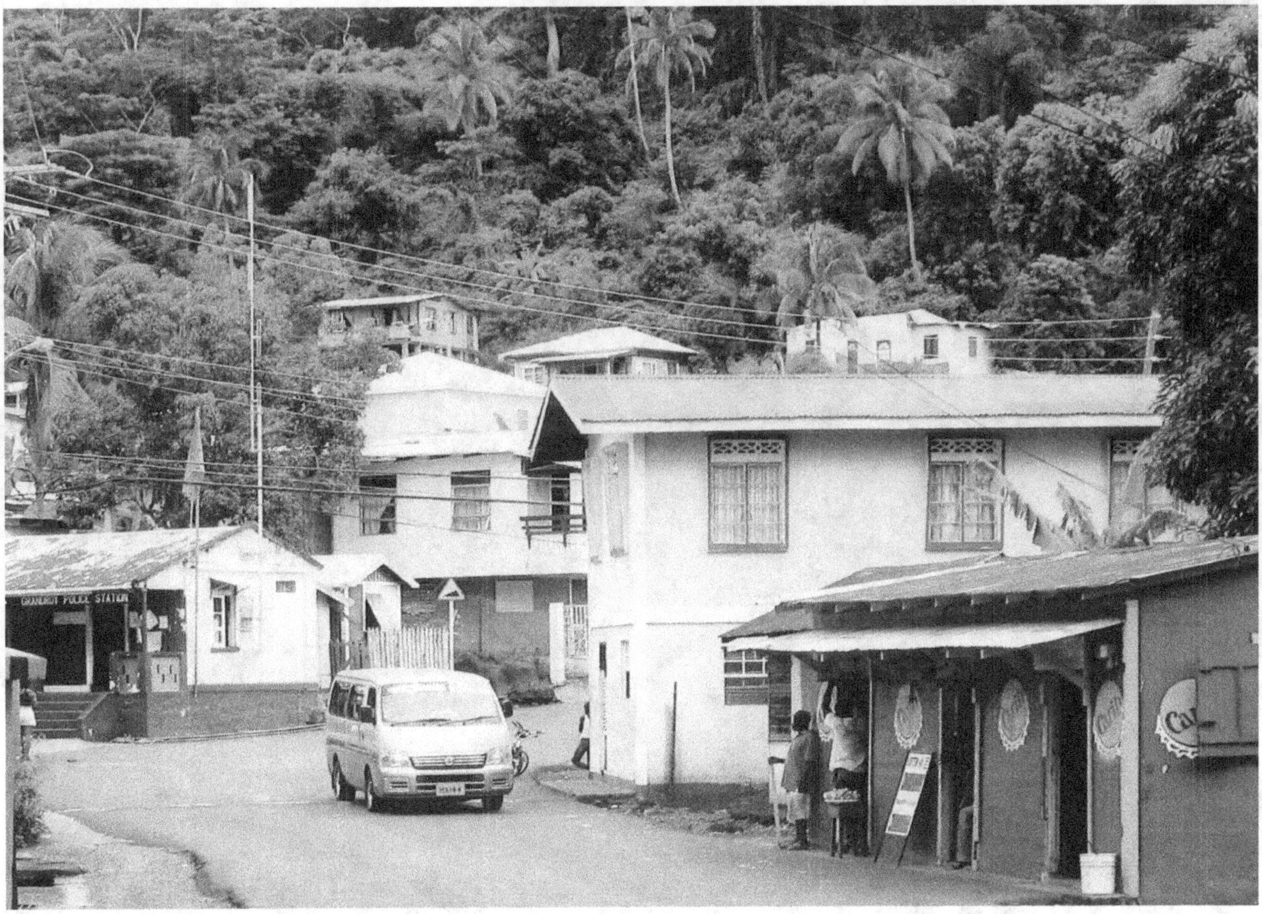

A passenger minibus leaves Grand Roy junction. Hamilton's grandfather drove a similar passenger bus.

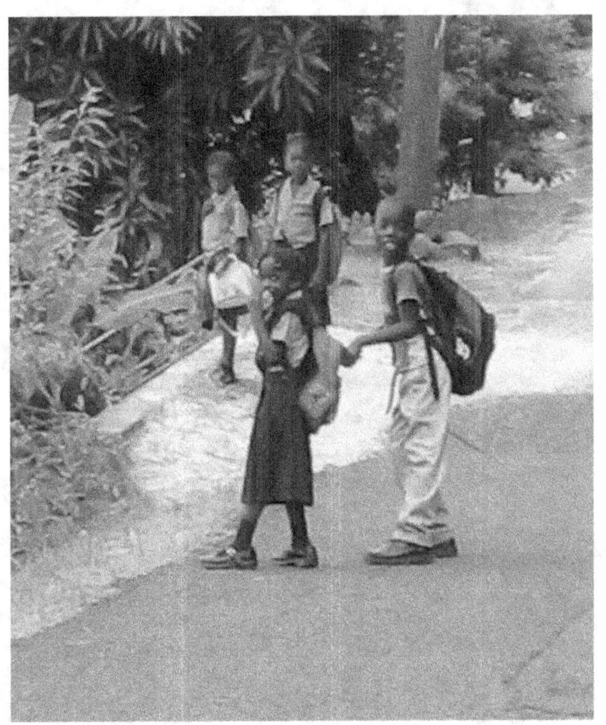

School children at Grand Roy. Are there more
Great kings in the making here?

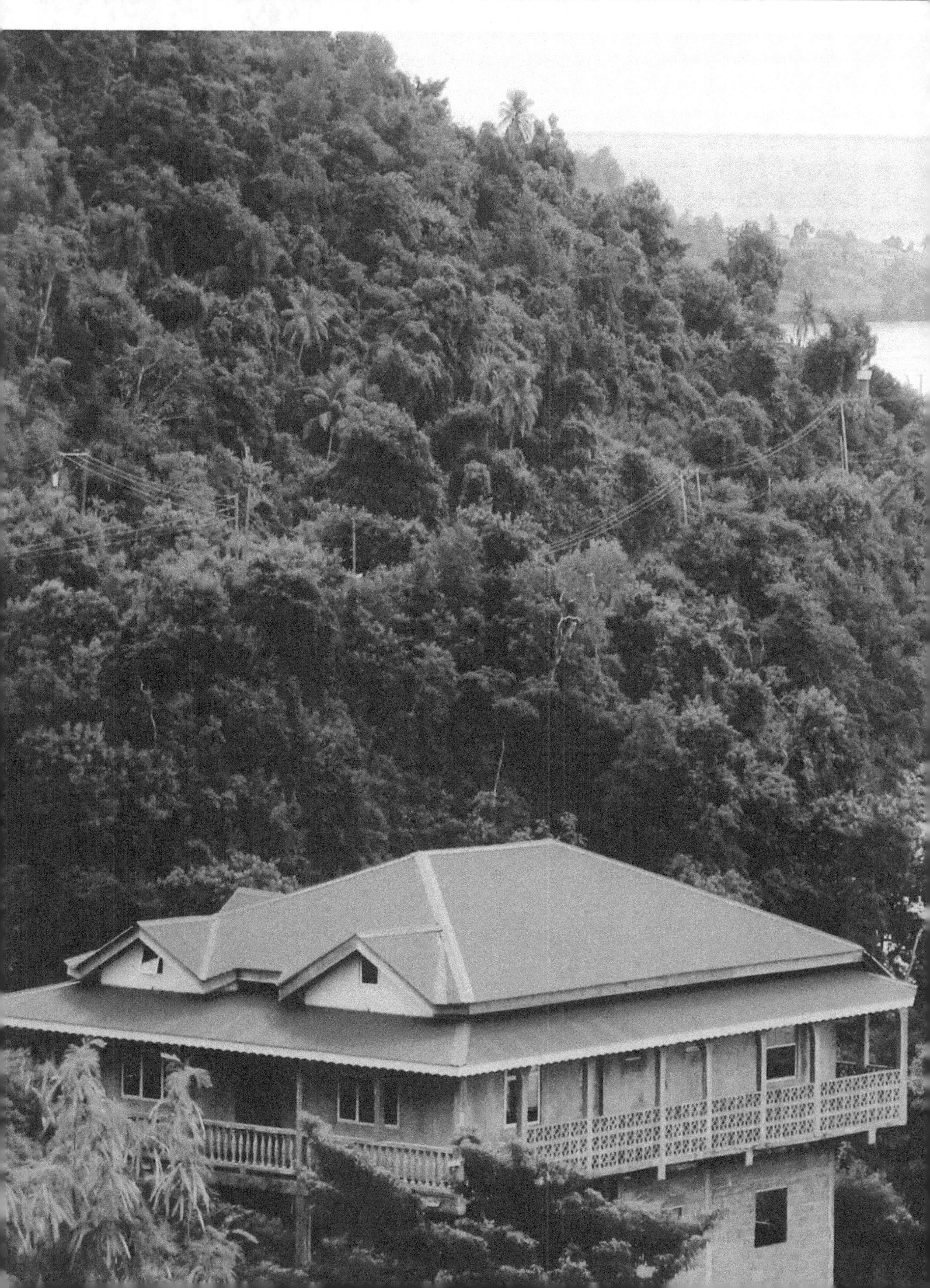

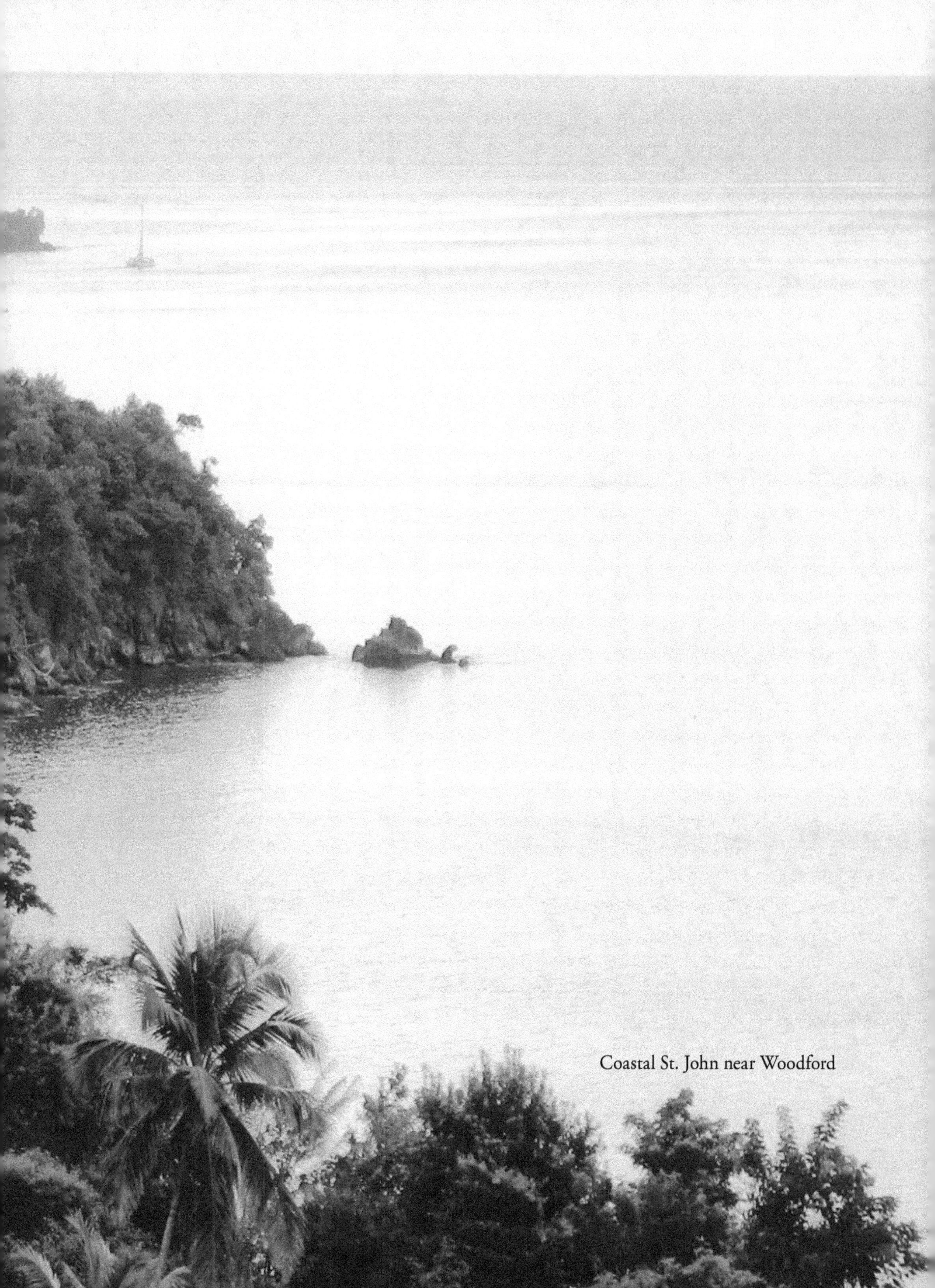

Coastal St. John near Woodford

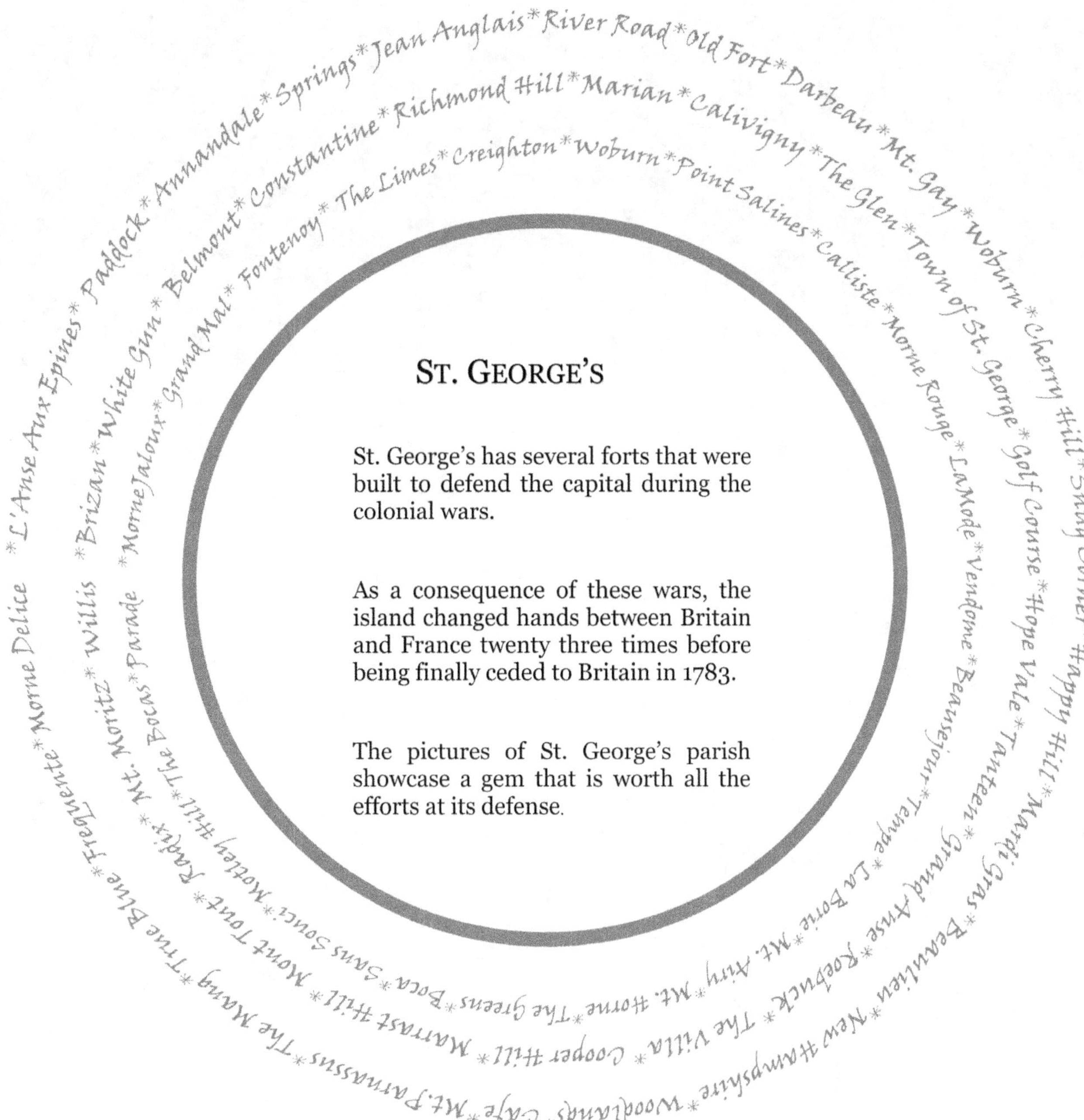

ST. GEORGE'S

St. George's has several forts that were built to defend the capital during the colonial wars.

As a consequence of these wars, the island changed hands between Britain and France twenty three times before being finally ceded to Britain in 1783.

The pictures of St. George's parish showcase a gem that is worth all the efforts at its defense.

A segment of St. George's Lagoon and yacht basin, part of old Port Louis

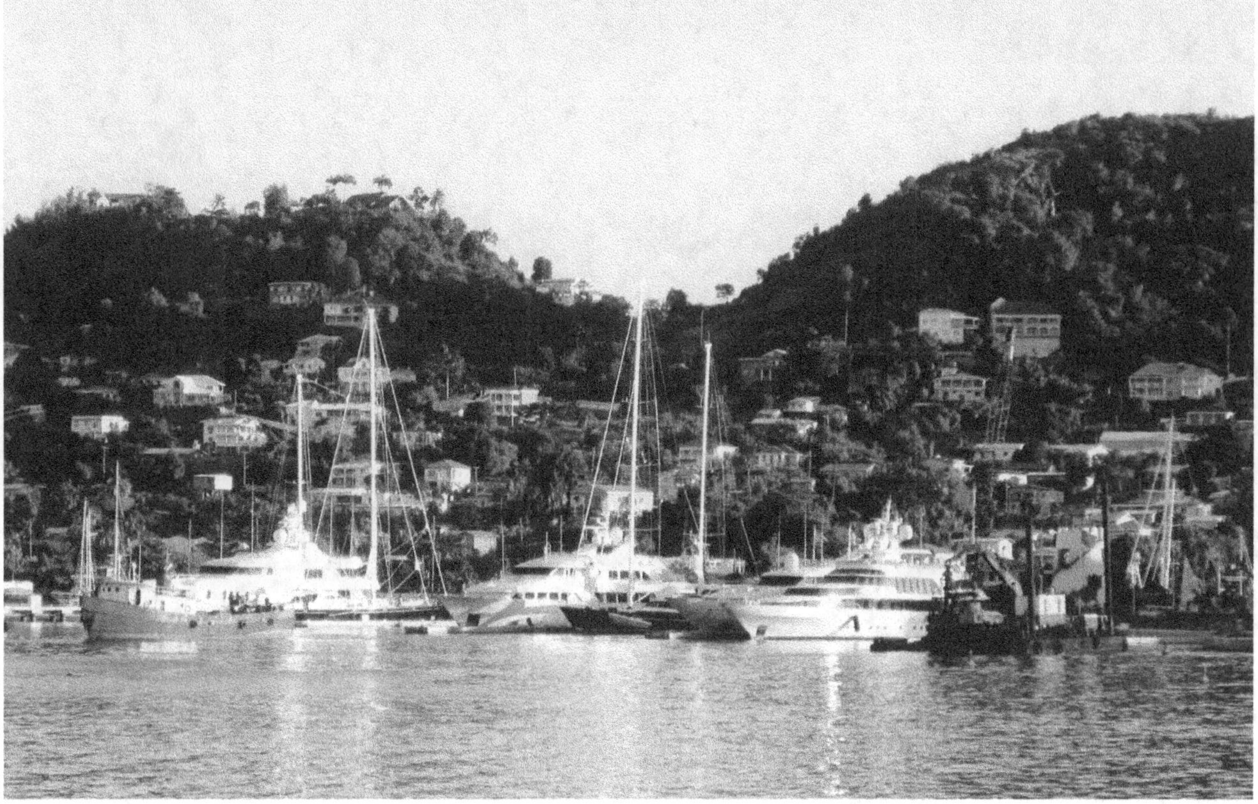

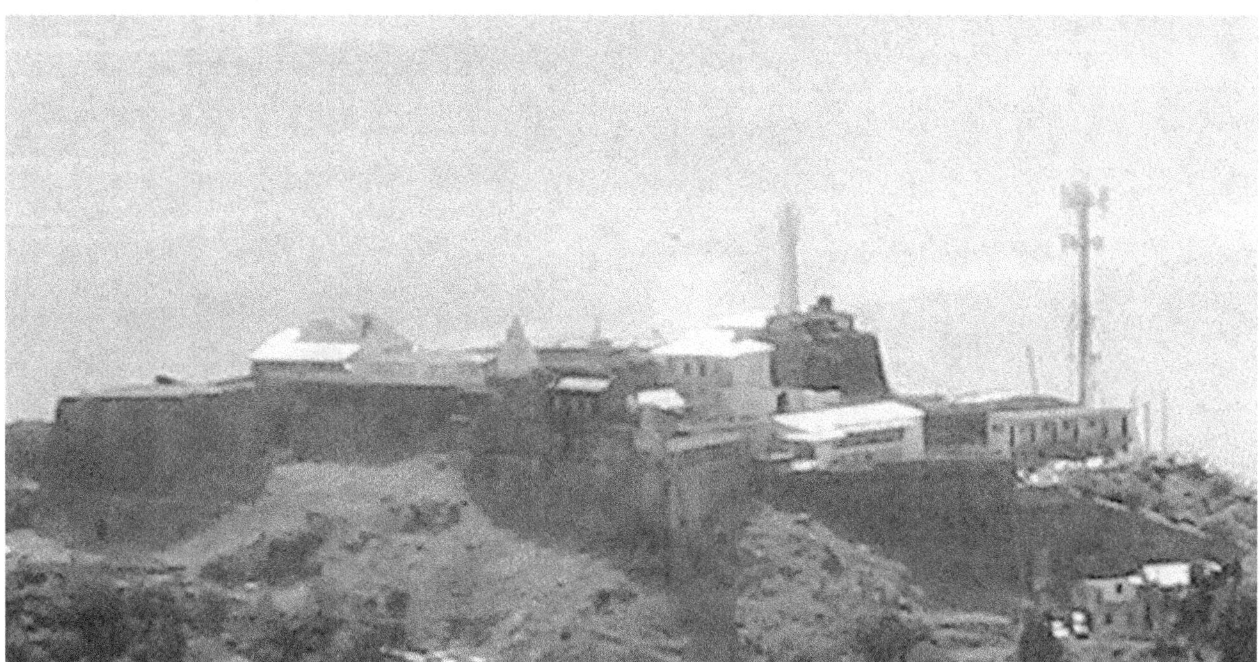

Before 1666, when Grenada's capital was in the lagoon area, the French colonizers erected The Great Fort on the hill overlooking the Lagoon (see pg. 89). By 1666 when the town grew and spread westwards, the Administration moved the fort to its current Hospital Hill location and called it Fort Royal. In 1705 the French rebuilt Fort Royal to provide the existing structure. In 1785, under their colonizing authority, the British changed Fort Royal to Fort George.

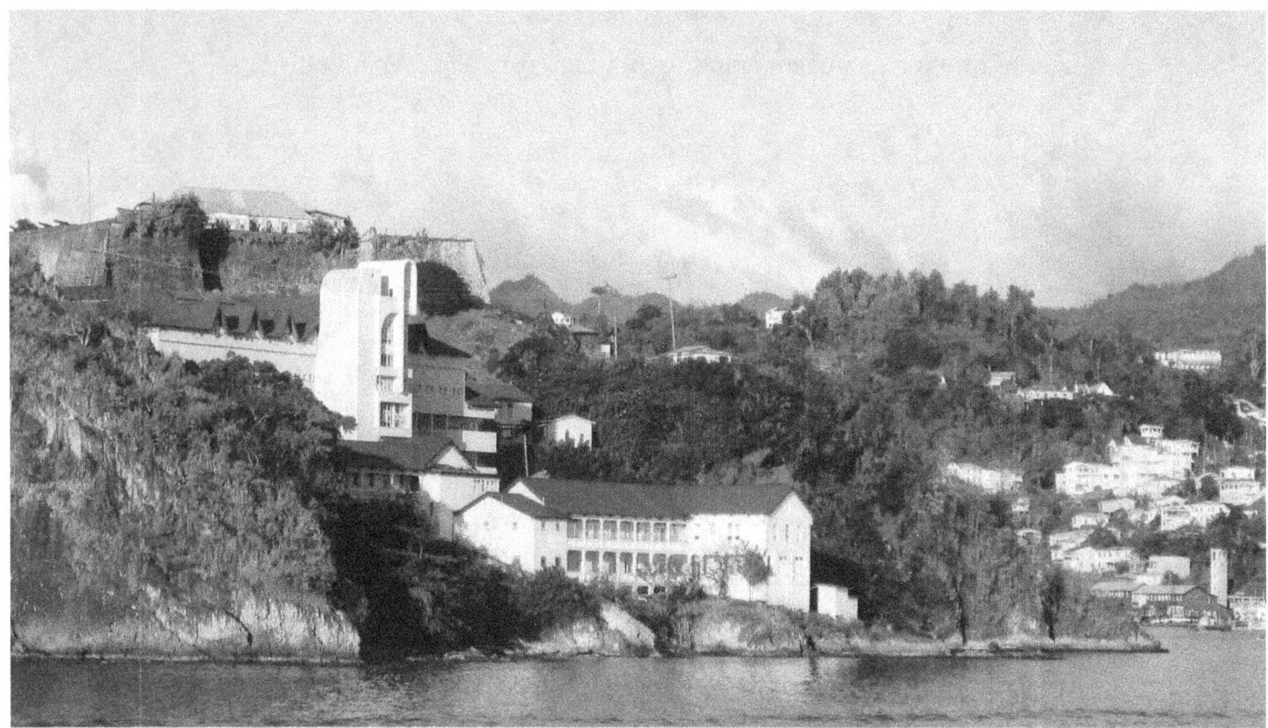

Fort George sits at the top of Hospital Hill, where it guards the harbor entrance. The Colony Hospital once occupied the area that is today the location of Grenada's General Hospital (red top buildings in the foreground). During the early colonial period, the Colony Hospital primarily served the British soldiers, many of whom served on the Fort.

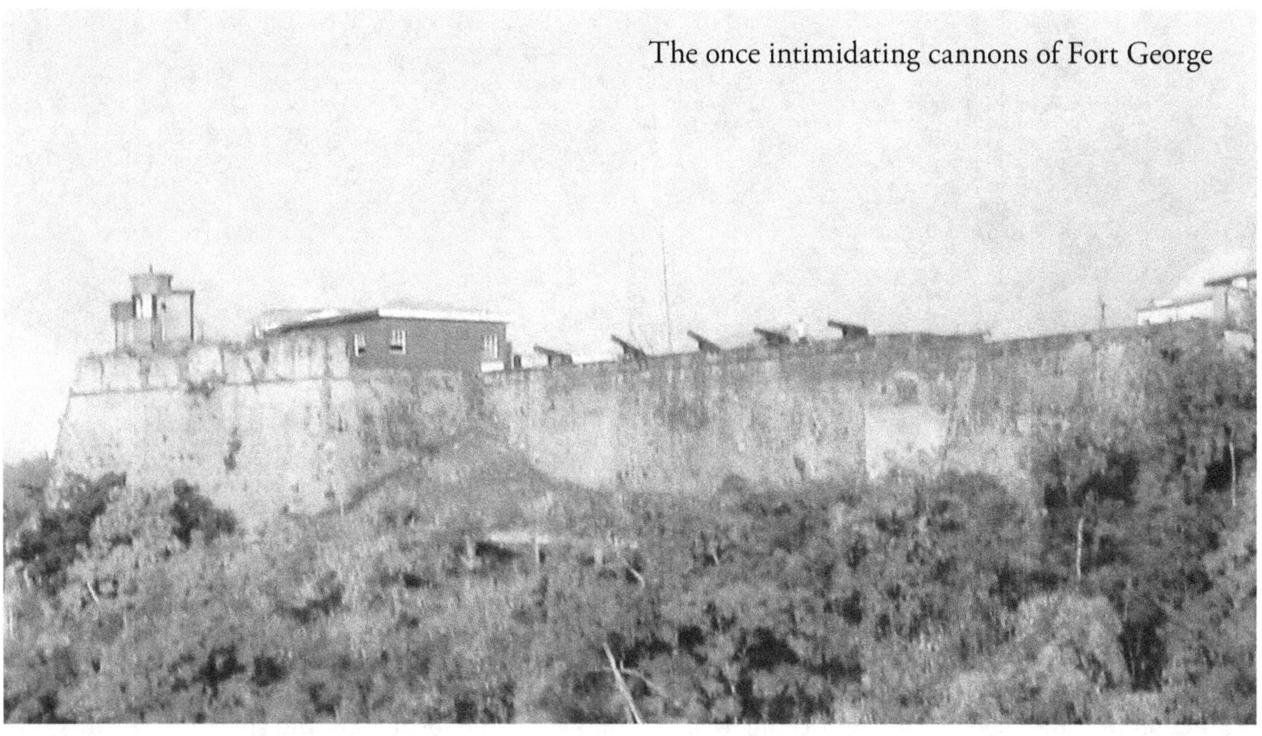

The once intimidating cannons of Fort George

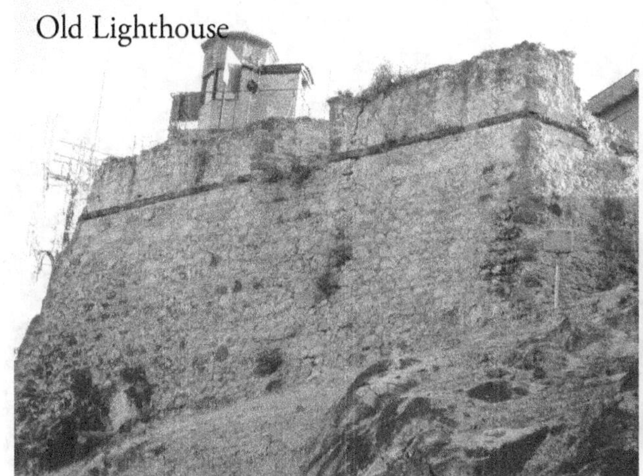

Old Lighthouse

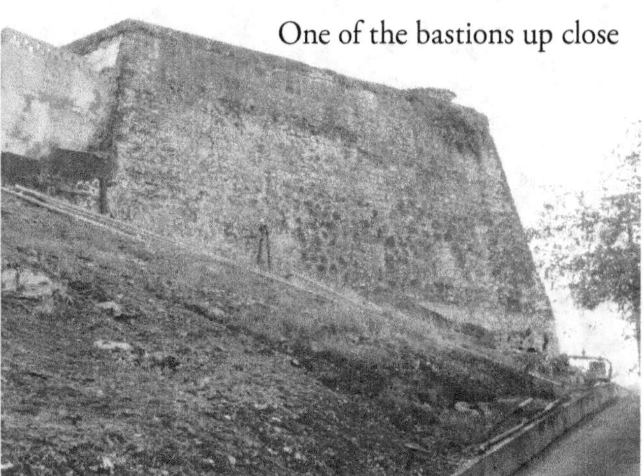

One of the bastions up close

Areas as far south as Quarantine Point in the front and Point Salines in the rear were within the protective range of cannon fire from the old forts of St. George's parish.

Grenada's international airport, Maurice Bishop International, is today located at Point Salines.

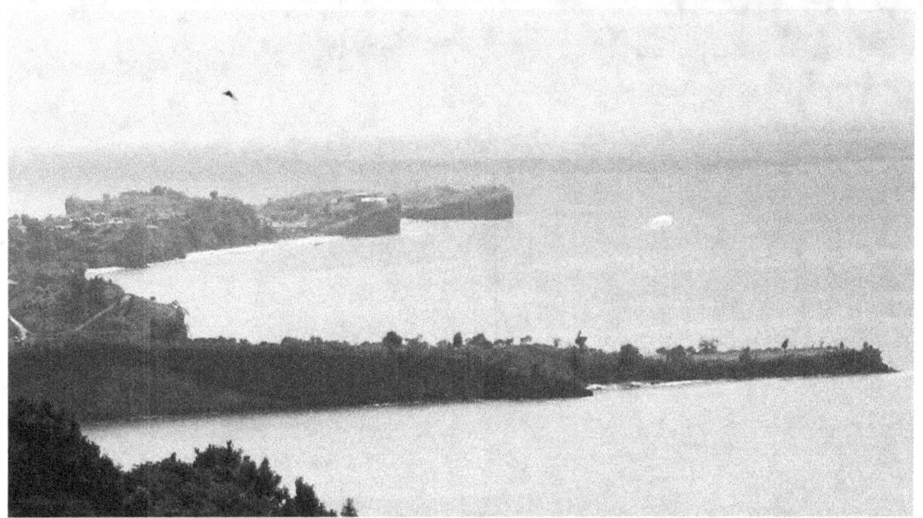

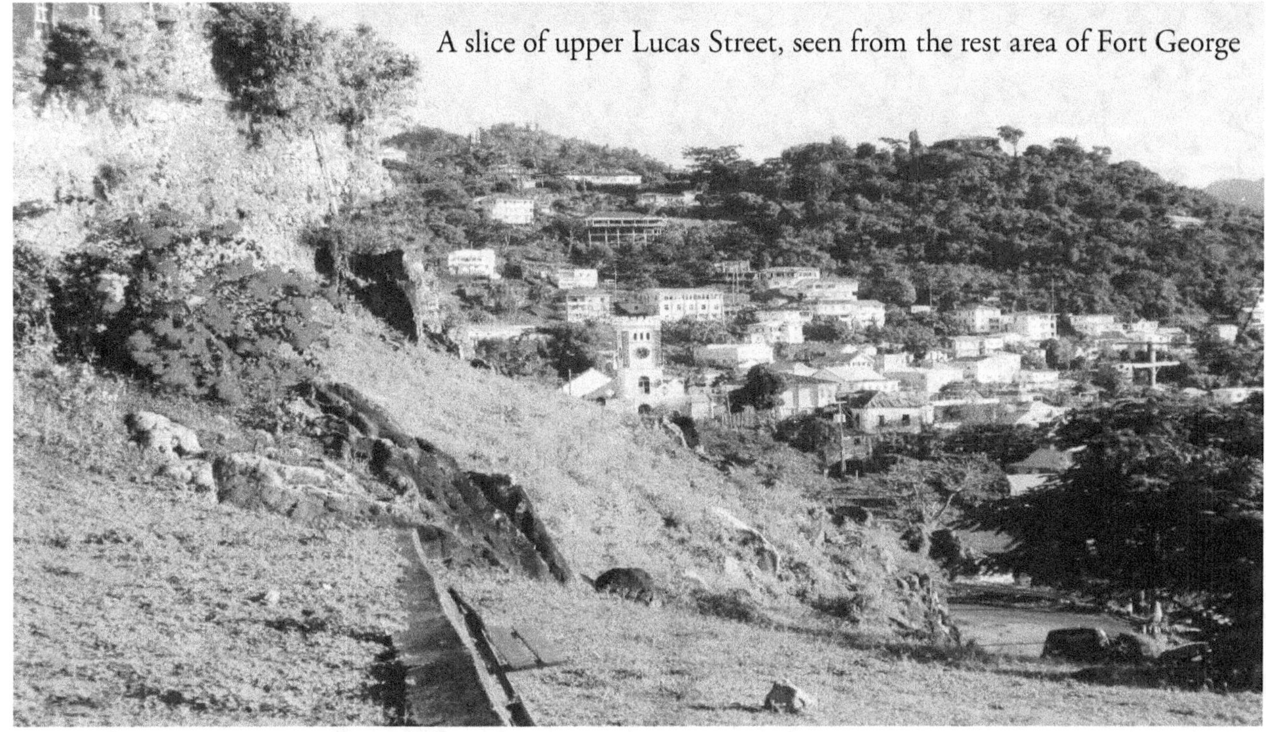

A slice of upper Lucas Street, seen from the rest area of Fort George

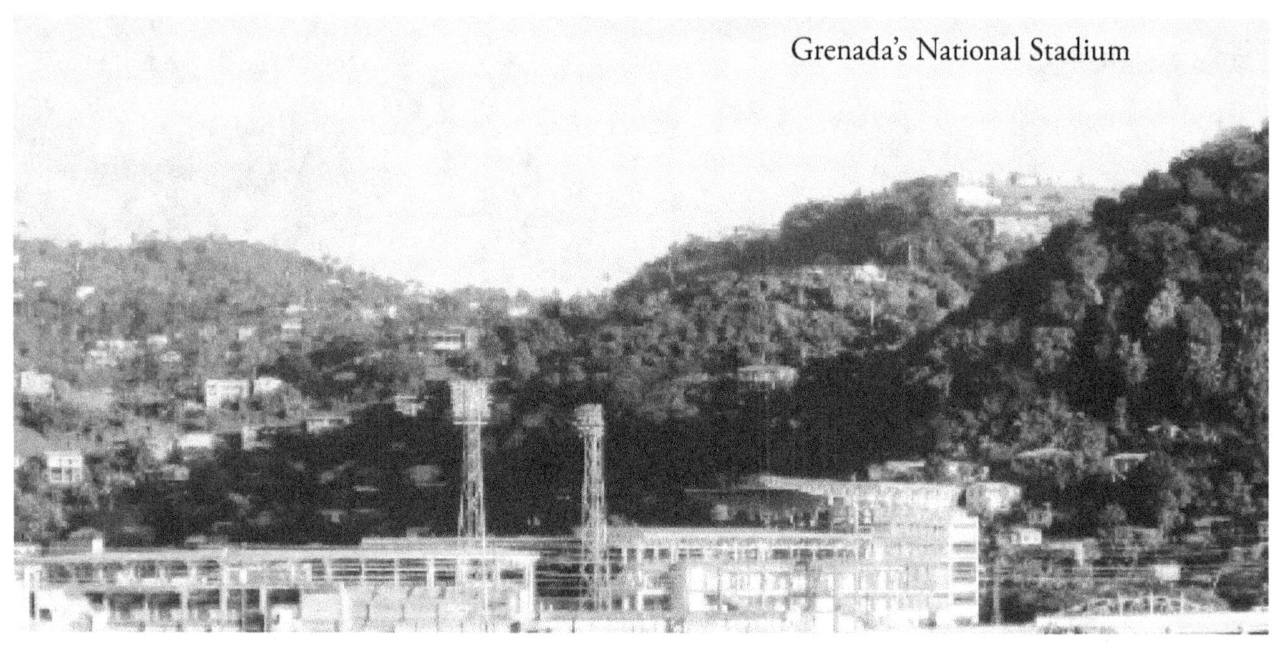

Grenada's National Stadium

National stadium while under construction

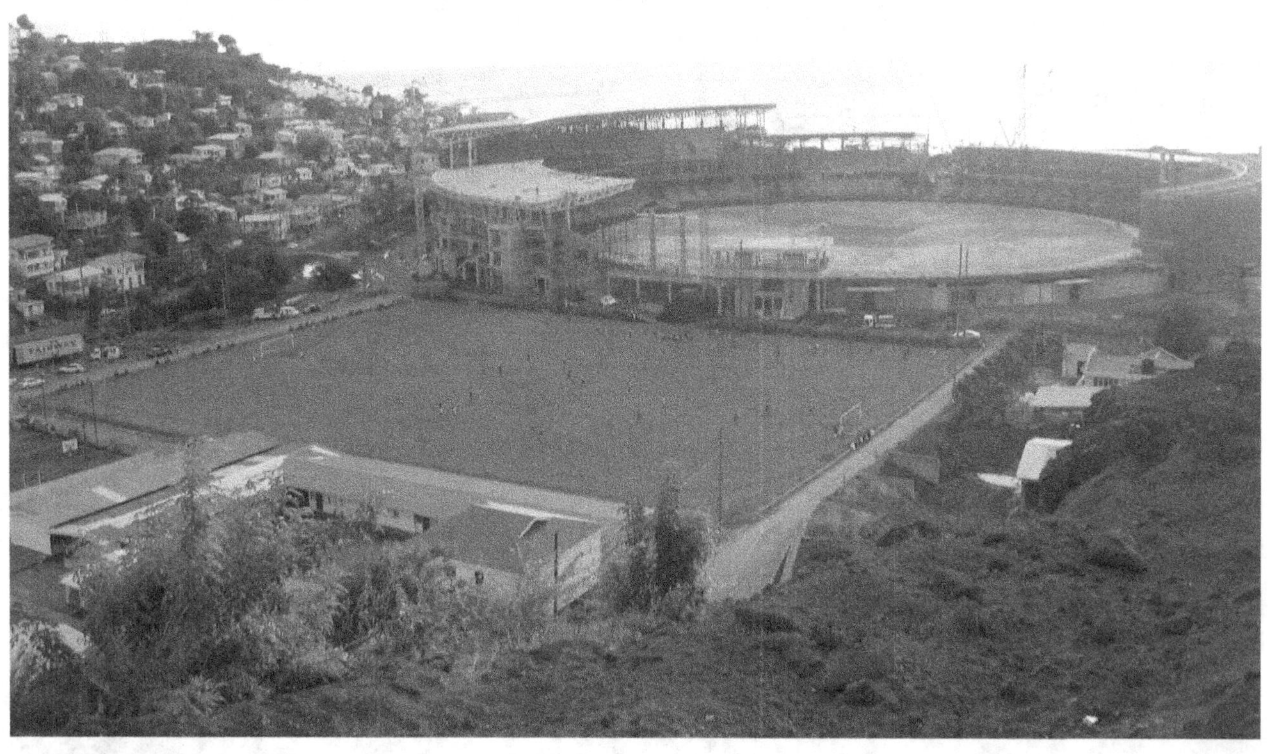

Fort Frederick

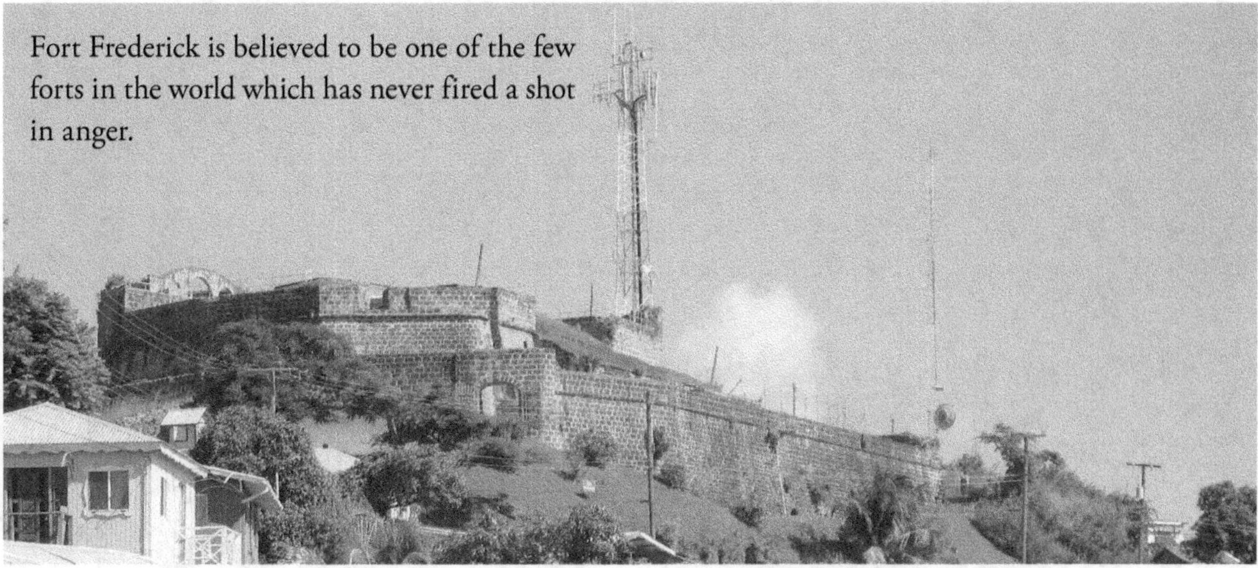

The French built Fort Frederick in 1787. It occupies a beautiful hilltop location where the capital St. George's, is in full view.

Welcome to Fort Frederick -- one of the few forts in the world which has never fired a shot in anger. It was built by the French, who had wrested the island from the British in 1779. The French realized that had such fortifications existed at the time of their assault on Grenada, their attempt to storm Hospital Hill and thereby capture the island could have failed. So, one of the first acts of the new French Government was to commence building a series of forts on Richmond Hill: Fort Frederick, and the neighbouring forts Matthew to the North, and Jolphus, and Lucas to the South. Mount George Estate, the property of the Hon. William Lucas, was forcibly appropriated for that purpose. Four years later, the Treaty of Versailles gave the island back to Britain, leaving the British to complete what the French had started.

Hospital Hill can clearly be seen down below and to the right, looking over the town of St. George's. Fort George stands guard on the promontory at the harbour entrance.

A plaque at the Fort's entrance, bearing some details of its history

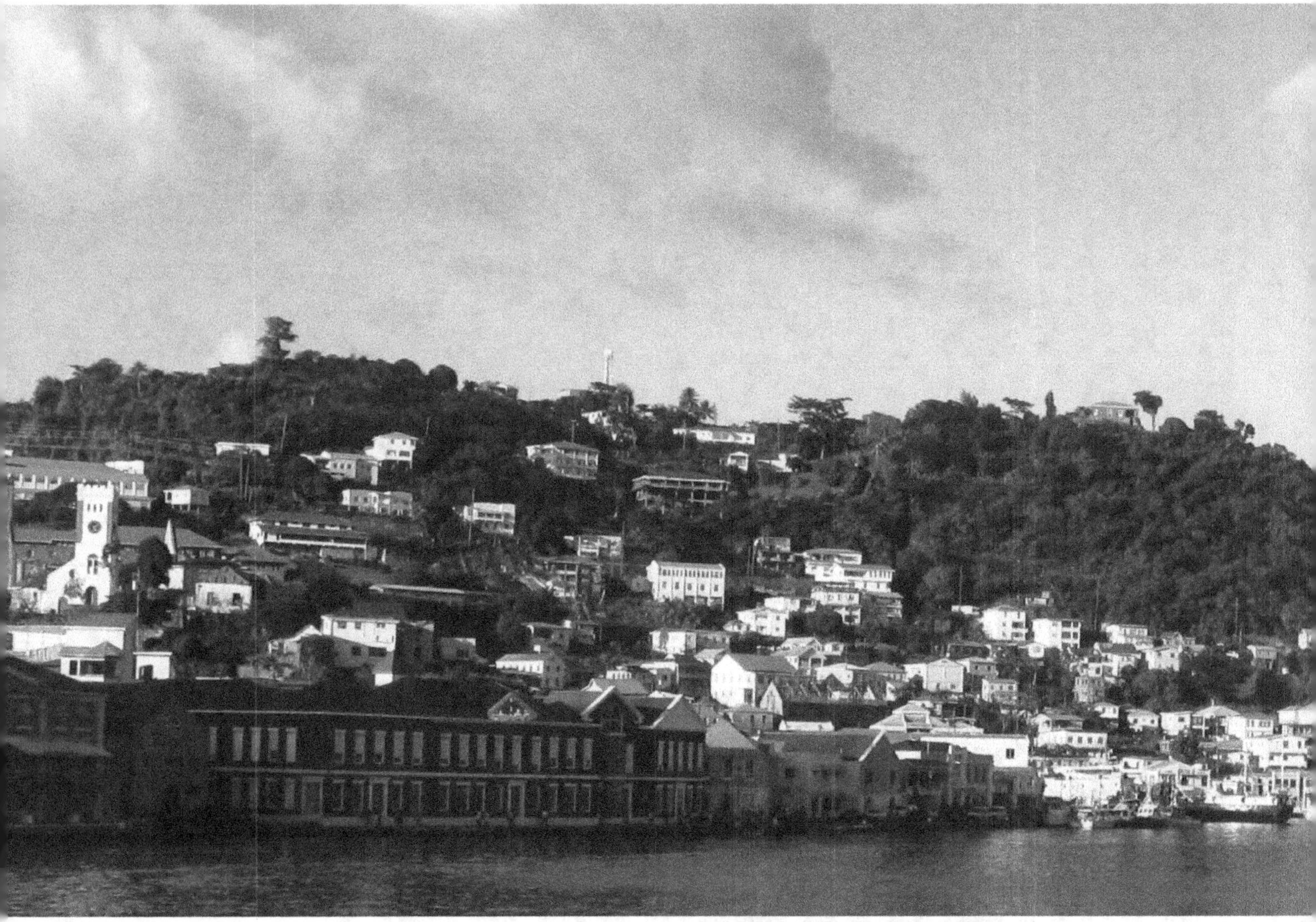

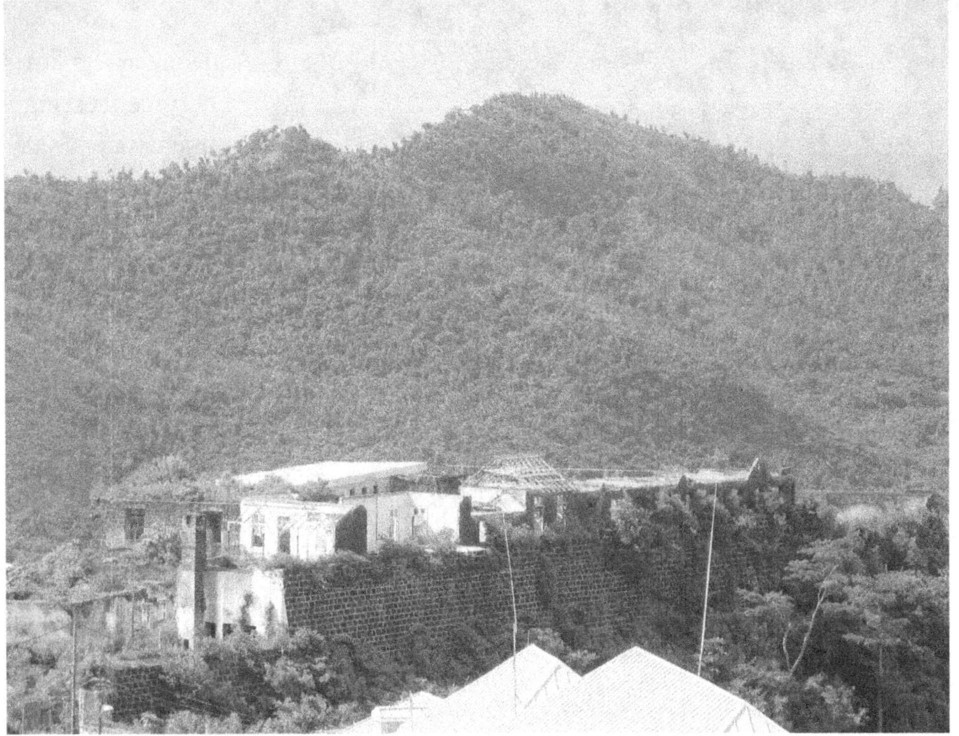

Here is another Fort structure built at Richmond Hill, which later served as a mental hospital, only to be devastated during the U.S. invasion of Grenada in 1983.

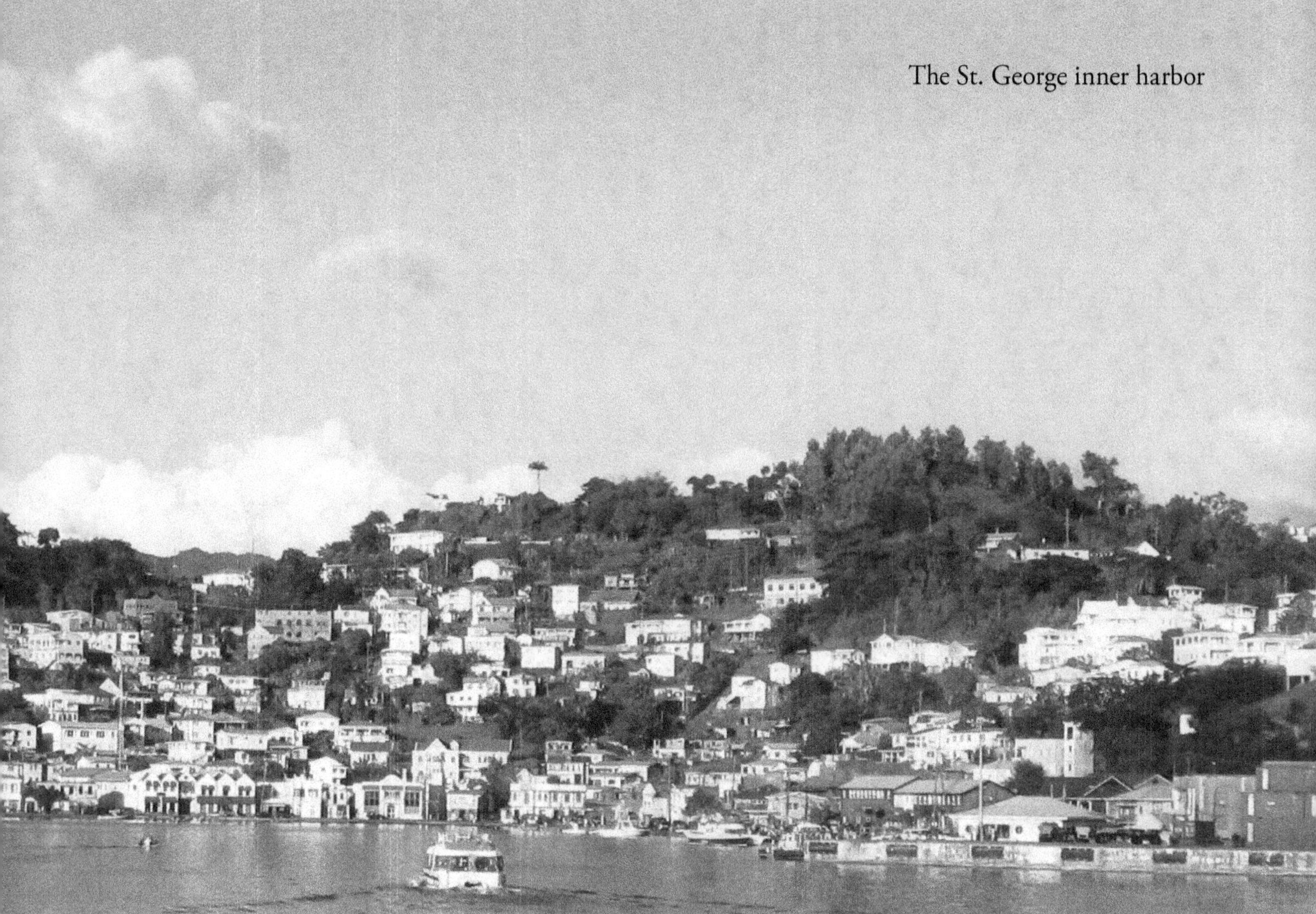

The St. George inner harbor

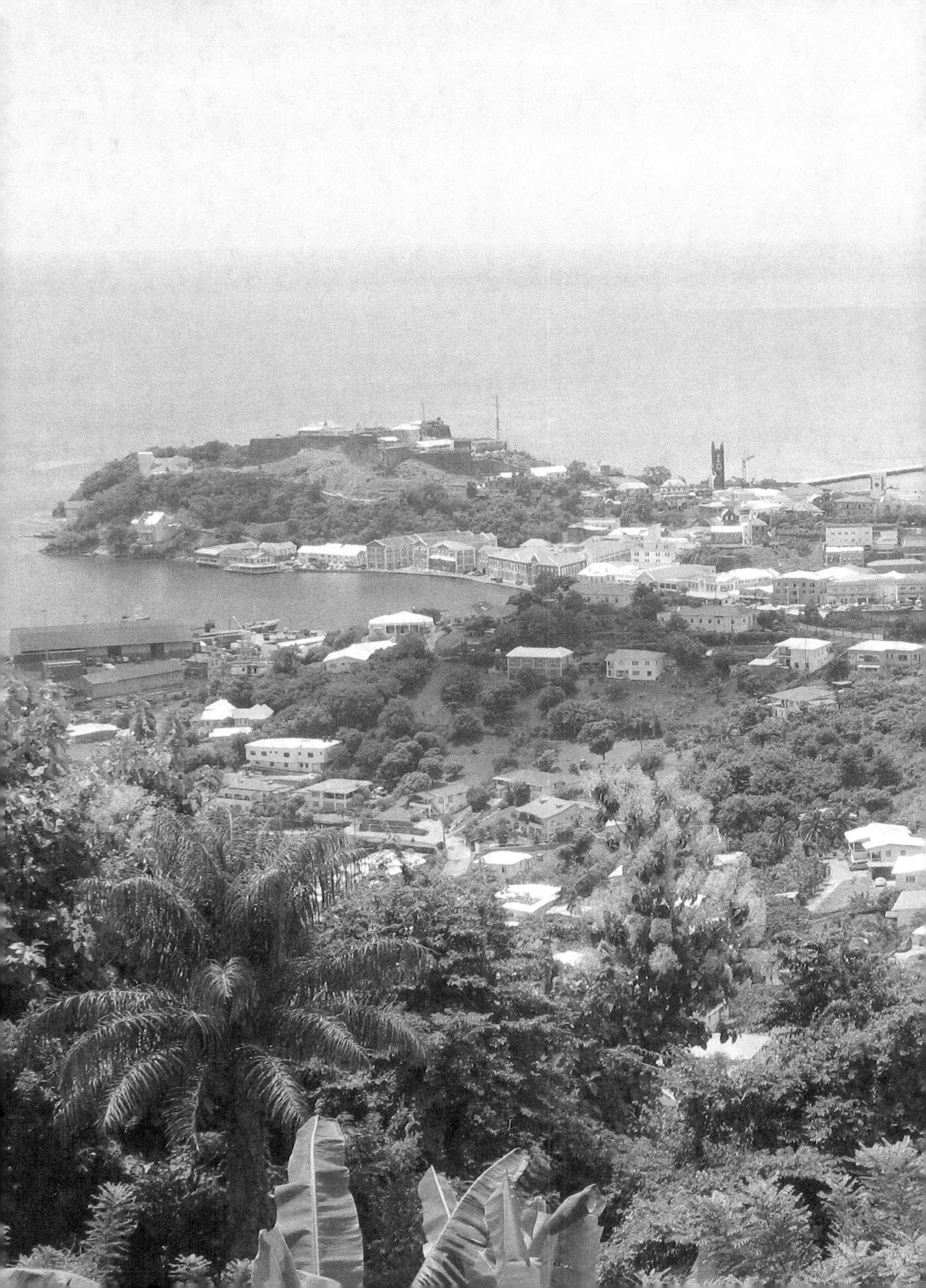

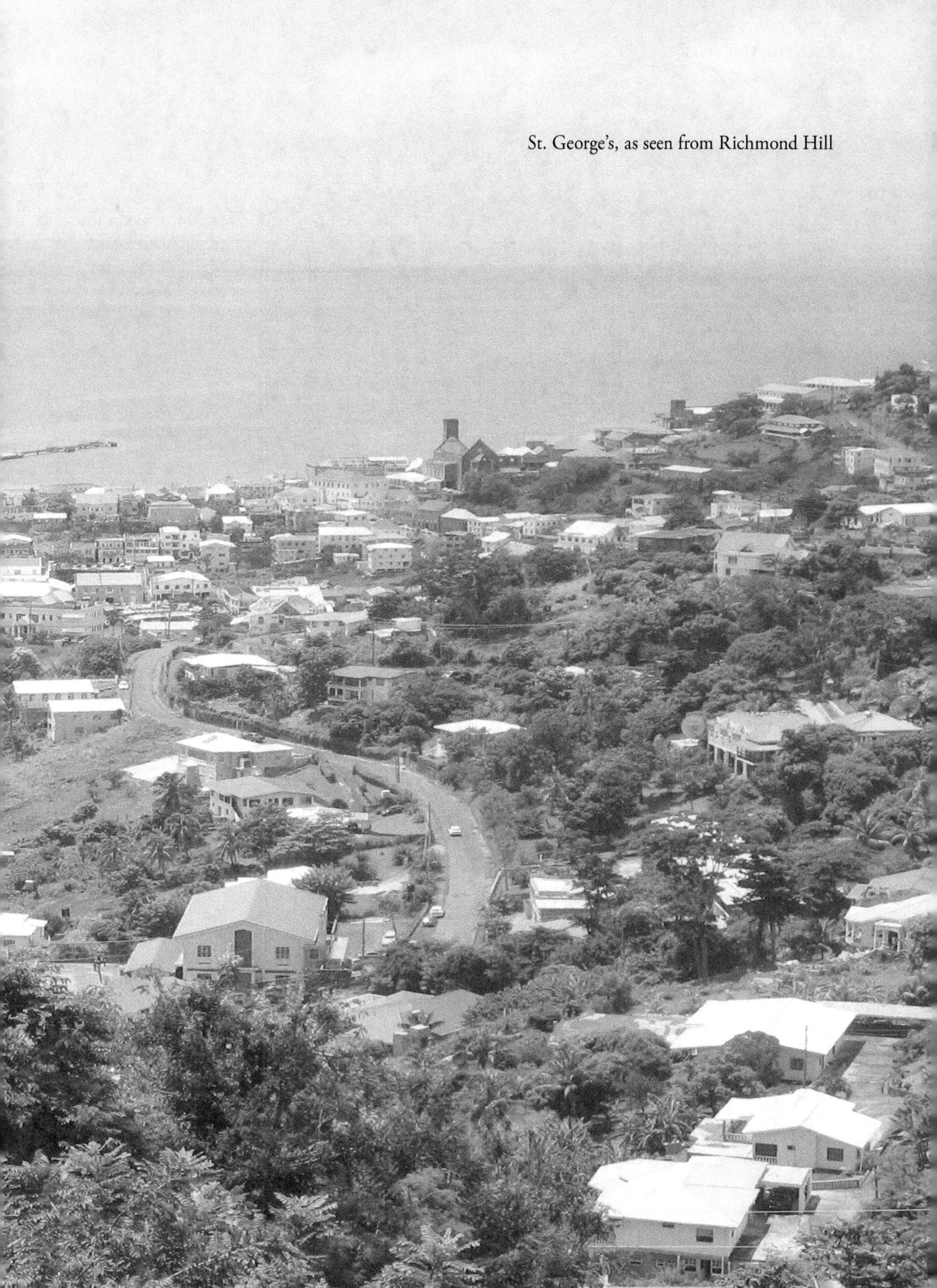

St. George's, as seen from Richmond Hill

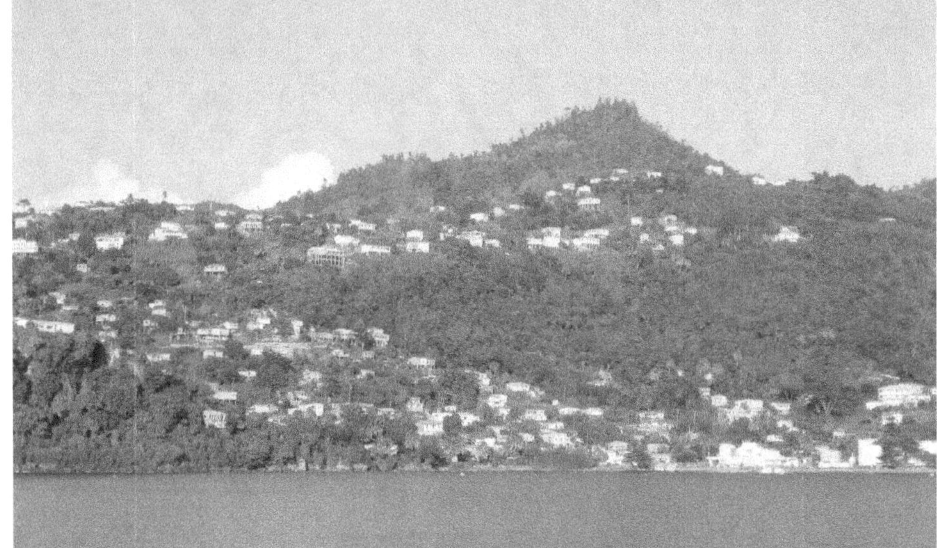

Mt. Moritz sits at the hilltop, with Grand Mal near the coast below.

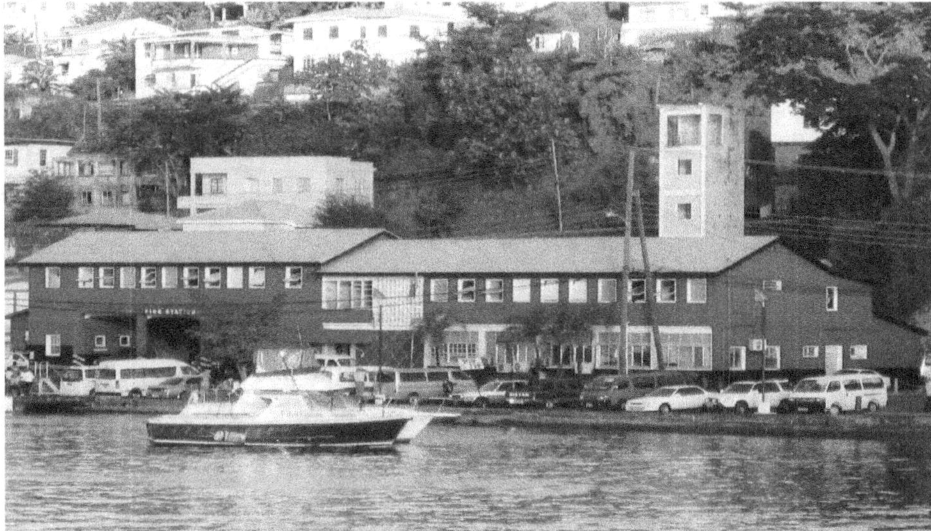

St. George's Fire Station

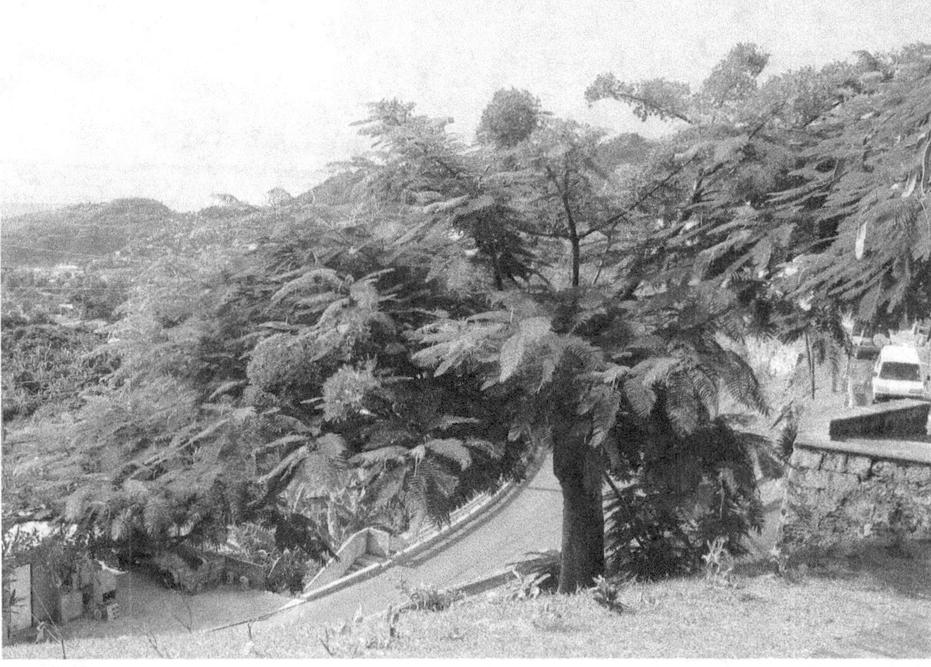

A flowering flamboyant tree

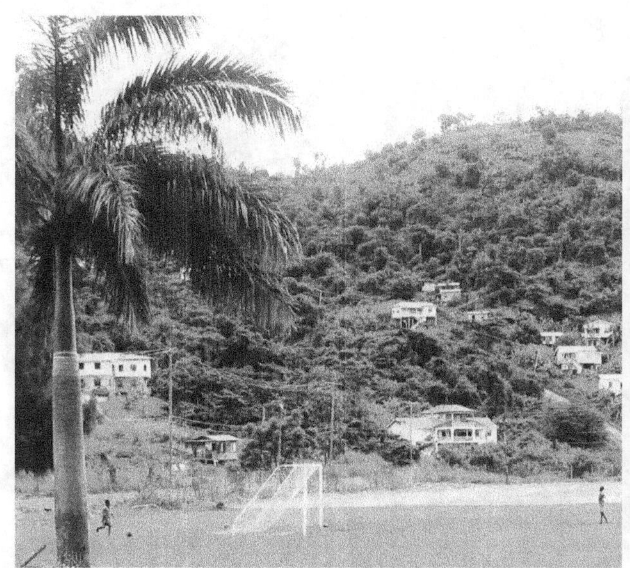

Kids playing soccer at Beausejour Park

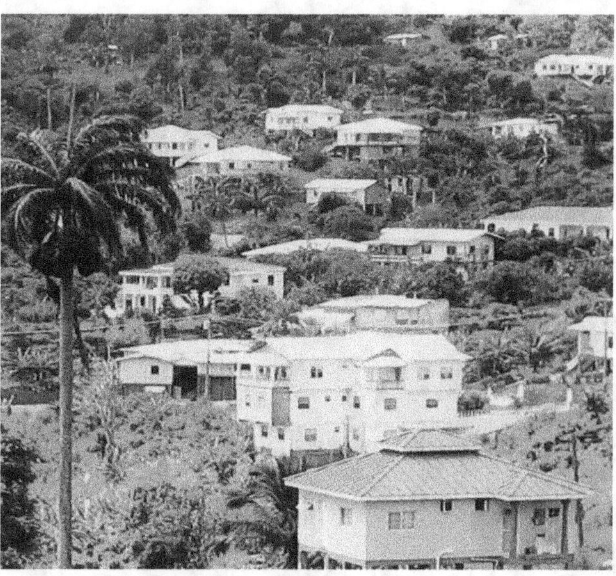

St. Paul's

T.A. MARRYSHOW, GRENADIAN HERO

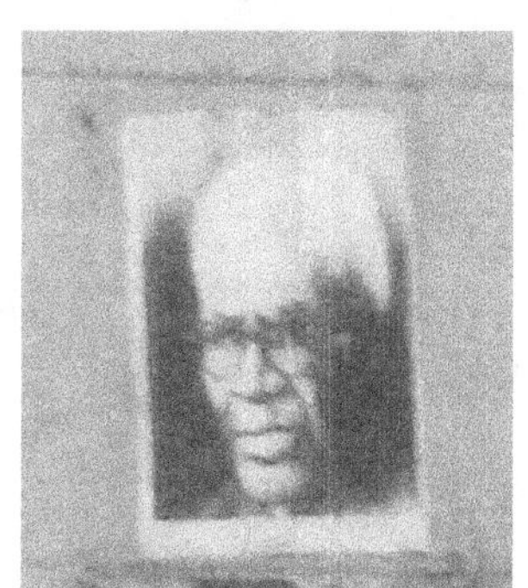

T.A. Marryshow

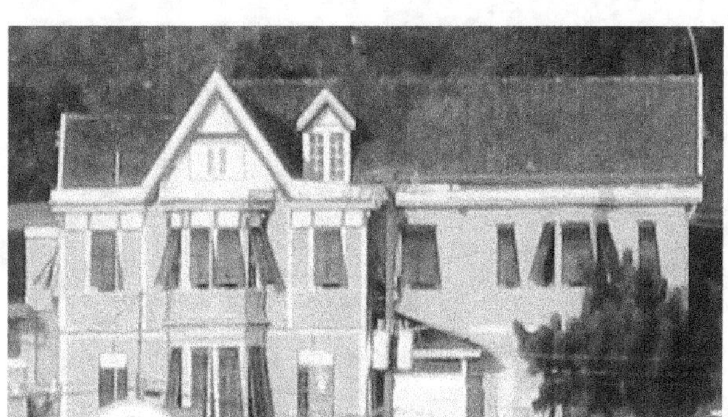

Marryshow House

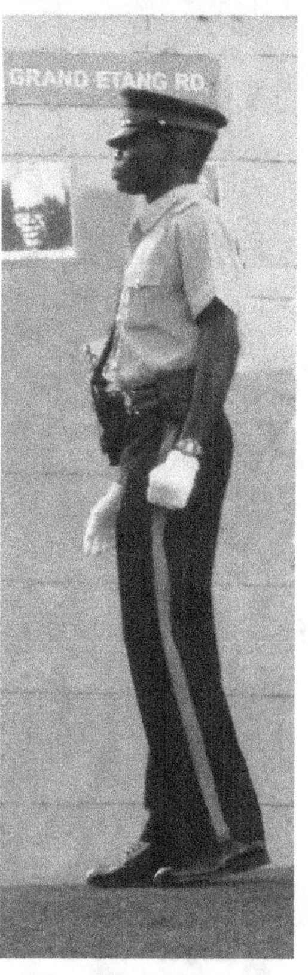

Theophilus Albert Marryshow (1887-1958) is a Grenadian hero. Born in St. George's parish, he was a politician, statesman, orator, and journalist. Grenadians respected him for his strident advocacy of West Indian federation and self-government. Grenada eventually achieved self- government in 1967. The island has honored T.A. Marryshow by Establishing Marryshow House and the T.A. Marryshow Community College.

A traffic officer on
Grand Etang Road,
near to a poster of
T.A. Marryshow

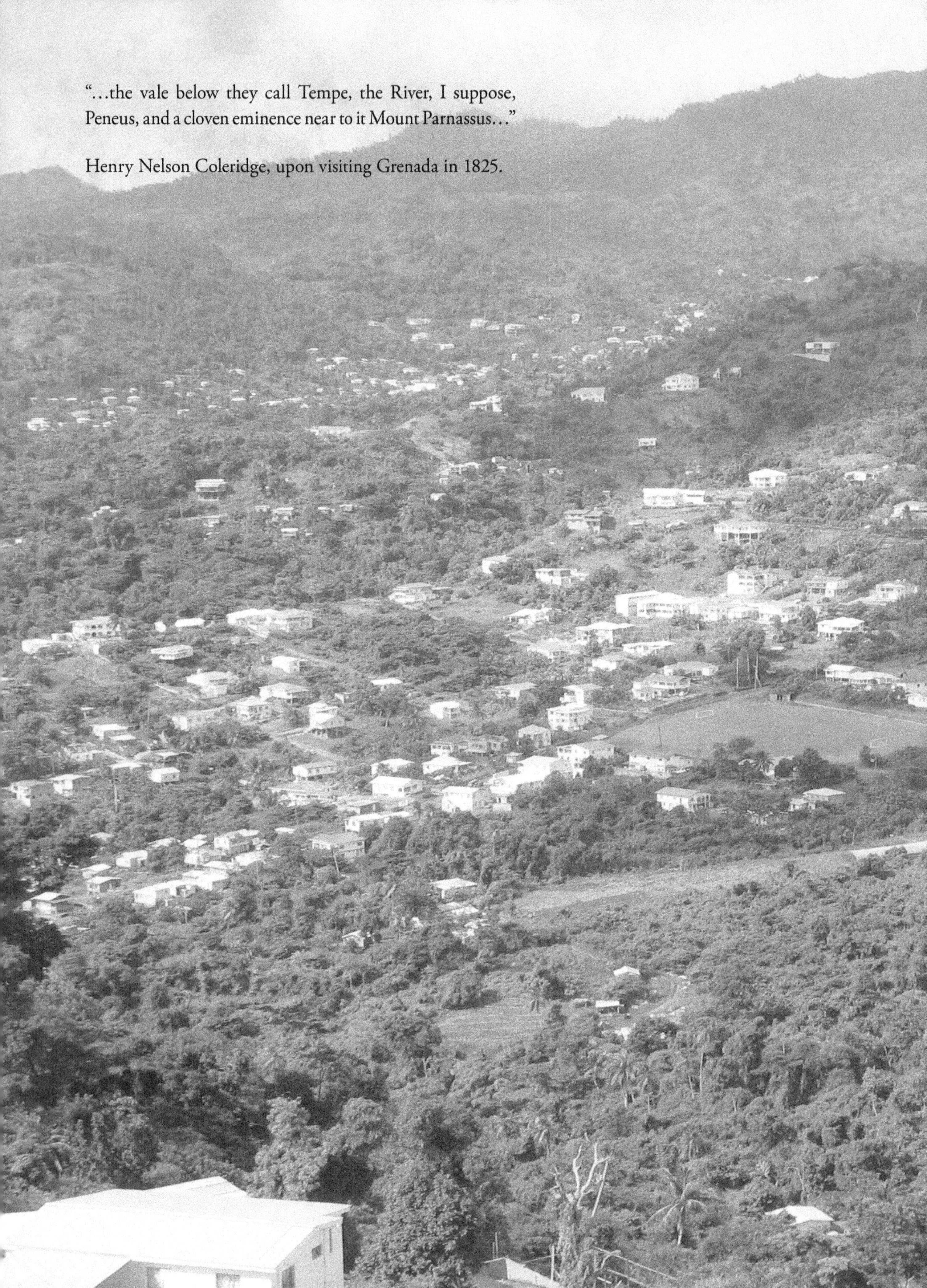

"…the vale below they call Tempe, the River, I suppose,
Peneus, and a cloven eminence near to it Mount Parnassus…"

Henry Nelson Coleridge, upon visiting Grenada in 1825.

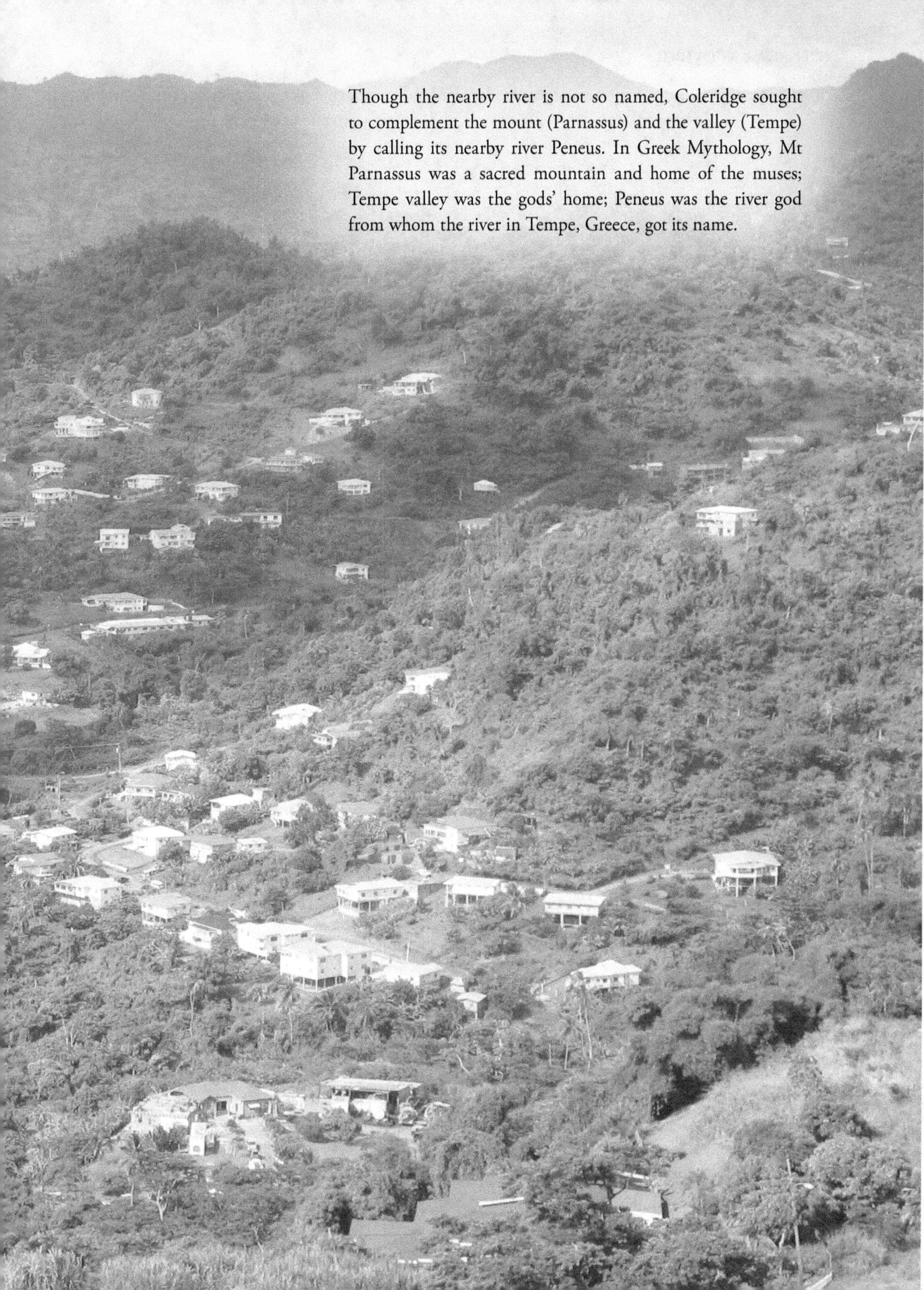

Though the nearby river is not so named, Coleridge sought to complement the mount (Parnassus) and the valley (Tempe) by calling its nearby river Peneus. In Greek Mythology, Mt Parnassus was a sacred mountain and home of the muses; Tempe valley was the gods' home; Peneus was the river god from whom the river in Tempe, Greece, got its name.

In some ways, the town of St. George introduces a Mediterranean look to the Caribbean. Below are downtown St. George, Darbeau, and different segments of the Carenage.

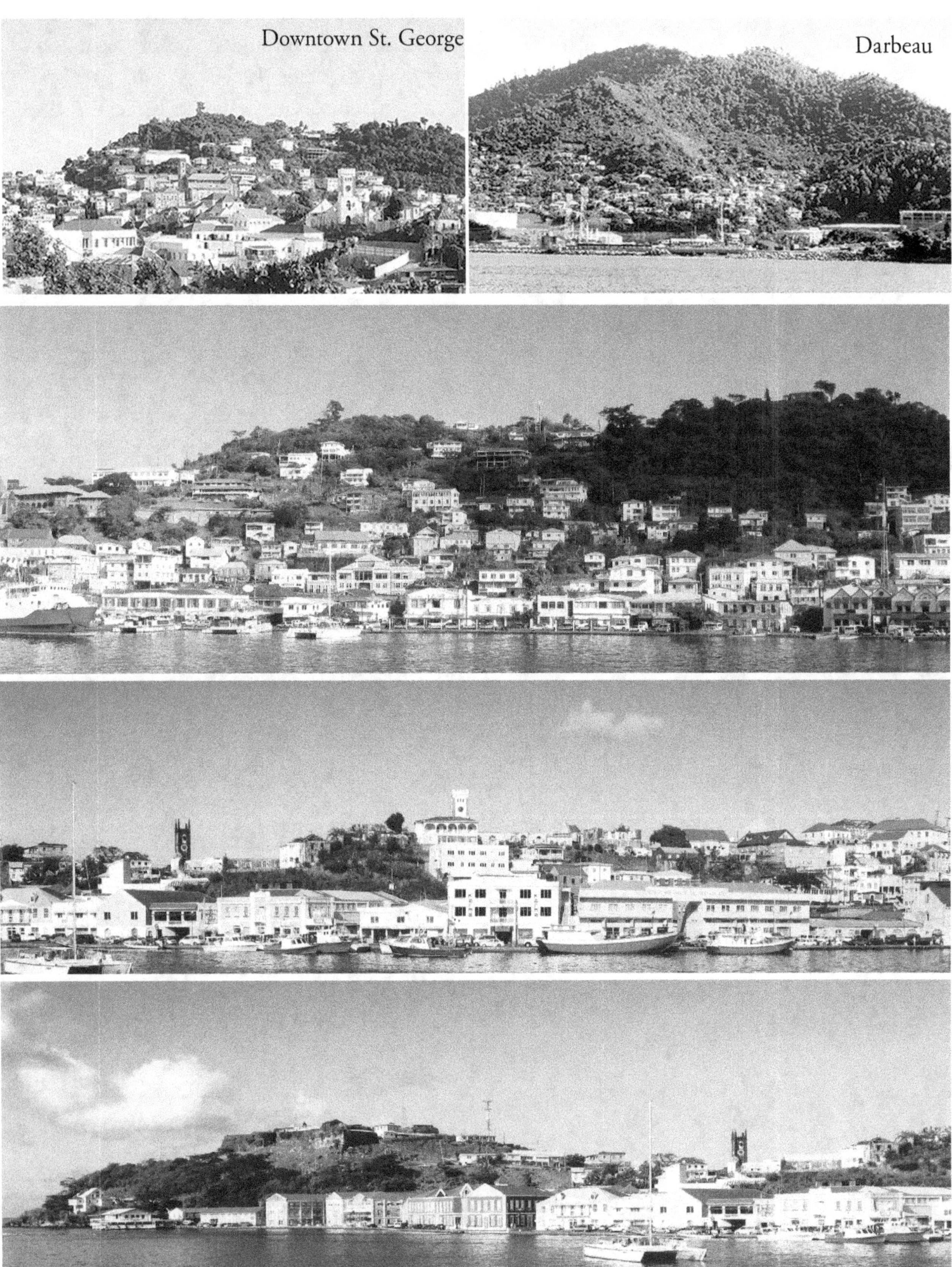

Mt. Moritz

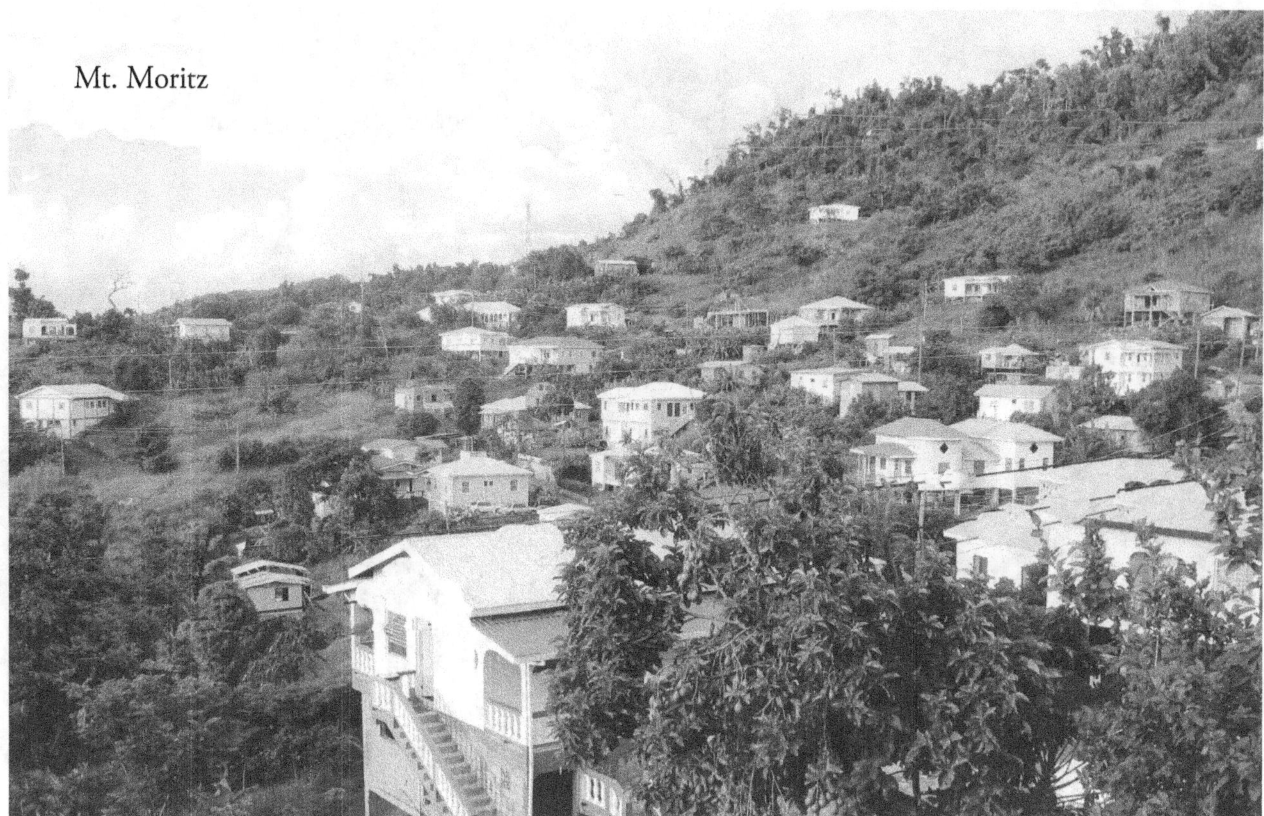

On the above hillside is Mt. Moritz. In the post-slavery 1800s, there was an influx of European immigrants who came there by way of Barbados. Some Grenadians still call the Mt. Moritz whites Bajans (Barbadians), but all live harmoniously here.

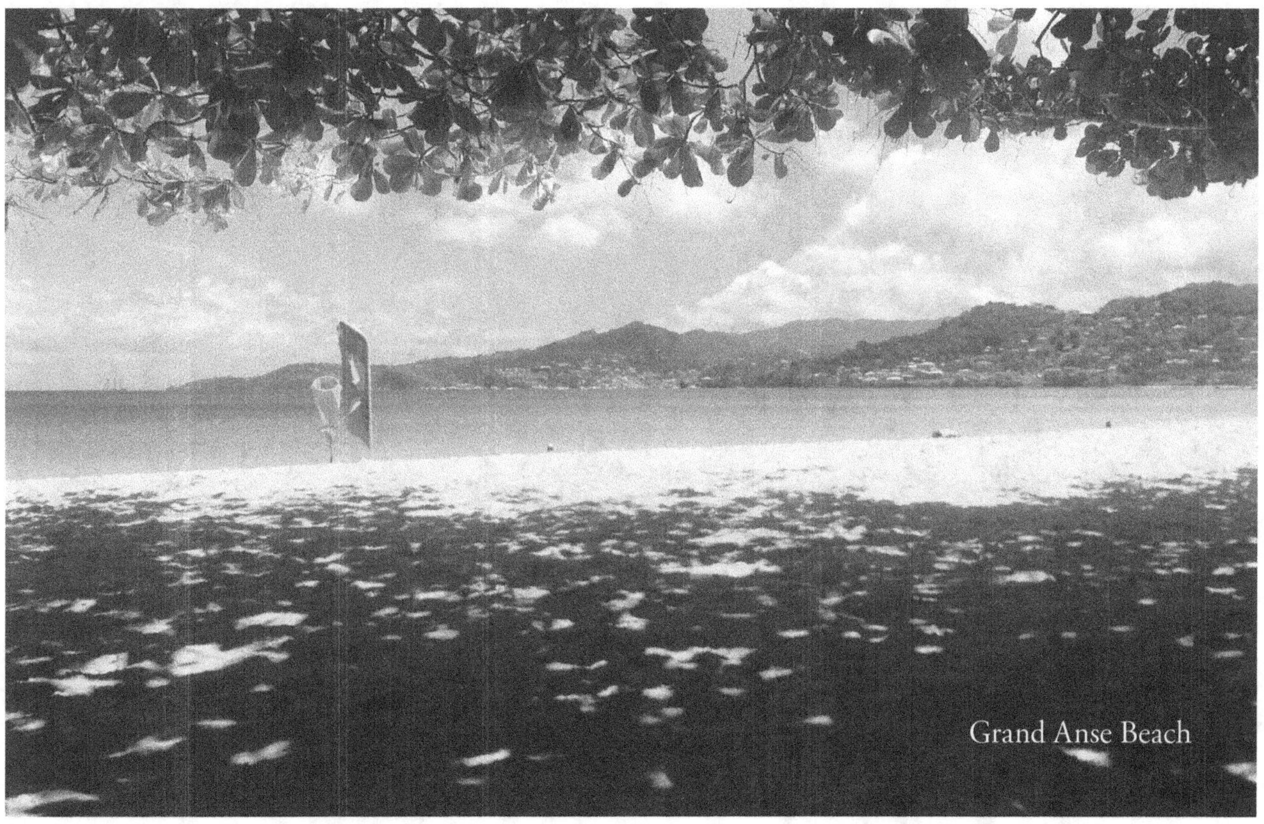

Grand Anse Beach

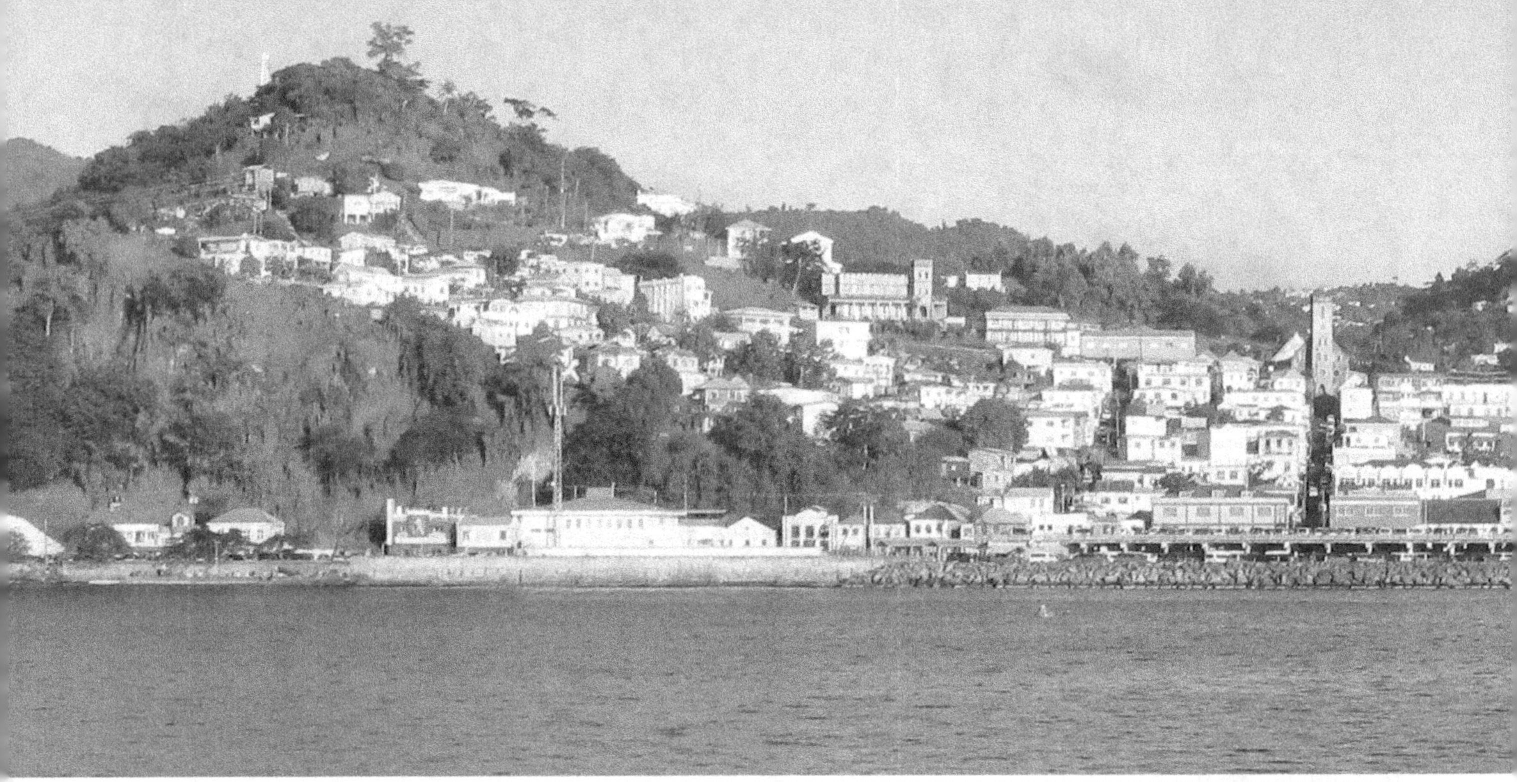

St. George's, along the Esplanade and Melville Street seafront, where the steeples along Church Street are evident

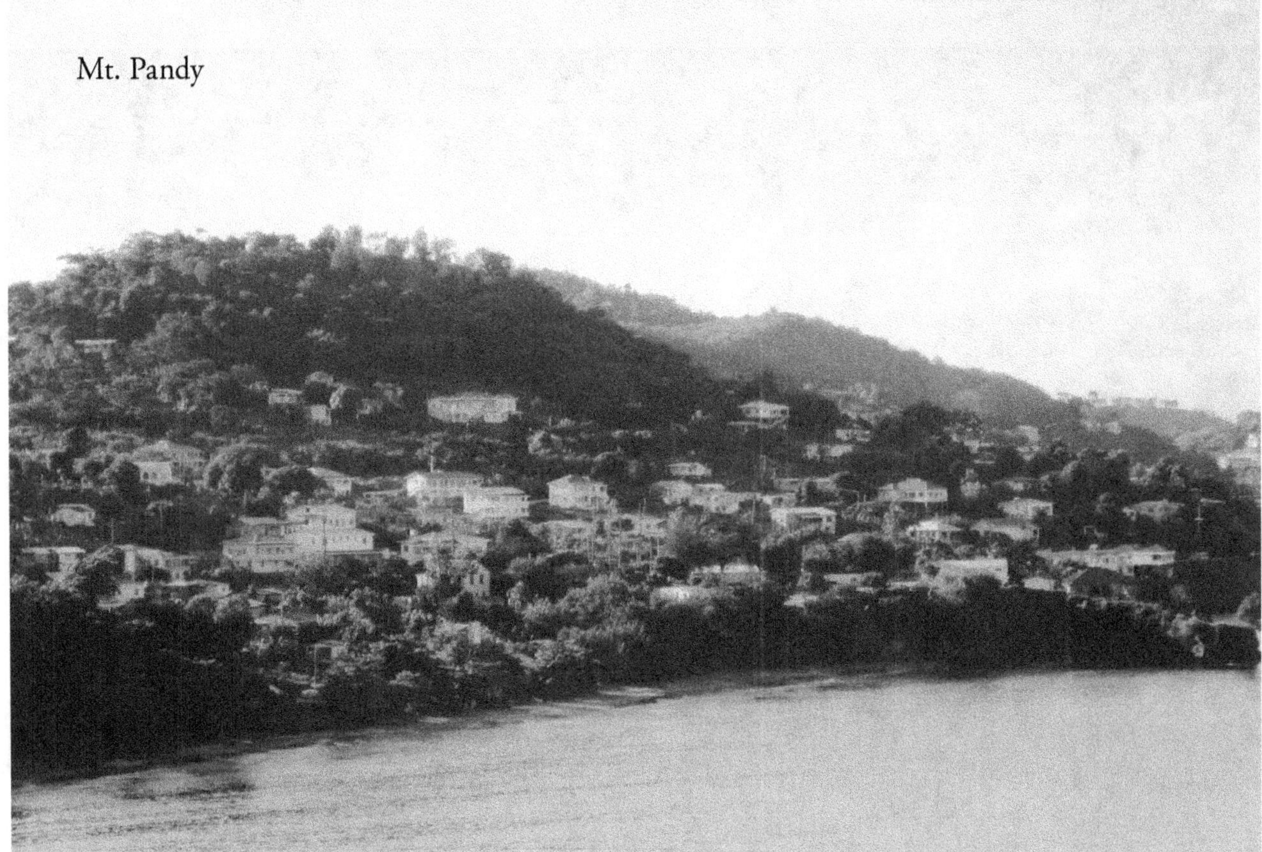

Mt. Pandy

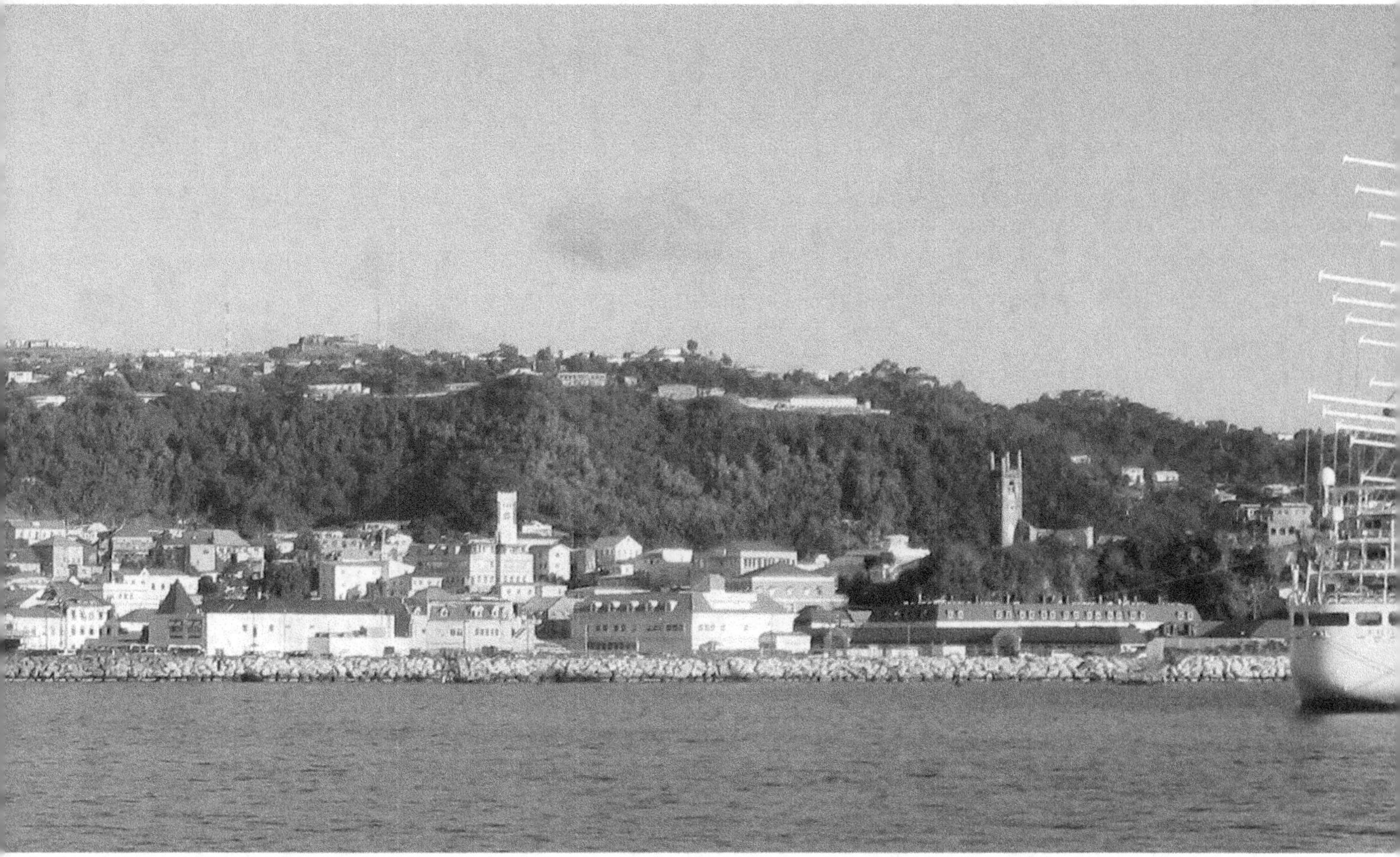

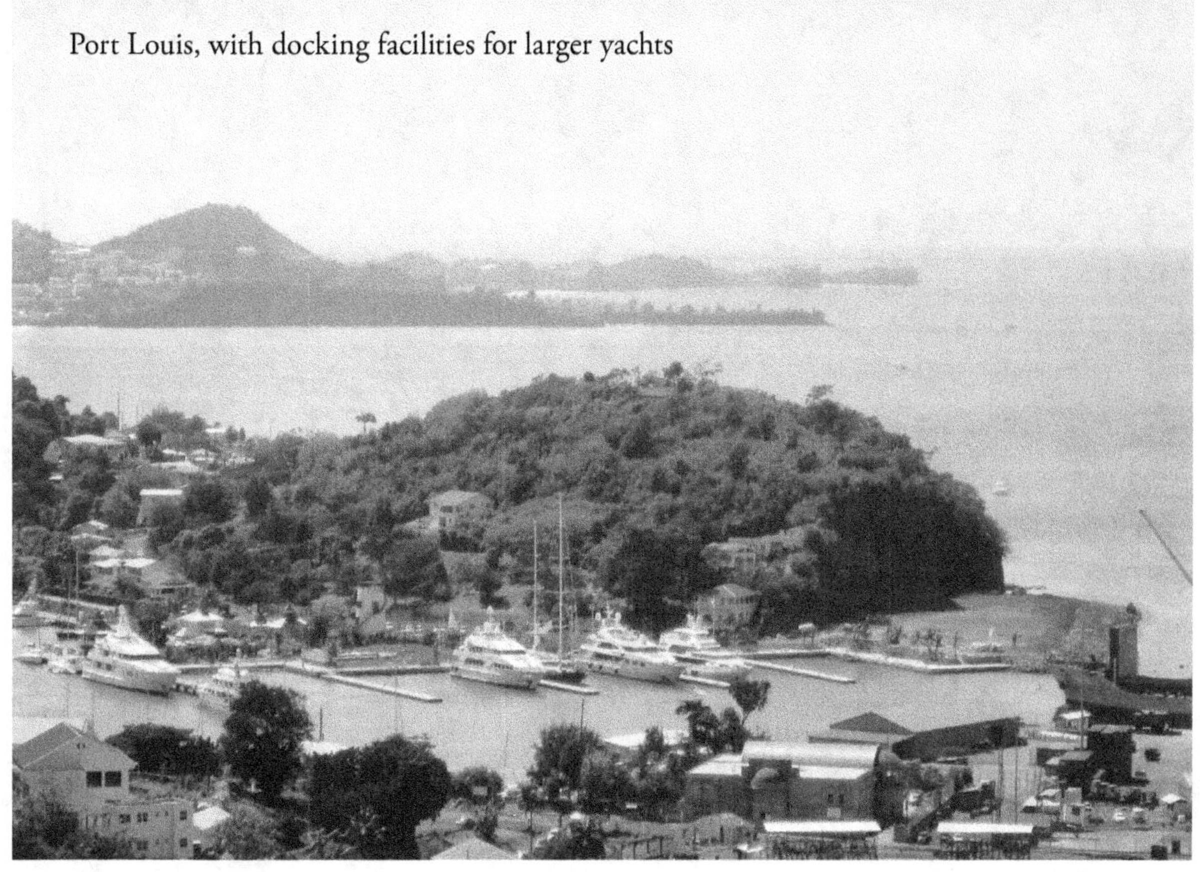

Port Louis, with docking facilities for larger yachts

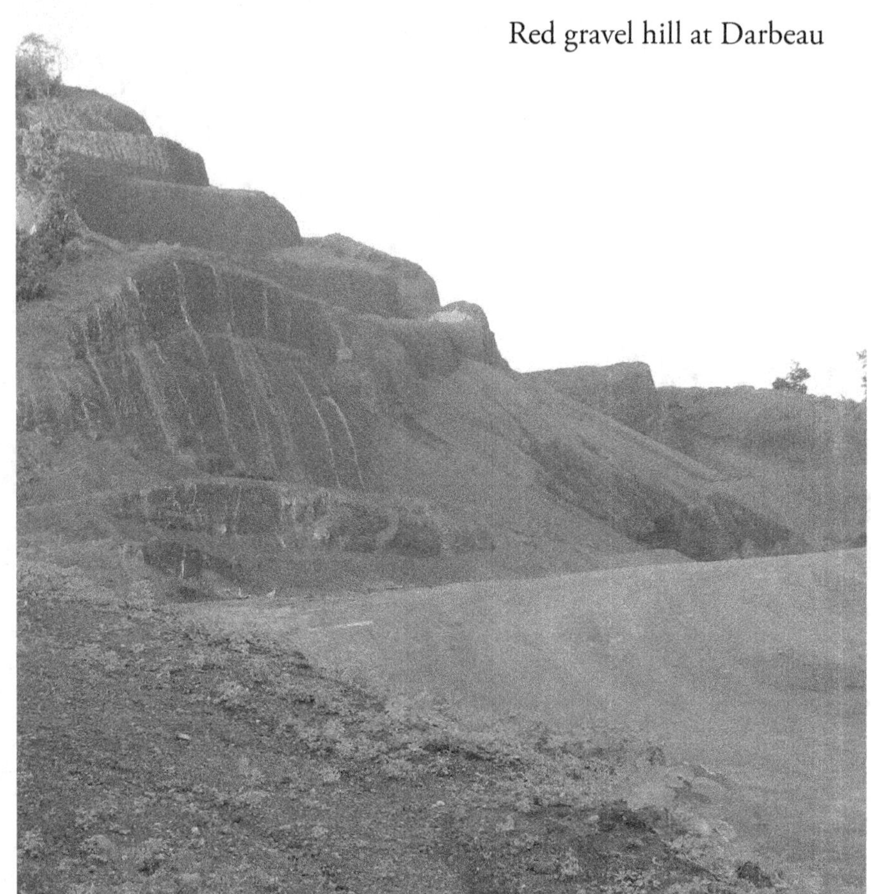

Red gravel hill at Darbeau

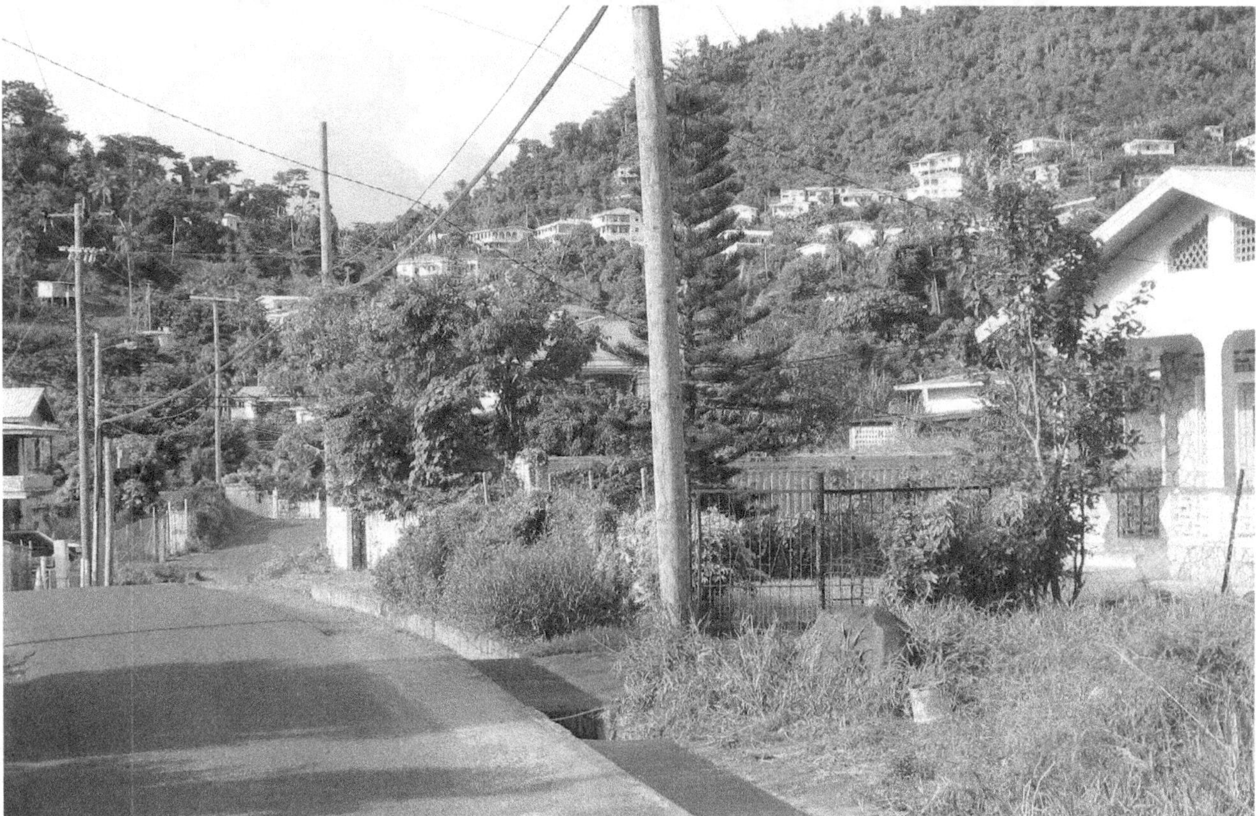

Roadside in Mt. Parnassus

2006

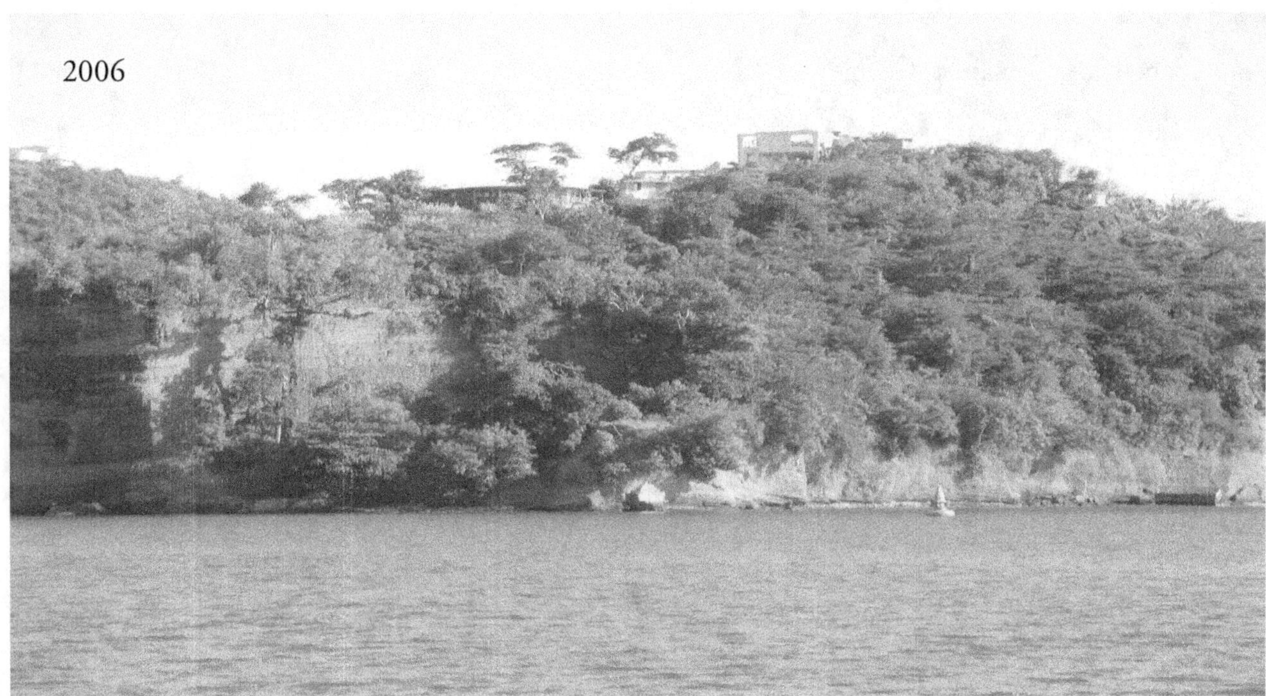

Above is the hilltop site of Grenada's 17th century French-built Great Fort, in what was then the Port Louis area. In the 20th century, it was the Santa Maria hotel site, which later became the Islander Hotel. The Santa Maria hotel was one of the 1957 movie locations of Island in the Sun, featuring Harry Belafonte, Joan Collins, Dorothy Dandridge, and James Mason. In 1979, Islander Hotel housed the Prime Minister's office. The government then renamed it Butler House in honor of Tubal Uriah "Buzz" Butler, a pioneering Grenadian trade unionist active in the Trinidadian oil industry. Now, in the 21st century, this site is being redeveloped as a yacht service under the original name, Port Louis.

2009

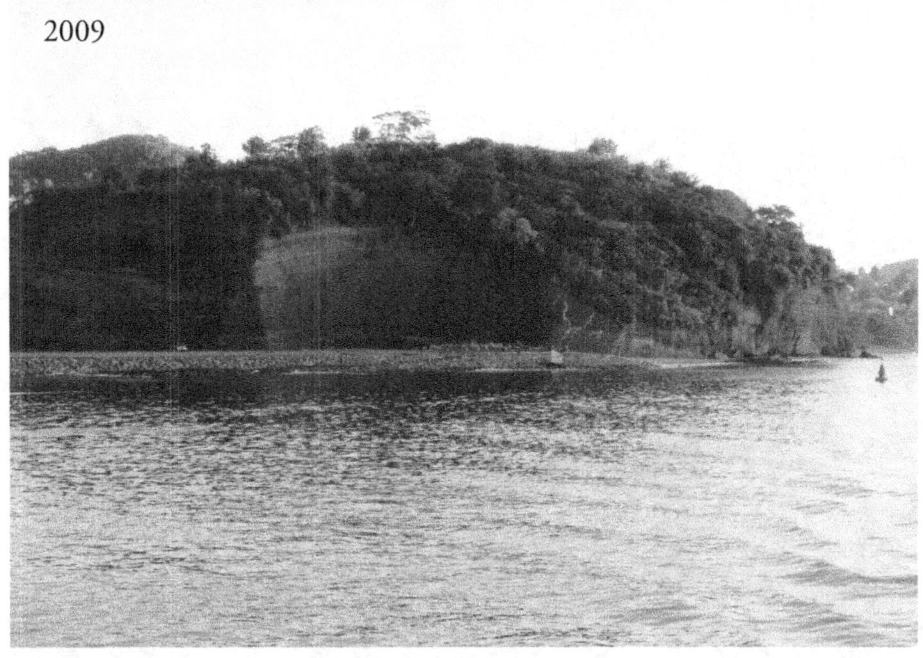

The coastline changed after work commenced on the new Port Louis project. To compensate for the small loss of coastal originality, it will be a good idea to integrate all the site's history into any new project on that site.

Catholic complex in St. George

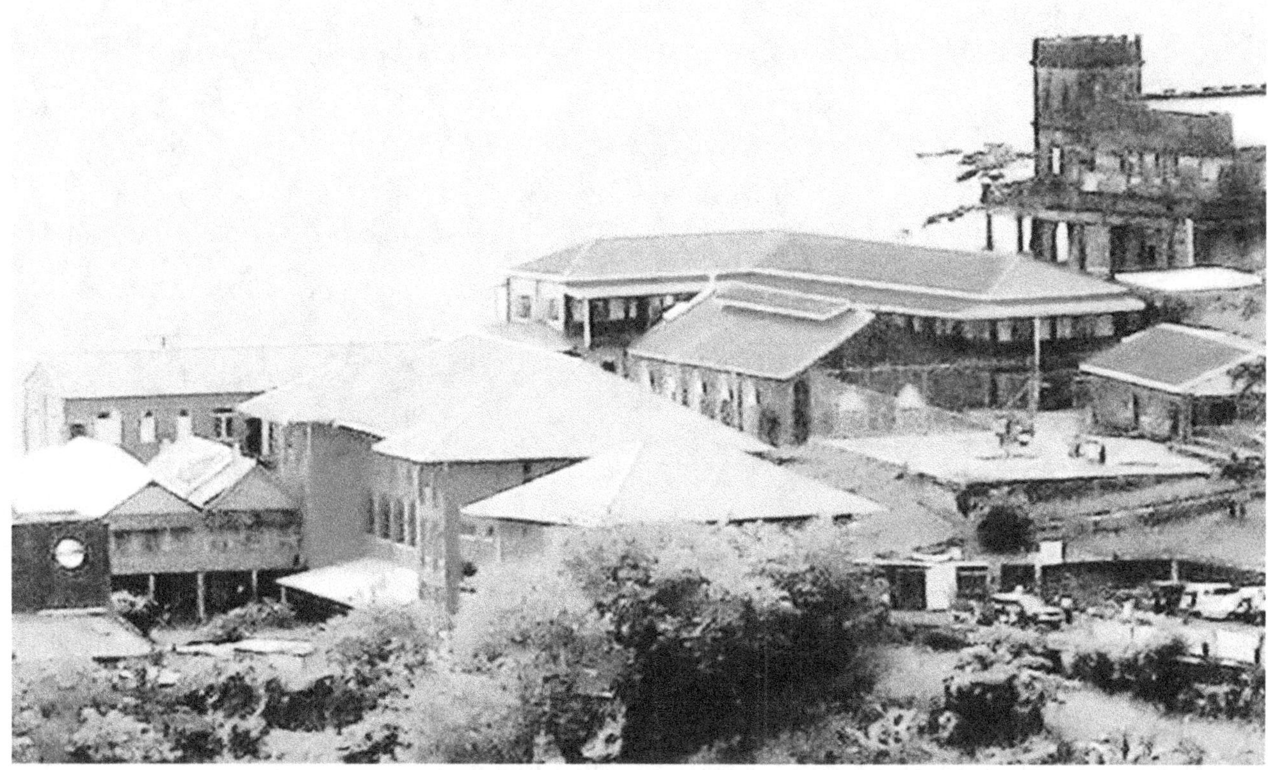

From L to R: St. Joseph's Convent; St. Louis R.C. School (Mother Rose School)

Willis

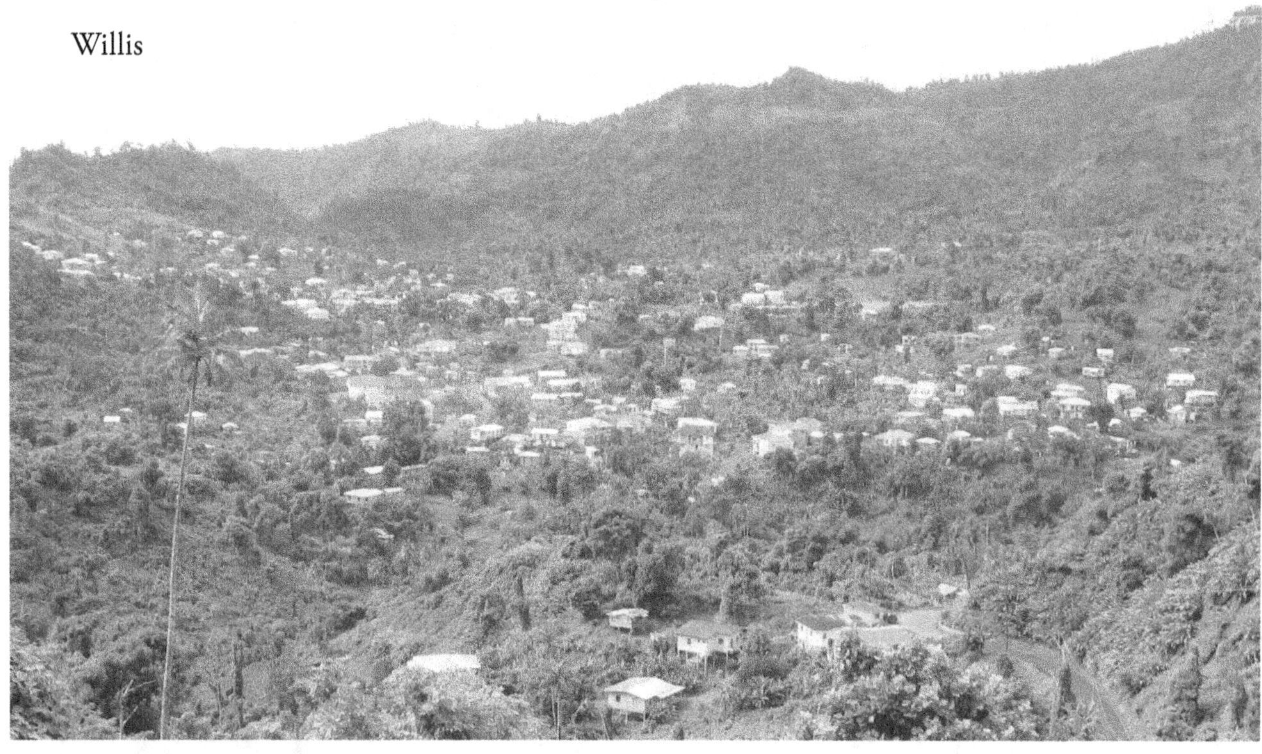

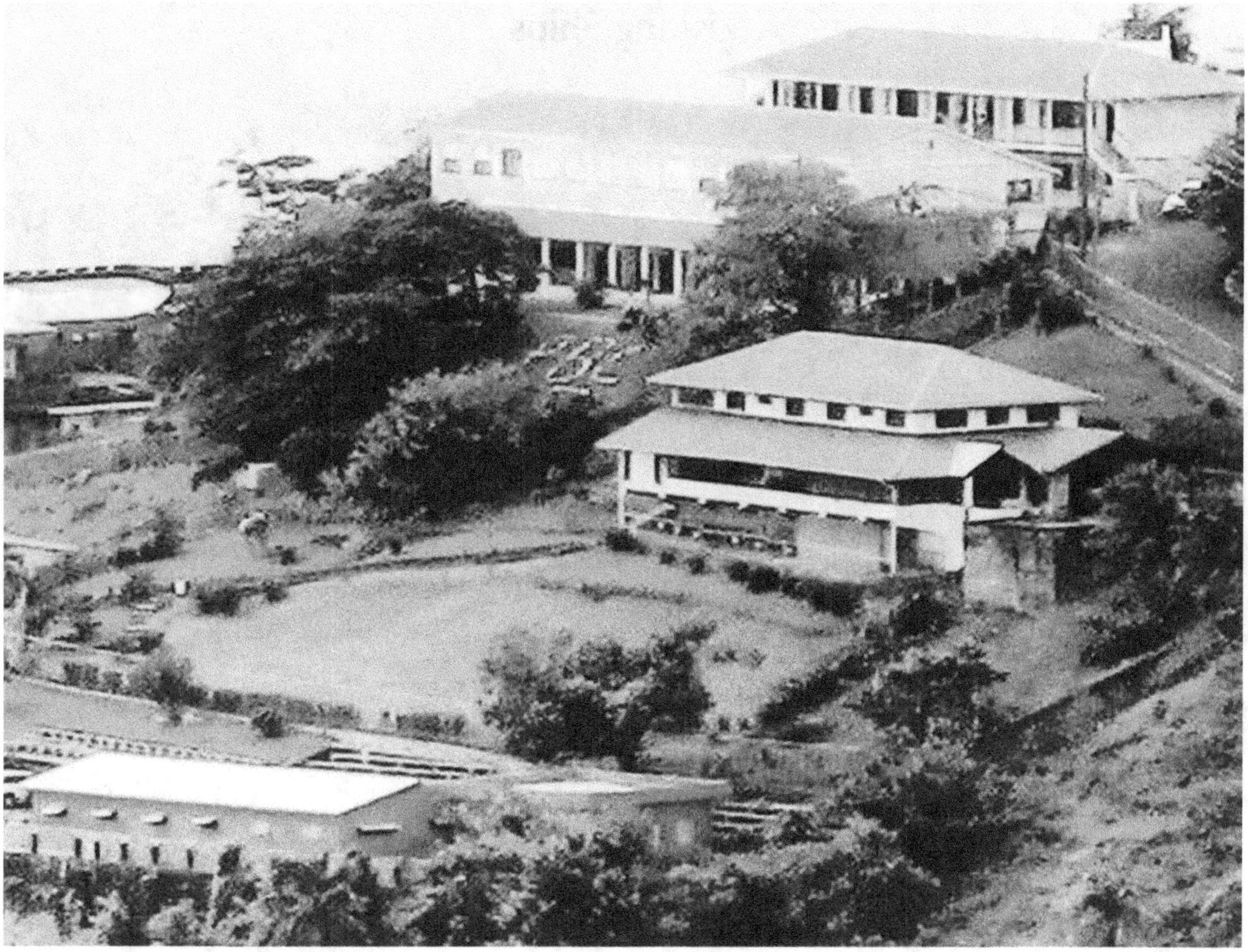

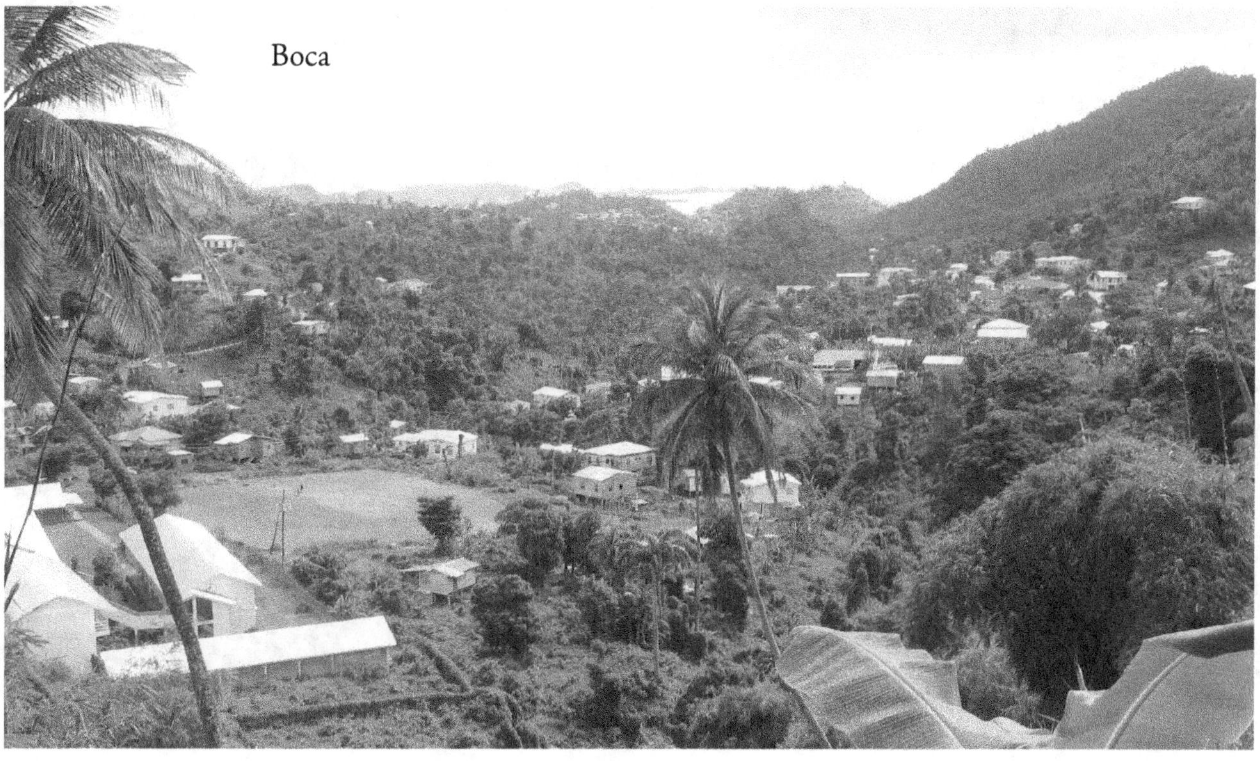

Presentation Brothers' residence; Presentation Brothers College; Sisters of Cluny residence

Boca

Visiting Ships

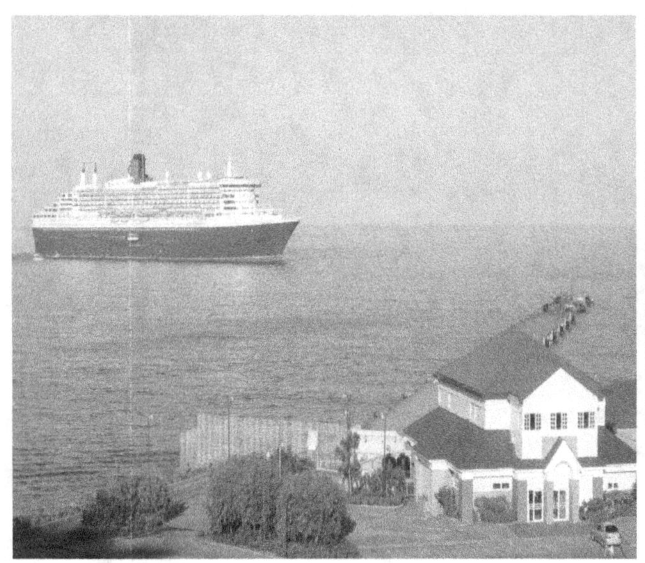

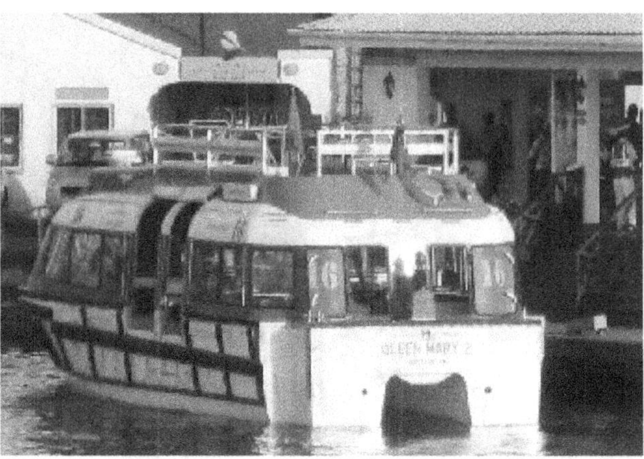

A lighter carries passenger ashore from the
Queen Mary 2 anchored offshore (left).

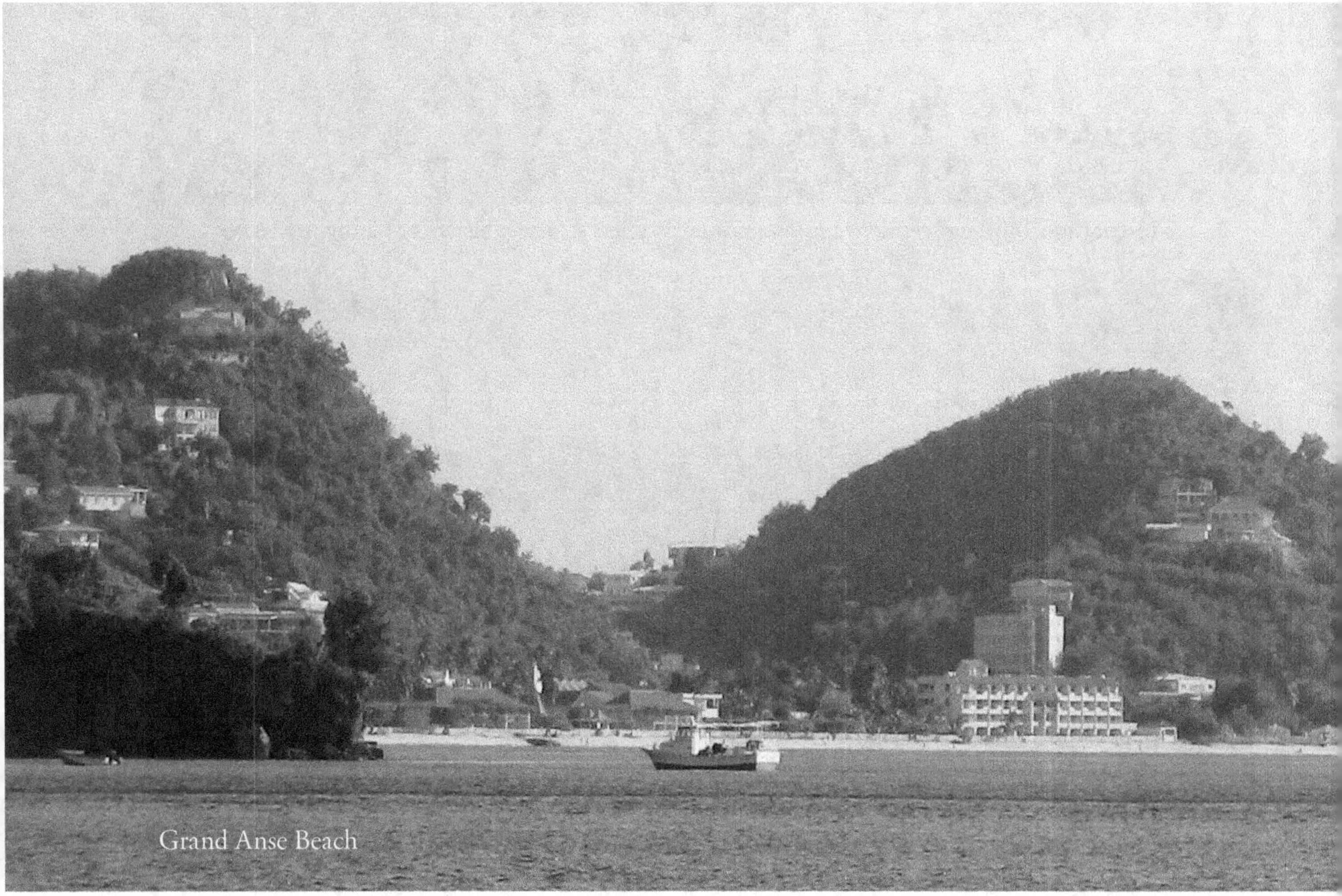

Grand Anse Beach

Visiting Ships

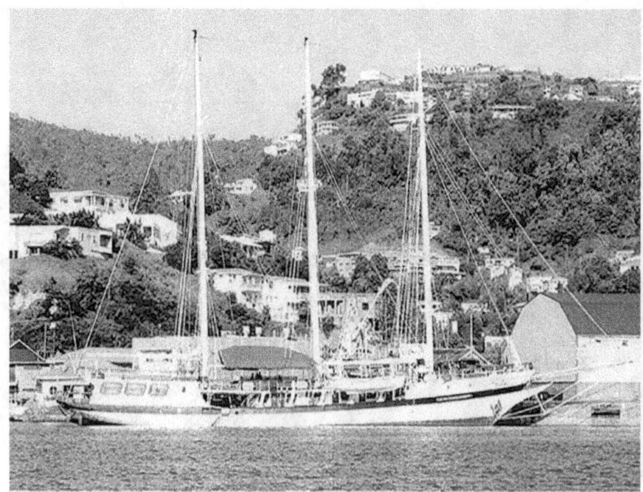

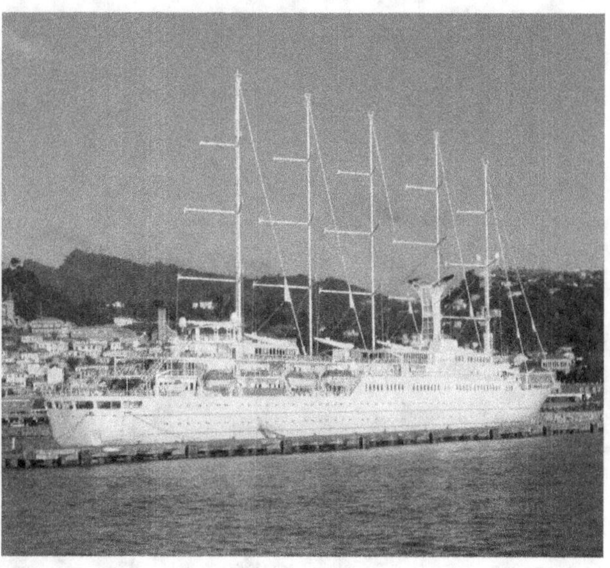

Some of the sailing ships that call in to Grenada's ports

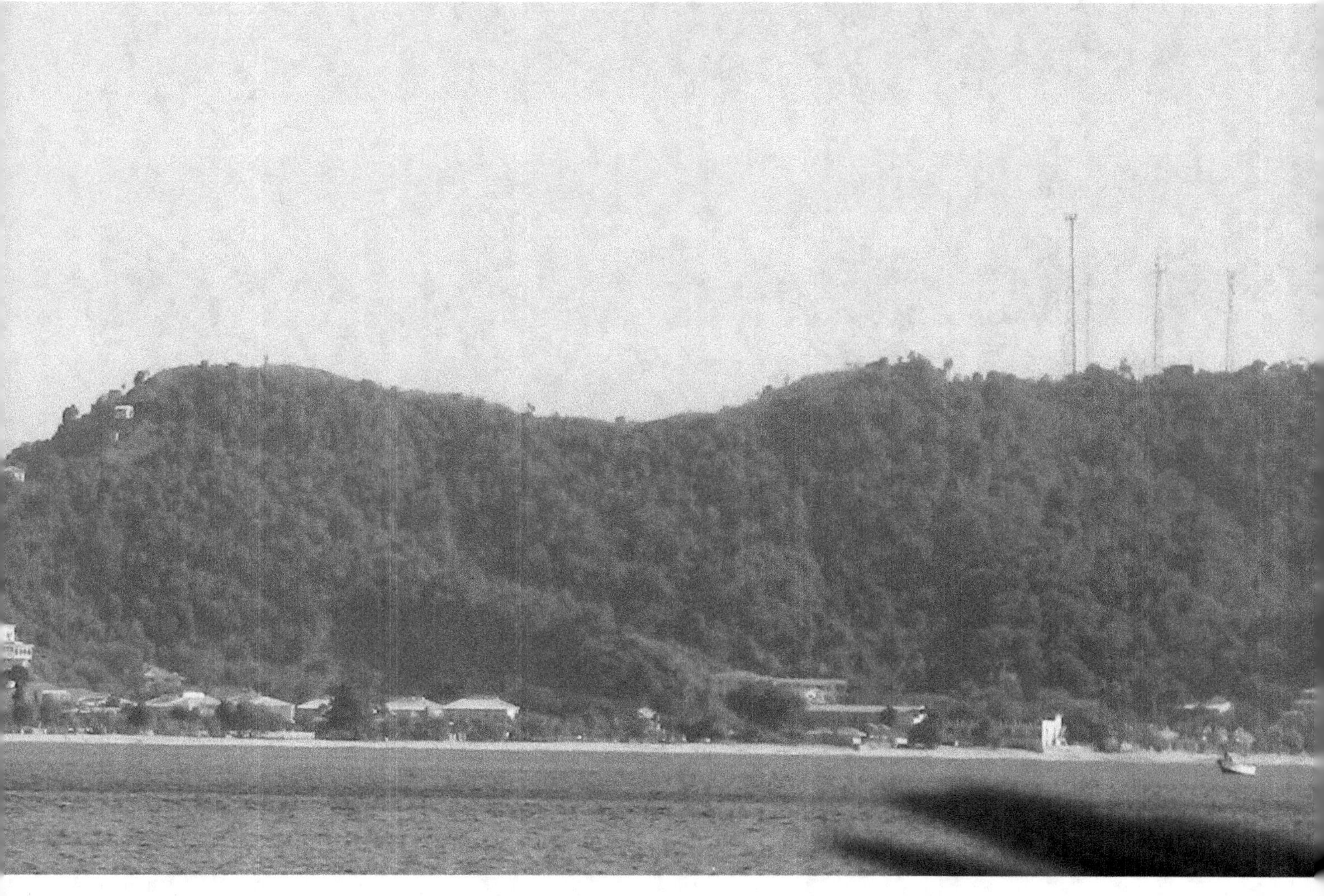

The hills overlooking Tempe and Mount Parnassus

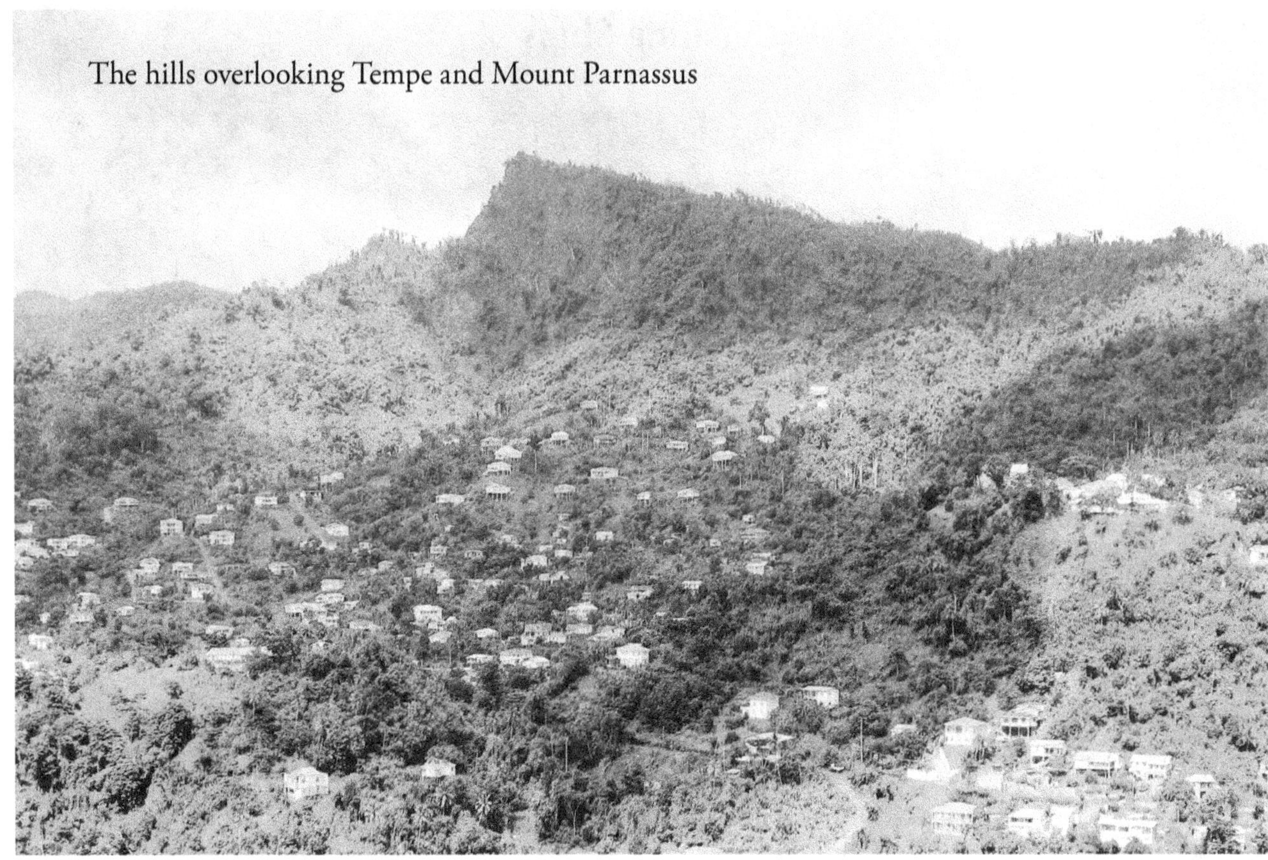

Creighton

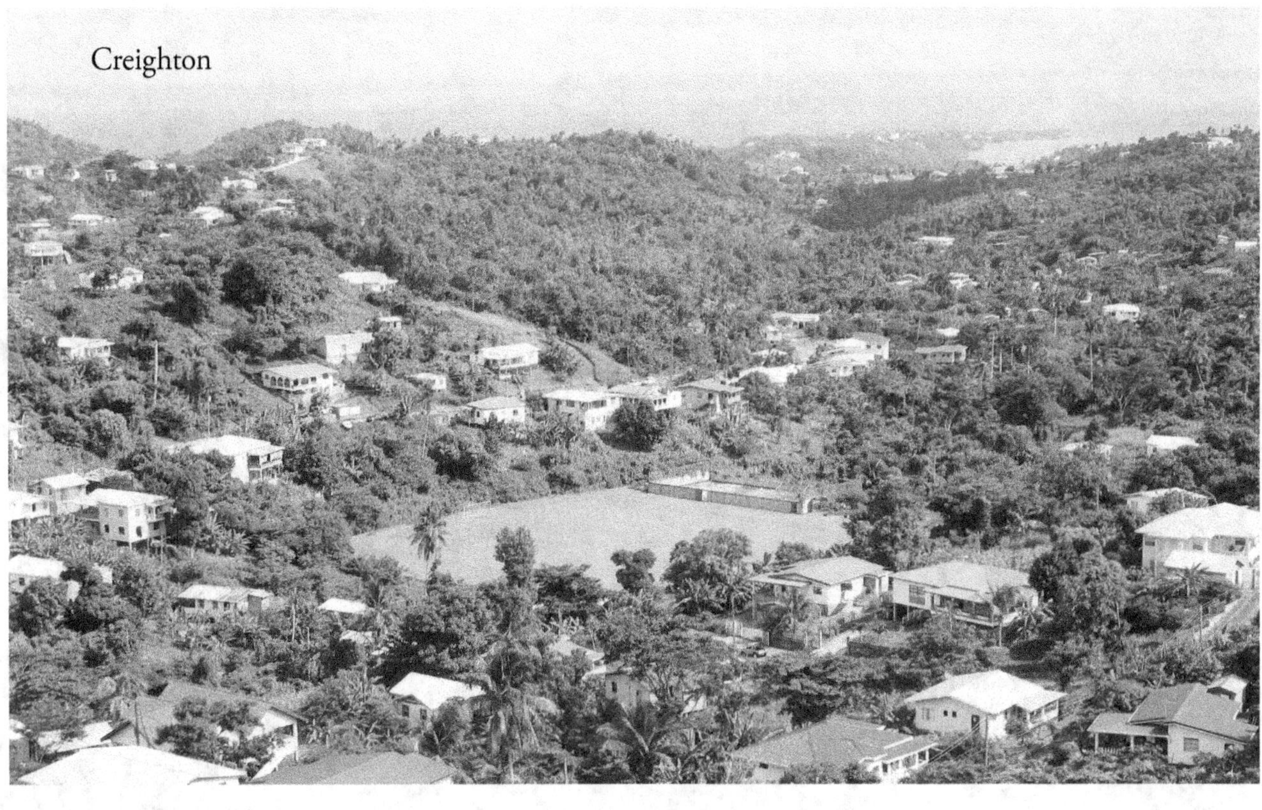

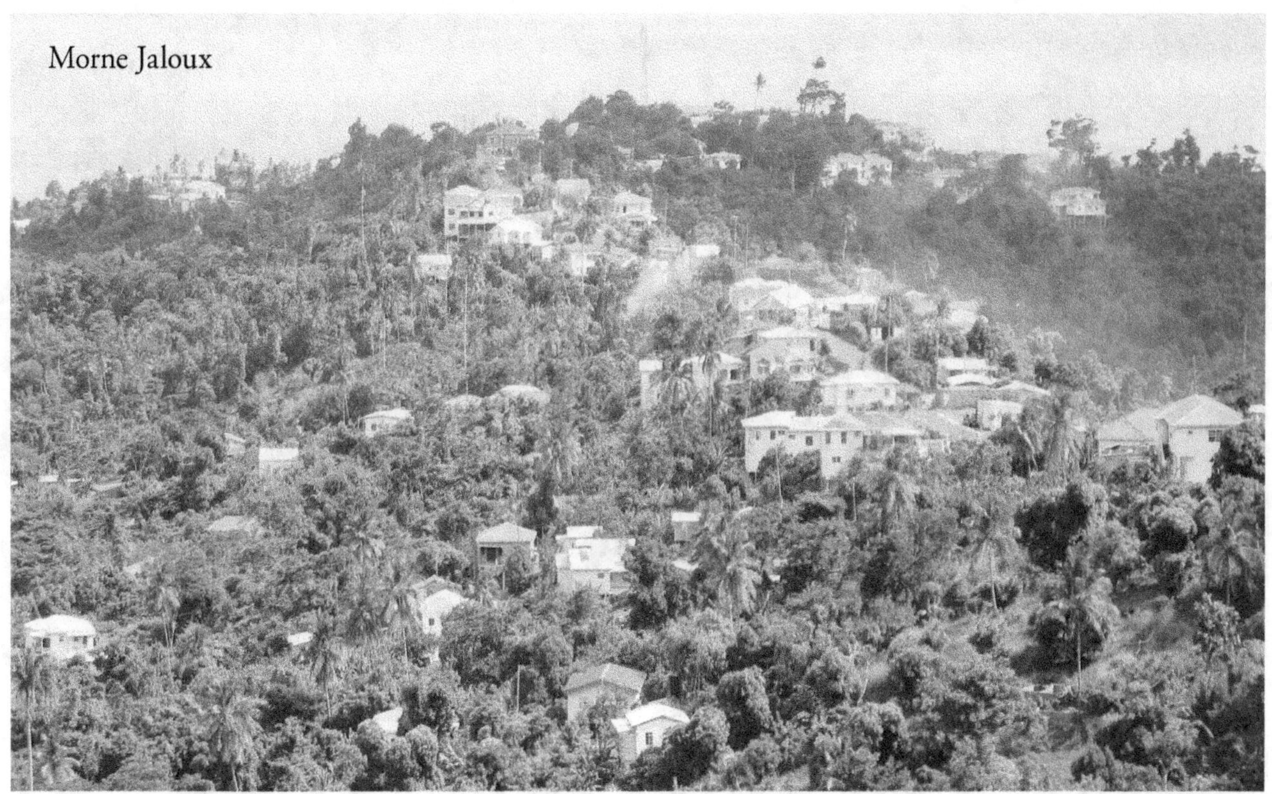

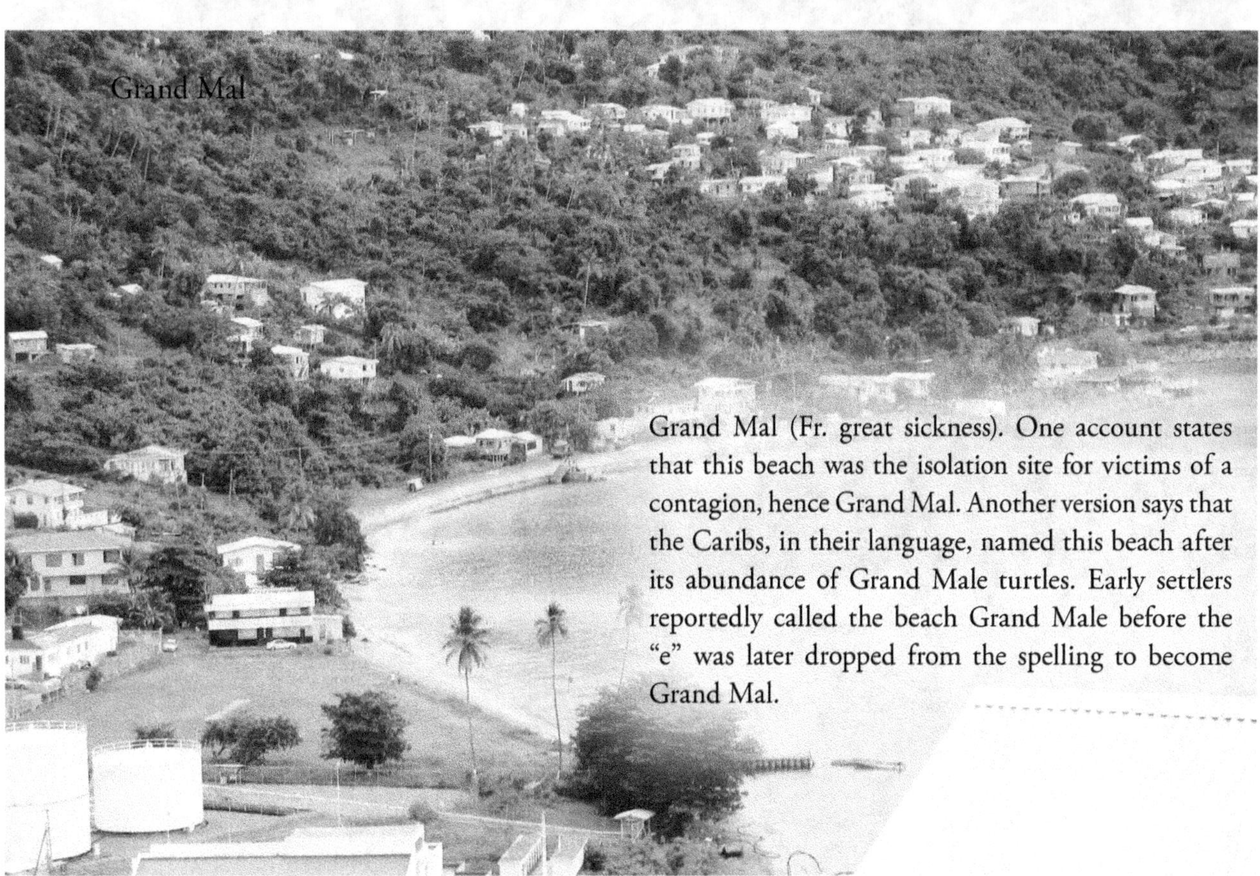

Grand Mal (Fr. great sickness). One account states that this beach was the isolation site for victims of a contagion, hence Grand Mal. Another version says that the Caribs, in their language, named this beach after its abundance of Grand Male turtles. Early settlers reportedly called the beach Grand Male before the "e" was later dropped from the spelling to become Grand Mal.

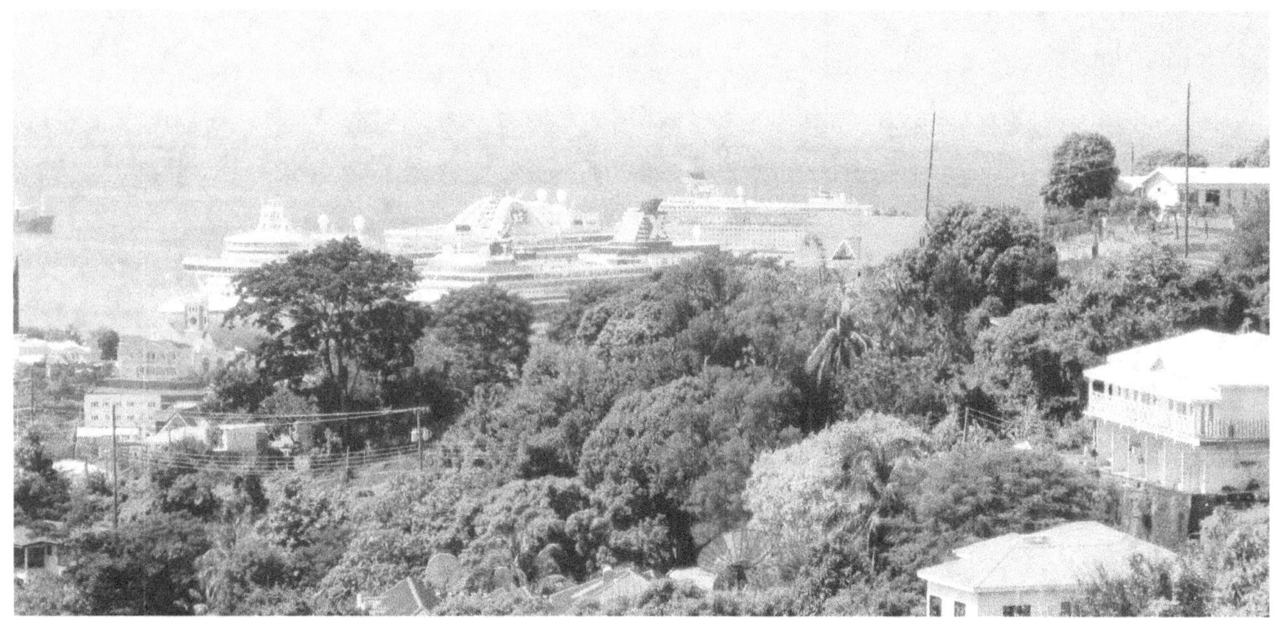

Above: Cruise ships berth at a port in St. George.
Below: Annandale Waterfall is one of the spots in the interior where the island welcomes visitors.

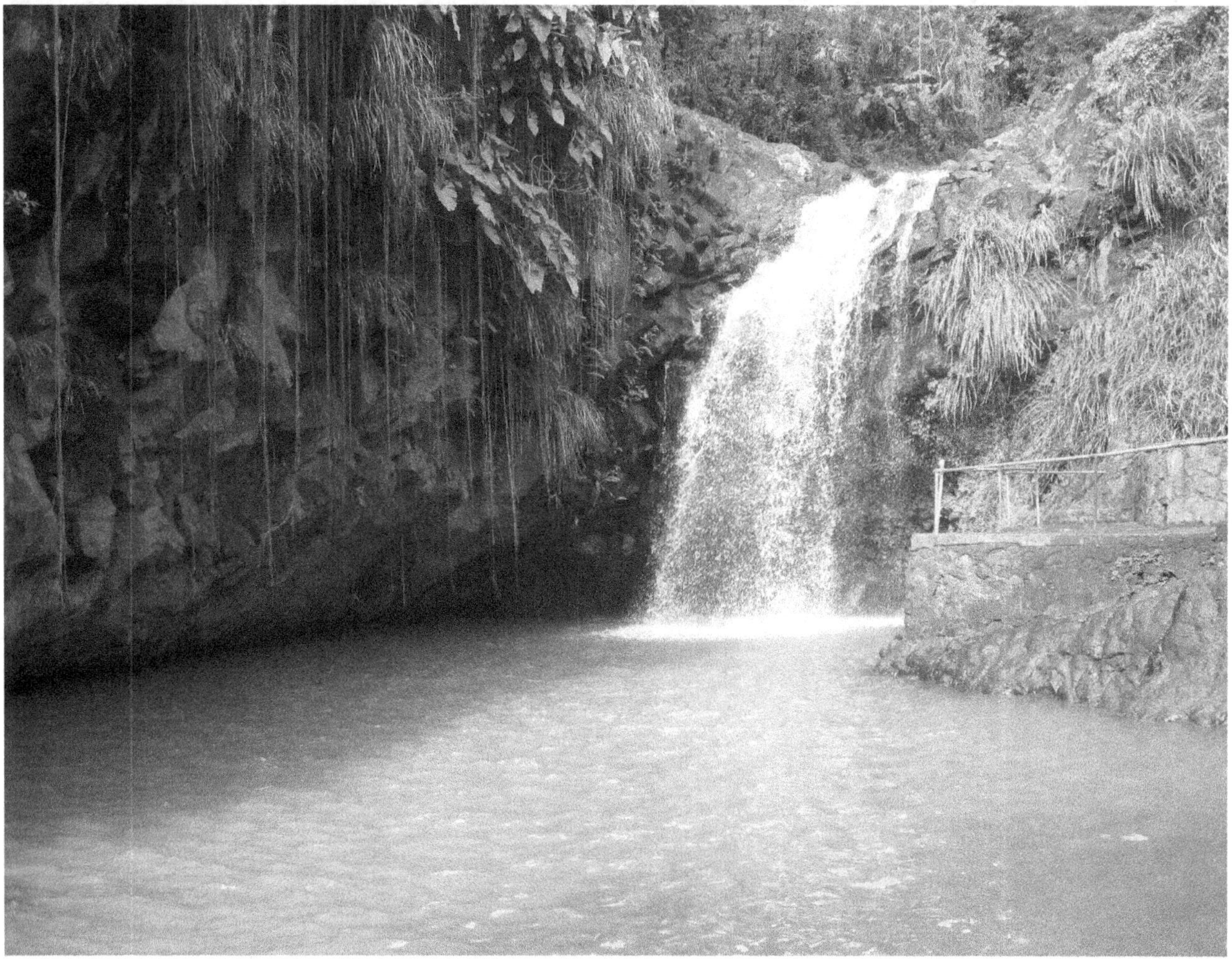

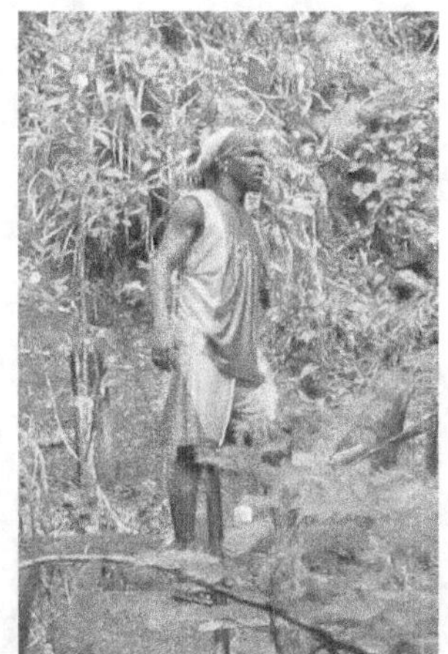

A cliff jumper at the waterfall

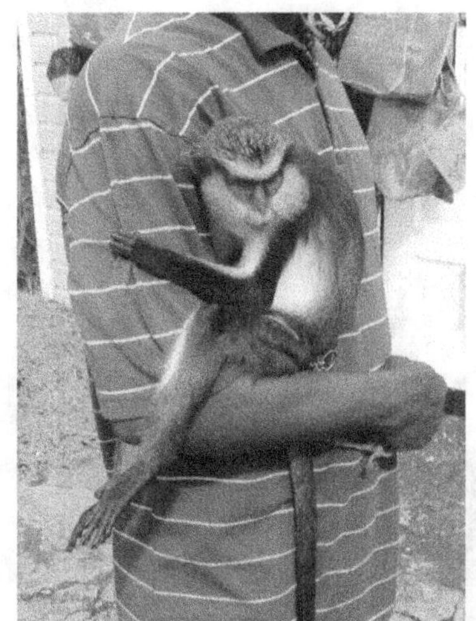

A Mona monkey sits on its owner's arm. The owner says that he has kept this monkey ever since it was a baby. He carries the monkey to the waterfall area to entertain visitors. Mona monkeys were initially found in West Africa but entered Grenada during the slave trade. Most of Grenada's Mona monkeys now inhabit the mountainous interior.

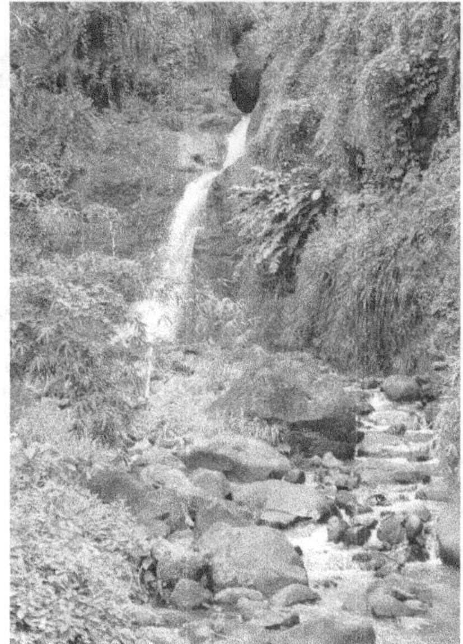

A smaller roadside waterfall along the Annandale route

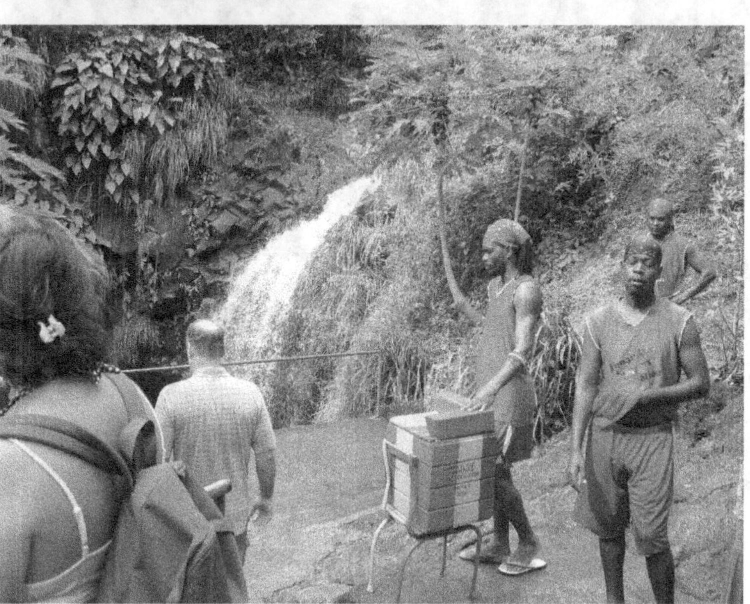

More uniformed jumpers. They entertain visitors by jumping over the roaring waterfall.

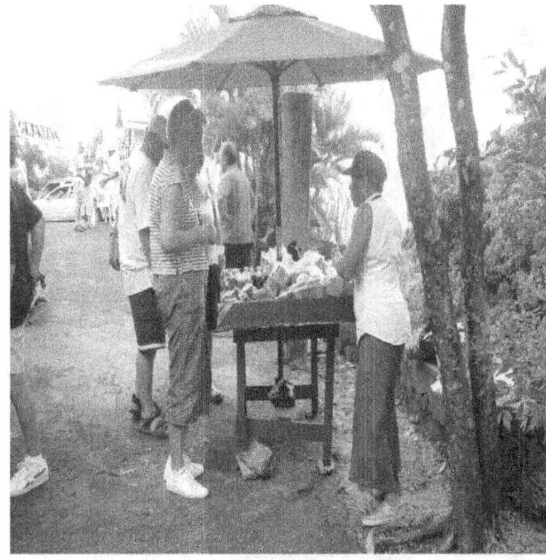

At a vendor's booth

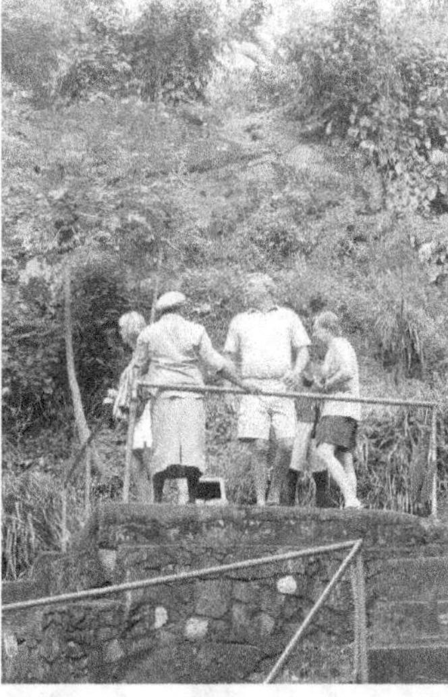

Visitors confer with a local guide.

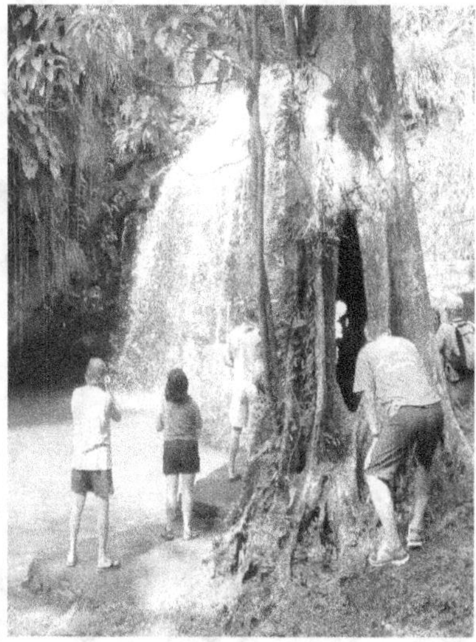

Having some fun exploring

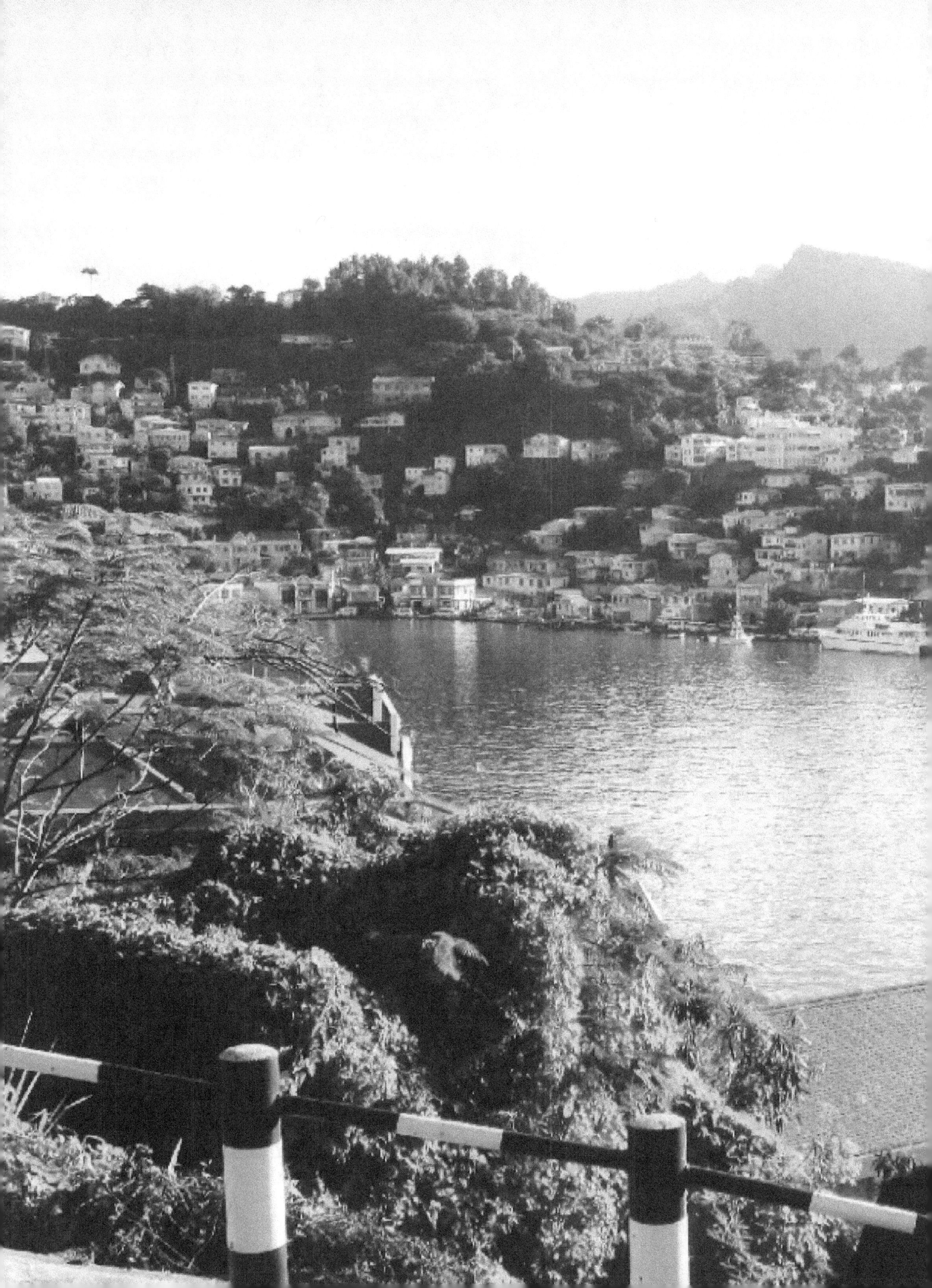

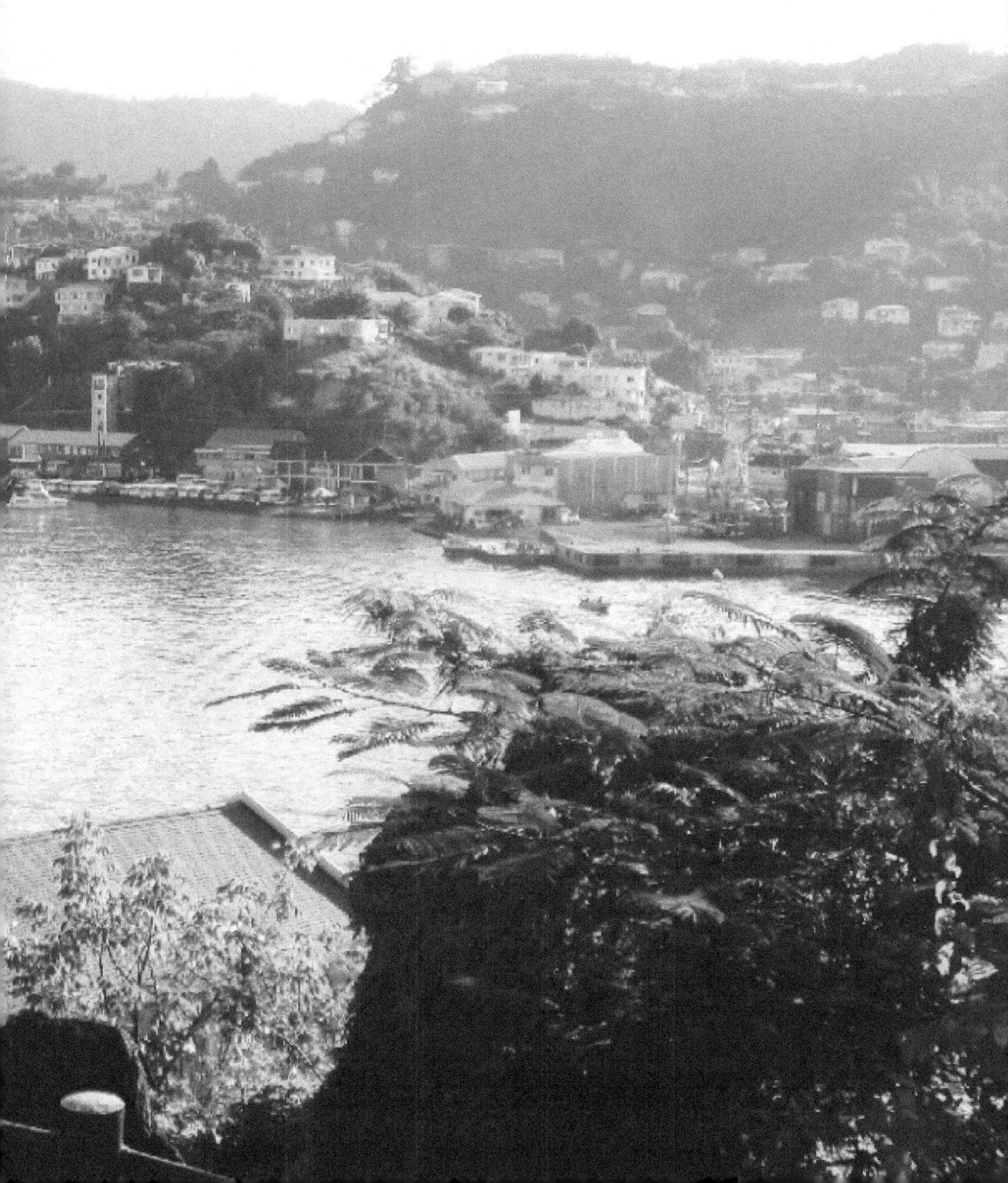

The morning sun begins to illuminate the St. George's Carenage.

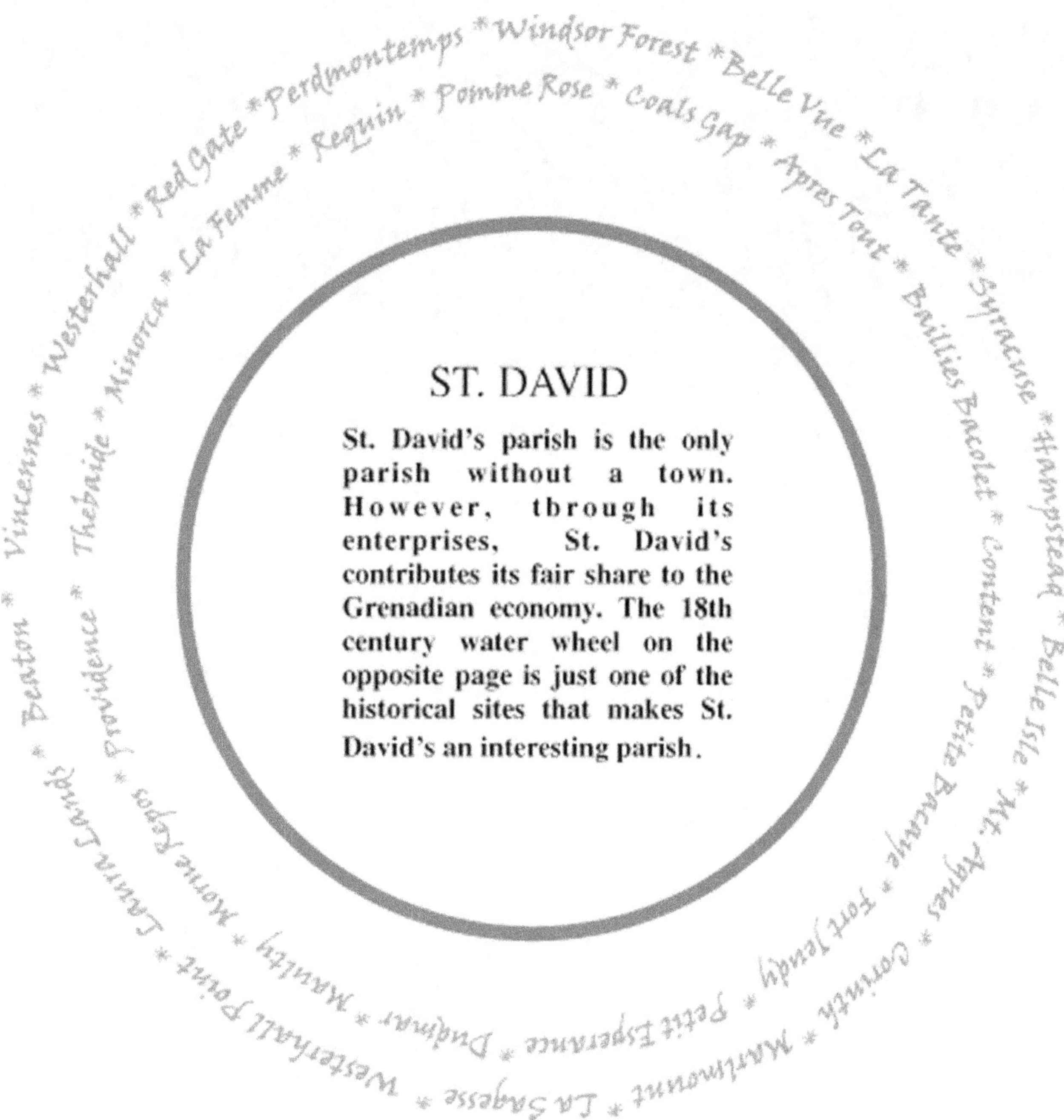

ST. DAVID

St. David's parish is the only parish without a town. However, through its enterprises, St. David's contributes its fair share to the Grenadian economy. The 18th century water wheel on the opposite page is just one of the historical sites that makes St. David's an interesting parish.

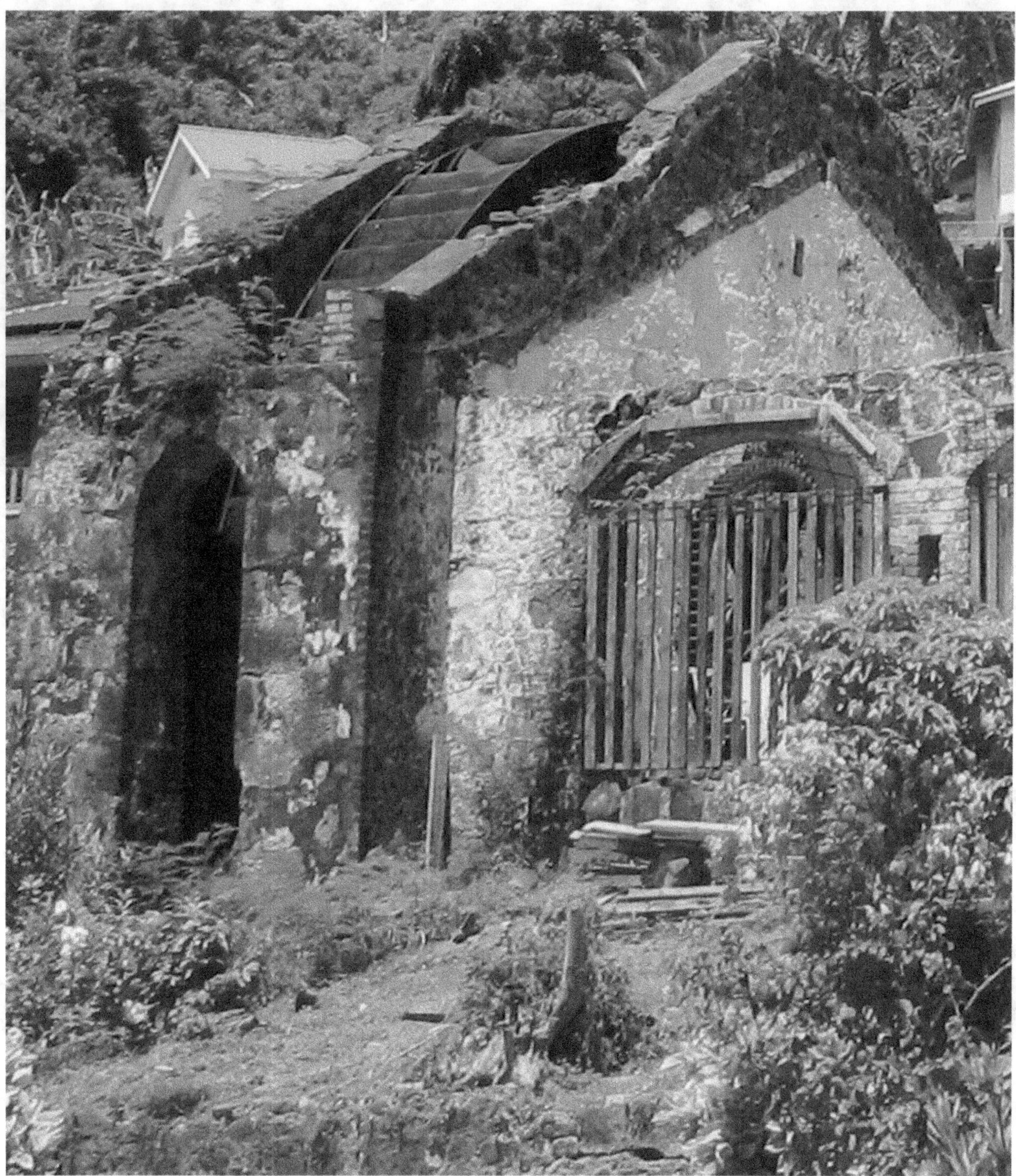

The water wheel of the old sugar-mill at La Sagesse Estate

The Estate once employed this waterwheel in the milling of sugar cane stalks. Water pressure turned the waterwheel, which activated the mechanical apparatus for milling the sugar cane. The juice milled from the sugarcane was boiled over a furnace, resulting in a constant stream of smoke from the mill's chimney (page 107). The most common products from the mill were sugar, rum, and molasses. The dried sugar cane stalks, called bagasse, were often recycled as fuel for the furnace. The water wheel provided a technological leap from the prior use of animal-driven mills.

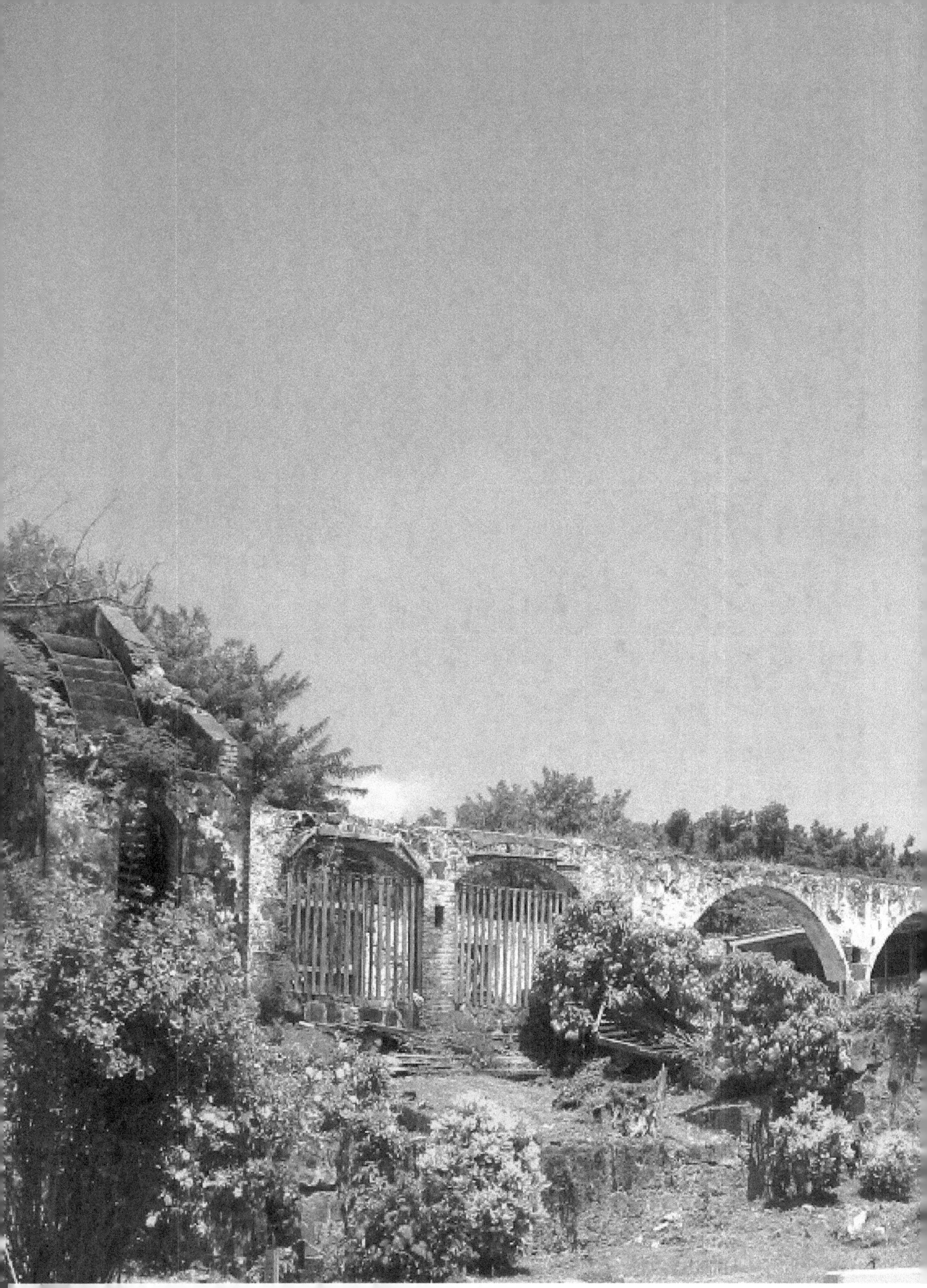

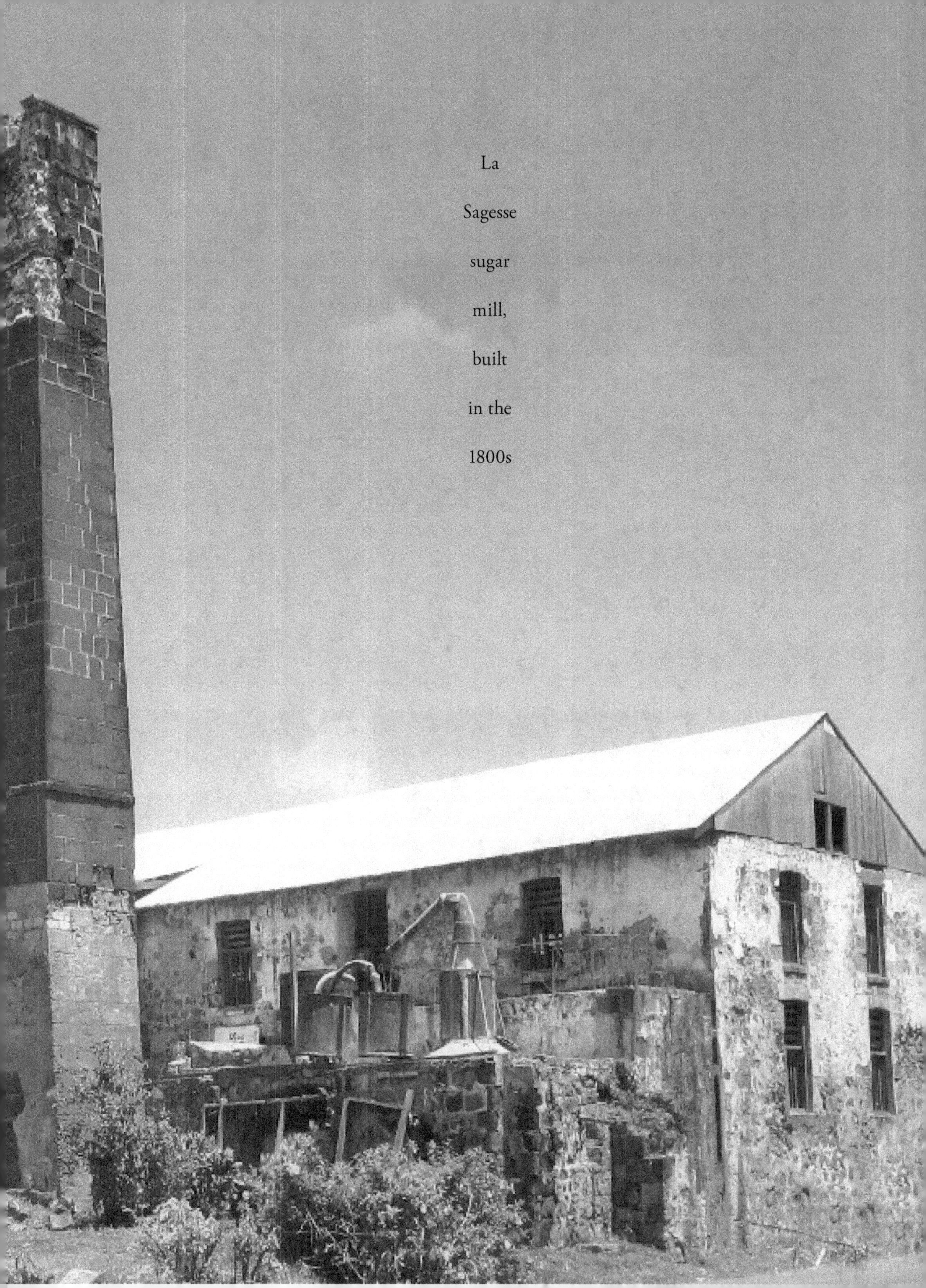

La
Sagesse
sugar
mill,
built
in the
1800s

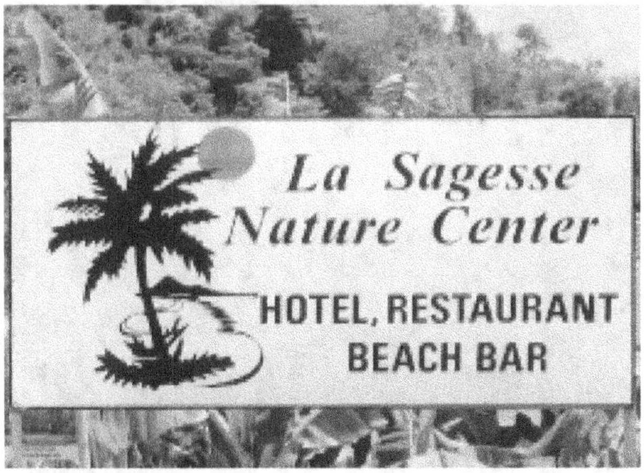

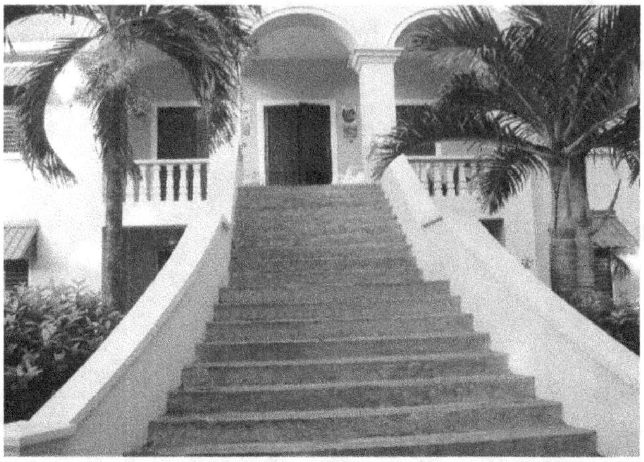

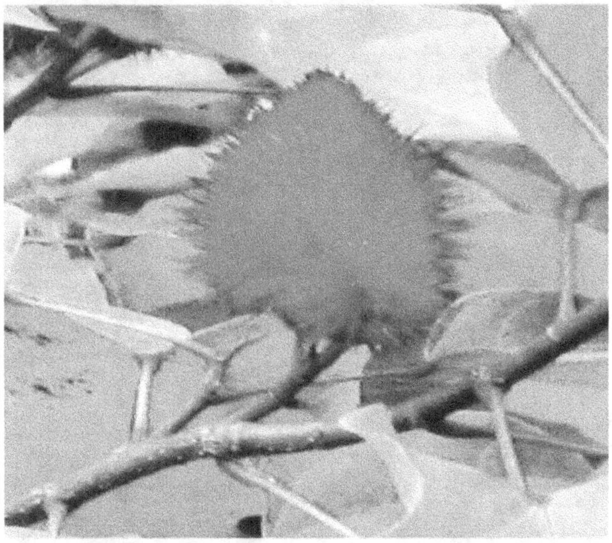

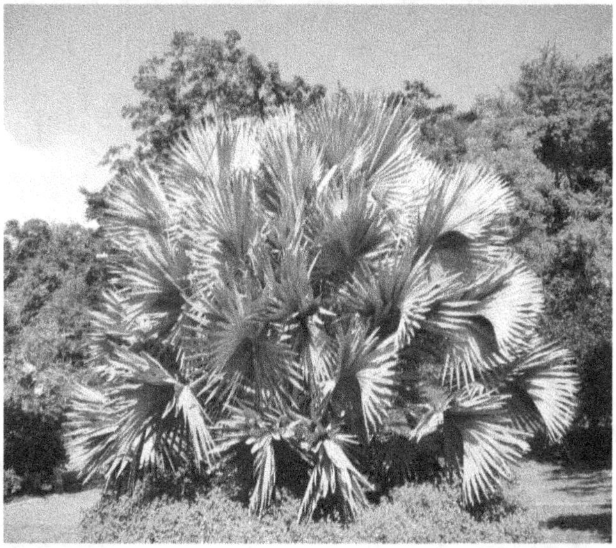

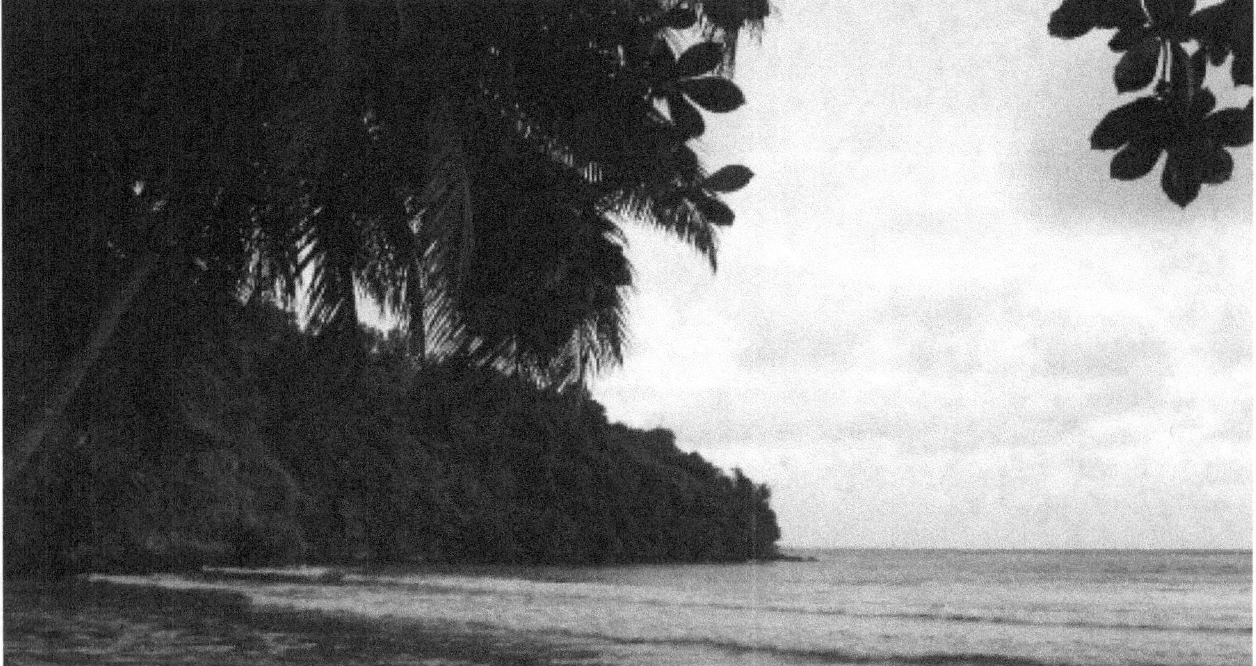

From bird watching to hiking, La Sagesse provides a peaceful communion with nature, compromised only by the homely comfort of its hotel.

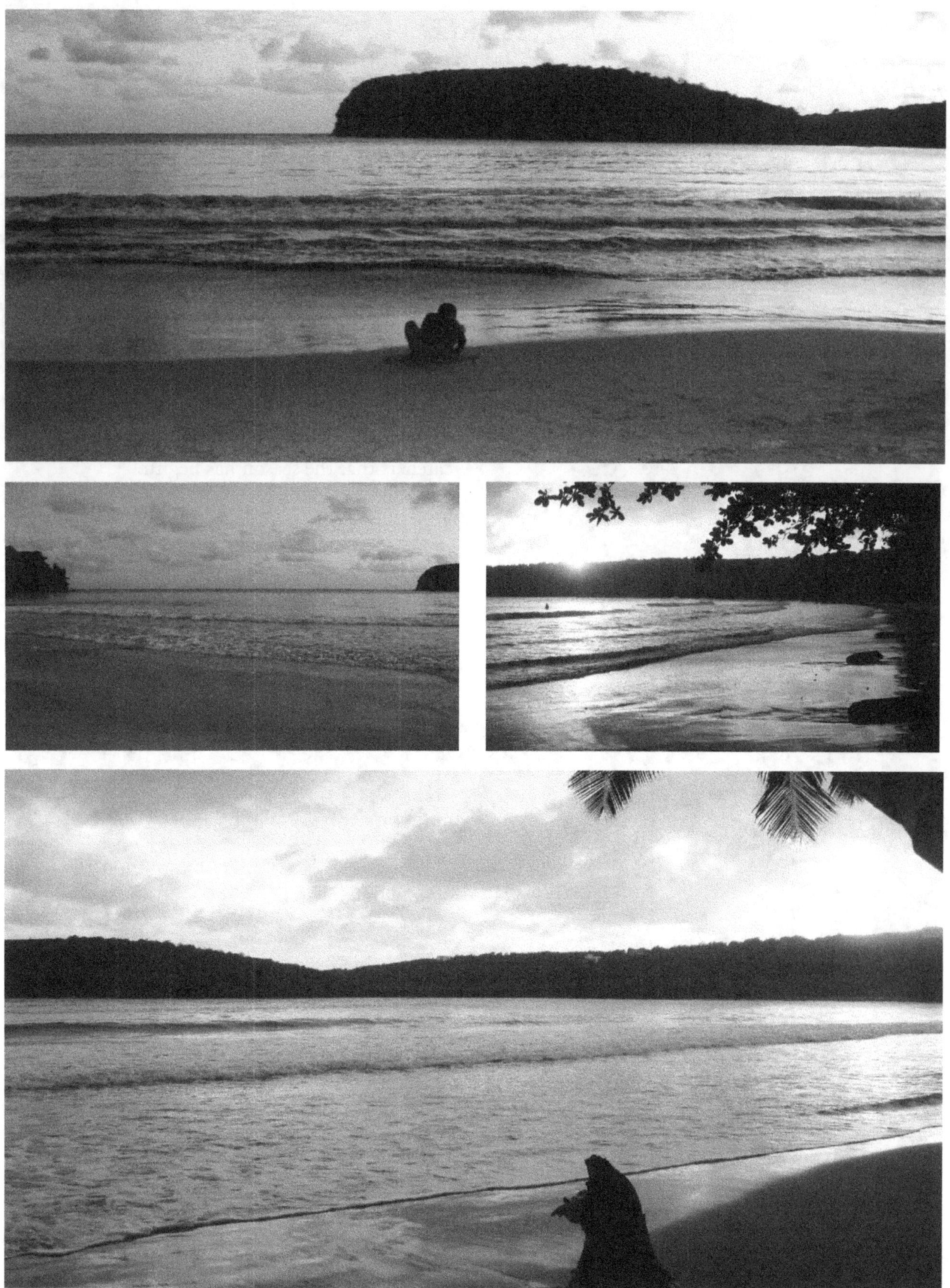

The pictures on both pages capture the beauty and serenity of La Sagesse Beach
both at dusk and in the brighter daylight.

TITIREE
(pronounced tee-tee-ree)

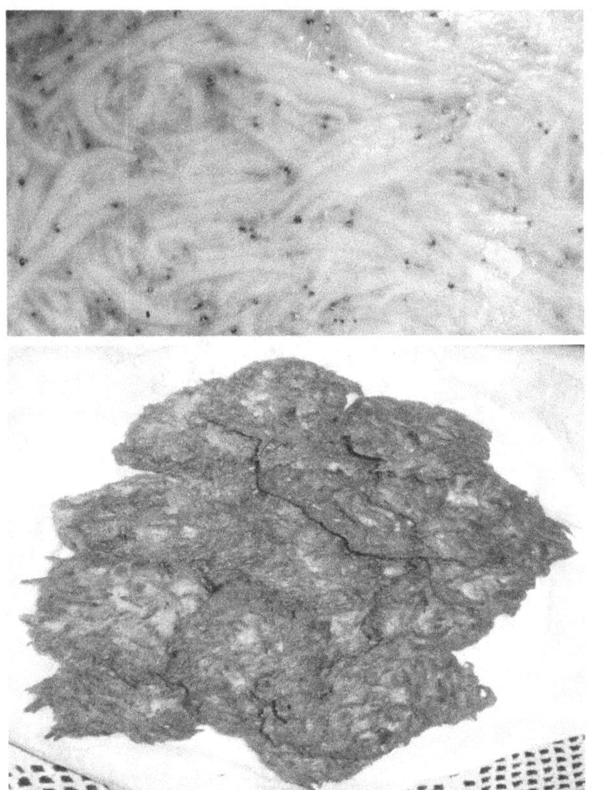

The titiree (top left) is a wingless, miniature fish less than one inch long and less than one-sixteenth of an inch wide; it is like silverfish in some parts of Asia. By the millions, titirees seasonally migrate upwards from the sea to spawn; they occupy the brackish waters of the Bushiree, where villagers catch them. The Bushiree is the area just before where the river meets the sea (see picture below).

There is often an episode of thunder-less lightning, called titiree lightning, that indicates to the titiree catchers that the season has begun.

Titiree fishcakes (left) are considered tasty and are immensely popular during the titiree season, usually around September. The fishcakes are typically made by seasoning the fish and making fishcake patties. Because the fish is so small, a fishcake can easily consist of a few dozen titirees.

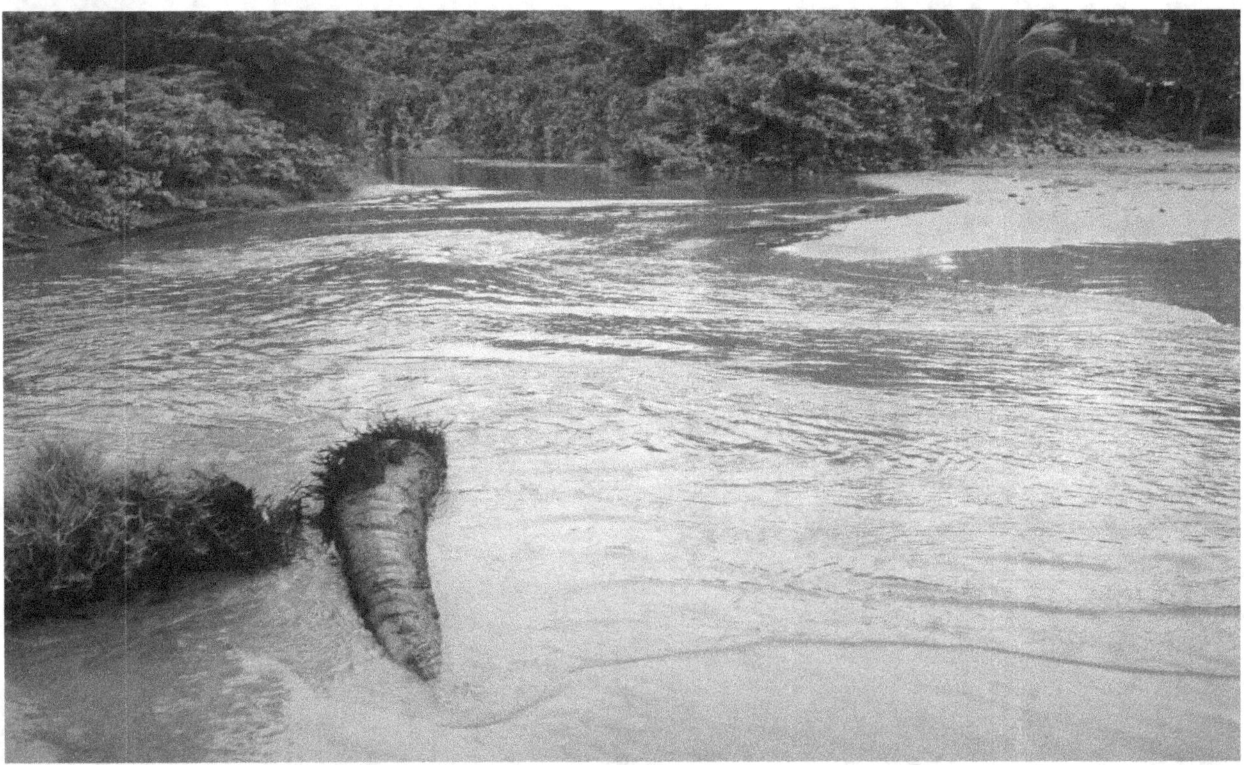

Here is the bushiree location where the river meets the sea at La Sagesse Beach. It is where someone can catch the titiree.

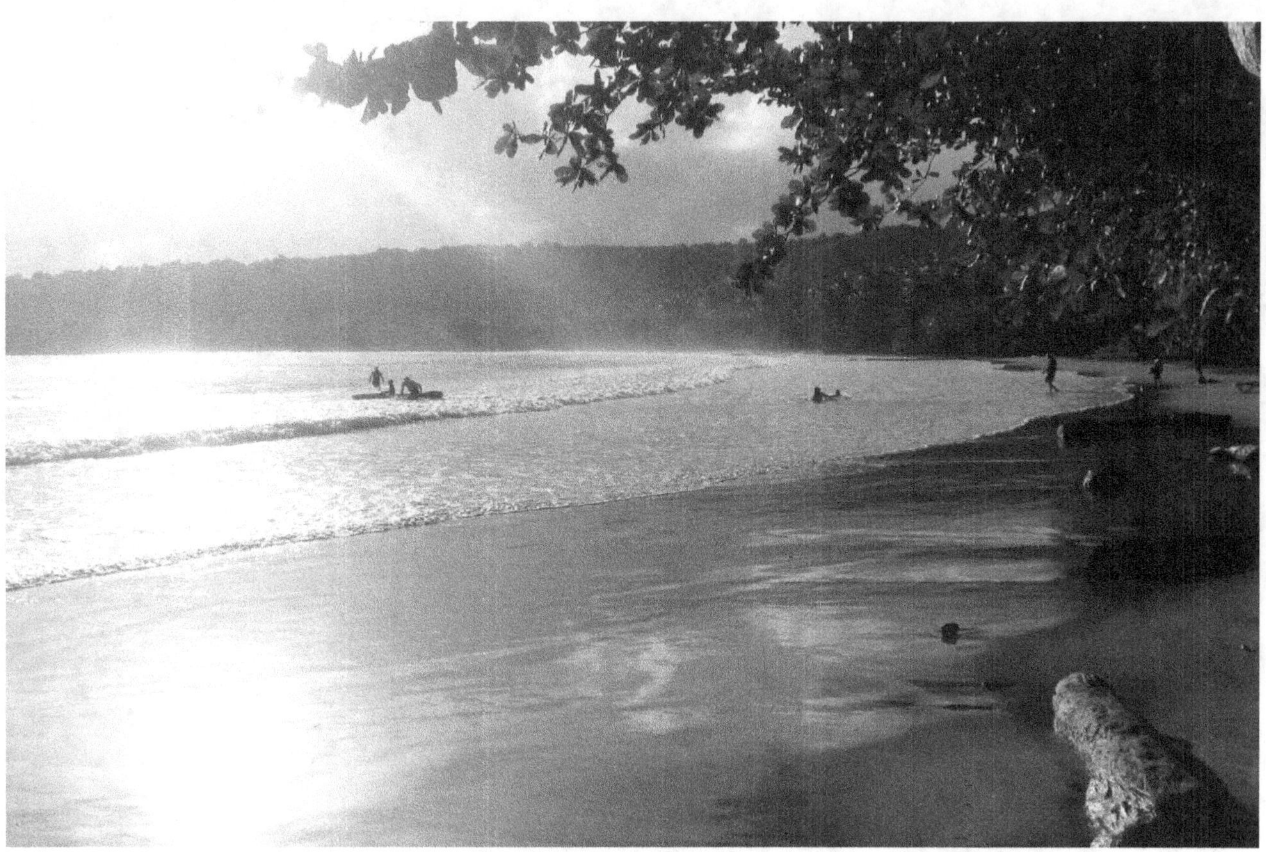

Quiet on La Sagesse Beach as the evening sun drops on the beautifully dark sands.

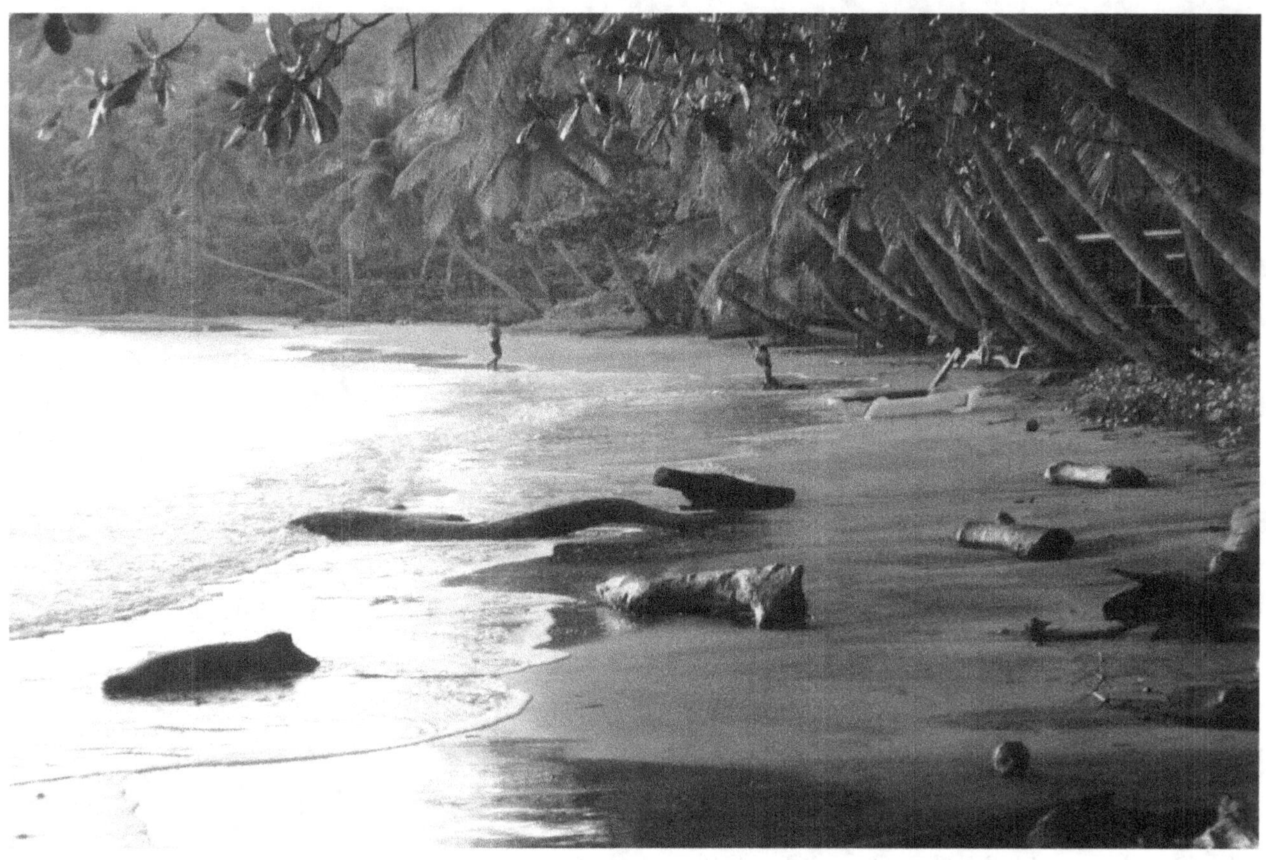

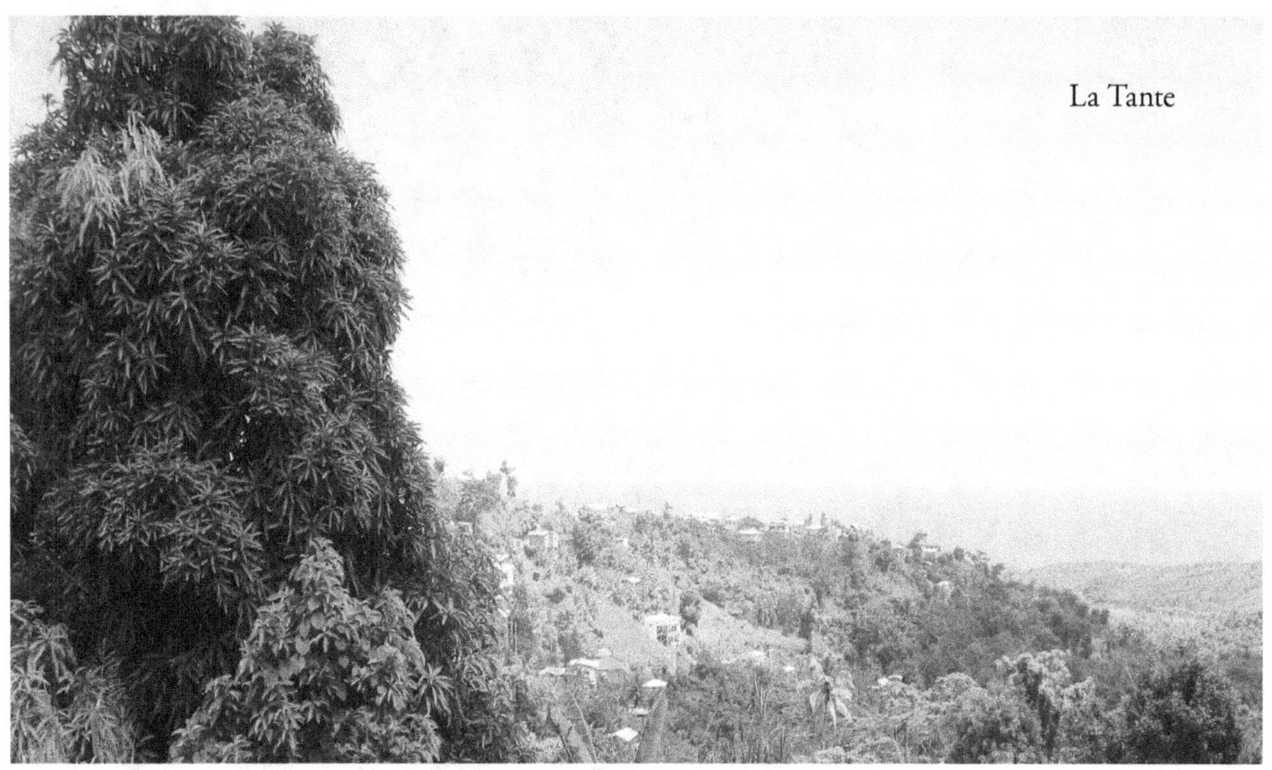

La Tante

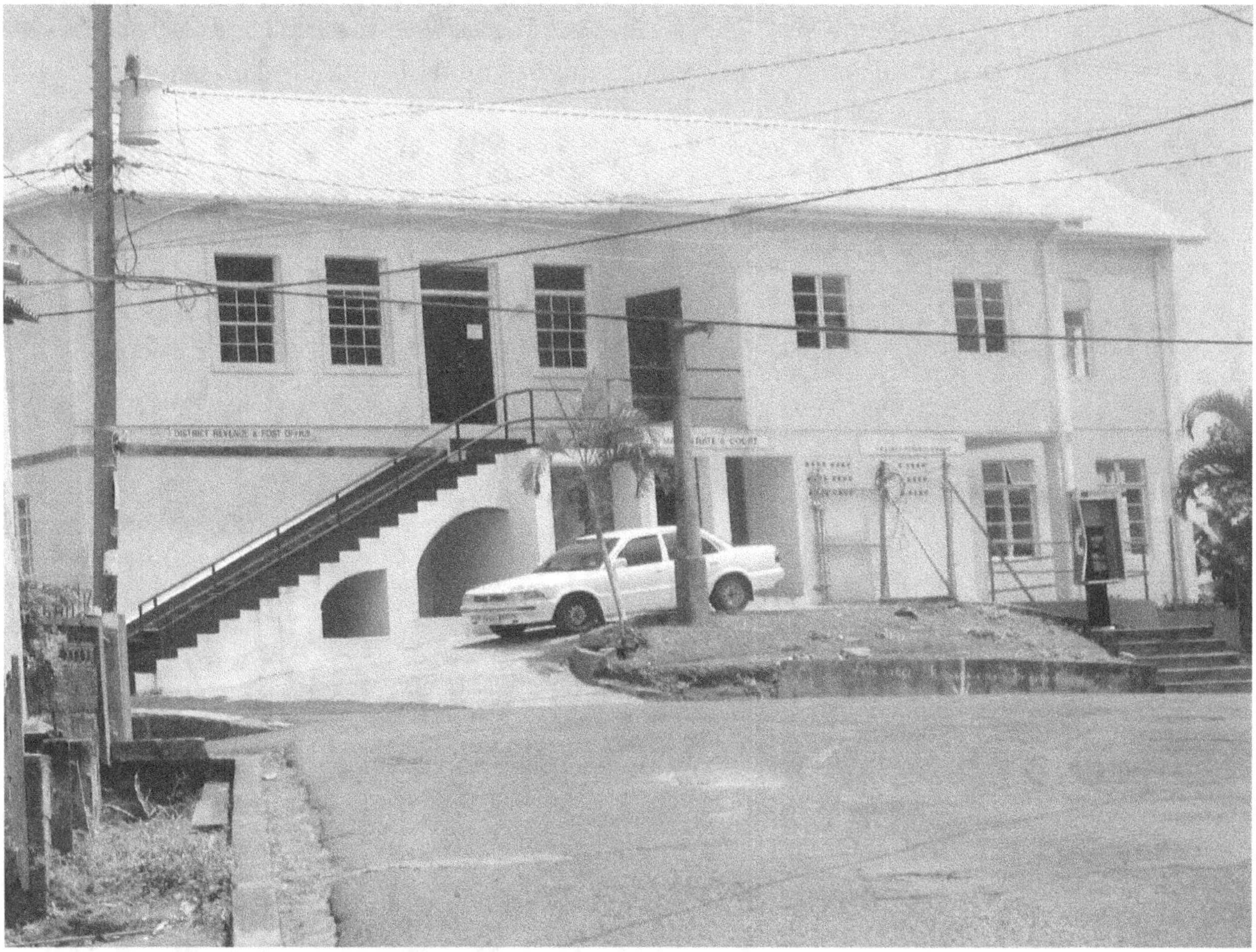

St. David's District Revenue Office, Post Office, and Magistrate's court are all housed in this facility.

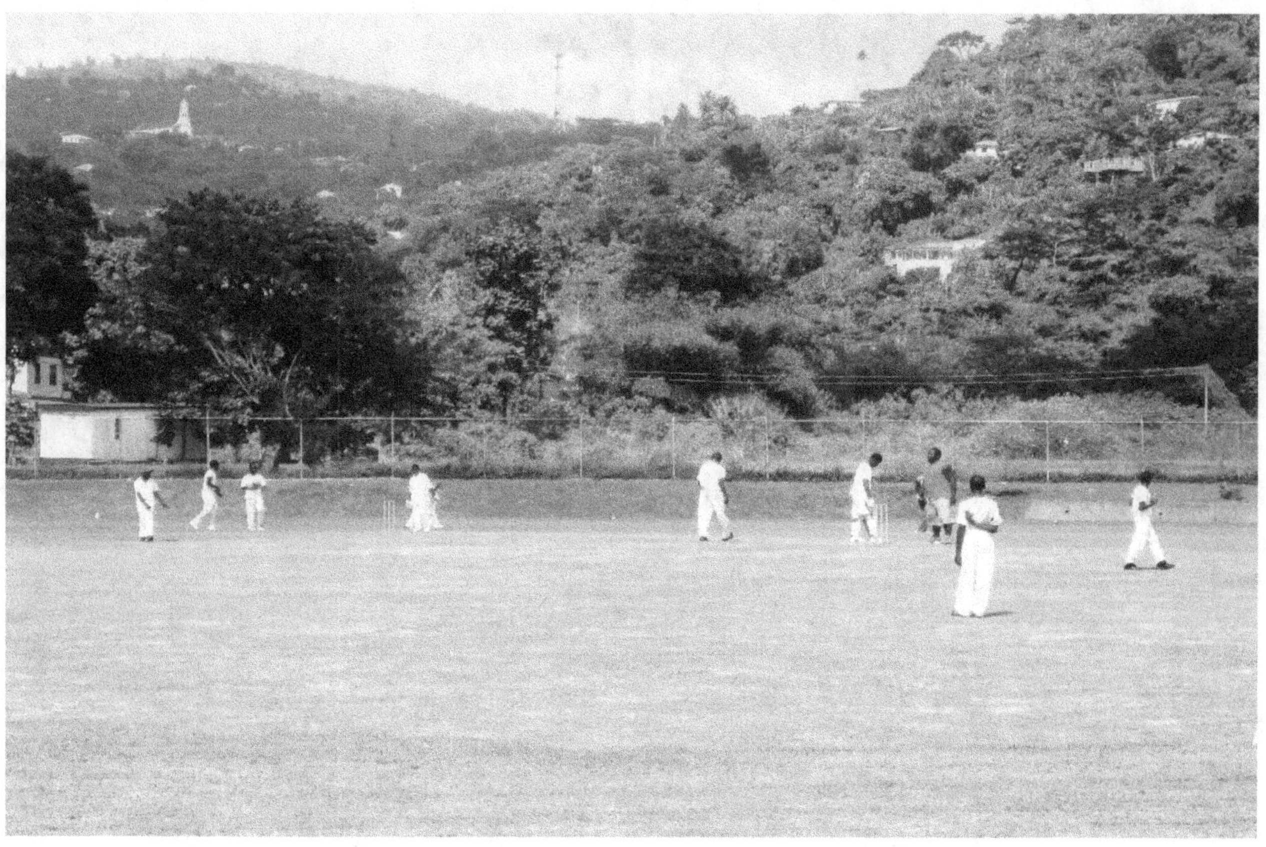

Playing cricket (above) and soccer (below) in St. David's parish

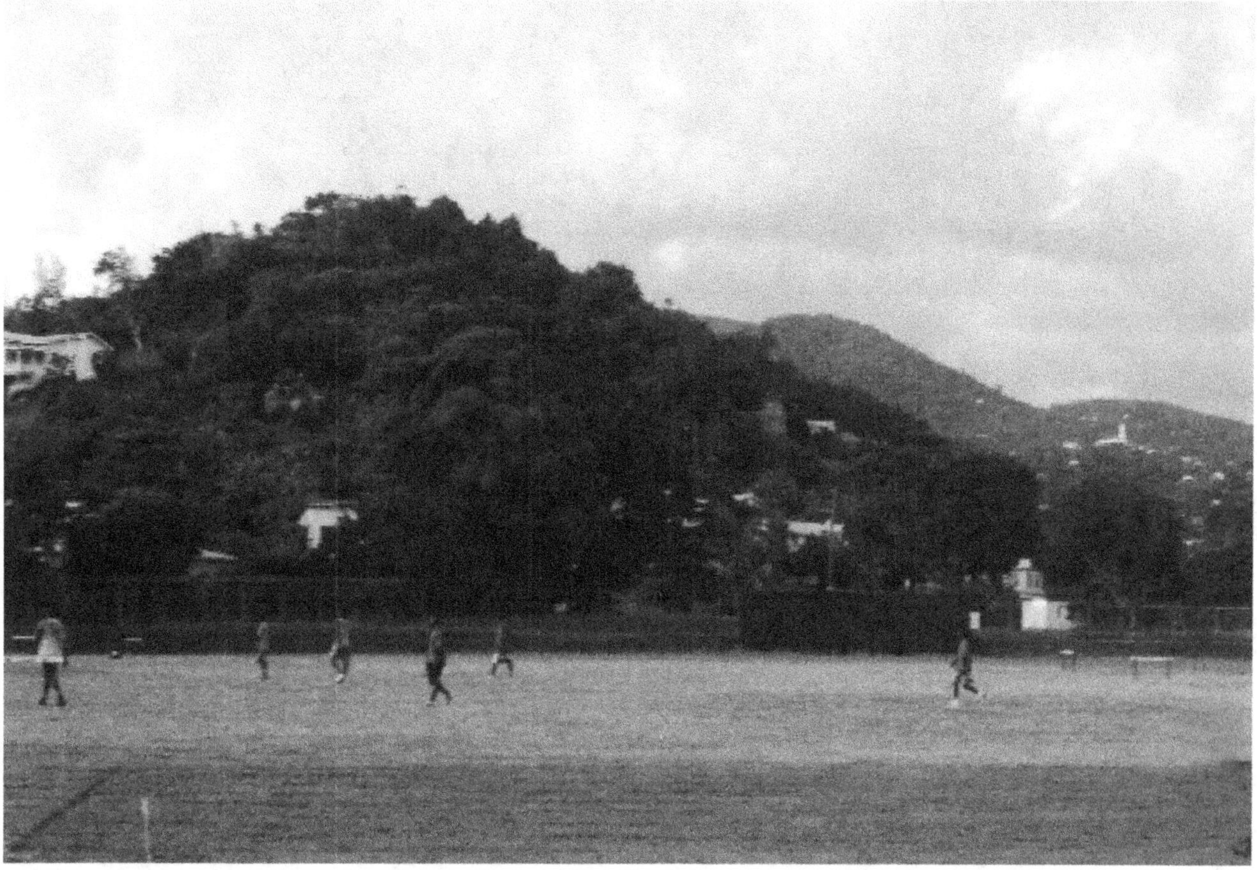

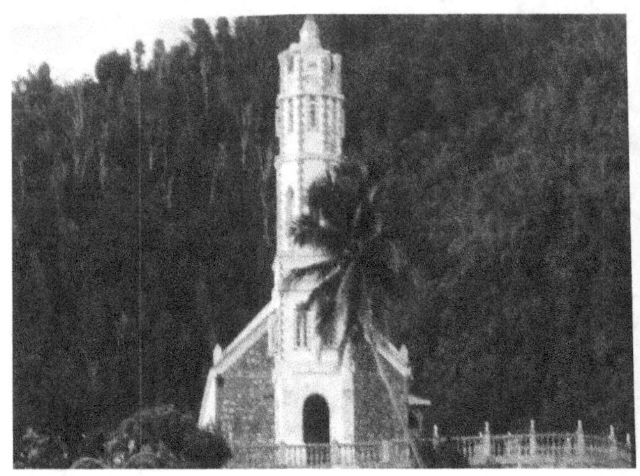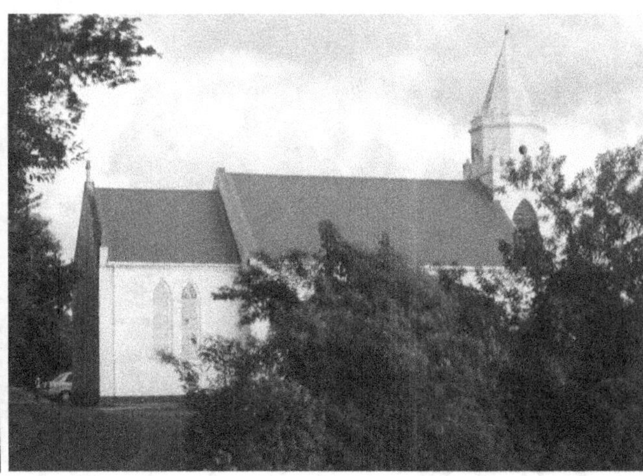

Churches in Bellevue

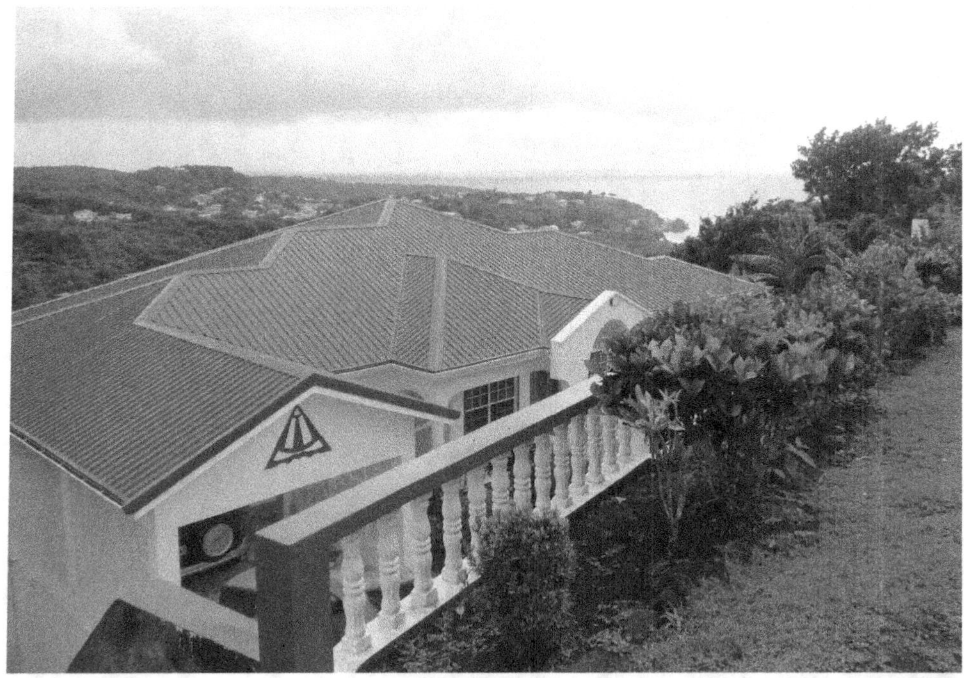

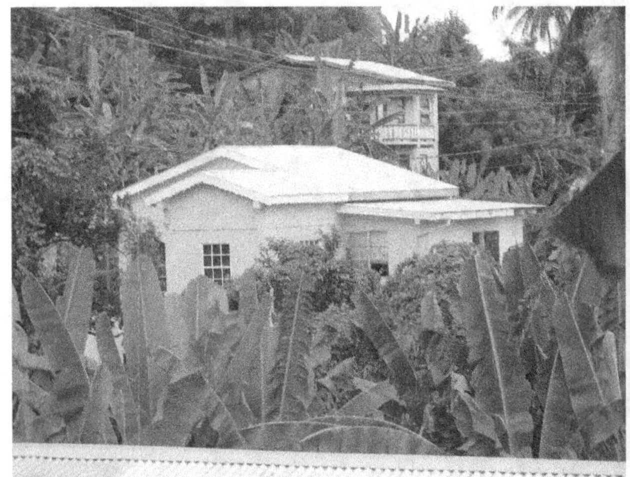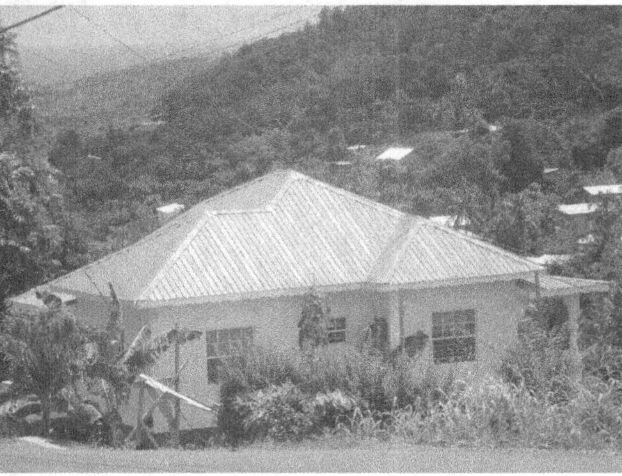

Homes in St David's Parish

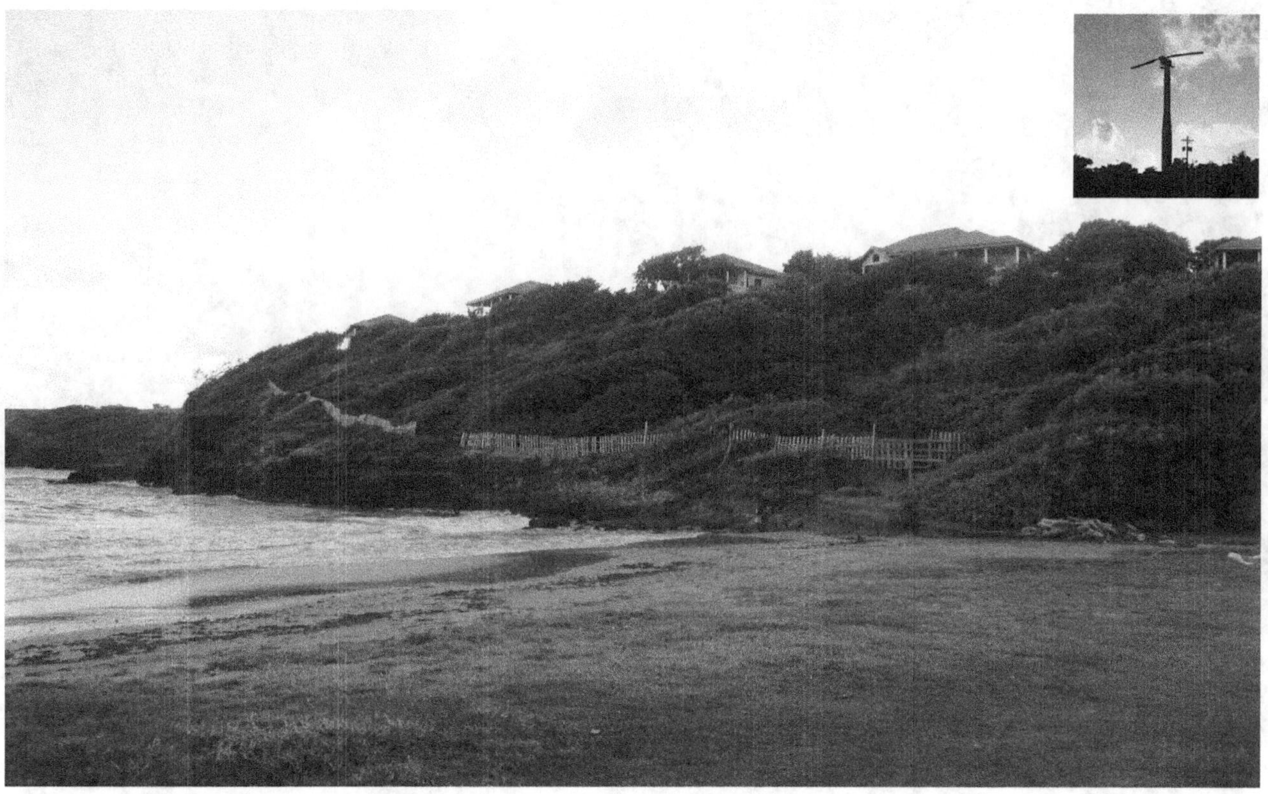

Above, the cottages at Paradise Bay Resort form a line along this coastal hillcrest in La Tante. The windmill, inset, provides electricity for the buildings. The opposite end of Paradise Bay is pictured below.

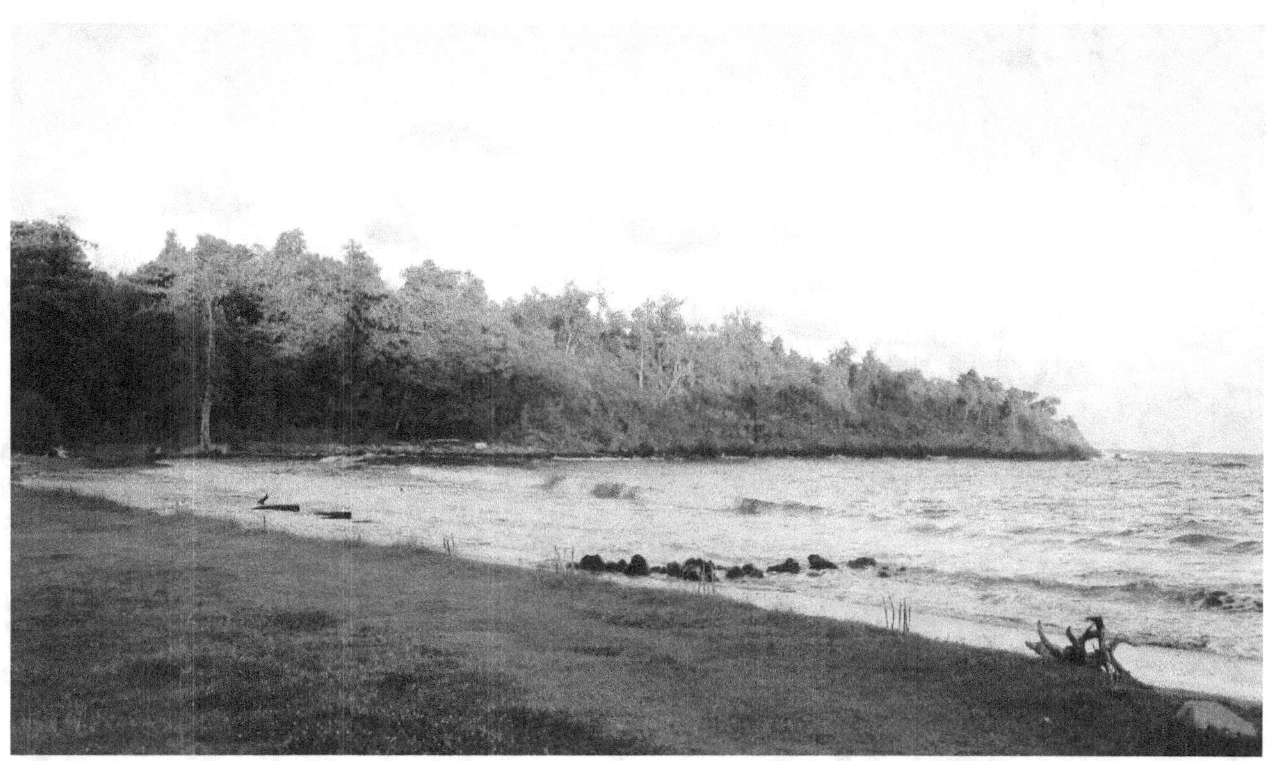

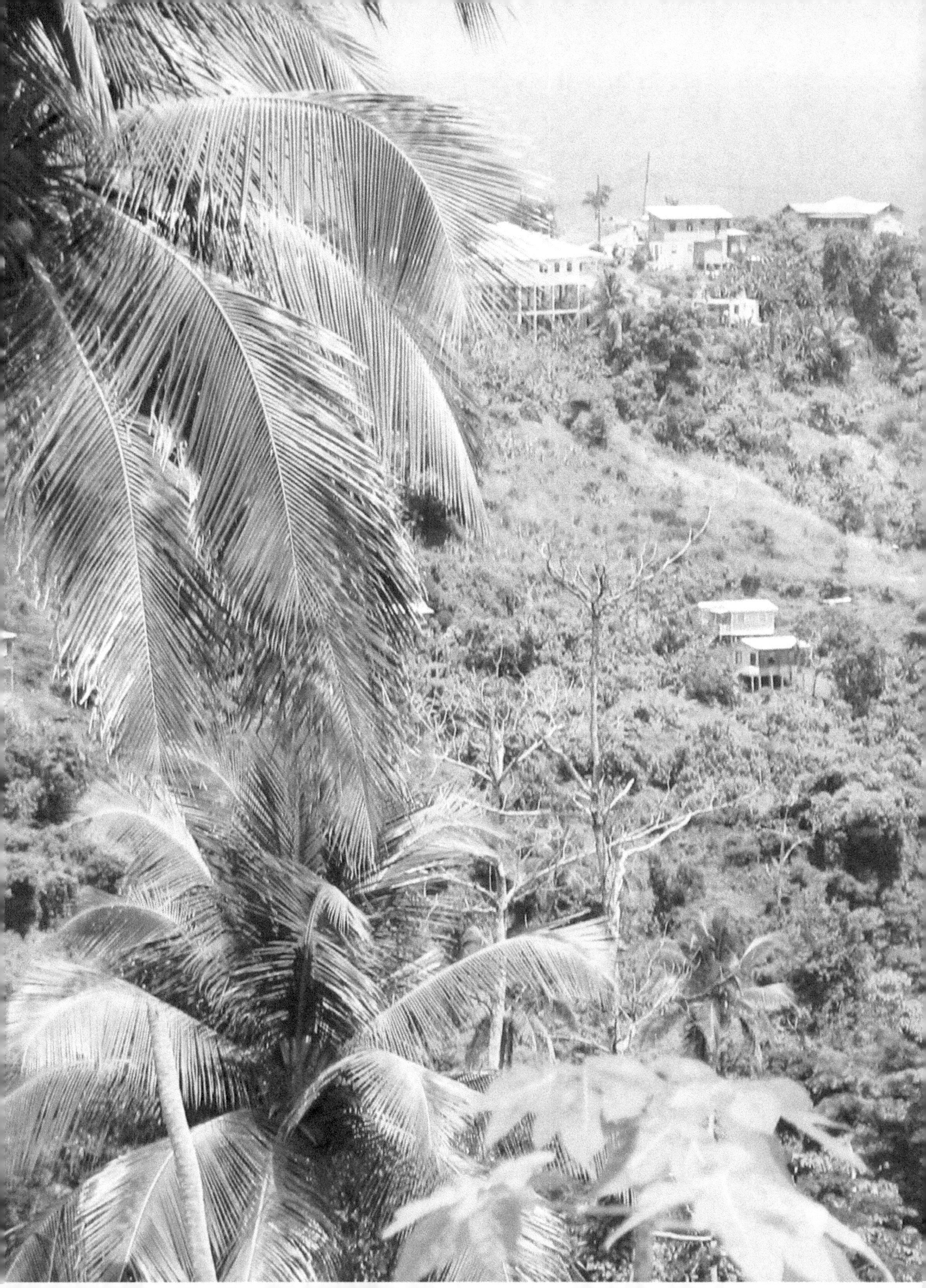

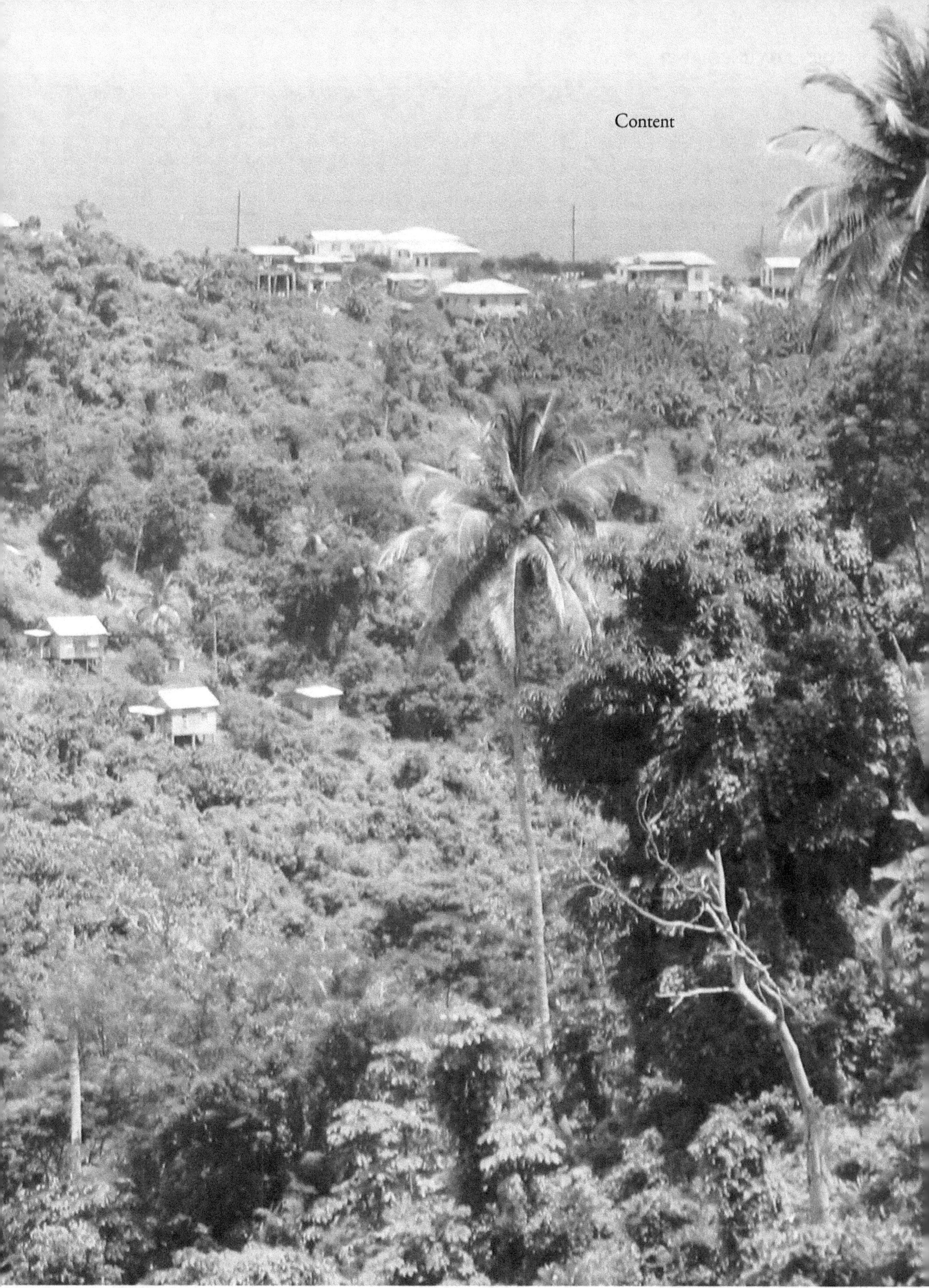
Content

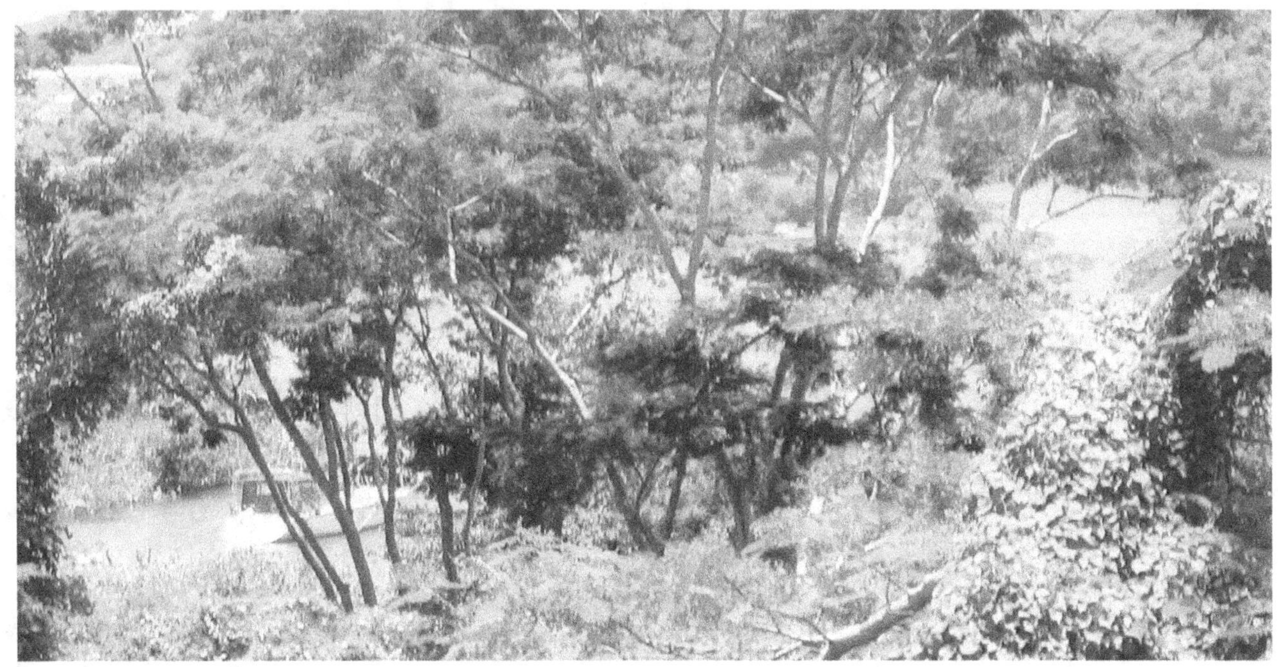

Egmont Harbour

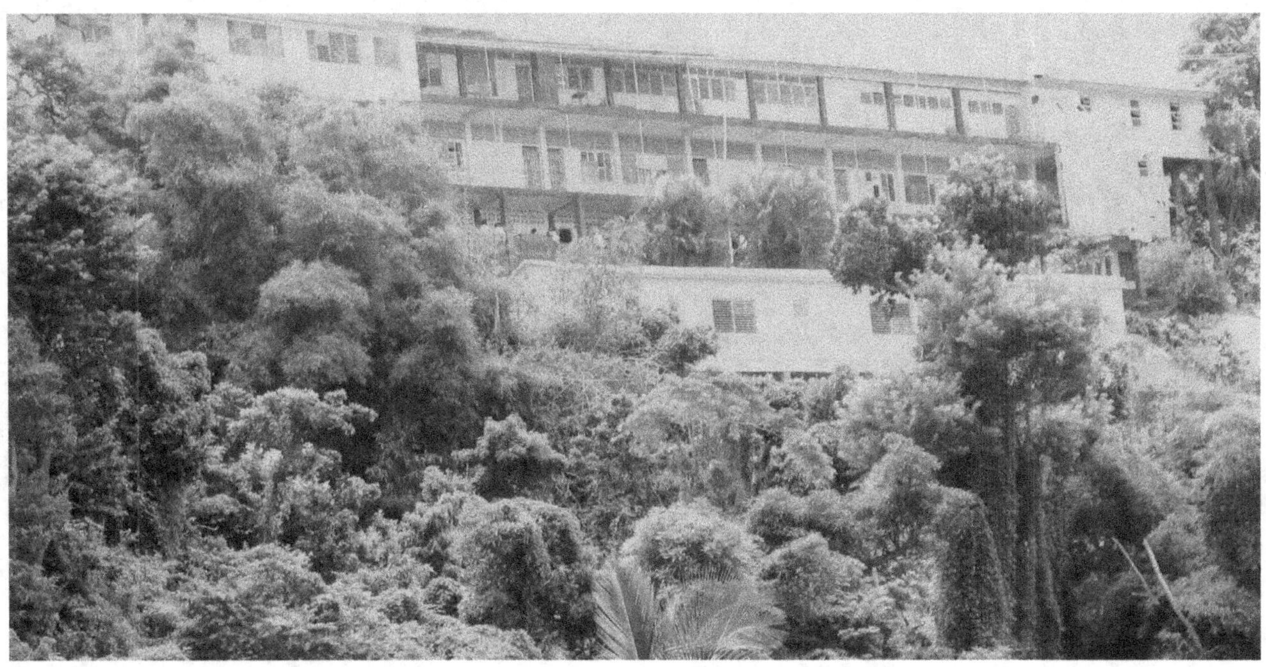

St. David's Christian Secondary School

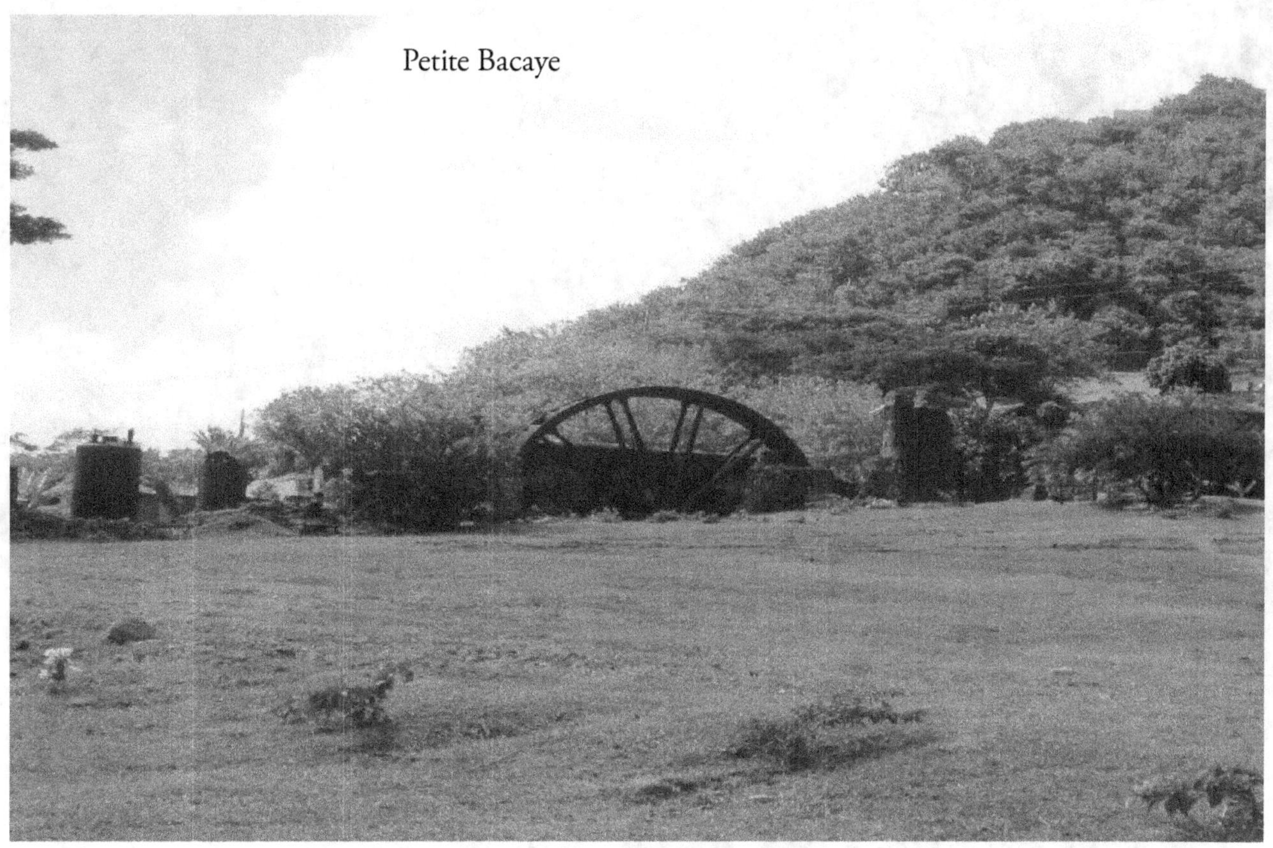

Petite Bacaye

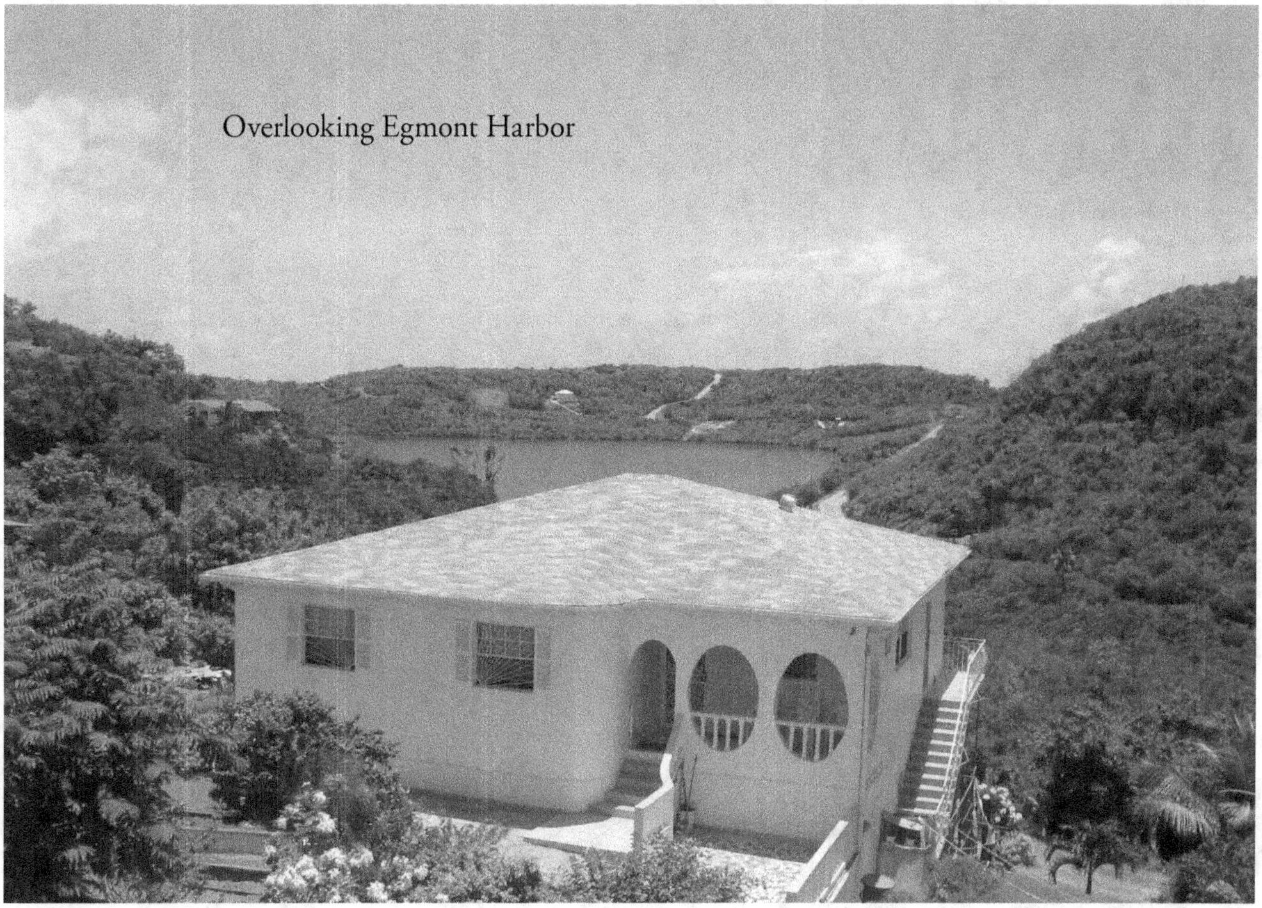

Overlooking Egmont Harbor

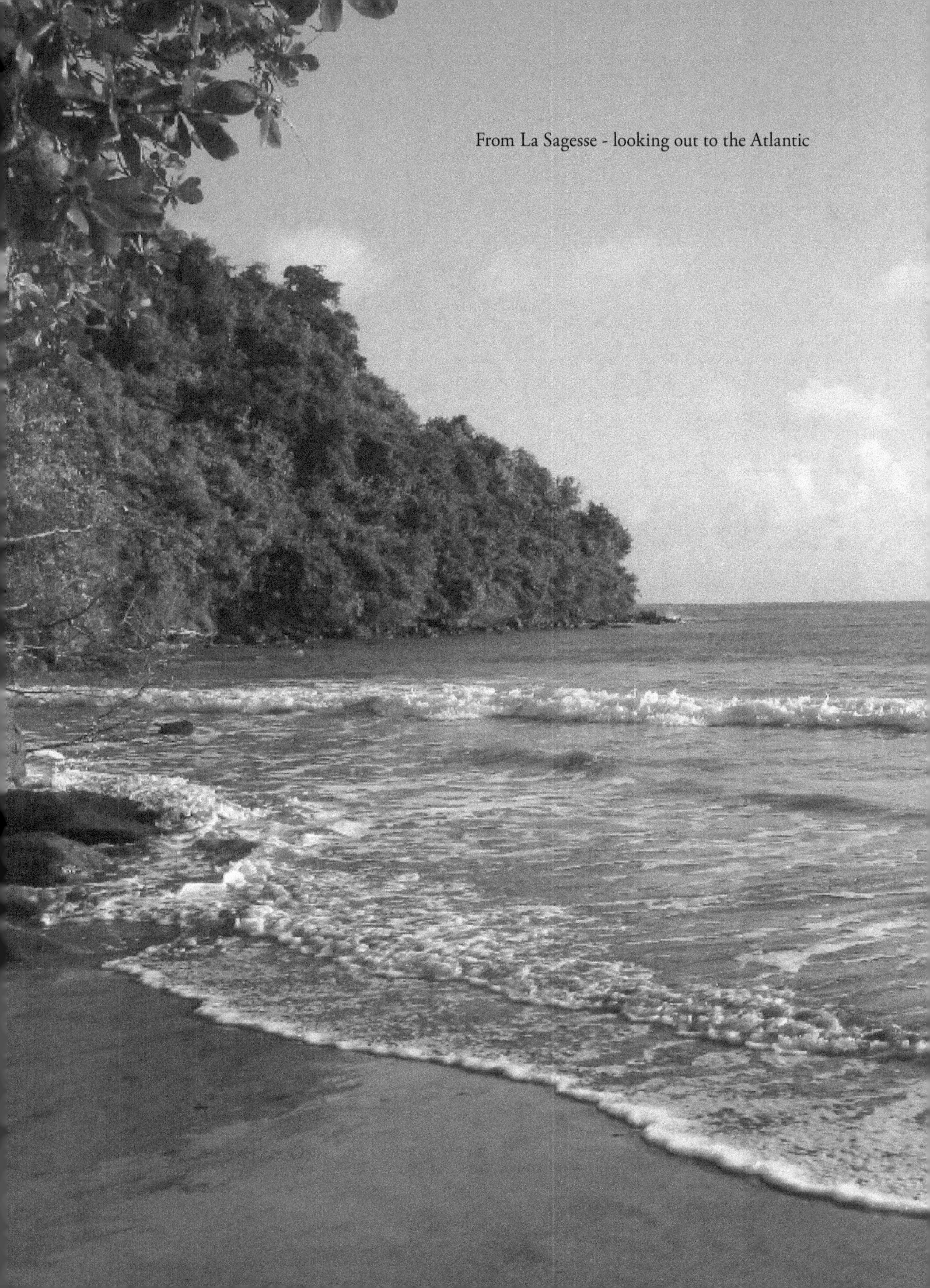

From La Sagesse - looking out to the Atlantic

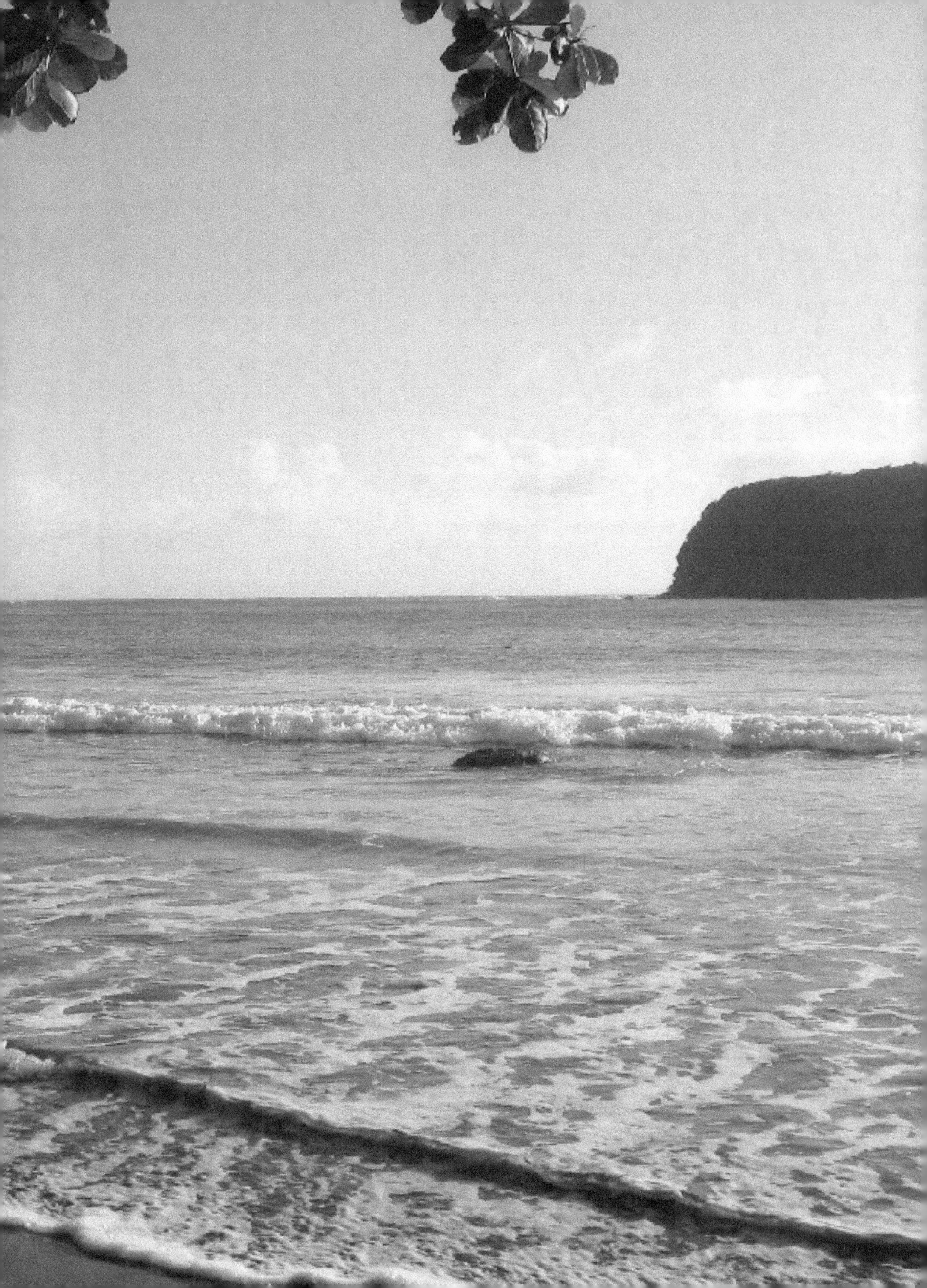

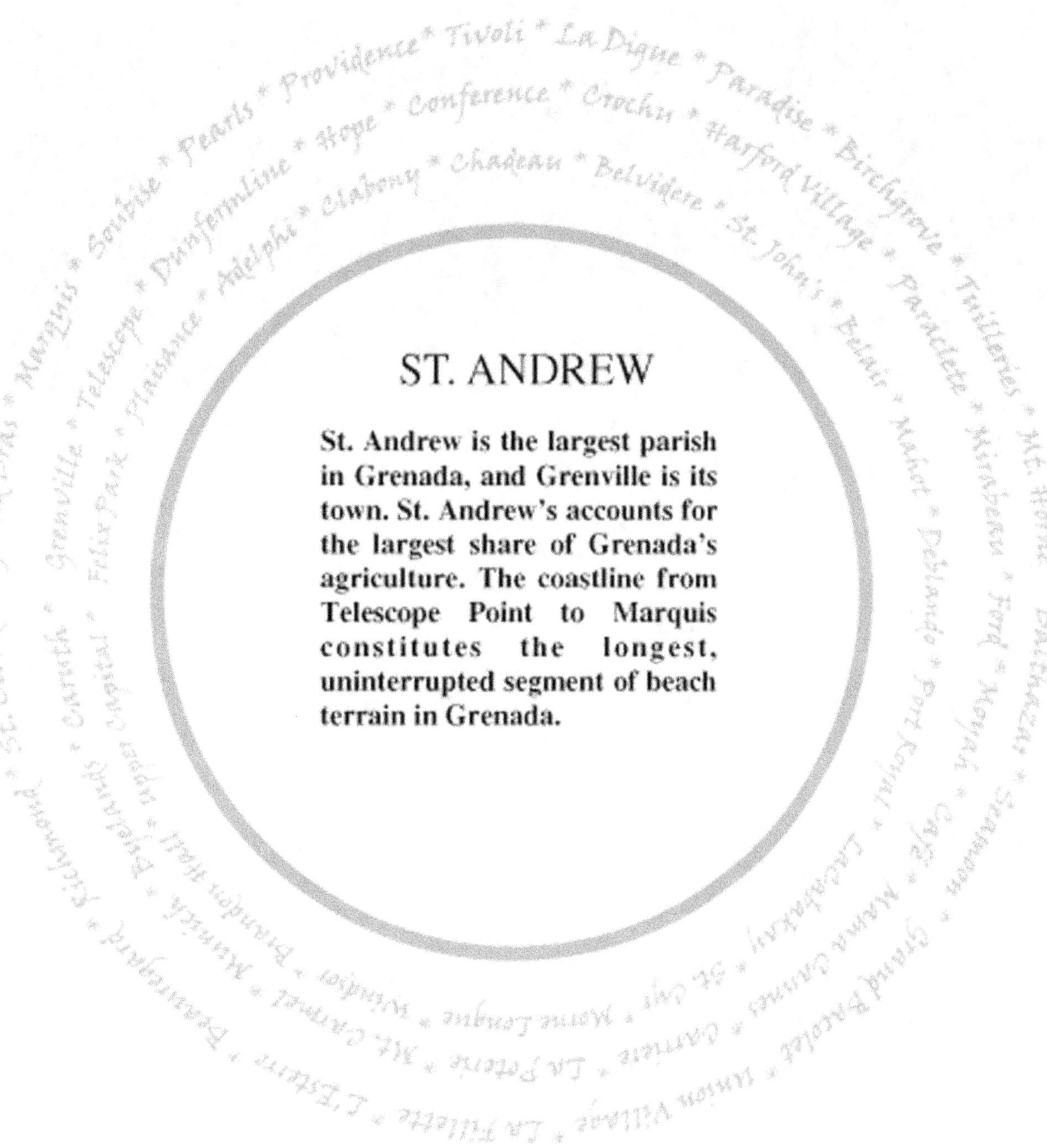

ST. ANDREW

St. Andrew is the largest parish in Grenada, and Grenville is its town. St. Andrew's accounts for the largest share of Grenada's agriculture. The coastline from Telescope Point to Marquis constitutes the longest, uninterrupted segment of beach terrain in Grenada.

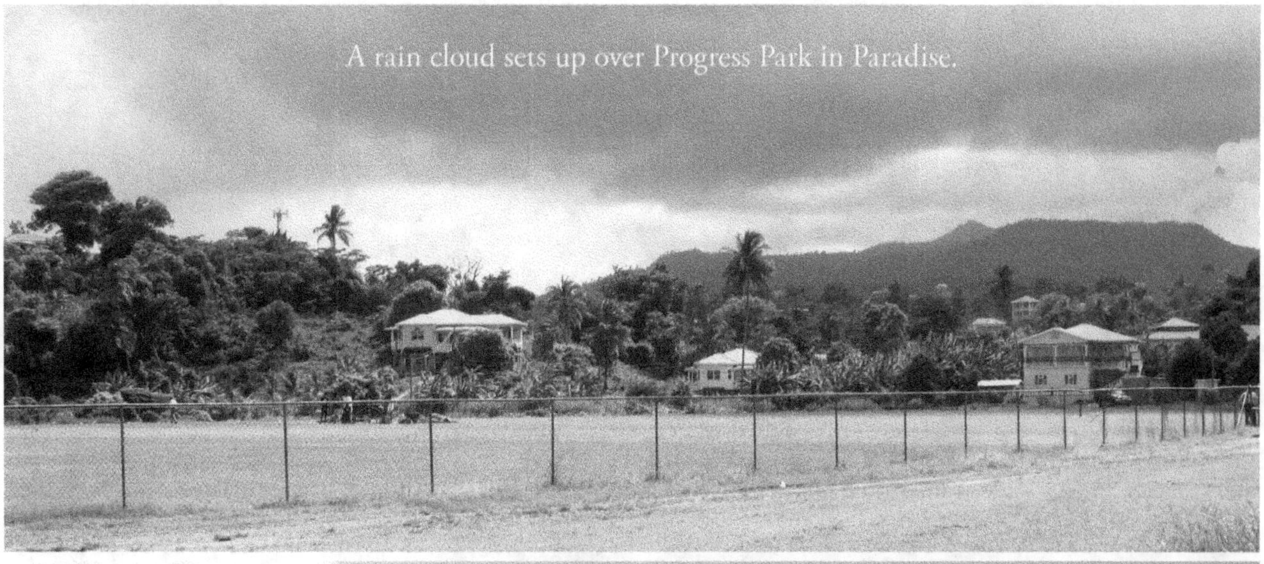

A rain cloud sets up over Progress Park in Paradise.

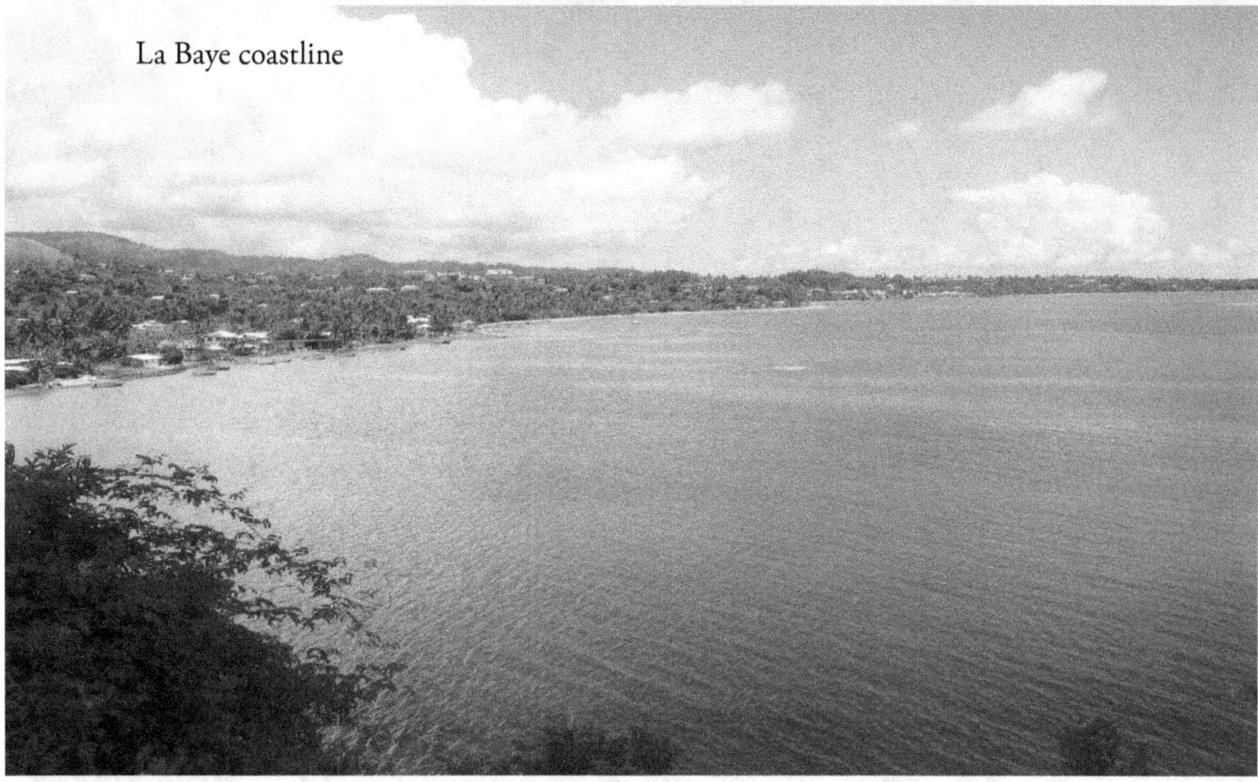

La Baye coastline

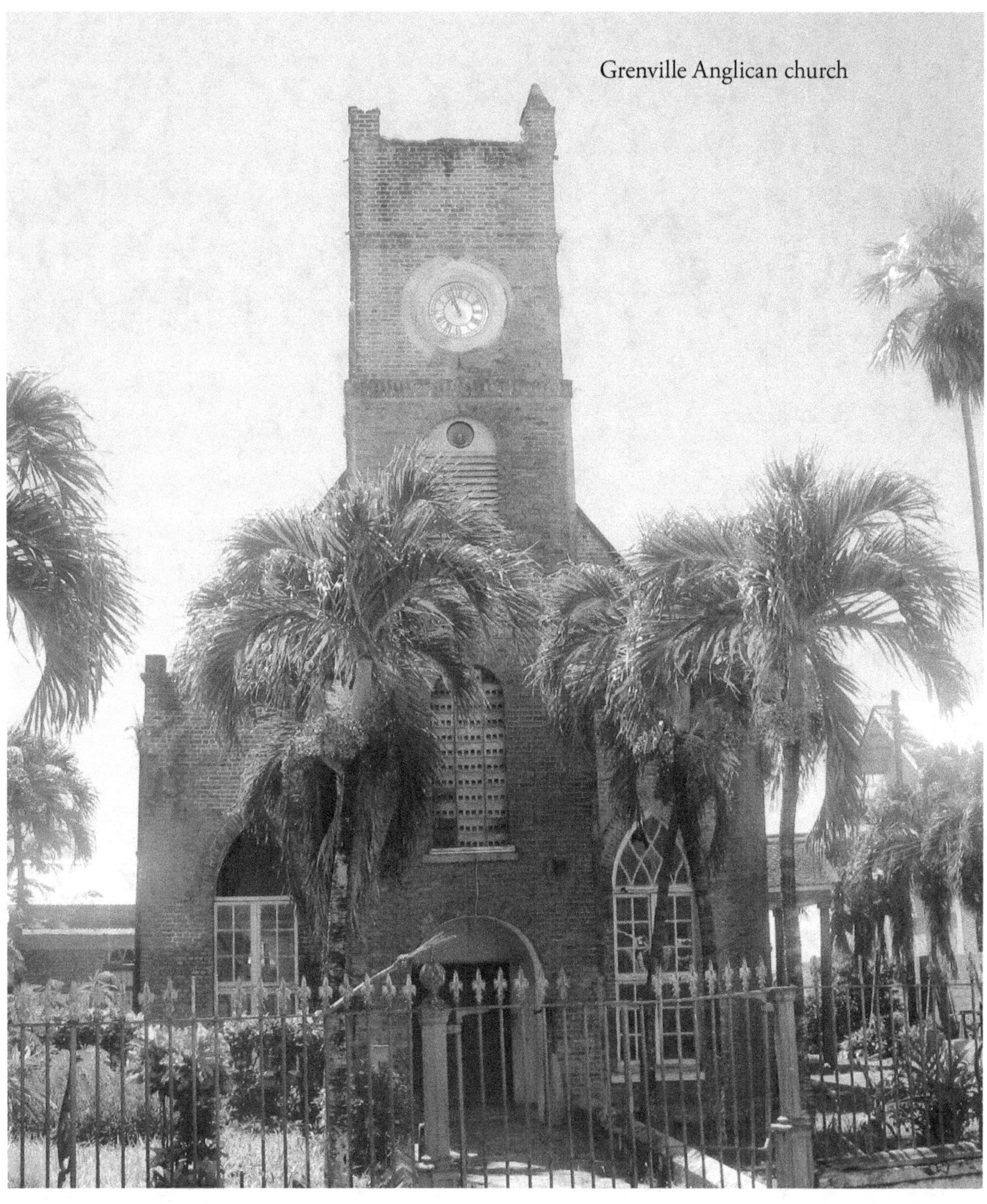

Grenville Anglican church

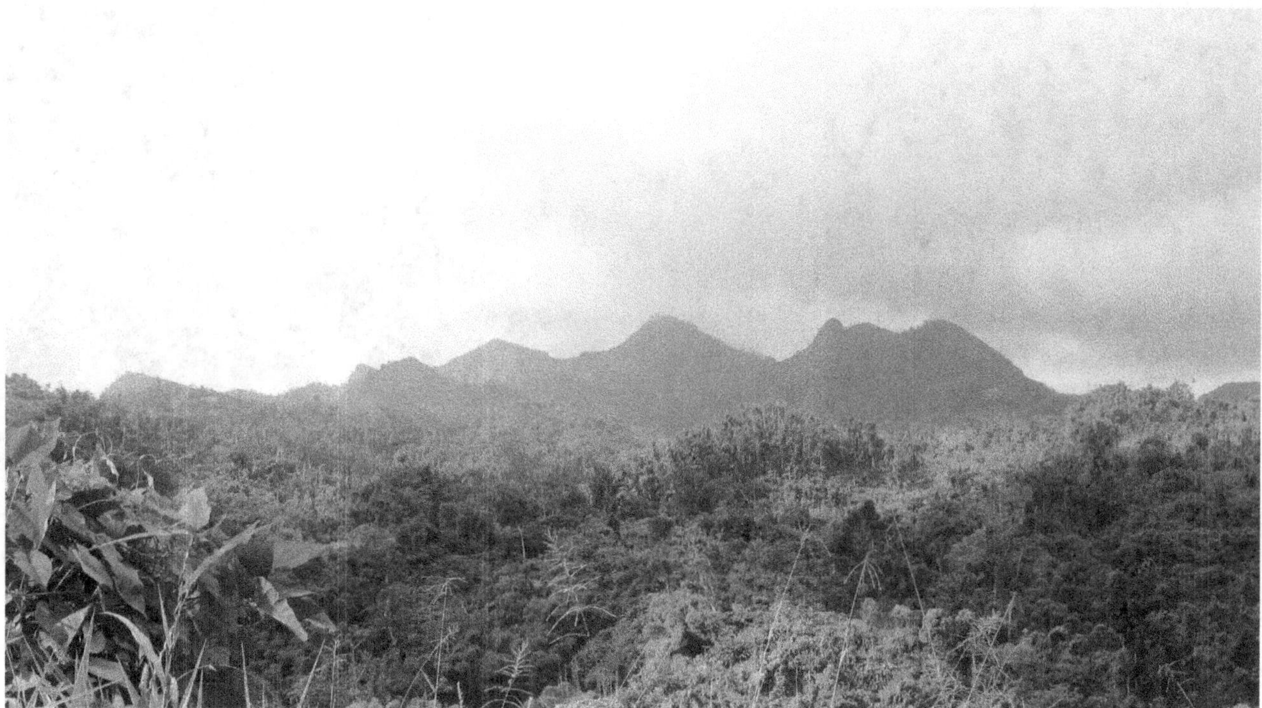

Above: The mountain range shows Grenada's highest mountains, including Mt. St. Catherine, Grenada's tallest mountain (2756 feet above sea level). Below: An antiquated bridge over a river near Belvidere, along the east-west roadway

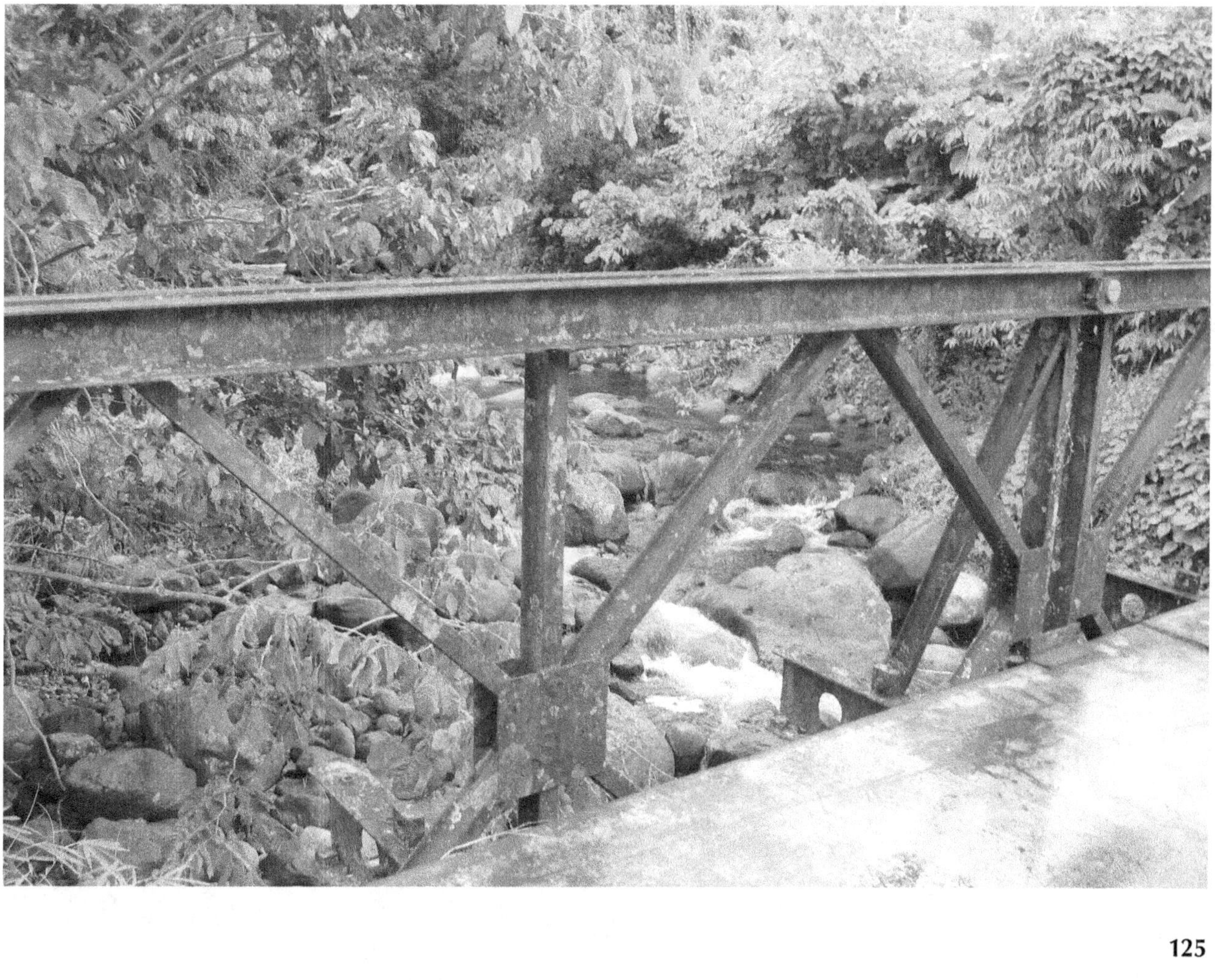

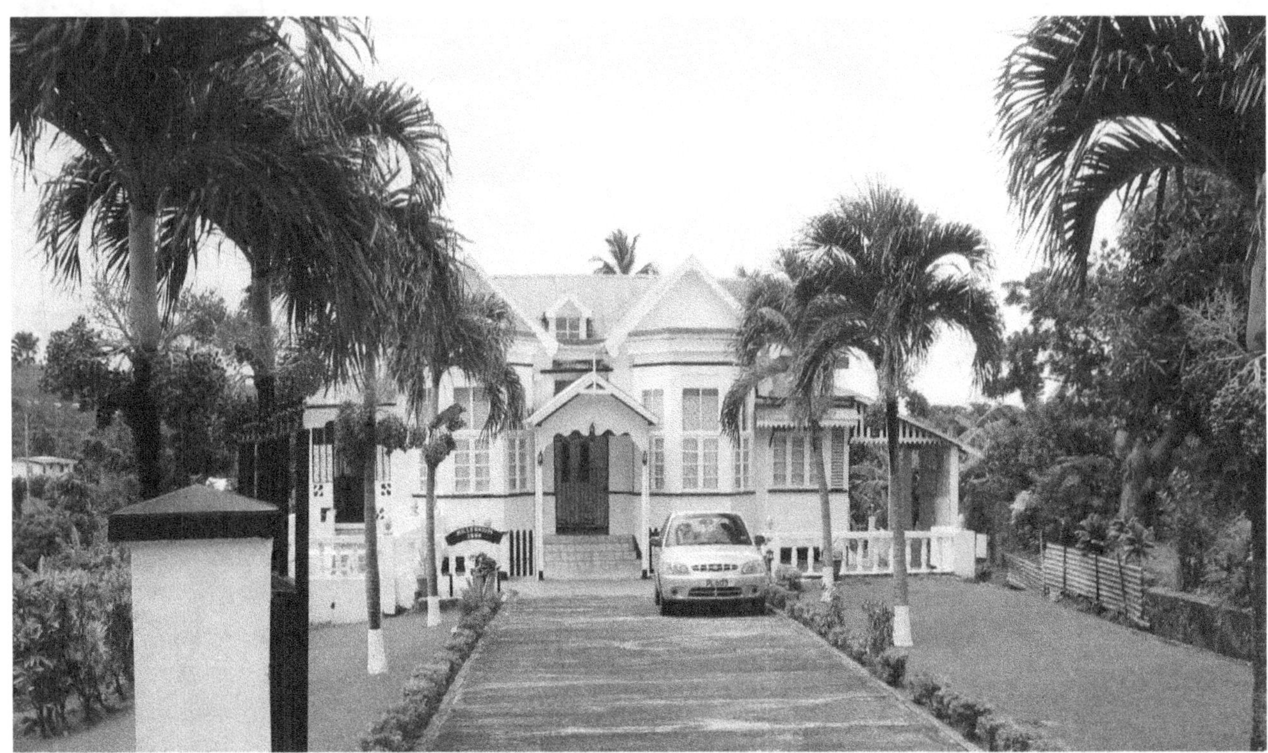

Above: Palms line the driveway to this Grand Bras residence. Below: Fishing boats near the jetty at Grenville

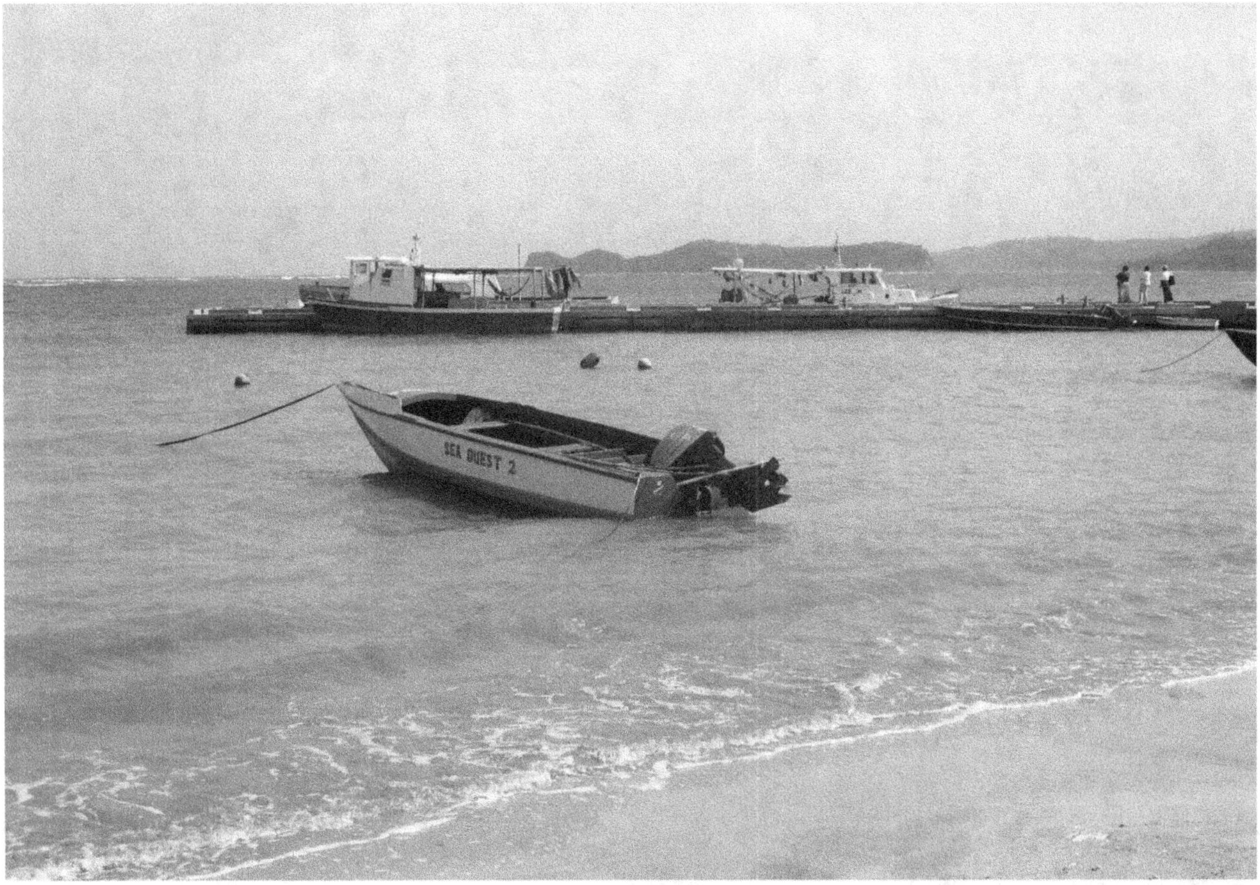

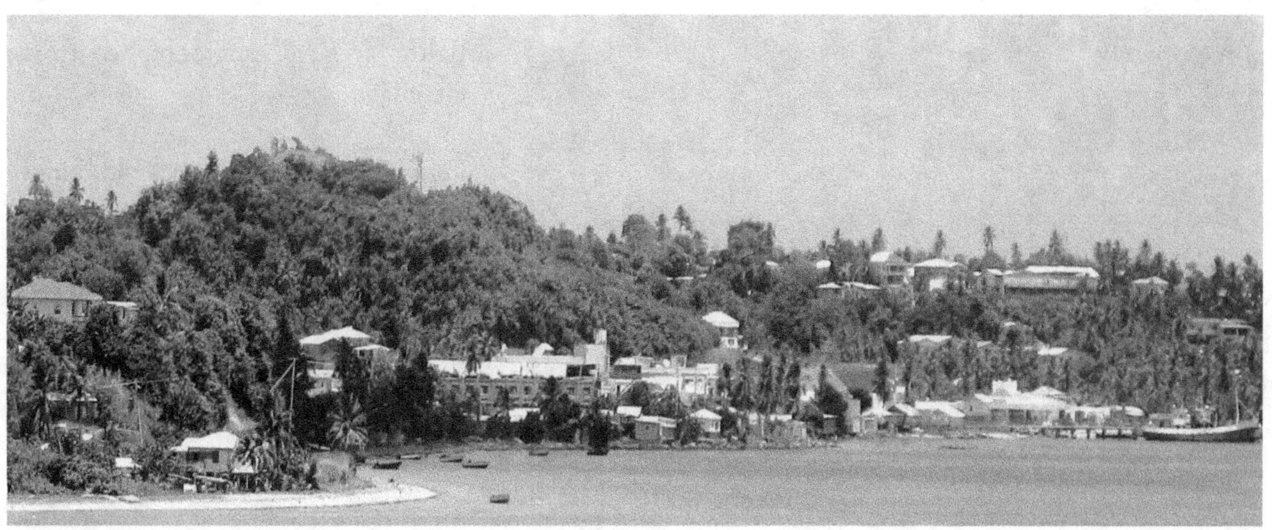

Grenville, called La Baye because of its location on Grenada's longest bay, is an important fishing and commercial town.

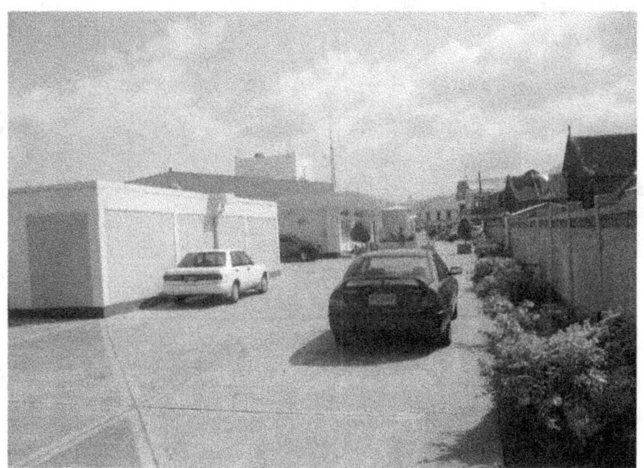

Grenville Fish Market area

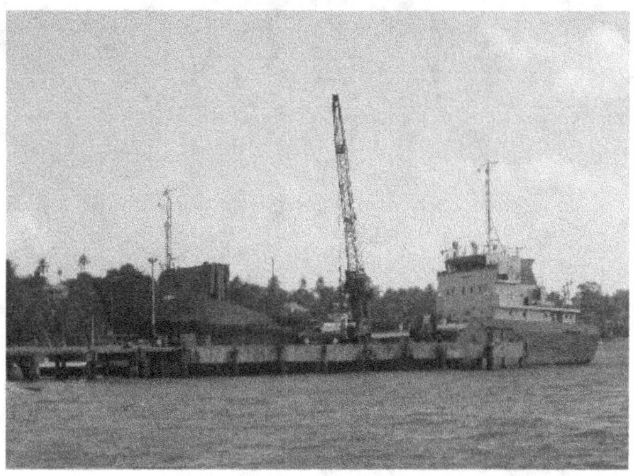

A cargo ship anchored at the Grenville jetty

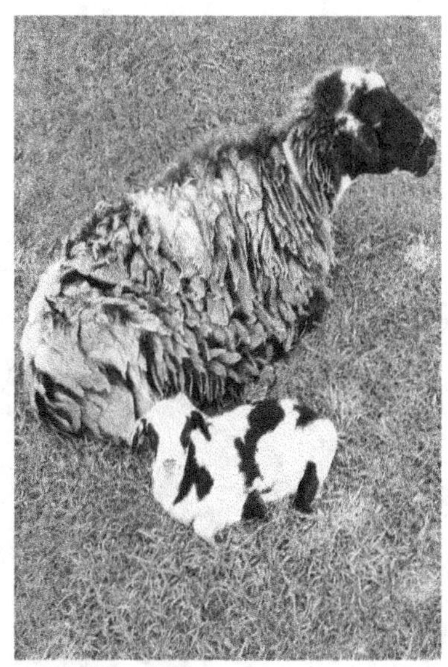

Ewe and lamb at La Poterie

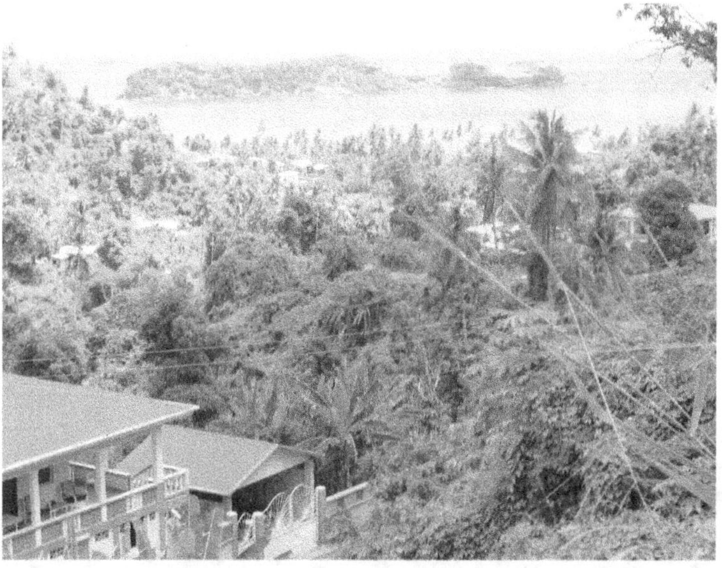

From Mt. Carmel, looking towards La Baye Rock

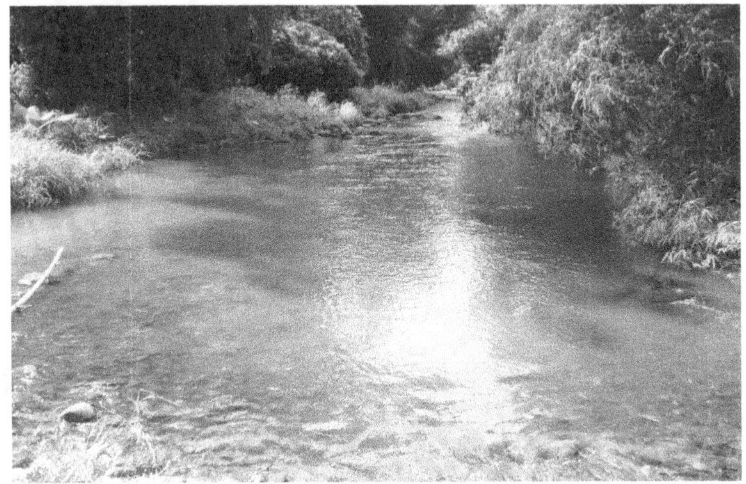

Balthazar River photographed from Conblaiere Bridge.

Left: The river approaches the bridge after passing through the mild rapids, where visitors enjoy white water tubing.

Below: The same river flows away from the bridge towards Grand Bras, Ford, and Paradise.

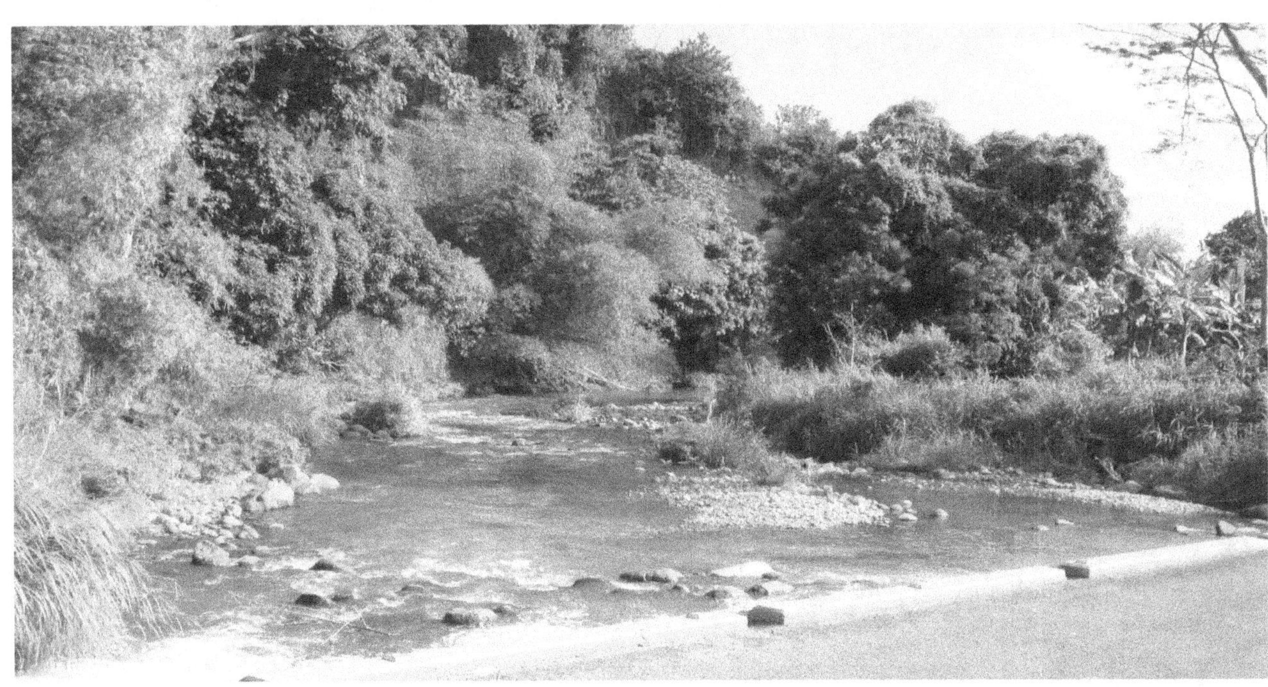

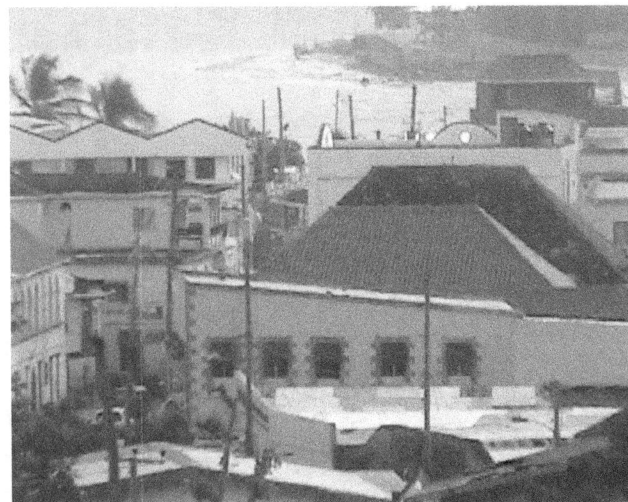

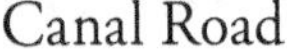

Canal Road

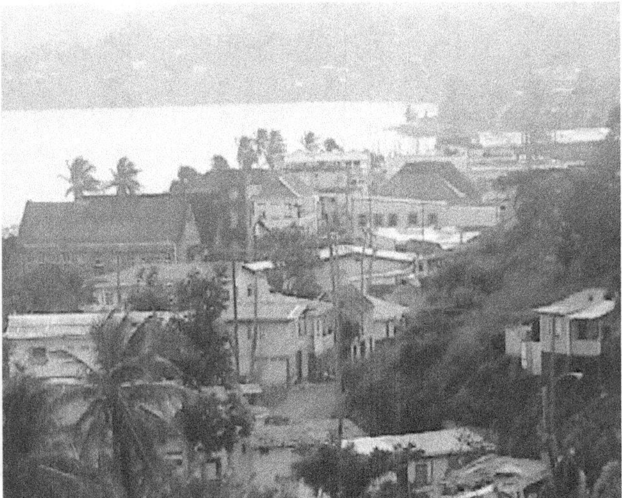

Downtown Grenville

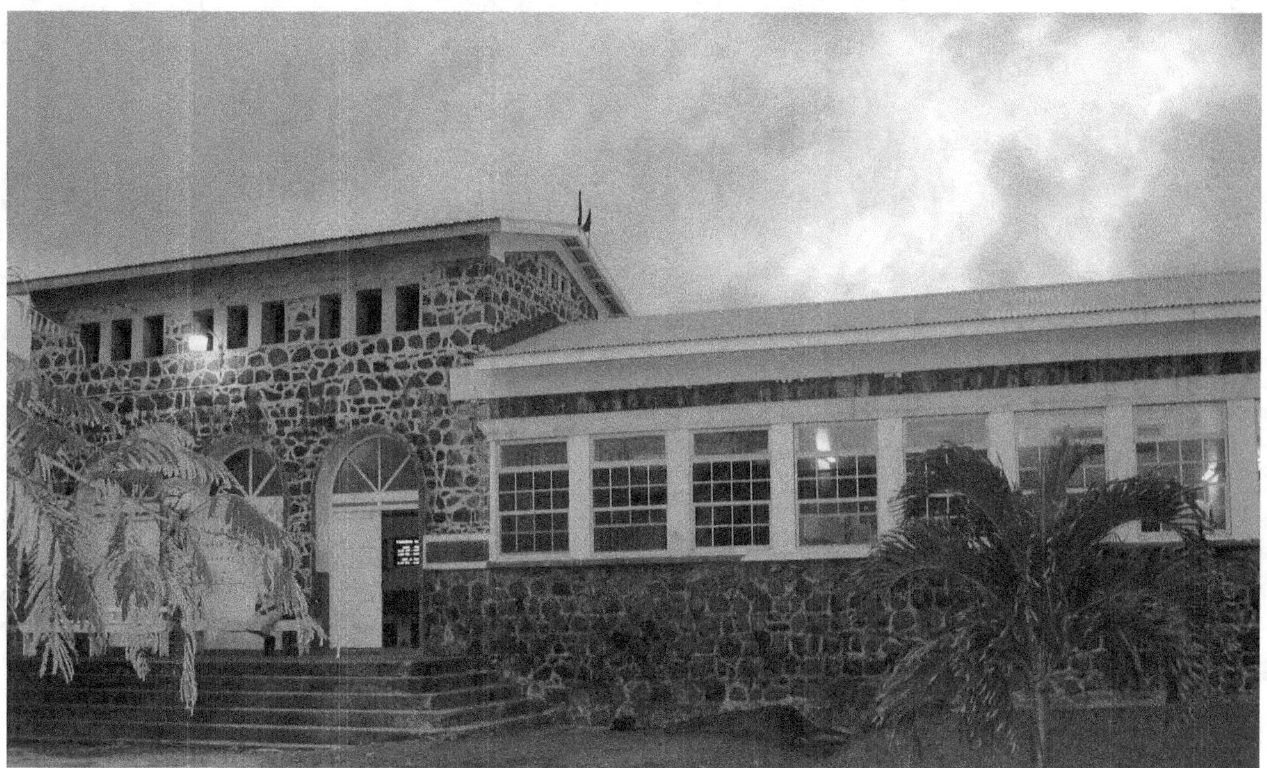

Princess Alice Hospital: Princess Alice opened the hospital while visiting Grenada on March 4th, 1950. Princess Alice (1901-2004) was the Aunt of Queen Elizabeth II.

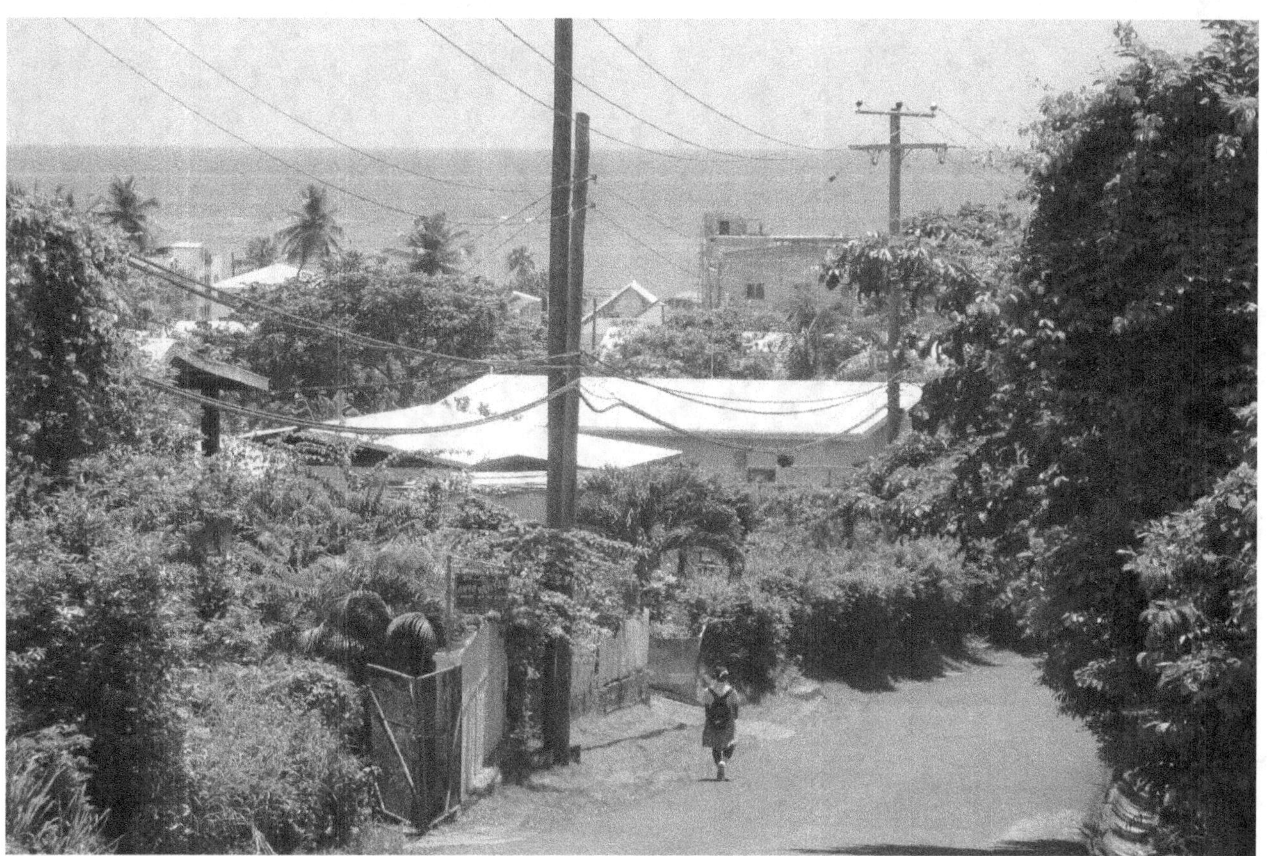

From Gladstone Road, Grenville, looking out towards the Atlantic

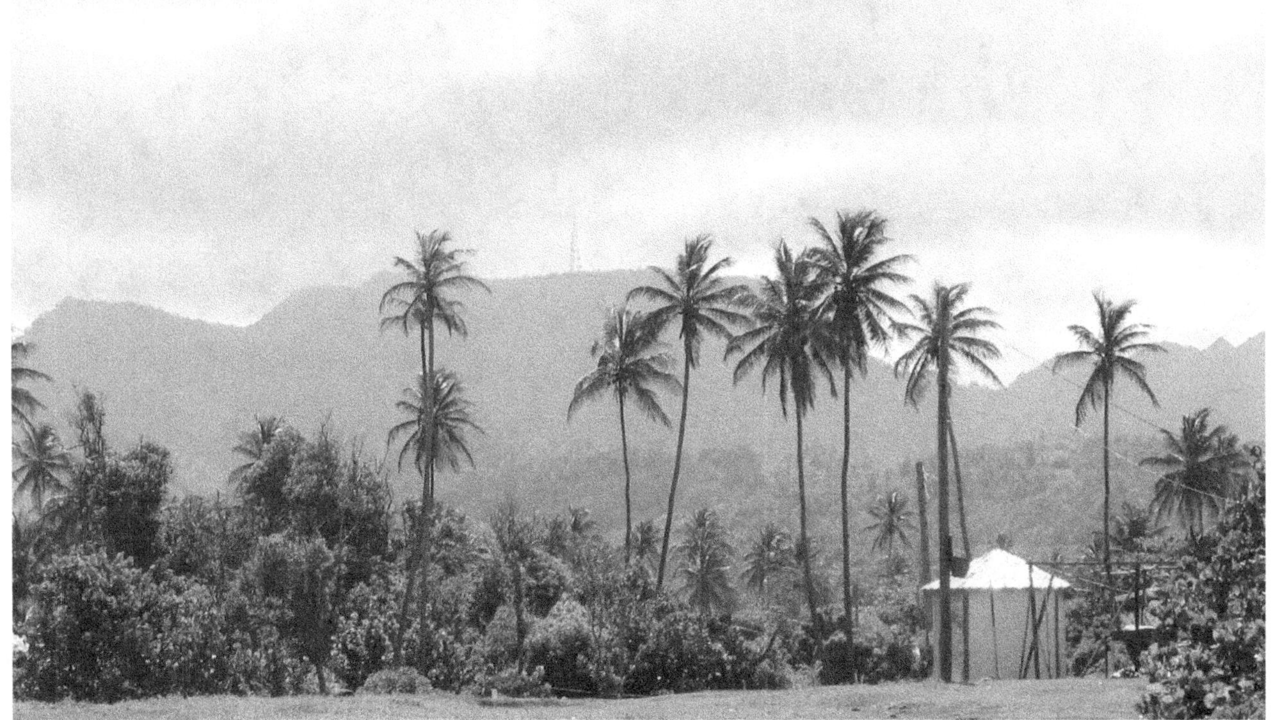

From La Poterie, we are looking towards the communications tower at Kooblal Mountain. There are heroic stories of the local truck drivers who drove up the steep hill carrying the tower to that site.

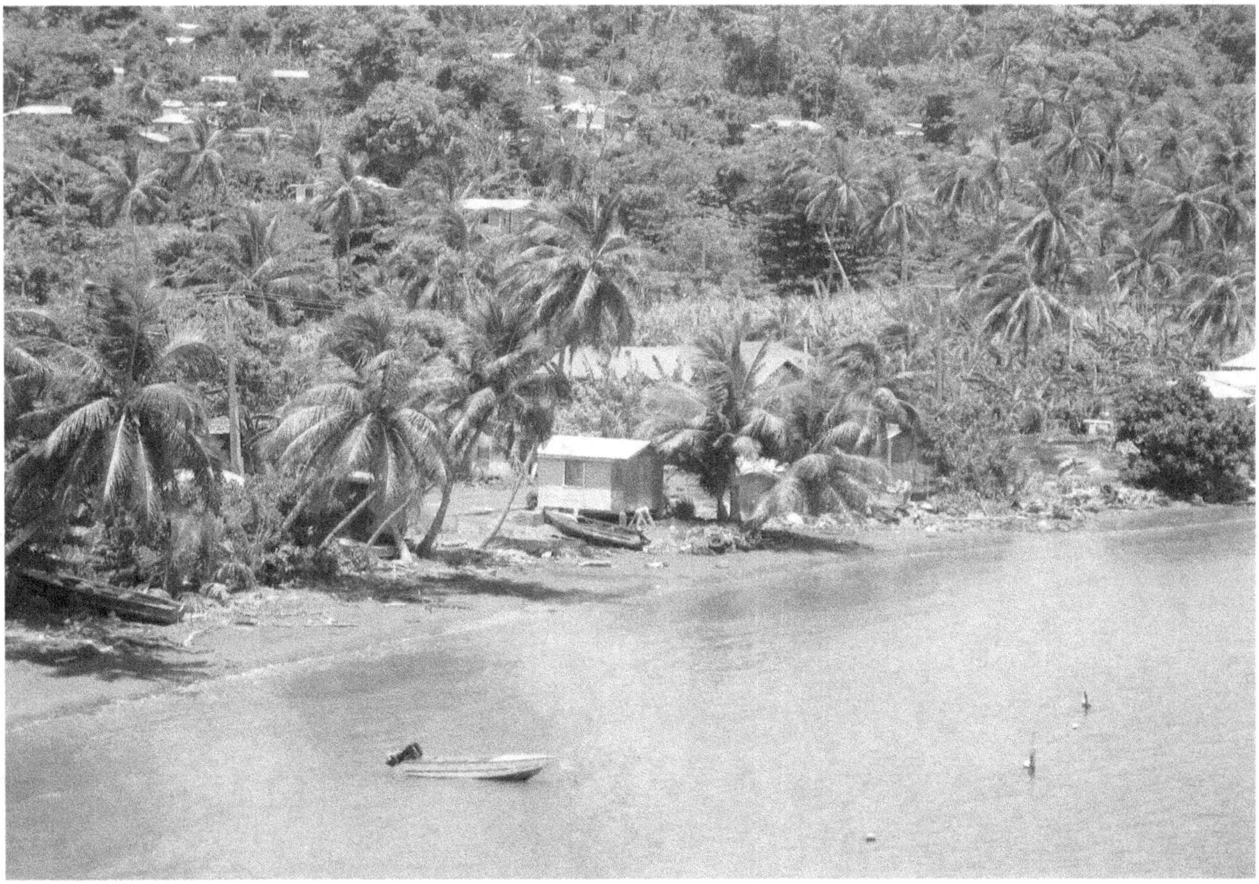

Marquis is a small fishing village in St. Andrew's parish.

GRAND ETANG LAKE

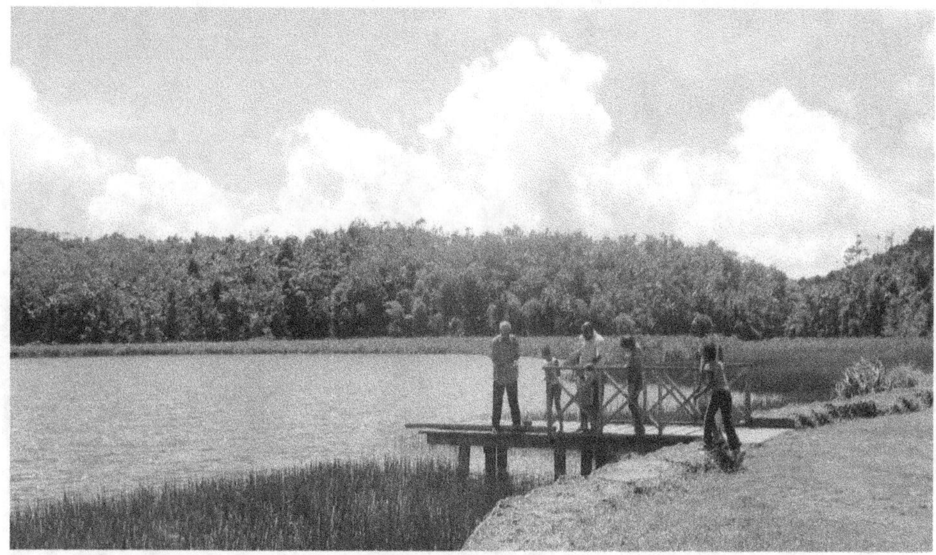

Grand Etang Lake is in a crater that was formed by a now extinct subterranean volcano. Together with its surrounding forest habitat and hiking trails, the lake environment provides an engaging attraction for eco-tourists.

Above and below: Visitors curiously examine the waterfront.

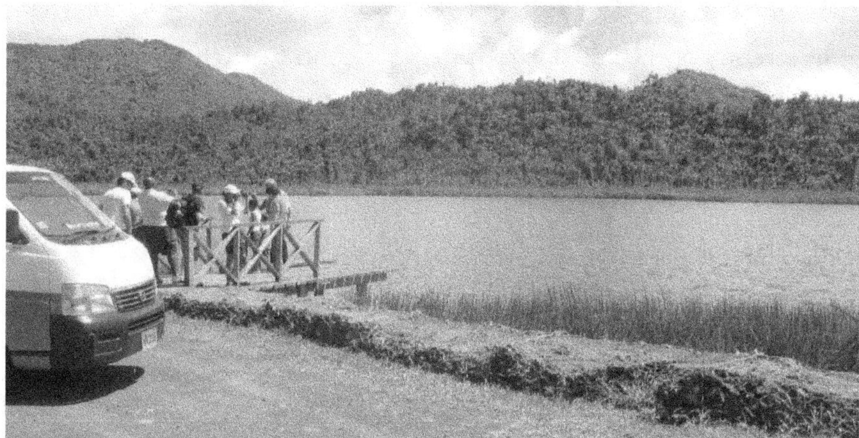

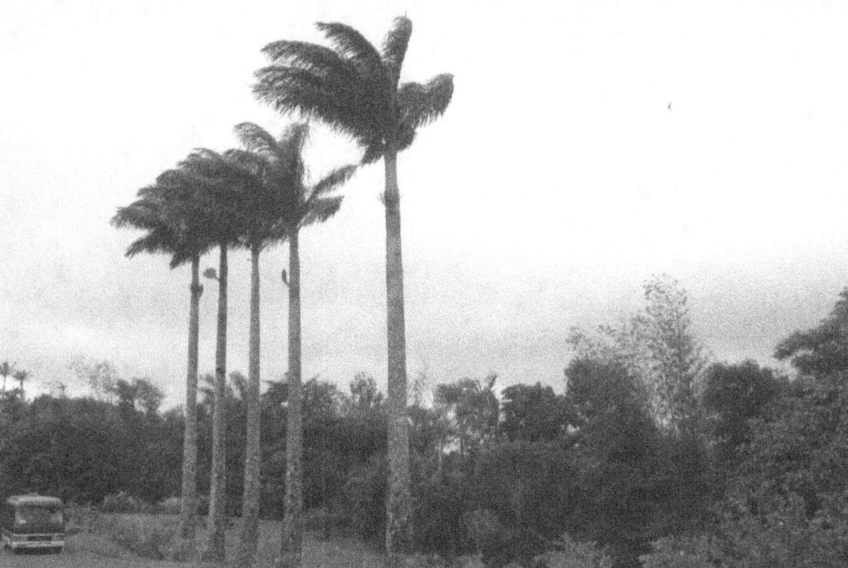

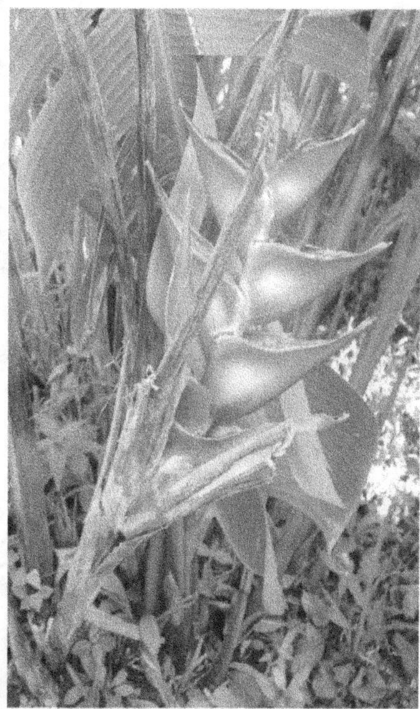

A Heliconia flower plant near the Grand Etang lakeside

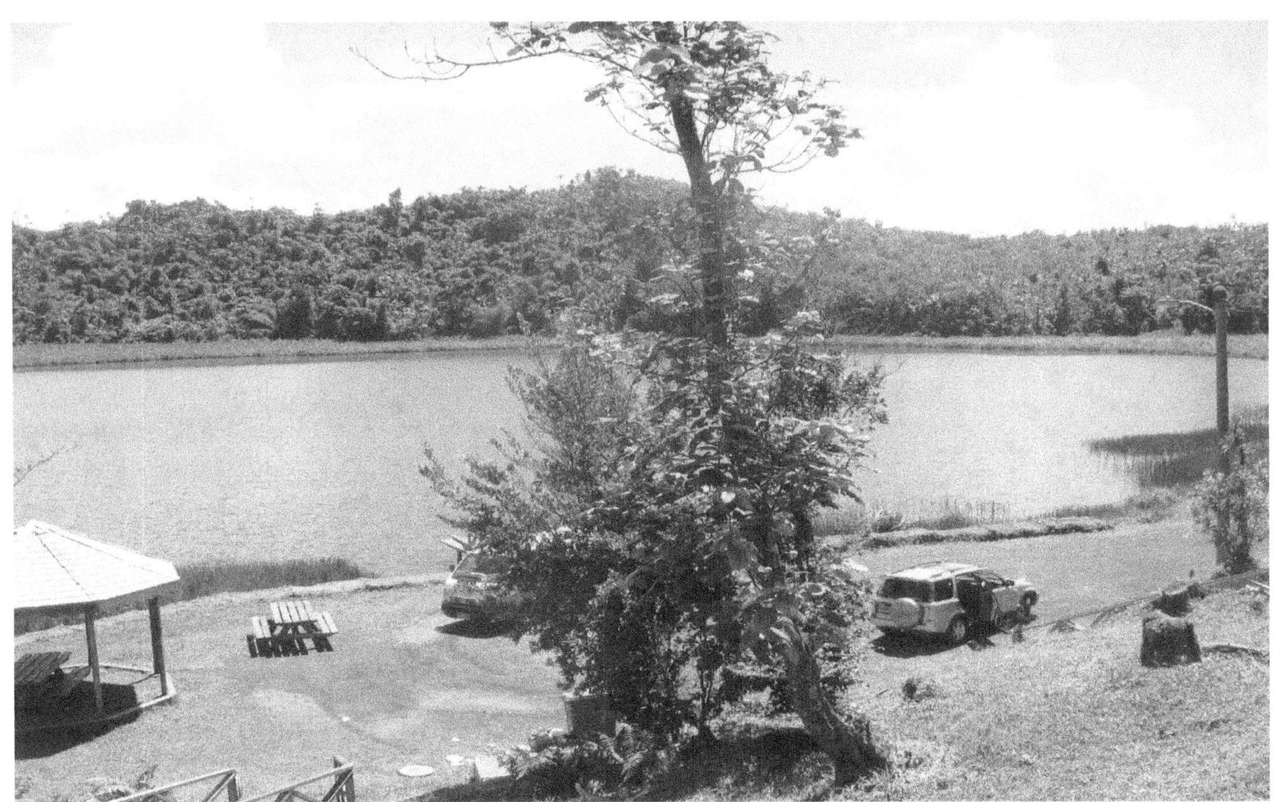

Above and Below: The serenity of the lakeside today is a far contrast to the past volcanic explosions that produced it.

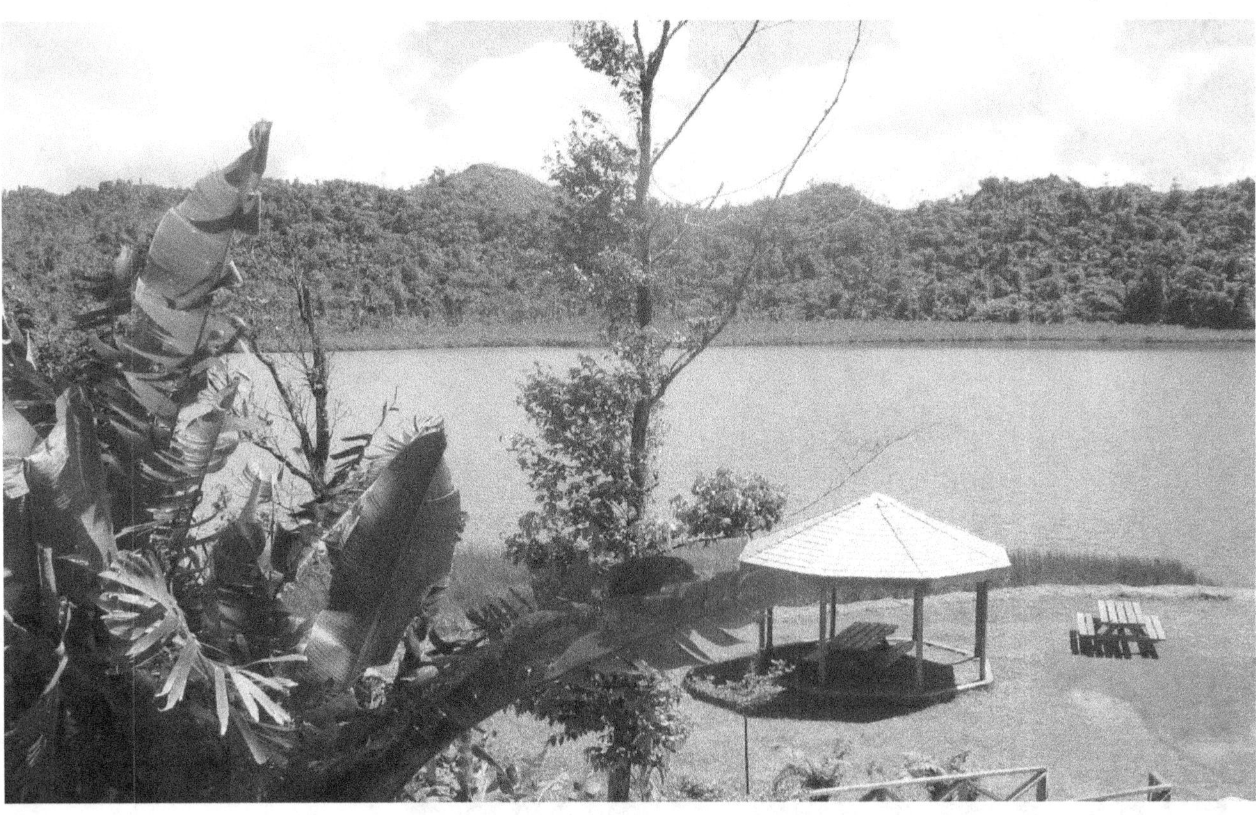

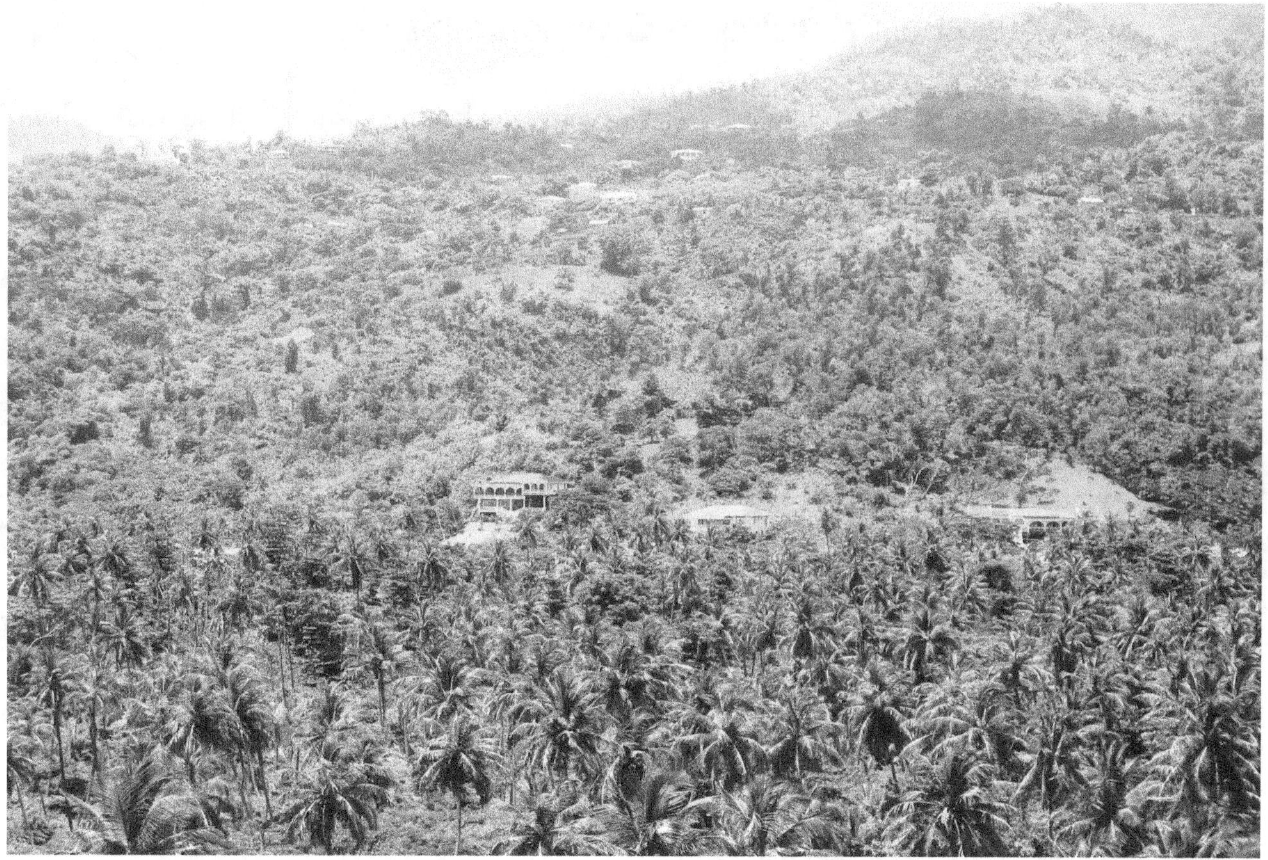

Part of the old Hope Estate has a large concentration of coconut trees that once supplied the Estate in producing oil, soap, and other coconut by-products.

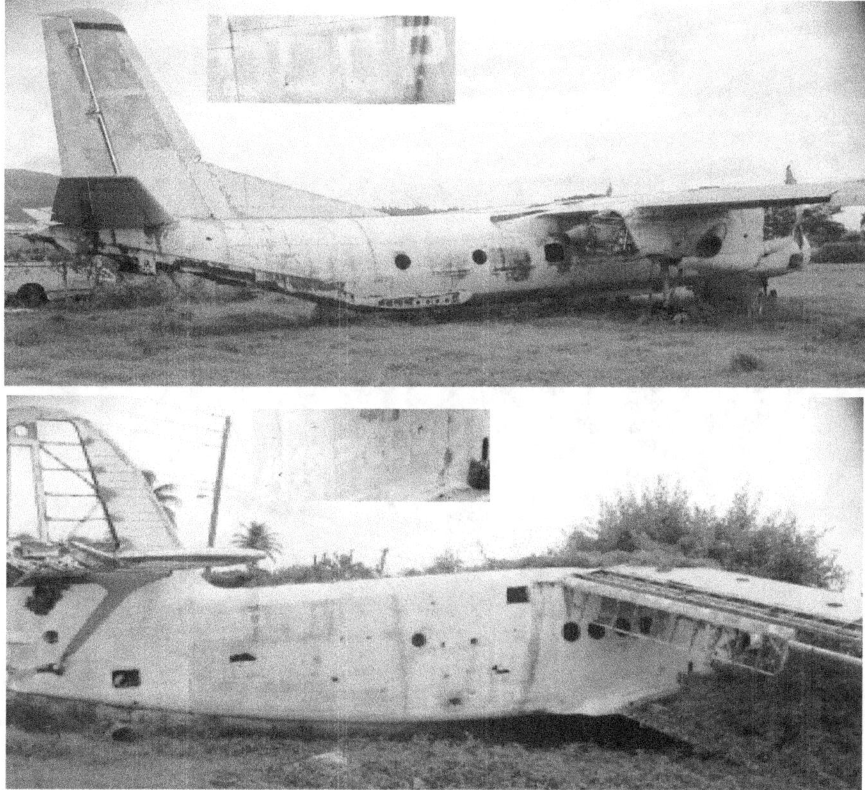

These are fuselages of old Soviet-era transport planes. Foreign forces abandoned them at Pearls Airport, following the U.S. invasion of Grenada in 1983.

Arguably, Grenada was the last place where the cold war became 'hot,' with Cuban and Grenadian forces fiercely responding to the U.S. military invasion. The remains of the Soviet planes are valuable relics of the cold war, defining Grenada's historical role as host. To that end, one hopes that efforts will commence in preserving these planes' remains before further deterioration.

Belair's relics of Grenadian history

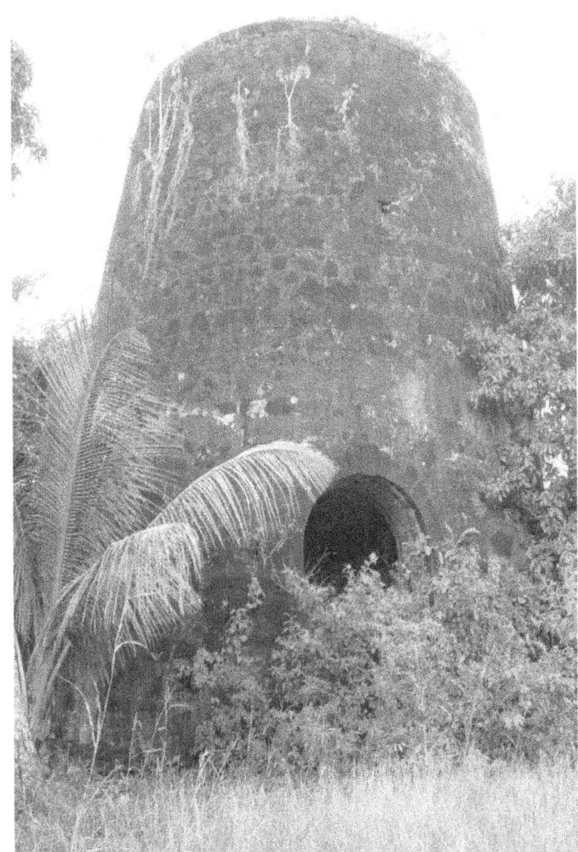

This once wind-powered sugar mill at Belair, where slaves toiled in 1770 (see MDCCLXX on its headstone separately shown below). They built the mill when America was still a colony of England. Dating back to just over 100 years after France first colonized Grenada, this mill is certainly among Grenada's valuable historical landmarks. Because the historic Belair Presbyterian Church (page 185) is directly on the opposite side of the street, this entire Belair location should be of high relevance to Grenada's history, culture, and geo-tourism.

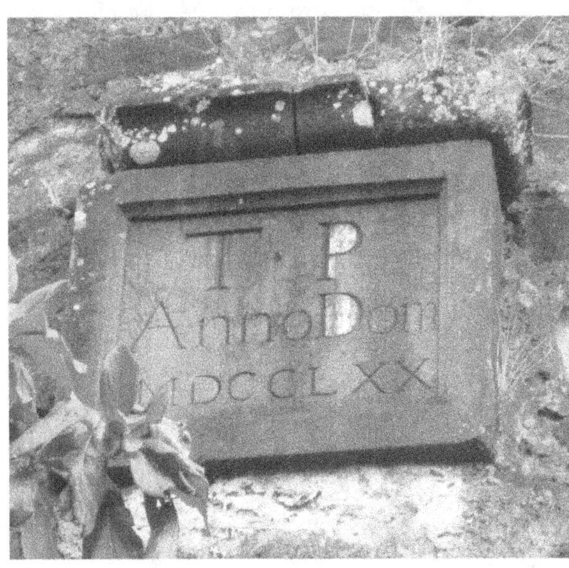

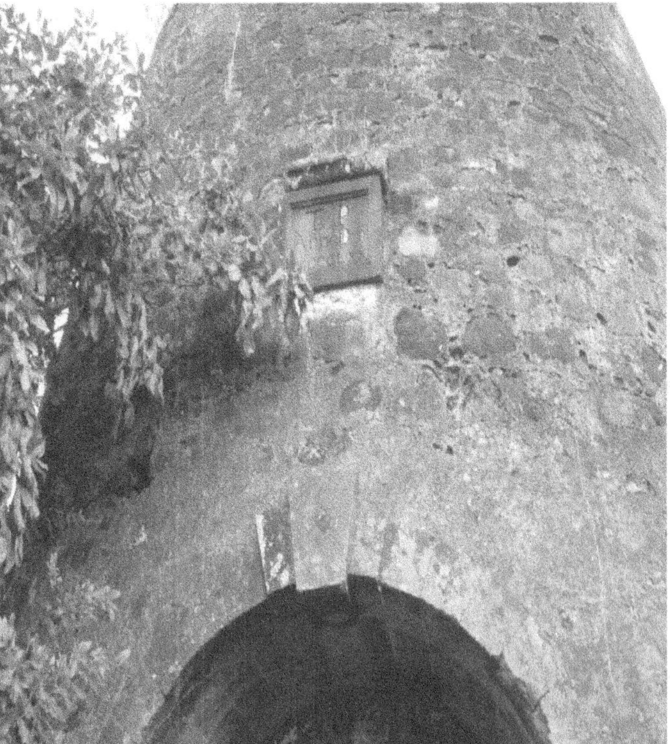

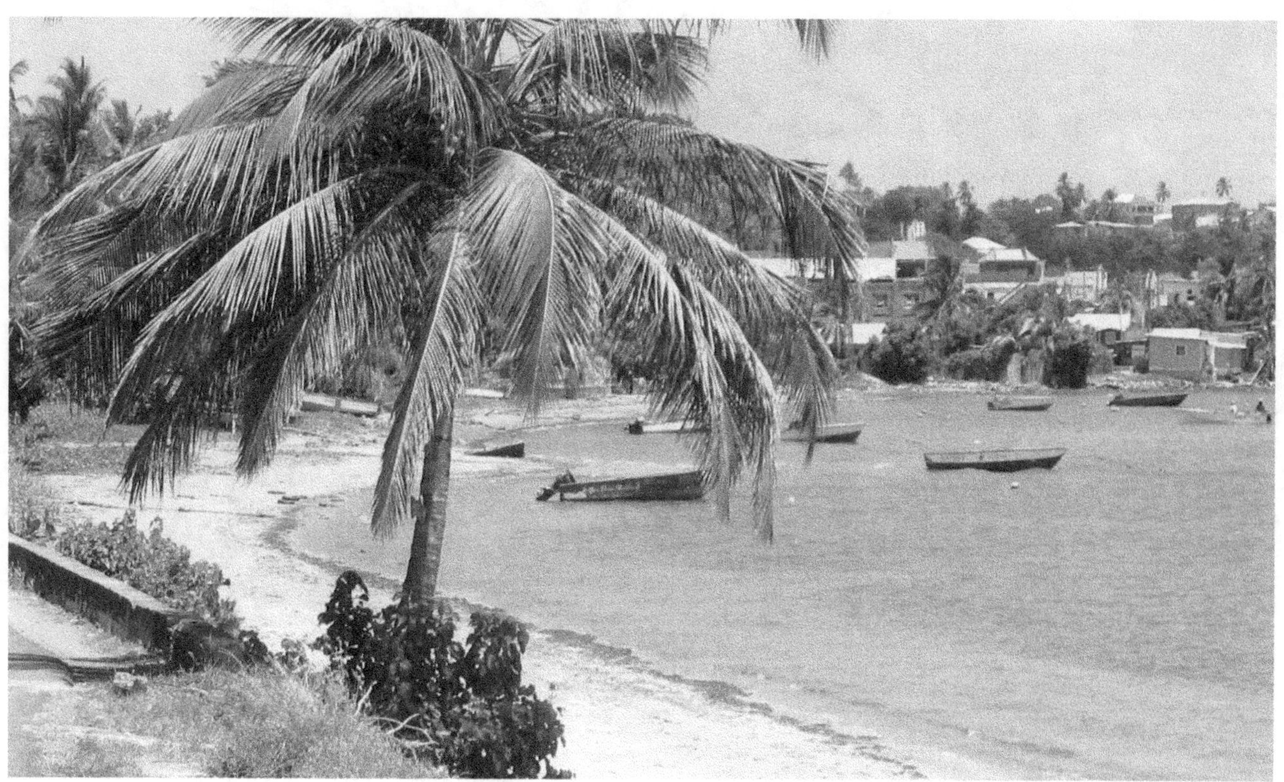

Fishing boats near Grenville

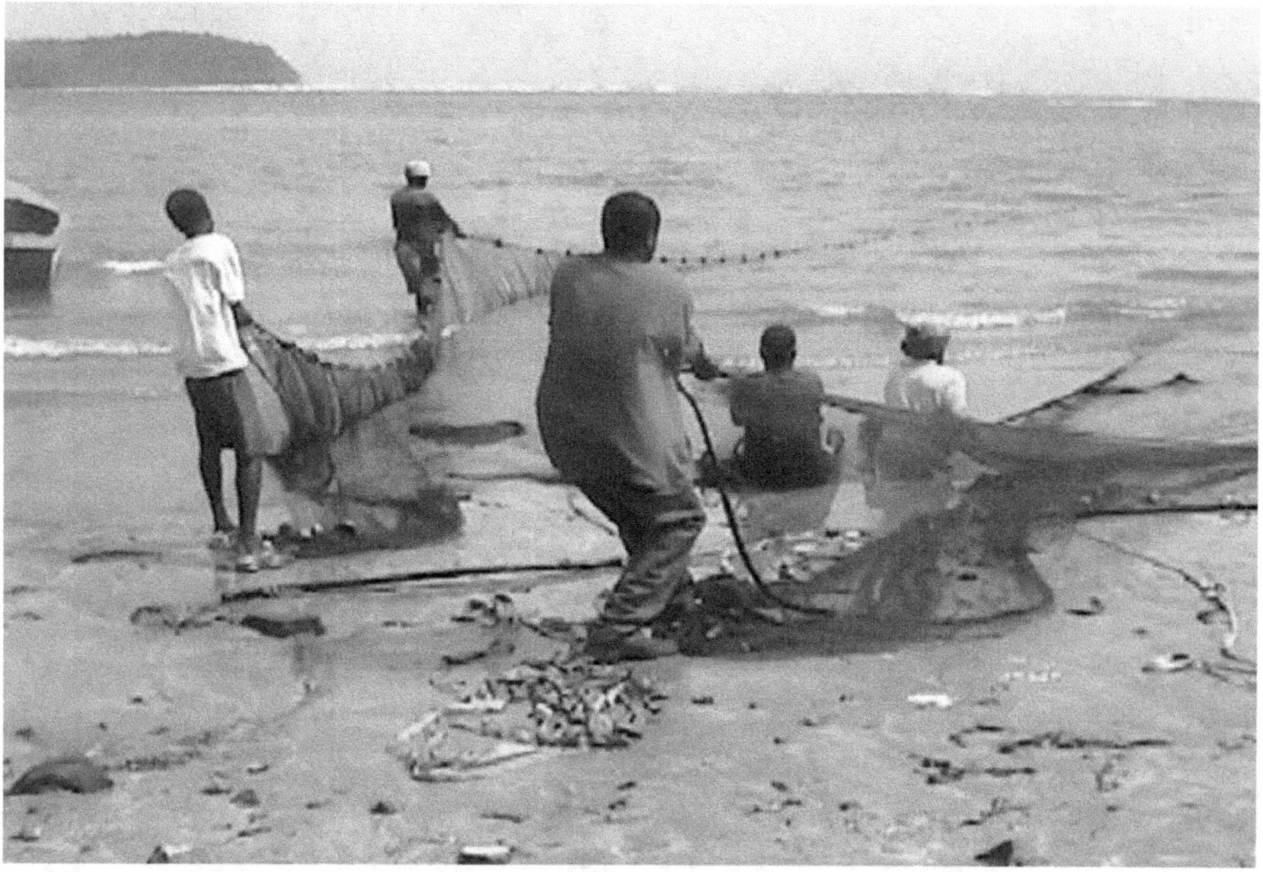

Pulling fishing nets at Grenville

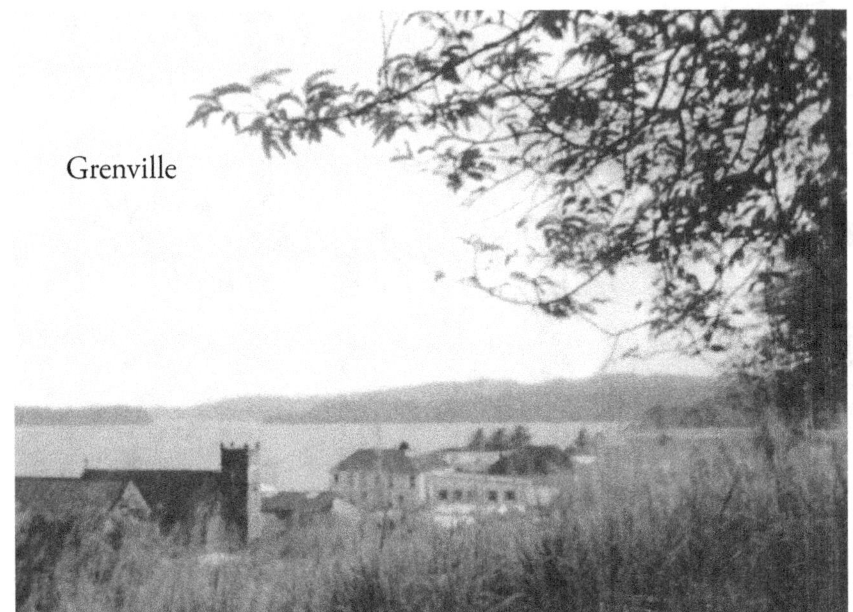

Grenville

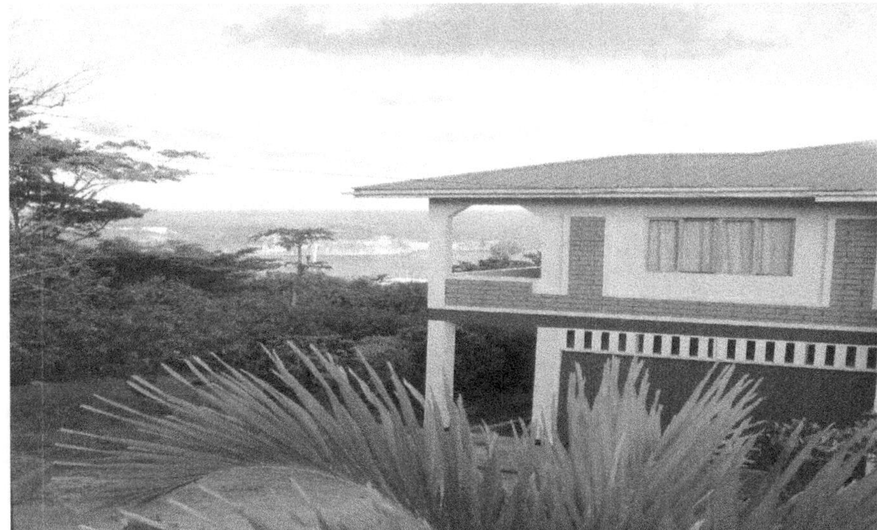

Because of the island's hilly terrain, many homes enjoy a beautiful view.

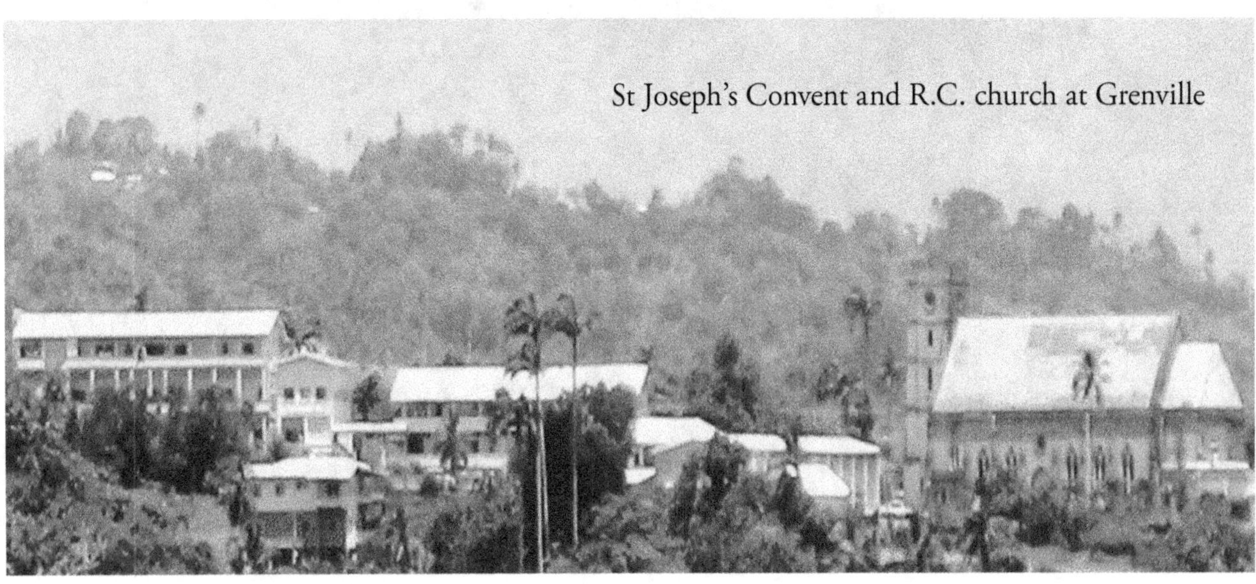

St Joseph's Convent and R.C. church at Grenville

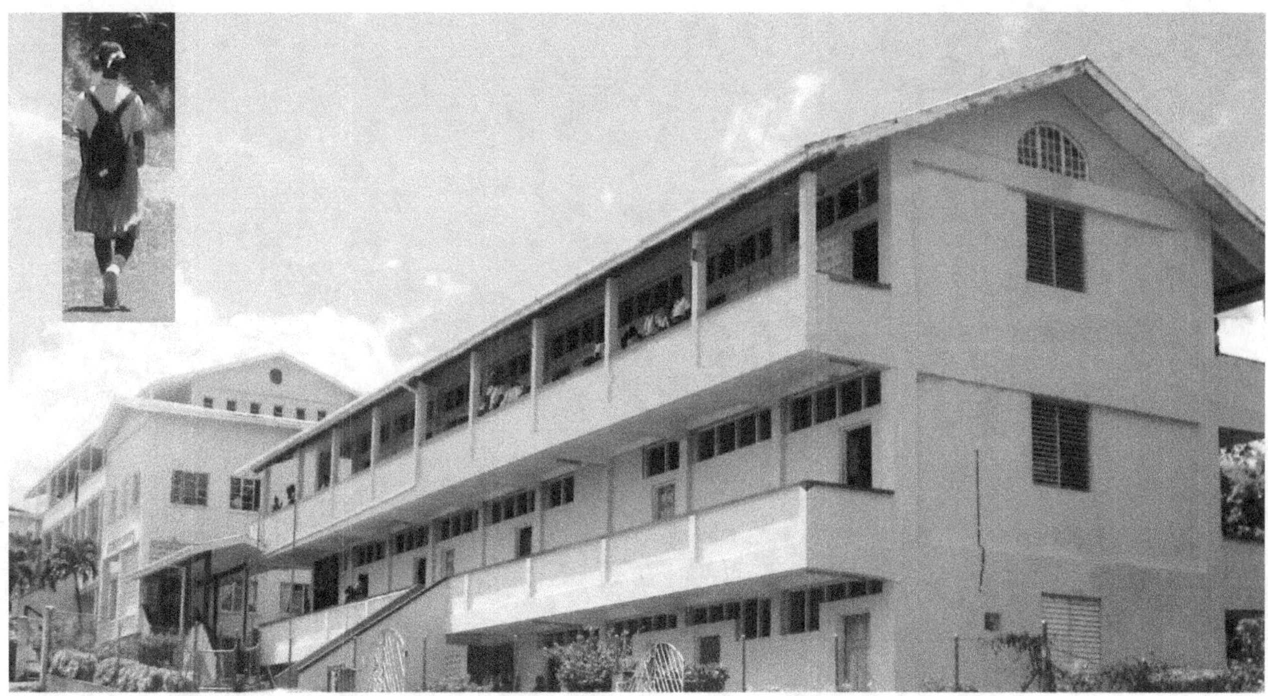

St. Joseph's Convent, Grenville   Inset: Convent student

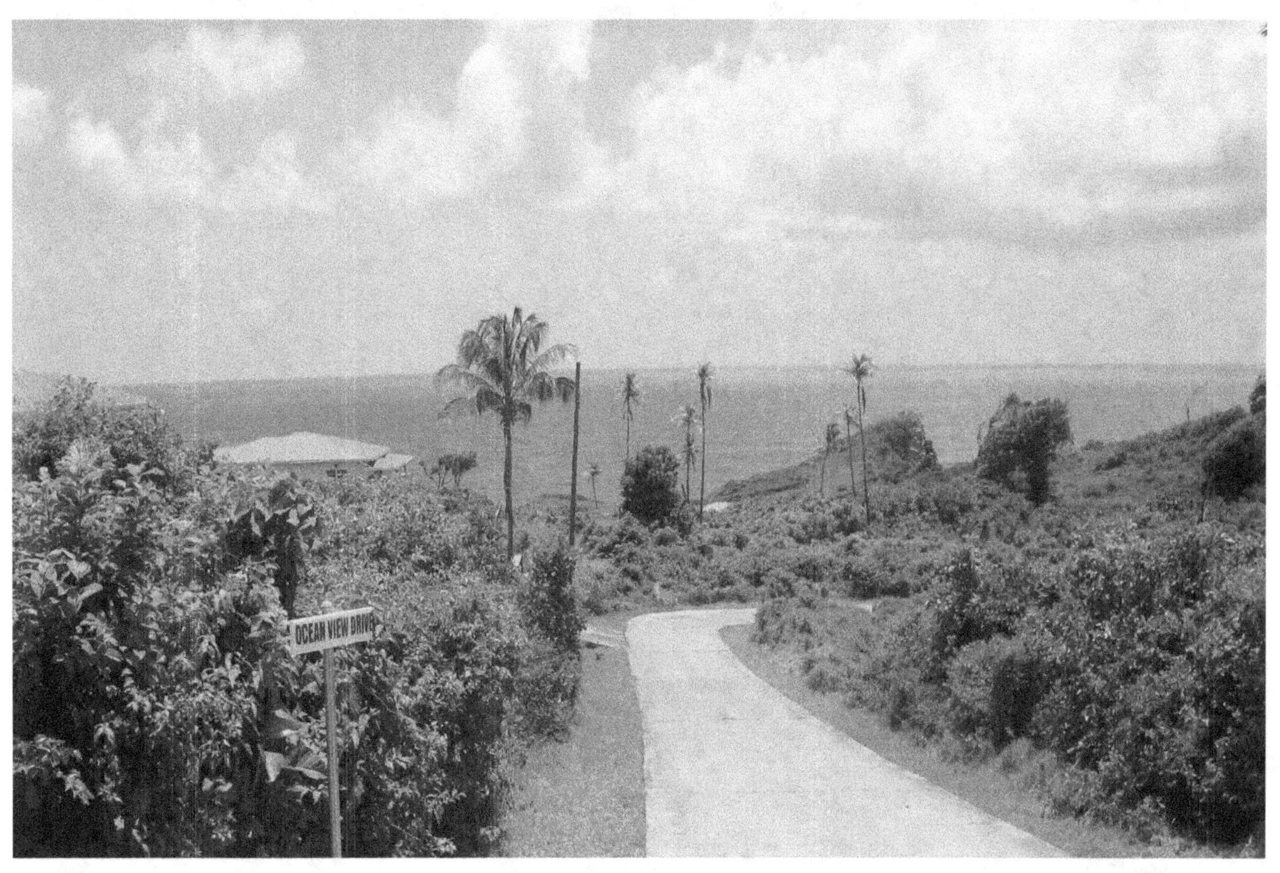

Ocean View Drive, Hope

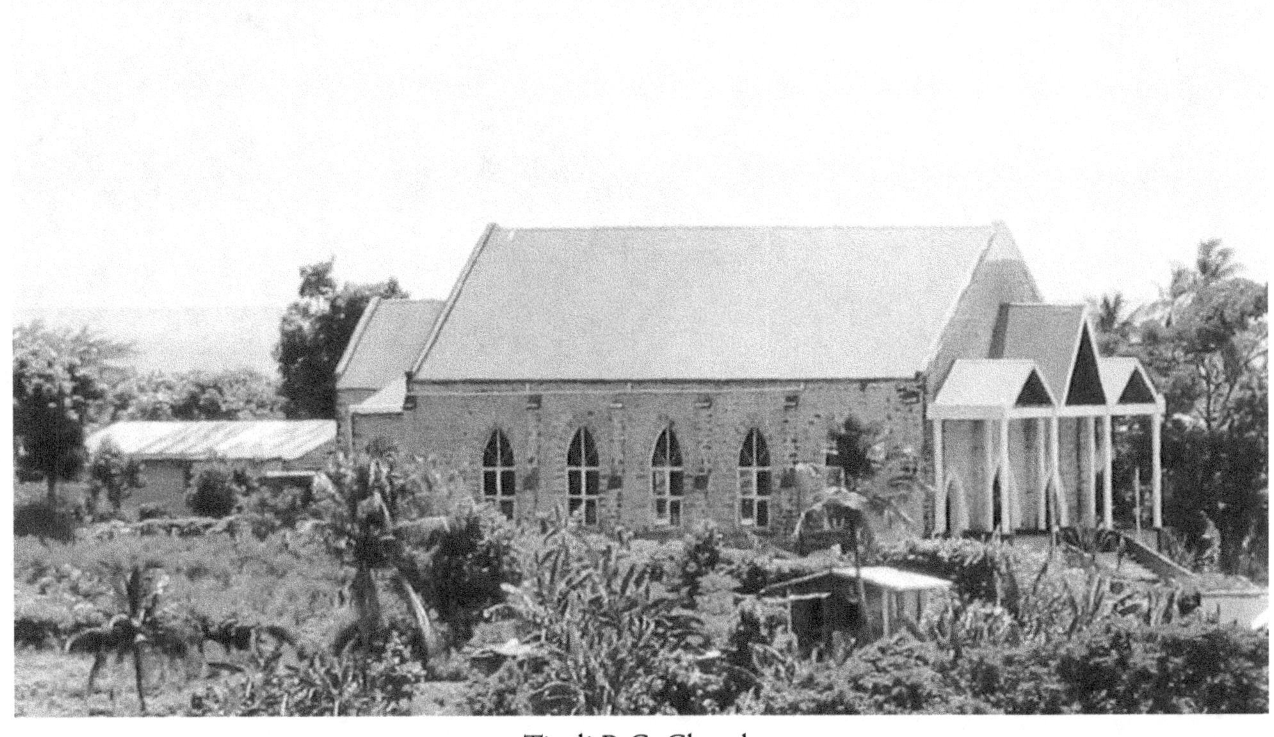

Tivoli R.C. Church

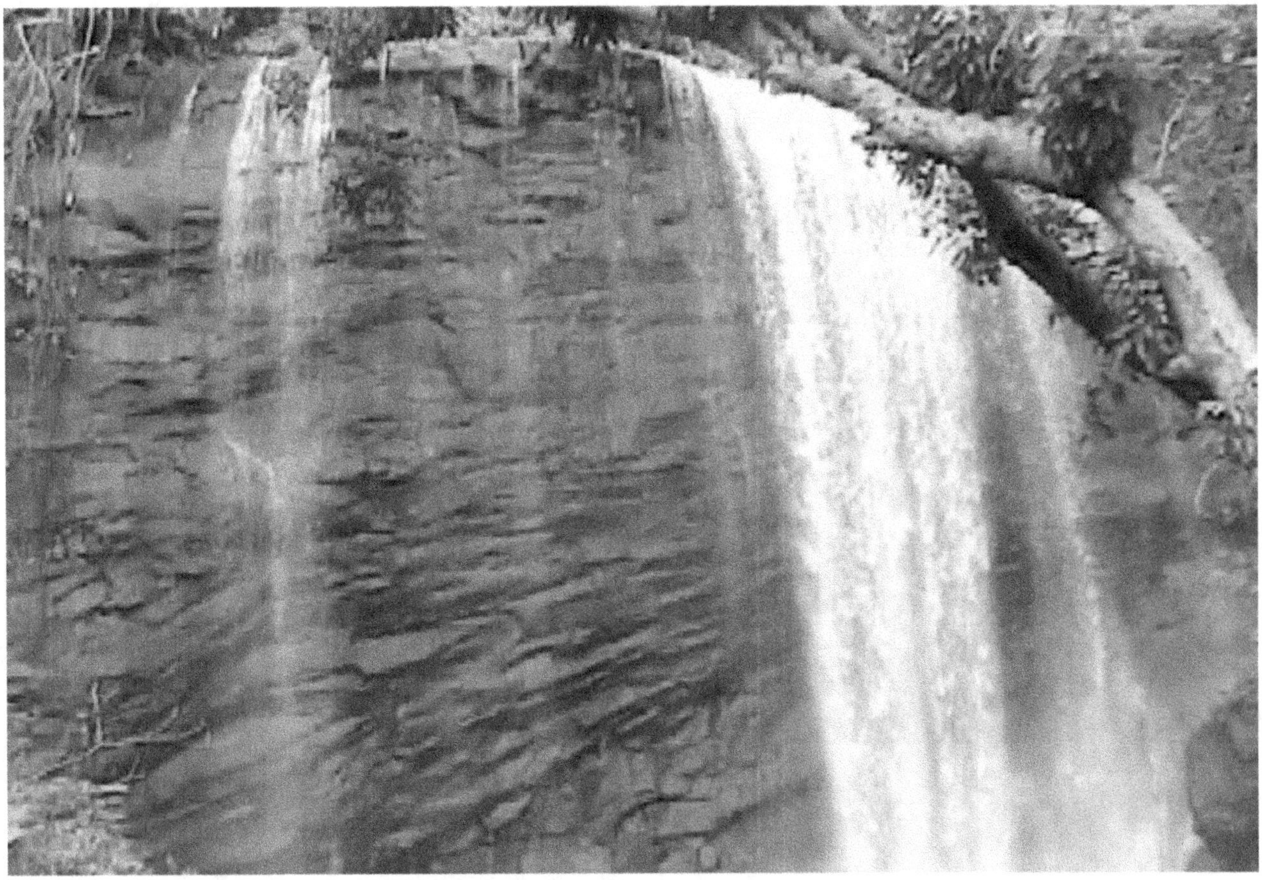

Marquis Falls, also called Mt. Carmel Waterfall

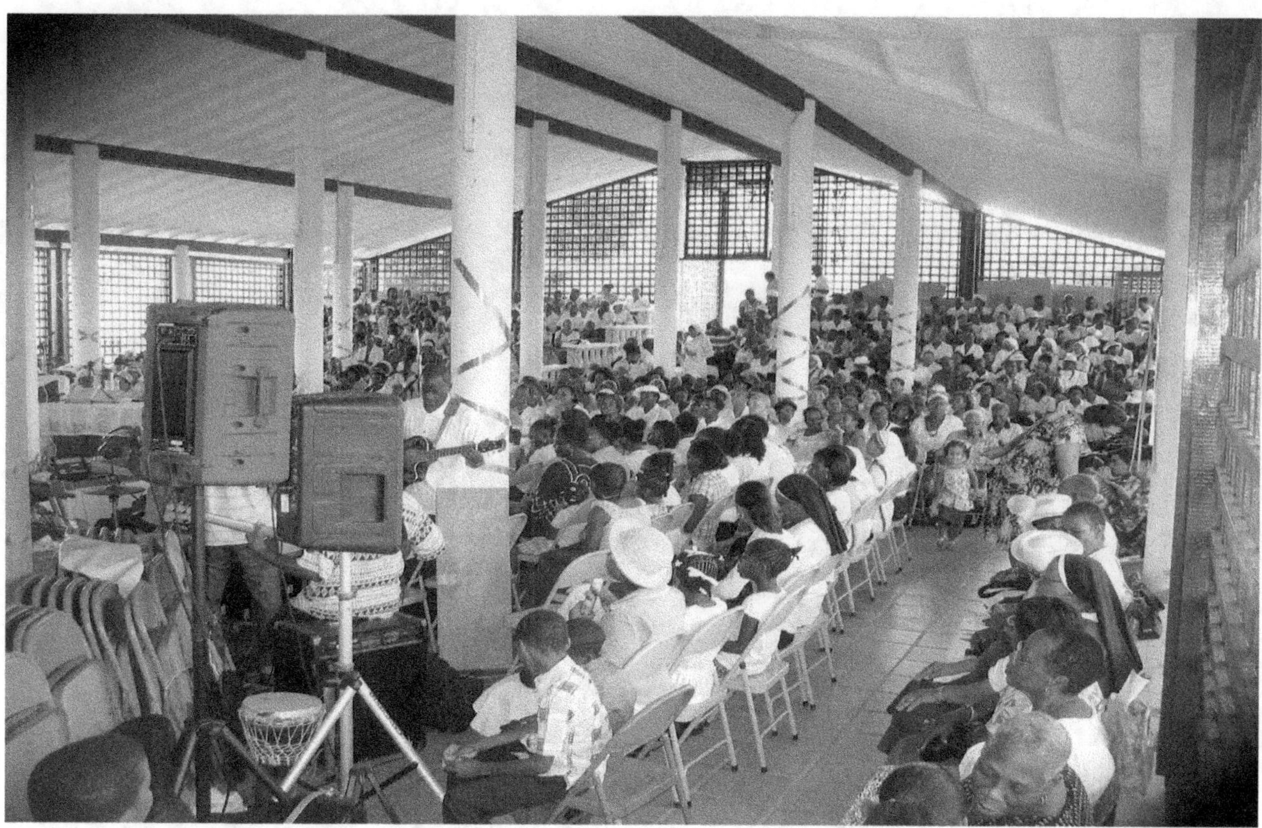

Battle Hill Catholic Church. Located at a colonial battle site, the church adjoins a Virgin Mary's shrine, the destination for many religious processions.

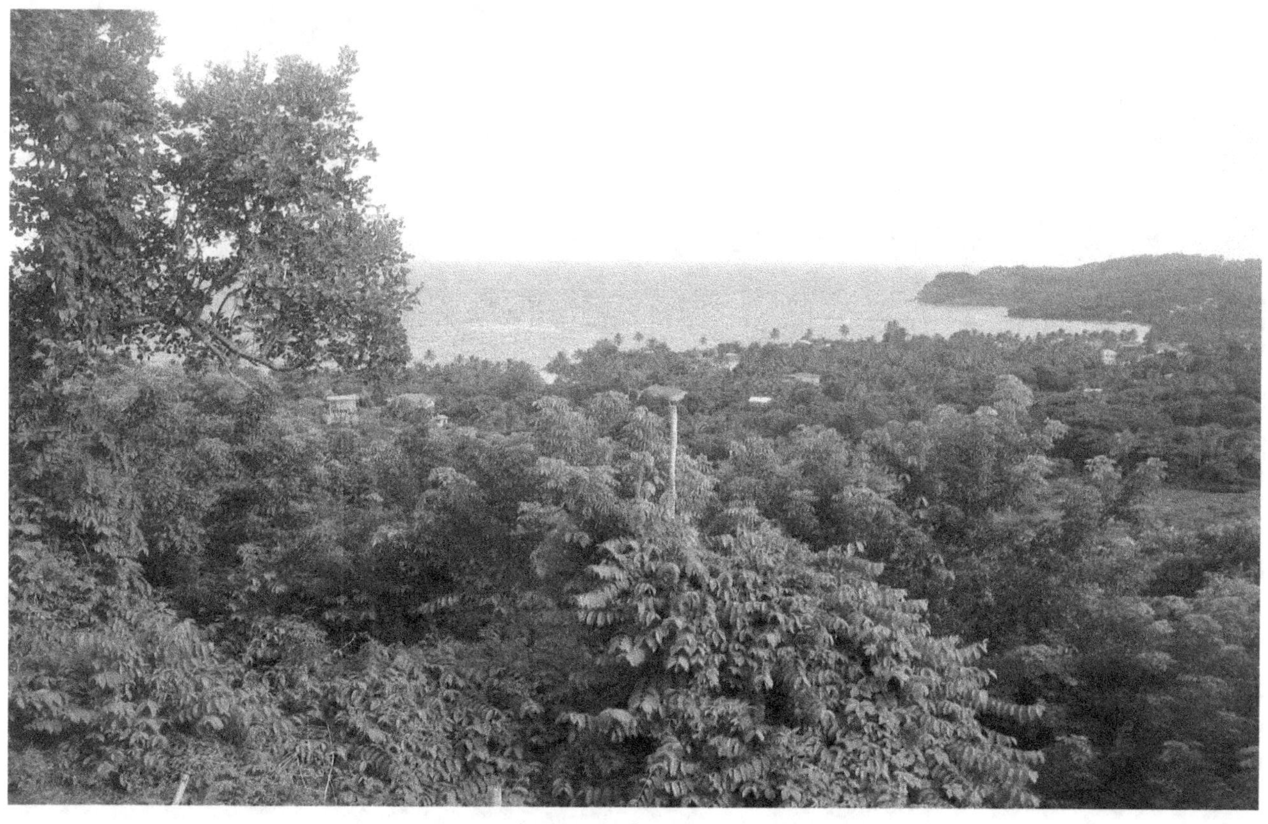

Another view from Battle Hill

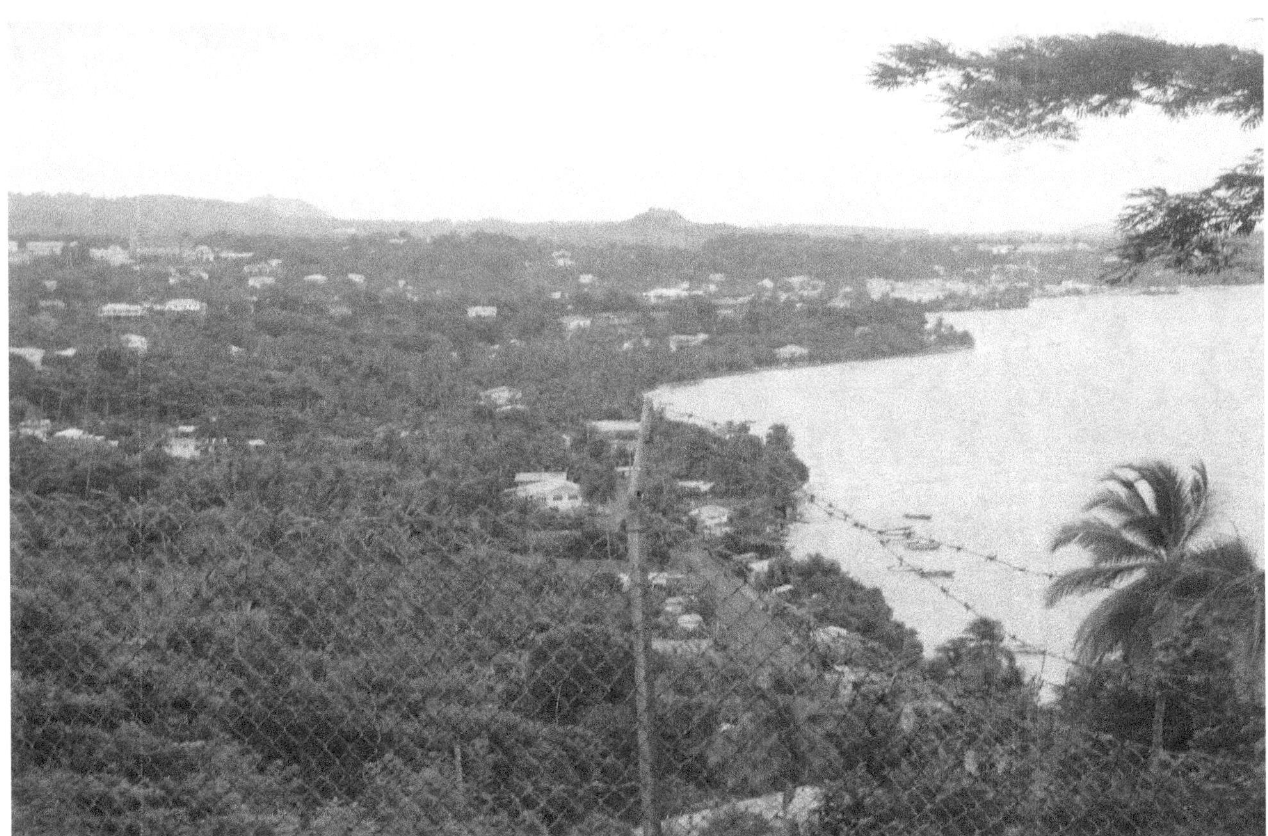

From Battle Hill, we see Grenville in the distance.

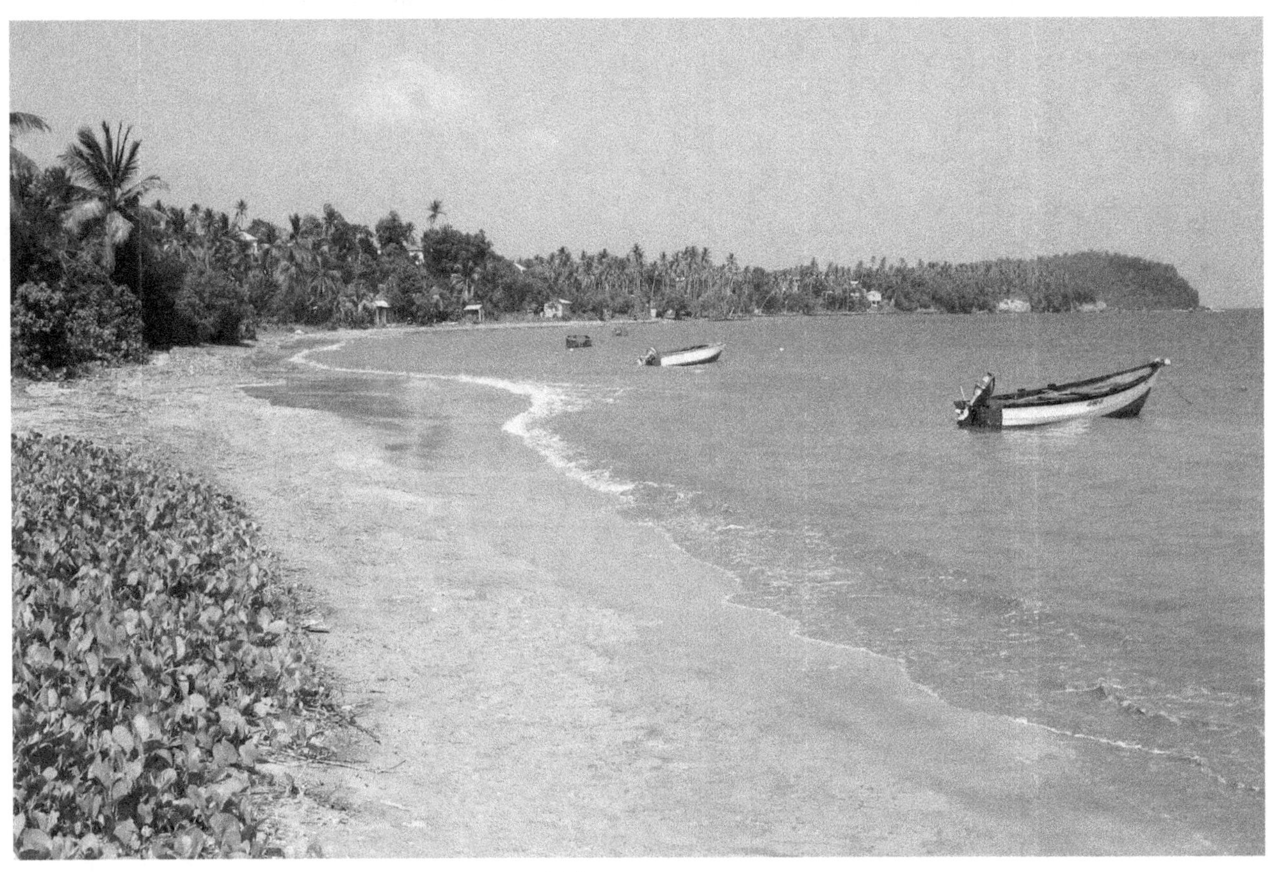

Telescope Point

Carriacou and Petite Martinique

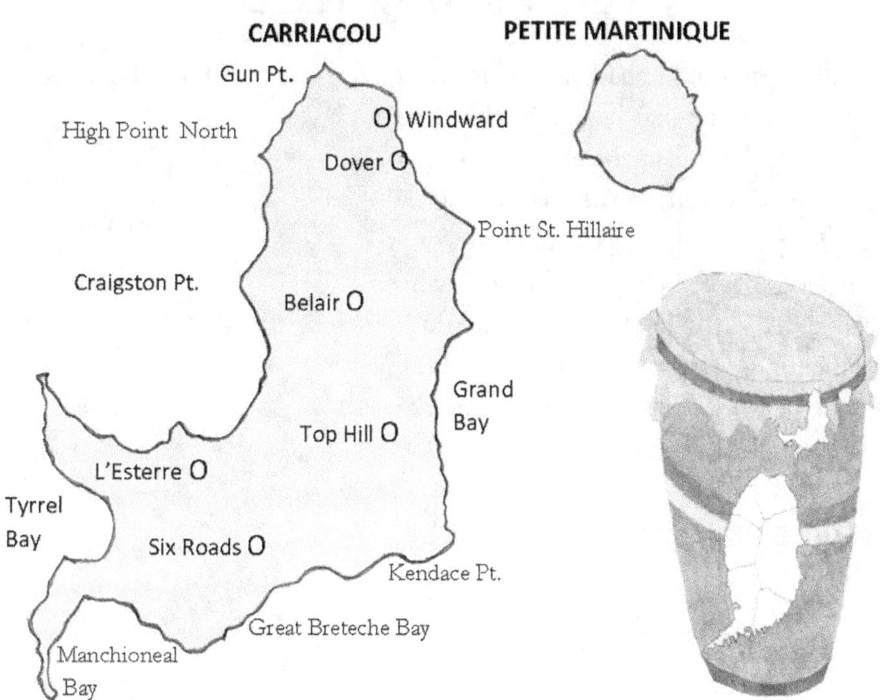

CARRIACOU

At 13 square miles, Carriacou is the largest of the Grenadine Islands, located just twenty miles north of Grenada, and it derives its name from an Amerindian Carib word, which means 'land of reefs.' Carriacou has 9,600 residents. Many are mainly self-employed in fishing, agriculture, and trading. Its reliable boat building traditions, in addition to its gateway location to the islands north of Grenada, provide Carriacou unique trading advantages. Grenada benefits from the port duties collected at the Carriacou port. As it was in Grenada, French colonialism brought the demise of Carriacou's indigenous Carib population. Carriacou's history developed in tandem with Grenada, changing hands between France and England during centuries of colonial rule, while African slaves constituted its mainstream population.

Visitors highly regard Carriacou for its geographical beauty. I have modestly sought here to capture that beauty. However, a fair appraisal of Carriacou must consider its European and African traditions. Carriacou's Scottish seafaring culture has influenced its boat building and launching culture. The African drum, which features prominently in Carriacou's Big Drum festival, seems an appropriate symbol of integration for Grenada, Carriacou, and Petite Martinique. The drum has traditionally accompanied Maroons and other communal celebrations on all three islands.

Historically, Maroons were runaway slaves who escaped into the woods to form communal societies. Today, a Maroon is a cultural event where the community works together to help one of its needy members, especially with house building, where they pool resources to support the event. Maroon-like activities, including Salaka in Grenada, Tombstone Festival in Petite Martinique, and the Carriacou Big drum festival, help us uncover a common culture expressive of beauty, freedom, and cooperation.

PETITE MARTINIQUE

Unlike the Amerindian pasts of Grenada and Carriacou, Petite Martinique has a history that begins in the effort of a Frenchman from Martinique in the early 1700s, Mr. Pierre, who first owned and settled the island to grow cotton crops. The largest village, Madam Pierre, was named in honor of Pierre's wife. The island is somewhat round in its coastal shape, with a 750 ft. high mountain in the center, from which most of the Grenadine islands are visible. Petite Martinique is 586 acres and has a population of approximately 960 residents.

From the onset, Mr. Pierre brought African slaves to the island, and over time the slave population increased. European seafarers also made Petite Martinique their home. Because of the closeness derived from its small size, Petite Martinique did not experience the harsher varieties of plantation slavery elsewhere in the Caribbean; its residents more readily practiced integration and intermarriage. There was less suppression of African practices, which has resulted in a rich culture today expressed in the Tombstone Festival, the Big Drum Dance, Cake Dancing, Flag Dancing at weddings, and boat launching rituals.

The local population learned boat building and other skills from the Europeans to the point that they have excelled in their maritime endeavors. Despite the suitability of the land for agriculture, Petite Martinicans derive a significant part of their livelihoods from fishing and sea trading. Given its small population and viable commerce, other islanders sometimes quipped that Petite Martinique has the highest per capita income in the entire Eastern Caribbean.

PETITE MARTINIQUE

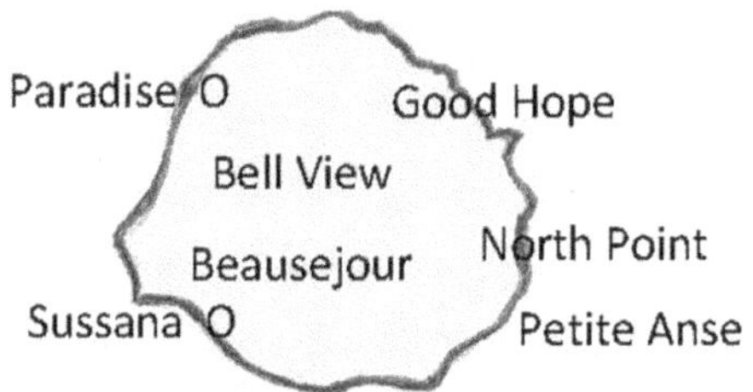

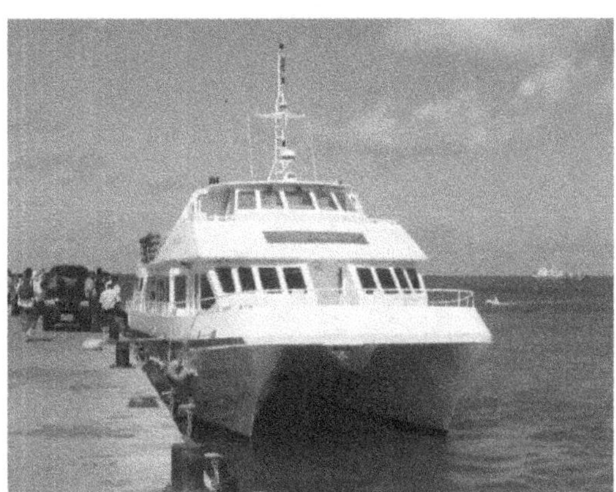

Osprey Shuttle carries passengers traveling to and from Grenada, Carriacou, and Petite Martinique.

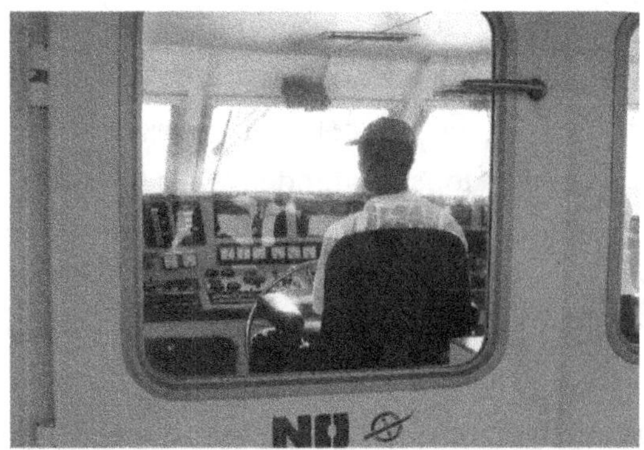

A Petite Martinican captain of the Osprey Shuttle

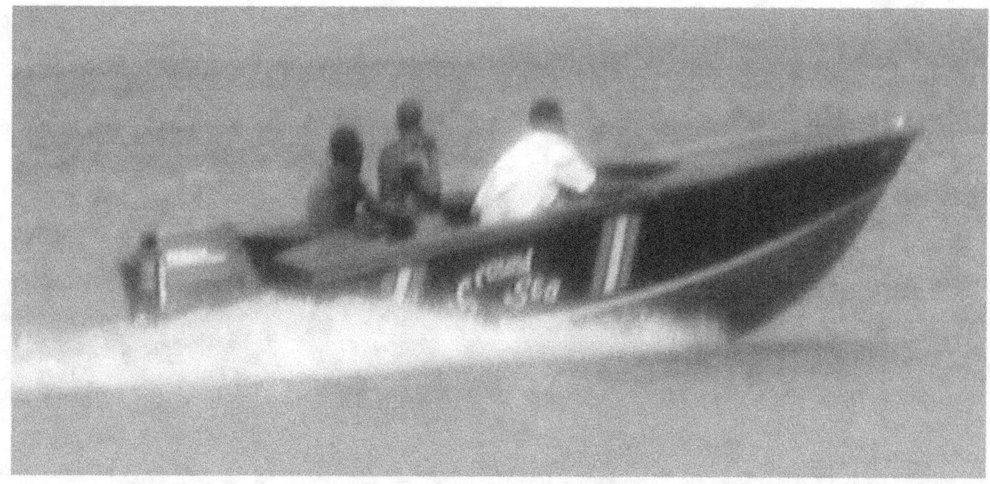

Ground Sea on the move

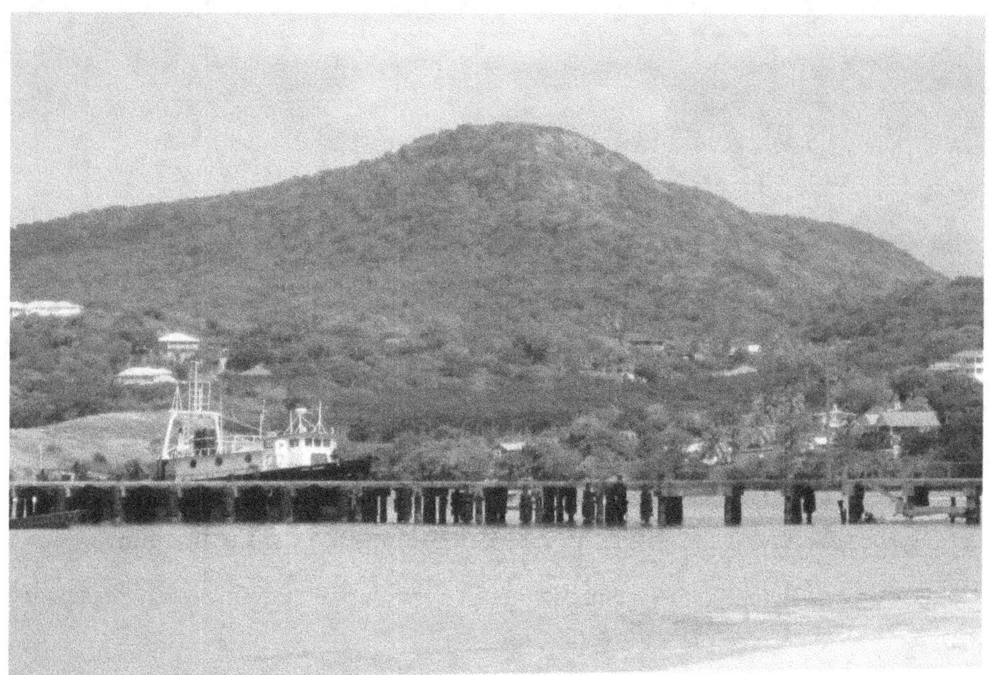

Belmont Hill

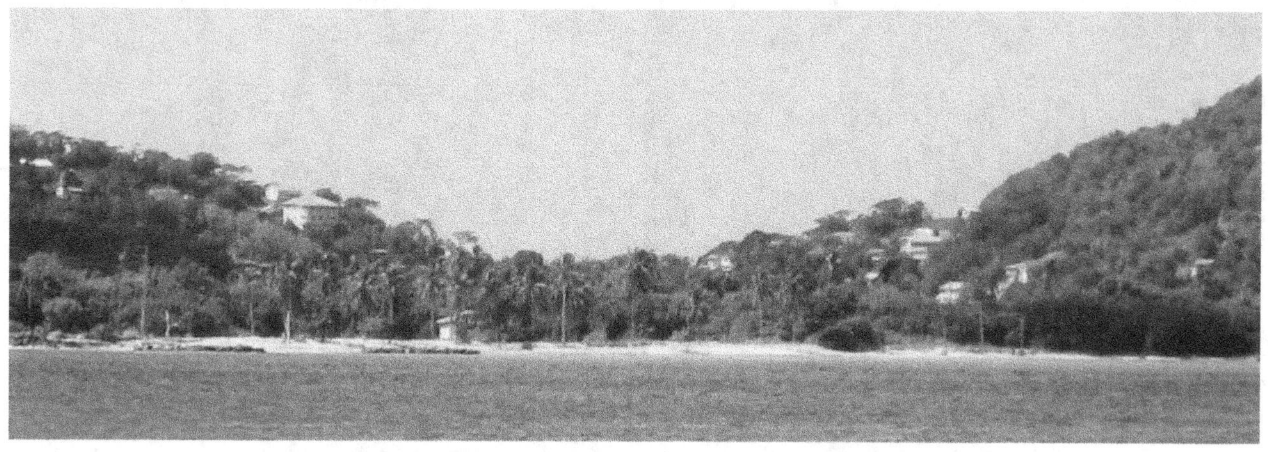

Coconut Beach with L'Esterre hidden behind the coconut trees

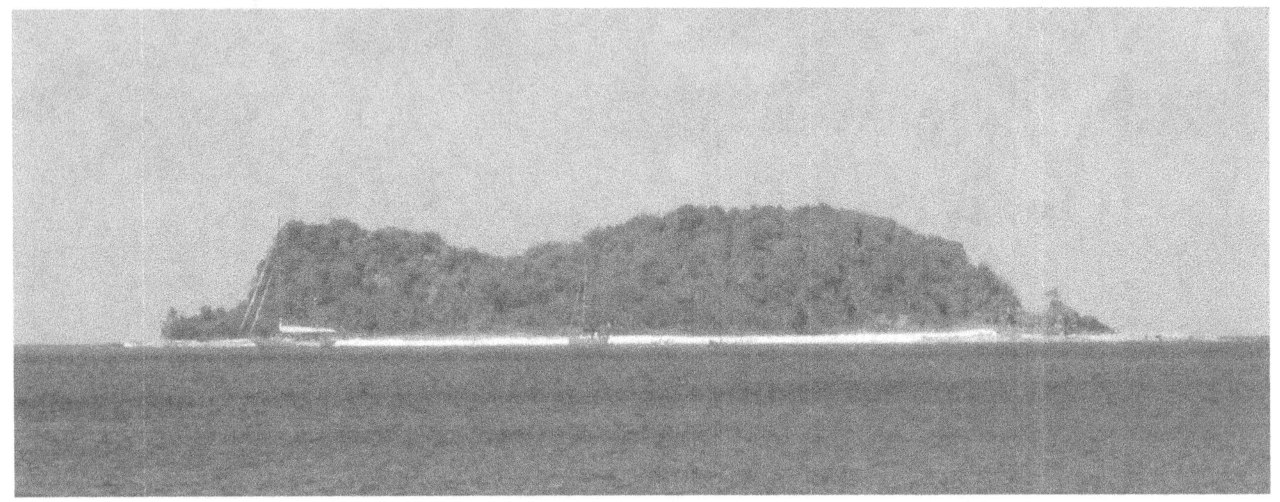

Mabouyah Island

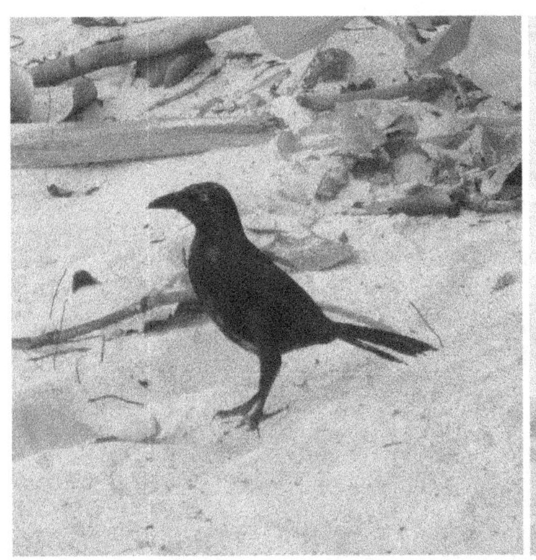

Surveying the seashore

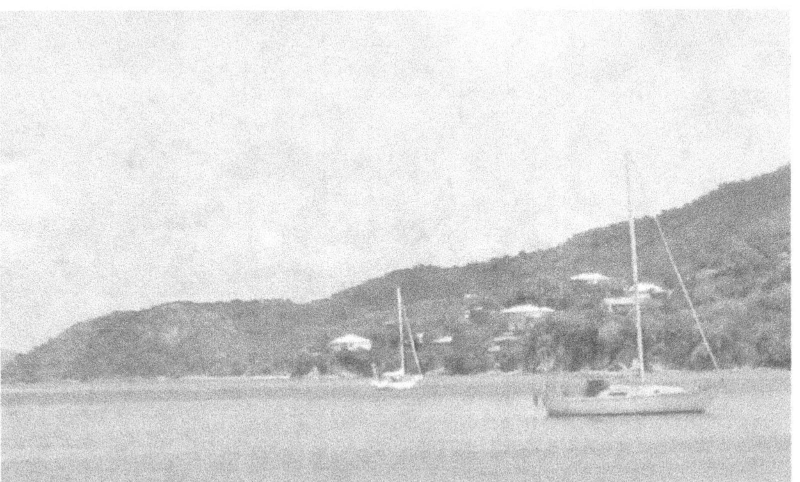

Craigston, once the site of a lime estate

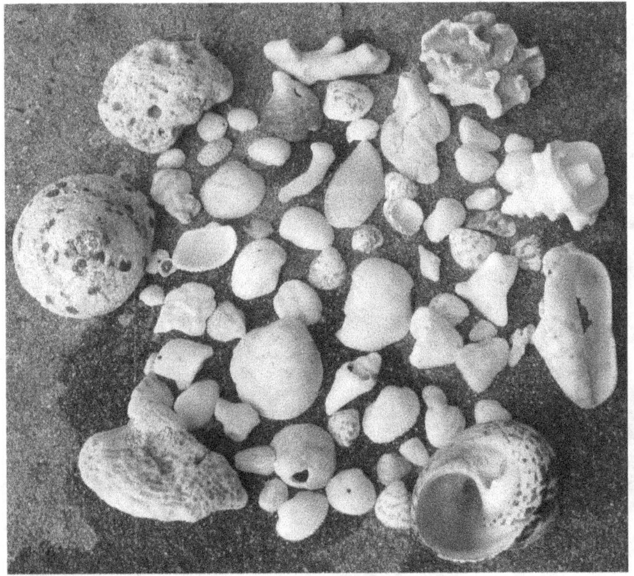

A collection of Carriacou seashells

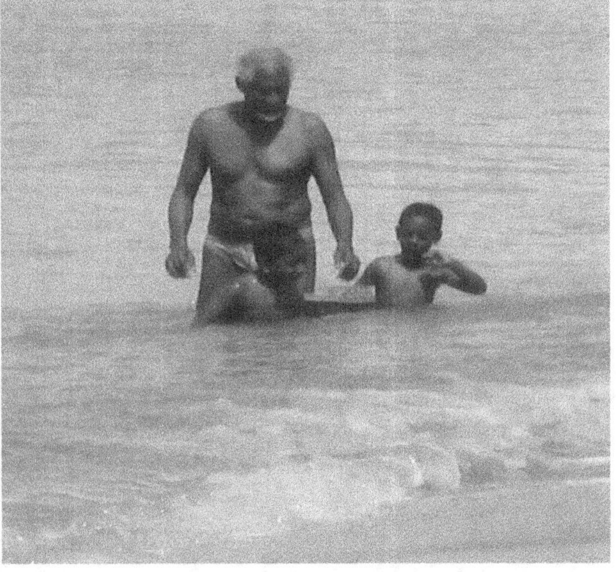

An adult supervises as kids play with a toy boat.

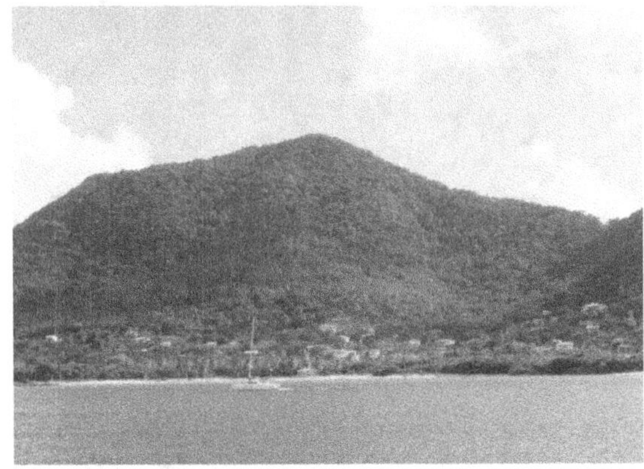

Chapeau Carre (Fr. Square Hat)
is the second highest peak in Carriacou.

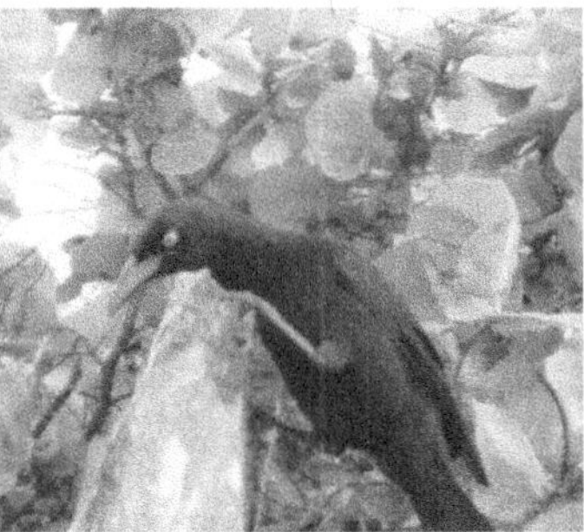

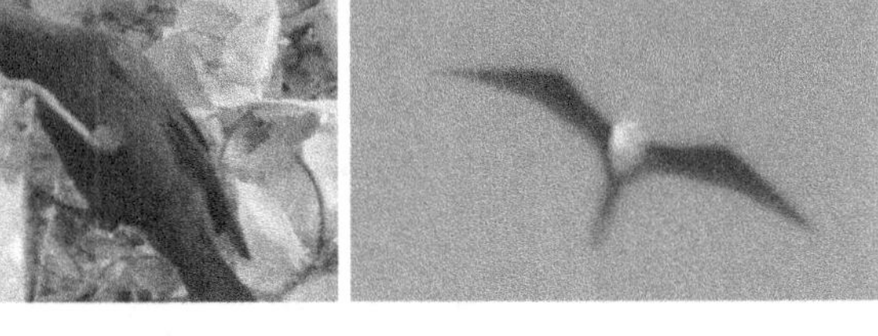

Two of the varieties of birds found on Carriacou

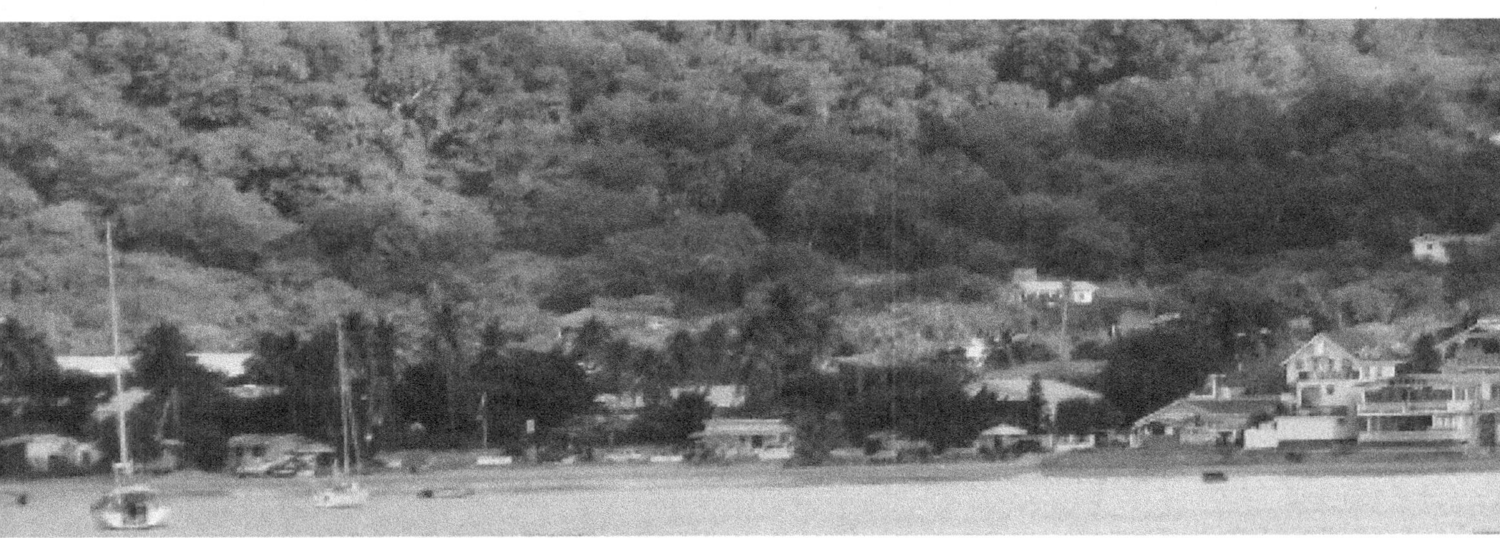

Sandy Island
is the atoll in
the foreground.
Morne Jaloux,
to the right, is
located on the
lower mount,
L'Aca Hosea.

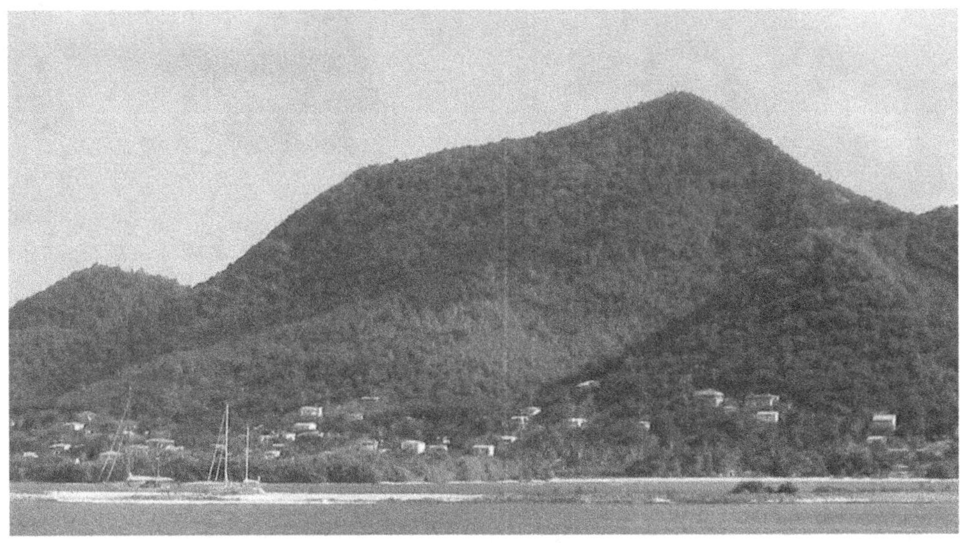

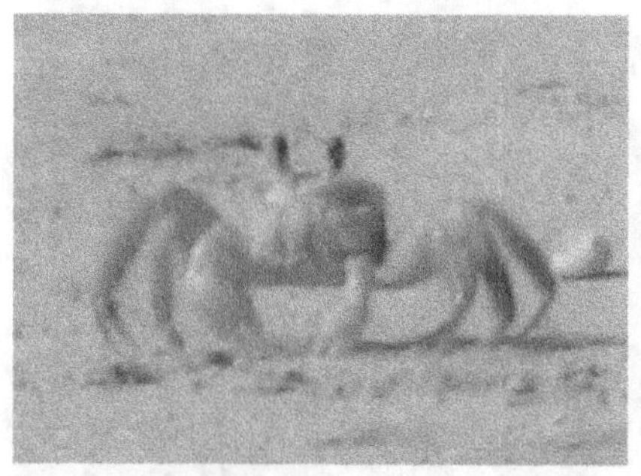
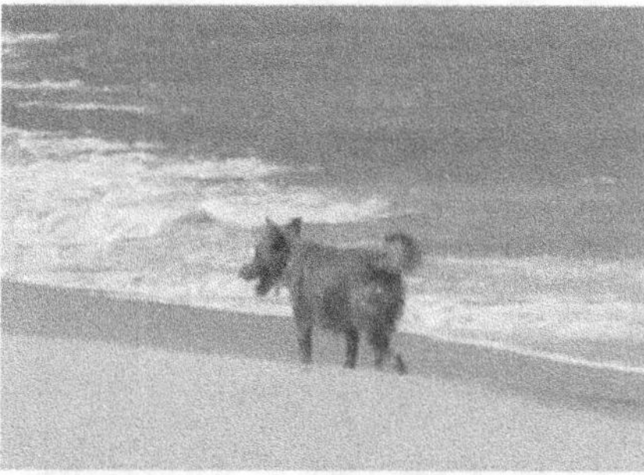
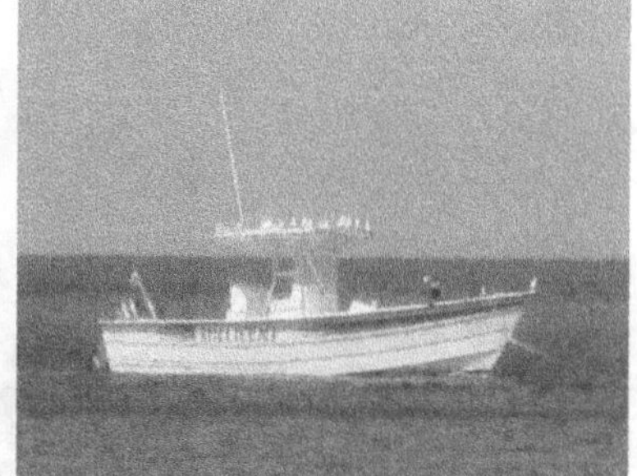

A dog strolls along the beach; a crab moves cautiously.

A boat named Millicent

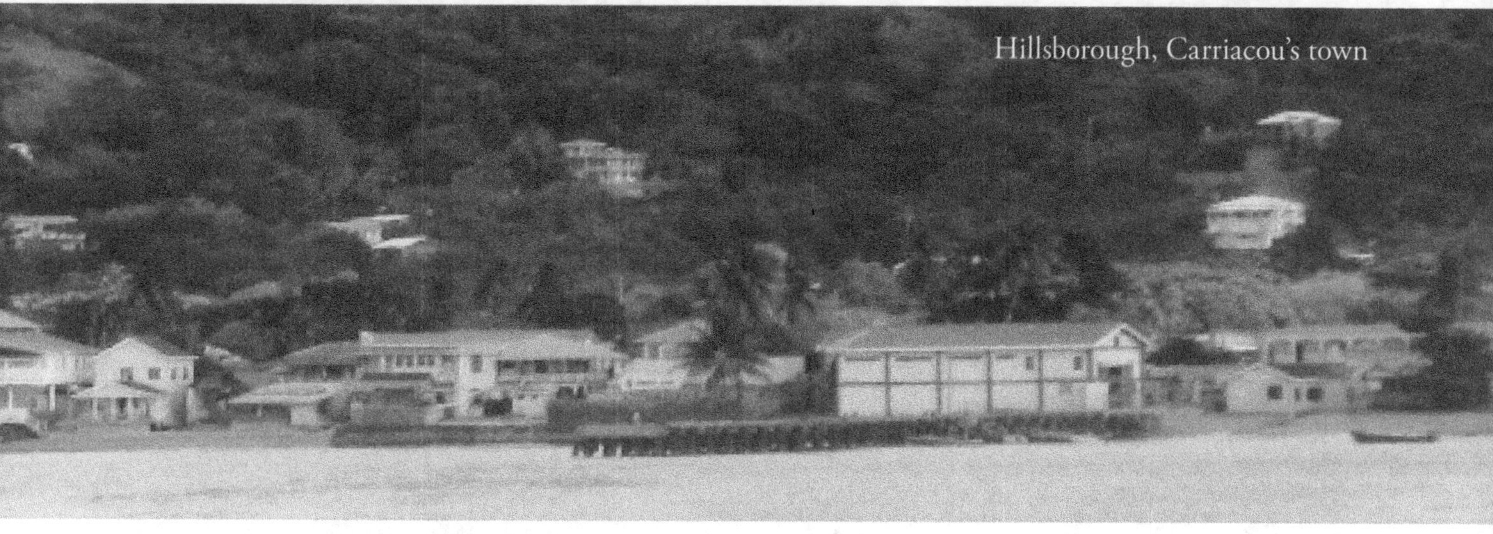

Hillsborough, Carriacou's town

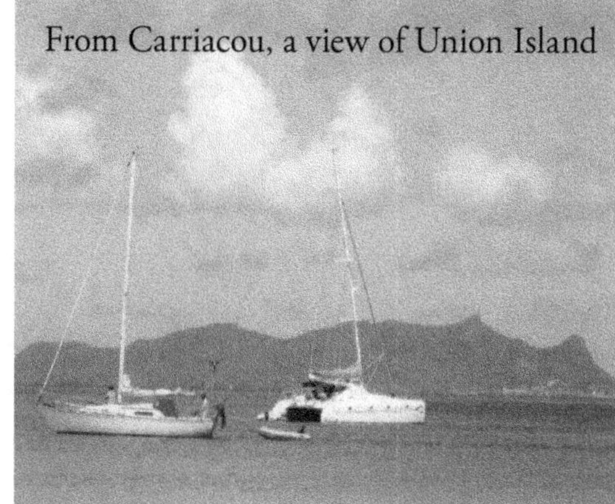

From Carriacou, a view of Union Island

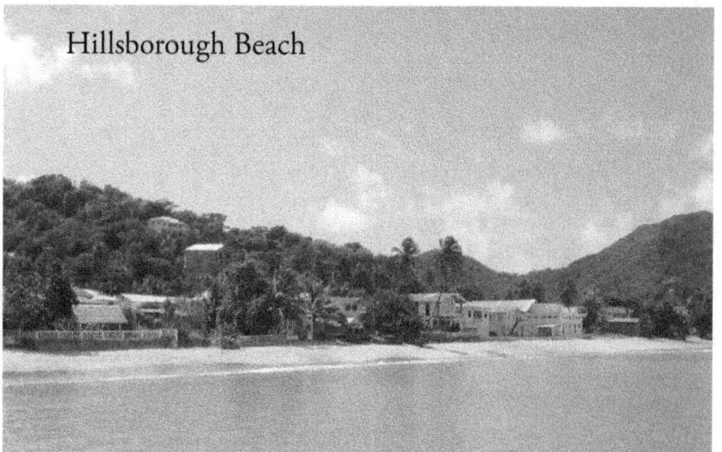

Hillsborough Beach

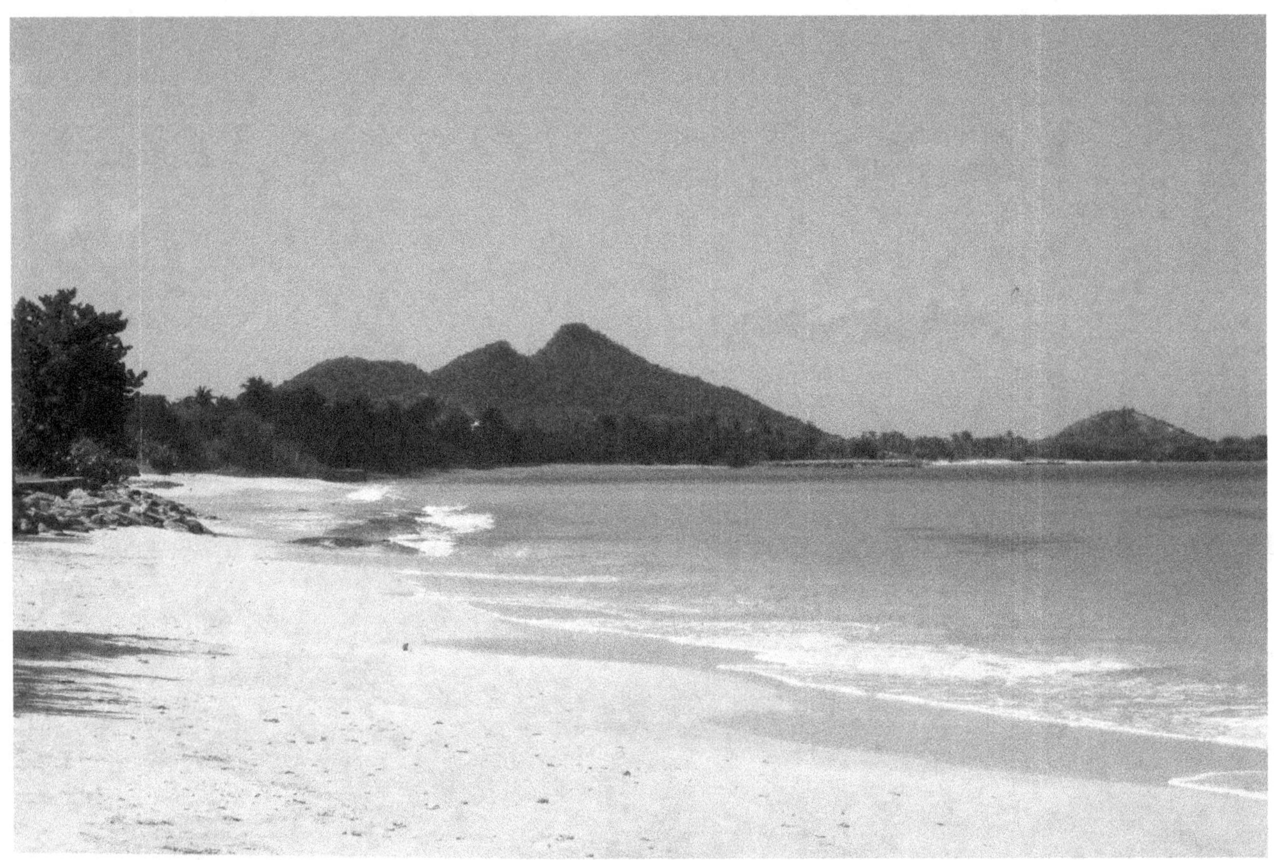

From Hillsborough, looking towards L'Esterre

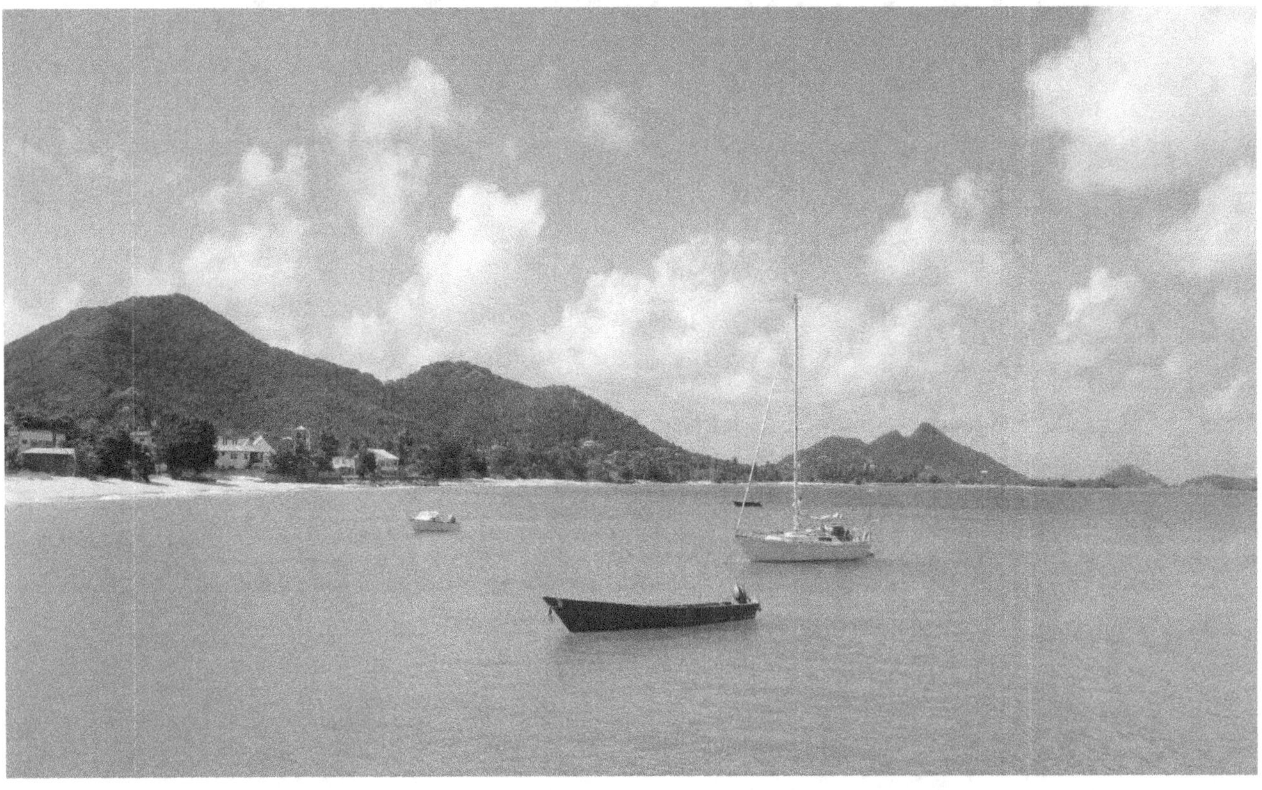

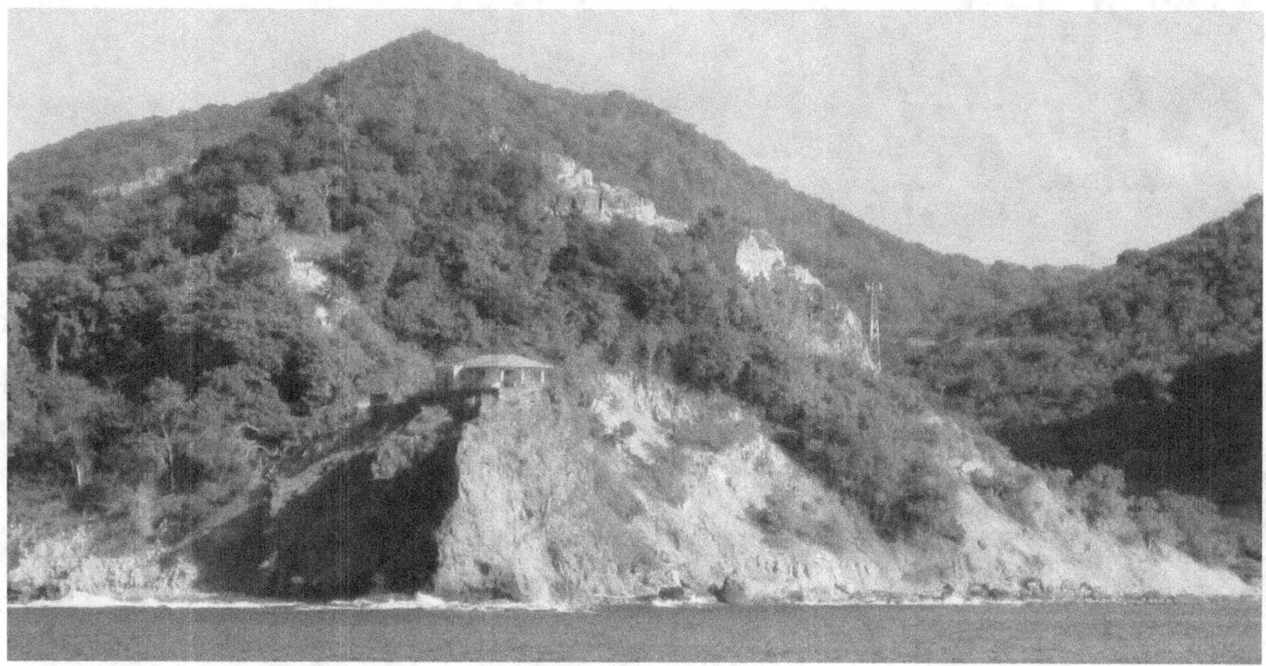

Jack Iron Point is a familiar landmark along the southward sea trip to Grenada. There is a robust white rum from Carriacou called Jack Iron Rum.

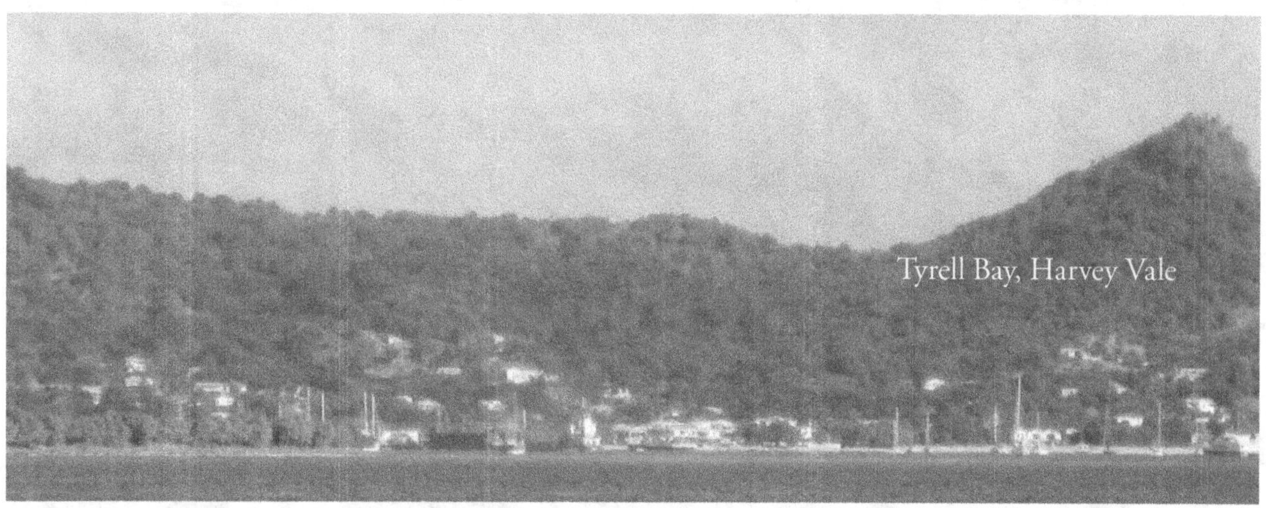

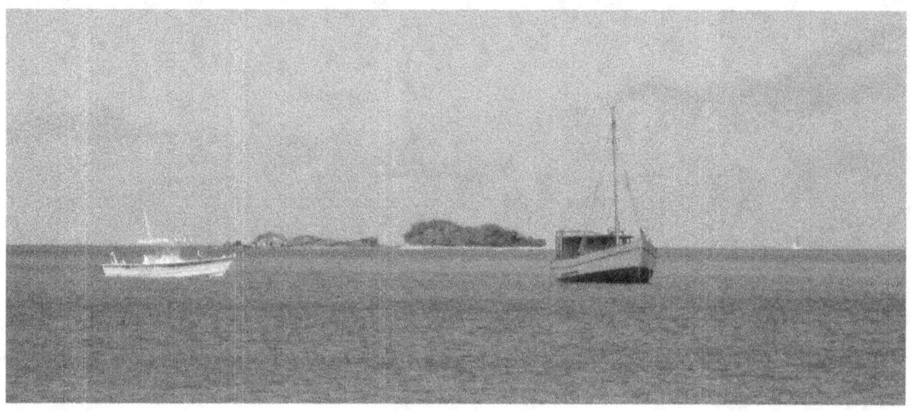

Fishing boats anchored just offshore

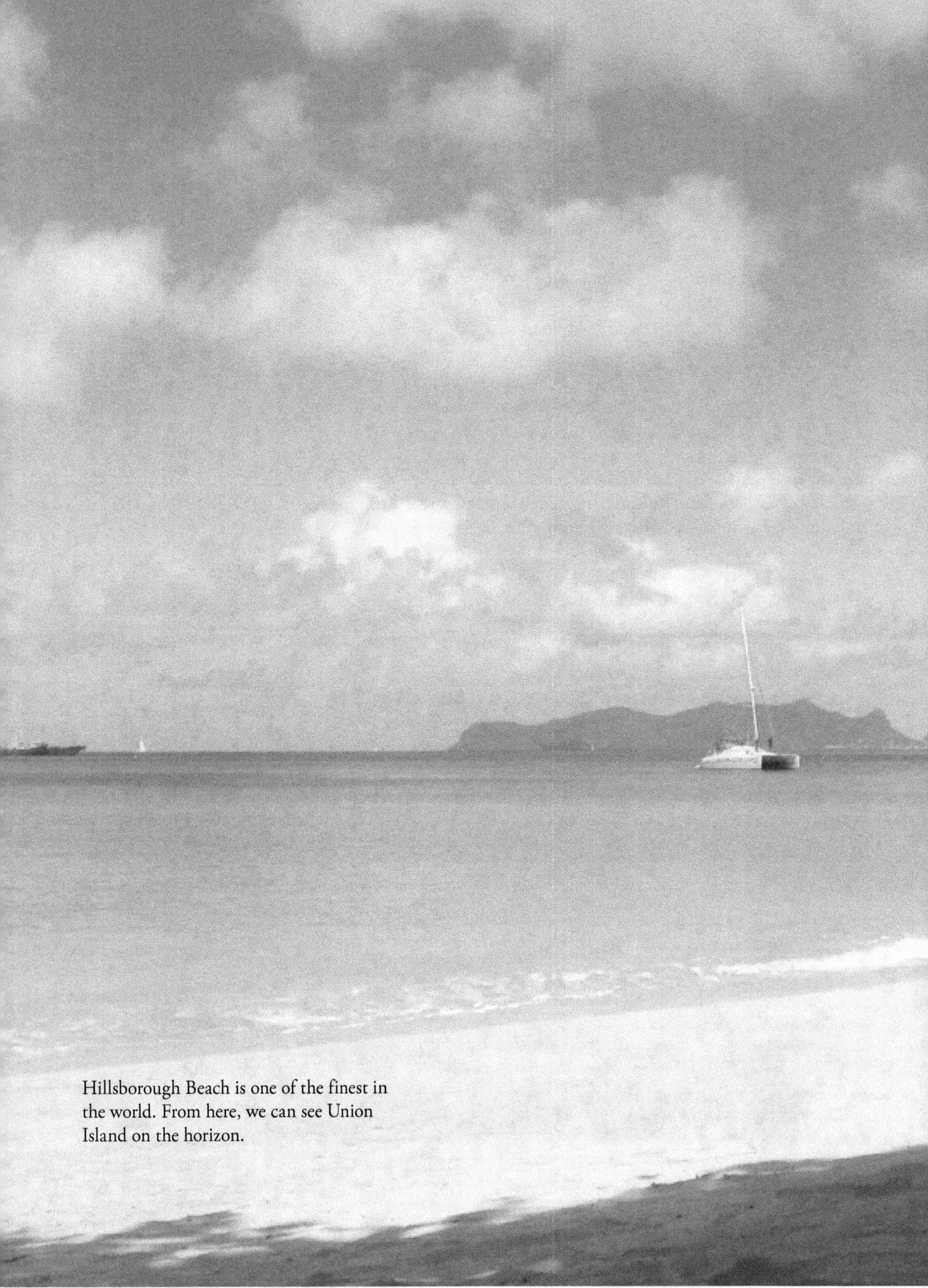

Hillsborough Beach is one of the finest in the world. From here, we can see Union Island on the horizon.

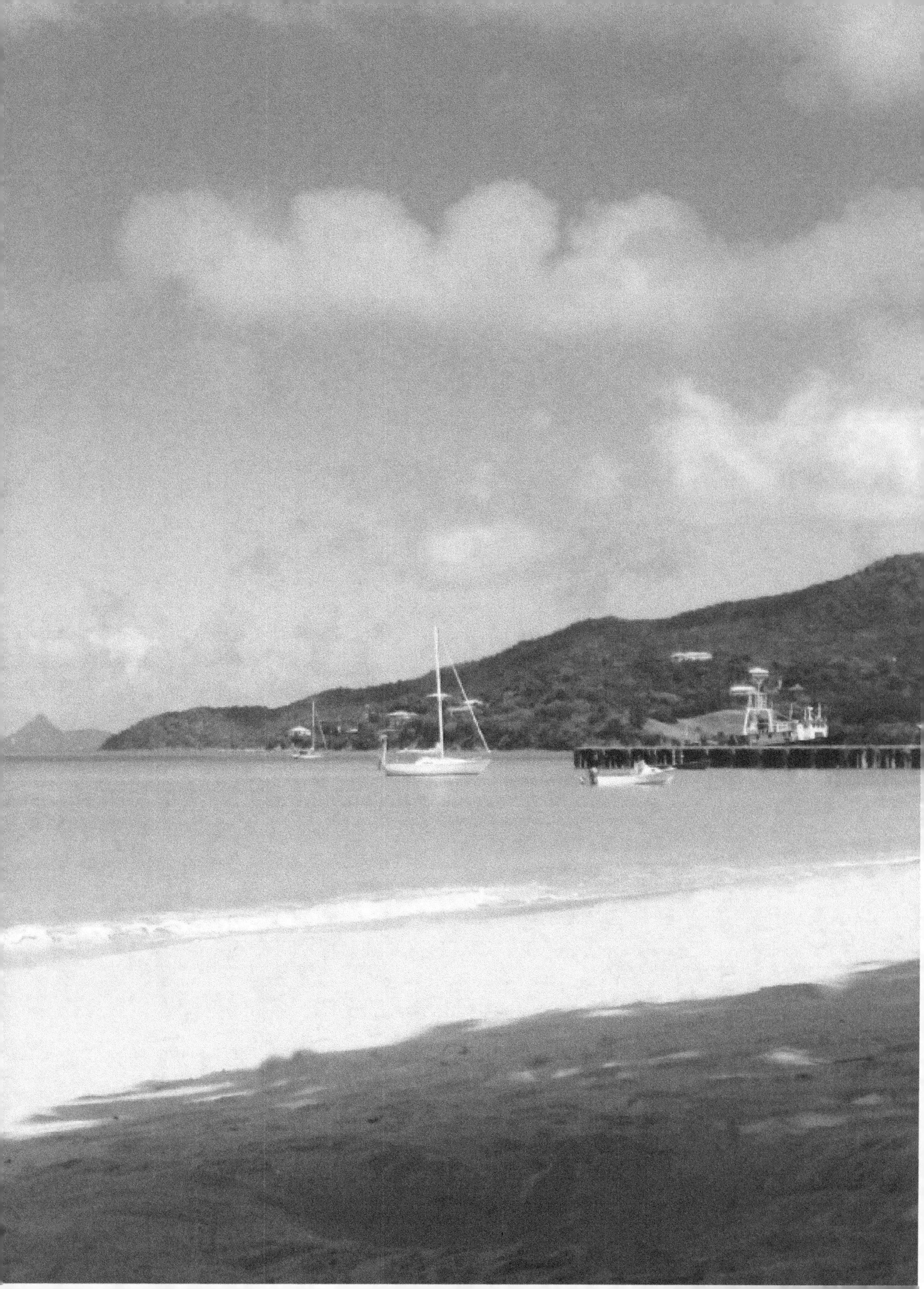

FRUITS, VEGETABLES, AND SPICES

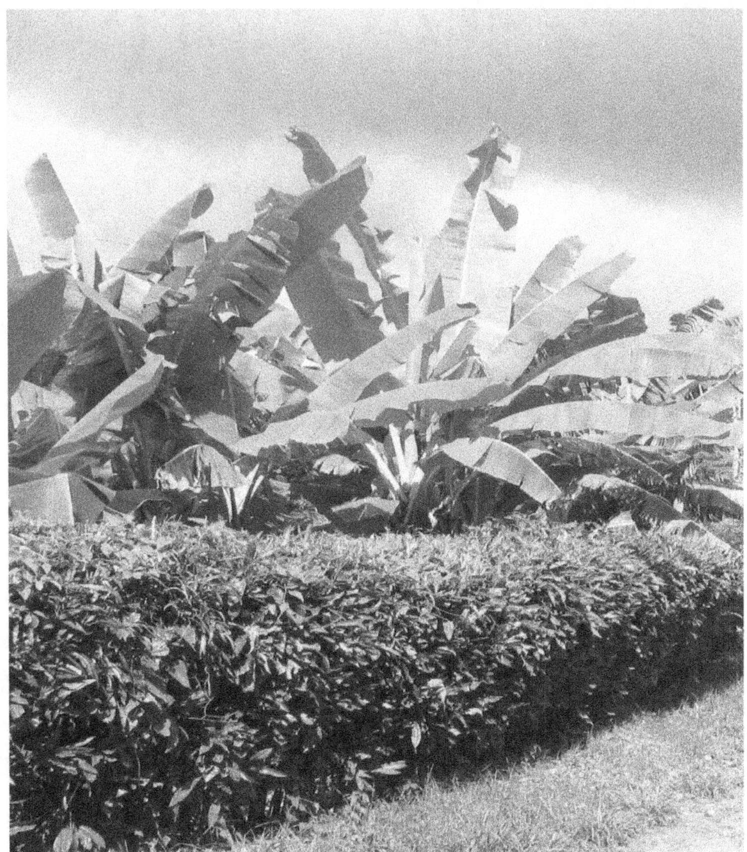

Banana trees near Paradise, St. John's. Cooked green banana is a popular food item in Grenada.
Cooked green banana is a popular food item in Grenada.

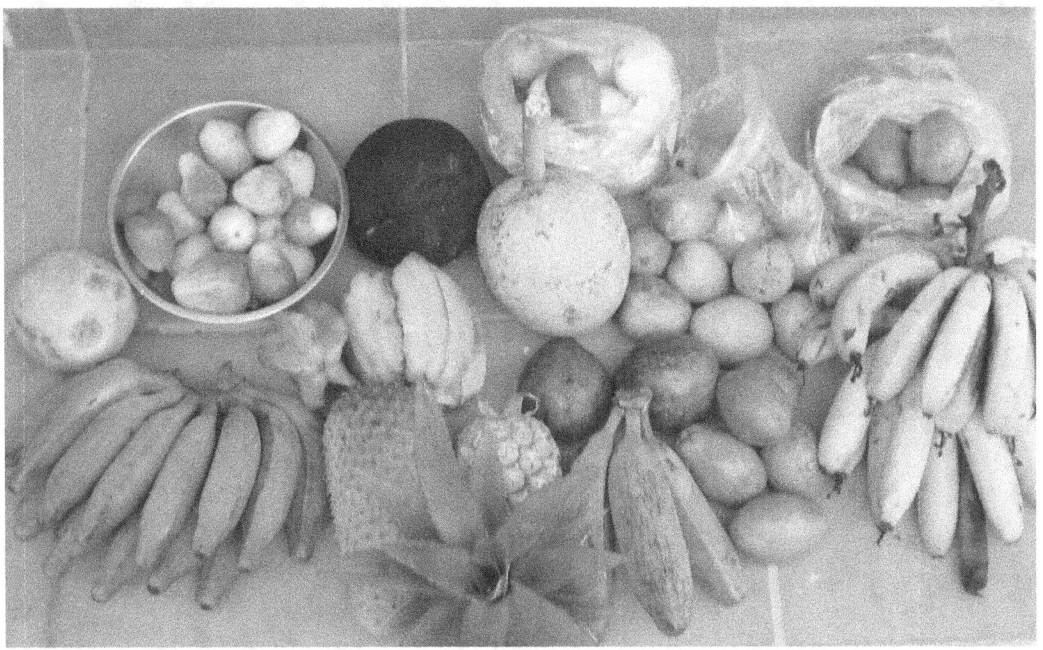

A casual assembly of Grenadian fruit

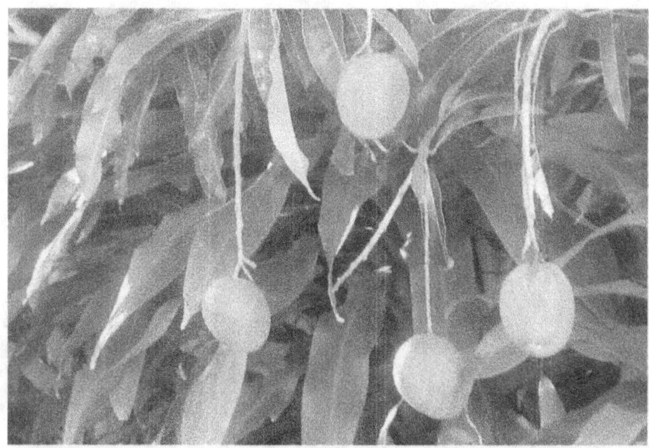

Here, Julie mangoes (also called Mango Julies) hang from a branch. Mangoes are locally given names that distinguish one variety from the other.

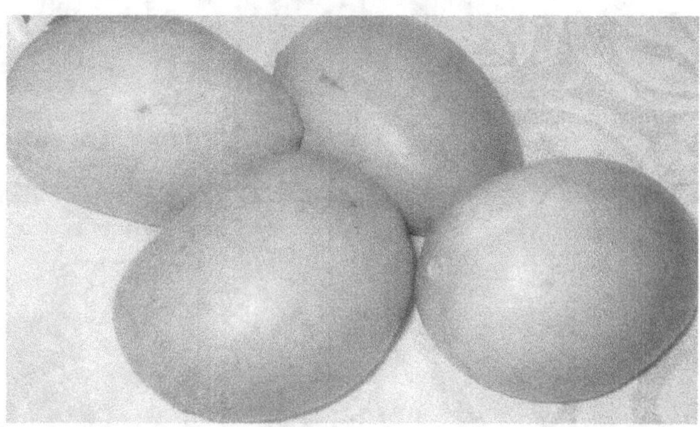

Julie mangoes are well known for their delightful taste.

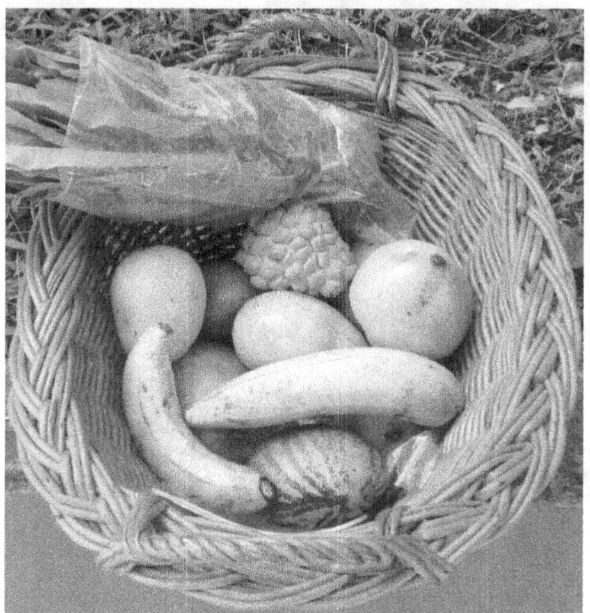

...and there are other types of mangoes, as we find in this fruit basket.

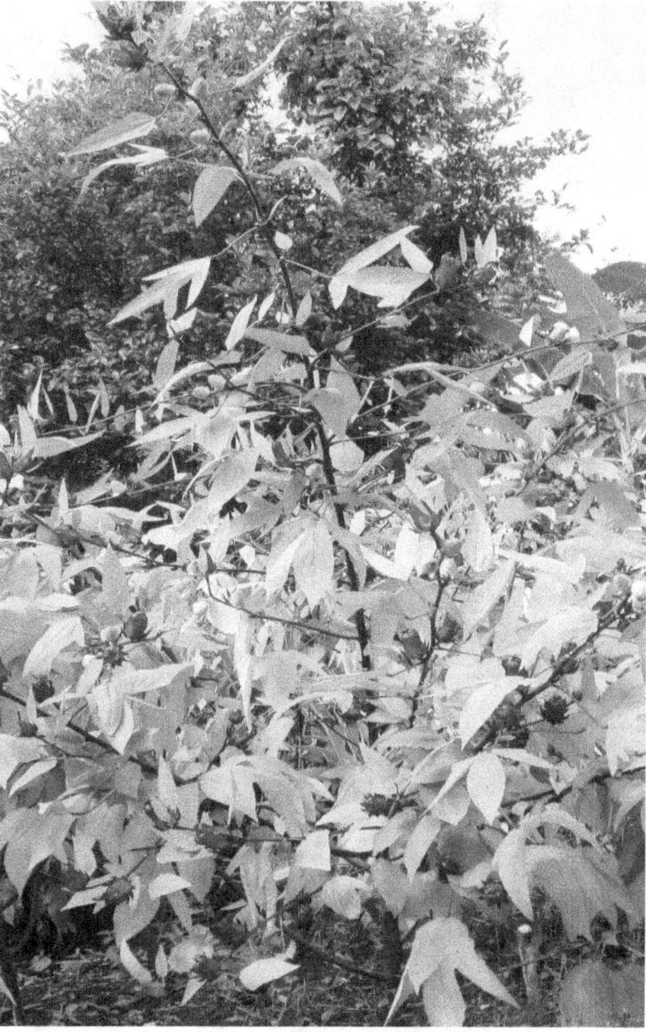

Sorrel: It is a plant (flower) that produces Grenada's most famous Christmas beverage (see page 160).

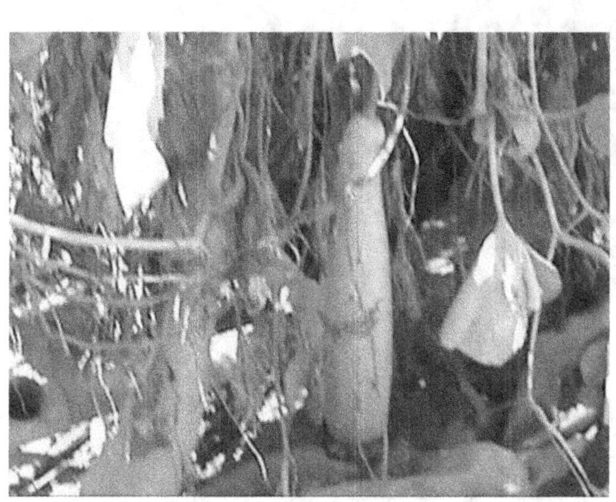

Squash

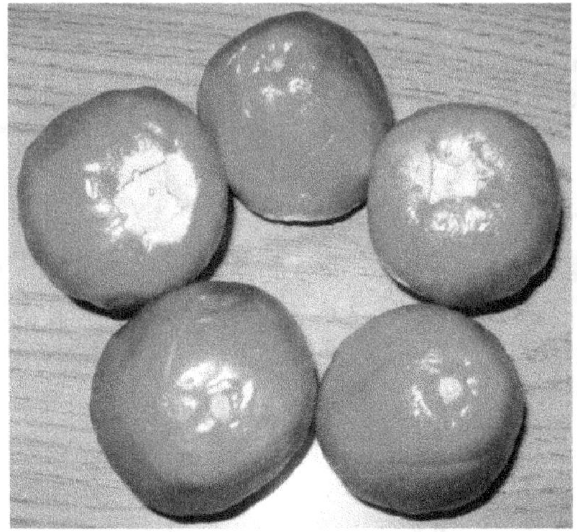
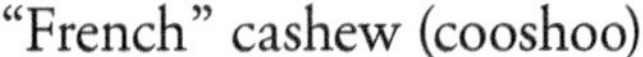

"French" cashew (cooshoo)

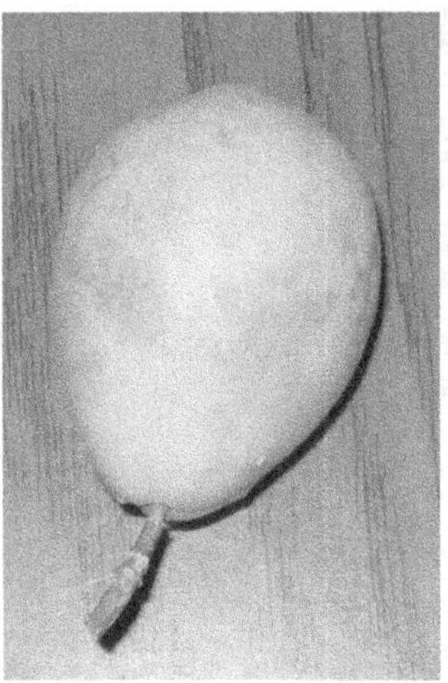
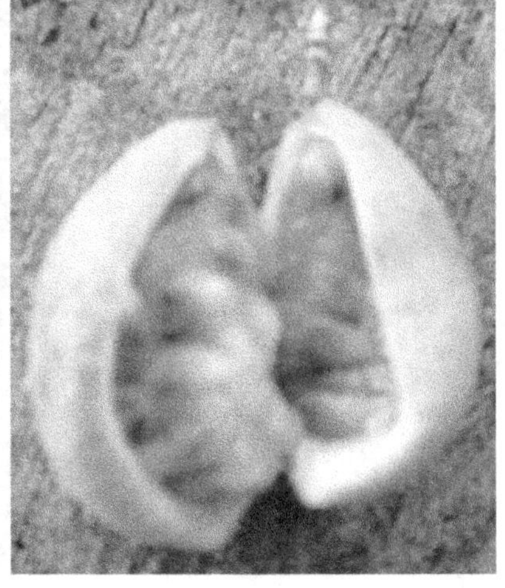

The granadilla is known locally as a water lemon.

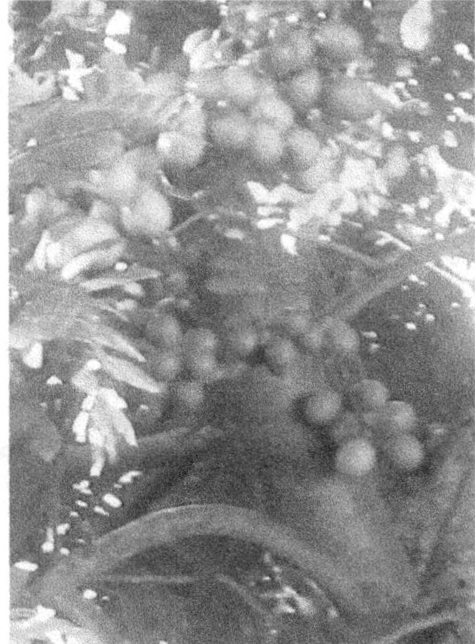
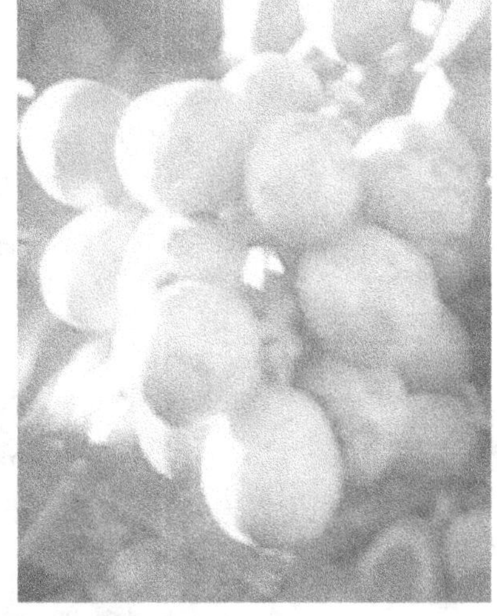

"Chinese" plums

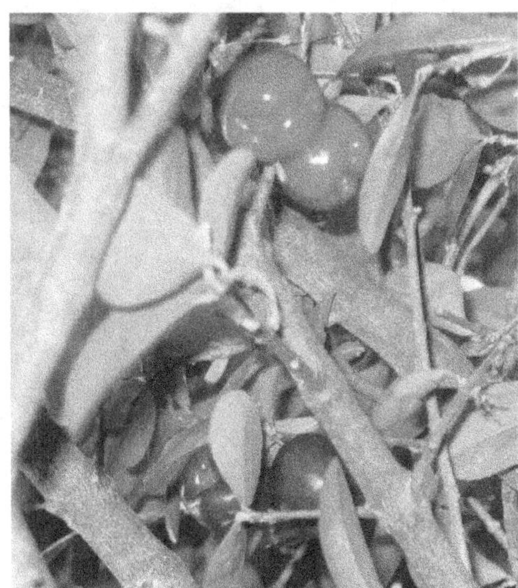

Cherries

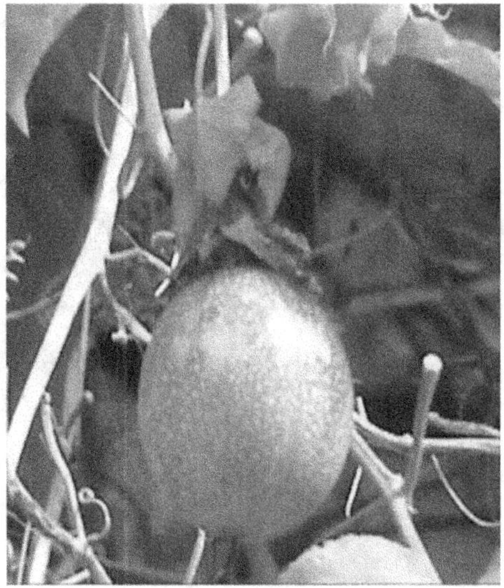

Passion Fruit

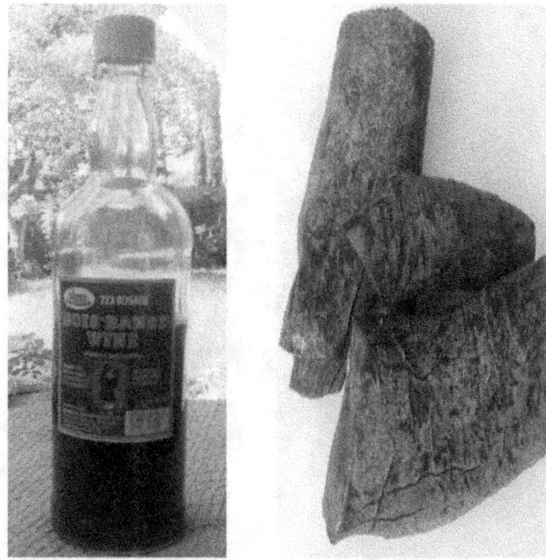

Bois Bande (hard wood): A tree root that they soak in beverages. Some Grenadians believe it to have aphrodisiac qualities. Long ago, Bois Bande was used by some Grenadian elders as a blood cleanser. Some have attributed a few medical 'miracles' to the use of Bois Bande. A locally made Bois Bande wine is also featured above.

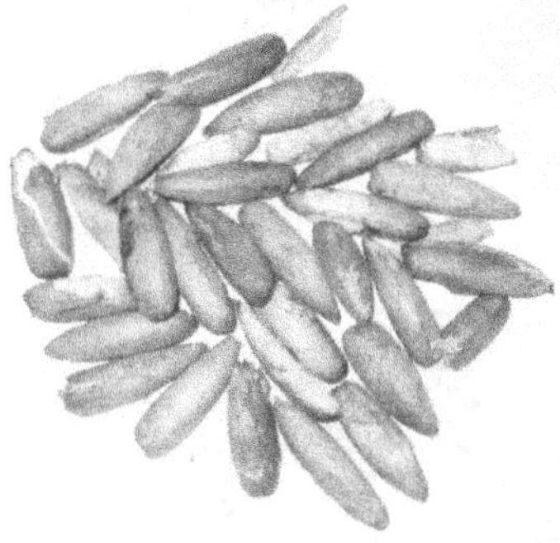

Almonds: These Grenadian Almonds are usually softer than those popularized on the international market. Grenadians generally harvest almonds for personal consumption.

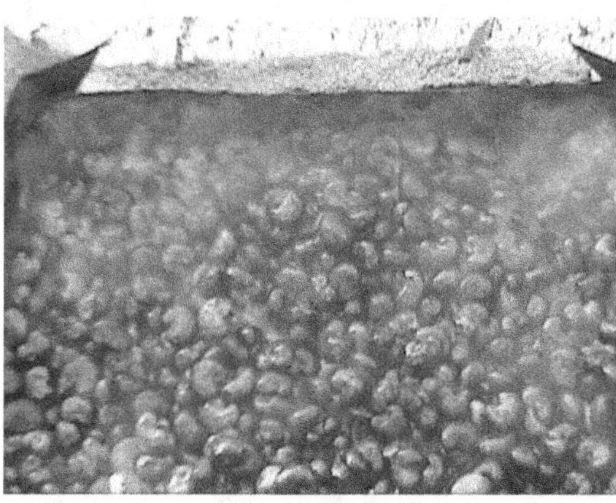

Roasting cashew nuts

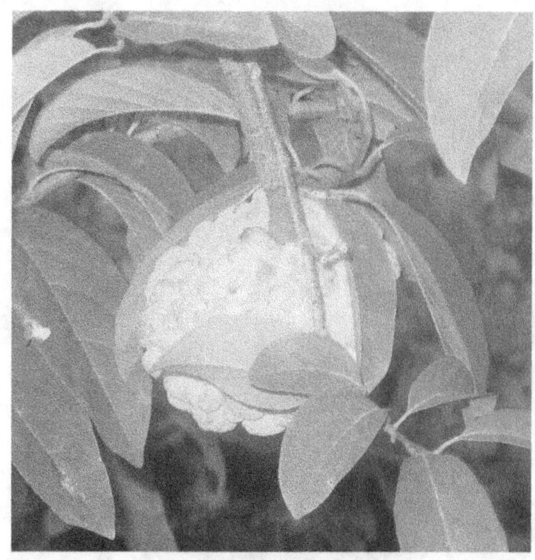

Sugar apple

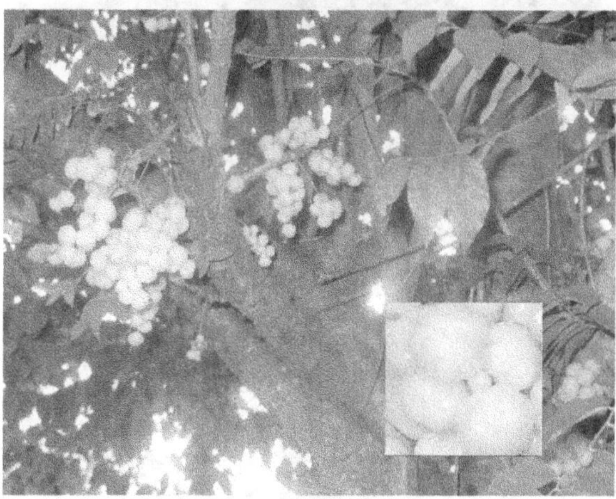

Damsons

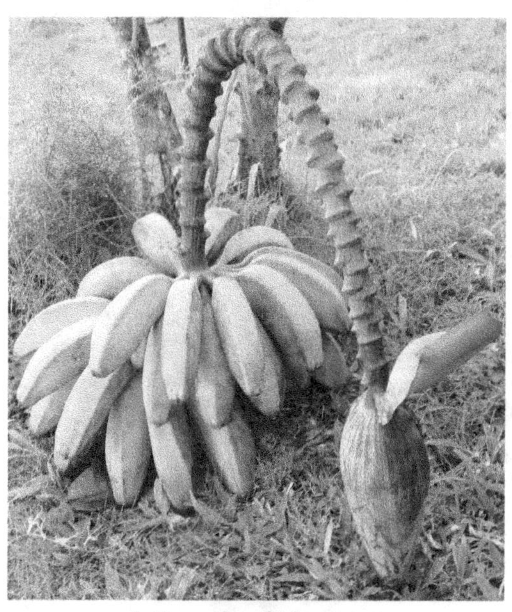

A Bunch of bluggoes
(not bananas)

SPICES

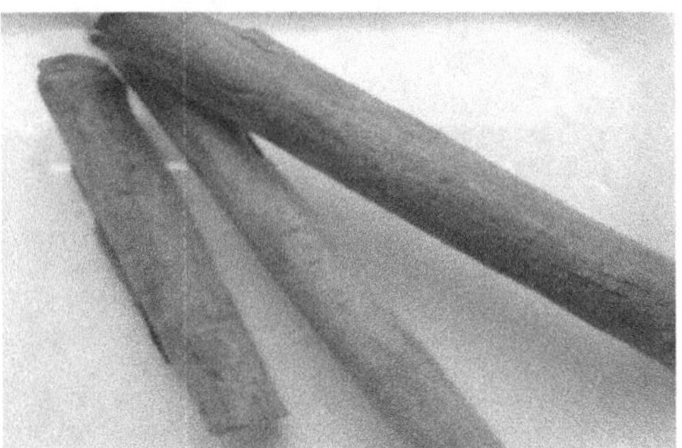

Cinnamon (above) is the bark of the cinnamon tree.

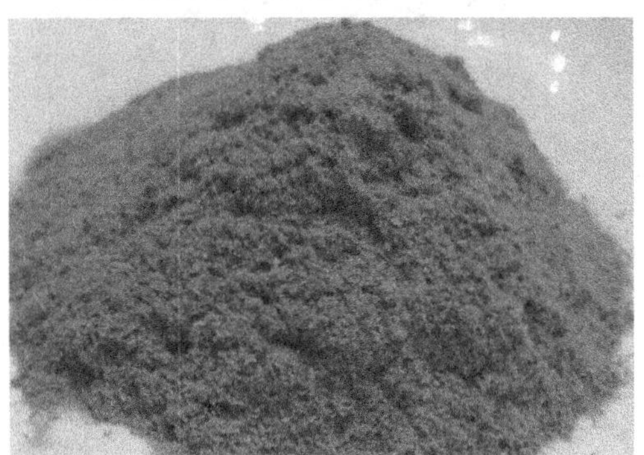

Cinnamon powder

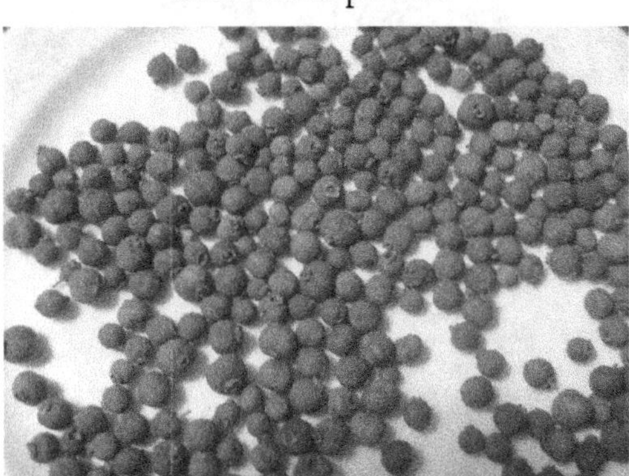

Allspice

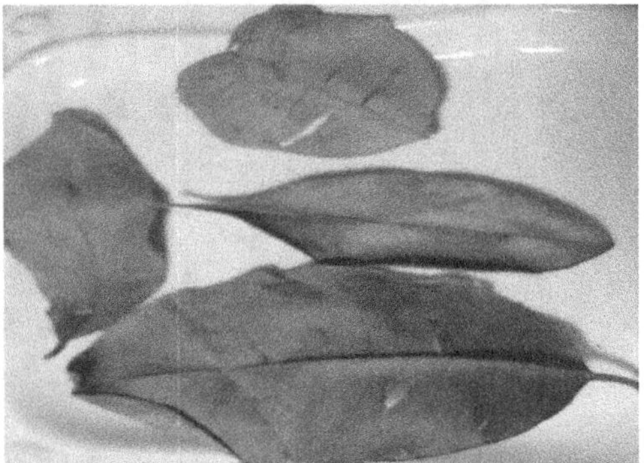

Bay leaves

Some of the reasons why Grenada is known as "The Isle of Spice."

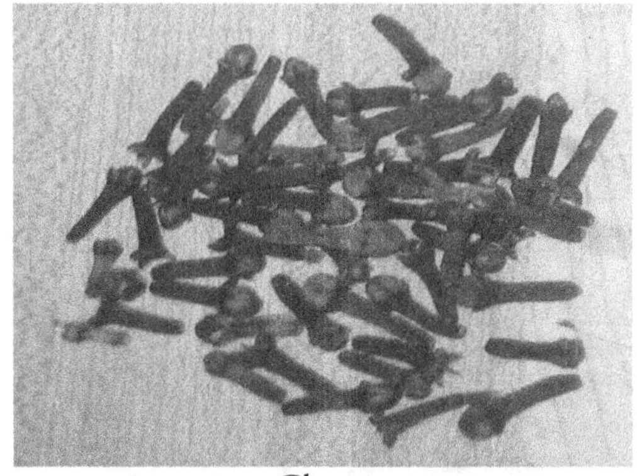

Cloves

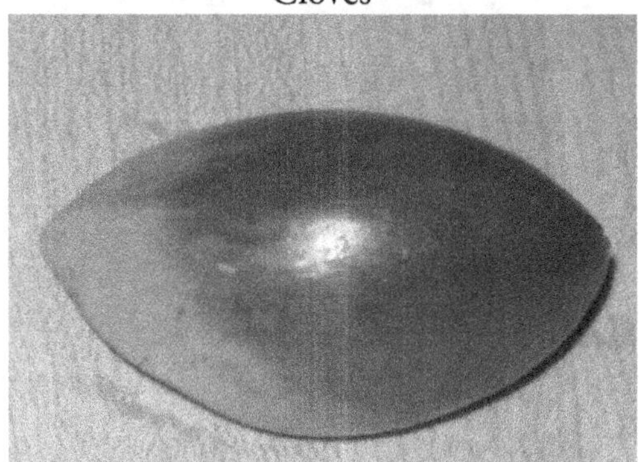

Sapot (above) and tonka (below) are aromatic beans used for flavoring pastries, ice cream, and milk beverages.

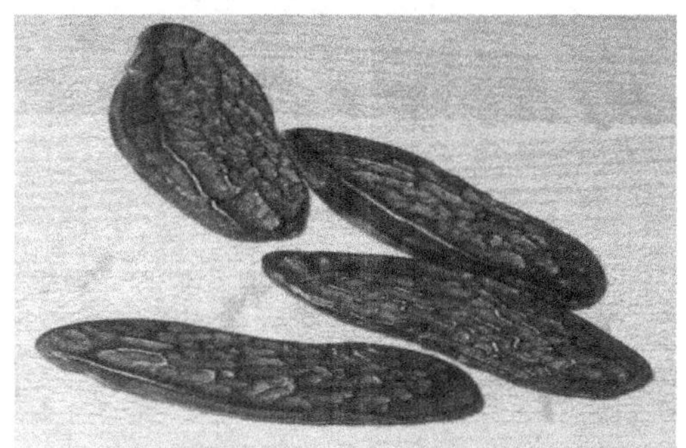

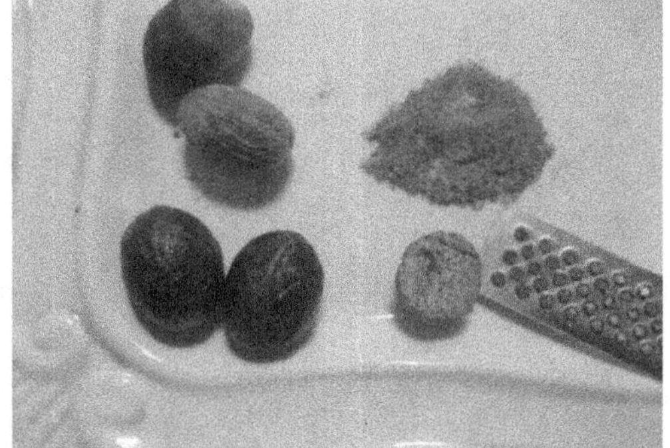

Nutmeg. Users remove the nut from the shell and grind it for use as a food or beverage flavoring.

NUTMEG

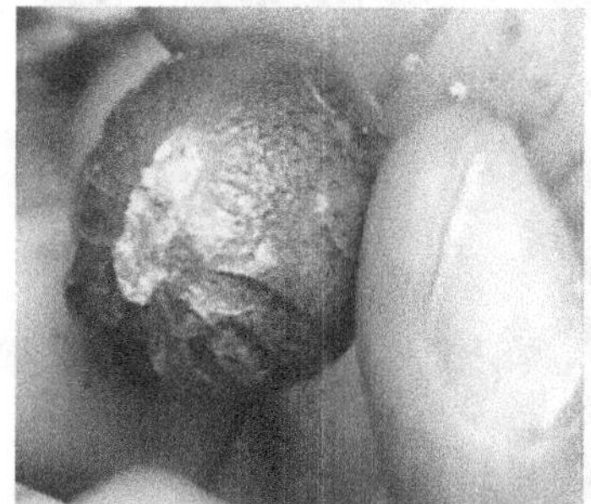

With mace removed, the nutmeg shell is revealed.

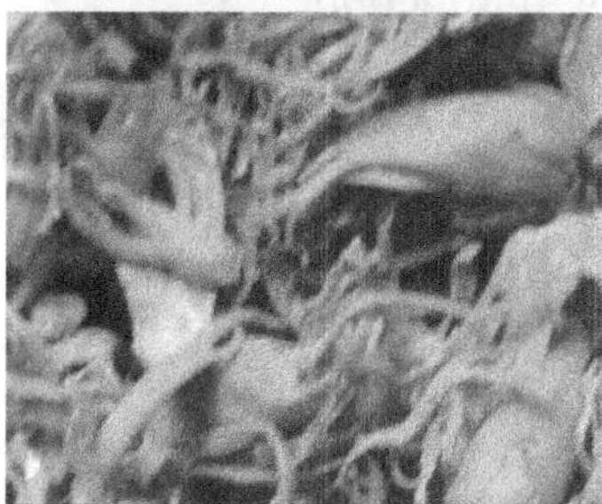

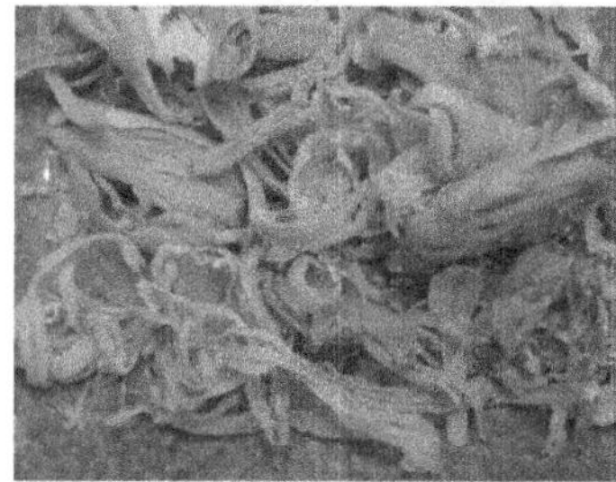

Above and Below: Varieties of mace, the velvet-like cover wrapped around the nutmeg shell. The mace is more profitable than the nut.

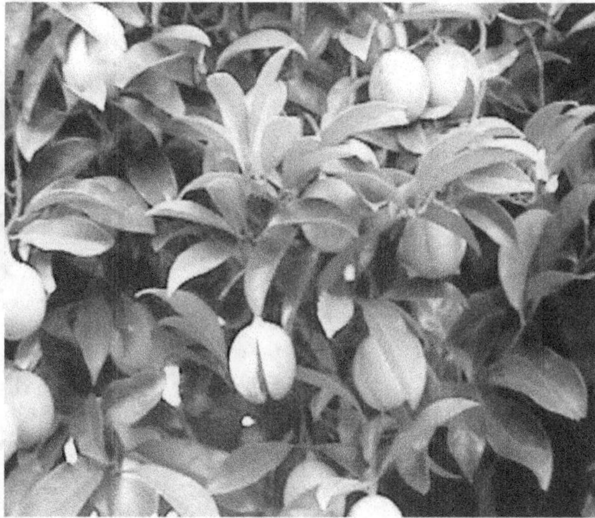

Nutmeg pods on a tree

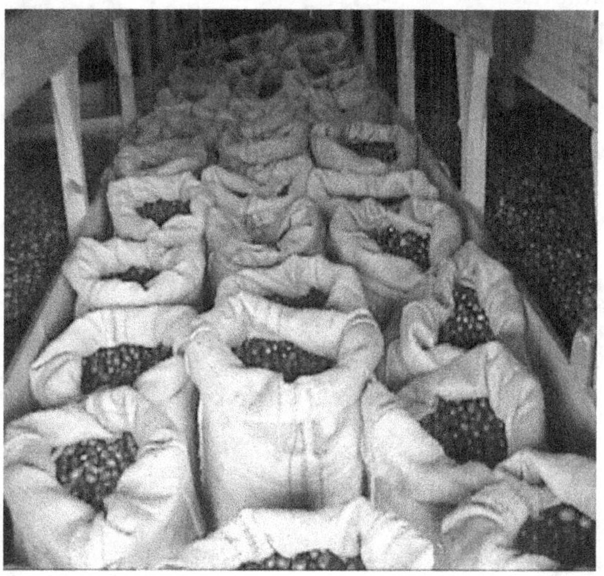

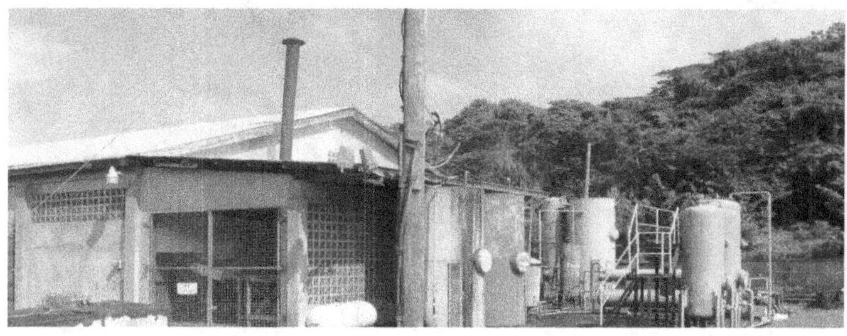

Nutmeg with red mace covering around the shell.

Center: Inside the nutmeg station, workers bag nutmegs for export. The Grenada Cooperative Nutmeg Association maintains nutmeg pools around the island to process the nutmegs for export. With a total of 120 sq. miles and a 1/3 supply of the world's nutmeg market, Grenada produces, per acre, the most nutmegs in the world. For this proud distinction, Grenada includes a nutmeg on its flag.

Nutmeg is Grenada's chief agricultural product, even after suffering disastrously under Hurricanes Ivan and Emily in 2004 and 2005. Grenada remains the second-largest producer of nutmegs in the world, mainly because of its ideal soil and climate. Apart from its use as a flavoring, they use nutmeg oil to produce cosmetics, preservatives, and pharmaceuticals.

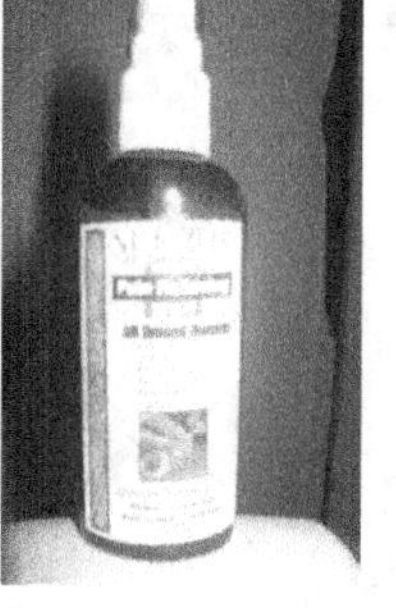

Nutmed spray (Left) is manufactured in Grenada and provides some relief from arthritis and muscular pains.

COCOA

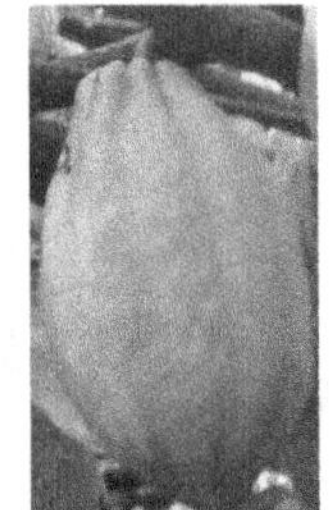

A single cocoa pod

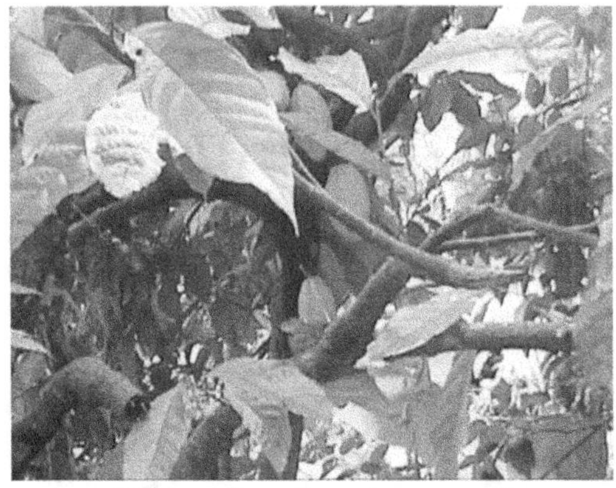

Tree with yellow cocoa pods

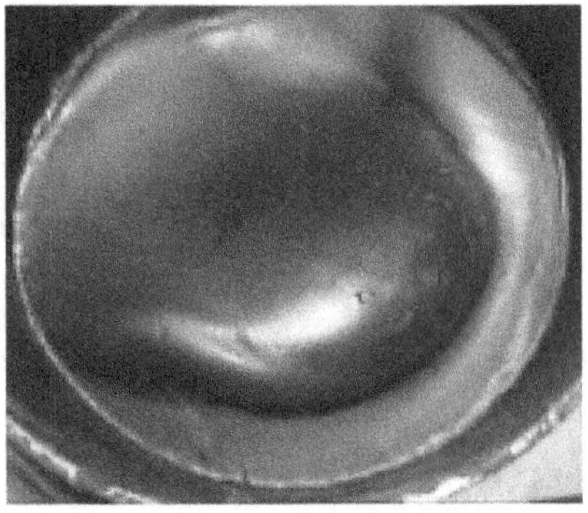

A thick chocolate paste emerges during production.

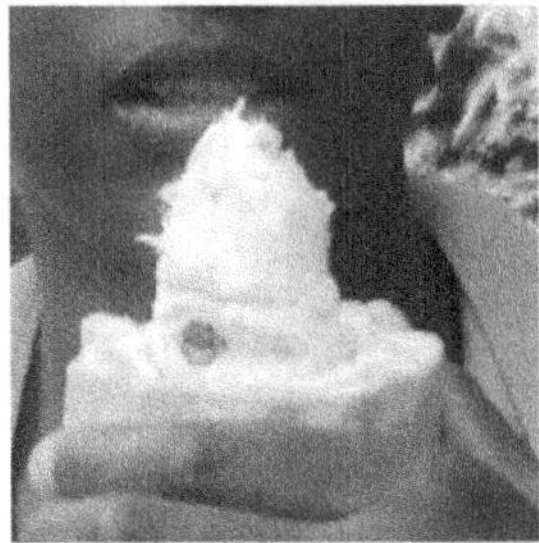

A juicy white covering protects the cocoa beans inside the pod, which aids the sweating process before drying. children sometimes enjoy sucking the juicy covering of the beans.

The production of chocolate at the Grenada Chocolate Company in Hermitage is an example of an environmentally clean and economically sustainable industry.

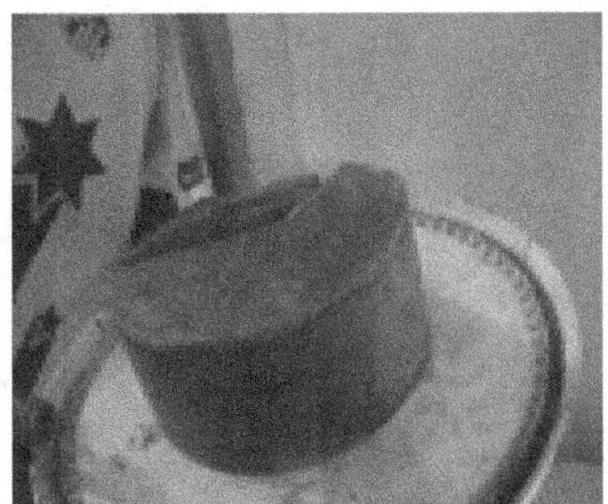

Dark chocolate piece

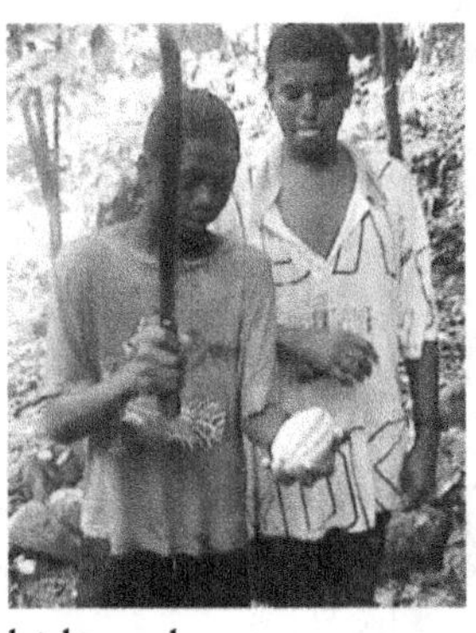

A kid cracks open a cocoa pod, a tropical starting point of chocolate products.

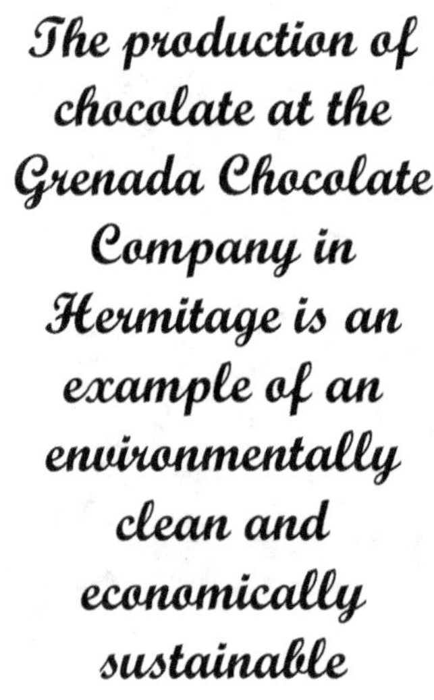

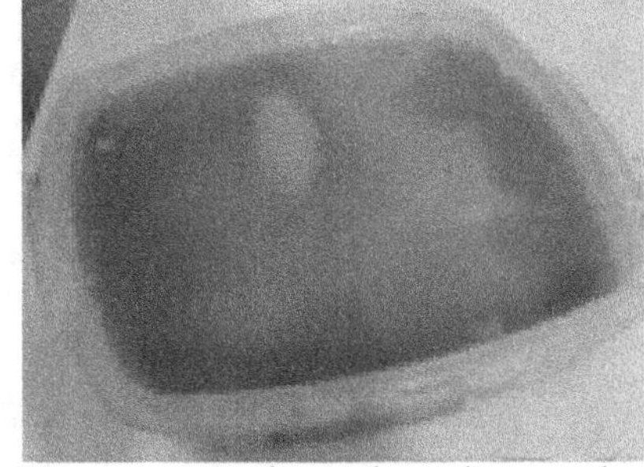

Processing white chocolate and cocoa butter from the cocoa fat

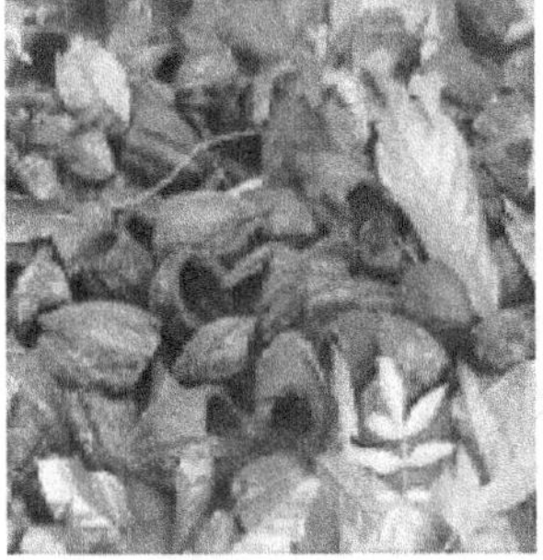

Cocoa pods are recycled into the soil as fertilizer.

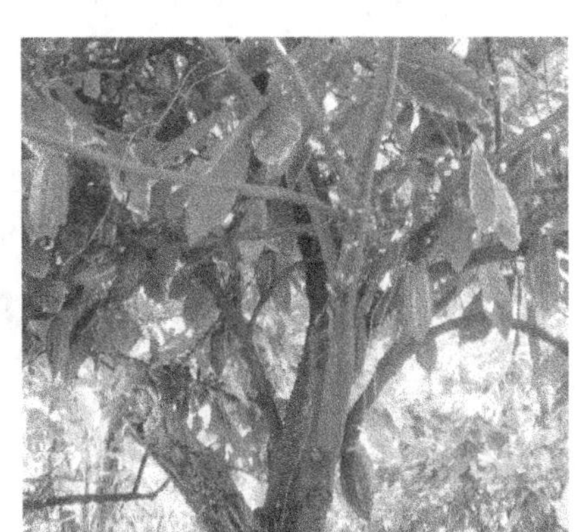

Tree with red cocoa pods

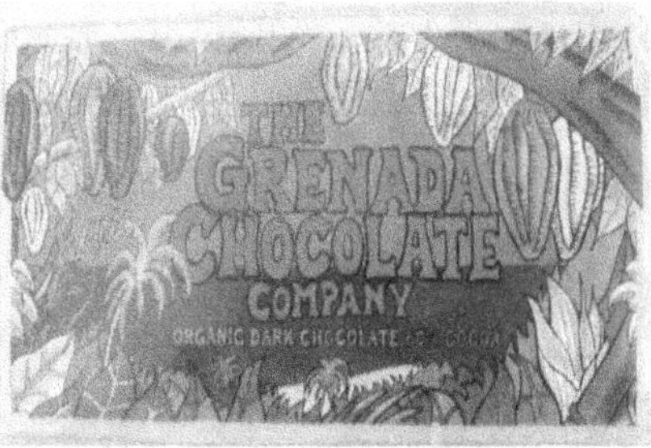

A locally produced dark chocolate bar at Hermitage, St. Patrick's.

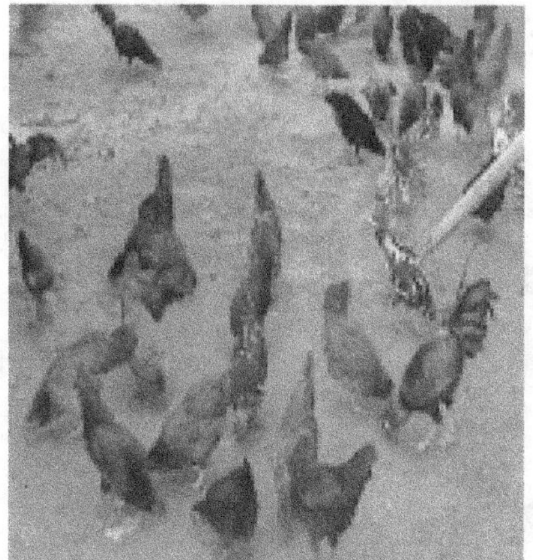

Chickens

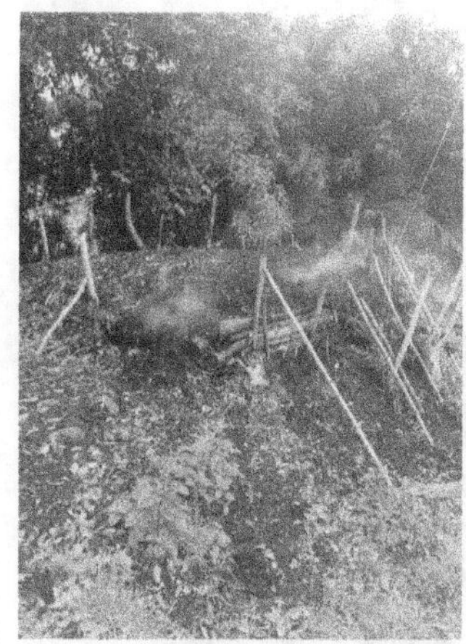

Burning wood to produce charcoal.

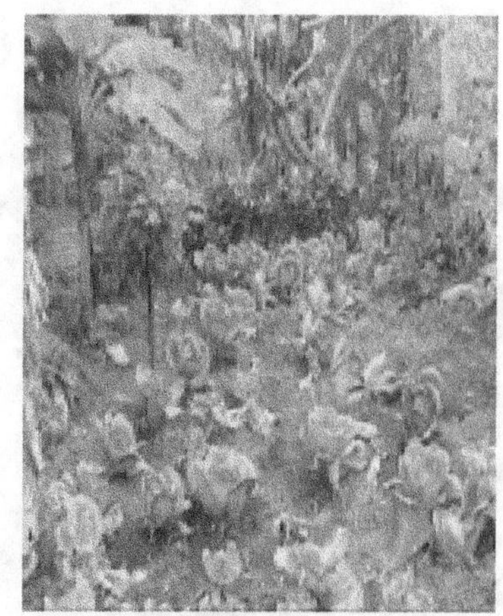

Cabbage patch

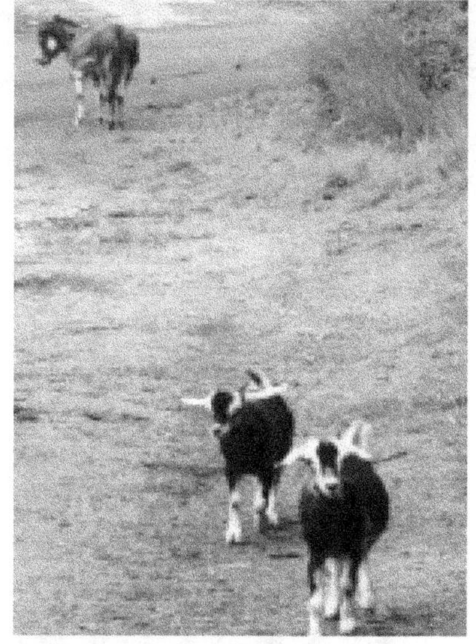

Two goats and a donkey

The agricultural environment

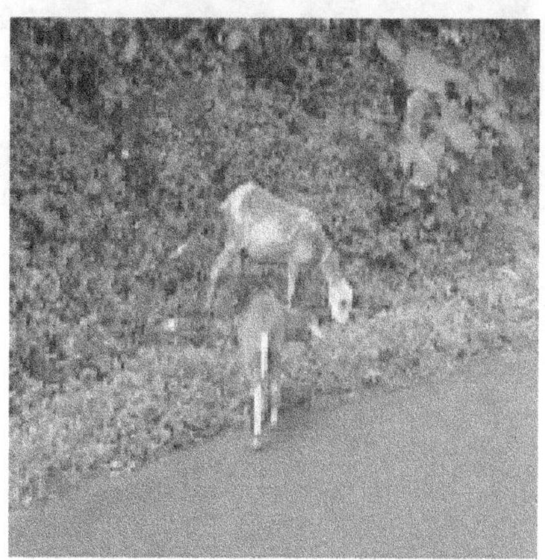

Sheep grazing by the roadside.

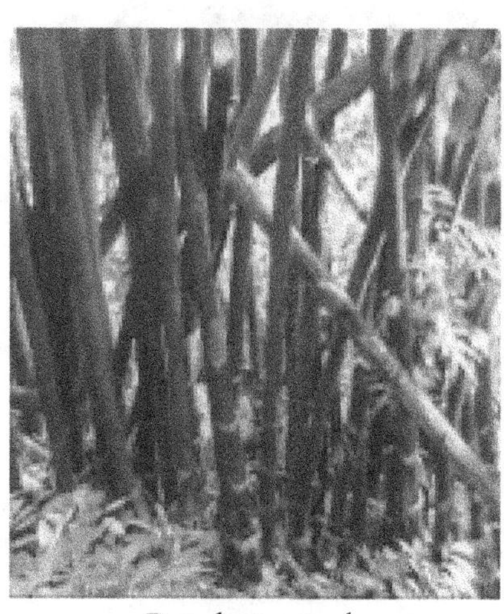

Bamboo stools

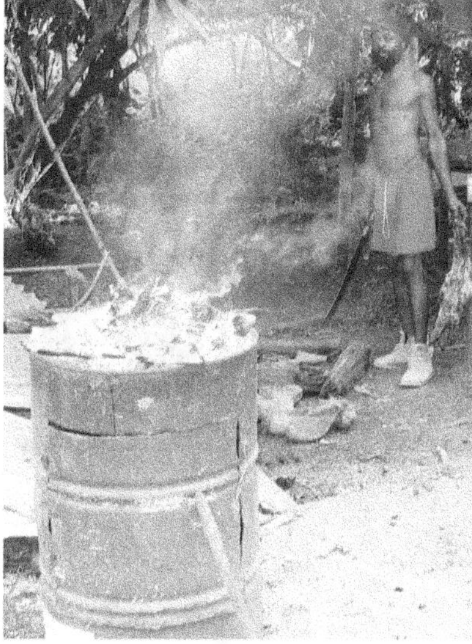

A young man is baking in an oven made from a steel drum that once contained oil. He uses wood and coconut shells as fuel.

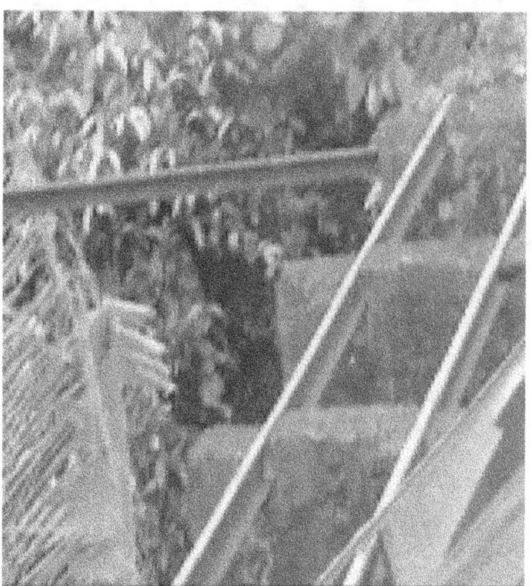

Agricultural laborers once used this rail to slide a drawer for drying cashew nuts, coconuts, cocoa, and nutmegs.

SOME GRENADIAN HOME BEVERAGES

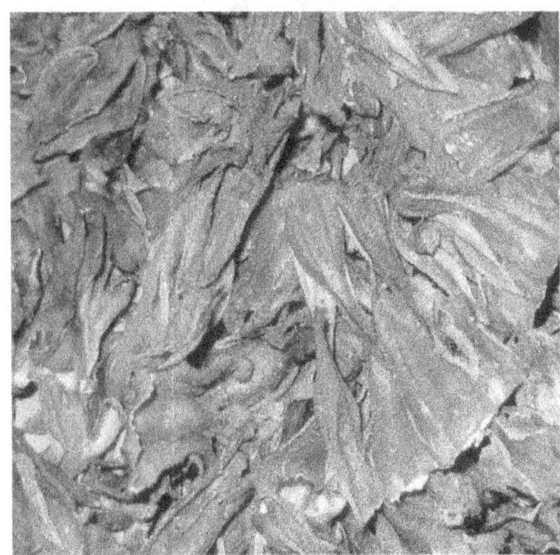

Sorrel

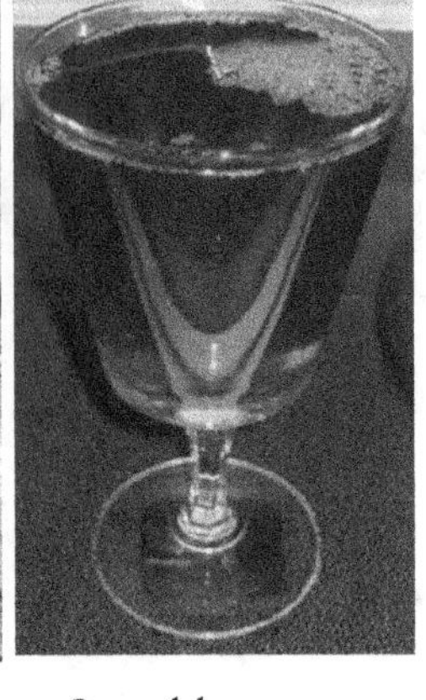

Sorrel beverage

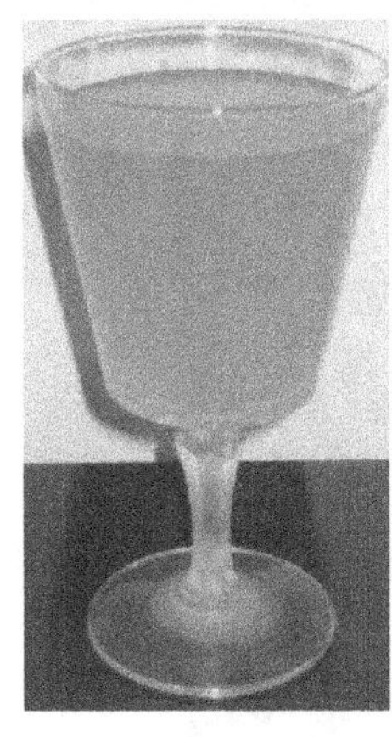

Ginger beer

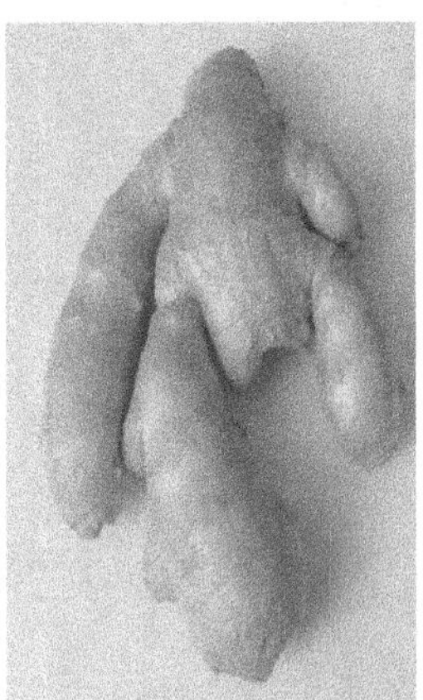

Ginger root

Sorrel is an annual plant of which you use the flower in making a delicious local beverage. One makes the sorrel beverage by either boiling or drawing the petals in water. You can use sorrel both when dried and when freshly picked. However, using dried sorrel is more prevalent. Sorrel beverage is a must for every Grenadian at Christmas time.

Ginger beer, also a must for every Grenadian at Christmas, is drawn from the water-soaked ginger root then sweetened.

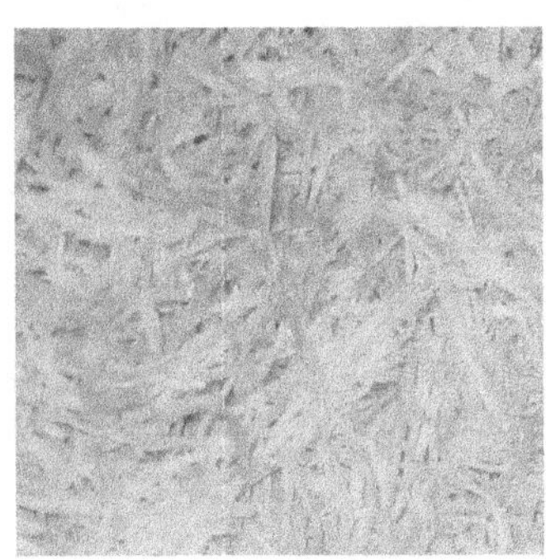

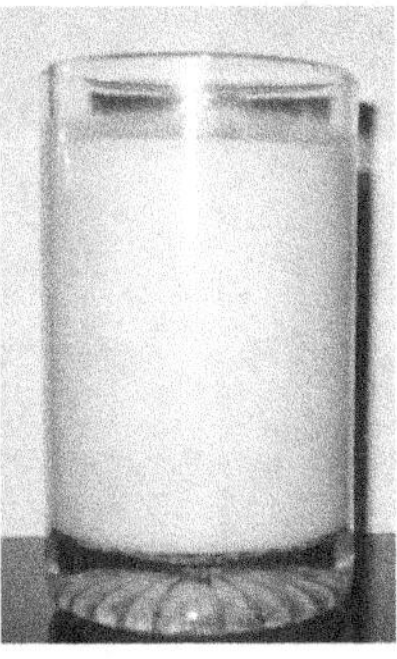

Sea moss is a seaweed variant used for making a milk-based drink, popular in Grenada.

Sea Moss beverage

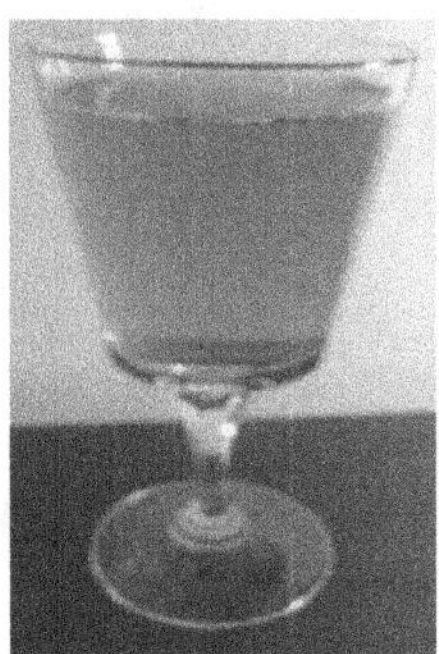

Mauby beverage

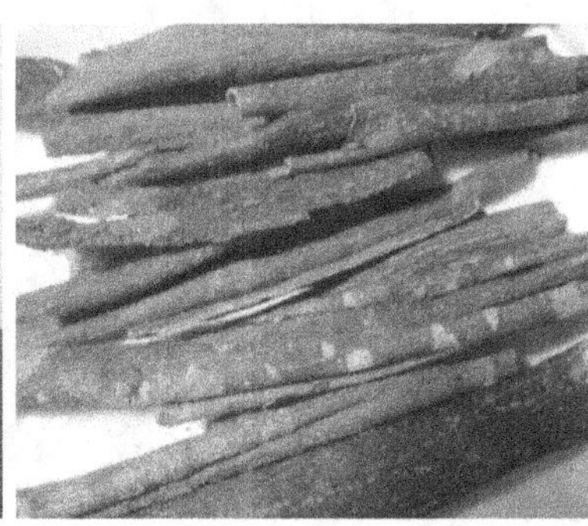

Mauby bark is boiled with anise seed essence and sweetened to provide a beverage with a bitter after-taste. Mauby beverage is an acquired taste.

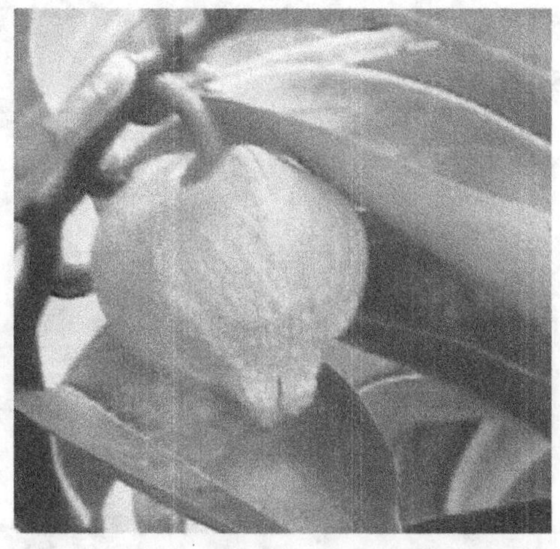

Young soursop

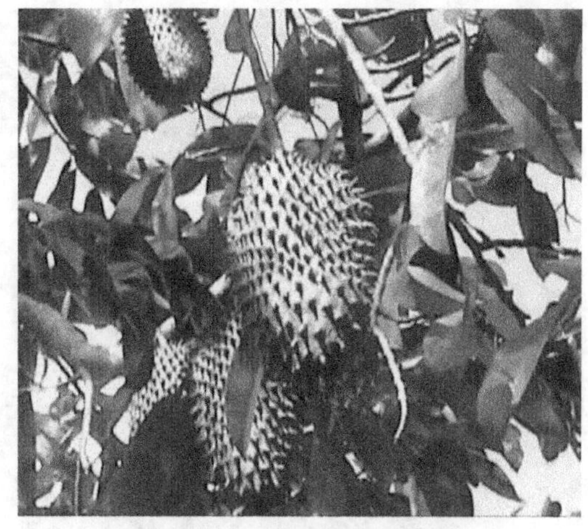

Matured soursop

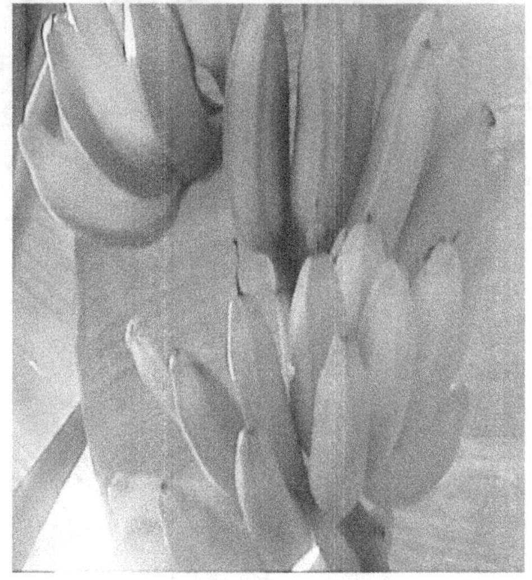

Bluggoe Bunch

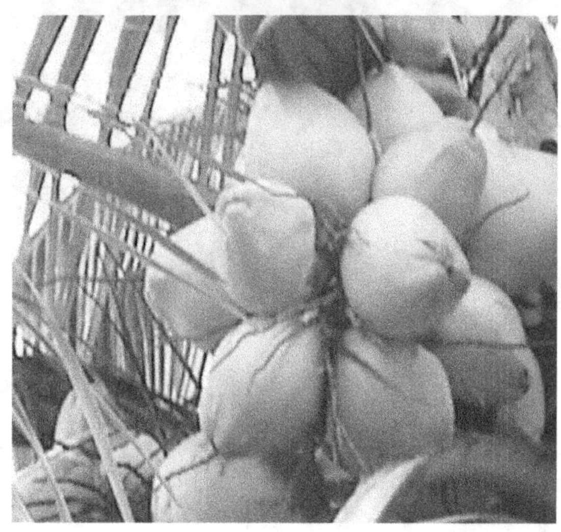

Coconuts

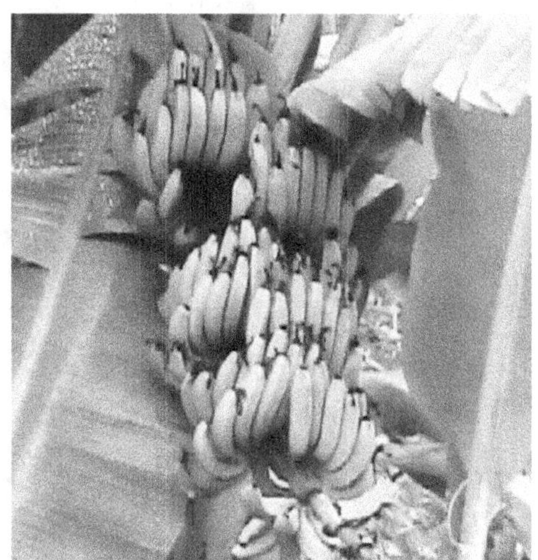

Banana bunch

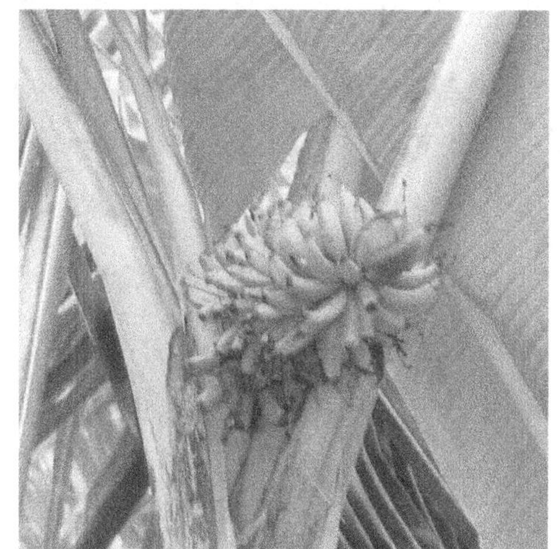

Young plantain bunch

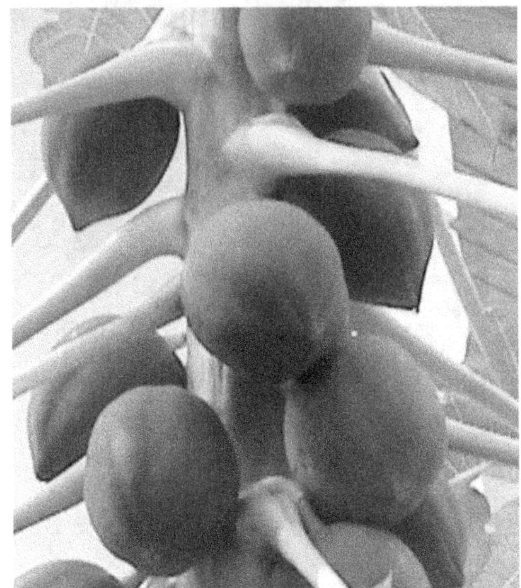

Top section of a papaya tree

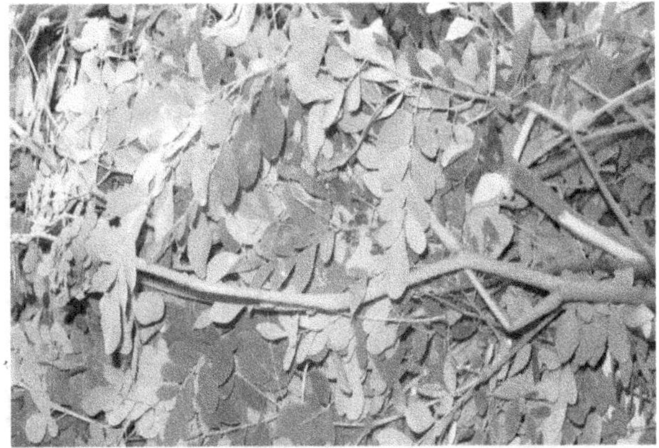

Moonga, also called moringa, is the name given to the plant that produces these branches. The leaves are stripped and cleaned, then cooked similarly to how we cook spinach or collard greens. East Indian Grenadians commonly use the tasty moonga green. `

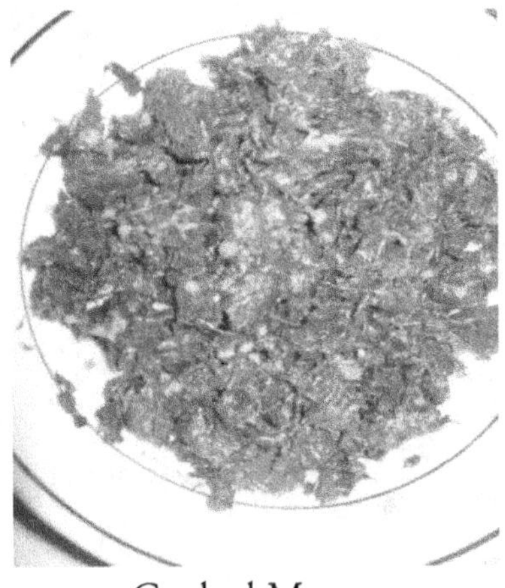

Cooked Moonga

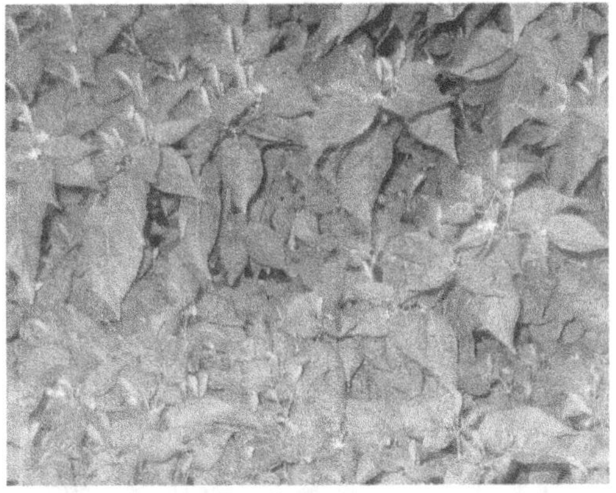

Bird peppers

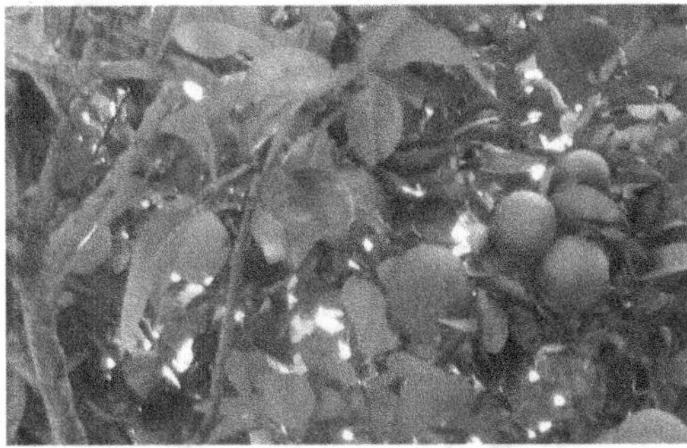

Gospo is a citrus fruit used both as a fruit juice, and in eliminating tough odors.

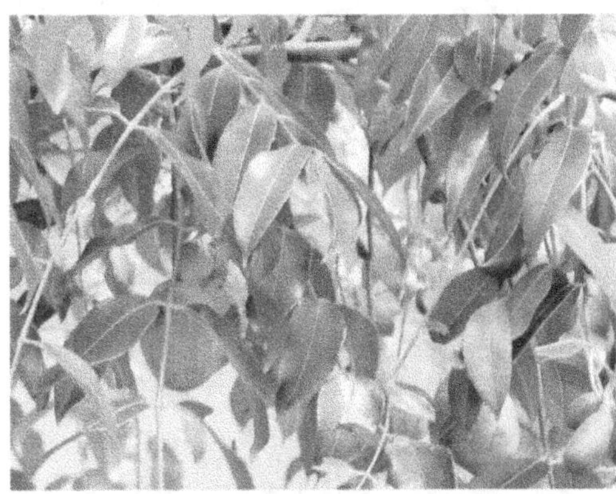

Golden apples

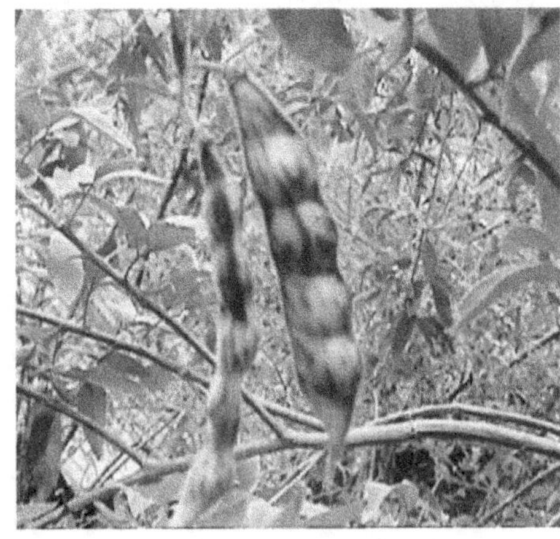

Pigeon peas

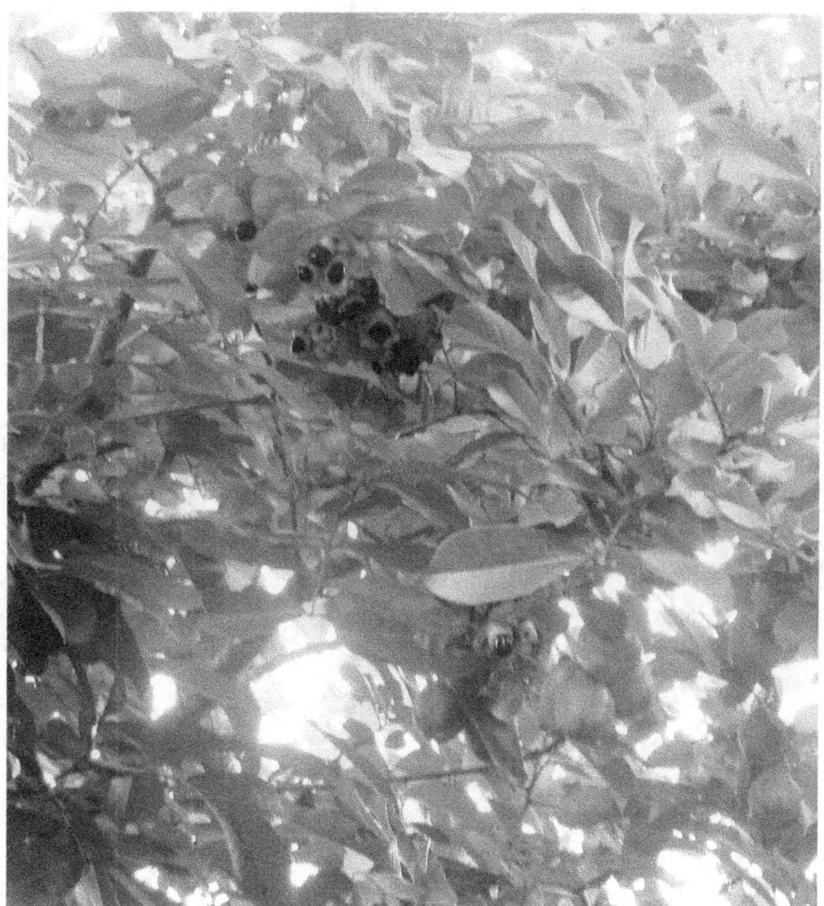

The branches of an ackee tree, laden with fruit.

Ackee is not common in Grenada, whereas in Jamaica, the ackee is so abundant that a dish made of ackee and salted codfish is considered the national dish. This ackee tree above is in Hermitage, St. Patrick's.

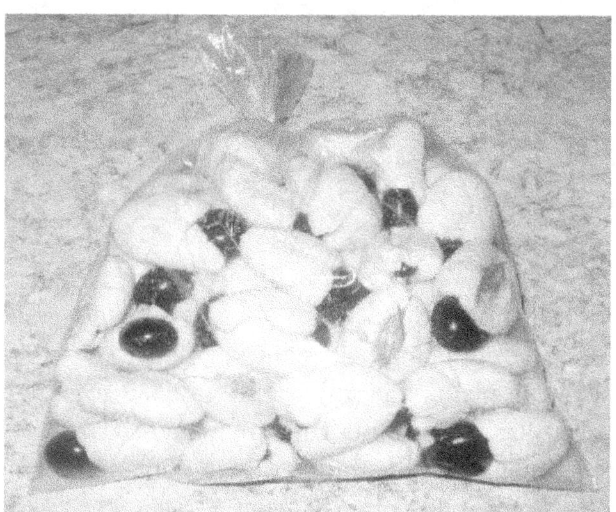

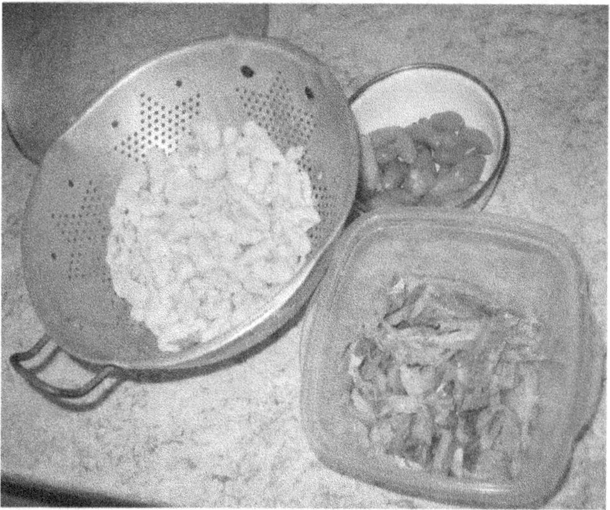

Above Left: Ackee fruit removed from the pod. Above Right: Ackee about to be mixed with codfish and peppers during the food preparation process.

BREADFRUIT

Breadfruit was brought to the West Indies from Tahiti by British naval officer Captain William Bligh (1790s). Breadfruit is one of the ingredients of Oil-Down, Grenada's national dish. Above, breadfruits are being sliced and peeled for cooking. Slave plantations introduced Breadfruit in Grenada as a cheap staple for feeding slaves. Today, Breadfruit is a popular food of choice for all Grenadians. Breadfruit can be boiled, steamed, roasted, fried, or baked.

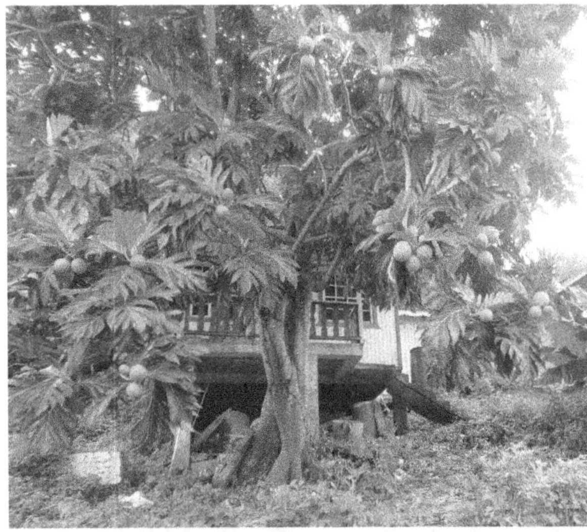

A breadfruit tree flourishes in this front yard.

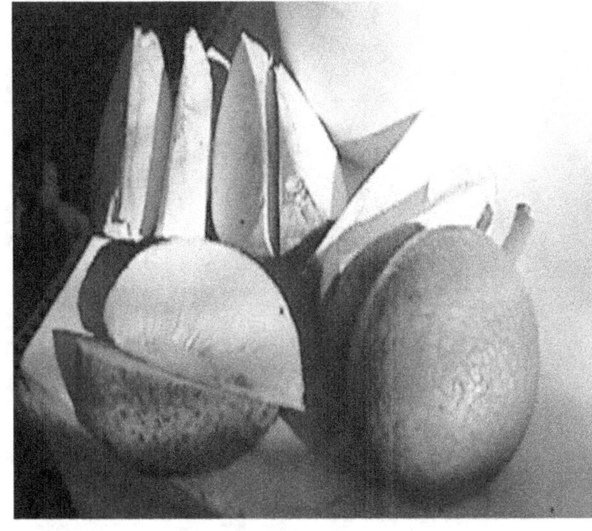

Breadfruit, peeled and sliced before cooking

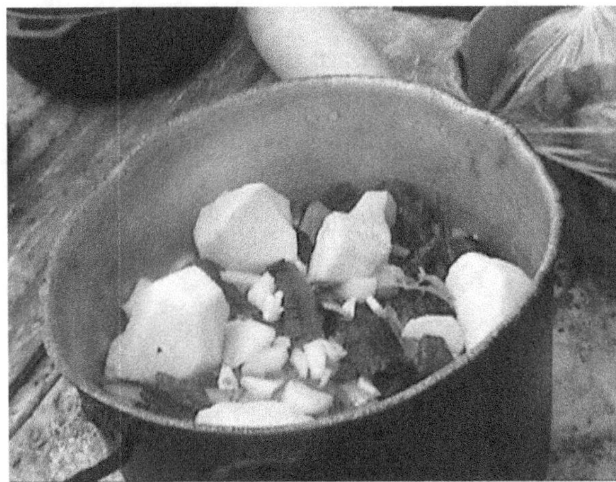

Farmers working in the woods have here prepared a pot of oil-down. Grenadians make oil-down by cooking the breadfruit in coconut milk, with meat and other vegetables, until the coconut milk boils down to coconut oil.

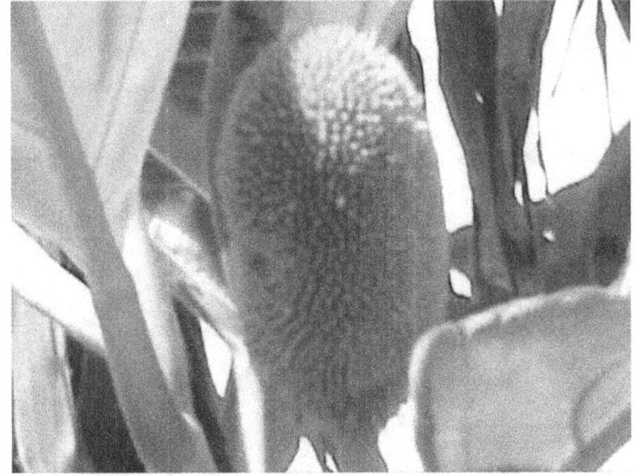

The breadnut plant looks somewhat like the breadfruit plant. The fruit is also similar, except that inside the breadnut fruit are many seeds, sometimes hundreds, which we can boil and peel before eating their bread-like kernel.

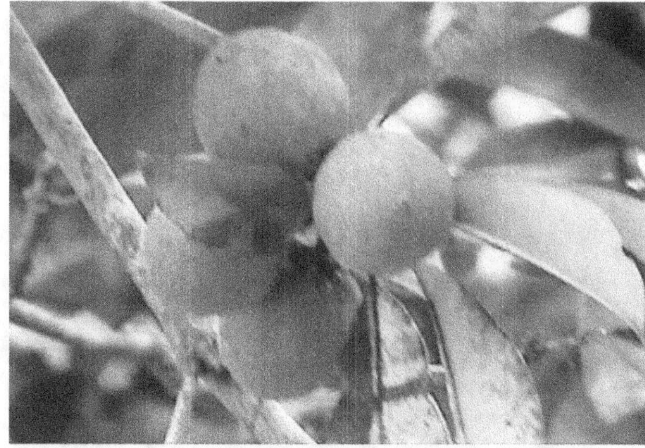

Sapodillas

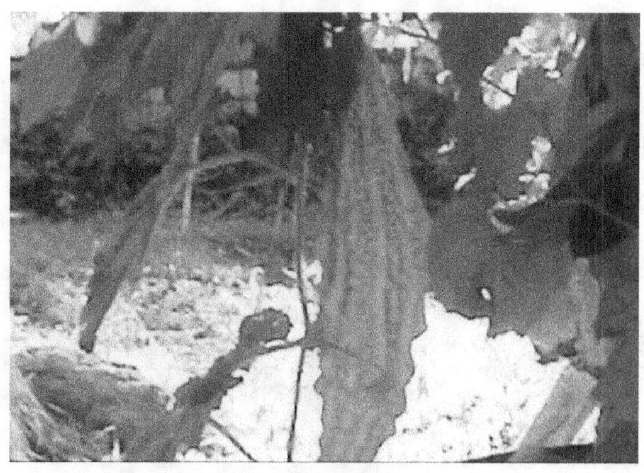

Karela, also called bitter melon,
can be curried to be eaten with rice.

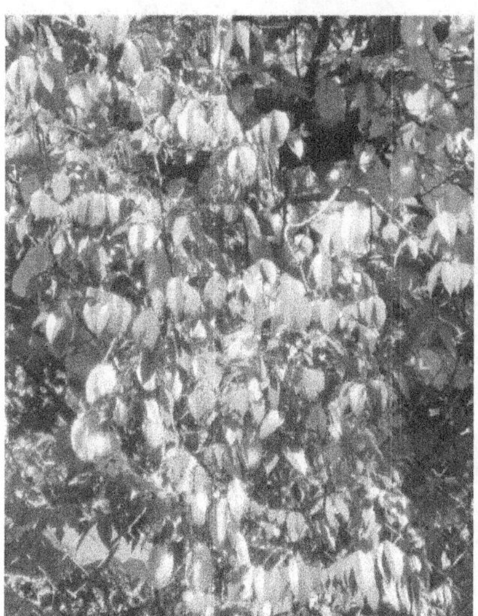

Carambolas on a tree

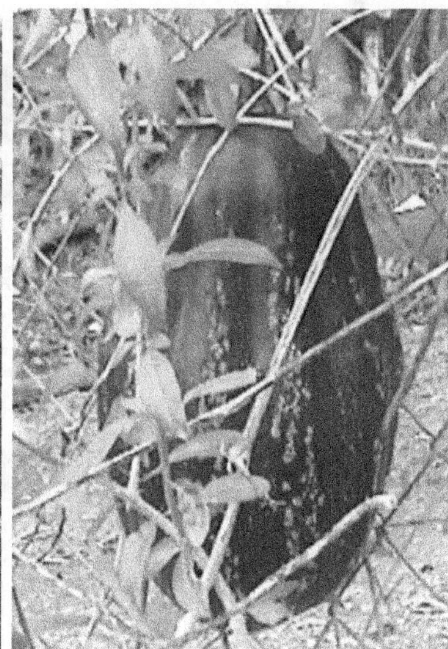

Pumpkin

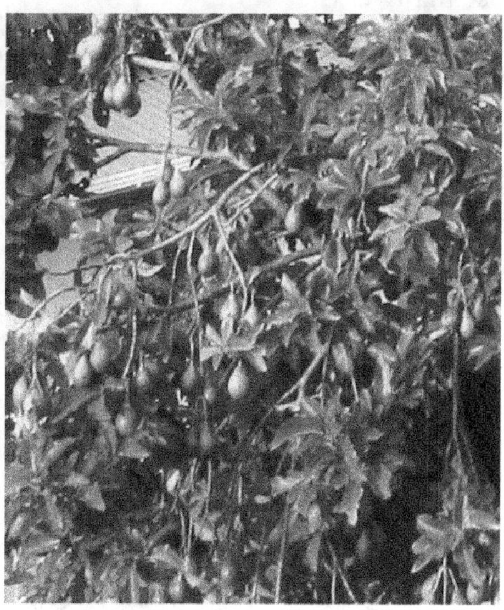

Avocado, locally called "pear." The
fruit is also called "zaboca," a patois
derivation of the French plural, les
avocats.

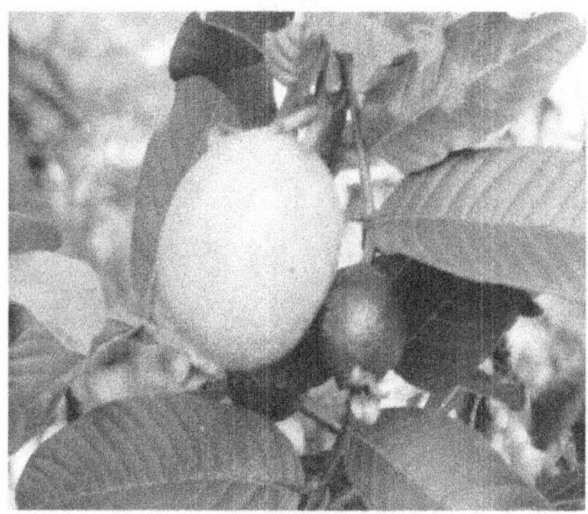

Guava

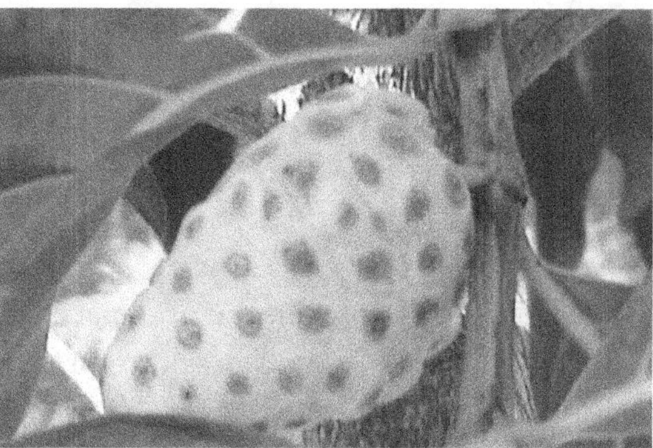

Noni

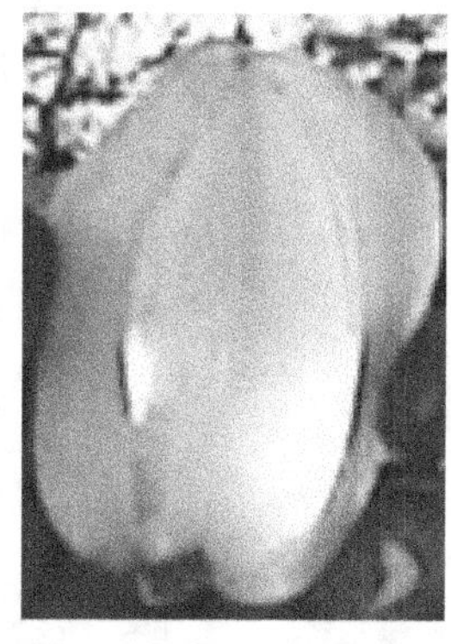

Carambola, also called
five fingers, makes a
delicious drink.

BUSH

Bush medicine, though more widely relied upon in the past, remains the choice of many Grenadians when faced with specific ailments. Some Grenadians use many of the bushes pictured here for a variety of colds and influenza. They use some for other illnesses. Here, I have assigned these bushes their local names.

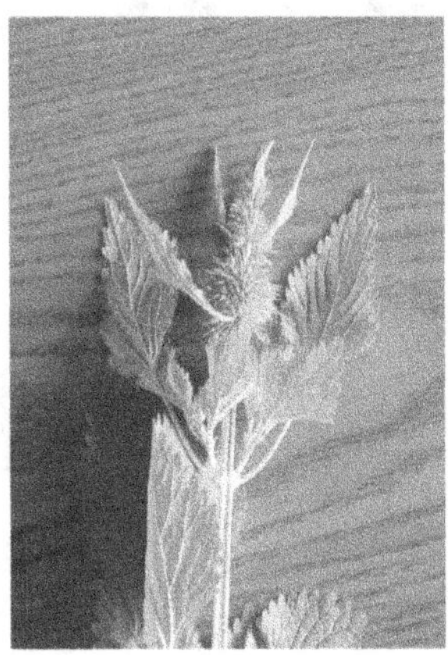

Honeysuckle

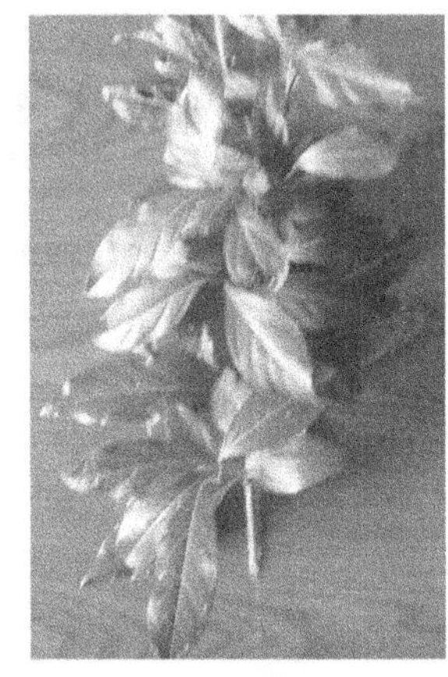

Cutlet

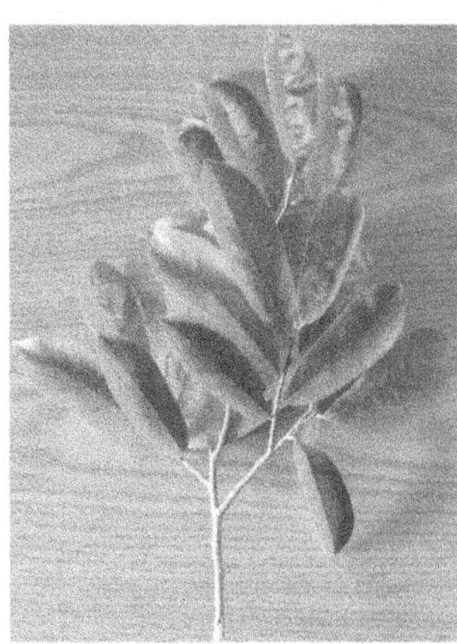

Soursop

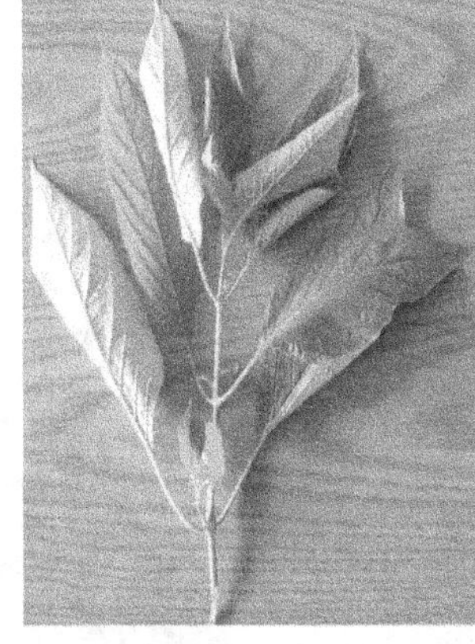

St. John Bush

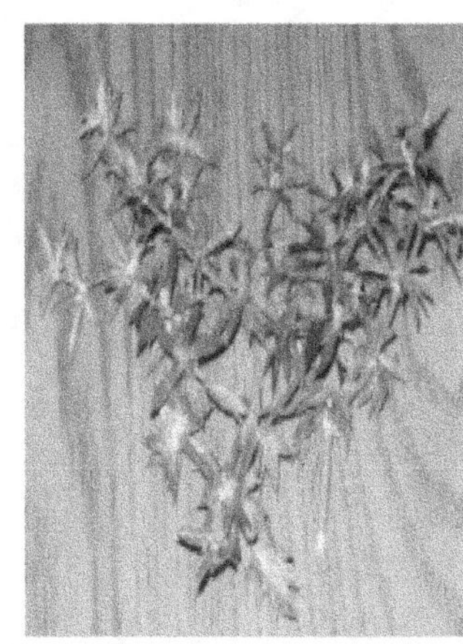

Shadow Benny

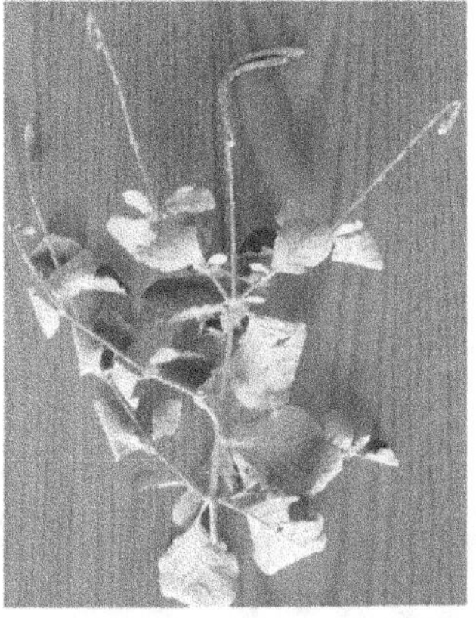

Man-better-man.

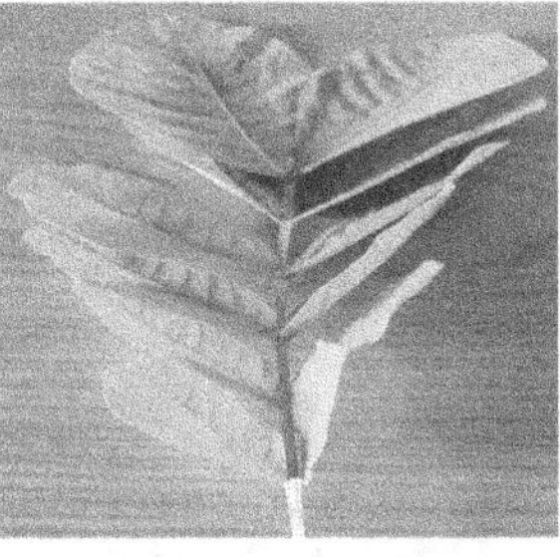

Senna

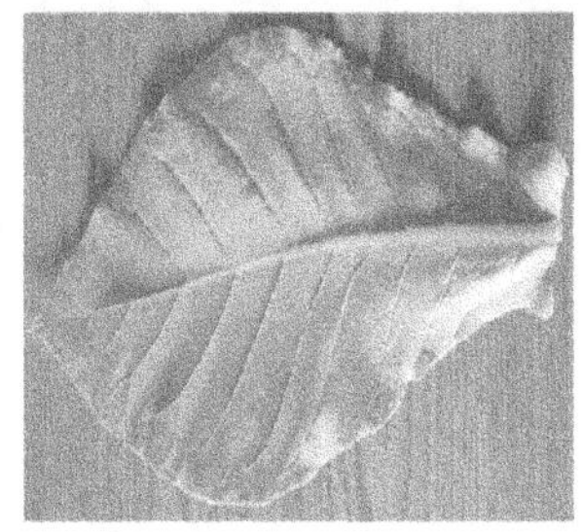

Tobacco

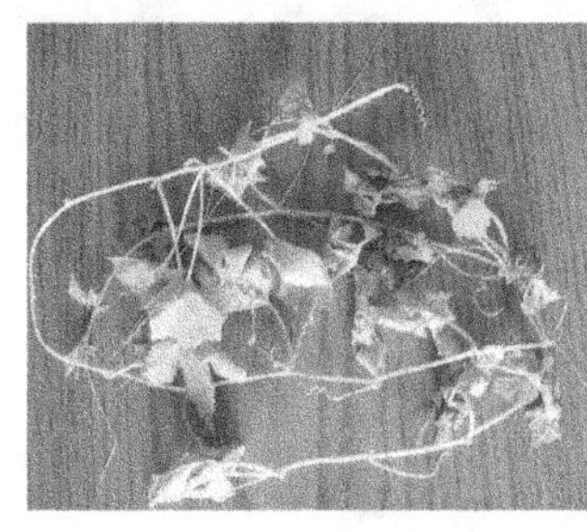

Karela

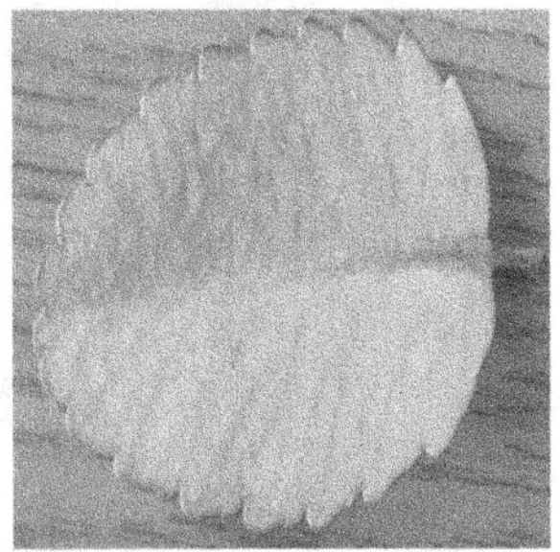

Zhay-oui-toot

Zhay- oui-toot, other than its use for colds, has been used by kids as a love 'medicine.' A young boy and girl in love would indent their names on a zhay-oui-toot leaf and place it inside a schoolbook. Over time, roots begin to sprout on the edges of that leaf. The sprouts are then considered testimony that their love, too, has sprouted.

MEDICINE

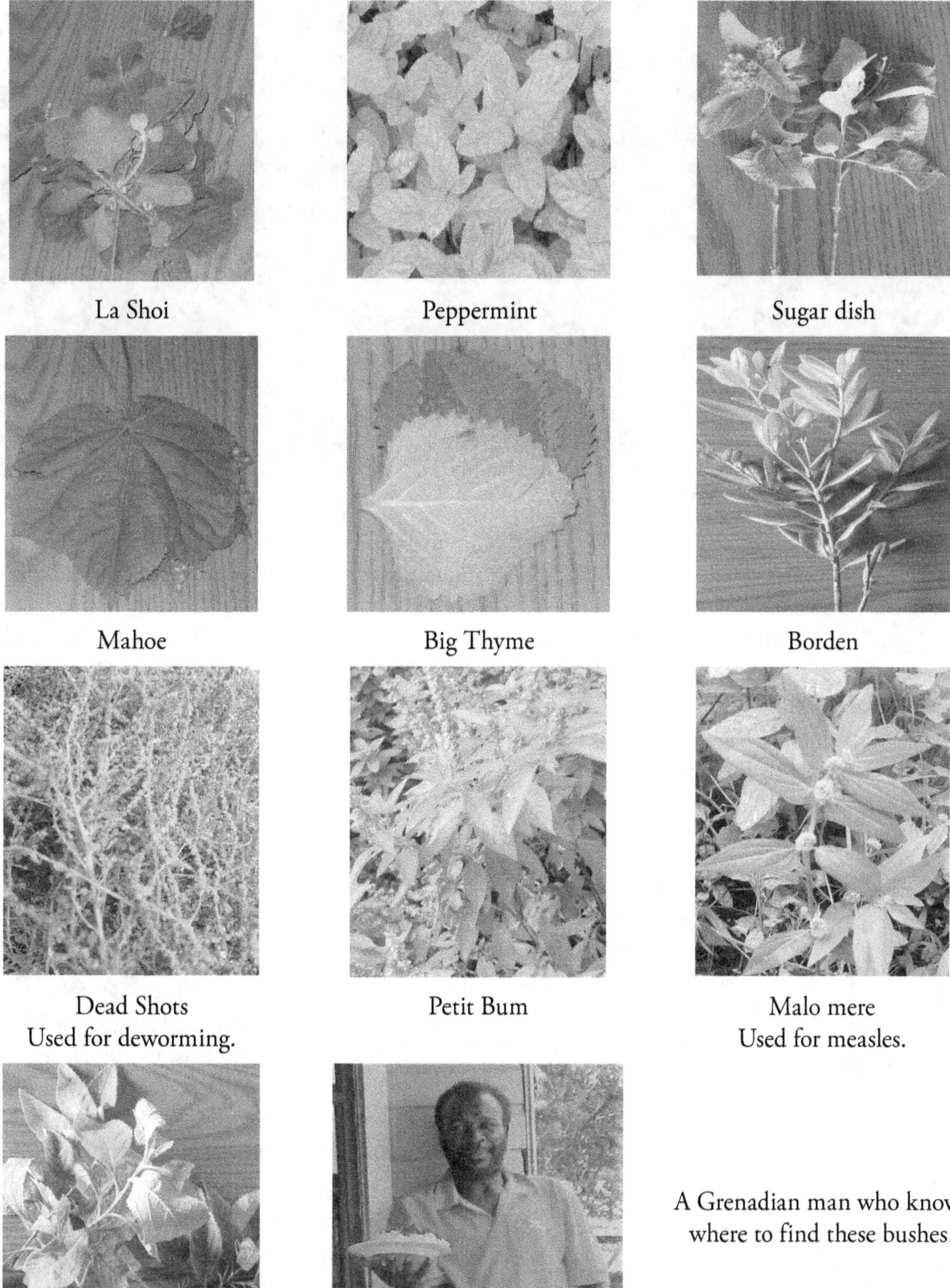

La Shoi

Peppermint

Sugar dish

Mahoe

Big Thyme

Borden

Dead Shots
Used for deworming.

Petit Bum

Malo mere
Used for measles.

Black Sage

A Grenadian man who knows
where to find these bushes.

CRAFT

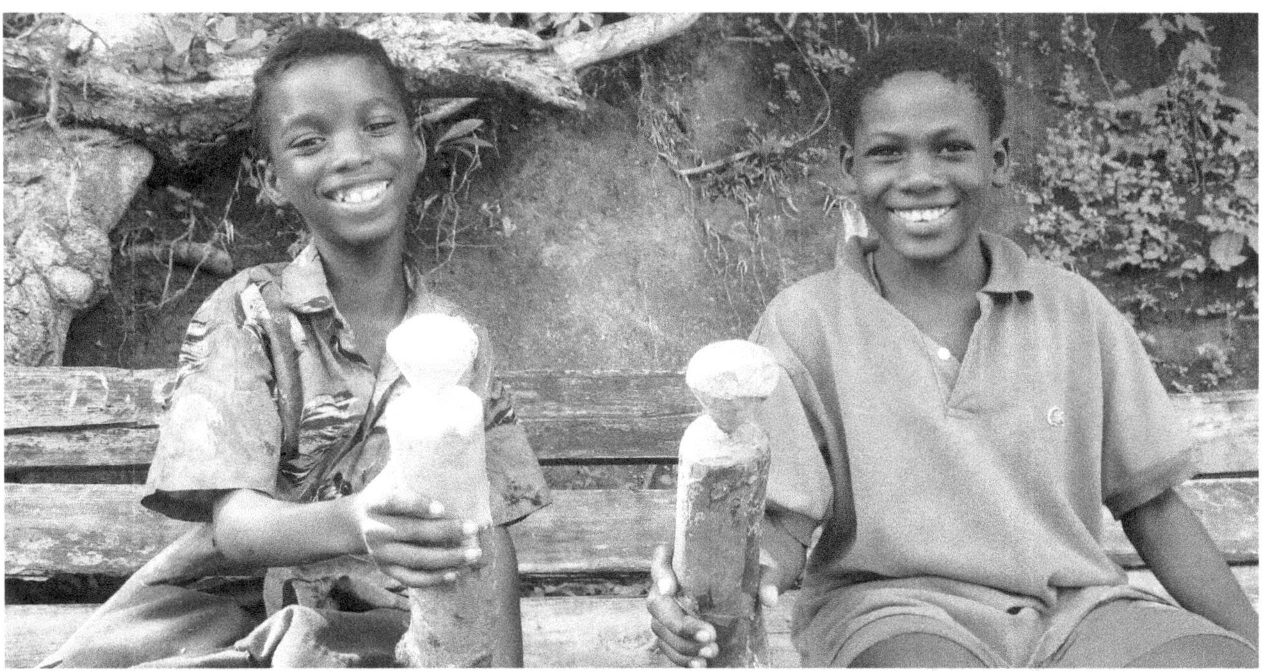

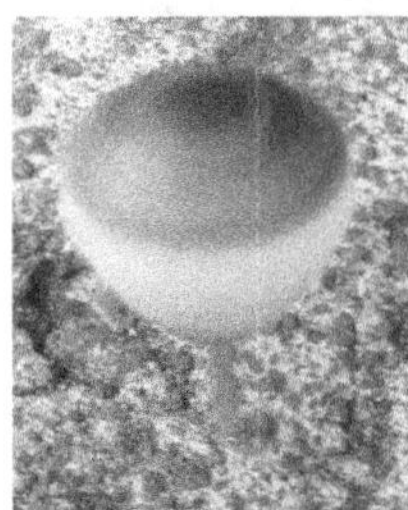

The above young boys from Hermitage village made the spinning top to the left.

Grenadian youngsters make a variety of toys from local materials. Here, these kids have put down their carving tools to show off the tops they are constructing from local cinnamon and guava woods. The cinnamon wood's bark is typically stripped and dried to produce cinnamon sticks, which they pound or grind to make the cinnamon powder.

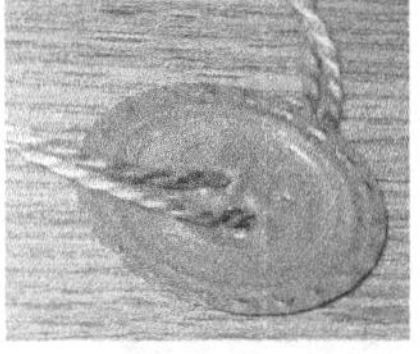

Kids make the zwill by looping a string through two holes in a flattened crown cap or lid of a can. They skillfully jerk the string to start an elastic series of extensions and contractions while the flattened cap rotates in clockwise and counterclockwise alternations. The zwill is just one of the many local toys made by Grenadian children.

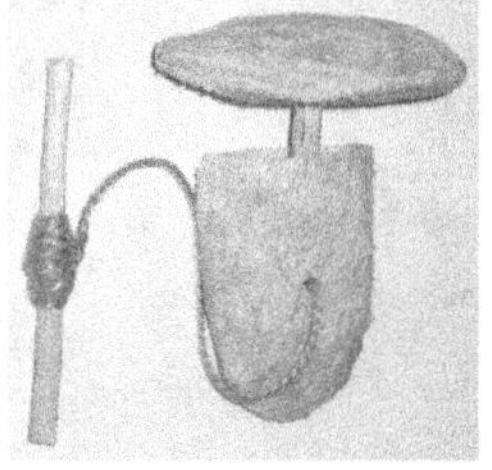
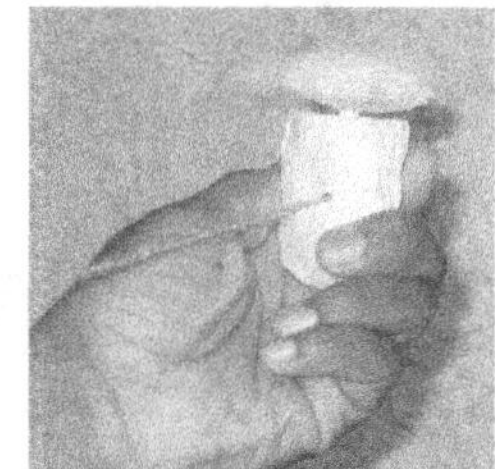

Ra-ra.: Youngsters make the ra-ra from two dry mango seeds, two small sticks, and a string. After being jerked into a start, the top seed is repeatedly pulled into a clockwise spin and released into a counterclockwise spin.

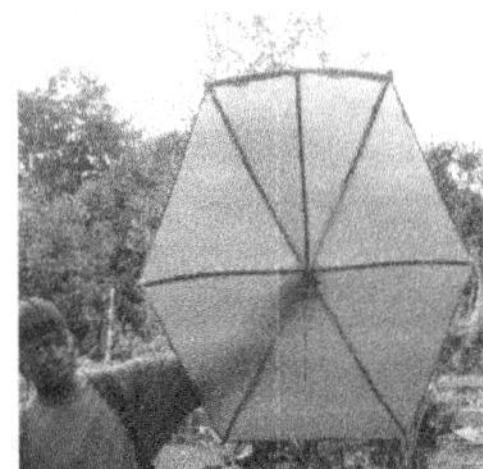

Here is a kite made of wood, plastic, and twine.

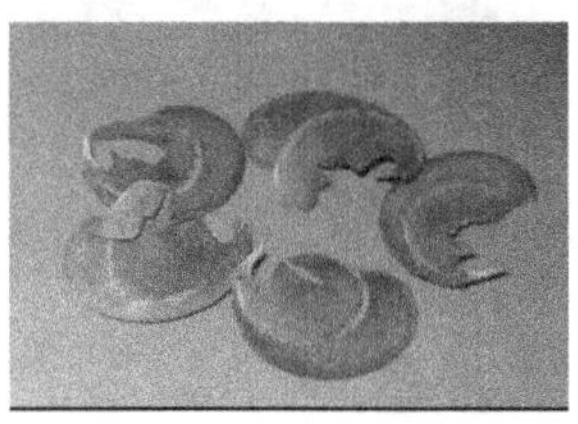

Artists sometimes carve the dried fruit of the sandbox tree (Hura-crepitans) as pendants for necklaces and other decorations.

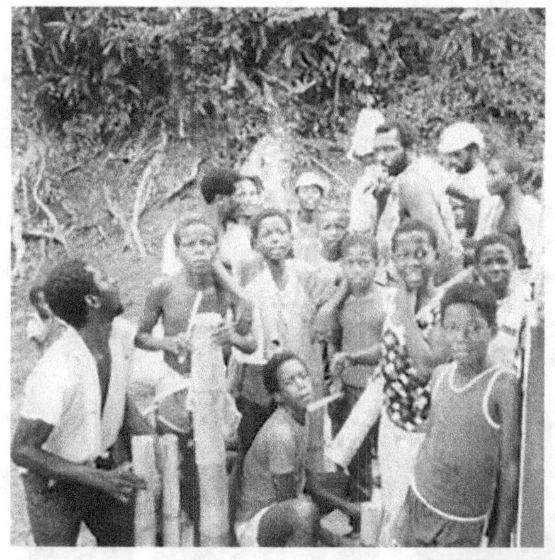

A Tamboo-Bamboo orchestra (left) at Christmas. The bamboos are cut in different lengths to produce different sounds when pounded on the ground. These players are here entertaining a Grenadian home.

This Grenadian man's clothing (right) including a hat, jacket, and pants, are all made of wist

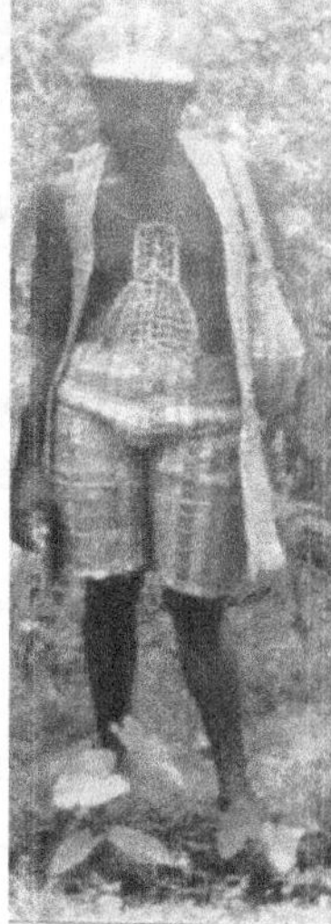

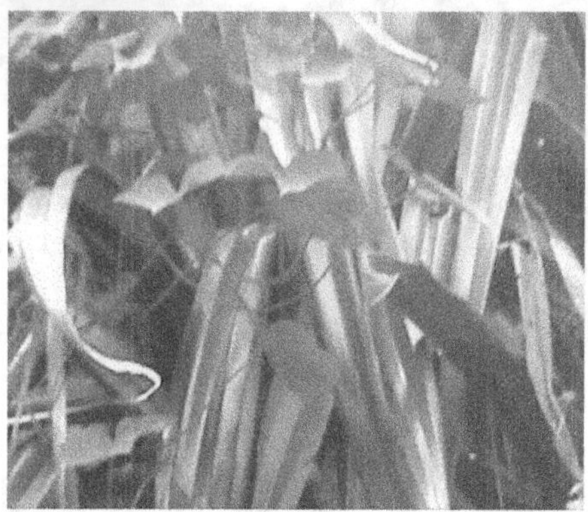

Wist: Vendors use the above sword-like reeds to fabricate bags, mats, and straw hats for sale in the stores and local markets.

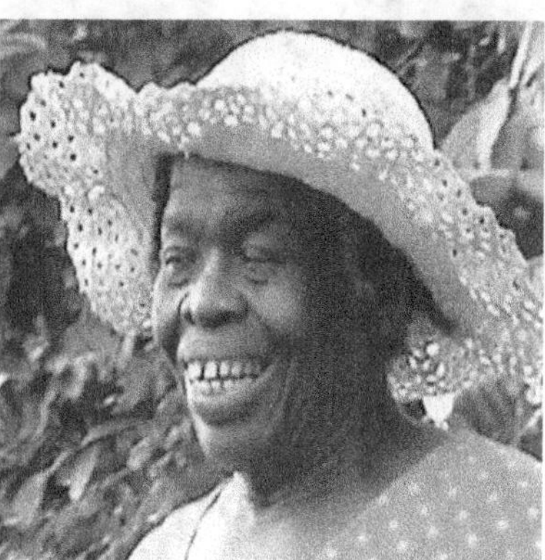

A straw hat made of wist

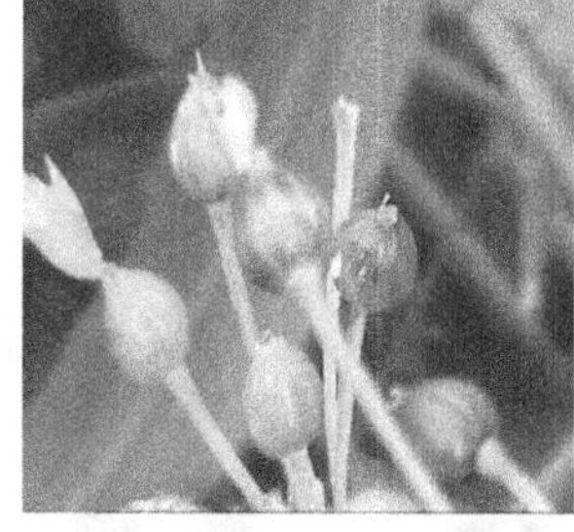

Job's Tears (Coix Lacryma-Jobi)

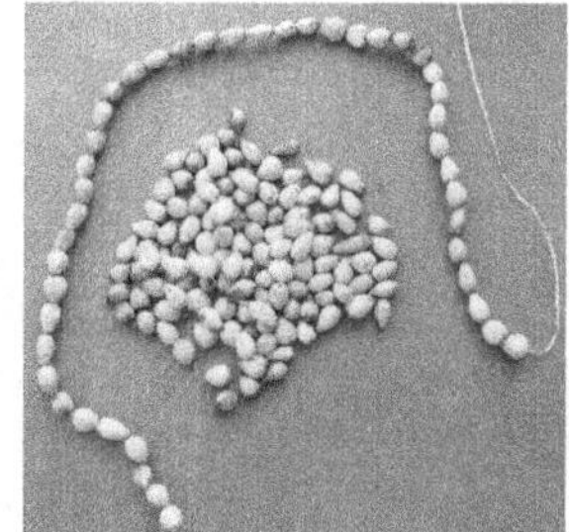

Necklace being made from dried Job's Tears

Job's Tears (coix Lacryma-Jobi), referring to the tears of the biblical Job, grow wild in Grenada. Sometimes the seeds, or involucres, are used to make decorative beads. Here, one has started to fashion a Job's Tears necklace. Many have made Rosaries with these beads. The beads' most popular uses are as anklets, bracelets, and necklaces for "wild Indian" masqueraders at the carnival festival. At the festival, Wild Indian masqueraders imitate the body adornments of our Amerindian, Carib predecessors.

FLOWERS OF GRENADA

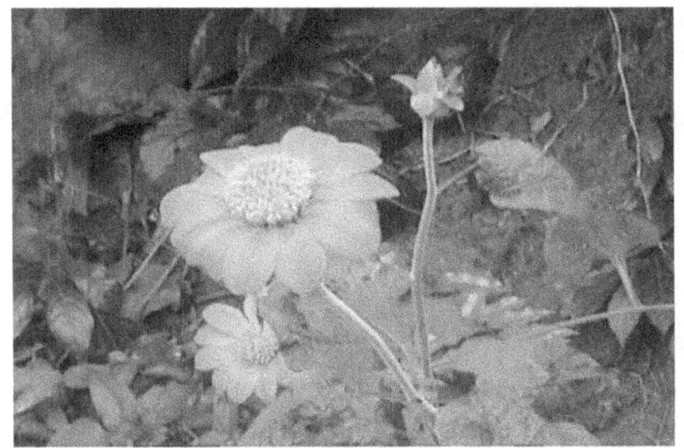

Mexican Sunflower (Tithonia rotundifolia)

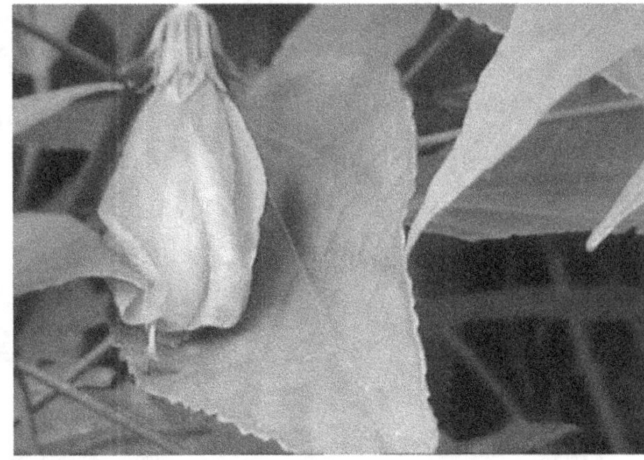

Parlor Maid or Chinese Lantern (Abutilon)

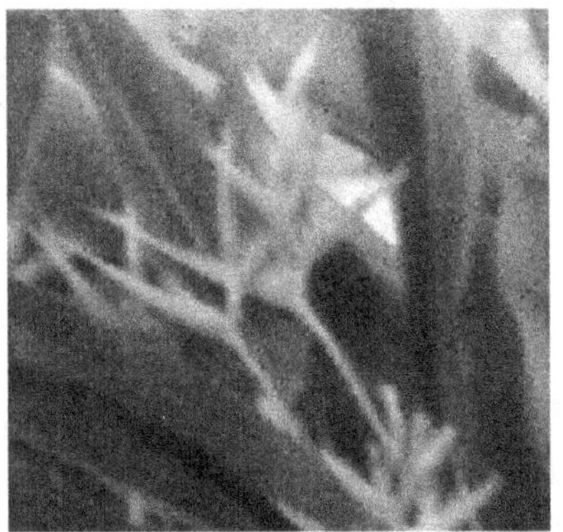

Heliconia Bihai

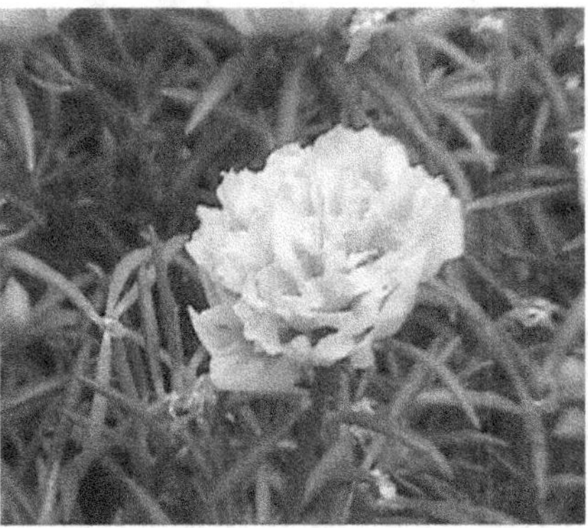

Carnation or Clove Pink
(Dianthus)

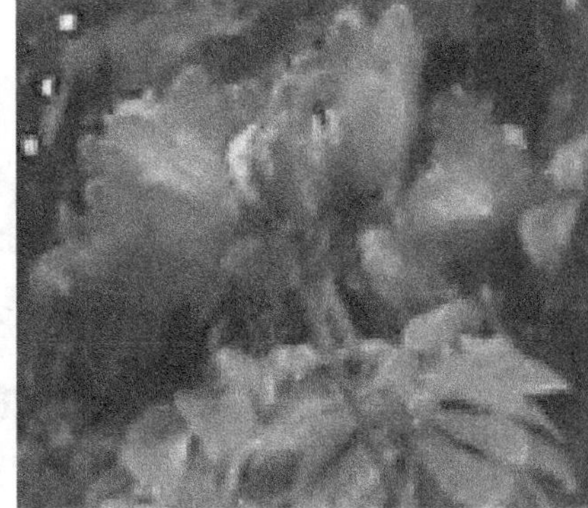

African Tulip (Spathodea
Campanulata)

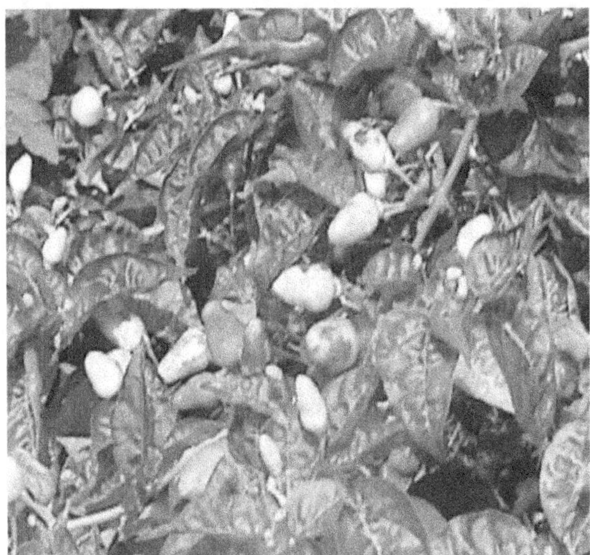

Cardinal's Guard (Pachystachys coccinea)

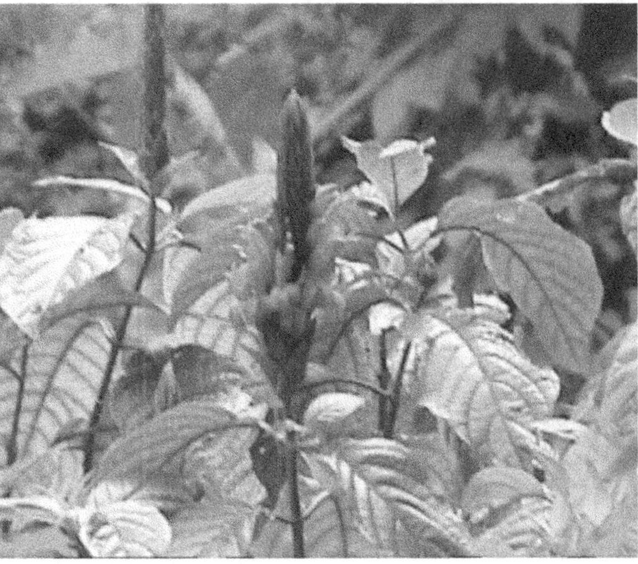

Bolivian Rainbow (Capsicum annuum)

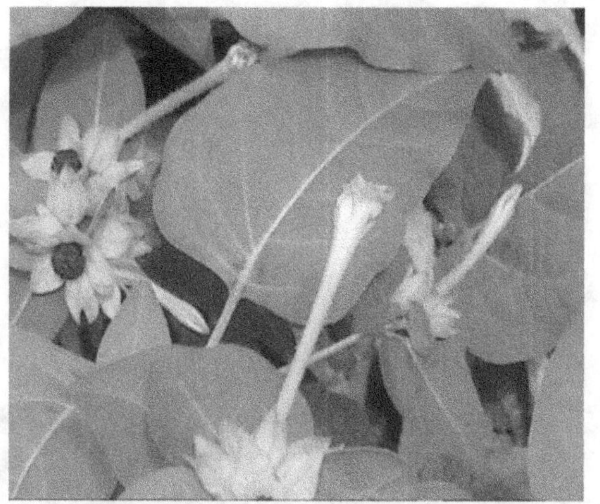

Four O'Clock or Clavillia
(Mirabilis Jalapa)

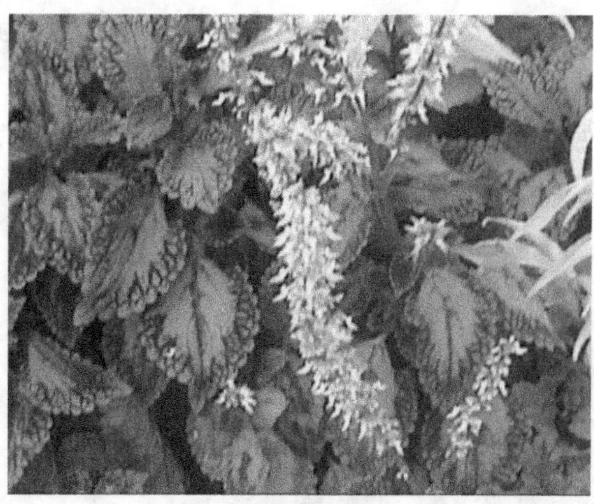

Coleus

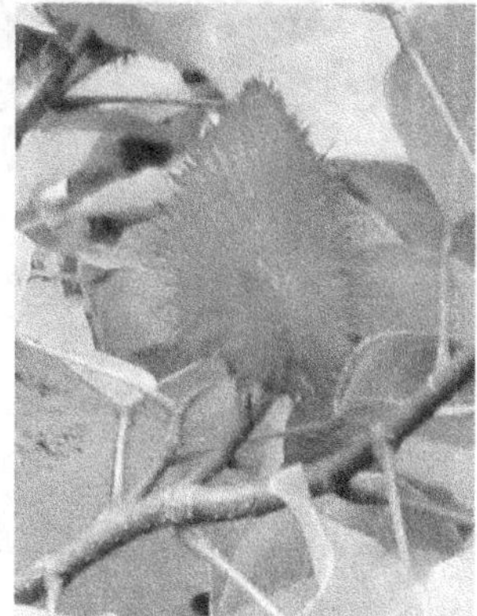

Roucou/Annato

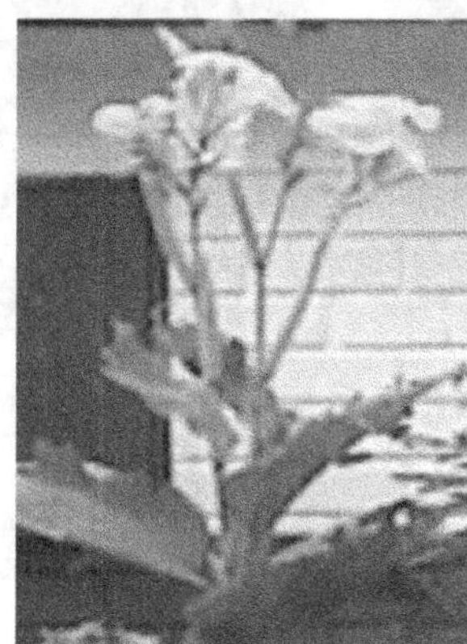

Carnation or Clove Pink
(Dianthus)

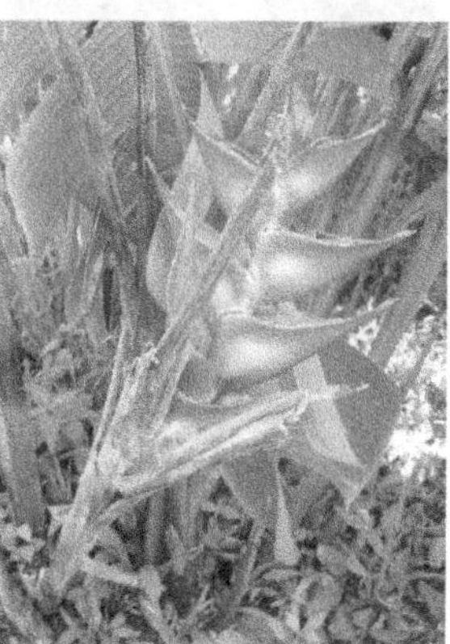

Heliconia Caribaea

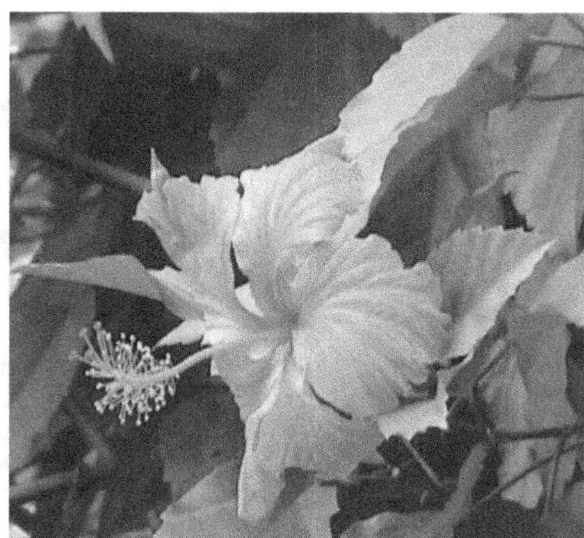

Hibiscus

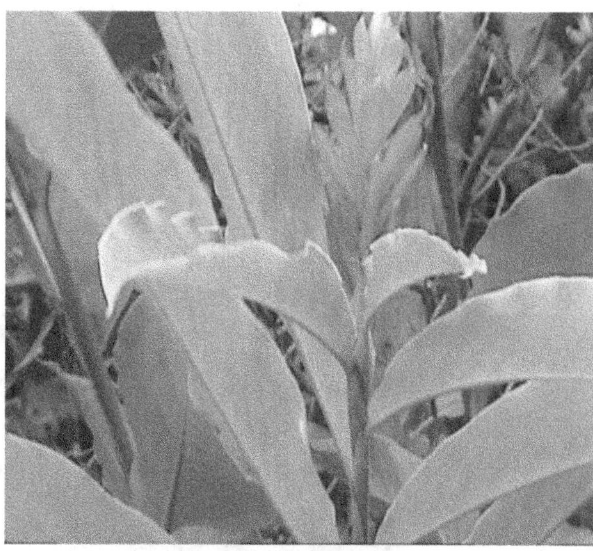

Ginger Lily (Alpinia purpurata)

Bougainvillea, Grenada's National Flower

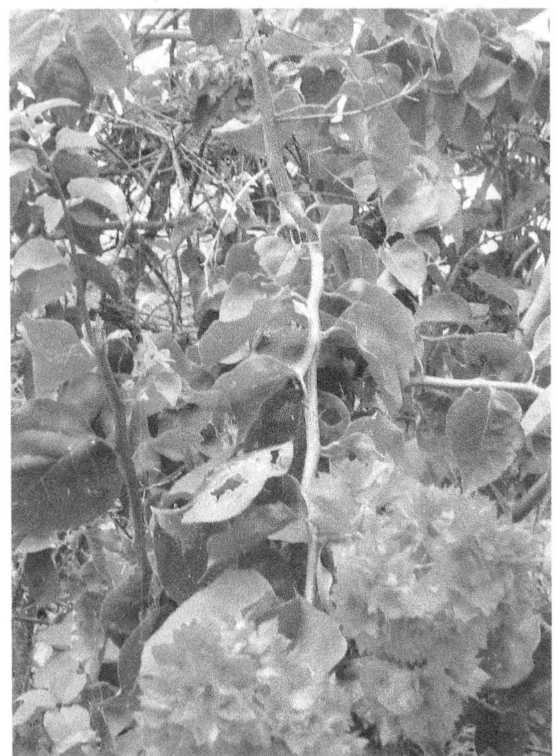

A sparrow at Hermitage has also shown its preference for a bougainvillea home decoration.

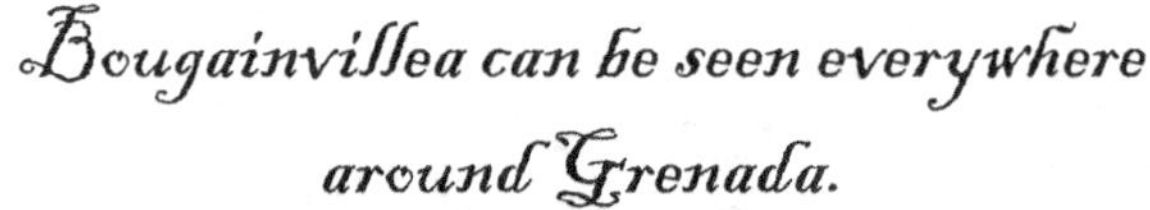

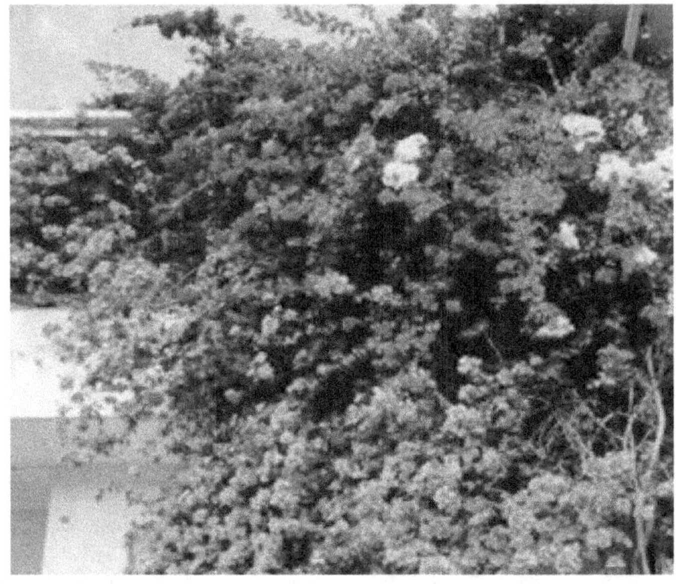

A multicolored patch of bougainvillea in Tanteen

The nest

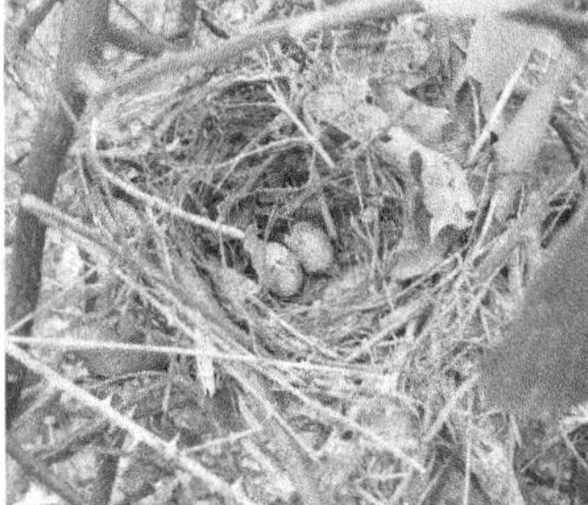

The sparrow's eggs add some more color to the occasion.

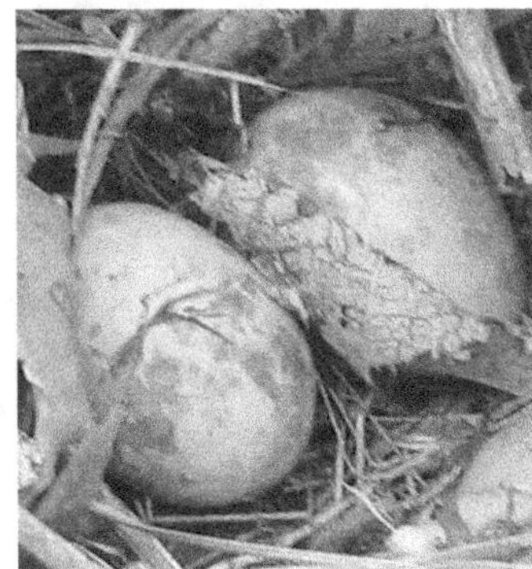

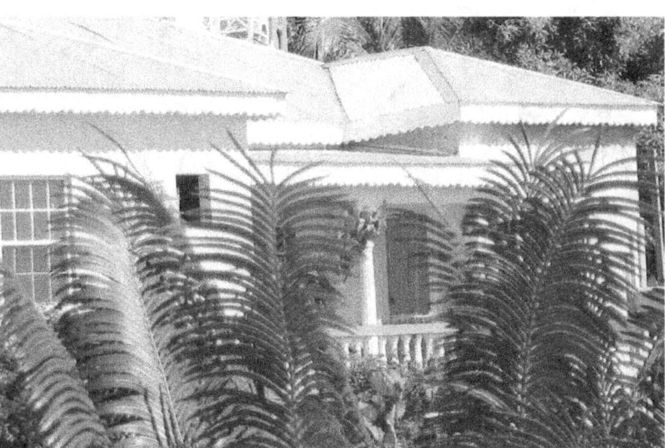

...and at Richmond Hill

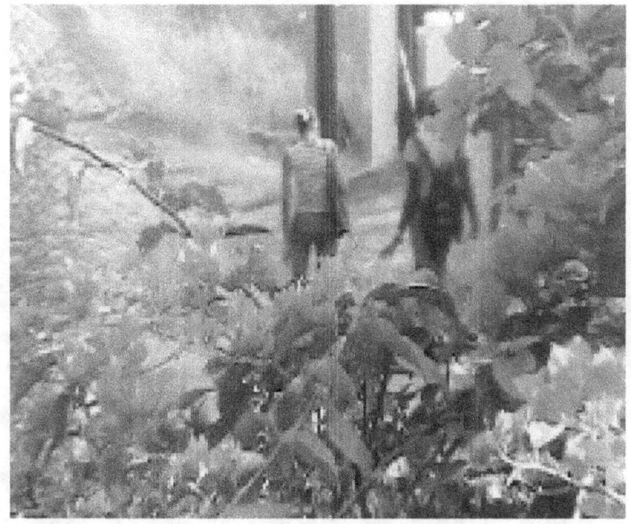

Clozier

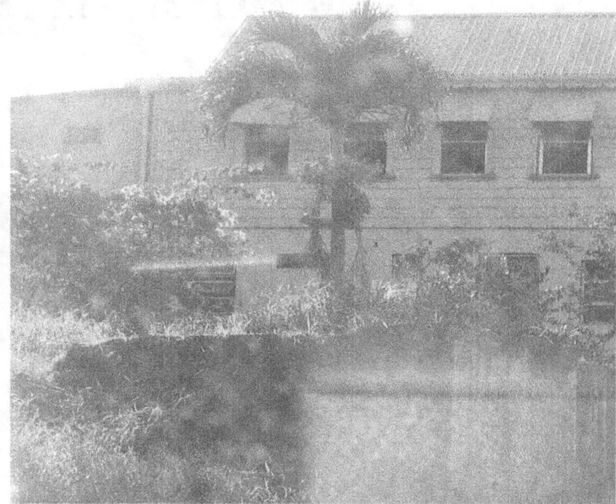

Telescope

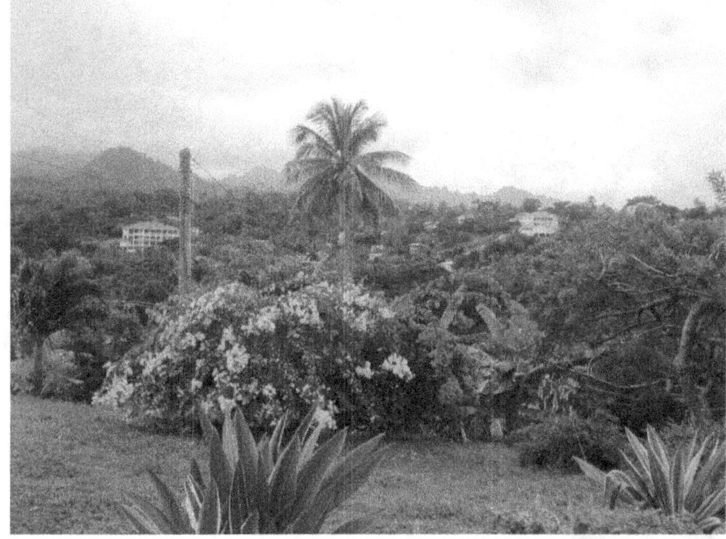

La Fortune

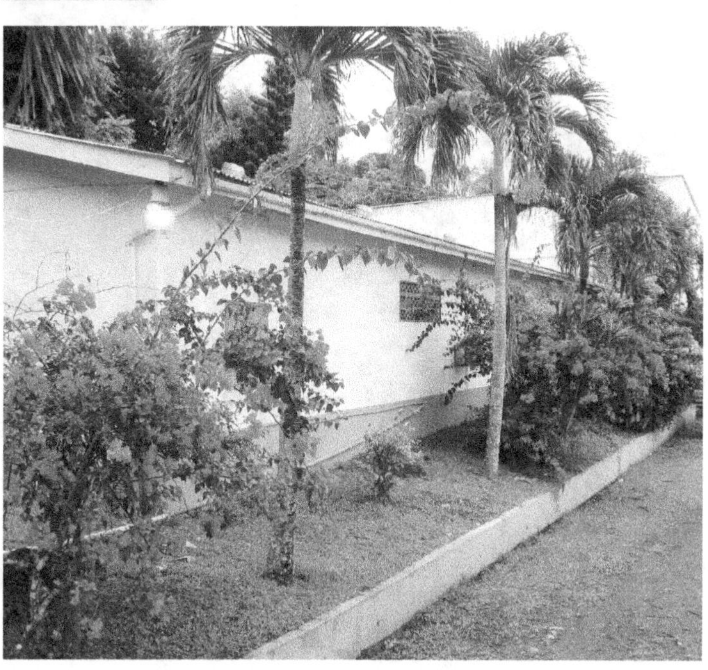

Mt. Reuil, at Glenelg spring water bottling facility

GRENADA'S CARIB PAST

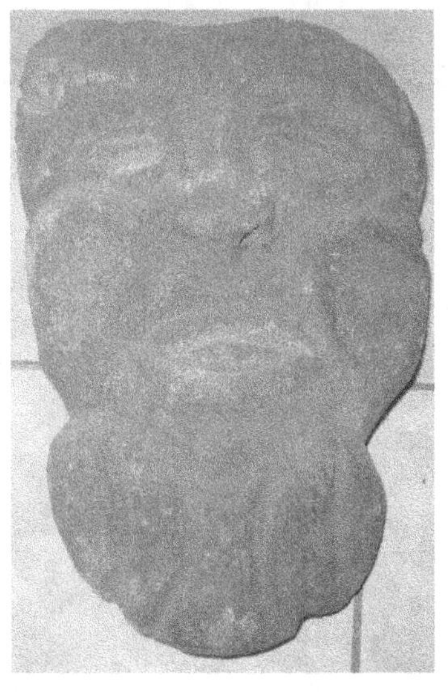

The artifacts on this page are among a huge collection located at the Sauteurs Museum. Most were discovered at an old Carib settlement in Pearls, St. Andrew. The 1940s ground-breaking activities at the site of the old Pearls Airport revealed many of these precious pieces of Carib handiwork.

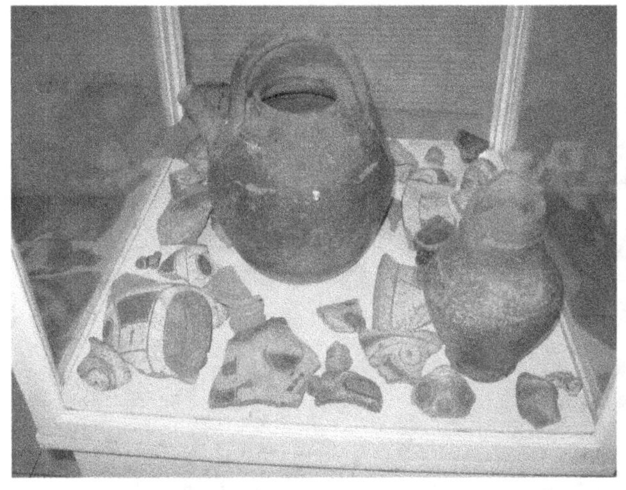

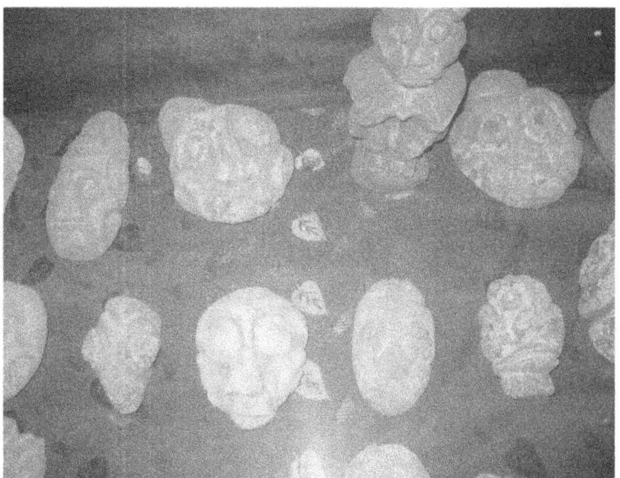

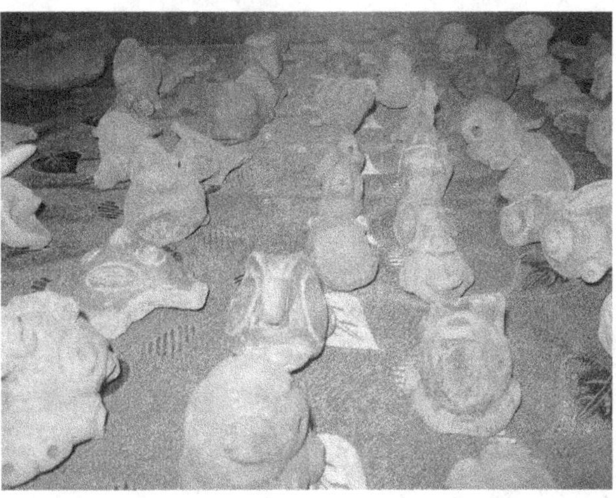

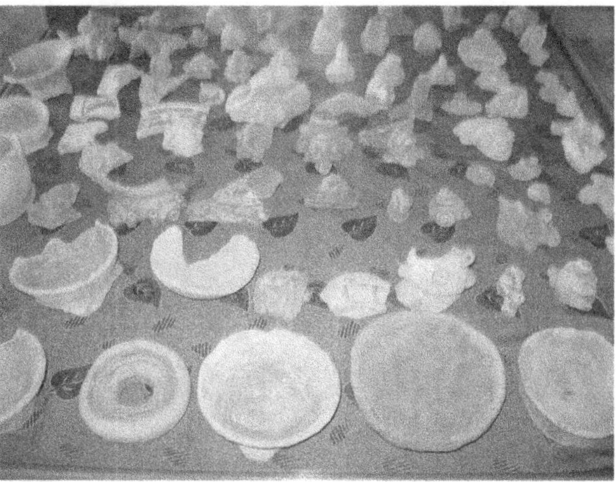

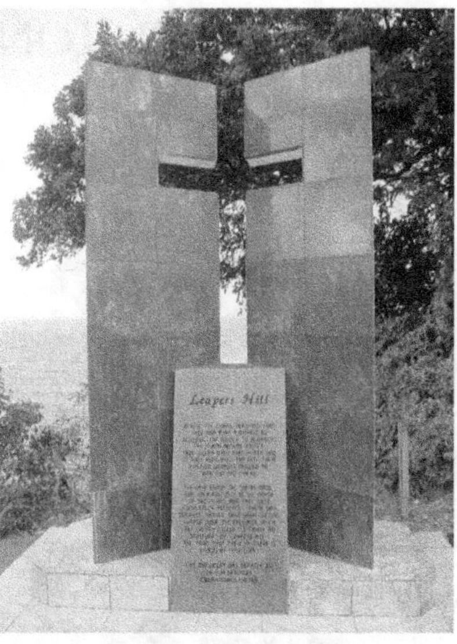

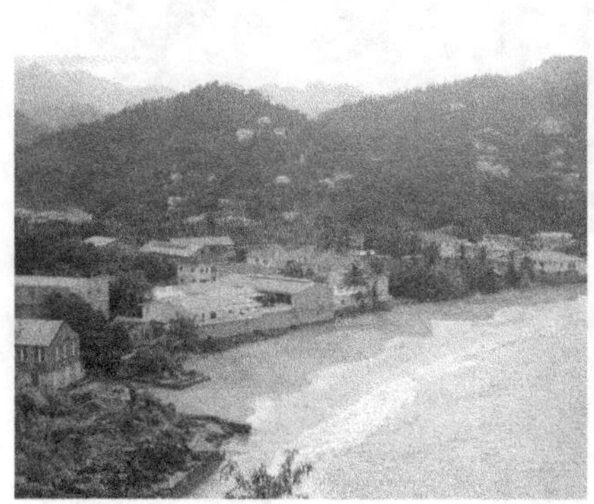

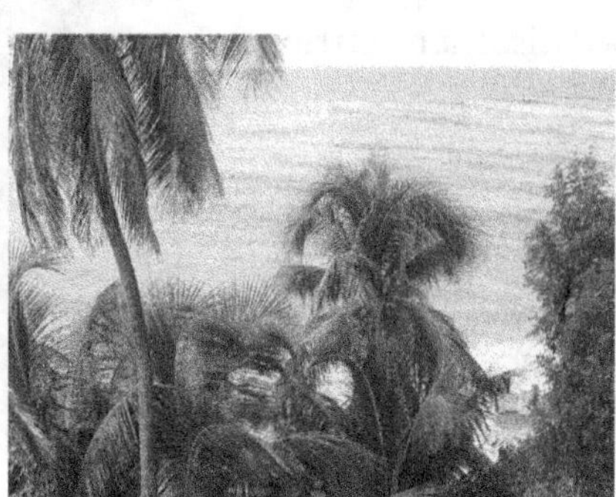

Leapers Hill Carib monument:
A Christian monument to
Grenada's Carib predecessors.
The surrounding pictures are
some of the sights from Leapers
Hill.

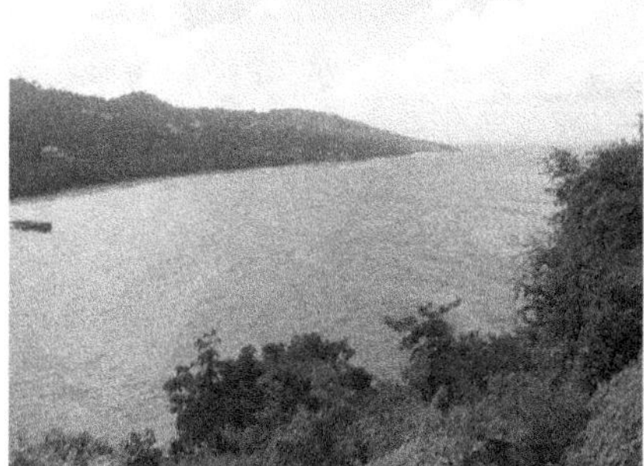

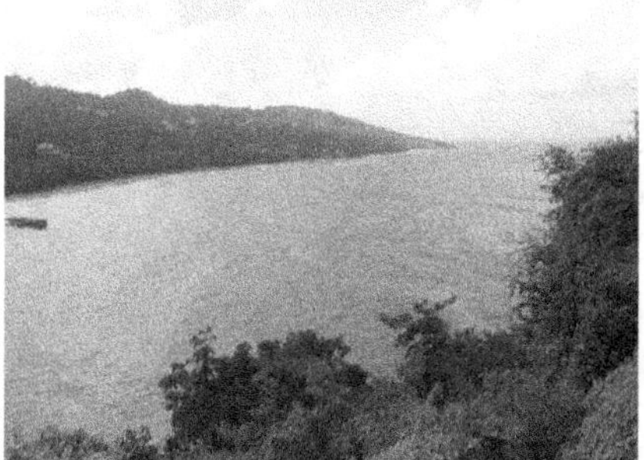

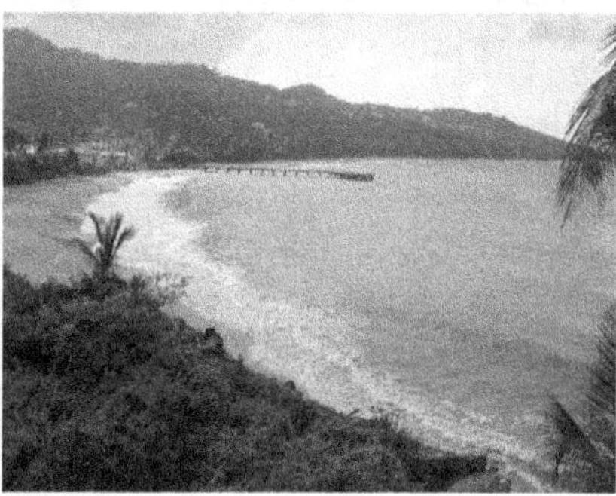

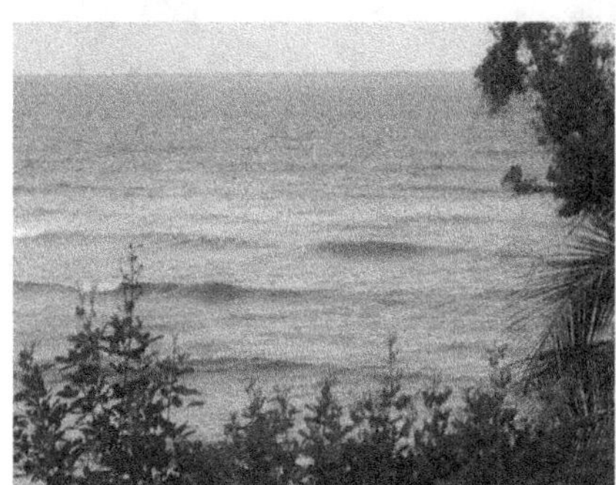

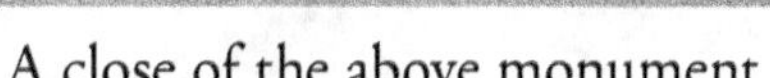

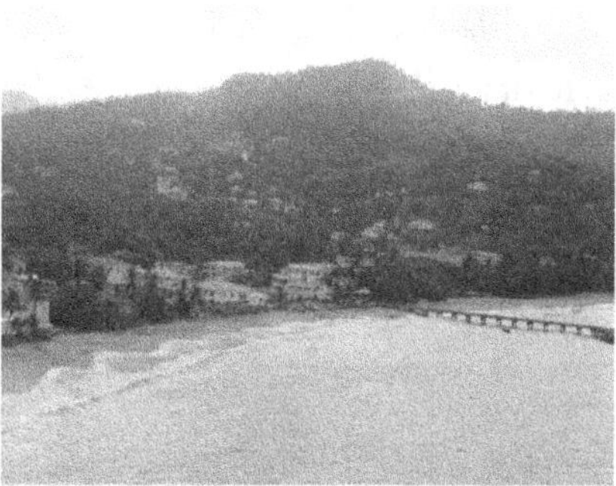

A close of the above monument

MT RICH CARIB STONE

The Carib Stone has dozens of petroglyphs that predate the French settlement of Grenada in 1650. Some historians attribute these petroglyphs to the Carib predecessors in Grenada, the Amerindian Arawaks. However, the majority view is that the carvings were the work of Caribs. Either way, the Caribs and Arawaks pre-existed Europeans, Africans, and East Indians in Grenada. These aboriginal Grenadians offer diversity and depth to the island's cultural expression through their art and history.

The Carib Stone rests over a stream at the bottom of a hillside in the village of Mt. Rich. It sits above a briskly flowing stream. A visitor would have to get close to observe its carvings.

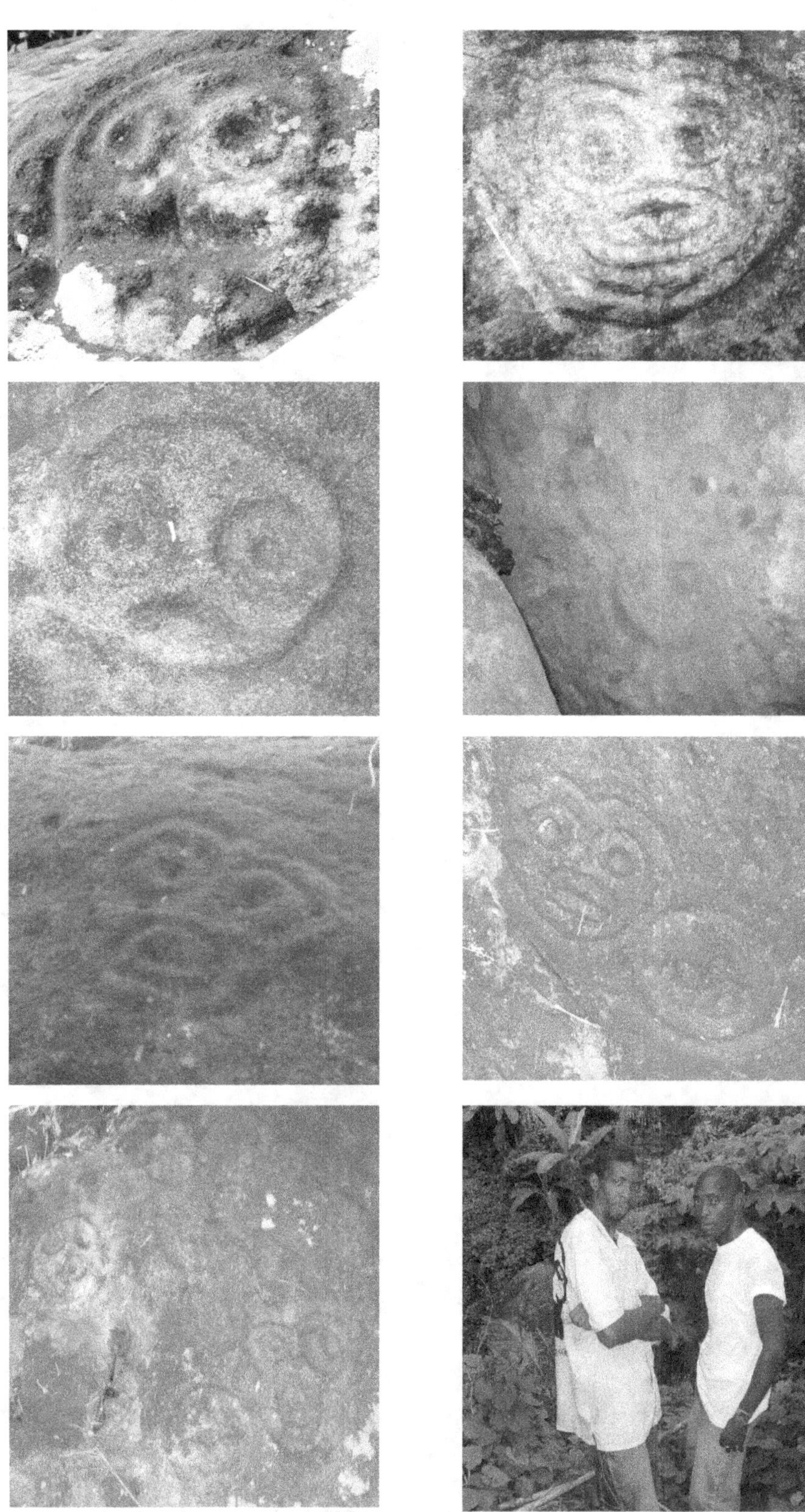

These men will gladly escort you to the Carib Stone.

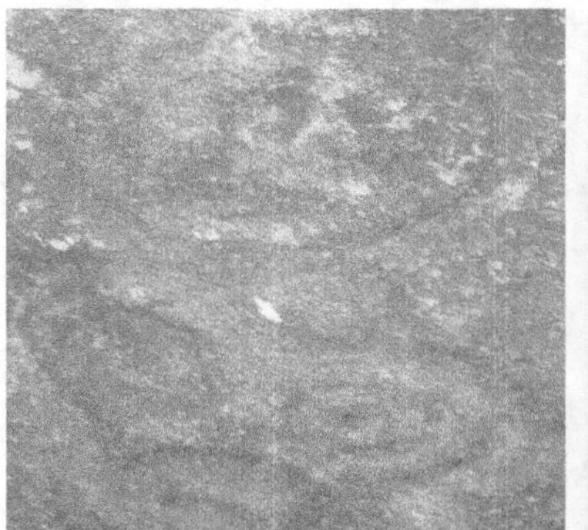
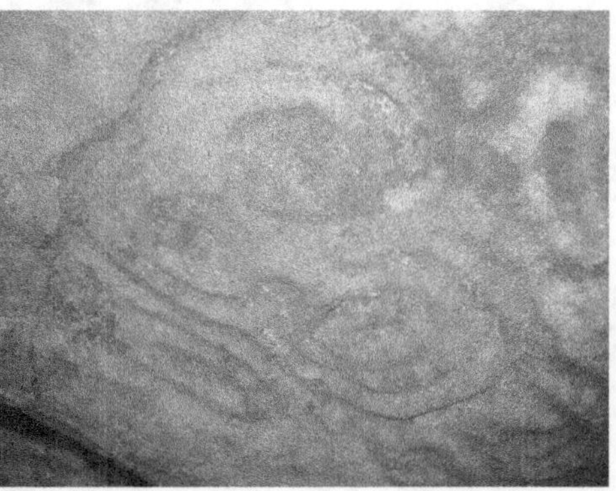
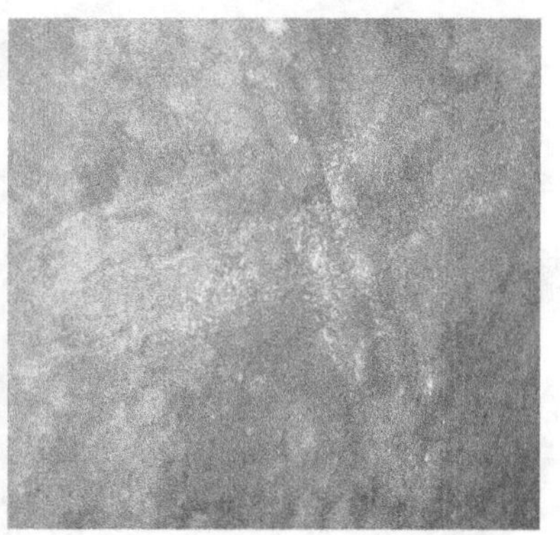

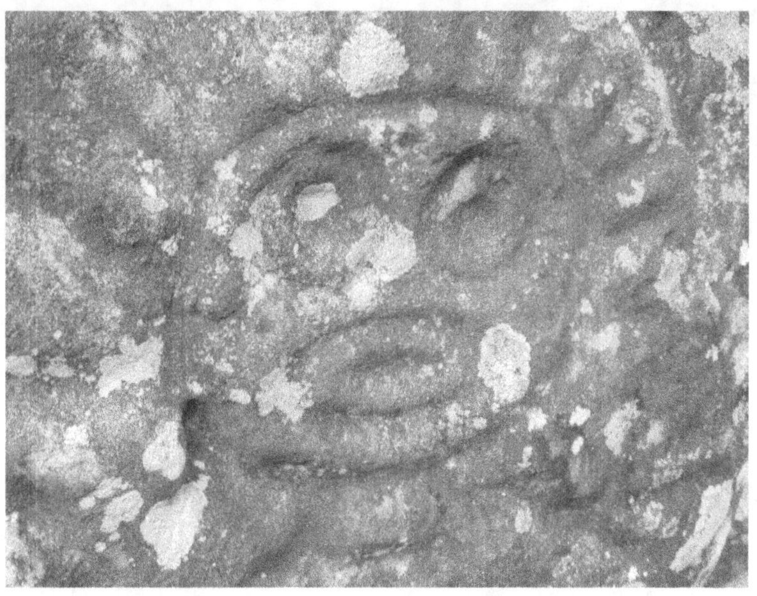

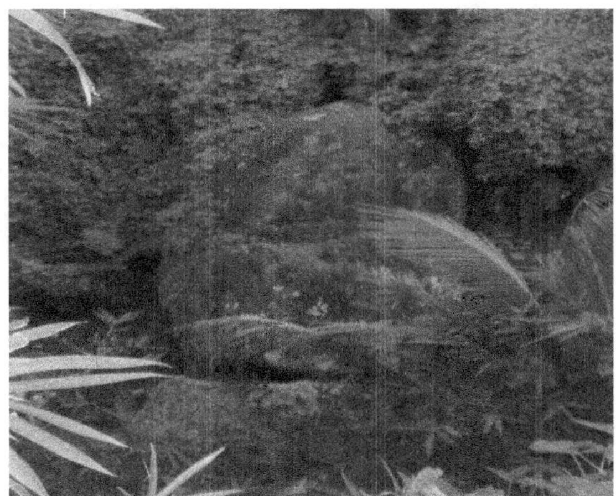

The Carib Stone is perched over a stream at the bottom of a hillside.

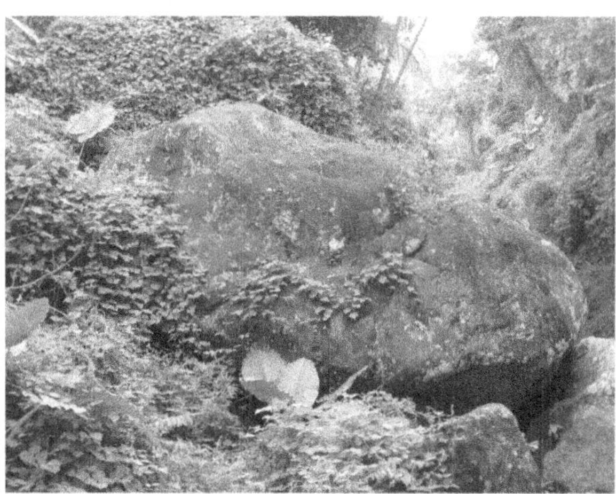

Approaching the Carib stone

Carriacou * Petit Martinique * Diamond Island * Les Tantes * Sandy Island * Hog Island * Calivigny Island * Marquis Island * Levera Island * Isle de Ronde * Isle de Caille * Green Island

Mabouya Island * Adam Island * Mushroom Island * Bacolet Island * Bird Island * Ramier Island * Conference Island * Saline Island * Gary Island * Glover Island * White Island * Hope Island * Jack Adam Island * Frigate Island * Kick 'em Jenny Rock * Kick 'em Jenny Rock

Grenada's Isles

Grenada has over 40 islands surrounding its coastline. The largest of these are Carriacou and Petit Martinique; both are inhabited and lie 20 miles to the north. The next larger set of islands is comprised of Isle de Ronde and Isle de Caille, both located just off the north east coast. These latter two are uninhabited, but people go there for long periods to hunt, farm and fish, and relax.

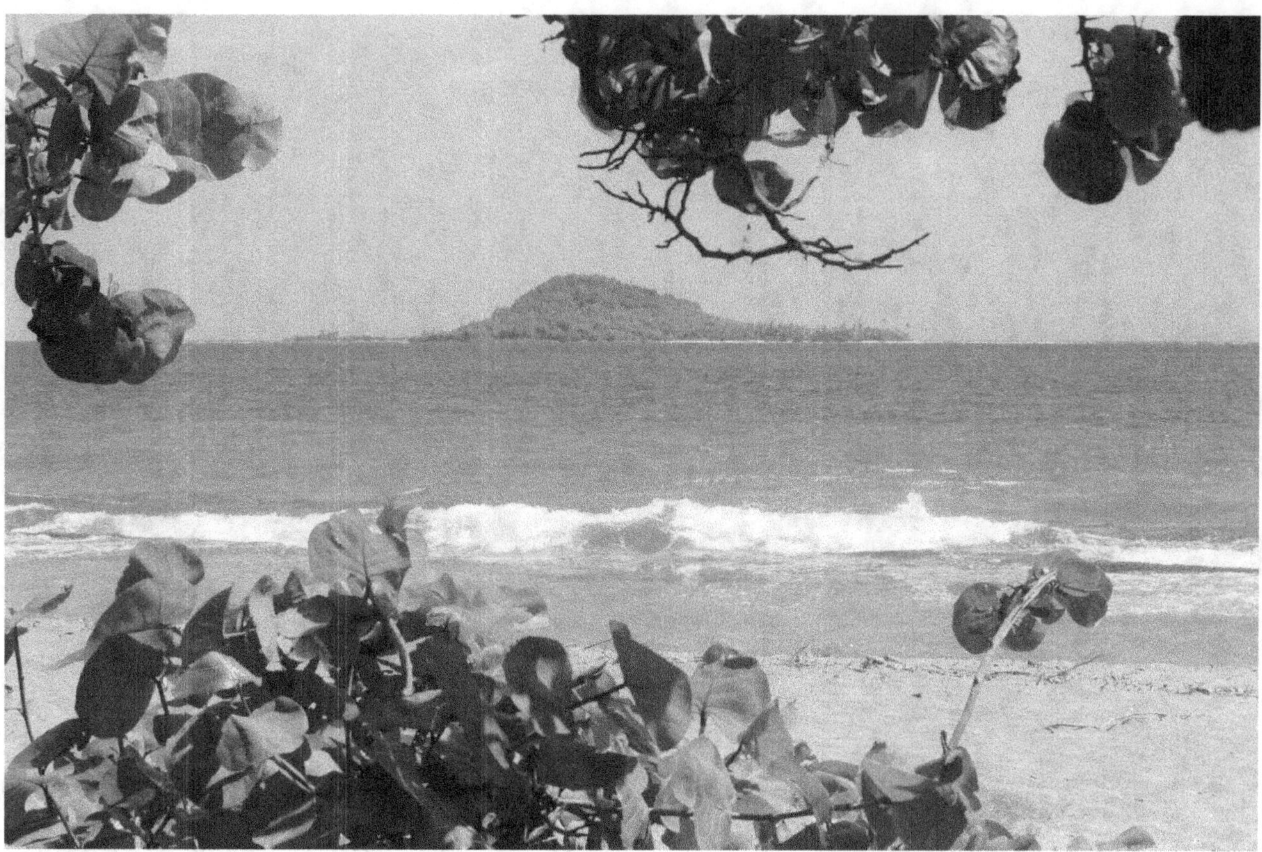

Above: Sandy Island, viewed from Bathway

Below: Conference Island, seen from Tivoli

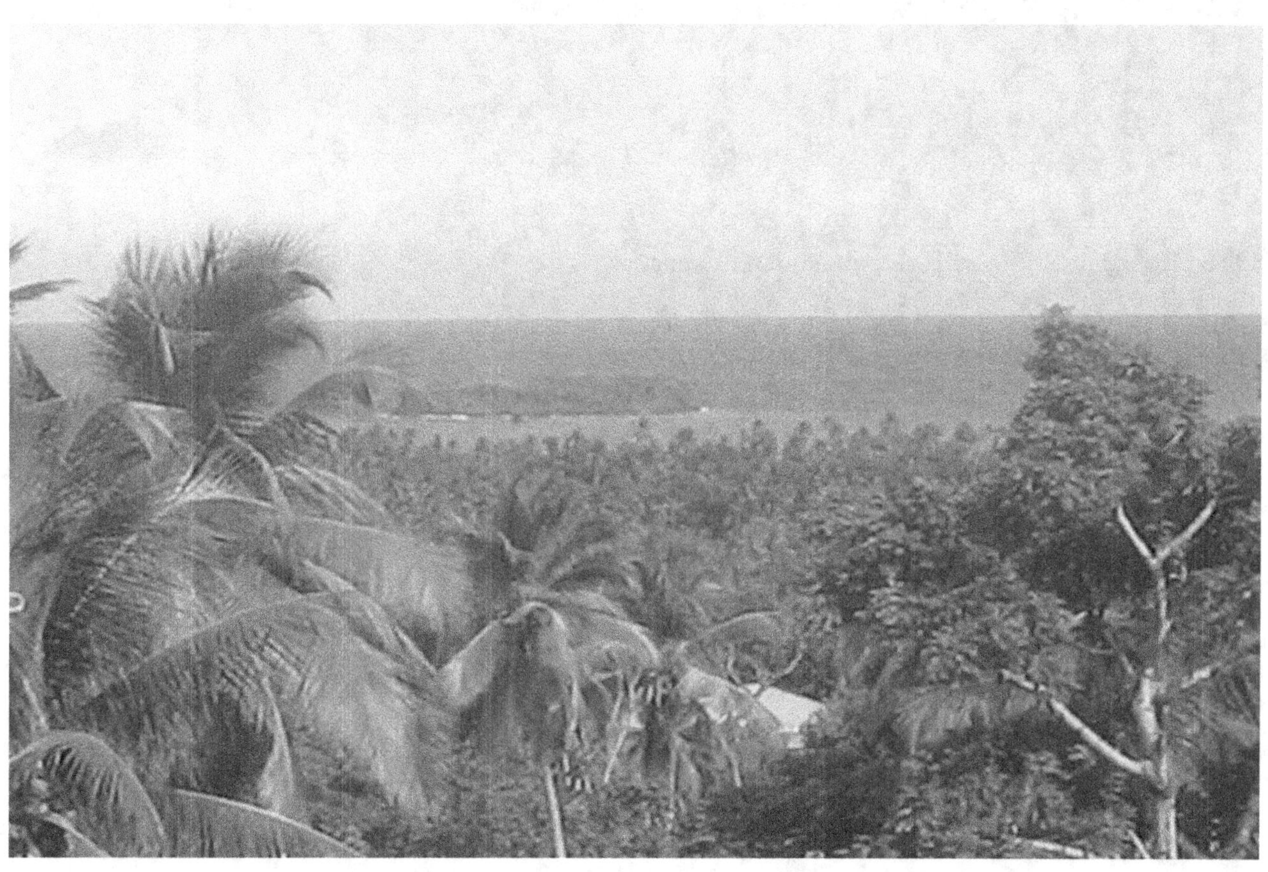

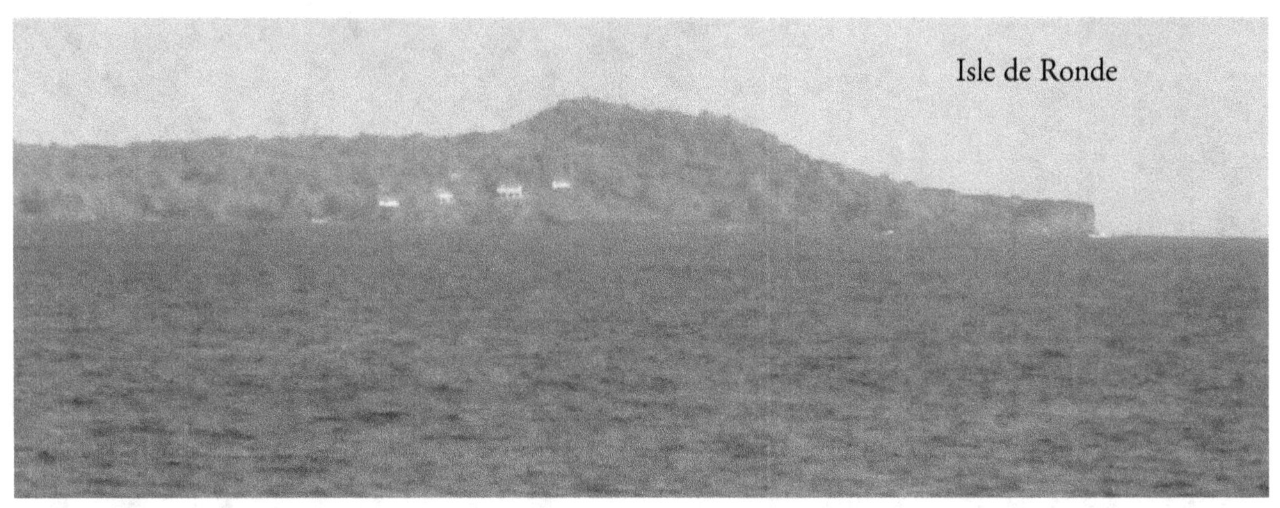
Isle de Ronde

Isle de Ronde

Seen from Mt. Rodney Beach on mainland Grenada

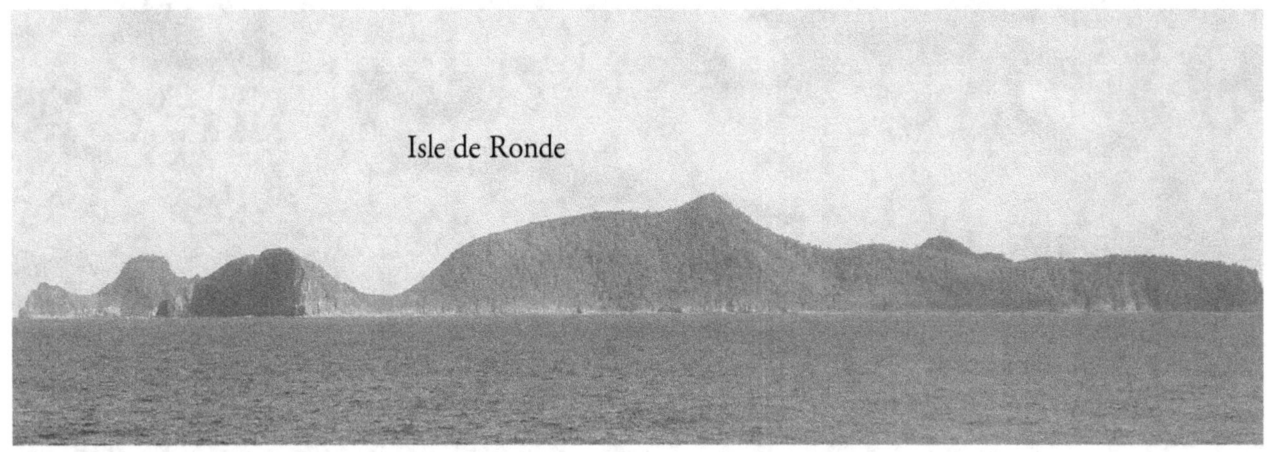
Isle de Ronde

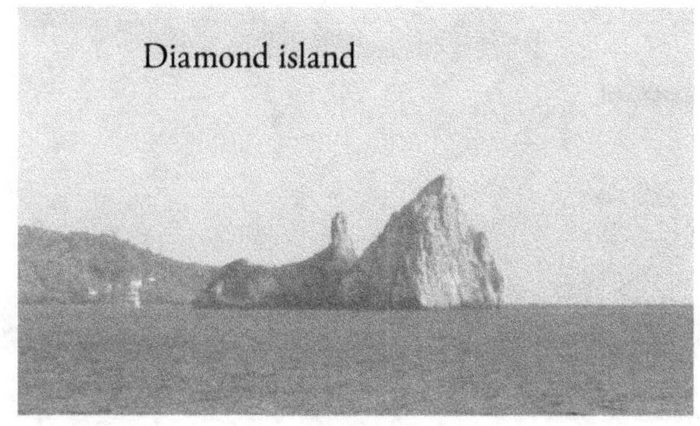

Diamond island

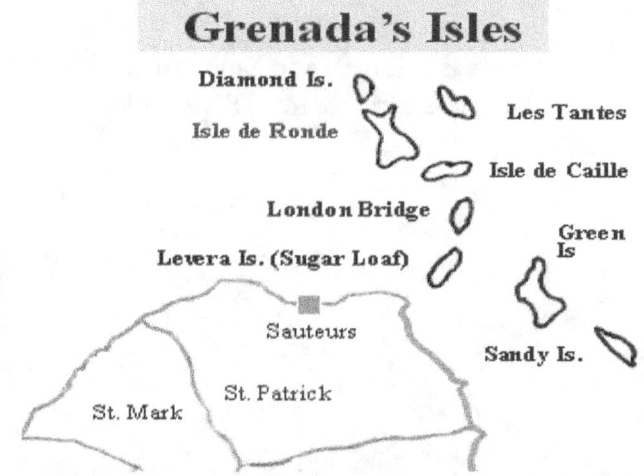

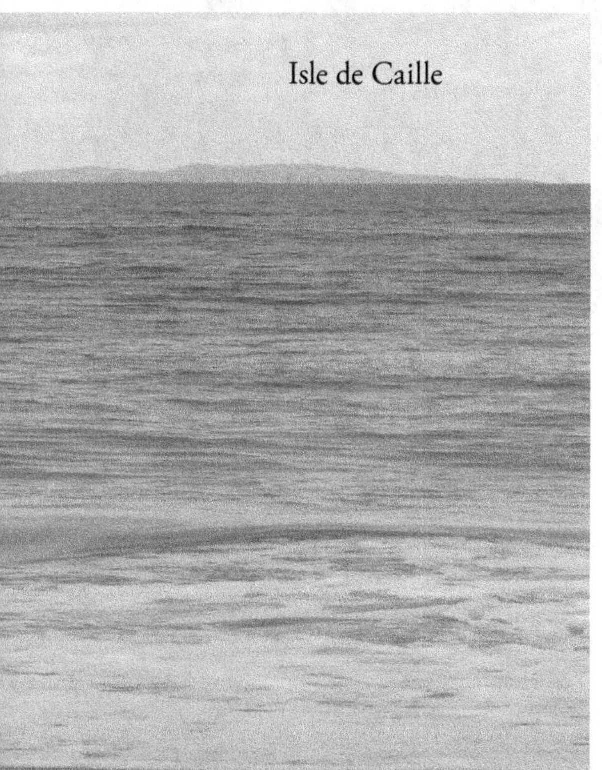

Isle de Caille

Isle de Ronde and **Isle de Caille,** seen in these pictures, are uninhabited. But a few mainland Grenadians farm, fish, and spend short periods on these isles. As illustrated above, the isles are the southernmost of the Grenadine chain of islands stretching between St. Vincent and Grenada. Closest to Northern Grenada, Ronde, and Caille Islands are the most regularly visited. Those who own properties on the isles also maintain houses there.

Isle de Ronde is the largest of the three islands shown. There is evidence of graves on the island, as well as the remains of colonial cannons. Maybe because of a colonial history of war and death on Isle de Ronde, visitors sometimes return to the mainland with supernatural stories of harmless but restless souls who wander the islands. Nevertheless, these visitors always return to Isle de Ronde. The island's Half Moon Bay is a lovely beach. And, farmers herd sheep and goats, as well as plant ground vegetables on Isle de Ronde. They once mined salt on Isle de Ronde.

Isle de Caille has an almost perfect little harbor and nice bathing spots, although it lacks a defined beach. There are about four houses on Isle de Caille. While the animals on Isle de Ronde are domesticated, the goats on Isle de Caille are wild. The vegetation on Isle de Caille is quite different from that of the mainland vegetation. From both islands, the moonlight is fantastic, casting a splendid glow on the far reaches of the surrounding water. The night lights of mainland Grenada, especially of the streets, the moving cars, and the houses, are a sight to behold from vantage points on the Isles. Diamond Island is essentially a picturesque rock that adds to the region's overall appeal.

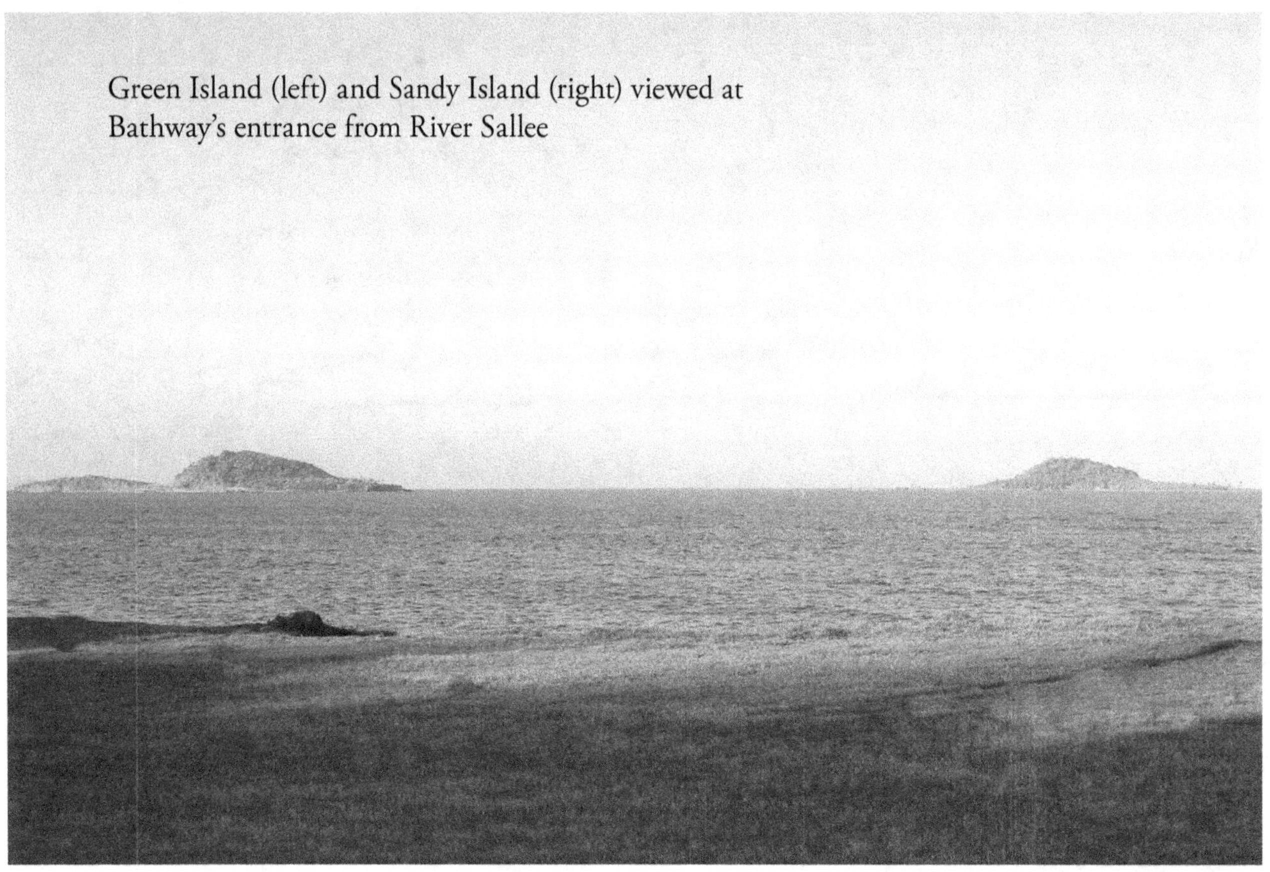

Green Island (left) and Sandy Island (right) viewed at
Bathway's entrance from River Sallee

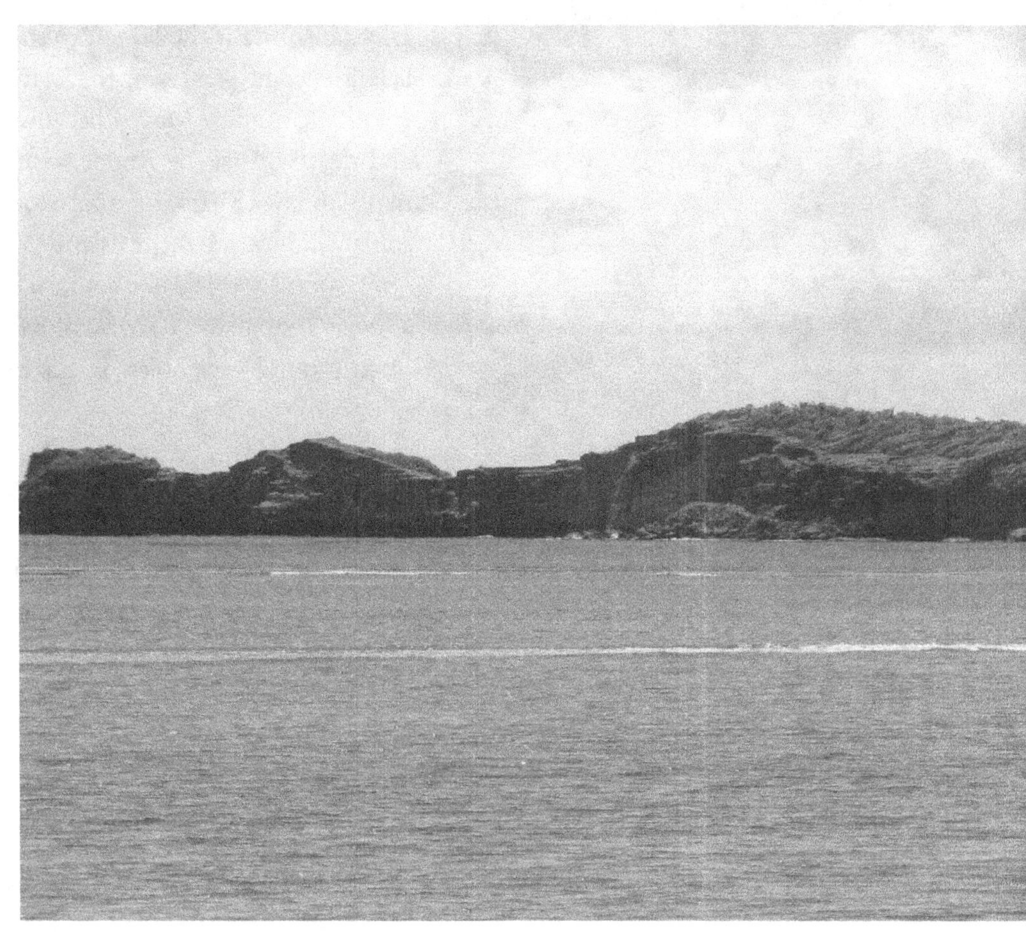

Marquis Island
also called La
Baye Rock

In local parlance,
"La Baye Rock"
describes an old
person or thing.
A person or thing
can be "as old as
La Baye Rock."

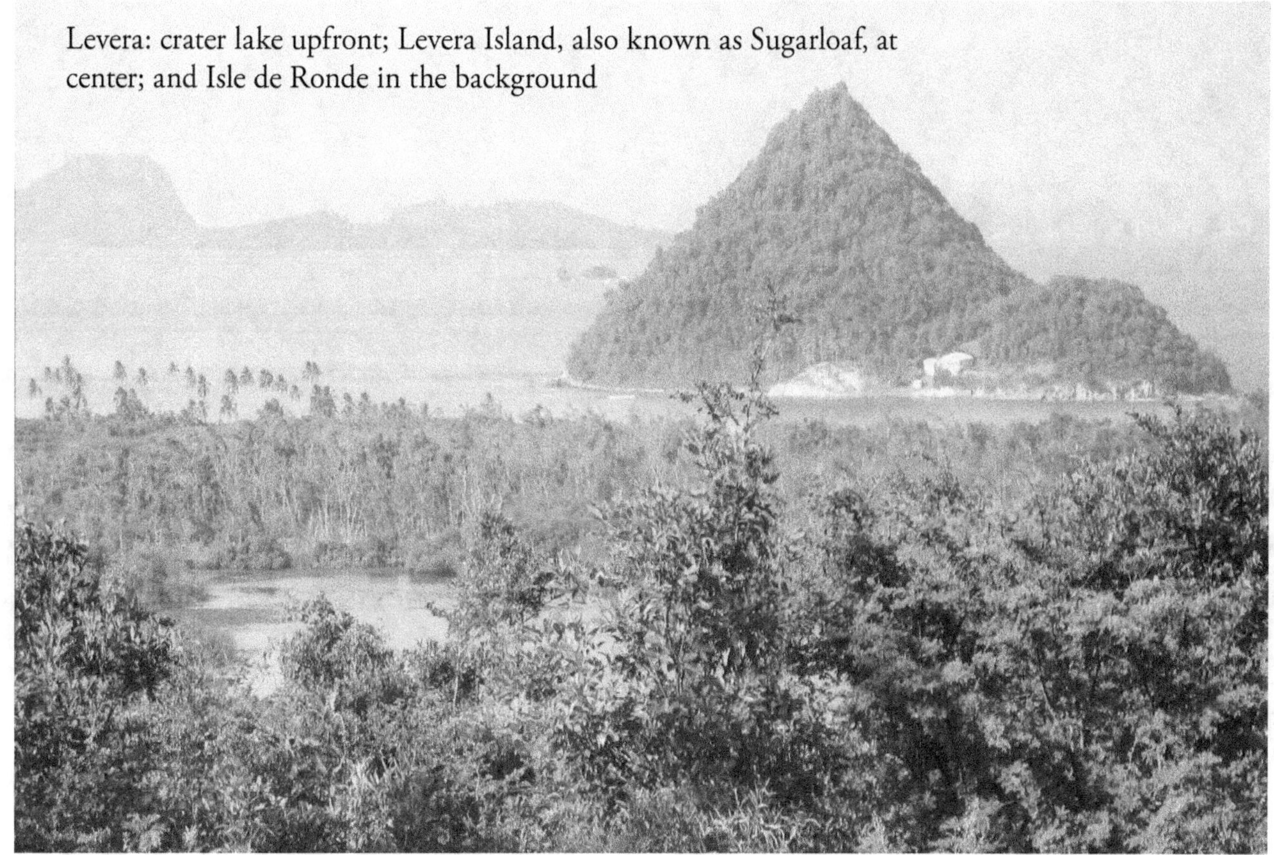

Levera: crater lake upfront; Levera Island, also known as Sugarloaf, at center; and Isle de Ronde in the background

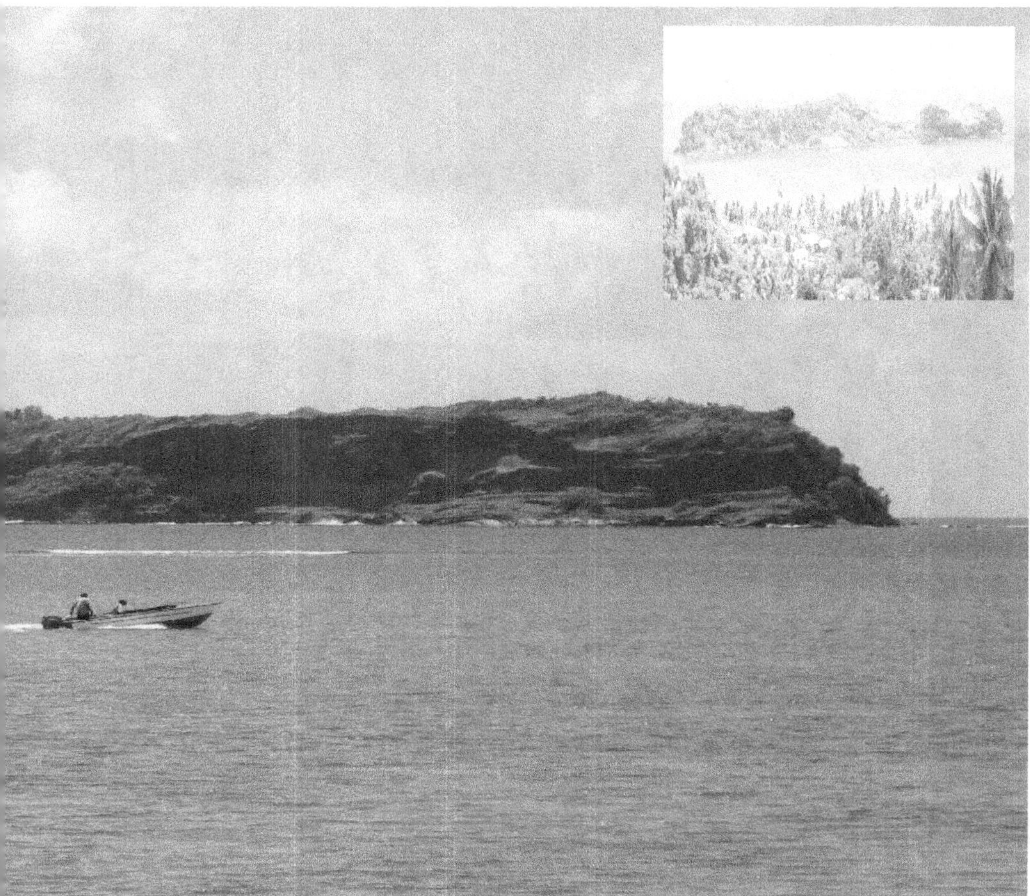

Inset: The back side of Marquis Island as seen from Mt. Carmel

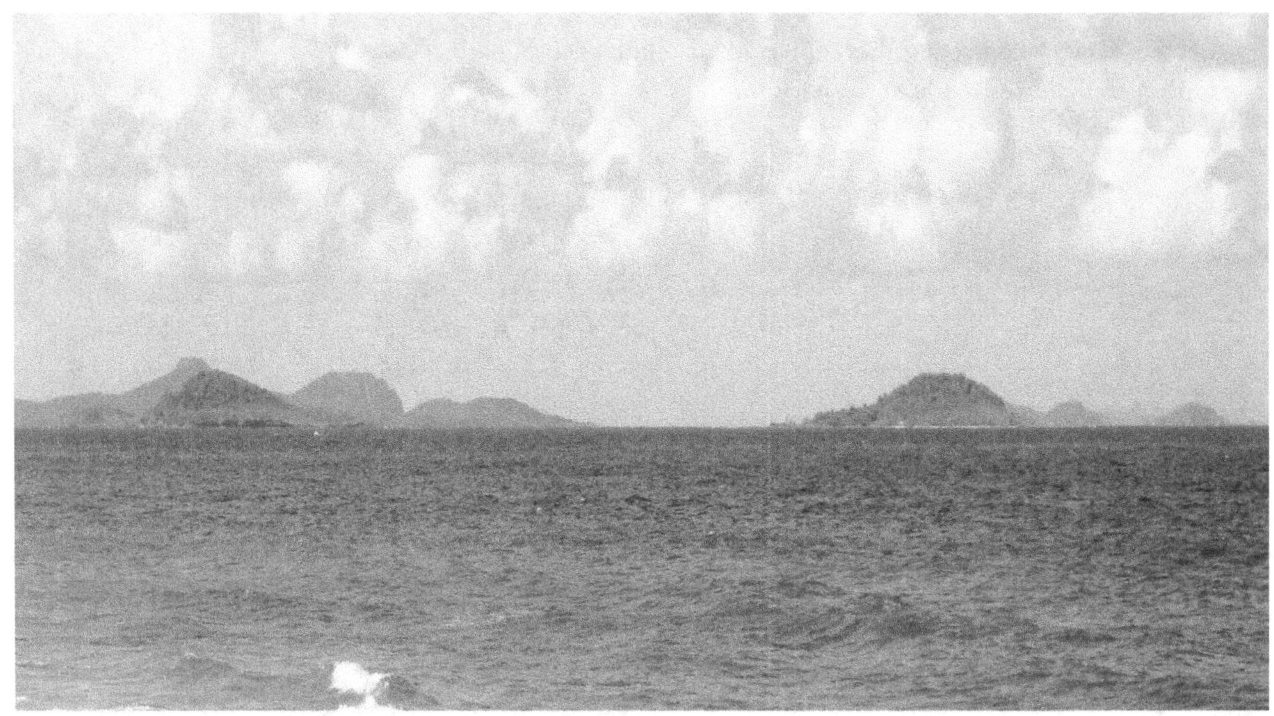

Above: From La Poterie, looking at the lower Grenadine Isles
Below: Hope Island

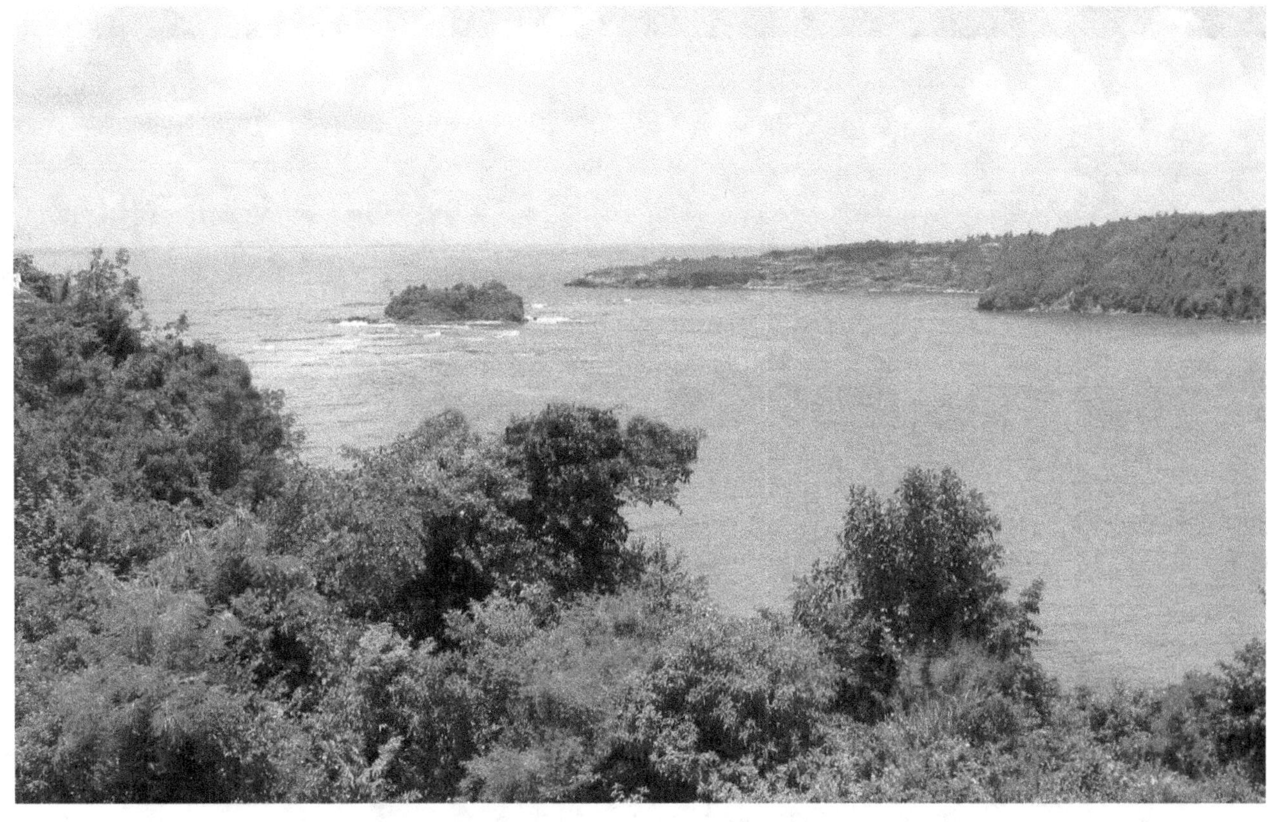

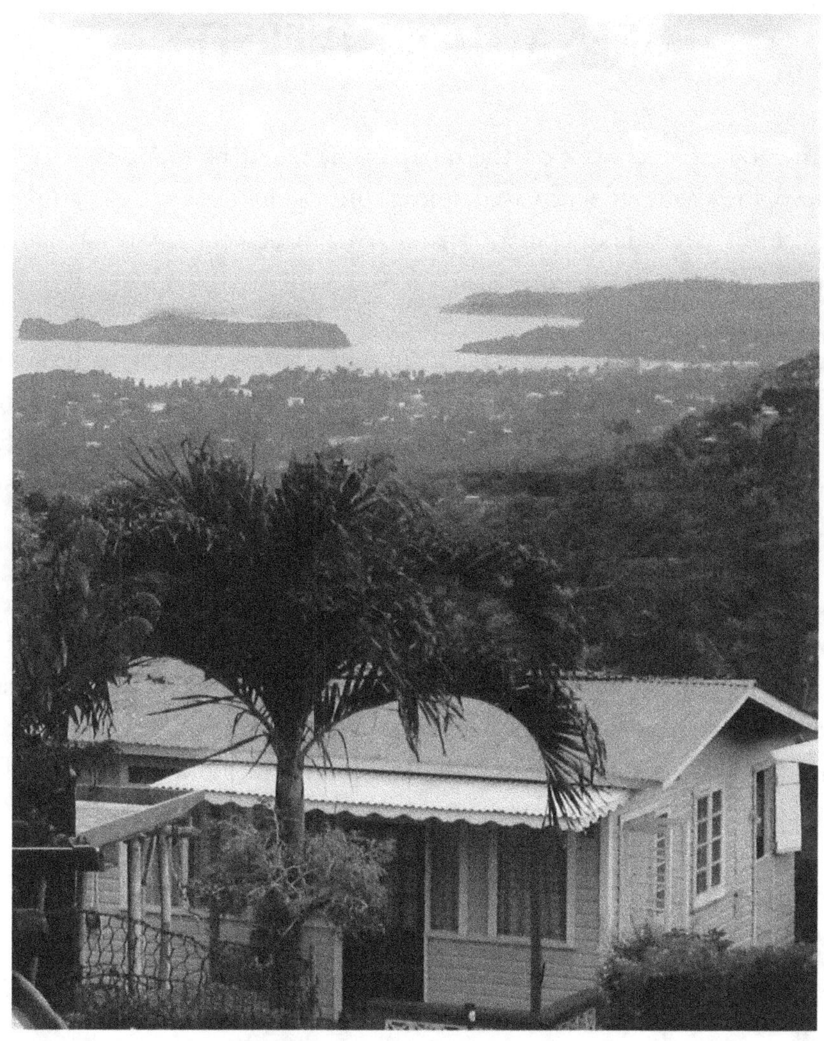

From Carriere, looking towards Grenville. Marquis Island is visible in the distance.

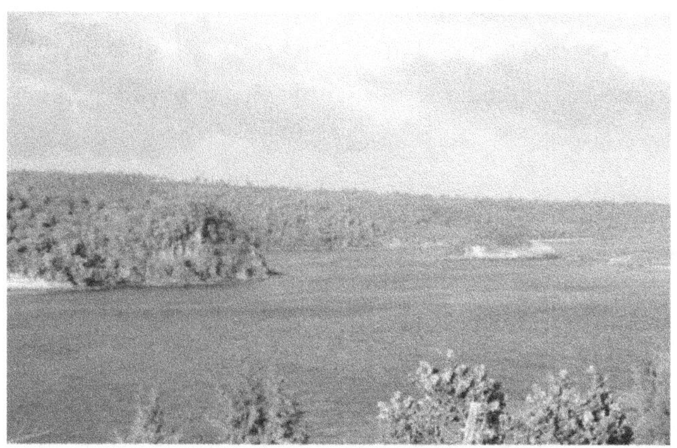

Petite Bacaye Island

Calivigny Island

GRENADIAN DIVERSITY

Africans first came as slaves to work on the tobacco and sugar plantations of Grenada. As sugar superseded tobacco, the slave trade increased, and so did the increase of African slaves to Grenada. Over ninety percent of Grenada's population is of African descent. Indo-Grenadians, the largest minority, is identifiably about five percent.

East Indians first came to Grenada in 1857 as indentured laborers to alleviate the labor shortage that resulted from the abolition of slavery. East Indians, like their African forerunners in Grenada, suffered the indignities of plantation servitude. In the same way that Afro-Grenadians suffered alienation from Africa, Indo-Grenadians suffered estrangement from their native India. Understandably, there is today a significant intermixture of Africans and Indians in Grenada.

Europeans first came to Grenada as colonizers, but many came later as migrants seeking farming opportunities. Although less than one percent of Grenada's population is ostensibly white, a larger percentage of Grenadians bear some European ancestry. Mt. Moritz once had the largest concentration of European descendants in Grenada, most having descended from a generation of farmers who came to Grenada by way of Barbados. Some Grenadians still refer to the white natives of Mt. Moritz as Bajans, a term used to describe Barbadians.

Lately, Grenada has begun to experience a broadening of its diversity in the form of a sprinkling of new Asian settlers in Grenada.

Diversity's Impact on Local Expression

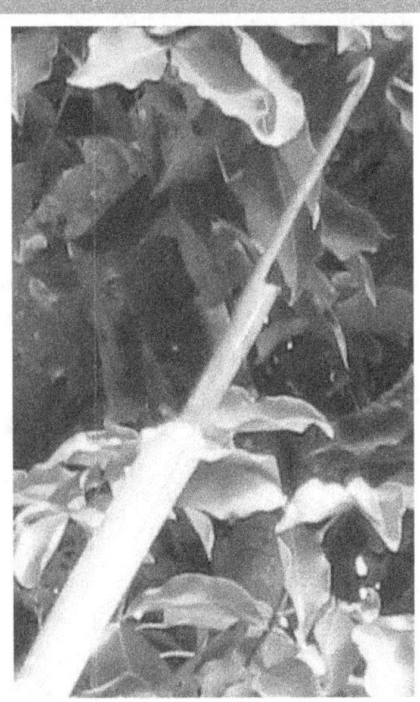

Banganet

Diverse language influences, European, African, and Amerindian, have impacted the colloquial tongue. Among Grenadian hunters, you may hear the expression: He jooked the manicou with a banganet. It means: He poked the opossum with a bayonet-like hunting weapon.

"Jook" is likely a word of West African origin and popularly used by blacks in the Americas. To jook means to stab or to poke. Manicou is a word used in Grenada for an opossum, and it is likely of Amerindian Tupi origin (manikuu). Amerindian Caribs introduced the manicou as food. Banganet is a local derivation of the French bayonet. A banganet is a long bamboo rod tipped with a metal point; it is used by Grenadian hunters to poke their prey out of hiding. Hunting is not as strong a tradition as in the past.

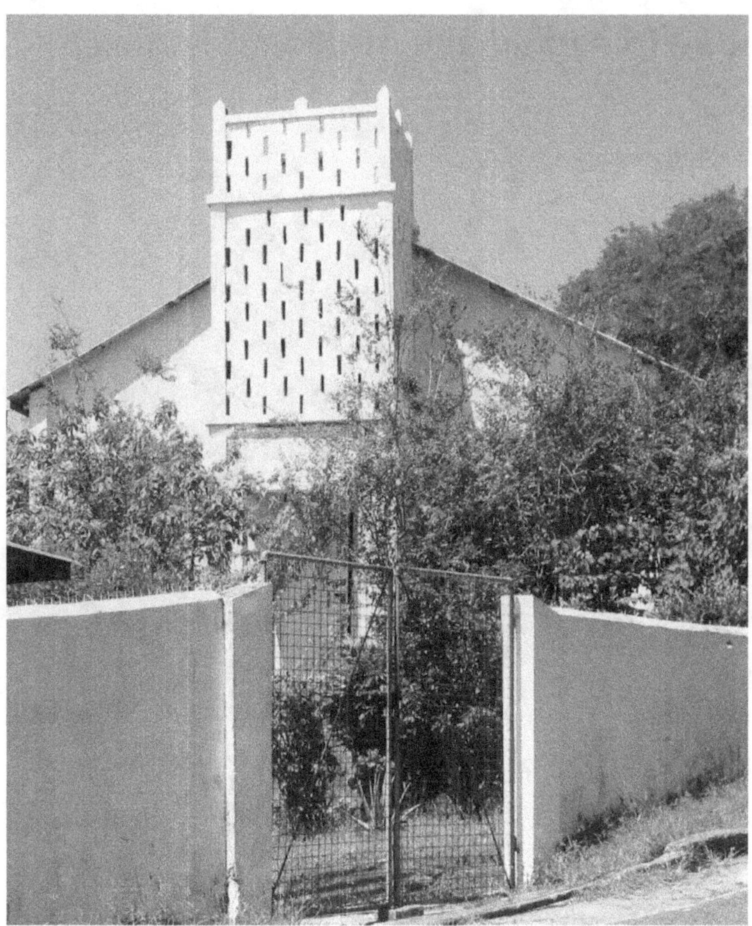

Belair Presbyterian Church

Present-day Belair Presbyterian Church (left) occupies the same general area as the original institution did in the 1860s when it was instrumental in Grenada's East Indian Hindu and Muslim religious conversions. Still today, many who attend this church are of East Indian descent. In the conversion process, many Indian names were Europeanized. Family names like Mahaday became Thomas and Jaegoo became Degale, for instance.

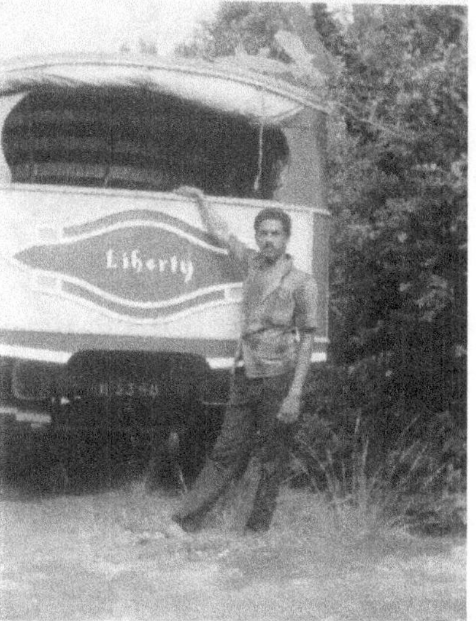

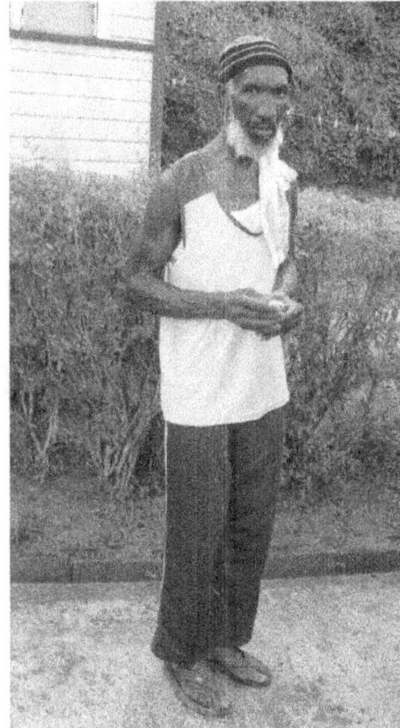

An Afro-Grenadian Muslim

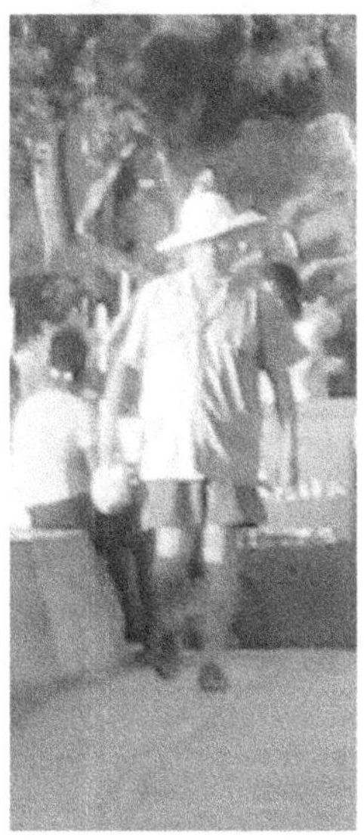

A Chinese man strolls along Fontenoy.

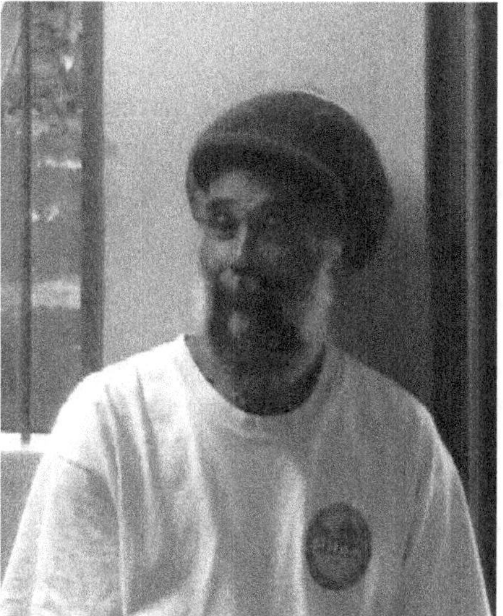

Indo-Grenadians (above 2 photos)

IRWIN'S BAY - where Indo-Grenadian ancestors first landed

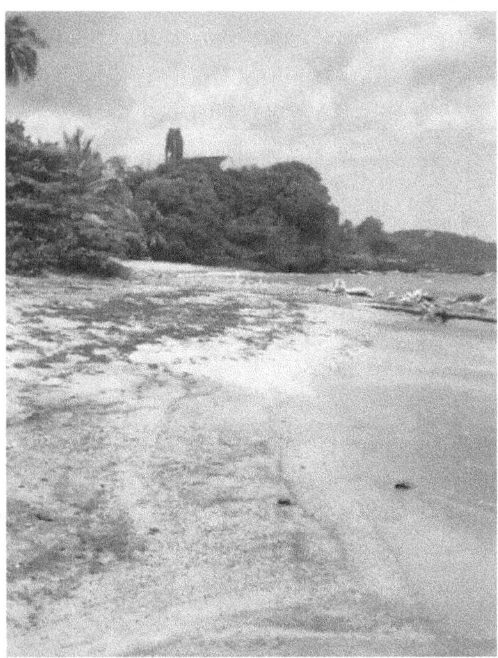

Irwin's Bay (Bushiree Bay)

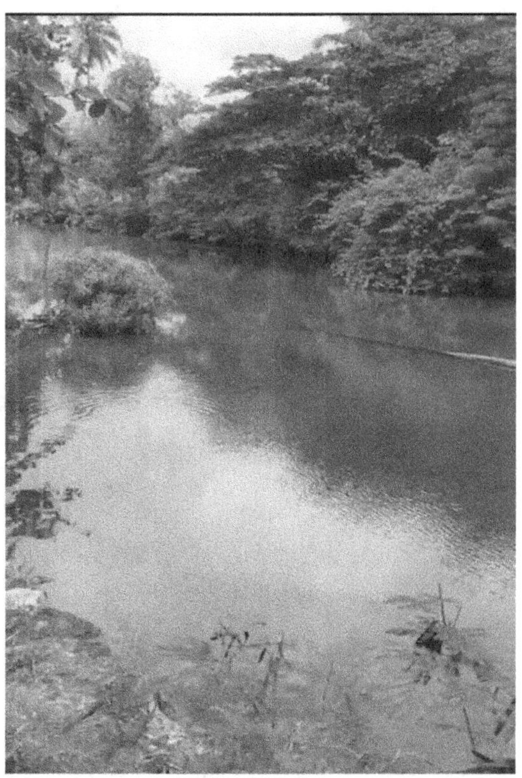

The river that pours into Irwin's Bay

Irwin's Bay, located in La Fortune, is the landing site of the first East Indian indentured servants who arrived in Grenada. Locally, the Bay is known as Bouchierre Bay. Bushiree (Boo-she-ree) is an informal derivation of the French word embouchure, which refers to a river's mouth. Here on Irwin's Bay, the mouth of the river pours into the sea.

On May 1st, 1857, a ship named Maidstone left Calcutta, India, with 304 passengers and arrived at Irwin's Bay on May 1st of that year with approximately 287 passengers. Many Indians died on that journey. Between 1857 and 1890, some 3200 persons from India arrived on Owen's Bay and other bays. Indian Arrival Day in Grenada is commemorated yearly on May 1st.

Residents refer to the road leading to the Bay as Bushiree Road, but it has been formally named Maidstone Road. Along Maidstone Road are the remains of a reported slave depot (right) where slave owners kept newly landed Africans. The depot will have pre-existed the arrival of the Indians. To some degree, Irwin's Bay symbolizes the shared experience of servitude by Africans and Indians in Grenada.

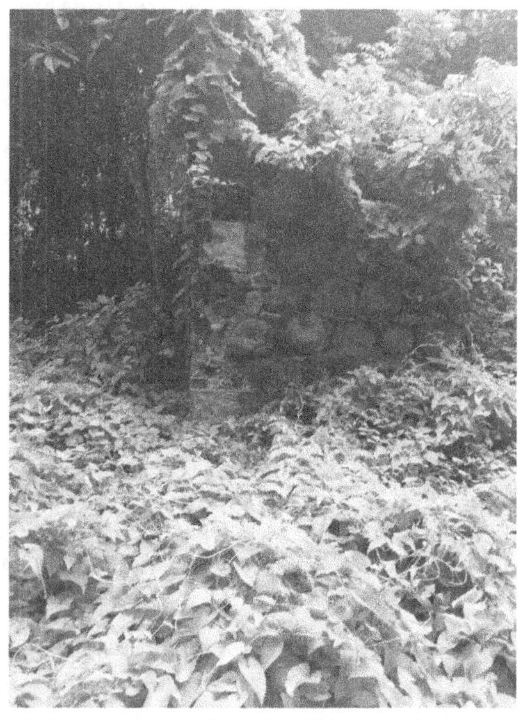

The remains of the Irwin's Bay depot is believed to have housed newly arrived African slaves to Grenada.

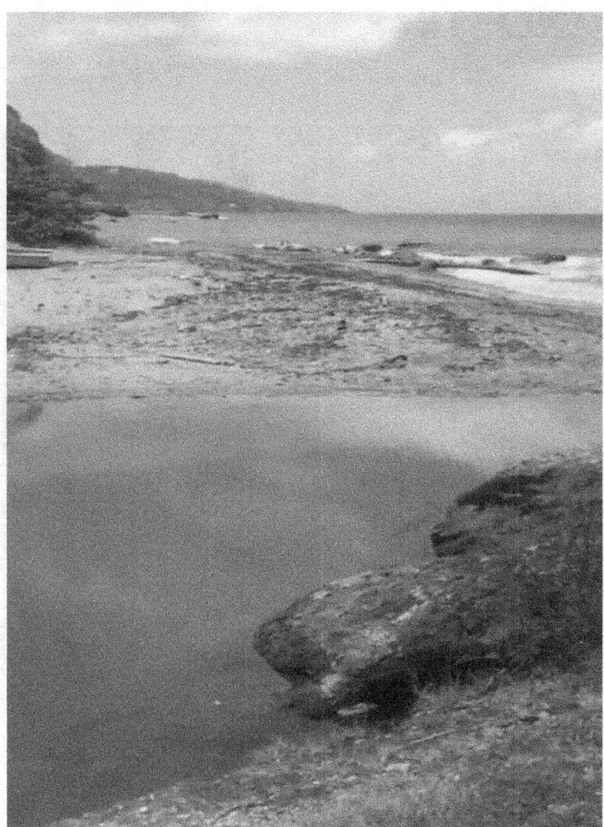

The river as it flows into the ocean

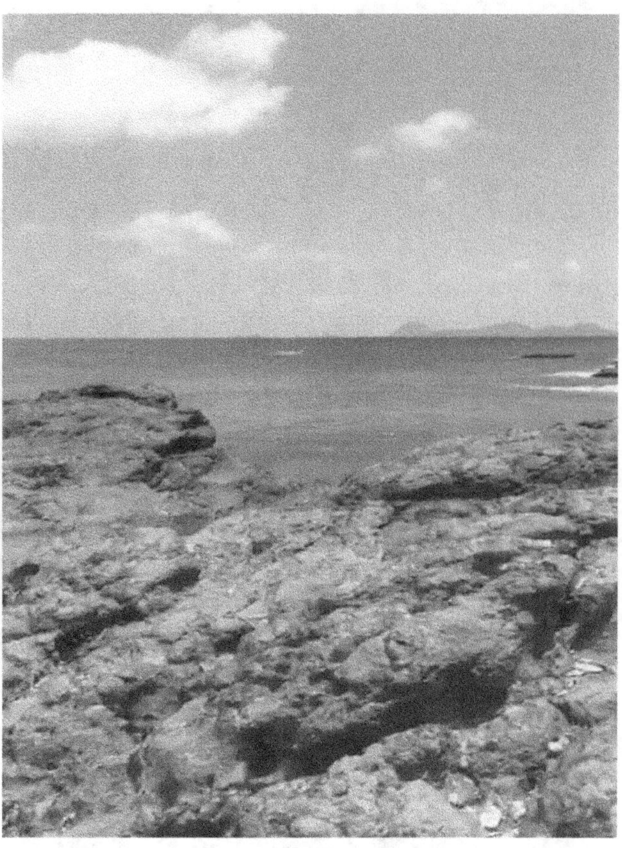

From Irwin's Bay, looking north towards the
Grenadines

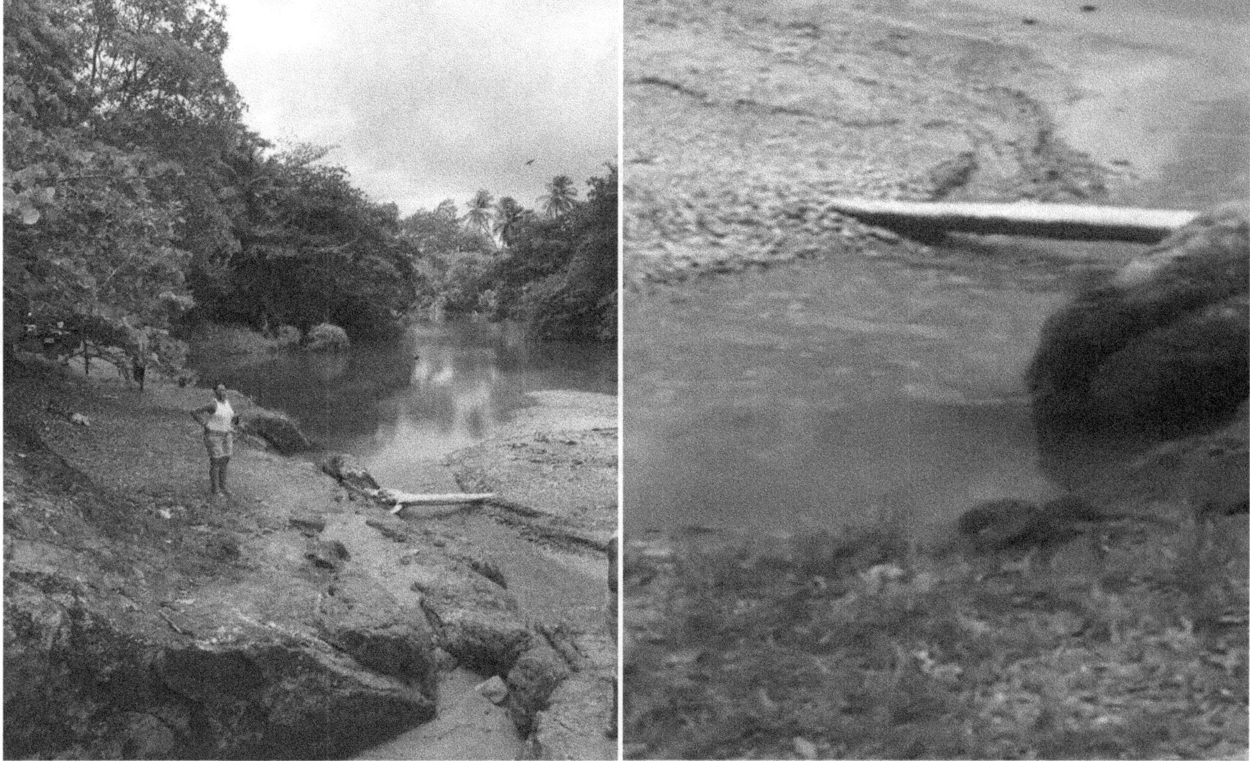

Makeshift bridges over the river where it drains into the bay

GRENADIAN ANCESTRY

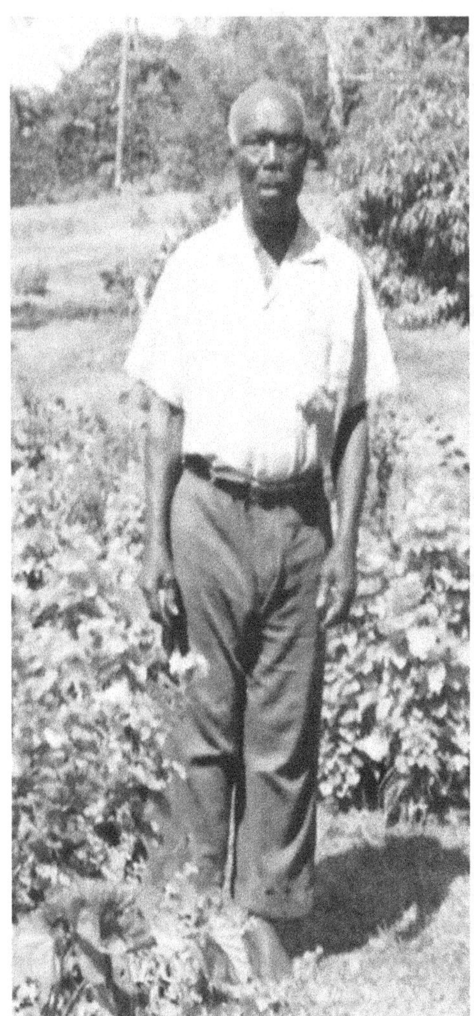

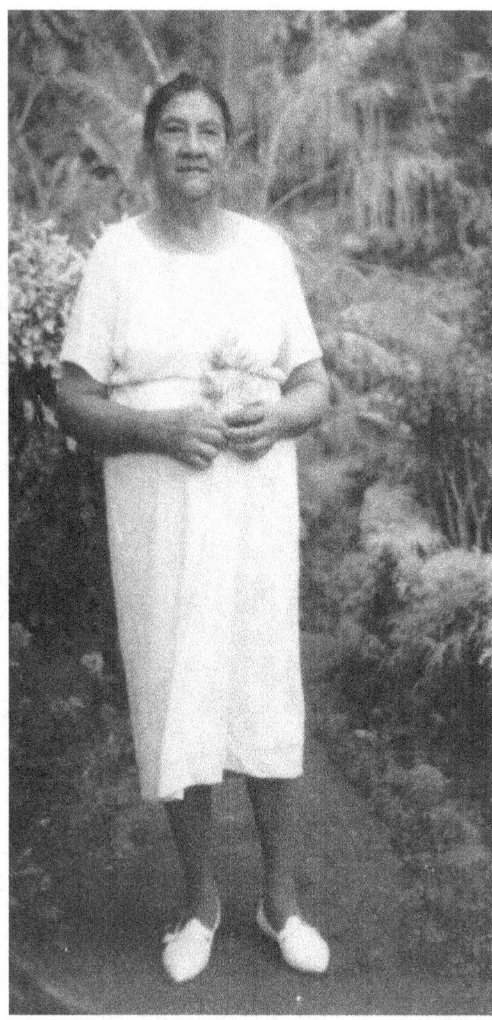

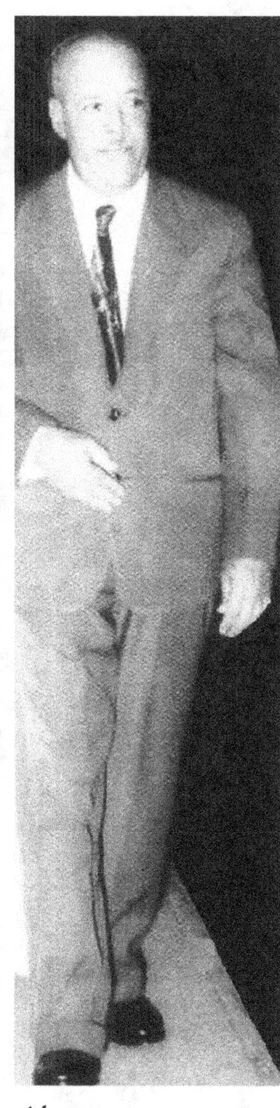

Over ninety percent of Grenada's population is of African descent.

About five percent is descended from East Indian indentured laborers.

About one percent is white

Above: Grenadians of yesteryear reflect the island's West African, East Indian, and West European ancestral origins. Today there is a fair intermixture of these original ethnicities.

We can observe Grenada's diversity among Grenadian merchants, some of whom have settled in Grenada for generations. Among these merchants are Grenadians of Arab descent, bearing names like Aboud, Bathik, and Nahous. Also, there are small generations of East Indians, descended from recent merchants to Grenada who, like the Arabs before them, were prominent store owners in Grenada. In the past, there were a few Chinese Grenadians. On one occasion in the 1970s, a Chinese Grenadian beauty queen (Diane Wong) participated in the Miss Grenada Carnival Queen Show.

Coo-coo

1-pound yellow cornmeal
6 cups of water
2 cups of coconut milk
Add salt to taste.
4 Tbs Margarine or butter
1/4 tsp black pepper

Pour into a pot 2 cups of water, with all the other ingredients, except the cornmeal. Bring to a boil and simmer for 10 minutes.

Meanwhile, in a bowl, pour 4 cups of water into the cornmeal and stir to a soft consistency.

Pour the cornmeal into the pot and mix into the simmered ingredients. Boil on low heat and continue to stir till the cornmeal thickens.

Can serve with corned fish and callaloo, Grenada's spinach-like green.

Curried Goat

2 pounds goat cut into small pieces.
2 tablespoons curry powder
2 tablespoons cooking oil.
salt
1/4 to 1/2 teaspoon pepper sauce or 1 small hot pepper
garlic or garlic powder
onion powder
Worcestershire sauce

Season goat well with salt, pepper, chives, thyme, garlic, onion powder & Worcester sauce.

Heat cooking oil in a heavy skillet. Mix curry powder in 1/4 cup of water, add to skillet, and fry for 2 to 3 minutes.

Add goat, stir well to coat all sides, and sauteed until liquid is absorbed. Add 2 cups hot water and cover. Cook on medium-low heat until tender.

Shepherd's Pie

1 lb. minced meat
1 egg
1 small onion
salt & pepper
chive & thyme
pepper
1 lb. (Irish/English) potatoes

Season minced meat well with above seasonings. Peel potatoes and boil. Mash potatoes with butter, salt & pepper, and a little bit of milk or mayonnaise if desired.

Sauté minced meat in a little oil in a skillet. When well cooked, remove from heat and add 1 beaten egg. Place the meat in a greased pie dish and place the mashed potato on top. The meat and potato can also be placed in four alternating layers with the meat first and potato last. Brown in a hot oven.

The dishes often reflect the diverse cultural influences upon Grenada. Here, we have an example of three recipes that reflect some of these various influences: Coo, West African; Curried goat, Indian; and Shepherd's Pie, European.

OTHER COASTAL SCENES

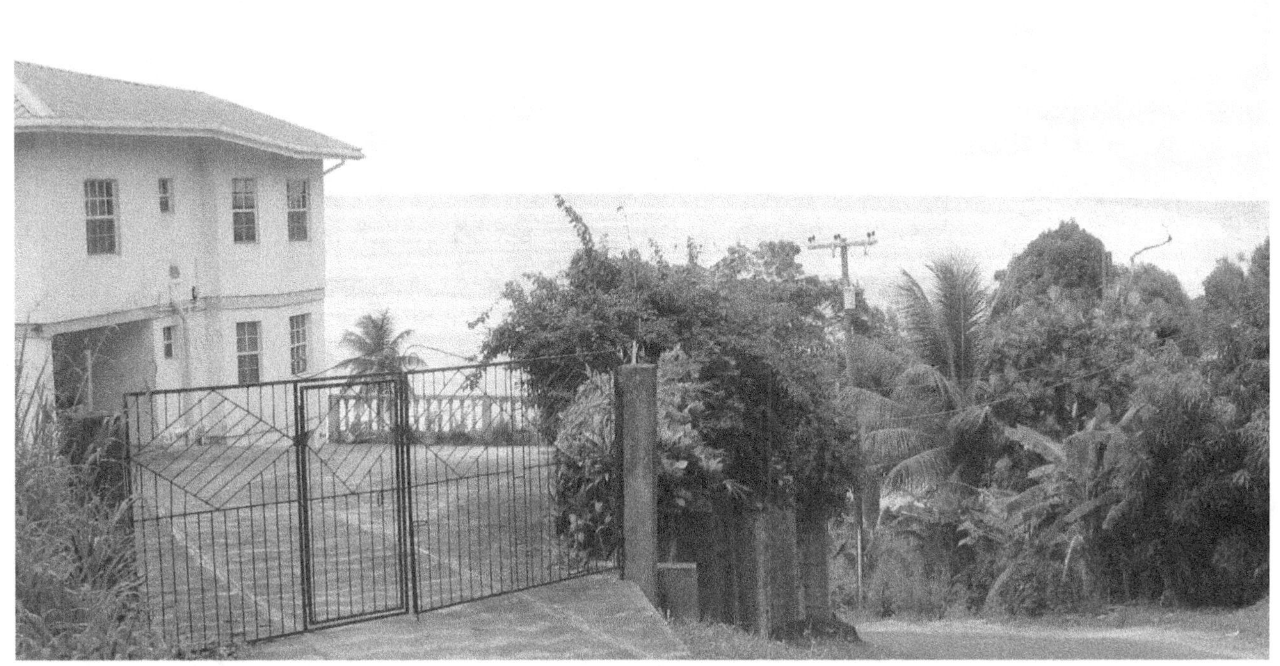

Above: View from Dougaldston
Below: West coast along Grand Roy

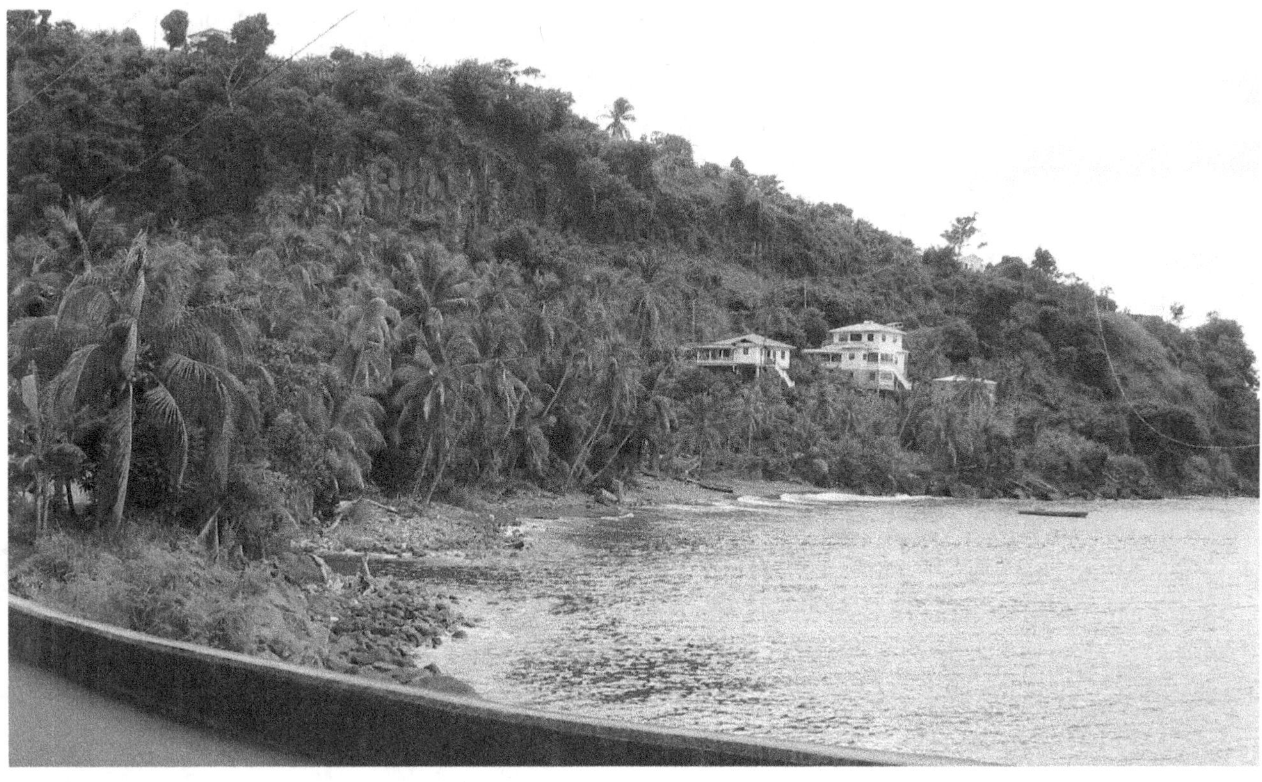

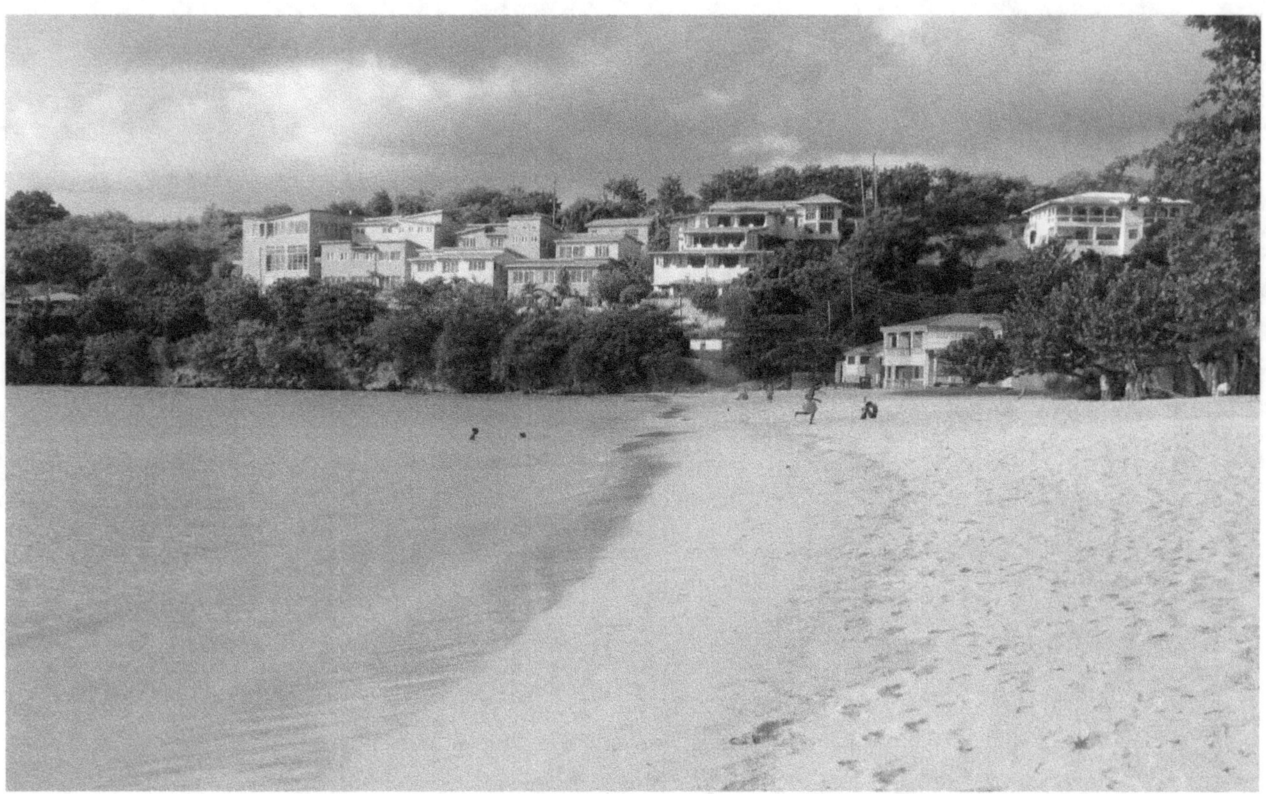

Above: The northern end of Morne Rouge Beach
Below: The southern end of Morne Rouge Beach

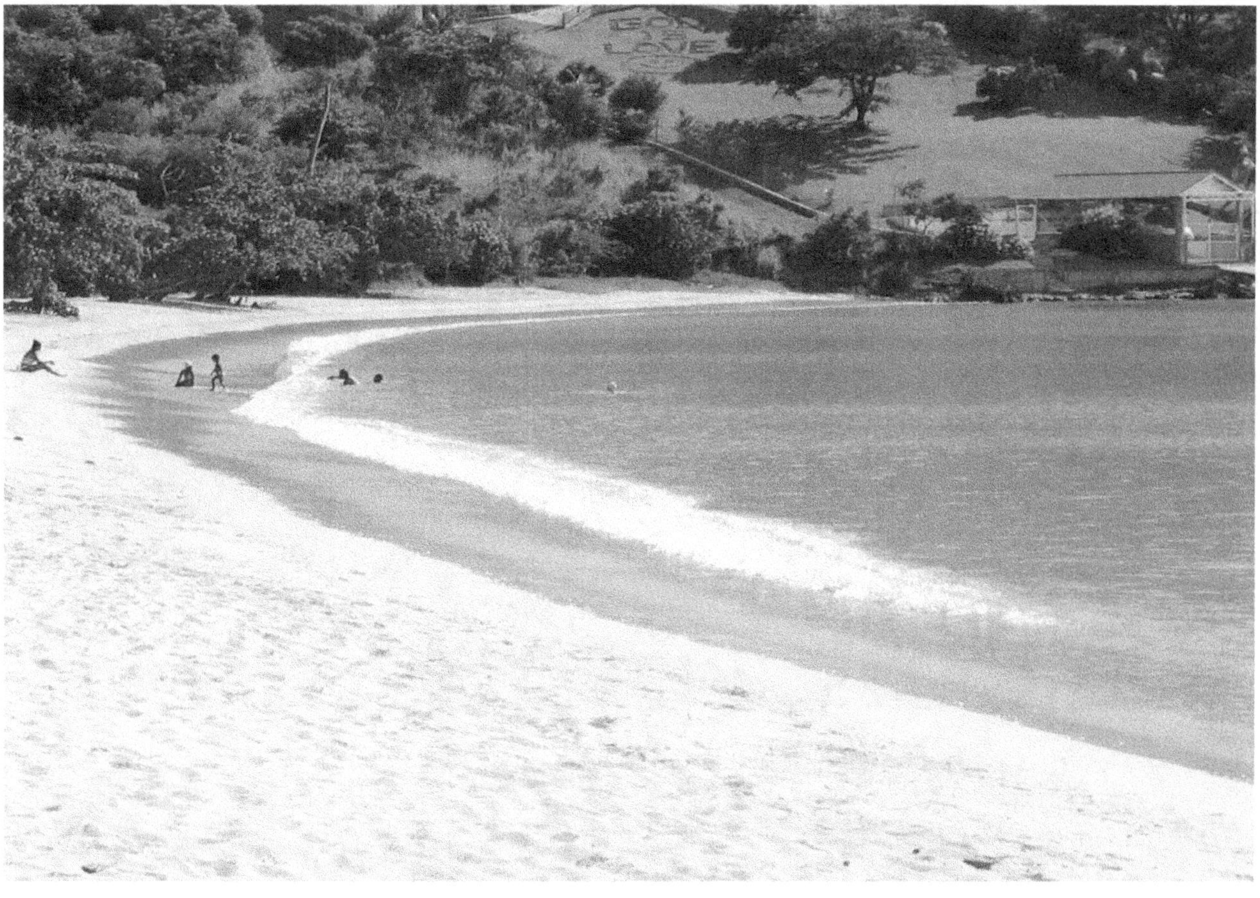

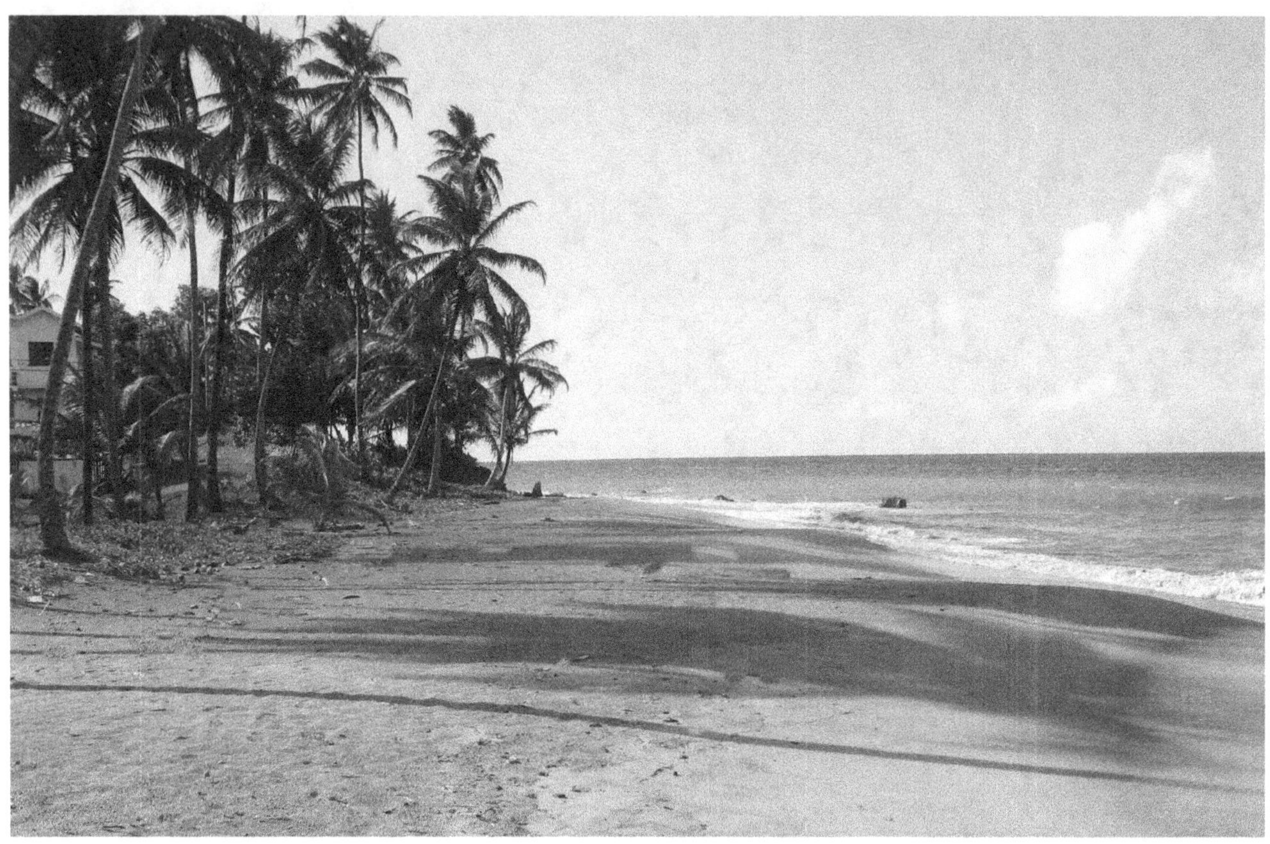

Above: Mt. Rodney's west end   Below: Palmiste Beach, a beautiful dark sand beach

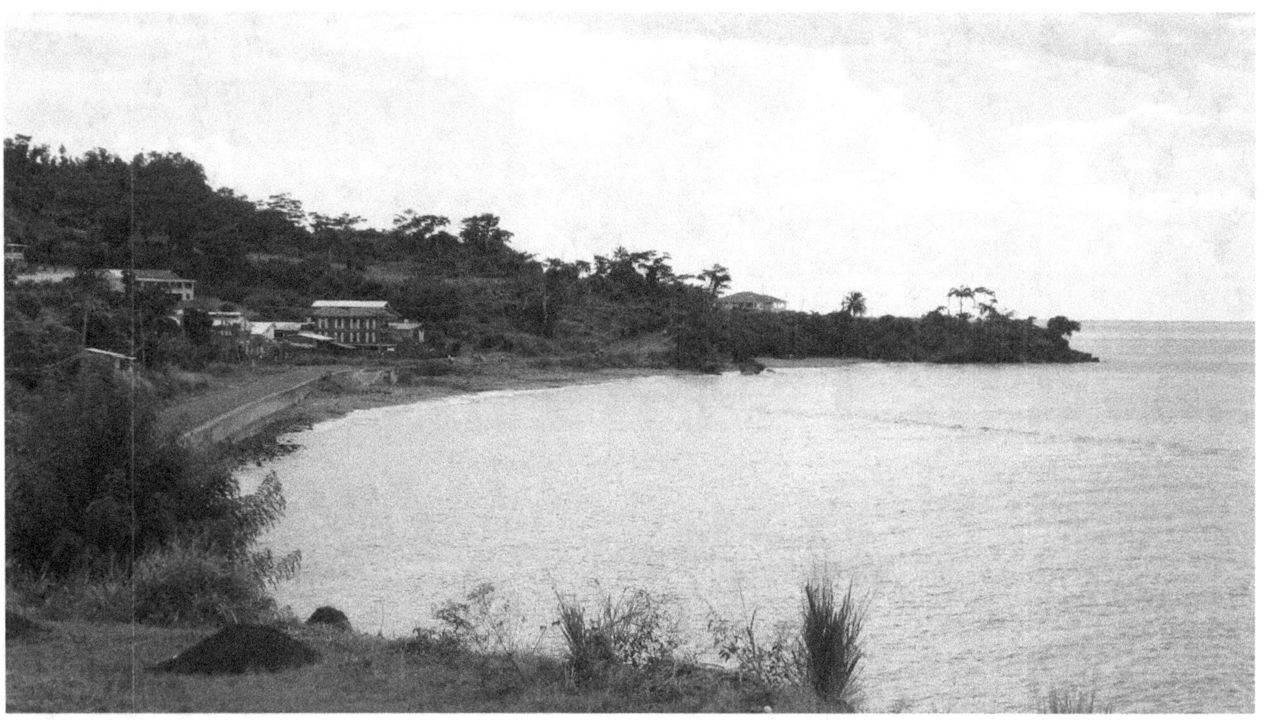

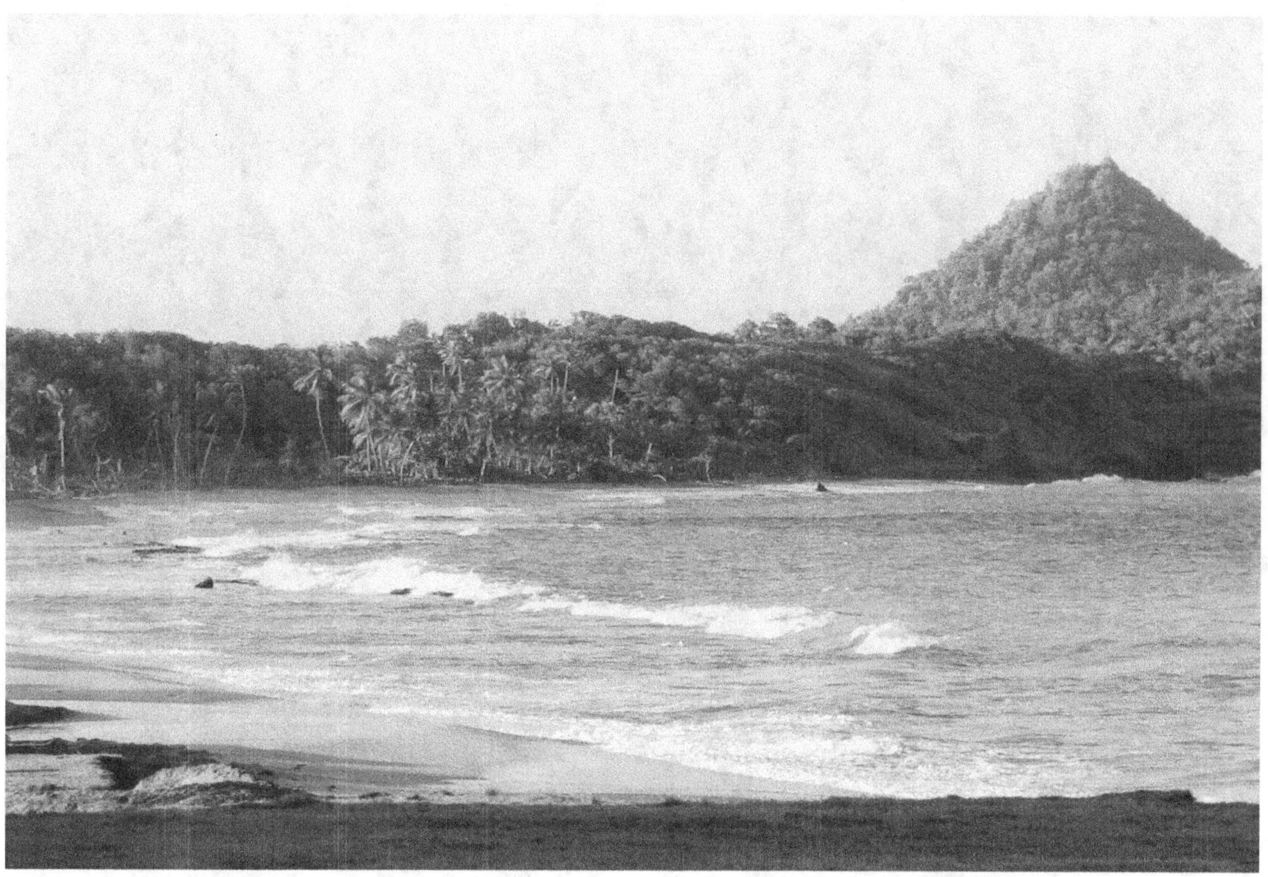

Above: Lively waves at Bathway

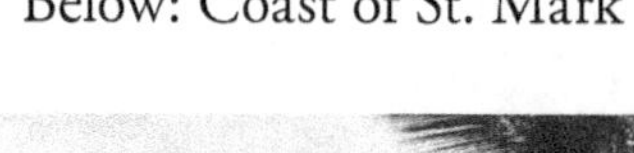

Below: Coast of St. Mark

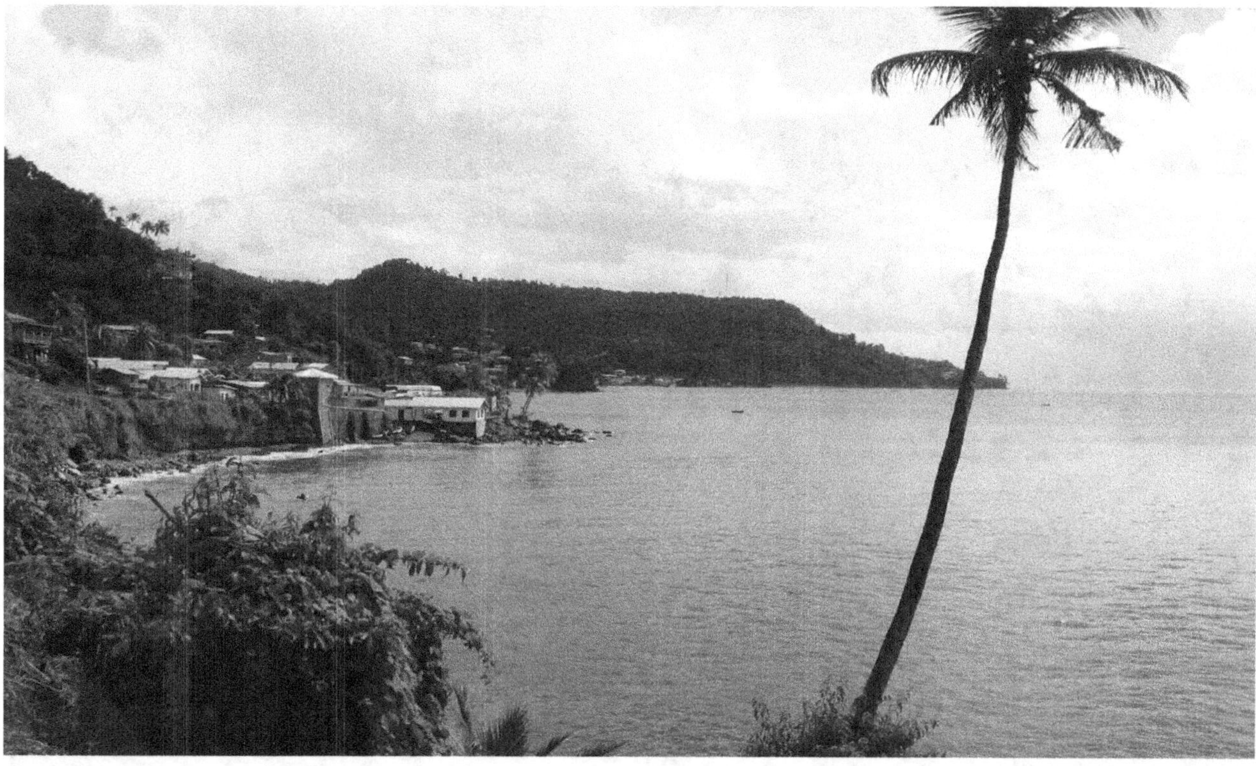

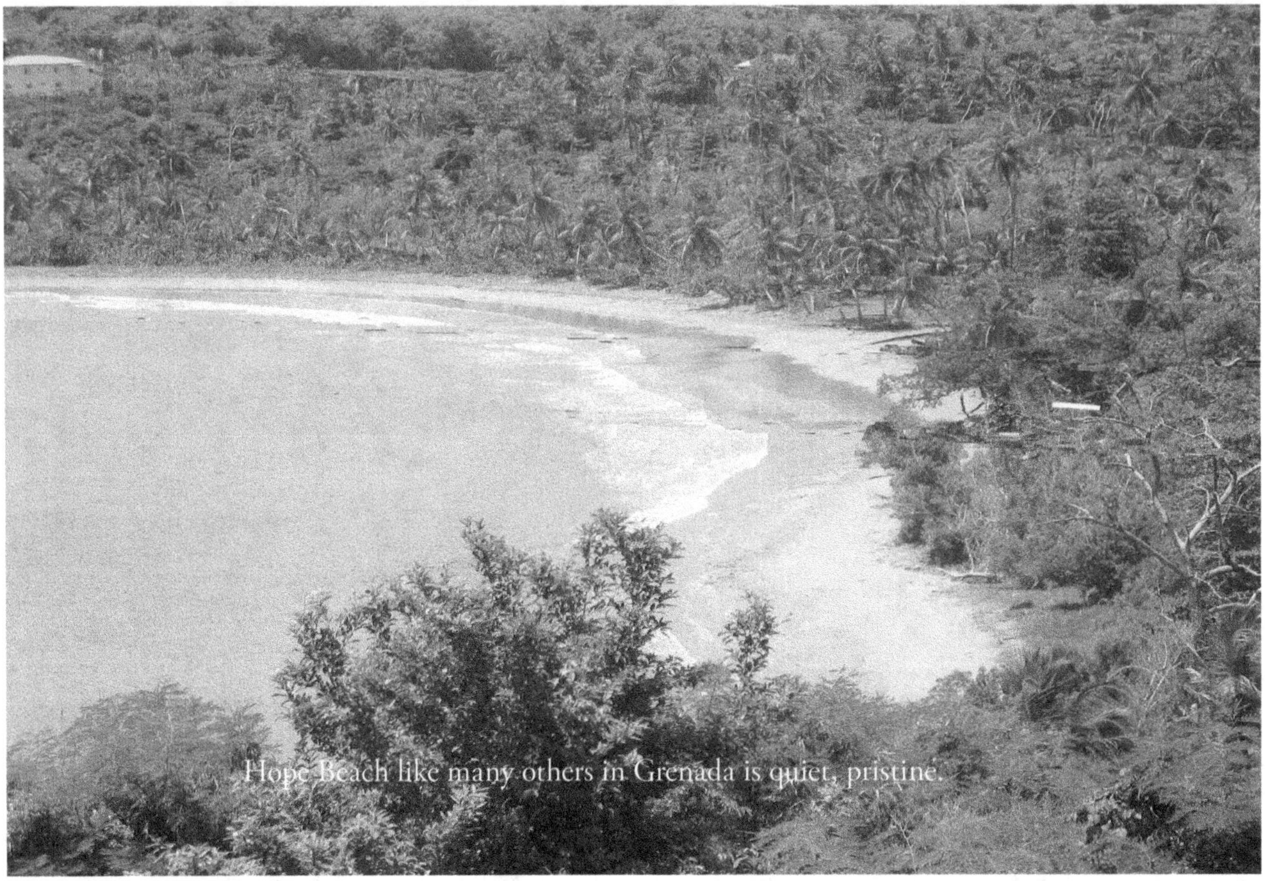

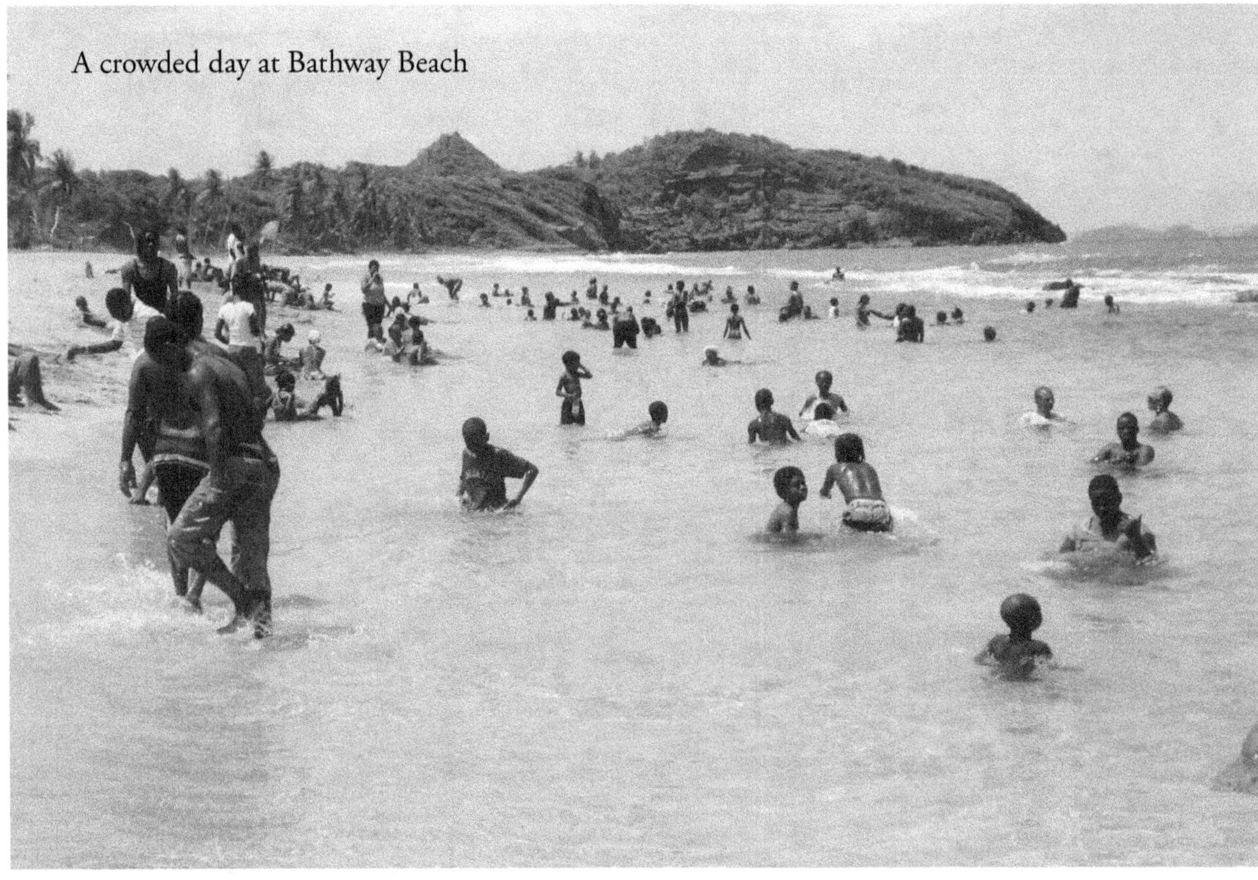

Hope Beach like many others in Grenada is quiet, pristine.

A crowded day at Bathway Beach

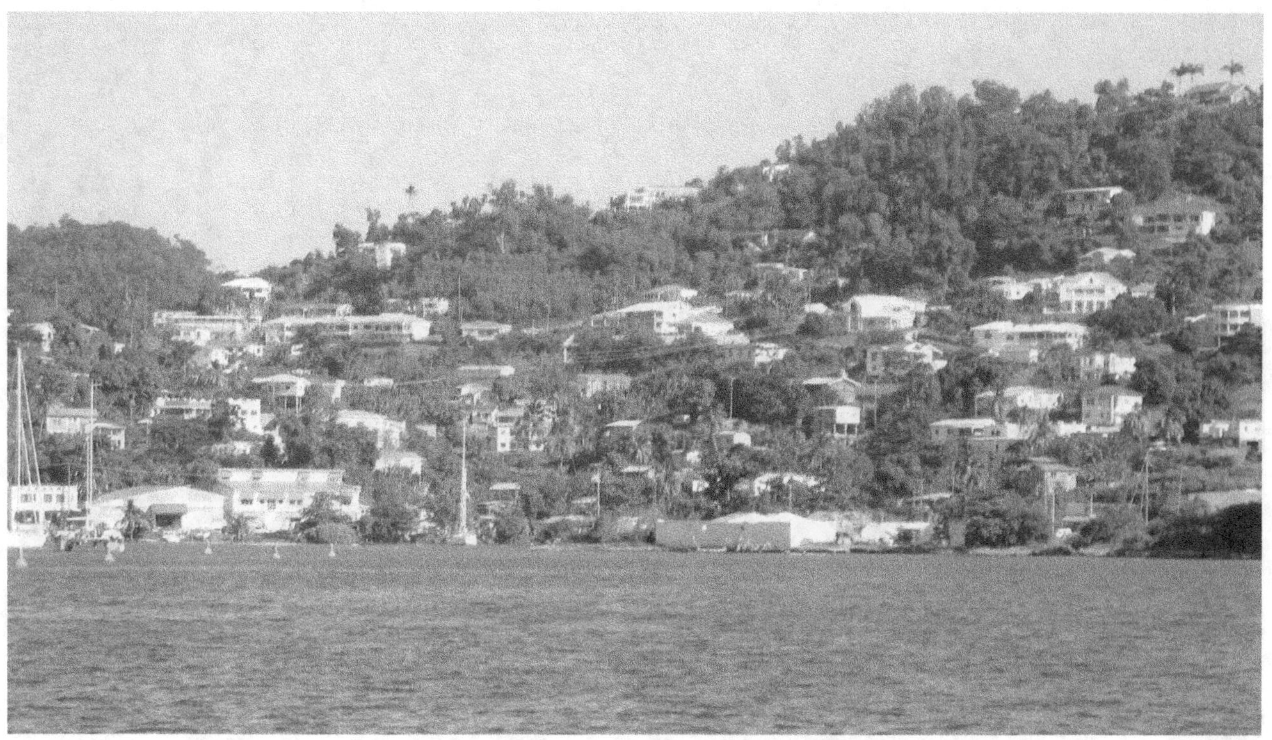

Here is a section of the lagoon area of St. George, along Kirani James Highway. The Government has named the road in honor of Kirani James, Grenada's 2012 Olympic gold medalist in the 400 meters.

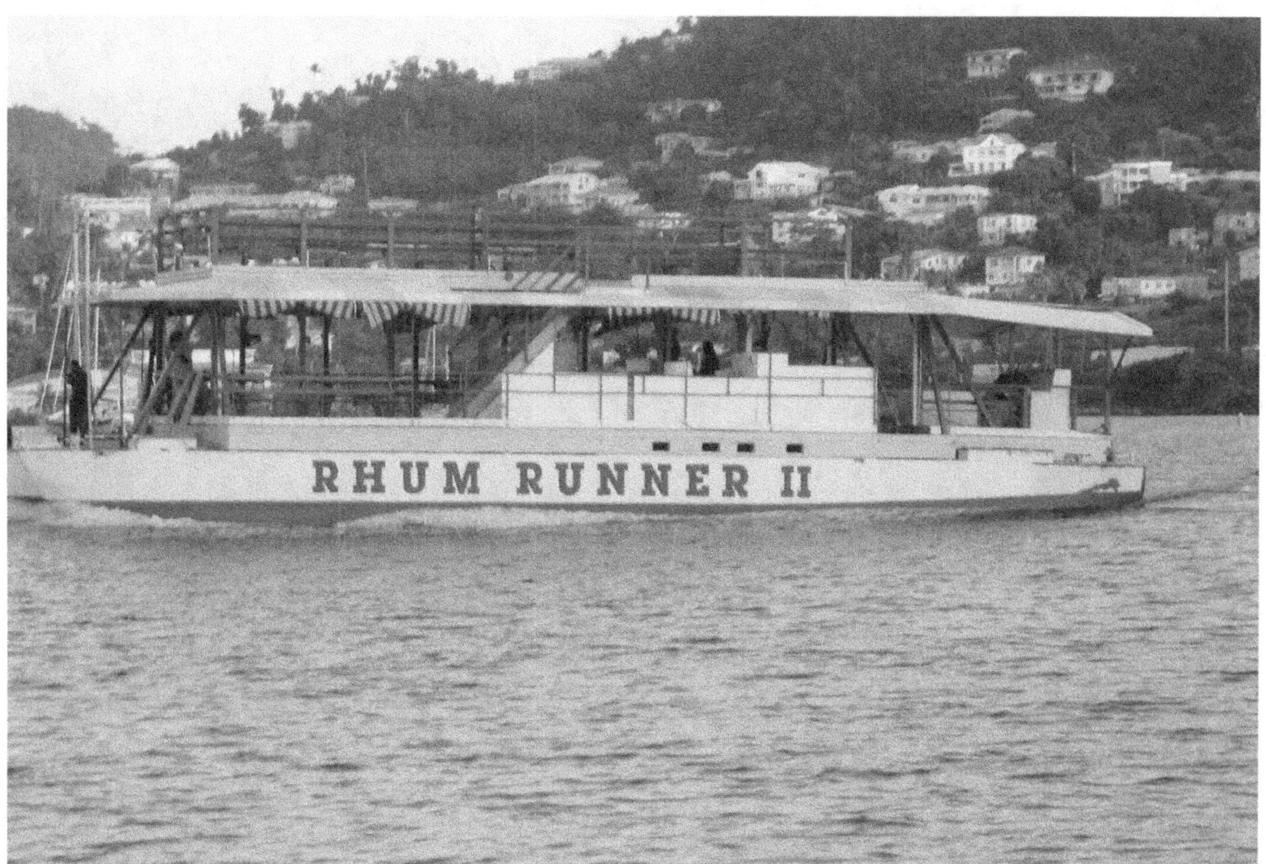

The Rhum Runner makes its way across the lagoon. The Rhum Runner hosts parties aboard as it cruises around the island.

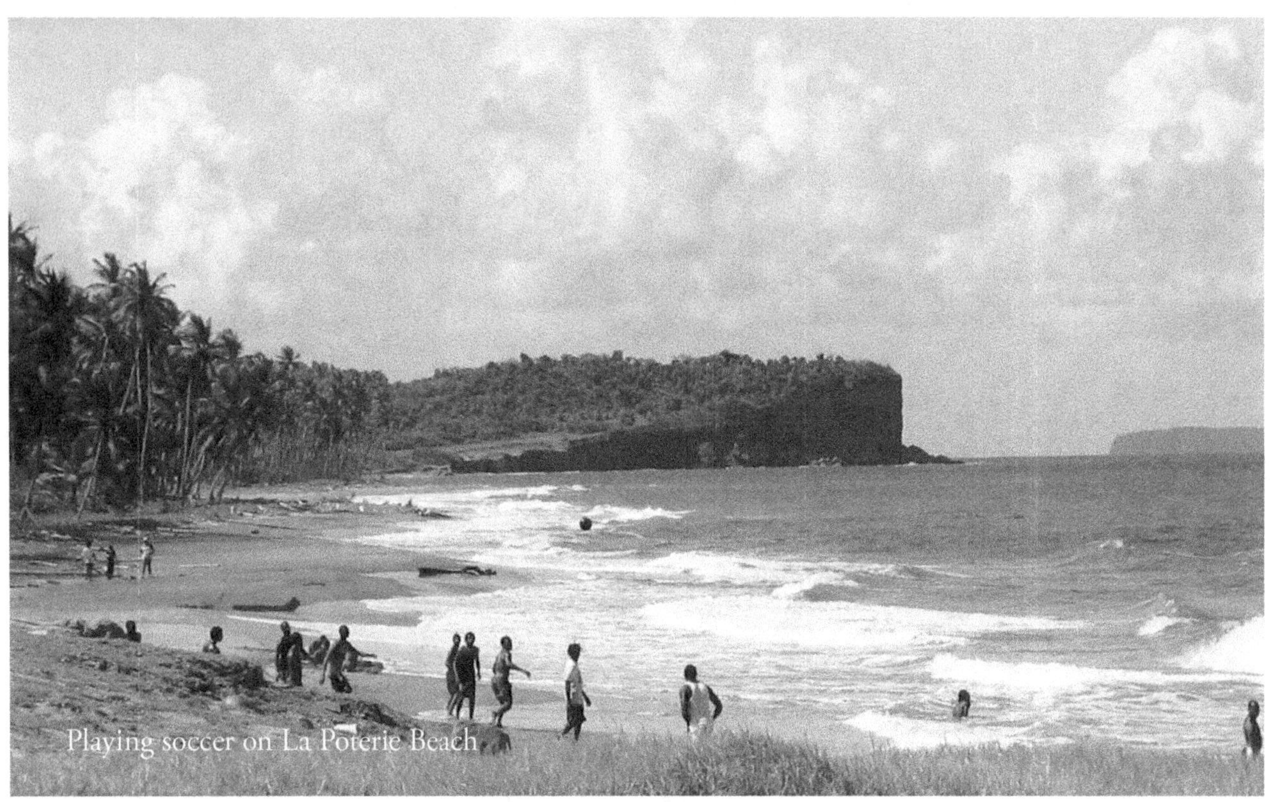

Playing soccer on La Poterie Beach

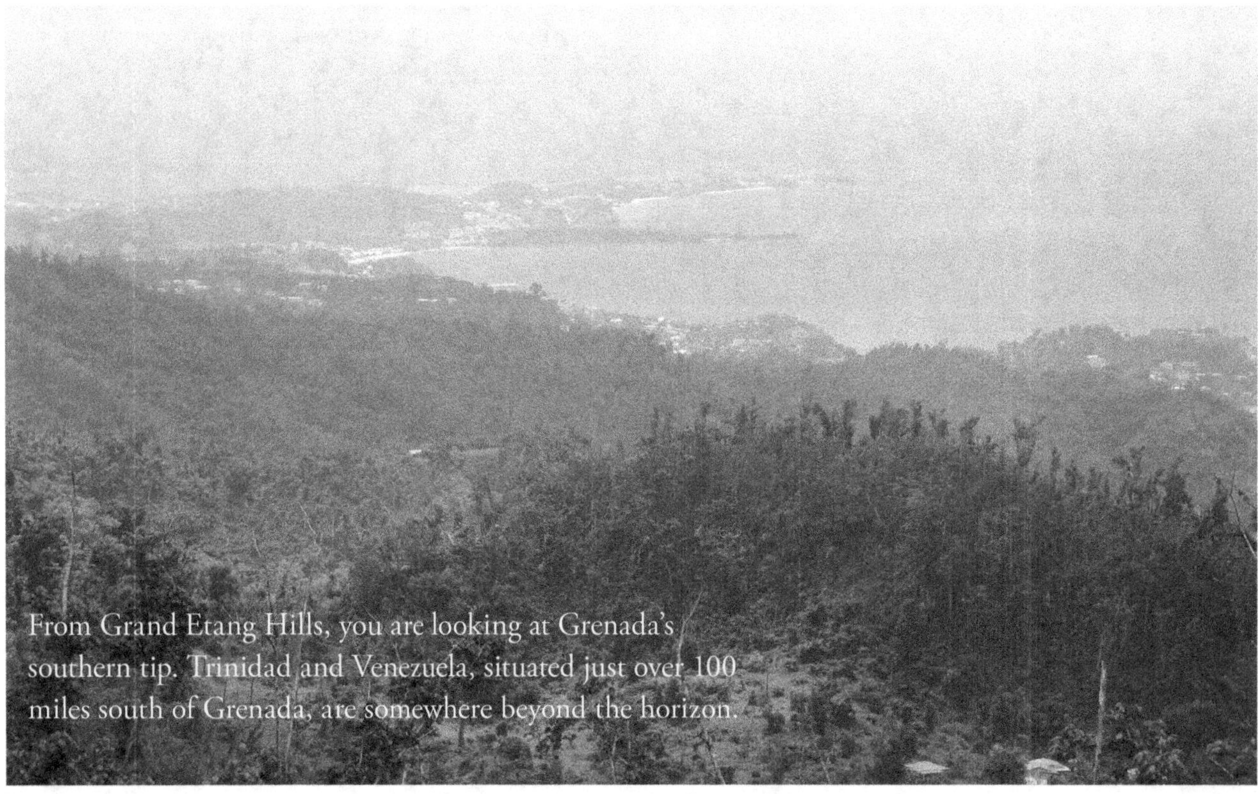

From Grand Etang Hills, you are looking at Grenada's southern tip. Trinidad and Venezuela, situated just over 100 miles south of Grenada, are somewhere beyond the horizon.

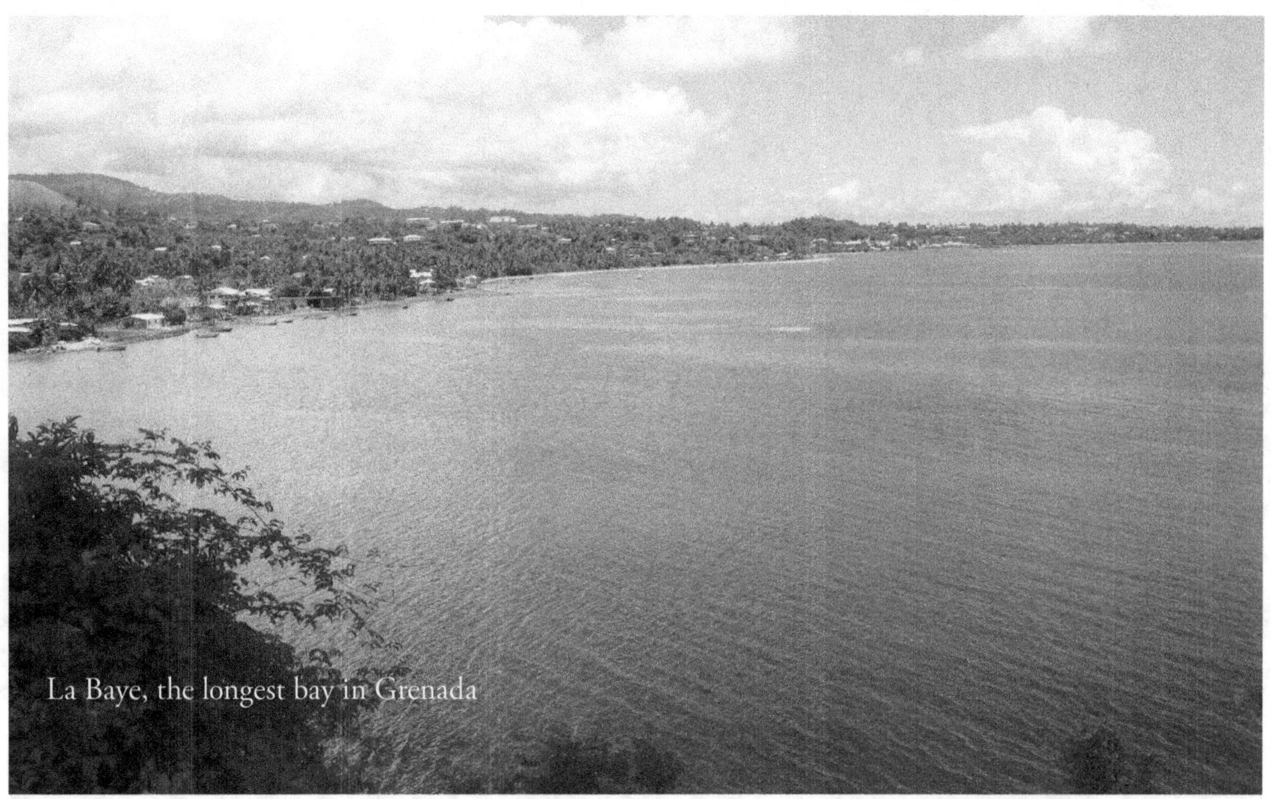

La Baye, the longest bay in Grenada

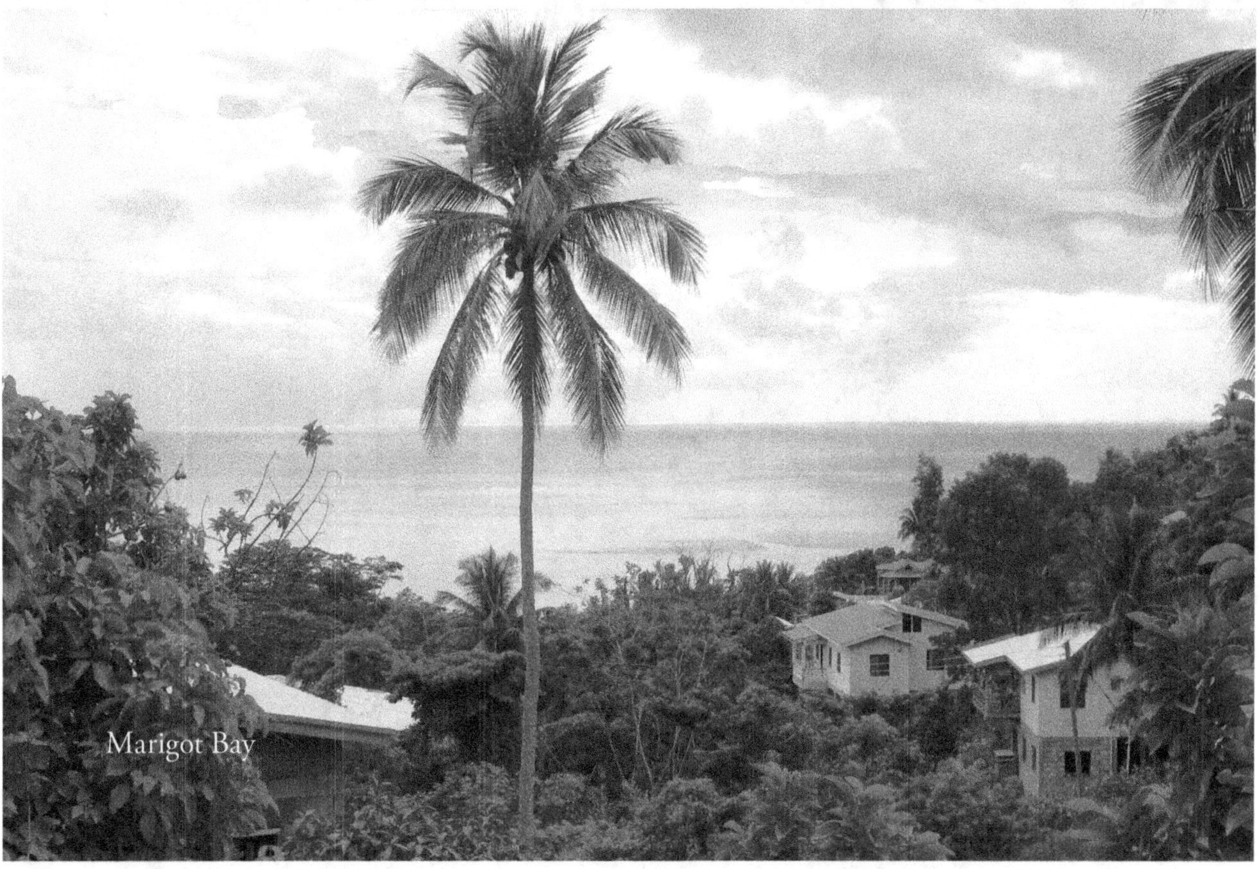

Marigot Bay

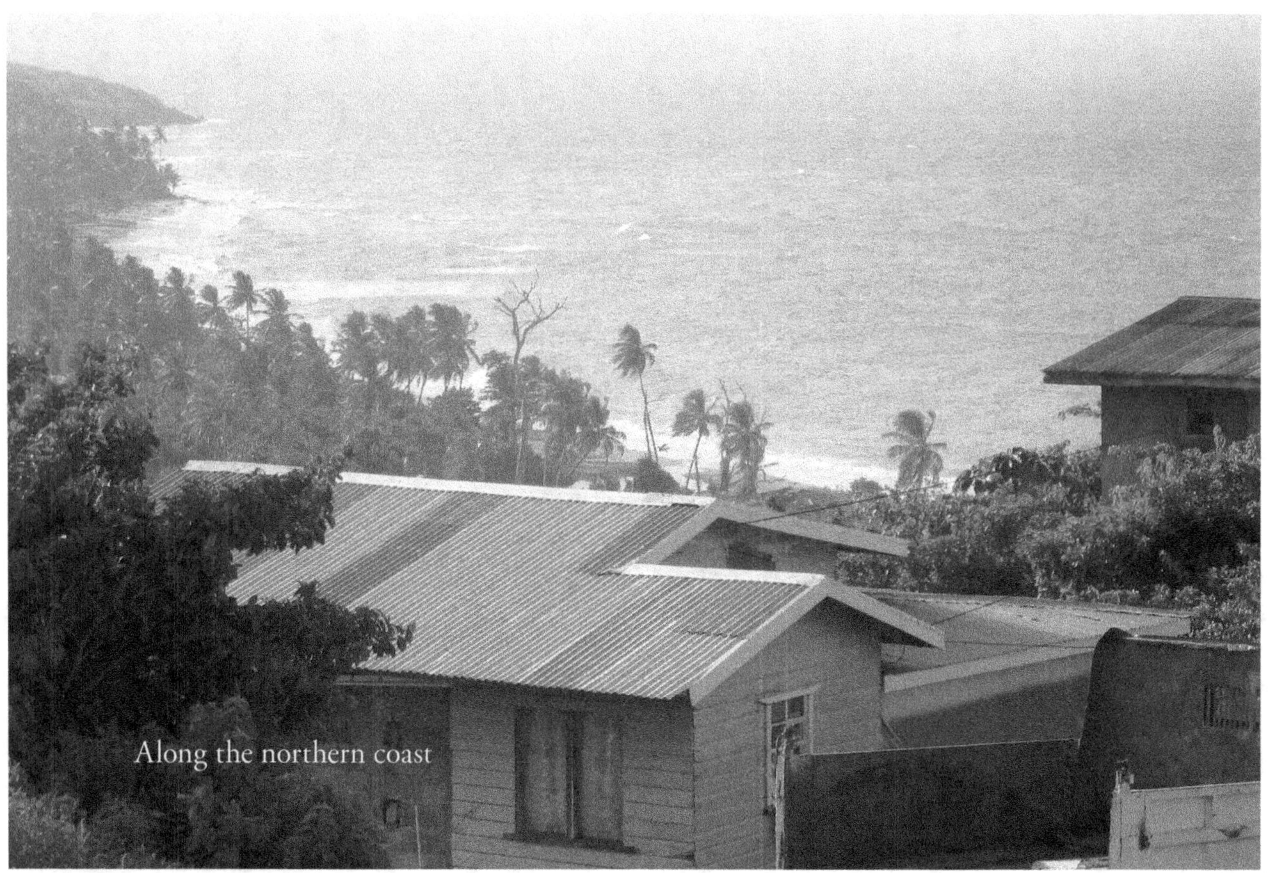

Along the northern coast

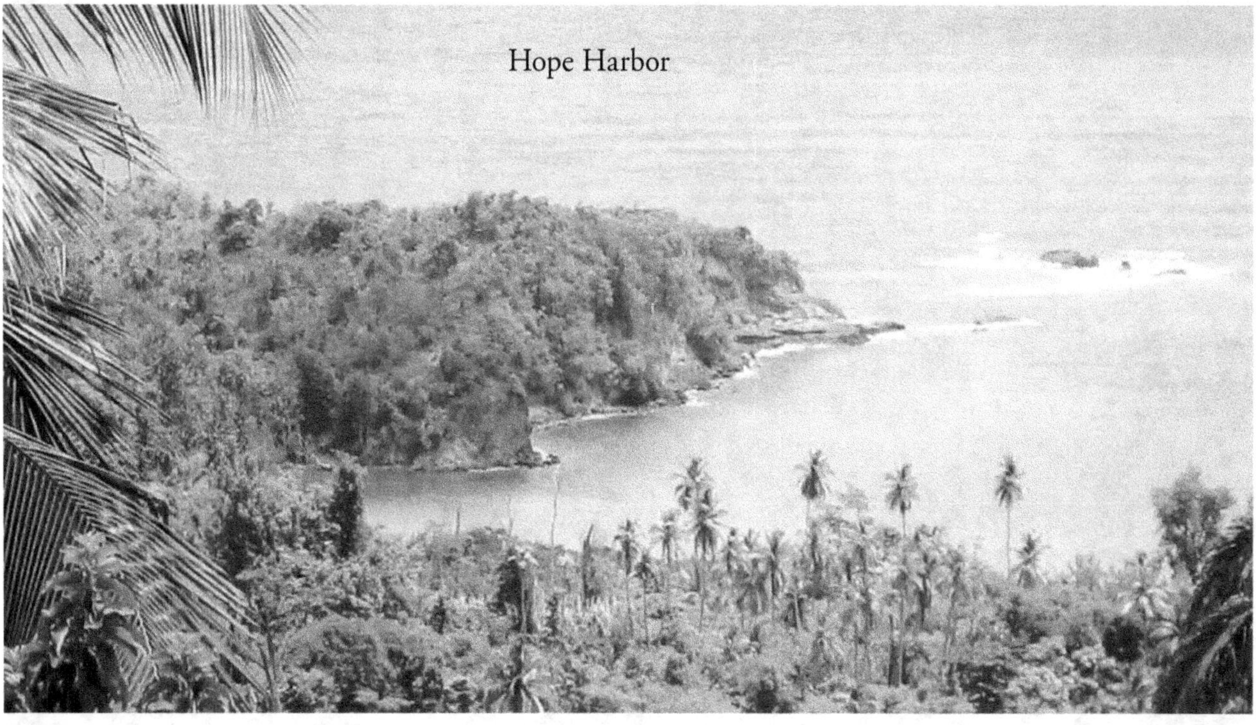

Hope Harbor

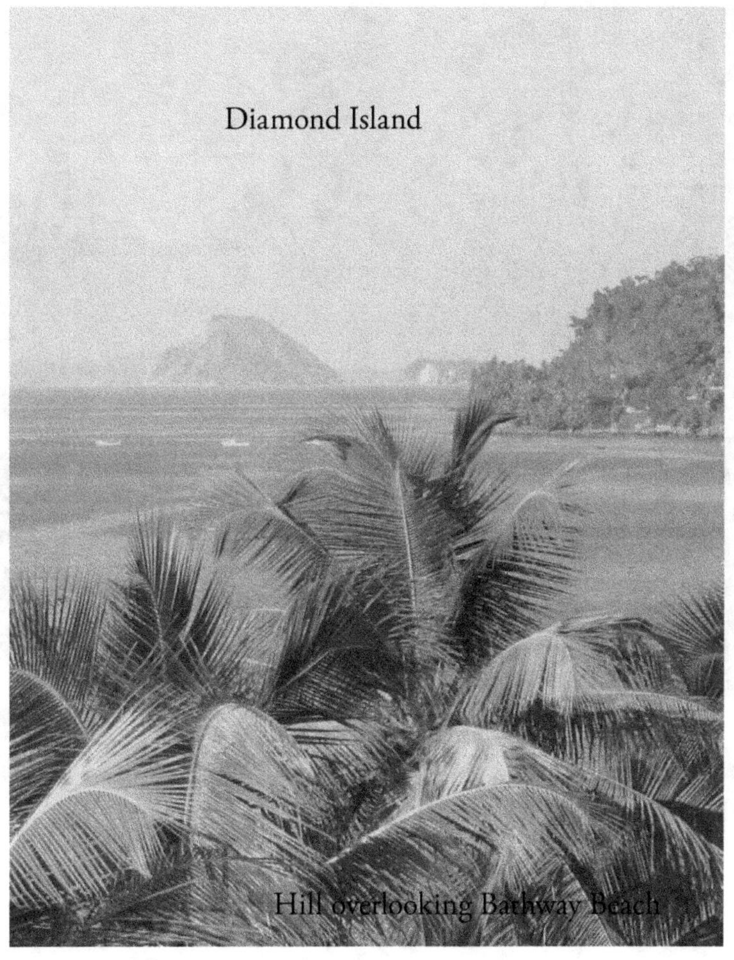

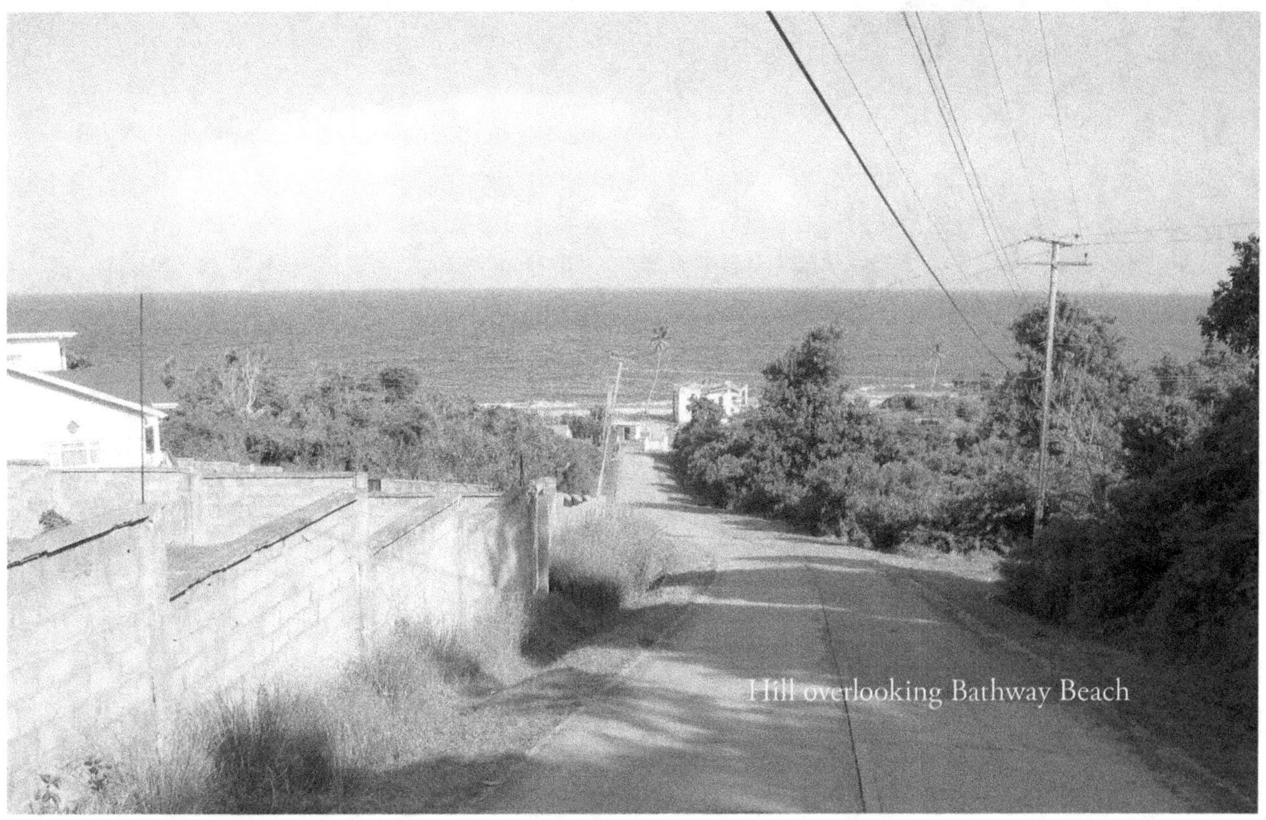

Hill overlooking Bathway Beach

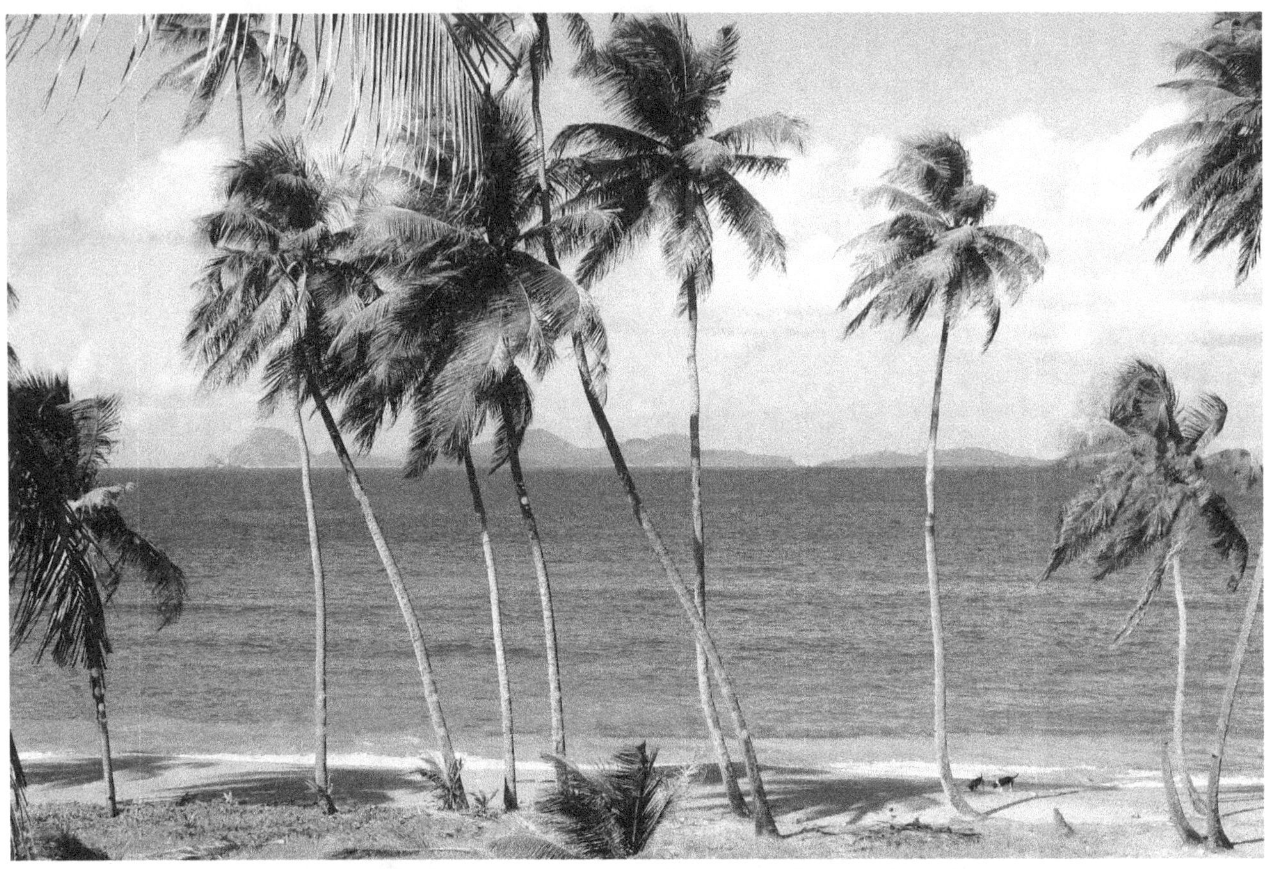

Above: From Mt. Rodney, another view of Grenada's isles
Below: Nonpareil, along the Western Main Road

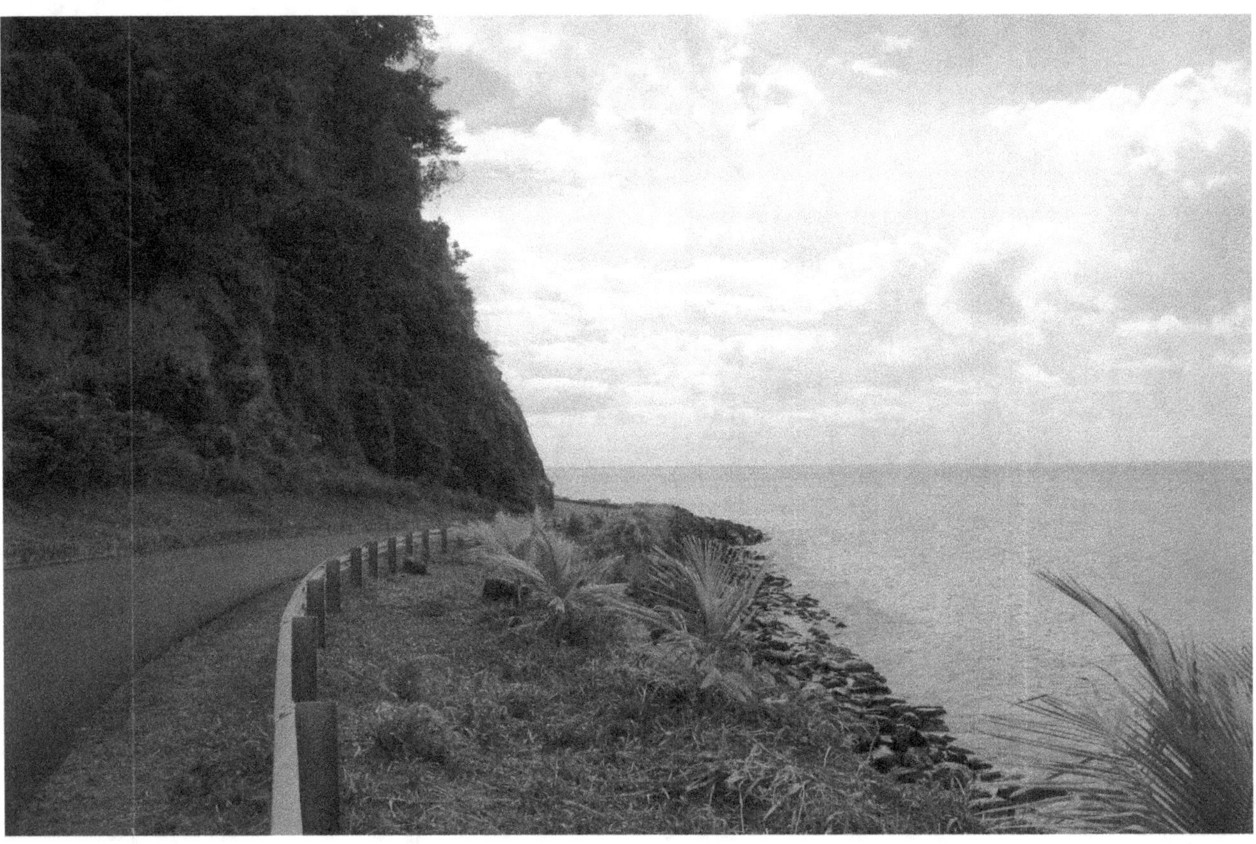

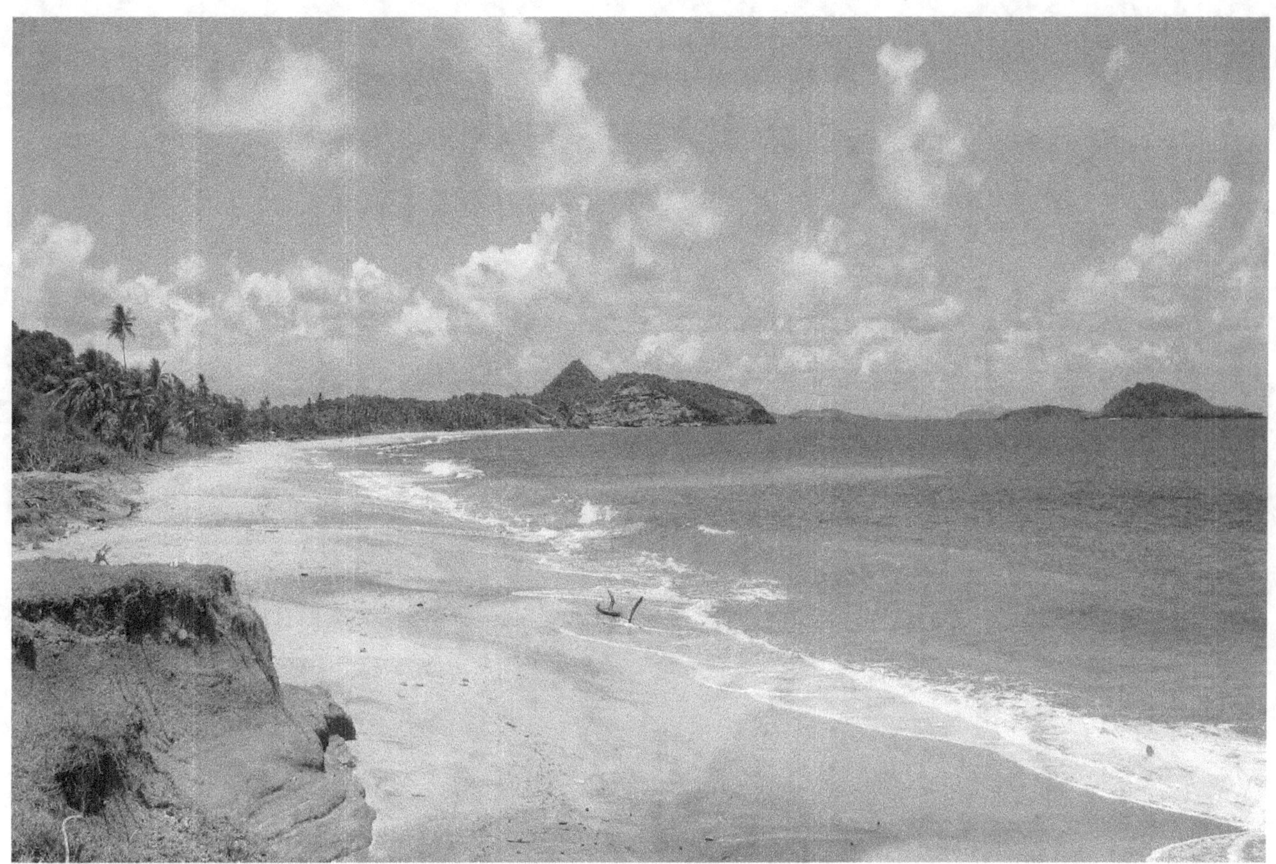

Above: Bathway Beach on a quiet day
Below: Ship docked at the Visitor's Port

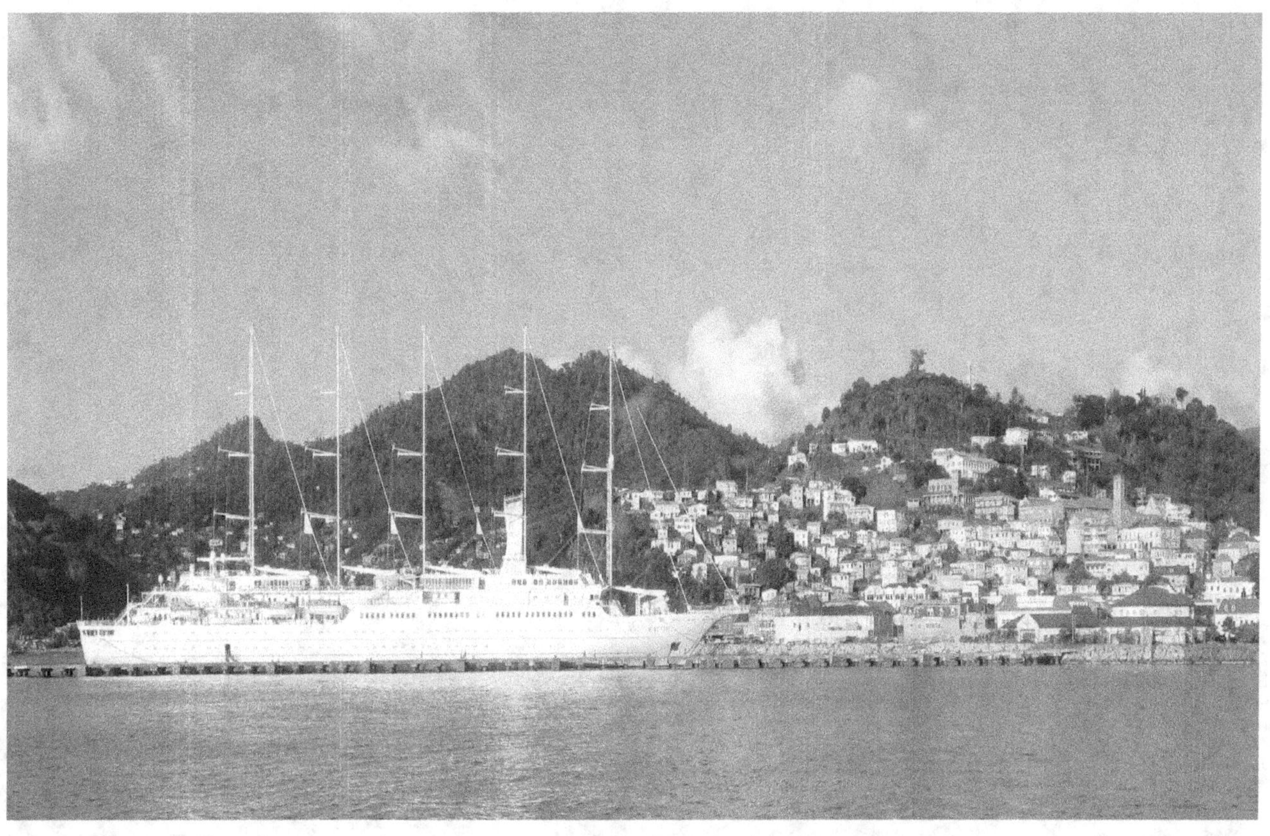

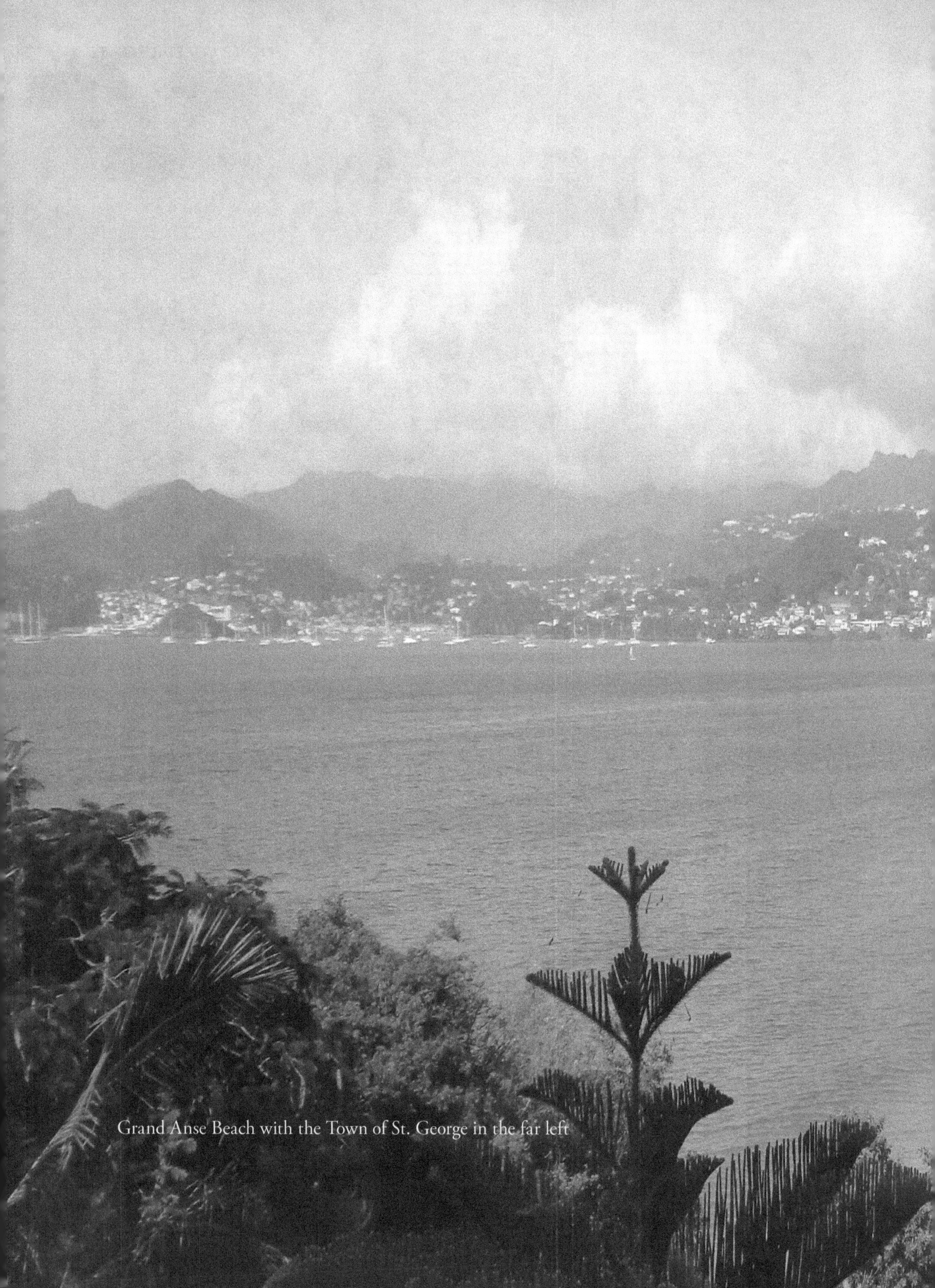

Grand Anse Beach with the Town of St. George in the far left

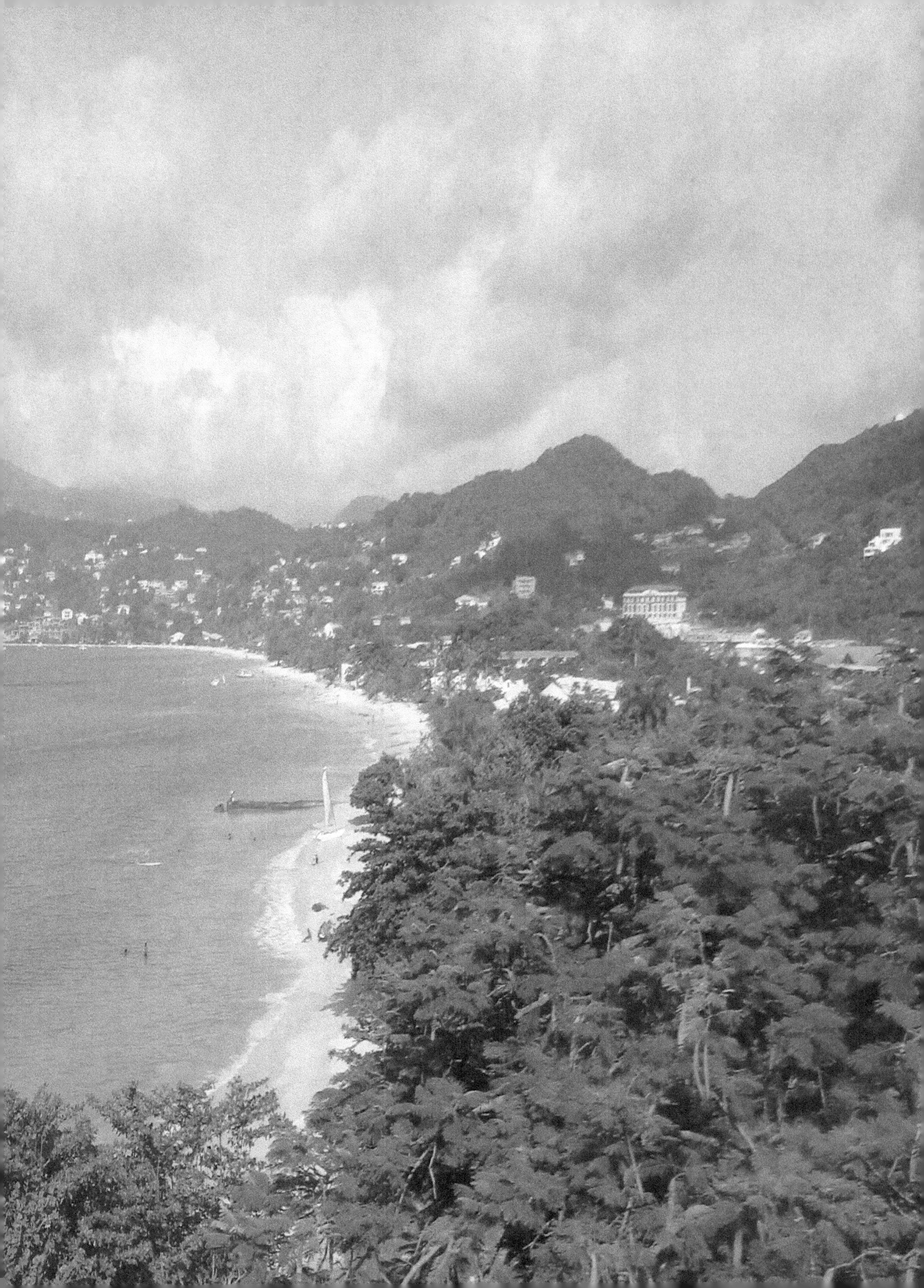

Final Curtain: Sun sets magnificently on
the coast near Victoria.

INDEX

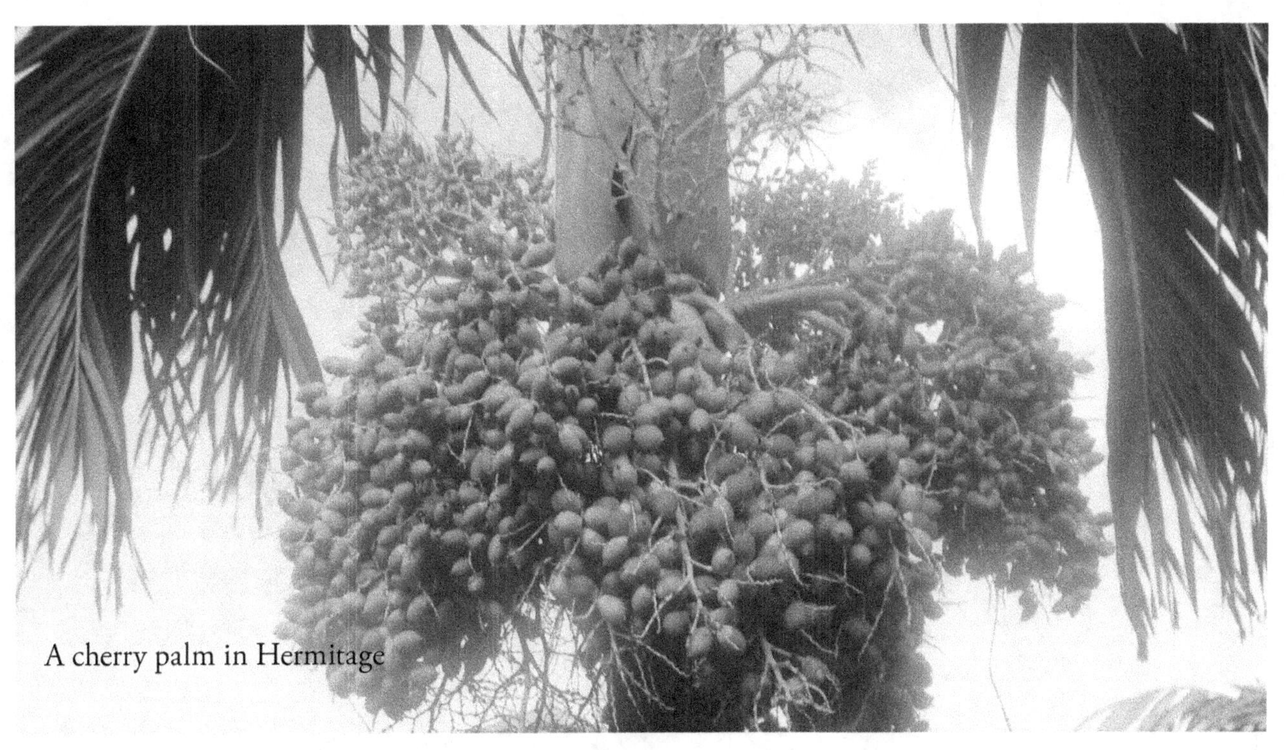

A cherry palm in Hermitage